# A THOUSAND AND ONE
# NIGHTS OF OPERA

Da Capo Press Music Reprint Series

MUSIC EDITOR
## BEA FRIEDLAND
*Ph.D., City University of New York*

# A THOUSAND AND ONE NIGHTS OF OPERA

BY

FREDERICK H. MARTENS

DA CAPO PRESS · NEW YORK · 1978

Library of Congress Cataloging in Publication Data

Martens, Frederick Herman, 1874-1932.
  A thousand and one nights of opera.

  (Da Capo Press music reprint series)
  "Tells the plots and 'places' the music of
some 1550 operas and ballets."—Foreword.
  Reprint of the ed. published by D. Appleton,
New York.
  1. Operas—Stories, plots, etc. 2. Ballets—
Stories, plots, etc. I. Title.
MT95.M23 1978        782.1'3        77-25416
ISBN 0-306-77565-4

This Da Capo Press edition of *A Thousand and One Nights of Opera* is an unabridged
republication of the first edition published in New York and London in 1926. It
is reprinted by arrangement with Josephine Martens.

Published by Da Capo Press, Inc.
A Subsidiary of Plenum Publishing Corporation
227 West 17th Street, New York, N.Y. 10011

# A THOUSAND AND ONE
# NIGHTS OF OPERA

# A THOUSAND AND ONE
# NIGHTS OF OPERA

BY

## FREDERICK H. MARTENS

AUTHOR OF "THE ART OF THE PRIMA DONNA"

D. APPLETON AND COMPANY

NEW YORK ♣ LONDON ♣ MCMXXVI

# FOREWORD

*A Thousand and One Nights of Opera* tells the plots and "places" the music of some 1550 operas and ballets, old and new, for the general reader, the opera goer, the music student and members of music clubs in search of musical program illustrations for some historic period. Encyclopædic in its nature, the volume makes no pretence to being an opera dictionary. Out of a possible repertoire of 50,000 titles, perhaps, it aims to present the operas worth notice from early times to our own.

As in every *Opera Guide* the fact that "the tale's the thing" has been borne in mind; and also that the tale in opera cannot well be disassociated from its music. The usual method of presentation which allows operas considered to follow the alphabet from *A* to *Z* has been abandoned for one which seems more logical, instead of "Ariane et barbe-bleue" following "The Apothecary" or "Benvenuto Cellini" and "La Bohème" appearing arm in arm, the present "book of the opera" follows a logical *historic* sequence in its arrangement of subjects, from the dawn of civilization to the present day.

In this "period" plan of presentation—aside from the inclusion of all the works of the standard repertoire, especially those produced in this country—certain special aims have been kept in view:

1. The claim to consideration of the greater works of lesser masters and the lesser works of greater masters. In every history and biographical dictionary of music the names of hundreds of operas are listed as *titles only*, and information regarding their plots and music is not always easily available.

2. A broader viewpoint than that which makes American performance the sole determining factor with regard to the operatic works considered. Limiting the operas considered to those performed in the United States would have excluded many modern works of great musical value and interest, and have defeated four objects the writer had in mind: (1) To give an idea of the principal operas of the Modern and Ultra-Modern Repertoire; (2) to give an idea of the principal American operas, that is, operas written by American composers; (3) to show, in the case of

operas and ballets produced during the nineteenth century and the first quarter of the twentieth, the reflection of actual human life and thought, movements and ideas, in musical dramatic works of the kind; and (4) to give the work an actual reference value for the music student and student of musical history or the history of opera.

The writer has tried to shape informative values in readable form and, while treating all which demanded reverence in music with reverence, has not attempted to present the patently ridiculous in text as the sublime. A variety of reasons have dictated the inclusion of certain individual operas (increasing revivals of older works on the opera stage both in Europe and America is only one) as well as the detail arrangement of works within their period outlines. All available published sources have been consulted in preparing the work and the author begs to express, in the same connection, his grateful appreciation to Dr. Theodore Baker, Mr. John Alden Carpenter, Sr. Eduardo Fuentes, Mr. Franke-Harling, Mr. Hans Gregor, Mr. Frederick Field Converse, Mr. Russell M. Knerr, Mr. Louis Mattfield (New York Public Library), Mr. Ivan Narodny, Mr. Herbert F. Peyser, Mr. Waldemar Riek, Mr. Cyril Scott, Mr. O. G. Sonneck and Mr. Oscar Thompson. It is the author's hope that the book may fill a place and voice an appeal in connection with an art form which, "the illegitimate child of the Middle Ages," continues to develop new phases and facets of interest with every passing year.

FREDERICK H. MARTENS.

Rutherford, N. J.

# CONTENTS

# ONE THOUSAND AND ONE NIGHTS OF OPERA

## CHAPTER I

### THE ORIENT

#### 1. *From the Land of the Pyramids*

The mysterious land of the pyramids, cradle of civilization, seems a logical point of departure for a period journey through the opera repertoire, but though Verdi's *Aïda* remains the Great Pyramid of Gizeh of its kind, there are other operas and ballets of Pharaonic Egypt. Among them are Paul Vidal's *Rameses* (Paris, 1908), and the Lett Medin's *Gods and Men* (Riga, 1922), philosophic rather than dramatic, telling an episode of the reign of Rameses III to music influenced by Richard Strauss. In Jean Nouguès' *Narkiss* (Paris, 1914), a spectacular, unoriginal ballet opera, the Pharaoh Narkiss, who is doomed if he sees his face, looks in a pool. He vanishes beneath the water, reappears as a lotus, and has his flower head cut from its stalk by a "woman of mystery" sent by the Egyptian priests to do away with him. *Khamma* (Paris, 1925), Claude Debussy's posthumous pantomime ballet, reflects musically "all Debussy's power of atmospheric evocation." Priests and people have vainly prayed the god Amon-Ra to aid war-threatened Egypt. Khamma, lovely dancer, moves the deity's granite heart. Stricken lifeless at the height of her frenzied whirl in his honor in token that she is accepted as a sacrifice, the sun god kisses the dead girl's face with a golden ray while the Egyptians exult in the foreknowledge of victory. *The Romance of a Mummy* (London, 1925), a Pavlowa ballet, tells Gautier's tale of the love of beautiful Princess Tahoser and the Pharaoh of the Exodus, according to the papyrus Lord Evandale found in her rock tomb with her mummy, asleep in a loveliness enduring for three thousand years. Tscherepnin's music has as outstanding numbers a "Dance of Nubian Slaves," a "Sacred Lotus Dance," and a Love Duet. None of these scores earned their composer, as did Verdi's *Aïda* when first given in Italy (Milan, 1872), an ivory baton set with diamonds, rubies and other gems and thirty-two recalls.

I

## "AÏDA"

GIUSEPPE VERDI. Original "story" by Mariette Bey, the famous Egyptologist; French book by Camille du Locle; Italian version by Ghislanzoni (Cairo, 1871). The first score of the composer's third period, *Aïda* was written for the dedication of the Cairo Théâtre Italien and the opening of the Suez Canal, among the royal guests of the Khedive of Egypt at the *première* being the late Empress Eugénie of France. Genuine Oriental airs are convincing examples of the use of Eastern local color in a score rich in beautiful melodies, outstanding in the famous romances "Celeste Aïda," "L'insana parola," and "O cieli azzurri," while the Finale to Act II ranks as one of the most grandiose scenic and musical conceptions of its kind.

In Memphian Pharaoh's palace, Rhadames, captain of the guard, is loved by Aïda, an Ethiopian slave (daughter of Amonasro, king of Ethiopia), and by Amneris, Pharaoh's daughter. Rhadames loves Aïda. Amneris, suspecting the slave girl's passion, feigns friendship for her to confirm her suspicions. When Rhadames, invested with consecrated armor in the temple of Pthah, leads the Egyptian army against the Ethiopians, Aïda mourns the fate which makes her lover her father's foe.

While Moorish slaves dance before Amneris, Aïda enters, mourning her father's defeat. When Amneris falsely tells her Rhadames has been killed, Aïda betrays her love for him; and Amneris makes Aida crouch on the steps of the throne when Pharaoh and his daughter receive the victors before the gates of Thebes, and Pharaoh rewards Rhadames with the unwelcome gift of Amneris' hand.

As Aïda waits for Rhadames to keep a nocturnal tryst on the banks of the Nile, her father Amonasro appears and threatens to disown her unless she makes Rhadames disclose the road the Egyptian army will take when it invades Ethiopia on the morrow. Then he hides. Rhadames now appears, tells Aïda he will refuse Amneris' hand and demands her own instead. Aïda assures him Amneris will not consent to be jilted. Rhadames promises to fly with her. Unwittingly he mentions the road the Egyptian army will take, Amonasro breaks triumphantly from his hiding place, and Rhadames realizes he has betrayed his country. About to flee with Aïda and her father, he is discovered by Rampis, the high priest, and Amneris, who raise the alarm. Aïda and Amonasro escape; Rhadames is made prisoner.

Golden light fills the judgment hall in Pthah's temple; gloomy darkness shrouds the subterranean vault of punishment opening from it (the stage shows both floors). While the priests above seal the tomb, Rhadames, condemned to be buried alive as a traitor, calls on Aïda—who comes to him out of the shadows. She has crept in to share his fate, not caring to live without him. The lovers expire in each other's arms, singing their swan song "O terra addio!" while above their sealed sepulcher the sighs of repentant Amneris mingle with the solemn chant of the temple priestesses.

## 2. The Serpent of the Nile

Cleopatra is a favorite heroine of the musical drama. Operas inspired by her include: the Spaniard Pedrell's *Cleopatra* (Madrid, 1881); Freudenberg's Wagnerian *Kleopatra* (Madgeburg, 1882); Leroux's theatrical *Cléopâtre* (Paris, 1890) after Sardou, showing her disguised as a boy in a ribald Alexandrian tavern scene (Act I) and preferring the serpent's tooth to the Roman triumph (Act IV); Findeisen's *Kleopatra* (Hamburg, 1897); Le Borne's *Cléopâtre* (Rouen, 1914) and Massenet's *Cléôpatre* (Monte Carlo, 1914) a score of his creative old age which has not materially increased his fame. *Kleopatra* (Copenhagen, 1893) by the Dane, August Enna, after Rider Haggard's novel, makes Harmaki, rightful claimant to the Egyptian throne, bury a dagger in his breast rather than kill the fascinating queen he has learned to love.

### "CLEOPATRA'S NIGHT"

Henry Hadley. Book by Alice Leal Pollock (New York, 1920), after Théophile Gautier's *Une nuit de Cléopâtre*. Cleopatra's Air, "I love you," the Intermezzo, the vivid, passionate Oriental dances, and final scene stand out.

Mardion, Cleopatra's maid, loves Meiamoun, an Egyptian lad, and is discussing with her companion, Iras, her own innocent and her mistress's scandalous love-life, when the queen appears. Lamenting her loneliness (?) Cleopatra is about to seek solace in the bath when an arrow falls at her feet. "I love you!" declares the strip of papyrus attached to its shaft. The archer is Meiamoun, who has swum through the conduit leading from the Nile and whose head now appears above the water. About to order his demise, Cleopatra remembers her loneliness and at the youth's ardent plea promises him a night of love, to end with his death at sunrise. As Meiamoun joyfully accepts her boon, Mardion kills herself and is flung to the crocodiles.

While Cleopatra lingers with her lover within the palace her guests wait on the terrace without. Then comes the orgy (Ballet) lasting till daybreak. The queen is half minded to spare her boyish lover but the fatal draught has been prepared. Why waste it? The "distiller of poisons" presents the horn goblet. Meiamoun drinks, falls dead at Cleopatra's feet and as trumpets announce Mark Anthony, Cleopatra rises to press on his living lips the kiss she has culled from slain Meiamoun's brow.

Massé's posthumous opera, *Une nuit de Cléopâtre* (Paris, 1885), tells the same tale, as does the Russian ballet, *Cléopâtre,* originally known as *Nuit d'Égypte* (Petrograd, 1900), in which Hebrew, Greek and Egyptian dancing girls swirl in a riot of white limbs, radiant color and frenzied movement in the orgy, by Arensky.

### 3. *Chaldea, Babylon, Assyria*

Herbert Spencer (*Some Musical Heresies*) asked why no composer ever proceeds from the complex to the simple in developing a composition, instead of vice versa. Vincent d'Indy answered his question in his symphonic variations depicting the old Chaldean myth, "The Descent of Ishtar," found on clay tablets of the library of the Assyrian King Assurbanipal among the ruins of Nineveh.

*Istar* (Paris, 1912) by Vincent d'Indy: Dance Poem. Dumuzi, the young sun god slain in the holy forest of Eridhu, has gone to the Chaldean Hades, "the land whence there is no return, where the shades of the dead dwell in the dark, clothed with wings, like birds"; and there the goddess Ishtar, his love, follows to claim him. At each of the seven gates of the Chaldean hell the keeper of the gate despoils Ishtar of one of her veils and the choregraphic action leaves her about to enter the realm of the dead. D'Indy's symphonic variations begin with the richest and most complex forms. They grow simpler and less involved as they proceed till, at last the theme only is revealed at the close. Each variation represents one of the seven stages of Ishtar's descent. Each loses in elaboration as Ishtar is stripped of her veils and jewels, until with the appearance of the theme unadorned the dancer is supposed to "stand forth in the full splendor of nudity." *Istar* (Prague, 1924), ballet, by the Czech Martinu, has been called "watered Debussy." Peter von Winter's *Babylons Pyramiden* (Vienna, 1797), Portogallo's mediocre *Semiramide* (London, 1808), made famous by Catalani's singing, and Catel's *Semiramide* (Paris, 1808) were cast in the shade by Rossini's genial Assyrian score whose brilliant Overture and the air "Bel raggio lusinghier" survive it.

*Semiramide* (Venice, 1823; New York, 1826) by Rossini, book by Rossi after Voltaire's tragedy based on Herodotus. Semiramide has murdered her husband Ninus, aided by her lover Assur. From him her fickle fancy turns to young Arsaces, who loves Princess Azema. When King Ninus' restless shade bids Arsaces seek his tomb at midnight, Assur, to prevent ghostly disclosures, hides in the tomb with dagger bared. But Semiramide has learned that the supposed Scythian boy is her own child, and the dagger meant for Arsaces is sheathed in her breast. Arsaces in turn slays Assur and temple gongs chime in honor of his wedding to Azema and his elevation to the Assyrian throne. The Duet, "Giorno d'orrore" (Act II) is reputed one of the finest examples of Italian *bel canto* melody.

The tragic end of Assyria's last king has called forth various scores. Aside from Famintsine's *Sardanapale* (Petrograd, 1875) and Duvernoy's *Sardanapale* (Liége, 1892), Victorin de Joncières' *Sardanapale* (Paris, 1867) after Lord Byron's poem, with a French

Wagnerian setting, has dramatic pages. Cruel Belasis, high priest of Baal, is about to knife on the altar Myrrha, the lovely Ionian slave, when Sardanapalus, the "man-queen," saves her to spend happy hours in his harem before it goes up in flame with its inmates. *Sardanapal* (Berlin, 1908) by Josef Schlar (music based on original Paul Taglioni score) is a spectacular ballet, *mise en scène* by the famous Assyriologist, Delitzsch, its climax a mad "Taumelbechertanz" ("Beaker Dance of Delirium") in which Sardanapalus' favorite slave, downing a golden beaker brimming with wine, tears off her jewels and falls senseless, thus typifying the breakdown of the Assyrian monarchy. Despite the personal interest of ex-Emperor William II of Germany it fell flat. *Assurbanipal* (Petrograd, 1916) by Albert Coates, its story based on the clay tablet "books" of Assurbanipal's (Sardanapalus') own Nineveh library, is musically interesting, since the composer is said to have "restricted himself to the ingredients of a *single chord*—but a chord of mighty dimensions."

### 4. *The Bible in Opera*

#### THE OLD TESTAMENT

Operatic creation is responsible for various Adams, among them *Adam und Eva* (Munich, 1870) by von Hornstein, and *Adam and Eve* (Christiania, 1924) by Torjussen, a "dance pantomime." Berlioz admired "the originality of melody, antique coloring and dreamy harmonies" of Lesueur's *La mort d'Adam* (*The Death of Adam,* Paris, 1809) ; but the *Eve* (Paris, 1875) of Massenet's sacred drama of that title (its prologue, "The Birth of Woman," is a fine page) is a neurotic Parisienne rather than a mother of mankind. *Die ersten Menschen* (*The First Human Beings*) by Rudi Stefan, an Austrian ultramodernist killed in the World War, presents the first family as a whole to a somewhat erotic book by Borngräber. An amiable Adam, a passionate, elemental Chawa (Eve), a gentle Chabel (Abel) and a savage Kajin (Cain) play the rôles assigned them in biblical narrative. "Musical color-complexes" are used to express moods and the "Thank Offering," "Love Magic," and "Mystic Close" scenes have been praised. Rubinstein's sacred opera *Das verlorene Paradies* ("Paradise Lost," Weimar, 1855), after Milton, contrasts light and darkness, heaven and hell in tone, the orchestra programmatically describing the fall, the expulsion, and the closing of Eden's gates on our hapless progenitors. Rubinstein died of heart failure while writing his opera trilogy *Kain und Abel,* but other composers survived to make earth's first killer the hero of their scores.

*Kain* (Berlin, 1900) by Eugen d'Albert, book by Bulthaupt. While Eve, Abel, and Hanoch (Cain's little son) recall happy days in Eden, Cain curses God and when Lucifer declares death only frees man from life's hardships, Cain plans to use death as a weapon against the Almighty. When Abel prevents his destroying God's altar, he kills him with an ax (Adam saves little Hanoch from the same fate); but Cain's wife makes him realize his awful crime and he departs with her and their boy to wander penitently about the world according to God's command. A symphonic opera, its most stirring musical moment is that in which God's voice calls the murderer to account.

*Kain und Abel* (Darmstadt, 1914) by Felix Weingartner gives the tale a modern psychological twist. D'Albert's Cain slays his brother to bring redeeming death into the world. Weingartner's Cain is a murderer for love. Lilith, according to old rabbinical legend, was Adam's companion before he met Eve. Abel, Lilith's boy, is born in the golden light and happiness of Eden. Cain, Eve's son, is the wretched offspring of the days of banishment. The two quarrel for Ada, Cain's half-sister. While Abel hunts the lost paradise Cain forces Ada to his will and when, in a passionate love scene, Abel tears the girl from him Cain uses his ax (off stage). In the dramatic score Ada's E flat major melody and Abel's heroic "Monologue" stand out.

Donizetti has told the story of the Deluge in his *Diluvio universale* (Naples, 1830) while *Noë* (Noah), Halévy's posthumous score, completed by Bizet, makes the angel Ithuriel entertain the patriarch in his heavenly mansion with a grand ballet of dancing girls in its concluding act. Noah's "Chanson d'ivresse" (Song of Drunkenness") might be mentioned. Claude Terrasse's *La petite femme de Loth* ("Lot's Little Wife," Paris, 1900), an *opéra bouffe* with happy musical numbers, illustrates French irreverence in the treatment of the biblical subject. Lot's wife, after leaving Gomorrah, turns back to look for her lover Melech. Both turn to salt but—a radical departure from Holy Writ—their crystallizations melting under the influence of mutual tenderness, they disappear together into a grove.

In *L'amico Fritz* ("Friend Fritz," Dresden, 1892) by Mascagni, a lighter score, Susel the village girl uses the story of Isaac and Rebecca to reveal her love for the bachelor landowner Fritz Kobus, as she gives his friend Rabbi David a drink of well water. Once this tale of patriarchal days has been told, Fritz (Act III) takes blushing Susel to his heart and both are happy. *Rebecca* (Paris, 1918) by César Franck is a one-act "biblical scene," with a book by Paul Collin, as is Charles Koechlin's *Jacob chez Laban* (Paris, 1925).

*Joseph* (Paris, 1807) by Méhul, the composer's greatest work and *the first opera without a love interest or a leading feminine rôle*, finds its dramatic climax in the recognition of Joseph by his father and brothers. It has "broad and vibrant harmonies, graceful accompanimental designs, and its expression always is genuine" (Berlioz). The sentimental "I was a youth" is the outstanding song. A more hectic Joseph than the hero of Méhul's innocent melodies has been presented by one of the most famous of modern dramatic composers in a ballet.

## "LA LÉGENDE DE JOSEPH"

### (*The Legend of Joseph*)

RICHARD STRAUSS. Book by Count Kessler and Hugo von Hoffmannsthal (Paris, 1914). The most elaborate, musically and scenically, of all modern dance dramas; Oriental colors and rhythms are prominent in the orchestral score. Outstanding are: the Intermezzo after the Banquet Scene; Oriental Dances (especially that of the "Sulamite," in which the *Salome* "ecstasy" motive appears); and the charming episode of "Joseph's Dream." The ballet is staged in Renaissance Italy (in the style of Veronese's painting "The Marriage at Cana"); the Egyptians wear Venetian dress of the Renaissance, and the merchants who sell Joseph, the garb of the sixteenth century Levant. A symbolic program makes Madame Potiphar represent the craving for the joys of this world, and Joseph innocence and the simple life. The actions of the Egyptian captain's wife are motived by her hope that if she can win the Hebrew shepherd boy's love, she will enter into *his* world of innocence and light.

In his palace hall Captain Potiphar watches a slave pour gold dust—Joseph's purchase price—into a golden bowl. Other slaves bring gifts to his wife, gems, rich rugs, Macedonian greyhounds. But she is bored. Potiphar beckons, and after Oriental dancers have depicted the unveiling of a bride on her wedding night in frankest pantomime, Turkish boxers fight until whipped apart by Potiphar's guards. Still Madame Potiphar is bored. But when Joseph, carried on in a litter, steps forth in his kirtle of white kid-skins (emblem of innocence) and dances, expressing his quest for the Divine, she is delighted and hangs a necklace of gems about his neck. Dusk deepens when the Potiphars leave the hall, and a servant, torch in hand, leads Joseph to the little room where he kneels in prayer before retiring. Alas, his rest is disturbed by the intrusion of Madame Potiphar! When she strokes his curls he thinks it a motherly caress; but when her lips touch his own his innocency is alarmed. Wrapping his mantle about him he runs from his cell, but the lady pursues, catches and presses him to her. At the cost of a torn mantle Joseph defies her blandishments, and in her rage she tries to strangle him. Then, handing him over to the slaves who enter, she faints. On Potiphar's advent she accuses Joseph of her own crime, and the torturers come in with the red-hot brazier and tongs. At this critical moment a golden archangel appears. As he touches the Hebrew boy, the latter's chains fall from him, and he moves off with the heavenly visitant leaving Madame Potiphar petrified with shame. Balked of passion, revenge, and penitence, the wretched woman strangles herself with her pearl necklace, Potiphar shrinking back in horror, and while her women cover her body with a black cloth, the Archangel and Joseph disappear.

Arthur Rahlwes' irreverent musical comedy *Madame Potiphar* (Halle, 1921), music in the style of d'Albert and Wolf-Ferrari, is a more recent version of the tale.

*Mosè in Egitto* (Naples, 1818; as *Moïse en Egypte,* Paris, 1827), by Rossini, book by Trottola, was one of Rossini's most successful operas. The music comprises effective dances, a sonorous "Warrior March," and the famous "Prayer" (Act III). Moses having cursed the Egyptians with darkness, Pharaoh Sesostris is about to let the Hebrews depart when he discovers his son Pherisis has secretly married Elcia, a Hebrew girl. Fearing to lose his daughter-in-law he forbids the tribal migration. At once thunder, lightning, storm, and hail (musical opportunities improved by the composer) strike the Egyptians. While Pherisis and Elcia flee to the interior of a pyramid, Moses threatens Egypt with the death of the first-born. Sesostris, hoping to save Pherisis, has him proclaimed Pharaoh; but Moses appears at the coronation ceremonies to curse, and poor Pherisis is struck by lightning when he tries to stab him. Singing hymns of praise Moses and the Israelites hurry to the Red Sea, followed by Pharaoh and his chariots. The prophet addresses his moving "Prayer" to heaven, and as it is taken up by the tribes on their knees, the waves pile mountain high on either hand, leaving a free passage for the fugitives to escape. *Moses* (Riga, 1894), Anton Rubinstein's undramatic "sacred opera," tells with occasional inspired pages the story of Moses' life from his finding among the bulrushes to his death in sight of the Promised Land. Musically Rubinstein's "brilliant description of the Ten Commandments is superior to Rossini's" (Act I).

Joshua has been immortalized musically in Moussorgsky's dramatic cantata, *The Fall of Jericho.* Kozeluch, the Bohemian, who succeeded Mozart as court composer in Vienna, wrote a *Deborah e Sisera* (Vienna, 1787), as did his fellow countryman Josef B. Förster, *Deborah* (Prague, 1893), a century later. Musically more important is the setting of *Debora e Jaele* (Milan, 1923) by a brilliant Italian modernist, Ildebrando Pizetti, no simple story of Deborah's prophecy and Jael's driving the iron nail through the temples of Sisera, the beaten captain, as he lies sleeping. Instead, in a fourfold conflict, figure: Deborah, the prophetess; Jael, the loving woman; Sisera, the kind-hearted soldier who opposes love's laws to Old Testament decrees; and the Hebrew mob, a composite creature of shifting passions. The struggle ends in Sisera's death and expiation. The score is dramatic, the melodies and rhythms of its music compressed in what d'Indy calls "thematic cells." The tale of Jephthah's daughter, whom he burned to death as a thank offering to Jehovah for his victory over the Ammonites, has been told in Giorgio Miceli's *La Figlia di Jepthe* (Naples, 1886); while the biblical idyl Ruth, principally represented in the field of cantata and oratorio, has at least one operatic setting by a composer of distinction, Michael Ippolitov-Ivanov's *Ruth* (Tiflis, 1887). The Czech Zamrzla's biblical music drama *Samson* (Prague, 1920) has not challenged the popularity of Saint-Saëns' great score.

## "SAMSON ET DALILA"

CAMILLE SAINT-SAËNS. Book by Ferdinand Lemaire (Weimar, 1877). Rameau, Graupner, and Handel wrote Samson operas, but Saint-Saëns' is the most widely popular score that treats the subject. It tells the dramatic Old Testament story in beautiful and passionate Orientai music. An effective ballet, the "Bacchanale," is included in the score; and the voluptuous air, "My heart at thy sweet voice," is world renowned.

When Abimelech boasts that Dagon, god of the Philistines, has overcome Jehovah, Samson gives the signal for revolt by slaying the boaster with his own sword. Israel conquers in battle, hymns of praise fill the air, and the loveliest maids of Philistia, among them bewitching Delilah, appear to move the victor's heart with song and dance. An old Hebrew warns Samson—but when have the young heeded the old? The Hebrew strong man falls a ready victim to Delilah's charms.

Delilah's hatred for Samson—she knows he really does not love her, and that he has a wife at home—is fanned by the high priest of Dagon. He bids her discover the secret of Samson's superhuman strength, so Delilah coaxes and caresses. At first Samson resists but finally, like many another man, tells her his secret against his better judgment. Then the seductress draws him into her chamber, uses her shears, and appears at the window, the shorn locks in her hand, to signal the Philistines that they may safely seize the hairless hero.

Samson, erstwhile pride of his people and terror of his foes, blinded, an object of derision, turns a treadmill in his dungeon prison. His bitter self-reproaches are too late. Finally, his enemies lead him to Dagon's feast of triumph, there to make a mock of him and his God, but seizing the mighty pillars that support the roof, Samson brings them crashing down on himself and his foes, sharing the death he visits upon them.

William Sutor's *David* (Stuttgart, 1812) and the Italian Amilcare Galli's *David* (Milan, 1904) deal with the shepherd king. Musically outstanding is the French modernist Arthur Honegger's *Le Roi David* (Jorat, 1921), book by Morax, presenting a series of tableaux, "David the Shepherd," "The Slaying of Goliath," "David before Saul," "The Witch of Endor," "David and Bathsheba," in music rich in exact and colorful orientalism. "Lamentations" on the battle of Gilboa, the "Dance before the Ark" and the tremendous final chorus, "The Death of David," are notable pages. *Saul and David* (Copenhagen, 1902), by Carl Nielsen, has a fine musical score and closely follows the Bible, with its climax in the battle of Gilboa. King Solomon in all his glory is well represented in opera. Alexiev Titov, a Russian cavalry general who wrote in Mozart's manner, composed *Zarya Salmona (Judgment of Solomon,* Petrograd, 1805) ; Rubinstein has written a biblical stageplay *Sulamith* (Hamburg, 1883) ; and the German modernist Paul von Klenau, among others, an opera *Sulamith* (Munich, 1914), oriental in color and Debussyan in style. Two well-known scores deal with the monarch of a thousand wives and the Queen of Sheba.

## "DIE KÖNIGIN VON SABA"

### (*The Queen of Sheba*)

KARL GOLDMARK. Book by Mosenthal (Vienna, 1875; New York, 1885). The composer's most famous score: it offers glowing, colorful pictures of the Orient, music of sensual charm, and a graceful Ballet, "The Dance of the Bee," in which the search for the insect supposed to be hiding beneath their garments is the theme of the dancers' variations. The music has been accused of lack of sincerity, and the tale has little to do with the Bible.

Assad, King Solomon's favorite, traveling in a far land, sees a lovely woman bathing in a forest pool. He returns to Jerusalem minus his peace of mind, but the author of the Proverbs assures him marriage to Sulamith, the high priest's daughter, will bring forgetfulness of the stranger. The Queen of Sheba appears at Solomon's court, drops her veil, and Assad recognizes her as his lady of the bath. When he passionately casts himself at her feet, however, she denies knowing him, for the Queen will not yield her crown to wed her Jewish lover. Meeting him by moonlight in the palace gardens, the loves of the forest pool are renewed, however, and the following day, at the wedding, Assad flings Sulamith's ring at her feet. But when he hastens to Sheba, she again disclaims all knowledge of him. It is not surprising that Assad curses God, and is led off by guards to be put to death as a blasphemer.

After the ballet, "The Dance of the Bee," the King coldly refuses

Sheba's request that Assad be pardoned; though he commutes his sentence from death to banishment.

In the desert she once more tempts Assad. But the desert has no pool and Assad, strong in virtue, curses her and begs heaven to bless his deserted bride. Entering on the scene after a sand storm which mortally wounds him, Sulamith arrives in time to let Assad's soul pass with the sigh "Released!" as cradling him in her arms she points out the eternal joys awaiting them above.

*La reine de Saba* (Paris, 1862) by Charles Gounod, book by Barbier and Carré, whose lyric melodies "Inspirez-moi" and "Plus grande dans son obscurité" endure, tells the love story of Adoniram, a famous Hebrew sculptor, and Balkis, Queen of Sheba. Though he refuses his workmen a raise and they vainly try to wreck his statue in the casting (Act II), he wins Balkis' heart (Act III) and drawing the engagement ring from Solomon's finger after she has put him to sleep with a narcotic, she hurries off to elope with her affinity (Act IV). Alas, Adoniram, hastening through the vale of Hebron on the same errand, is stabbed by three strikers (Act V), and Balkis arrives only to fling herself on the beloved corpse and curse the murderers!

Variations of the Judith story include Götze's *Judith* (Magdeburg, 1887); Serov's *Judith* (Petrograd, 1862), a Meyerbeerian score with effective dances; George Whitfield Chadwick's *Judith* (Worcester, 1900); and the German modernist Max Ettinger's *Judith* (Nuremberg, 1922), a music drama based on old Hebraic themes in which stand out "a brutal march full of rattling armor and swords," and the aria "Liberation of Jerusalem." In *Holofernes* (Berlin, 1923) by E. N. von Rezniček, after Hebbel, the heroine in Holofernes' tent (Oriental Ballet) cuts off his head as he lies in a drunken stupor and (Epilogue) when her fellow-Hebrews refuse to kill her, dies by her own hand. Suggesting *Aïda* in its Oriental color, the score employs the whole-tone scale and (thematically original) is Straussian in style.

*Judith* (Mezières, Switzerland, 1925) by Arthur Honegger is a biblical drama in a fine modernist "mosaic" score, in which the "Lamentations" (Act I), the Incantation Scene (Act II), and the "Chant of Victory" (Act III) stand out. The familiar tale ends with the departure of the heroine, carrying off in a kind of breadbasket the head she is obliged to sever to preserve her virtue, and with the triumphant defeat by the Jews of their enemies who, like their leader, have lost their heads.

*La chaste Suzanne* (Paris, 1839) by Moupou irreverently handles the episode of the virtuous bather and the shameless elders and charmed *boulevardiers* in the days of the "Citizen-King."

Rubinstein's *Die Makkabäer* (*The Maccabees,* Berlin, 1875), after Joarim, Benjamin and Eleazar Maccabaeus have been burned before their mother's eyes (Act III), rises to a climax in her death while Antiochus, King of Syria, etc., goes mad (Act IV), as Judas Maccabaeus, acclaimed King of Israel, enters the royal tent. Fine old Hebraic melodies and an erotic song of three slave girls, "one of the most voluptuous original melodic blossoms of Rubinstein's genius," stand out.

*Esther* (Kiel, 1922) by Albert Mattausch, after Grillparzer, a modern grand opera with fine choruses, preceded Antoine Mariotte's *Esther, Princesse d'Israël* (Paris, 1925). King Assuerus of Persia selects Esther (brought up by Mordecai as Israel's hope) among Persia's loveliest maids as his new queen; and her fascinations enable her to get the better of the Amalekite minister Aman (Haman) and bring about his death and the destruction of his people. The Overture, containing the "musical psychological substance" of the drama, Esther's duets with Mordecai and Assuerus (Finale), the thrilling chorus of the Jews as they storm the palace in Susa and massacre the Amalekites, and a great Choral Ballet (Act II) stand out.

*Nabuco* (*Nebuchadnezzar,* Milan, 1842; New York, 1848) by Verdi is remembered only as his first great success; *Nabuchodonozor* (Paris, 1911) by the French impressionist Grovlez, contains dances which might have delighted the Babylonian king before his salad days. Kastalsky, one of Russia's leading church musicians, wrote a *Furnace of Nabuco* (Moscow, 1909), a biblical opera presented with "Chaldeans in costume and a glowing furnace"; his compatriot Korestchenko has composed *Belshazzar* (Moscow, 1891). *Daniel in der Löwengrube* (*Daniel in the Lion's Den,* Hamburg, 1914) is a clever comedy opera by Amalie Nikisch.

## THE NEW TESTAMENT

### "SALOME"

RICHARD STRAUSS. German music drama in one act. Book after Oscar Wilde's play (Dresden, 1905). Oscar Wilde's perverted, erotically degenerate Salome, who "like most of the women of her time was suckled with the venom of serpents and reared among corpses," is realistically expressed by an orchestra of 120 players. The singers are incidental, intoning rather than singing. It is the most offensively effective opera of the modern repertoire. Some forty leading motives are used in the score, notable for unity of color and passion. Its outstanding musical numbers are: Salome's passionate "I will kiss thy mouth, Jochanaan"; the grotesque, naturalistic "Hebrew Quintet" of the Jews quarreling before Herod; the "Jewel Aria," and the "Dance of the Seven Veils."

Narraboth, captain of Herod's guard, keeping watch on the terrace of the palace at Tiberias, shudders to hear a mysterious voice sound in the night. It is Jochanaan (John the Baptist) from his cistern prison cursing the sinful Tetrarch of Judea and his court. His voice lures the Princess Salome from banquet hall to terrace. Wearied of familiar vices she yearns to indulge in novel, unknown lusts . . . her erotic fancies turn to the holy man in the well. But when she has coaxed the infatuated captain to hale forth his prisoner, and by her shameless wooing of the man of God has driven love-mad Narraboth to fall on his sword, the indignant prophet curses her and returns to his pit. Now Herod and his drunken courtiers stagger out upon the terrace, and while the Tetrarch's devouring glances sweep her, Salome begs that Jochanaan be slain. Herod hesitates, while fanatic Jews quarrel as to whether Jochanaan is or is not a prophet. Again the voice sounds from the well, rousing Herod's rage and Salome's lustful desires. The Tetrarch bids her dance and Salome dances the "Dance of the Seven Veils," casting them from her one by one with erotic abandon, and finally demanding the Baptist's head on a charger. Reluctantly Herod hands the executioner his signet ring; he descends into the pit. Salome listens greedily till a great black arm rising above the cistern rim holds out Jochanaan's head on a silver platter. Triumphantly Salome flings herself upon it, passionately mumbling the dead lips. "As Salome kisses Jochanaan's head, the organ sounds a low C minor chord, cut by second-intervals, bloodily dripping with Salome's red leading motive, suspended from the silver threads of the violins." Herod shudders. Even his base soul revolts. "Kill me this woman!" he commands, and his guards crush the wanton between their brazen shields.

The success of Strauss's opera made dancing Salomes an almost obligatory feature of the dramatic and musical stage for several years, and for a time no self-respecting *café chantant* was without one. More important than Antoine Mariotte's lyric tragedy, *Salomé* (Lyons, 1908), after Wilde, and Gabriel Pierné's lyric pantomime *Salomé* (Paris, 1895), and antedating Strauss's, is a pantomime score by Florent Schmitt, *La tragédie de Salomé* (Paris, 1907), book (mute drama) by d'Humières (danced by Loie Fuller, 1912; Trouhanova; 1913, Karsavina). A "Dance of Pearls," in which Herodias hands her daughter pearls from a brimming chest on the palace terrace, precedes a scene of sorcery on the Dead Sea. Sodom and Gomorrah beneath the waves breathe forth evil suggestion to Salome. Schmitt's music evokes fragments of drunken song, strangled by a rain of bitumen and cinders, snatches of dance tunes, clapping of hands, stifled passion-sighs, maniac laughter. Suddenly, born of the dreams of

ancient sin, Salome's dance begins. As lightnings flash Herod
seizes her veils and tears them away, but the Baptist appears and
covers Salome's white form with his mantle. Herod's gesture of
rage summons the executioner who leads John off, reappearing
with his head on a brazen charger. Salome seizes it, then as
though the dead lips had murmured in her ear, casts it from the
terrace into the sea. The waters turn blood-red and Herod, Herodias, slaves, guards and executioner flee while Salome swoons.
When she regains consciousness the gory head rises everywhere
before her. She whirls into a mad dance of terror. The storm
whips the Dead Sea into monstrous waves. Pillars of sand crash
on the desert. Cypress trees are torn asunder by furious winds,
lightnings strike, and stones fly from castle walls. Mount Nebo
spits living fire and the hills of Moab glow red as the dancer
is whirled away in delirium. D'Humières' *Salomé*, like Wilde's,
is a perverse, cruel woman, but there is no fondling of the dead
head. The poignantly beautiful prelude, the "Dance of the Pearls,"
a barbaric "Dance of Negroes" (Ethiopian slaves with ostrich
plumes about their loins and in their hair), and an effective Oriental three-part chorus stand out. *The Vision of Salome* (London,
1908), dance drama by Maude Allan to a musically graceful score
of Marcel Rémy, reveals Salome as "an innocent girl of fourteen." She dances to please father Herod and mother Herodias
and kindly Herod bids her ask a boon. "Pray, mamma, what shall
I ask?" whispers guileless Salome and prompted by her parent
puts the historic demand. Then the child victim of a sinful mother
kisses the cold lips of the head, *not* with voluptuous fervency, but
as "a mute prayer for the spiritual aid of a Christian prophet,"
her chaste caress calling up a fleeting vision of salvation, and
dancing a frenzied dance of infantile joy she falls exhausted to the
ground. Between the ghoulish Salome of Strauss and the incred-
ibly innocent one of Rémy stands the Salome of Massenet's opera.

## "HÉRODIADE"

JULES MASSENET. Book by Millet and Grémont (Paris, 1881). The
Temple's "Holy of Holies" is shown on the stage, but the work is secu-
lar in spirit. Herod's "Vision fugitive" and Salome's lovely Air "Il est
doux, il est bon" are lyric pages which endure.

Salome in search of a mother (she has been mysteriously parted from
Herodias as a child) tells her troubles to Phanuel, a young stargazer,
as the caravan moves toward Jerusalem. There Herod sees and fancies
her, but Salome yearns for John the Baptist, "who was kind to her"
in the wilderness. John has called Herodias a Jezebel, and she demands

his head, which Herod refuses. When entering the palace the prophet's fiery curses drive the royal pair in terror from the hall. Salome flings herself at his feet and confesses her love for him, only to be sternly rebuked.

King Herod cannot turn his thoughts from Salome. The dances of lovely Greek, Nubian, and Assyrian slave girls (Ballet) only make her seem fairer by contrast, till mentally he is so overwrought he conspires against his Roman masters (great mob and legion scene in the square of Jerusalem).

Herodias learns from Phanuel that Salome is her daughter only to repudiate her as her rival, and Herod follows the girl to the Temple, where she goes to pray for the imprisoned Baptist, who is tempted for a moment to murmur "I love you" to Salome. Herod's love is repulsed with horror, and he condemns the maiden and the Baptist to death.

In the palace Salome begs that John—whose head already has fallen—be spared, then seeing the executioner's bloodstained sword she raises her dagger against Herodias, learns she is her mother and sheathes it in her own breast.

The Christ ideal is reflected in Rubinstein's *Christus* (Bremen, 1895), his most ambitious biblical opera, meant to make Bremen a "sacred Baireuth." Its musical high moments are: the scene of the Magi Kings, the baptism of Christ, the raising of Lazarus, and the Last Supper—in which connection Richard Wagner's "biblical scene," *Das Liebesmahl der Apostel* (*The Apostles' Love Feast,* Dresden, 1843), should be mentioned. The Christ ideal is also reflected in Gabinetti's *Il Nazzareno* (Buenos Aires, 1911) and Franco Vittadini's *Nazareth* (Pavia, 1925), book by Adami, after Selma Lagerlöf's novel. *Les vierges folles* (*The Foolish Virgins*), a Swedish Ballet, by Atterberg (Paris, 1921) is a pantomime presentation of its subject, and the Belgian Désiré Paque's opera *Judas* (Warnemünde, 1910) deals with that deservedly unpopular apostle. The Prodigal Son and Mary Magdalen are operatic favorites.

*L'enfant prodigue* (Paris, 1850) by François Auber handles the tale of the Prodigal Son in lighter vein. A "March of the Bull Apis"—the White Way along which the prodigal sported being located in Egyptian Memphis—its melody progressing above the ingenious bellowing of an ophicleide accompaniment is noteworthy. *Il figliuol prodigo* (Milan, 1880), Ponchielli's spectacular biblical opera, book by Zarnandini, is musically superior to *Gioconda*. A fine Prelude to Act IV and a Chorus, "Pasqua del Signor," stand out. The orgies of the eater of husks are staged in ancient Nineveh, and a Babylonian Ballet and the burning of Nineveh are dramatic high points. *L'enfant prodigue* (Paris, 1897) by André Wormser, a graceful ballet pantomime, modernizes the biblical parable. A youth, bored to death at home, flees to the great city with Phrynette, after going through his father's safe. Driven to cheat at cards to keep Phrynette as she would be kept, he returns with gold to find she has left him for a wealthy *roué*. Broken bodily and in spirit, he hastens home to the fatted calf and enters the army to refurbish his tarnished honor. *L'enfant prodigue* (Paris, 1910) by Claude Debussy, a one-act lyric scene, adheres to the biblical original. While Simon and Leah mourn their wayward boy, Azaël enters tattered and torn, and falling on his knees is forgiven by his parents who praise God for having restored him to them.

*Die Toten Augen* (*The Dead Eyes*) by Eugen d'Albert, book by Ewers and Marc Henry (Dresden, 1916), Myrtocle's "Cupid and Psyche," an outstanding song, combines erotic, brutally realistic, and religious motives. Arcesius, a hideously homely Roman, has married a lovely Corinthian blind girl. She yearns to see the handsome husband of her imagination but her eyes are "dead." Hosannas announce the Christ on his way to the Holy City (Palm Sunday) and Myrtocle hastens to him to be healed. As the dead eyes He touches come to life, He murmurs, "Verily, woman, you will curse me before the going down of the sun!" Arcesius' friend, Galba, had advised her to appeal to the Nazarene. Myrtocle, hastening home mad with joy meets Galba and thinks him her husband. As he passionately returns her caresses Arcesius strangles him and Myrtocle flings herself on his body crying that her husband has been slain by a monster. Undeceived, she realizes the gift of sight has destroyed her happiness, and exposing her eyes to the sun-glare she again becomes blind. Arcesius, seeking her out filled with remorse, finds he has regained his wife of old, now content to live unseeing in the bright light of her dreams. The Magdalen appears only incidentally, her rapt announcement of Christ's coming bringing Myrtocle to Him.

*Maria di Magdala* (Milan, 1924) by Arrigo Pedrollo, book by Rossato, makes Publius, a Roman centurion, the Magdalen's lover and depicts the conversion of a "Thaïs" of old Judea. The suicide of Publius (typifying paganism) affirms the triumph of the Christian ideal. The music, "opalescent with Levantine tints," has highly dramatic moments. Striking is Mary's scene with Publius, close of Act I, where she cries, "Bite me on the mouth . . . give me death!" while a Christian anthem echoes ,purity and peace. *Marie-Magdalène* (Paris, 1873), Massenet's "sacred drama," created a sensation at its première. The composer and the librettist, Gallet, saw the biblical tale as a poetic legend. The French point of view is shown in a critic's mention of "Jesus' very successful stage entrance." Though the "Bible is doctored up to suit the taste of impressionable Parisian ladies" (Hervey) Massenet treated the love of the Christ and the Magdalen with delicacy, and Tschaikowsky says: "I was so moved by the emotion of the music in which Massenet depicts the Saviour's compassion that I shed many tears."

## 5. *Ancient Persia and Carthage*

*Zoroastre* (Paris, 1794) by Rameau tells the victory of the Persian god of light and his prophet over the god of darkness to noble, colorful music. The tone picture of the nether world of Ahriman (Act IV) has been called "a grandiose demoniac ensemble painting." In *Le Mage* (*The Magian,* Paris, 1891) by Massenet, book by Richepin, after Marion Crawford's novel *Zoroaster,* the holy man escapes the amorous pursuit of shameless Varedha, the priest Amrou's daughter, by taking refuge on a sacred mount. When the Turanians overcome the Persians, destroying their king and their temple, Zoroaster, returning to clasp his true love, the Turanian queen, Anahita, in his arms, finds Varedha's enchantments have surrounded them with a ring of flames. At his "Prayer" (the best musical number) the god Ahura-Mazda puts them out and Varedha, balked of love and revenge, "expires with a cry of jealous rage as he escapes with his sweetheart." Of Rossini's *Ciro in Babilonia* (*Cyrus in Babylon,* Ferrara, 1817) only the charming air "T'abbraccio" survives.

### "LA PÉRI"

#### (*The Peri*)

PAUL DUKAS. *The first lyric poem danced on the stage* (Paris, 1912), introduced "a new principle in the ballet: a free-form musical work, intimately united with mimic action, in which the mere picturesque had no part" (Robert Broussel). An idiomatic Oriental leading motive "courses through the score like the blood in an organic body, giving birth to the most varied and ingenious harmonic and contrapuntal combinations." (An earlier *Péri* [Paris, 1843], ballet pantomime, scenario by Théophile Gautier, music by Burgmüller, deals with the less poetic adventures of a péri who leaves the skies to supplant earthly beauties in a young Oriental's harem.)

The youth of Iskender, king of Iran, was drawing to an end. The Magians saw his star grow pale in the vaults of night. So Iskender, alarmed, traversed all Iran in search of the flower of immortality. At the uttermost limits of earth, where it merged with sea and clouds, on the great stairway leading to the abode of Ormuzd, Source of All Good, he saw a Peri slumbering in her jeweled robes. Above her head gleamed a star, her lute reposed on her breast, and in her hand glistened the lotus of immortality, green as an emerald, undulant like the wave beneath the sun of dawn. Iskender, bending noiselessly over the dreamer, drew the sacred flower from her grasp and it flamed in his hand like the noonday sky above the forests of Ghilan. Then the Peri, opening her eyes, smote together her palms in despair and uttered a great cry. The sacred flower ravished from her, she could no longer ascend toward the light of Ormuzd. Iskender admired her loveliness, surpassing that of Gurda-ferrid, and coveted her.

Then the sacred lotus in his hand blushed purple and glowed like the face of desire. And thereby the Peri, servant of the Pure One, knew the flower of immortal life was not destined for Iskender. She darted forward but Iskender withheld it from her, torn between thirst for eternal life and the delectation of his eyes. The Peri danced the "Dance of the Winged Ones," drawing nearer and nearer to Iskender until her face touched his face, and he yielded the lotus to her without regret.

Once more the Peri held the lotus, now a thing of snow and gold, like the summit of Mount Elborus in Mithra's dying ray; and she melted into the clear light rising from the lotus chalice, until naught remained but a hand, holding a flower of flame, which finally vanished in the upper regions. Iskender, seeing the Peri disappear, knew her departure betokened his approaching end, and as shadows gathered about him realized he had bartered the eternal delights of paradise for a fleeting moment's sensuous joy.

*Les Troyens* is a vast drama comprising two operas, *La prise de Troie* (elsewhere considered) and *Les Troyens à Carthage,* by "the father of modern orchestration," the latter the greatest operatic work dealing with ancient Carthage. *Les Troyens à Carthage* (Paris, 1863) by Hector Berlioz, book by Mérimée, after Virgil, has been called "the national opera of the Latin peoples" as Wagner's "Ring" cycle is that of the Germanic. In it Berlioz strove to attain purest beauty of form, and among its great pages are: the "Trojan March," the Septet, and Dido's and Æneas' Love Duet. Irabas' wooing rejected by Dido (Act I), Æneas, cast ashore at Carthage, reveals himself as King Priam's son, defeats Irabas and his Numidians and wins the heart of the Carthaginian queen. Nymphs bathing in a forest pool hide as Tyrian huntsmen appear (Act II), and when these scatter as the tempest breaks Dido and Æneas take refuge in a grotto. But neither stolen moments of passion nor festivals and dances (Act III) can hold the hero. The shades of Priam, Hector, and Cassandra urge him to set sail for Italy. Deaf to Dido's prayers he boards his ship and when she sees it dwindle on the horizon she mounts the funeral pyre. Prophesying the birth of Hannibal, her avenger, she kills herself with Æneas' sword, and above the sonorous strains of the "Trojan March" echo the curses of the people of Carthage on Æneas and the Roman race, whose founder he is destined to be. *Dido and Æneas* (London, 1675) by Purcell tells Virgil's story in three short acts, and Dido's death song, "When I am laid in earth," with its chorus of mourning Cupids, ranks as one of music's finest portrayals of the despair of a broken heart.

## "SALAMMBÔ"

ERNEST REYER. Book by du Locle after Flaubert (Brussels, 1890). If not always inspired, Reyer's music is lofty and sincere, his local color convincing, but the score has been accused of lacking the musical brilliancy Flaubert's theme demands. Salammbô's Aria (Act IV) in which, while doves of Carthage flit through evening skies, she sings sad presentiments of her love, is one of the finest lyric pages.

As revolted Carthaginian mercenaries revel in Hamilcar's palace gardens Salammbô, has daughter, appears to rebuke their license, only to find that the Libyan Matho, their leader, insists she marry him.

On the temple terrace Salammbô, to save her native city from the rebels is about to wrap the goddess Tanit's holy veil around her, though Shahabarim, the high priest, warns her it is death to do so, when Matho rushing up tears the veil from her and wrapping it round himself, escapes with it to his companions.

Hamilcar, appointed general of the Carthaginian army, demands a human sacrifice for Moloch, and the high priest (change of scene) seeks out Salammbô. She is to go to Matho and, pretending love, wrest the holy veil from him.

Narr'havas, King of Numidia, in Matho's tent, is treacherously offering to aid the rebel when Salammbô appears. Natt'havas tries to induce her to leave with him, but she stays with the Libyan to be caught with him in the toils of a true and passionate love. Matho yields the veil, yet when Salammbô wraps it about her, the tent blazes up in flame and drives them out (change of scene). Thanks to Narr'havas' treachery, Hamilcar has defeated the mercenaries, Matho is a prisoner, and the holy veil restored to Tanit's temple.

Matho is to be sacrificed to Moloch, and Salammbô is to kill him with her own hand. Yet loving Matho and unable to take his life, she stabs herself, and the Libyan, catching her as she sinks to the ground, falls on his own sword.

Flaubert's novel also has called forth a *Salammbo* (unfinished) by Moussorgsky, one by the Czech, Karl Navratil, and one by Niccolò Massa (Milan, 1880). *Moloch* (Dresden, 1906) by Max Schillings, after Hebbel, musically original, is cursed with "an impossible book." Hieram the Carthaginian saves Moloch's image from his burning natal city and bears it in a Punic galley to Ultima Thule. The gods' gifts (southern fruits and wine) shall voice the call of the sunny South to the primitive Gothic sons of the North, and draw them on to destroy Rome and avenge Carthage. Hebbel's cultural idea is the background for the love story of Theoda and Teut, which ends tragically owing to the intervention of Hieram and his idol.

### 6. *Vedic, Brahmin, and Buddhist India*

Many opera composers have paid tribute to the spell of Indian poesy, musical color and mystic thought, whether in connection with a vaguer, prehistoric background or a definite historic period. *La figlia del re* (*The King's Daughter*, Turin, 1922) by Adriano Lualdi is a tragic love tale of prehistoric India by an Italian ultramodernist. *Ikdar* (Dresden, 1921) by Gustav Mračzek is by a German modernist. Saothi, a sculptor of Vedic India, sees the Princess Riana, whose husband is insanely jealous, unveiled at a religious festival. The love of his dreams, he models her statue from memory. But the face betrays to Riana's husband the "psychic union" existing between the sculptor and his wife and he has the artist blinded. While the statue, obeying Ikdar, goddess of love, falls upon and crushes the Prince, the sculptor finds solace in visions unseen by mortal eye. *Le dieu et la bayadère* (*The God and the Bayadere*, Paris, 1830) by François Auber, an opera ballet after Goethe, in which Taglioni created the mimic rôle of the Bayadere, has effective numbers: the Overture, Elifour's Air "Le vin" and a charming nocturne, "O bords heureux du Ganges!" The god Mahadeo, descending to earth, is entertained by a temple girl. The "lost child's" meretricious interest in her divine visitor soon yields to a deep, pure love. In the morning the stranger is dead and when she leaps into the flames of his funeral pyre despite the Brahmins' objection that he was not her husband, the god rises with her in his arms to paradise. *Mahadeva* (Düsseldorf, 1910) by Felix Gotthelft, a Wagnerian dream of Brahmin gods, tells the same tale; while *The Temple Dancer* (New York, 1919) by John Adam Hugo, book by Jutta Bell-Ranske, shows the effect of religious prostitution on the intellect. A temple bayadere curses god Mahadeo when he refuses to interest himself in her love affairs, with a snake dance charms the guard about to slay her, then poisons him with water he brings her to drink, and again cursing Mahadeo as she tries to steal his jewels, is felled by lightning from the Hindoo heavens. In *Izeyl* (Hamburg, 1909) by Eugen d'Albert, book by Lothar, its music theatrically effective, Prince Scyndia brings the Hindoo courtesan Izeyl the tripod with the holy temple fire to show his love. Seized by the priests and only released when Scyndia's mother declares her *beneath* punishment, scorned Izeyl swears revenge. But Scyndia's father, a forest hermit, instead of falling a victim to her charms (Act II) converts her to a life of purity. When Scyndia brutally assails her new-won virtue Izeyl stabs him and, about to be killed, dies happy in the royal hermit's platonic embrace, while he sings his spiritual love for her. The Hindoo temple girl who turns into a religious rite what Christianity regards as a deadly sin occurs also in Catel's *La Bayadère* (Paris, 1810); Le Borne's *L'idole aux yeux verts* (*The Green-Eyed Idol*, Rouen, 1912); and the ballets *Mallika* (Paris, 1911) by Mathé; *Djali* (Paris, 1913) by Menier, and Pougin's *Les princesses de Rana* (Monte Carlo, 1913).

## "LES PÊCHEURS DE PERLES"

### (*The Pearl Fishers*)

GEORGES BIZET. Book by Carré and Cormon (Paris, 1863; London, 1887, as *Leila*). A tale of Ceylonese passion in prehistoric times, Narid's Air, "I hear as in a dream," and Nadir and Leila's love duet (Act II) stand out in a score whose charm of oriental color is confined in traditional Italianate forms.

Leila, the veiled priestess who comes to pray to Brahma that lustrous pearls may reward the divers' toil, lets Nadir know she loves him, and not his comrade Zurga. The joys of earthly love, however, Nourabad, the high priest, tells Leila (Act II) are not for Brahma's priestess. Bidding her mind her vows he has no sooner left her than Nadir enters, and the two lovers at once ardently sing their forbidden passion. Noura-bad who has returned and overheard, sternly tears Leila's veil from her guilty head and Zurga, Nadir's rival, sees that Leila is the same woman whom both he and Nadir solemnly swore never again to meet, in order to remain friends. Zurga, as captain of the pearl fishers, condemns to death the priestess who forgot her god and the man for whom she forgot him. About to be led to their doom the divers' camp goes up in flame (Act III). Zurga, noble fellow, has set it afire to allow the lovers to escape. Yet Nourabad has seen him, so Zurga takes the place of the guilty lovers on the flaming pyre while the people fling themselves down adoring Brahma.

From the Sanscrit epic poem, the *Mahabharata*, the Hindoo poet Kalidasa took and retold the story of "Sakuntala." The translations of this most charming of all East Indian love stories have inspired the musical versions.

## SAKUNTALA

Sakuntala, daughter of the nymph Mekana and King Viswami-tra, has been brought up in Father Kanva's hermitage, where "fearless fawns move softly on the close-cropped forest lawns."

During Kanva's absence King Dushyanta, hunting in the woods, chances on the sacred grove and laying aside his royal garb, is received by Sakuntala, "in maiden loveliness," as a simple traveler. Charmed by her beauty the king makes love to the hermit maid, marries her by "the simple, voluntary rite" which dispenses with "priest and witness" and giving her his signet ring departs, promising to return in three days' time. Alas, poor Sakuntala, lost in yearning for her absent husband, forgets to show due reverence to a bigoted pilgrim, and the latter lays a curse on her! She shall be forgotten by Dushyanta until he once more sees his ring upon her finger. The curse goes into effect. Dushyanta forgets his woodland love and falls into a melancholy, while Sakuntala, leaving the green hermitage of her childhood makes her way to the royal palace. There Dushyanta treats her as a stranger, and to her terror Sakuntala finds she has lost her betrothal ring while bathing in holy Mother Ganges. In despair she flees from Dushyanta's court, and taken in by a pious hermit, is carried up by Apsares to god Indra's paradise. Meanwhile a fisherman has found Dushyanta's signet ring in a carp's belly; and brought before the monarch, the latter, seeing the golden band, suddenly remembers his deserted wife. Then Indra, pitying his longing, sends down his own golden chariot to take him to paradise where he finds his beloved with whom he returns to his kingdom.

Ballet developments of the story include Ernest Reyer's *Sacountala* (Paris, 1858), romantically Oriental, and Bachrich's *Sakuntala* (Vienna, 1866), with graceful music suggesting Johann Strauss's Vienna rather than Brahminic Benares. Karl von Perfall's opera *Sakuntala* (Munich, 1853); Felix Weingartner's Wagnerian *Sakuntala* (Vienna, 1884), and Balduin Zimmermann's *Sakuntala* (Erfurt, 1905) seem musically less significant than *La Leggenda di Sakuntala* (Bologna, 1921) by Franco Alfano, an Italian ultramodernist's score, whose music, anti-veristic, yet dramatically vibrant and lyrically passionate, has been termed the essence of expressive pathos. It presents its tale beneath "a sky eternally lucid, serenely illuminating a life transfigured and, as it were, immaterial" (G. M. Gatti).

*Malawika* (Munich, 1866), by Weingartner, in which a vocal septet stands out, is after Kalidasa's drama, the *Malavikagnimitra*. King Agnimitra, who has two wives, makes room in his heart for Malavika, maid to his first queen. The two wives try to oust the intruder, but she turns out to be a princess born and becomes the third person in Agnimitra's bridal trinity.

*Urvasi* (Dresden, final version, 1909) by Wilhelm Kienzl, after Kalidasa's drama, an opera rich in colorful lyric music, shows Urvasi, loveliest of the Apsares (nymphs the god Indra sends to

earth to tempt saints from the narrow path) caught in a grove by
a demon. King Pururavas appears, rescues and falls in love with
her. But despairing of seeing his celestial sweetheart again, despite her promise, his lack of faith condemns her to an existence
in another shape. After seeking his lost love the wide world over
the King draws sword to slay himself when a rosebush is pointed
out to him. Kissing its flowers he prays Indra to restore his lost
love and Urvasi, who was the rosebush, stands before him. After
an exalted love duet her lover dies at her feet, and their souls
united, ascend to Svarga, Indra's paradise.

*Sita* (London, 1906) by Gustave Holst, after Kalidasa's drama,
*The Dynasty of Raghu,* tells the adventures of King Rama, torn
between love for his wife and duty to his subjects, and beautiful
Sita, faithful to the husband who rejects her. *Savitri* (London,
1921) by Gustave Holst, its dialogue developed in melody rhythmically and tonally free, is a "chamber opera" (small orchestra, female chorus, and three principals). Among its finest pages is
Savitri's "Appeal to Rama," a passionate invocation to the god of
death. The woodman Satyavan and his faithful wife Savitri are
in the forest when the former is stricken down by Rama. Savitri
dogs the god's footsteps till he promises to grant her a boon. When
she begs for a life free from *maya* (illusion), which obscures all
things, and he grants her request she claims Satyavan's life, without which his gift is incomplete. Moved by her constancy Rama
allows Satyavan to wake to life again in her arms. The Wagnerian
Hermann Zumpe in *Savitri* (Schwerin, 1907) also has set the
tale.

## "LE ROI DE LAHORE"

### (*The King of Lahore*)

JULES MASSENET. Book by Gallet, after the *Mahabharata* (Paris, 1877).
The clever handling of the exotic note in Massenet's first great success,
a tragic Hindoo tale, made the score popular. The Overture, "Marche
Celeste," the Chorus of Priestesses, and the Love Duet, "a thousand
times more beautiful and melodious than the one in Goldmark's *Queen
of Sheba*" (Tschaikowsky) yield in popularity to the lyric solos "Pro-
messe de mon avenir" and "Je cours après le bonheur."

Scindia, King Alim's minister, loves his niece Sita, a temple priestess.
When, in Indra's temple, Timour the high priest refuses to release her
from the vow of celibacy, Scindia threatens to ruin her by accusing her
of keeping love trysts before the altar with an unknown. Since she refuses to yield to Scindia's base desires he rings the gong, Timour enters,
and Sita is condemned to death on perjured testimony. At this moment King Alim enters. He was the innocent unknown lover, and

declares himself ready to lead his men against the Moslems at once if Sita will accompany him. The diplomatic high priest, eager to have the king strike a blow for the threatened temple fires, hands the maiden over to him.

In the desert of Thol Sita's gloomy forebodings are realized. The beaten Hindoo soldiery flood the stage, and when King Alim appears, mortally wounded by Scindia's traitor hand, he finds the latter has won over the army. Alim dies in Sita's arms, and the defeated host surges off to the cry of "On to Lahore!" dragging along the girl in its flight.

In the ballet, Indra's paradise, where the blue water walls of the god's palace are arched with living fire beneath domes of rainbow cloud, is the background for voluptuous dances of black-eyed nymphs of delight, the Apsares, whose tiny feet leave lotus prints in golden sands as they move to the dulcet strains of the god Nareda's flute. Yet Alim's soul, though celestial choirs sing the joys of its new home, is not happy. When Indra learns that unappeased longing for Sita turns paradise into hell for Alim, he allows him to return to earth with the proviso that when Sita dies he, too, must die.

In Lahore Scindia, crowned king, meets the living dead man on the temple steps and orders him slain. But Timour, who believes Alim divinely inspired, has his priests hide him in the temple.

It is there Sita has fled from Scindia, preferring to die rather than marry her uncle. But she no sooner has cast herself into Alim's arms than torches gleam and Scindia enters. As soldiers advance to seize Alim she stabs herself, and, dying in each other's embrace, the lovers leave Scindia foiled, their souls taking flight to Svarga, revealed in a vision of golden and jeweled splendor.

## "PADMAVATI"

ALBERT ROUSSEL. Book by Louis Laloy (Paris, 1923). A moving tale of a wife's fidelity in thirteenth century India. The music has noble choruses, ardent lyric pages, and stylistic affinities to Berlioz. Tonally outstanding is the great "Sacrifice Pantomime" in which the gods of the nether world mingle with human officiants.

Ferocious Alaouddin, Sultan of the Moguls, a guest in the Hindoo King Ratan-Sen's palace in Tchitor, has watched the dancing girls, "graceful as golden creepers, their eyes beneath the shadow of their lashes holding the distant glow of temple lamps" (the dances carry out the idea of the Pshari frescoes in the Anjuta temple), weave voluptuous rounds for his pleasure. He then insists on seeing Ratan-Sen's wife Padmavati, and having feasted his eyes on the Hindoo Helen, Alaouddin threatens that if she be not surrendered to him, his Moguls will attack the city and put every living soul to the sword. His demand refused, the city is at the point of surrender (Act II). But when Ratan-Sen, distraught by pity for his people, bids Padmavati sacrifice herself for their sake she kills him with her dagger, preferring death to dishonor. At night, as the Brahmins invoke the god Siva in his temple with magic rites, she joins her dead husband on the flaming pyre. Alaouddin, entering the city at the head of his hordes, forces the temple gates to win his desire, but only a red glow shows in the crypt whence his dream of love has vanished.

## "LE DIEU BLEU"

### (*The Blue God*)

REYNALDO HAHN. Book by Cocteau and Madrazzo (Paris, 1912). A legend of a fabulous Bakstian India, said to have been inspired by the stupendous temple ruins of Angkor in Cambodia. The score is sensuously and effectively Oriental and the outstanding musical pages those describing Krishna's "Scene with the Monsters."

Towering orange cliffs overshadow a temple shrine and pool. Brahmins and yogis appear. A youth is to be initiated into the priesthood. He sees the girl he loves, steps toward her, but—it is too late. Bayaderes swing into a frenzied dance, white kids are brought forward for sacrifice. As her lover, now a priest, strides by the girl drops sobbing at his feet. He spurns her, but her "Dance of Memories" (charming music with a vague Mozartian tinge) undermines his self-control. Tearing off his white robe symbolic of purity, he clasps her to him. The priests tear her away; chain her to the dark cavern haunted by reptile demons and leave her. When the moon rises upon her, she shrinks from the circling monsters, and her impassioned prayer to Krishna, the Blue God, evokes a miracle.

The giant lotus in the temple pool unfolds rosy petals, azure light illumines the sleeping waters. Krishna, silver flute in hand, steps from the sacred flower. Raising the trembling girl he drives off the reptile rakshas with a solemn dance of exorcism, and Rhada, his consort, when the Brahmins return to gloat, motions the girl to embrace her lover. True love, even without benefit of clergy, has come into its own, and while the happy maid dances a "Dance of Ecstasy," the lotus petals enfold Rhada, and she disappears beneath the waves. As Krishna steps forward a huge section of the orange cliff melts away, revealing the golden stairs leading to Indra's paradise. Slowly the Blue God ascends them as his worshipers lie prone.

Buddha is not so well represented in opera as the Brahminic gods. *Kunala's Eyes* (Prague, 1908) by Ottokar Ostrčil after a *Sutras'* legend, develops exotic color possibilities telling how Kunala, son of King Asoka, Buddha's protector, blinded by cruel intrigues of his stepmother, regains his sight by a miracle of faith. In *La colombe de Bouddha* (*Buddha's Dove*, Cannes, 1921) by Reynaldo Hahn, a score with novel exotic effects, old Kobe, gardener of the god's pagoda in Japan, loves a young mousmee. Other singing girls lure her off and the elderly victim of the Asiatic Cupid dies of the passion he hides in his breast. Echoing the

song the mousmee sang when she took to the broad and easy road,
Buddha's dove coos sadly on the dead man's body. *Prinzessin
Girnana* (Frankfort, 1921) by Egon Wellesz, a Schönberg dis-
ciple, sets a legend by the German novelist Wassermann, in music
reflecting the influence of Bela Bartók and the French modern-
ists. Prince Sidho lifts the veil of his bride, Princess Girnana,
and flees in horror, so repulsive is she. He married for ambition's sake; she to gratify sensual longings. Each has betrayed the
higher self. But since the Princess suffers with patience her curse
of ugliness Buddha appears to her in a dream, and when Sidho
enters her chamber she stands revealed in all her loveliness. *Anjuta's Frescoes* (London, 1923) by Tscherepnin, a Pavlowa ballet,
makes the frescoed gods of the famous Hindoo temple descend
from the walls and revel while worshipers sleep, till Buddha leaves
the orgy to seek the higher life.

### 7. Under the Pagoda Tree

Various operas reflect the glamour India exercised on the Occidental imagination during the eighteenth and early nineteenth centuries, when French, English, and other adventurers shook "the
pagoda tree" and gleaned its golden fruit. *La reine de Golconde* is a tale by the Chevalier de Boufflers (1768). A young
officer robs rustic Aline of her innocence. Dropping her milk
pail she wanders from the village, is captured by pirates, sold to
the Rajah of Golconda, and succeeds him as queen when he dies.
Her betrayer, become a French governor, calls on Aline for political ends, and in the palace garden, in her village dress, sees the
girl he had deceived. But when he mentions love the injured
innocent who has achieved Asia's most opulent throne turns from
him saying: "I am the Queen of Golconda!" Monsigny's *Aline,
reine de Golconde* (Paris, 1766) is a "heroic ballet"; Berton's
*Aline* (Paris, 1803) is one of the best of his many operas. Doniz-
zetti's *La regina di Golconda* (Naples, 1828) is musically inferior
to Boieldieu's *Aline, reine de Golconde* (Petrograd, 1804). Dedicated to the Czar Alexander I, its graceful music is innocent of
Oriental color. A modern elaboration of the tale is Raida's comic-
fantastic opera *Die Königin von Golkonda* (Berlin, 1897).

The Frenchman Lemierre's tragedy (1770) *La veuve de Malabar* (*The Malabar Widow*) took Paris by storm because of its
suttee scene, the custom then being unknown to Europeans. In
*Jessonda* (Cassel, 1823) Spohr wrote an attractive lyric opera on
this drama. Jessonda, a charming Hindoo girl, meets and loves a
Portuguese captain, Tristan d'Acunha. Her father finds a white
man has been tampering with his brown child's heart, hurries her

from Goa to Malabar and marries her to the rajah of Malabar. Her husband dies. Tristan, commanding the Portuguese army, arrives to besiege the city. During a truce, as she steps blushing from her bath in a holy well, Jessonda meets him, but Tristan has promised no Hindoo bather shall be detained and she is led away. Then, storming the walls Tristan snatches his love from beneath the high priest's dagger and all is well. Jessonda's Air, "Hast thou known silent anguish" (Act I), the bayadere melodies, and a Portuguese "Military Polonaise" are among the best pages of the romantic opera.

*Indra* (Vienna, 1852; as *L'esclave de Camoëns,* Paris, 1843) by Flotow, book by Pulitz, "has one admirably achieved number, the 'Cigarette Duet'" (Bie). In Lofala, Portuguese East Africa, the poet Camoëns, serving as a soldier, uses gold meant to buy his freedom to rescue Indra, an innocent girl, from Kudru the procuress. Deserting with her, her herbs save wounded King Sebastian's life (Act II) in Lisbon, but she repulses his improper advances, and when the King has read Camoëns' *Os Lusiade,* she reveals the identity of its author (Act III), obtains his pardon, and is clasped to his breast. *Vardhamana* (Cassel, 1892) by Bernard Oelsner is veristic, with the outstanding song "Give me one tender word." As Vardhamana, a Brahmin, prays his god not to let a stranger rob him of Sita's love, she reports her betrothal to Ralph, an English captain. When Vardhamana clutches her, Ralph wrests her from his arms, and is stabbed in the back. The Brahmin rushes off with his victim, but Ralph tracks his love by white lotus petals she has dropped to Brahma's hollow statue. It opens and he clasps Sita as Vardhamana leaps from the precipice the statue masks to death in a raging stream below.

## "LAKMÉ"

Leo Delibes. Book by Gille and Godinet (Paris, 1883). A sensuous, gracefully Oriental score. Lakmé's famous soprano aria, the "Indian Bell Song," "Où va la jeune Indienne," enjoys perennial popularity.

In British India Nikalantha sings a song of hatred in his breast against the conquering race while Gerald, an English officer, breaks through the bamboo fence of the Hindoo's ruined temple home to teach Lakmé, his daughter, the lesson of love. Nikalantha, however, discovers the hole in the fence.

Dagger in hand and accompanied by Lakmé disguised as a street singer, he hunts her unknown lover. Lured by Lakmé's singing of the "Bell Song" Gerald appears, is recognized by Nikalantha and stabbed in the street while bayaderes dance.

In the Indian forest whither Lakmé and Mallika, her slave, have borne wounded Gerald, his convalescence progresses to songs of deathless love. But his regimental messmate Frederick appears. The drums are calling: Gerald must go. In despair Lakmé eats the poison flower, begging Nikalantha, who kneels beside her, to let her lover depart unharmed. As Gerald hastens to join the British forces, Lakmé's dying sighs are lost in the tramp of marching feet.

*Le paria ou la chaumière Indienne* (*The Pariah or the Indian Hut*), Gaveaux's opera, telling Saint-Pierre's tale of the Hindoo outcast and the Brahmin widow who prefers his love to incineration with her husband's corpse (Paris, 1792), preceded Carafa's *Paria* (Venice, 1826) and Moniusko's *Paria* (Warsaw, 1870), whose Hindoo widow sings Lithuanian folk songs. In Membrée's *Les parias* (Paris, 1874) St. Francis Xavier, apostle to the Indies, saves Gadhy, the pariah, and Maia, the Brahmin widow; but when he is about to be burned by the Brahmins with his converts, the Ganges rises in flood and the funeral pyre, now a raft, floats them to the shelter of a Portuguese man-of-war. God moves in a mysterious way His wonders to perform! More modern and less miraculous is Görter's *Der Paria* (Strasburg, 1908); while Marschner's *Der Babu* (Hanover, 1837) offers a fine musical portrait of an Oriental rascal type in early nineteenth century British India.

## 8. *Purée Mongole*

### TURANDOT

The Venetian Carlo Gozzi, "the sardonic nobleman whose bones have been moldering by the blue lagoons for over a hundred years," reshaped (1762) the story of cruel Princess Turandot and Prince Calaf, a Persian tale from the *Thousand and One Nights*. *Turandotte* is one of those *fiabe* or "fairy tale" satires on the life and society of his time, with which he delighted his Venetian theatre audiences; and later Schiller went to Gozzi for his *Turandot*.

Suitors of Princess Turandot of China, who are unable to answer three riddles, must die. Their heads top iron spikes above the Pekin gates. When Calaf, Prince of Astrakhan, appears to try his fortune, the roll of distant drums declares another spike crowned. But Calaf has seen Turandot's picture . . . Turandot, upon entering the palace hall to the sound of tambourines, asks: "Which twin doves bring man tidings from the Land of Heart's Desire?" Calaf replies: "Hope and Faith!" "Which twin pillars uphold Paradise?" "Knowledge and Power." "Which magic flower hides the riddle of the World?" "Love!" Calaf has solved the riddles. Yet when shamed Turandot says she would rather die than marry him, he offers to release her if she can tell him the name of the king's son (himself) who became a beggar, and was most fortunate (guessing her riddles) when fortune favored him least. Turandot's slave girl Adelma tricks Calaf into admitting he is the beggar prince, driven from his father Timur's realm when the latter fell in battle against the Sultan of Tashkent.

The next day as the Emperor Almoun bids the priests begin the marriage rites, Turandot rises from the throne and cries: "Calaf, son of Timur, go seek another wife!" In despair the Prince tries to slay himself, but Turandot stays his dagger realizing she loves him and as she turns it against herself, Calaf takes her into his arms.

Franz Danzi's *Turandot* (Karlsruhe, 1815) lacks Chinese musical color in the modern sense; but Weber's overture for Schiller's *Turandot* has a genuine Chinese theme. Vapid is Reissiger's *Turandot* (Dresden, 1853); Theodore Rehbaum's *Turandot* (Berlin, 1888) with an effective sextet, "Oh, day of joy," makes the Mongol girl a Kashmir princess. The important settings are modern. Ferrucio Busoni's *Turandot* (Zurich, 1912) secures the feeling and color of Chinese music in a brilliant orchestration; outstanding are the grotesque "Truffaldino's March" and the "Danza alla Turca." Giacomo Puccini's posthumous score *Turandot*, book by Simon and Adam, after Gozzi's *fiaba,* is his second "Mongol" opera. It is based on intensive study of primitive Chinese music, developed in accordance with his statement while working on his score, that "without melody there is no music, and melody is the one thing that gives life to opera."

## "LE ROSSIGNOL"

### (*The Nightingale*)

Igor Stravinsky. Book after Hans Andersen's fairy tale (Paris, 1914). *Le Rossignol,* an opera ballet, is musically a modern opera development of Mongol color. The arias of the "true" and the "artificial" nightingales; the Entr'acte "Shadow Dance," "Les courants d'air," and the effective "Chinese March" stand out. Underlying the music is the idea that machinery is the enemy of man, and its most interesting musical departure is the placing of the coloratura voice in the orchestra.

A little brown bird sings so beautifully that the Emperor of China coaxes it to dwell in his palace. But envoys of the Emperor of Japan bring an artificial nightingale whose music-box trills so delight the Son of Heaven and his courtiers that the little brown singer is forgotten. When the Emperor happens to ask after the bird, it has flown away, whereupon the angry ruler banishes it from his realm. Then Death comes, seats himself on the Emperor's bed, steals his scepter and crown, and is about to lay his icy hand on his brow when the little Nightingale flies in, and sings with such eloquence that Death is touched and fore-goes his prey. When the courtiers enter the Emperor's chamber in the morning, thinking to see his corpse, they find him alive and well. *Le chant du rossignol* (Paris, 1920) is the composer's rewriting of his opera as a Ballet Russe. The first episode shows the Emperor's palace with walls and floors of porcelain, golden lamps, and bell flowers tinkling in the "Currents of Air"; the second the contest of the live nightingale and its rival, covered with pearls, sapphires and rubies (here occurs the "Song of the Fisherman"); the third that of Death's defeat.

In *Des Kaisers Dichter* (*The Emperor's Poet*, Hamburg, 1920), by Clemens von Frankenstein, China's Omar Khayyam, Li-Tai-Pe, despite intoxication's handicap wins his sweetheart Yang-Qui-Fe and bests enemy intriguers at the Emperor's court. The music is expressionistically modern, the final Love Duet standing out. *Das Nush-Nushi* (Stuttgart, 1921) by Paul Hindemith, a brilliant ultramodern score, is wedded to an offensive tale, in which the Nush-Nushi, a Burman river-monster, an Asiatic Figaro, a drunken general and four faithless imperial wives play unedifying rôles. The "Nush-Nushi Dances" have been played by the Philadelphia Orchestra (1925). *Le vieil aigle* (*The Old Eagle,* Monte Carlo, 1909) by Raoul Gunsbourg is a family tragedy of the fourteenth century Crimea. The old Khan Asvez has promised his son Tolak, victorious over the Russians, his heart's desire. The boy begs for lovely Zina, his father's favorite concubine. She prefers the "old eagle" to the young one, and when she flings herself into the sea to escape flaming youth, her romantic old lover follows her to a watery grave.

*Die Heilige Ente* (*The Holy Duck,* Düsseldorf, 1923) by Hans Gal has modern yet melodic music in which the "Dream Scenes" stand out. It is a Chinese play of gods and men, turning on an exchange of brains, love, and personality in the intoxication of a coolie's opium debauch. *Siang-Sin* (Paris, 1924) by Georges Hue, a ballet of exotic charm, is the tale of a Chinese emperor's faithless favorite, turned into an old hag by the sorcerer who re-stores her master's youth. But the Mongol Faust's second bloom-ing is poisoned by remorse at having destroyed the lovely creature's beauty, so he has the sorcerer restore it. *Tamerlano* (London, 1724; Karlsruhe, 1924) by Handel has fine arias and a noble trio, "Voglio strano." The Mongol conqueror is so inflamed by the beauty of Asteria, daughter of his captive, the Turkish Sultan Bajazet, that he determines to marry her. Bajazet's convenient suicide solves a struggle between honor and duty and brings about the union of Asteria and her lover, the Greek Prince Andronikos.

*Fay-Yen-Fah* (*The Land of Happiness,* Monte Carlo, 1925) by Joseph Redding, book by Crocker, is an American opera whose music contrasts Chinese exotic with western harmony in a tale showing the influence of an Occidental education on an Oriental mind.

In *Le paravent chinois* (*The Chinese Screen,* Brussels, 1925), by Guido Sommi, a ballet set to charming mock-Chinese music, a girl and her lover, an intriguing old woman who stirs up a bonze to part the two, and other characters step from the panels of a rich Coromandel lacquered screen. When the old mandarin has stopped the hurly-burly in which enemies and sympathizers of the amatory pair indulge, the two lovers cannot be separated and enter the same panel together.

## 9. *From the Land of the Chrysanthemum*

### "MADAM BUTTERFLY"

GIACOMO PUCCINI. Book after John Luther Long's novel, dramatized by the author and David Belasco. Italian text by Illico and Giacoso (Milan, 1904). "A Japanese blossom-grove of singable and tonally happy motives, feelingly and intelligently transplanted from exotic into European art . . . its peculiar eastern Asiatic intervals . . . animated by the most intense Italian passion" (Bie). "Ancora un passo" (Act I), "Un bel di vedremo" (Act II), and "Butterfly's Death Scene" (Act III) are among the loveliest pages.

The *Abraham Lincoln* is stationed at Nagasaki. Lieutenant Pinkerton, U. S. N., has Goro, a Japanese marriage broker, provide him with a "port wife." When Sharpless, the American Consul, points out little Butterfly's youth and innocence, Pinkerton cynically drinks to the bona fide American girl he hopes to marry some day. In the love nest whither Butterfly brings a sinister heirloom, the suicide sword once sent her father with a hara-kiri hint by the Mikado, the advent of the girl's uncle, a fanatic bonze, breaks up the wedding feast. He curses her for renouncing her gods, but as friends and relatives abandon her Pinkerton draws her to him. The curtain falls as they sing "Ah, night of rapture" oblivious of all save love.

Three years later—Pinkerton's ship ordered home, he has left Butterfly, promising to return "when robins nest again"—the *Abraham Lincoln* is due at Nagasaki. But Sharpless had received word from Pinkerton that he is bringing with him an American wife. Poor Butterfly, meanwhile, has begged Sharpless to write Pinkerton that her baby (the image of his father) named "Trouble," shall be rechristened "Joy" in honor of his return. Not knowing of her husband's desertion which automatically frees her, dagger in hand she threatens Goro, who is trying to marry her to old Prince Yamudori. A salute announces

Pinkerton's ship has cast anchor; for sheer happiness Butterfly cannot sleep in anticipation of her lover's coming.

He comes next day, with his wife; but leaves it to Sharpless to break Butterfly on the wheel of anguish. She enters as Pinkerton's kindly wife is trying to induce her maid Suzuki to surrender the child whom she is eager to adopt. Thus Butterfly learns the terrible truth. With the calmness of despair she blesses the rival who has asked her forgiveness and promises to deliver her baby boy to his father in half an hour if he will call for him. Then, her visitors gone, she thrusts a tiny American flag into little "Trouble's" hand, kisses him farewell with frantic tenderness, and kills herself with her father's sword of honor. When Pinkerton enters and, falling on his knees beside the dying woman, calls her name, she points to the blindfolded baby, crooning and waving his flag.

*Madame Chrysanthème* (Paris, 1893) by André Messager after Pierre Loti's novel, with charming lyric pages, extracts tragedy from the "port-marriage" situation, leaving tender sentiment. Pierre, a French navy lieutenant, port-bound in Nagasaki (Prologue) enters into qualified matrimony with Chrysanthème (Act I). The bride's friends serenade the newly wedded pair in their cottage (Act II). Pierre rages to think his mate, Yves, may have been flirting with Chrysanthème (Act III); but when his cruiser is ordered to sea, the little Japanese near-wife is vindicated (Epilogue) by her farewell letter, and Pierre drops a sentimental tear on the quarter-deck in memory of Chrysanthème's innocence as the scene of his fleeting love dwindles on the horizon.

*Iris* (Rome, 1898) by Pietro Mascagni, book by Illica, had sufficient musical charm to win qualified favor for its unpleasant story, a tale of veristic horror Mongolized. The "Hymn to the Sun," is an outstanding number. Iris, her doll still in her childish arms, is lured from her blind father Cieco's garden by the rich young rake Osaka and his procurer Kyoto, and is drugged and dragged to Yoshiwara, Tokio's "red light" district, to wake in a house of ill fame (Act II) where geishas sing, innocently thinking she is in the Japanese paradise. Osaka's ardent wooing is powerless against her uncomprehending purity, and disgusted with her ignorance he rushes out, ordering Kyoto to auction Iris off as a slave. But Iris' voice betrays her to her blind father. Thinking the worst he bespatters her with mud and curses till the frenzied girl flings herself from a window to perish in the sewer. There ragpickers squabble over the dress they tear from her body (Act III) while dying Iris, passing from earth's vileness, hears the Sun's voice welcome her to eternal bliss with a hymn of joy.

*La princesse jaune* (*The Yellow Princess,* Paris, 1872) by Camille Saint-Saëns, book by Gallet, a "facile, cold, and elegant score," counts among its best pages an Overture and the exotic "Scientist's Dream" music. Kornelis, a Dutch scientist, loves a Nipponese princess painted on a fan. In a Japanese book of magic he finds the recipe for a potion giving the drinker his heart's desire. He drinks, sleeps, and in his dream lovely Ming steps from her ebony frame. The exotic charm of the Orient weaves about their love-making, but Kornelis wakes to find his pretty, flesh and blood cousin Lena has been impersonating his dream girl, and is content to exchange the impalpable for the real. In *Lili-Tse* (Mannheim, 1896), by Franz Curti, a mirror, its function unknown to simple Japanese villagers, is used as a means to shake Lili-Tse's faith in her husband Kiki-Tsum, and his in her; till the explanation of the mystery of refraction by a young Englishwoman restores happiness to loving hearts and foils the naughty bonze Ming-Ming's hopes of winning the supposedly injured wife. *The Rivals* (Chicago, 1925) by Henry Eichheim is a Chinese ballet whose music has the actuality of true Mongol city and country folk tunes heard, noted down, and developed by the composer in China.

### "THE MIKADO"

ARTHUR SULLIVAN. Book by W. S. Gilbert (London, 1885). *The Mikado* may be called the tragic *Madame Butterfly's* comic opera twin, in so far as popularity is concerned. A surface musical exoticism adds to the charm of its melodies, including the famous song, "The flowers that bloom in the spring."

In a Japan of fantasy ruled by Pooh-Bah under the Mikado, Ko-Ko, guardian of state wards and lord high executioner, plans to marry Yum-Yum, most charming of his charges. She prefers Nanki-Poo, the Mikado's son who, disguised as a minstrel, has fled court to escape marriage with Katisha, an elderly maiden. Ko-Ko who is threatened with loss of office because of too few executions, accepts Nanki-Poo's offer (Act II) to give his head for a month's wedded bliss with Yum-Yum. But when the Mikado, to whom Ko-Ko has described the execution, learns that his own son has been beheaded, he orders that Ko-Ko be immersed in boiling oil. The Mikado rescinds his order as the lovers are restored to him alive, Ko-Ko is only too happy to turn over Yum-Yum to Nanki-Poo for good and all, and his punishment is reduced to marriage with Katisha.

*Taëfun* (*Typhoon*, Mannheim, 1924) by Theodor Szanto after the Hungarian Lengyel's play uses exotic themes with dramatic effect to tell a struggle between love and duty in a Japanese diplomat's heart. Infatuated with a Parisian *cocotte,* he is saved by friends from betraying his country's military secrets to her, and in a moment of rage he strangles her. A countryman takes the blame for the murder and the hero dies of heart failure, his *Parisienne* appearing to him in a vision as a geisha girl after the "typhoon" of passion succeeding his garroting. *Die Dorfschule (The Village School,* Vienna, 1920) by Felix Weingartner, after the Japanese tragedy *Terakoja,* has effective koto themes underlining dramatic high moments, particularly the "Burial Music" on a Japanese tune. Genzo, a village schoolmaster, hides among his pupils the dethroned emperor's son, entrusted to him by Matsuo, now in the usurper's service. The secret discovered, the new emperor demands the boy's head. Matsuo brings a new lad to the school and with his consent Genzo kills him (the little head is heard falling off stage) and learns that Matsuo and his wife have sacrificed their own child, now lying headless on his bier, to save the little prince. *Namiko-San* (Chicago, 1925-26) by Aldo Franchetti, book by Durand, is based on Japanese folk tunes. The choral scene of the "Japanese Wake" stands out. Sixteen-year-old Namiko-San, gathering flowers, meets a wandering monk and, as love flames in their hearts, she forgets the Prince, her betrothed. The latter surprises her with the monk that night, and she flings herself on the sword he has drawn to pierce his breast. Then, as the folk of the countryside mourn the dead child on her bier of white chrysanthemums, the Prince learns that she was innocent of wrong.

### 10. *The Thousand and One Nights in Opera and Ballet*

*Les mille et une nuits (The Thousand and One Nights,* Paris, 1914) by Armande Polignac is a symbolic ballet, "a translation of music into color and light," that illustrates the cruel and luxurious character of Saracen civilization in a general way. Neither Planquette's melodious operetta *Le paradis de Mahomet* (Paris, 1906) in which Parisian beauties played the parts of houris, "fair as the sheltered egg," nor the Swedish ballet *Derviches* (Paris, 1920) by Glazounoff, a "giratory display of dazzling white robes against a dull gold background," is religious.

### "SCHÉHÉRAZADE"

NICOLAI RIMSKY-KORSAKOFF. Choregraphic drama. Decorations by Léon Bakst and action by Mikail Fokine after *The Arabian Nights* (Paris, 1910). Rimsky-Korsakoff's beautiful symphonic suite of the same name ("The Ocean and Sinbad's Vessel," "The Story of Prince Kalendar," "The Young Prince and Princess," "The Festival in Bagdad," four tales of Scheherazade) has been adapted to tell another story, and the negroes are massacred to music describing the wreck of Sinbad's vessel. New York performances drew a color line, making harem slaves brown instead of black, after the police, alarmed for public morals, had thrown cold water on their too realistic transports of passion.

Sultan Shariar, lord of India and China, extols to his brother, Shah Zeman, the faithfulness of Zobeide, princess of Samarkand, his sultana. Shah Zeman's skepticism, when the dancing of three odalisques fails to cheer his brother, suggests a departure on a hunting expedition and an unexpected return as a practical test of Zobeide's faith.

As the sound of the Sultan's hunting horn dies in the distance, the cloistral peace of the harem, basking in the rosy luster of hanging lamps, yields to uproar. The women bully the doddering chief eunuch into unlocking the great doors of bronze and silver, leading to the quarters of the stalwart negro slaves. Through them crowd blacks in garments of gleaming copper and silver brocade, the secret lovers of the Sultan's women. When the golden door is opened a gigantic negro, Zobeide's paramour, in cloth of gold, bounds into the room. The slaves seize their mistresses, who struggle wildly only to relax in ebon arms. Dancing girls and boy cupbearers run in, are caught up in the choregraphic whirl and merge in its design, the music keeping pace with the riotous development of the orgy, until . . .

Shariar, a silent, sinister figure, suddenly stands in the portal, startling the guilty carousers into immobility. While his guards cut down the fleeing harem beauties and the sable lovers with relentless scimitars, Zobeide pleads for mercy. But Shah Zeman touches her black lover's body with his foot, and looks at his brother. Zobeide reads her doom in Shariar's eyes, and anticipates it by plunging a dagger into her breast.

*Schazrade* (Mannheim, 1917) by the German modernist Bernard Sekles, book by Bassewitz, is an opera exotically colorful and rich in tragic sentiment. In the Caliph Schahryar's palace on one of the isles of India and China over which he ruled when the Prophet's word was law on earth, his vizier tells him he has found a maid fairer than all her predecessors to share his couch. A hundred of the loveliest maids of the kingdom already have lost their heads by the sword after a night of love, for since his sultana betrayed him the Caliph trusts no woman. But when Saad, an emir's lovely daughter, is brought in, Omar, the Caliph's captain of the guard, who loves her, tries to stab his master. The latter forgives the youth but denies him the girl; and after the Caliph returns from the chamber where he has been closeted with Saad, Omar kills his love and himself. Meanwhile, in his villa, the Vizier tells his daughter Schazrade—kept hidden from Schahryar's eye—of the Caliph's vow to visit all virgins with dishonor and death because his sultana deceived him with a black slave. But Schazrade rejects her father's advice to leave the land as the wife of a rich merchant, Musair. Secretly she loves the gloomy Commander of the

Faithful, and is ready to dare death to win his heart. In the Caliph's gardens (Act III) she yields to his embrace; and in the morning he is her willing slave: her affection has restored his faith in woman's fidelity.

## "MAROUF, LE SAVETIER DU CAIRE"

### (*Marouf, the Cobbler of Cairo*)

HENRY RABAUD. Book by Lucien Népoty after Dr. J. C. Madrus' French translation of *The Thousand and One Nights*. A brilliant and orientally colorful musical and dramatic exploitation of the Egyptian variant of the story of "Aladdin and the Wonderful Lamp" (Paris, 1914). The scene of action is Cairo, Khaïtan, a city "somewhere between China and Morocco," and a plain without the city. "Each scene is constructed like a piece of 'absolute' music, on a principal theme used like a symphonic theme rather than a leading motive" (Carraud). Outstanding are the humorous "Scene of the Bastonnade" (Act I), the "Wedding Festival" Ballet and the splendid fugal final chorus.

Fattoumah, the cobbler Marouf's wife, is a shrew untamed. When Marouf brings her a sugar instead of a honey cake, she falsely accuses him of brutal treatment, and drags him to court. There the Cadi prescribes two hundred blows on the back, and the unfortunate cobbler, abandoning his home fires, leaves Cairo with some passing sailors.

The merchant Ali appears in the Khaïtan market place, followed by slaves bearing the unconscious body of the shipwrecked Marouf. Ali—richest man in Khaïtan and once Marouf's schoolmate—bids the cobbler play the rôle of a wealthy man in the bazaar, and boast of his "caravan," soon to arrive. Marouf overplays his part, and the Sultan of Khaïtan (wandering through the streets in disguise with his Vizier) impressed by Marouf's glittering fables, asks him to the palace.

The Sultan yearns for a millionaire son-in-law, and Marouf's marriage to the Princess Saamcheddine is soon announced. When the groom pleads poverty till his caravan arrives, the Sultan places the treasury at his disposal. Marouf empties it, flinging gold pieces to the crowd in honor of his wedding. Alone with Saamcheddine, he swoons with delight when she doffs her veil while she—a case of love at first sight—stoops and kisses him as the curtain falls.

The caravan does not arrive. The suspicious Vizier urges the Sultan to have his daughter question Marouf, and the latter laughingly admits to her that he is but a cobbler, his golden caravan a dream. Fearing exposure Saamcheddine (disguised as a youth) decides to flee with him. They go out, and the galloping of horses sounds off stage.

In a plain near Khaïtan, Marouf and his wife meet a fellah. While he goes to prepare food for them Marouf guides his plow. The plowshare catches in a ring attached to a flat stone, the entrance to a magic treasure cavern. The fellah (when the Princess rubs the ring, which

Marouf has torn from its socket) turns into a serviceable *djinn*. Marouf has come into his own, and bids the *djinn* provide the caravan of his boasts. When the Sultan and the Vizier, in pursuit of the runaways, appear, and Marouf is about to be executed, lo, the caravan—a thousand camels, fourteen hundred mules, laden with rich stuffs, gold and jewels, with drivers and Mameluke guards—draws near. The repentant Sultan releases Marouf, and the happy lovers leave the stage to the music of the bastinado the hateful Vizier receives.

Aladdin operas include *Aladdin* (London, 1825), Sir Henry Bishop's "only opera"; Isouard's *Aladin ou la lampe merveilleuse* (Paris, 1822), and the Dane Hornemann's *Aladin* (Copenhagen, 1888). Ali Baba has been remembered in Cherubini's last score, *Ali Baba ou les quarante voleurs* (Versailles, 1833), with a fine "Robbers' March" and "Sleepers' Trio"; and in Max Brauer's musical but undramatic *Morgiane* (Karlsruhe, 1899) with the climax (Act III) in Morgiane's stabbing of Kosru, the drunken robber captain as she dances for him, thus removing the obstacle to her union with Ali, her lover. *Abu Hassan* (Munich, 1811) by Carl Maria von Weber, tells the tale of "The Sleeper and the Waker." The sparkling overture, and the contralto solo, "Oh, Fatima, gift sent from heaven," stand out. Abu Hassan and his wife Fatima have spent the Caliph's gold in riotous living, and hounded by creditors he tells the Caliph Fatima has died, while she tells the Caliph's wife that Hassan has passed away. While they feast on the money obtained for each other's funeral expenses, the Caliph Haroun and his wife Zobeide compare notes, and unable to agree as to which is dead, follow their messengers to Abu Hassan's home, where both lie on a bier in their winding sheets. But when Haroun cries he would give a thousand gold pieces to know which died first—for he and his wife have made a wager—Hassan leaps from the bier with a cry of joy, and after due explanation the ingenious rascals are pardoned. Ludwig Hess's *Abu und Nu* (Danzig, 1919), a charming lyric dance opera, is a modern version of the tale. *Frauenlist* (*Woman's Wiles*, Sondershausen, 1911) by Emil Robert Hansen after an *Arabian Nights* tale, is a piquant score in "conversational" style. Turning on the merchant Abdallah's store sign, "Man's Cunning Is Greater Than Woman's," the action proves the contrary in the course of amatory intrigues which end with Fatima's marriage to the young Persian Ahmed, despite her uncle the Cadi's objections. Johann Strauss, Jr., also has set the story of Ali Baba as a comic opera with attractive unoriental waltz melodies as *Indigo* (Vienna, 1871) a score revived as *1001 Nächte* (*1001 Nights*, Vienna, 1906) to a new text by Reiterer.

## "DER BARBIER VON BAGDAD"

### (*The Barber of Bagdad*)

PETER CORNELIUS. Book by the composer, after "The Story of the Tailor" (Weimar, 1858). A score based dramatically on Wagner and musically, in part, on Berlioz. Outstanding are: two Overtures (the original a graceful comedy introduction, the second a brilliant concert piece), the symphonic Intermezzo based on the muezzin's call to prayer; Noureddin and Margiana's lyric Duet; and the final chorus, "Salamaleikum," a masterpiece of vocal counterpoint.

Noureddin, ill of longing for the Cadi's beautiful daughter, is restored to health when Bostana brings word that Margiana expects him at noon when her father has gone to pray in the mosque. First, however, he must see a barber, for reasons obvious to every lover. Abu Hassan, Bagdad's incomparable tonsorial genius, "a giant as a talker," appears. Instead of shaving Noureddin he casts his horoscope, and when the despairing lover's pleas induce him to do his duty he insists on accompanying him to his rendezvous.

In the Cadi's harem he, Margiana, and Bostana sing "He comes, he comes!" But the greedy old judge means Selim, Margiana's rich suitor, who has given her a chest of costly gifts. The muezzin's call to prayer resounds and the Cadi's departure to the mosque is followed by Noureddin's advent. The lovers fall into each other's arms, but their love duet is interrupted by the cries of a slave the returned Cadi has ordered bastinadoed. In the street the Barber hears the cries. He thinks Noureddin is being murdered, and incites the Bagdadees to storm the house. The frightened lovers are at their wit's end. Flight is out of the question; Noureddin hides in Selim's chest. Too late, when the Barber appears, Bostana discloses the lover's hiding place, and begs him to remove the chest. The Cadi prevents it. A tremendous uproar (choral ensemble) ensues, and so great is the public commotion that the Caliph is drawn to the scene. The Barber now accuses the Cadi of murdering his friend: the Cadi declares the Barber has attempted to steal his daughter's chest. The chest is opened and, to every one's surprise, Noureddin is disclosed. He has fainted. But Morgiana's rose in the Barber's hand recalls him to life, and the Caliph decrees the Cadi must give his daughter the "treasure" found in the chest. The Barber is to follow the Caliph to court. All praise the sovereign's verdict in the chorus "Salamaleikum," to which the curtain falls.

*La Statue* (Paris, 1861) by Ernest Reyer, unjustly accused of "salon orientalism," is a free operatic version of an *Arabian Nights* tale in which stand out an "Opium Smokers' Chorus" and Margyane's "Romance." The king of the *djinns* weans young Seyd the Damascan from the ignoble pursuit of fluttering harem veils by promising him the missing diamond statue in his father's subter-

ranean treasure vault.   Even when the girl he is to yield to the
*djinn* in exchange turns out to be lovely Margyane, whom he
met in the desert and passionately loves, Seyd keeps his word.   His
fidelity is rewarded by the discovery that Margyane is the missing
statue, worth her weight in diamonds to him.

*Fatme* (as *Zilda,* Paris, 1866; as *Fatme,* Berlin, 1925) by Flotow, book by Saint-Georges, revised by Bardi, in which Fatme's
*arioso* numbers stand out, is based on an *Arabian Nights* tale, of
Fatme, sent to Bagdad by her husband to collect a debt due him from
Dr. Babuk.   He demands the sacrifice of her virtue as a preliminary to payment, and her appeal in succession to the Cadi and
Grand Vizier for protection proves their minds run in the same
channel.   Fortunately the Caliph Haroun has heard and seen all
disguised as a dervish.   In the guise of a corsair captain he ter-
rifies the three wretches who seek to take advantage of Fatme,
and as the Caliph he forces each to pay the whole amount of the
debt originally owed her by Babuk.

## "HASSAN DER SCHWÄRMER"

### (*Hassan the Dreamer*)

WILHELM KIENZL.   Book by Bauer after *The Arabian Nights* (Chem-
nitz, 1925).   A score lacking Oriental color but rich in effective, ingra-
tiating melodies.

Hassan the cobbler yearns to make his fellow human beings happy.
Once a year he entertains the world (personified by a chance acquaintance whose features reflect a noble inner life) as his guest.   When he
seats the Caliph Haroun at his board unawares, thinking him a passing
merchant, and flushed with wine, says he longs to be Caliph for a day,
the Commander of the Faithful has the intoxicated cobbler carried to
the palace, where he wakes to find all paying homage to him.   When he
realizes, however, that he is being made a fool of he turns the tables
on his mockers with revolutionary commands until the Caliph is glad
to have him put to sleep with a powder and carried home.   Wakening
there to actuality, he hears Fatme—the lovely harem girl to whom he
lost his heart, and the Caliph's parting gift to him—singing, and realizing that in her his soul has at last found the "guest" for which it
longed, clasps a whole world of love to his heart by taking her in his
arms.

A multitude of operas present original stories in the *spirit* of the
*Arabian Nights* tales.   *La rencontre imprévue* (*The Unexpected
Meeting,* Paris, 1704) by Gluck, revived of late on German stages
as *Die Pilgrime von Mecca,* shows Prince Ali finding his lost love
in the Sultan of Egypt's harem—still true to him!   They plan flight

with the Mecca caravan and the Sultan, apprised of it, confronts them in a caravanserai. Instead of having them beheaded he is moved by their faithfulness to bless their union. *Zémire et Azor* (Paris, 1771) by Grétry is said to have brought tears to Du Barry's lovely eyes; and Spohr's romantic opera *Zemire und Azor* (Frankfort, 1819) survives in the air "Rose, wie bist du so reizend." Azor, King of Kashmir, whom a sorcerer has changed into a fell monster, is disenchanted by Zemire, an Ormuz merchant's daughter, who finds the needed magic ring and joins her lover on the throne. *La caravane du Caire* (*The Cairo Caravan*, Paris, 1782) by Grétry, book by Marie-Antoinette's brother-in-law, Louis XVIII of France, when he was Count of Provence, shows St. Phar, an admiral's son, and Zelime, a nabob's daughter, improving a slave caravan's halt on the banks of the Nile by making love. In Cairo (Act II) the keen-eyed Pasha picks Zelime for his harem from among Dutch, English, Persian, and other girls, but his sultana, Almaide (Act III) helps Zelime escape with her lover. Recaptured, they are brought before the Pasha as St. Phar's father is thanking him for permission to repair his fleet on Egypt's coast, and the young noble is released to clasp Zelime, the Pasha's gift, in his arms.

*Axur, re di Ormus* (Vienna, 1788), the most famous opera of Gluck's pupil Salieri, once rivaled Mozart's *Don Giovanni* in popularity. In Ormuz, on the Persian Gulf, Tarar's virtuous wife is foully abducted to make a harem holiday for King Axur. Rejecting Axur's addresses, faithful Asteria is about to be flung into a negro's black arms in punishment when the negro is unmasked as Tarar, who has entered the palace gardens disguised as an Ethiop, bent on revenge. A revolt of the palace guards saves Tarar from instant cremation and when Axur, disgusted with Tarar's nobility of soul, stabs himself, Tarar ascends the throne with his rescued wife. In Boieldieu's *Le calife de Bagdad* (Paris, 1800) its pretty airs innocent of Eastern color, the Caliph Isauun, wandering through Bagdad streets in disguise, arrested by the widow Lemaide when he makes love to her daughter Zeltube, reveals himself in royal robes and receives a son-in-law's welcome. *La fiancée du roi de Garbe* (*The King of Garbe's Betrothed*, Paris, 1864), a tuneful Auber score, tells Boccaccio's tale of the Oriental princess who passed through many hands before coming to rest on her fiancé's breast. *Thamara* (Paris, 1891) by Bourgault-Ducoudray, the French musical Orientalist, tells how Thamara, loveliest virgin of Baku, the Caspian petroleum city, stabs the Moslem invader Noureddin (a seductive melody pictures him basking in his harem) when he tries to add her to his conquests, then slays herself on the temple steps because she has shed another's blood.

*Der Rubin* (*The Ruby*) by Eugen d'Albert after Hebbel is an earlier pseudo-Wagnerian score. Bedura, the Caliph's daughter, ravished from her rose garden and imprisoned in a ruby by an evil *djinn*, is released by the fisherman's son Asaf who, after many misadventures, rather than part with the stone he loves, flings it into the Tigris and clasps Bedura in his arms as the executioner's sword is about to lay his head at his feet. In *Der König von Samarcand* (*The King of Samarcand*, Dessau, 1910) by Franz Mikorey, a modern opera after Grillparzer's play *Life a Dream,* the Caucasian huntsman, Rustan, sleeping after his evil black slave Zenga has coaxed him to follow the lure of Samarcand's distant golden towers, sees unrolled a vision of falsehood, murder, and shame in which he plays the villain's part, and opens his eyes to find it a prophetic dream. Cured of his longing for adventure Rustan clasps his pretty cousin Mirza to his heart, bent on finding happiness in her love amid familiar surroundings. *Der Traum* (*The Dream*, Berlin, 1912) by Gustav Mraczek, a modern Oriental score, varies the same tale, powerfully underlining the character of Zenga, the black Mephistopheles, in music.

*La source lointaine* (*The Distant Spring*, Paris, 1912) by Armande de Polignac, a mystic pantomime "rich in grace and color . . . unfinished melodies and efflorescent chords, bathed in the aura of skies we never shall see" (Laloy), tells of the Peri Allah sends to Iran's divine spring, who forgets her mission and instead of filling her bowl with water sips the wine cup with a young prince she meets hunting and to whose embrace she yields after having danced a dance of Allah's paradise. The wayward Peri, dead to all but love, sees the Prince sink to the ground overcome with wine. A troop of *djinns* invade the grove, but as the lovely sinner is about to be dragged to Gehenna the Archangel Gabriel saves her—there is still enough water in her bowl to gain Allah's forgiveness. *Maïmouna* (Paris, 1921) by Gabriel Grovlez, a fantasy ballet, ". . . limpid scenic music, bizarre rhythms" (Banès), shows the Caliph Hassan downing a love potion because his captive Maïmouna rejects him. In a dream he sees her deny herself to an emir, and to an athlete to favor a musician, and wakes to find Maïmouna actually in a musician's arms. Dismissing his annoyance, he unites the lovers and returns with a sigh to the accustomed embrace of his favorite sultana. In *Hagith* (Darmstadt, 1923), Karol Szymonowski's opera, musically "a development of *Elektra's* dramatic expression," a royal Oriental Faust must possess Hagith, his son's betrothed, to regain his youth. He dies in the attempt to gain by violence the youth on which his own depends, and Hagith is stoned to death singing a love song. Her betrothed, hastening to save her, finds only her corpse. *Boudour* (Chicago, 1919) by

Felix Borowski, a graceful Persian ballet, might also be mentioned
here.

## "DIE FRAU OHNE SCHATTEN"

*(The Woman without a Shadow)*

RICHARD STRAUSS. Book by Hugo von Hoffmannsthal (Vienna, 1919).
An endeavor to provide Mozart's *Zauberflöte* with a sequel, stressing
moral instead of political equations, this is a problem opera of modern
marriage and motherhood, showing how "the guilty, by means of inward
purification may attain redemption and purest happiness" through sacrifice and suffering. The work takes four hours to perform. Strauss
uses the giant orchestra of *Elektra,* and the score is notable for beautiful
melodic numbers, many suitable for concert use (especially the great
soprano solo scene of the Empress).

The Emperor, hunting with his falcon, catches a white gazelle, but
his spear raised she turns into a beautiful woman, and making her his
Empress he is happy in her love. Yet the Empress—daughter of Keiko-
bad, king of the *djinns*—casts no shadow and bears no child. And the
falcon (its whistling cry a recurring musical theme) wails: "The woman
casts no shadow! The Emperor must turn to stone!" The Empress
knows that unless she can obtain a mortal shadow, her dream of love
is done. Her nurse takes her to Barak, the dyer's wife. Tempted
by jewels and rich robes, Barak gives up her unborn babes (when the
Nurse conjures fish into the frying pan for Barak's supper they wail
with infant voices while sizzling) and agrees to sell her shadow.

But sorrow for honest Barak drives sleep from the Empress' eyes,
and when the faithless wife abjures motherhood with magic rites and
stands forth shadowless, the Empress nobly renounces her claim. The
walls of Barak's dwelling burst; a tidal wave sweeps off the dyer and
his wife as the Nurse carries the Empress away on her magic mantle.
(The vocal difficulties of the exciting close of Act II have made singers
call it "The Ride to Death").

In the temple hall where her husband, only his eyes alive, sits turned
to stone, the Empress steels herself against the tempting murmurs of
the water of life, bubbling at her feet, and promising her husband salvation if she claim the shadow sold her. But as she struggles in
anguish of soul, human pity and renunciation release her husband from
his magic bonds, and they stand together with the reunited dyer and
his wife in an Edenic landscape, while the song of the unborn babes
vouchsafed them fills their cup of joy to overflowing.

*Der türkisenblaue Garten (The Turquoise-Blue Garden,* Leipzig,
1920) by Aladar Szendrei, a symbolič modernist opera of love and
death, tells of Nayeláh, captive in a Shah's magic garden, the blue
turquoises of whose necklace reflect her master's unrequited passion.
Young Haidar climbs the garden wall and youth calls to youth, but
Nayelah, fearing the distant magician, rejects Haidar's love, till, plunged
in a deathlike trance by a narcotic, slaves bear his rigid form to her and

she, filled with irresistible yearning, kisses him alive and knows love's hour of ecstasy. But from afar the Shah by hypnotic power compels the girl to stab her lover. Returning to his garden, where Haidar's corpse and the blue turquoise stones lie upon the grass, he is about to torture Nayelah when she kills herself with the dagger which slew her lover and joins him, her soul freed by suffering.

## 11. *The Bedouins and Lalla Rookh*

Opera has not neglected the tented Bedouin. In Orefice's *L'Oasi* (Vincenza, 1866) the tent, musically, is redolent of cologne rather than musk; but Bruneau's *Kerim* (Paris, 1887) tells a desert tale to native themes, and Francesco Santoliquido's modern verist score *Ferhuda* (Tunis, 1920) is a tragedy of Arab love based on Tunisian folk tunes. Veristic also is Isidore De Lara's *Naïl* (Paris, 1912). Naïl, the Moorish dancing girl, flees from Emir Kantara with her Bedouin lover, Hadjar, and when Kantara nails captured Hadjar to a cross, foils the Emir's passion by burying a dagger in her breast. Anis Fuleihan's *Arab Fantasia* (New York, 1924) in which scenes from Arab life are set to a score based on desert tribal melodies, contrasts in the authenticity of its themes with Maillart's *Lara* (Paris, 1864) after Byron, whose musically piquant but surface Oriental characterization of the Arab slave girl, Khalid, who follows her lover disguised as a boy, stands out.

## "ANTAR"

GABRIEL DUPONT. Book by Chekri-Ganem, after the *Siret Antara* (*Adventures of Antar*), the Arab *Morte d'Arthur* (Paris, 1921). "Since *Carmen* the most purely human as well as musical work mounted on a government subventioned stage . . . music of meridional emotion, ardent, quivering" (Collet). Outstanding are: an "Arabian Song" (Act I); Arab Ballet, "veritable rhythmic orgies celebrating the wedding"; Antar's and Abla's Love Duet (Act II); the orchestral Nocturne (Act II); and "Antar's Funeral Oration," an orchestral page which compares with the "Funeral March" from *Die Götterdämmerung*.

Antar, son of an Abyssinian slave captured by a desert chief, grows up a daring warrior and rescues Abla, daughter of the Emir Malek, from enemy raiders. Loving her madly he asks her hand in marriage. In "The Desert" (Act I) Malek hears his suit. But the Emir Amarat is also a suitor for Abla's hand. So Malek decides Antar must make good the words of the Arab "Song of Desires." He must bring him the white, sapphire-collared camels of the Persian king's stud, his famous steed Ophir, shod with gold, and his royal diadem, sparkling with diamonds, if Abla is to be his. The hero undertakes the superhuman task. Antar returns to "The Oasis" (Act II) with camels, steed, and diadem to claim his reward. Received with rapture by the tribe, he marries Abla and the wedding is celebrated with tribal dances ("Spinners' Dance," "Fire Dance," "Rose Dance," and the "Dance of Thirst," grisly pantomime of desert agony).

In a "Defile in the Mountains" (Act III) at night, gleam the fires of Antar's camp. He and Abla appear in the darkness, hand in hand, and sing their passion. But Amarat, loser in love's game, has sworn revenge. At his instigation Zoheir, chief of an enemy tribe, who falsely believes Antar has wronged him, speeds an arrow in the darkness and wounds Antar in the shoulder.

It is day in Antar's camp. The hero's own shaft has stricken down Zoheir; but he learns that the latter's arrow was poisoned. He is doomed. He sends off Abla and his caravan not knowing that he must die, and in an eloquent speech to his confidant the gist of which is "Better a well filled morning than an empty day!" resigns himself to his lonely death in the rocky waste.

Thomas Moore's *Lalla Rookh, an Oriental Romance* (1817), either as a whole or in part, has inspired various operas. Whether composers found "the interest existing in the poem chiefly due to the undercurrent of Irish patriotism cleverly worked into it," is open to question.

## LALLA ROOKH

The Princess Lalla Rookh (Tulip-Cheek), daughter of the Mogul Emperor of India, Aurungzebe, betrothed to Aliris, the young King of Bokhara, has set out from Delhi across the continent with a spendid caravan for the Valley of Kashmir, there to meet her future husband. The journey is long. The chatter of Lalla Rookh's women, the conversation of Fadladeen, the Grand Chamberlain of the harem, bore the Princess, till the Chamberlain recalls a young poet of Kashmir, Feramorz, among the attendants sent on by the bridegroom. Feramorz shall recite his lays before the Princess at the stopping places and beguile the tedium of her journey. He does so, and of the four tales or legends he recites, the first is set to tuneful and vigorous music by Charles Villiers Stanford, *The Veiled Prophet of Khorassan* (Hanover, 1881), book by W. B. Squire. Mokanna, the false prophet, hides behind a veil of silver gauze "features horribler than hell e'er traced." The tragedy of the tale is his betrayal of poor Zelica, her death and her youthful lover's agony. Mokanna himself, besieged by the Caliph's armies, finally leaps into a copper cauldron filled with burning drugs. Two melodious, unimportant scores, *Il Profeta Velato di Koraso* (Naples, 1893) by Daniel Napoletano, and the opera-ballet *Mokanna,* by Guglielmo Zuelli (since 1911 Director of the Paris Conservatory) represent Italian reactions to the theme.

The young poet's second narrative tells of a Peri, "one of those beautiful creatures of the air, who live upon perfumes," standing at the gate of Eden, eager to enter in. In vain she brings to gain admission the drop of blood shed by a dying hero, the last sigh of a maid whom love leads to share the death of her betrothed. But finally a repentant sinner's tear unbars the crystal gates and "Heaven is won." *Das Paradies und die Peri* (*Paradise and the Peri*), by Robert Schumann, a cantata (1843), is the only outstanding musical setting of this subject. It has little Oriental color but its wealth of beautiful melodies and choruses (among them a "Dance of the Houris") makes its music sound "as though the angels of Botticelli were singing."

Feramorz' next narrative tells the love of a Mohammedan Emir's daughter and the young chief of the fire-worshiping Guebers of Persia. The Emir, Al Hassan, storms the fire worshipers' mountain fastness, but when Hinda, the Moslem girl, sees Hafed, "her soul's first idol and its last," disappear in the flames of his burning shrine, she leaps from the mountain top to find death in the abyss "whose waves . . . foam 'round the frightful caves" below. *Gli Adorati del fuóco* (Venice, 1891) is a forgotten Italian opera on this theme; but the most important setting is a choral one, *The Fire Worshipers,* by Granville Bantock, whose music is filled with Byronic passion.

Feramorz' last tale is that of "The Light of the Harem" ("Nourmahal"), the graceful story of a lovers' quarrel between the Mogul Emperor Jehangir and his favorite sultana, Nourmahal, in which the Light of the Harem sings her way back into her master's heart at the Feast of the Roses in the enchanting Vale of Kashmir.

*Nourmahal oder das Rosenfest von Kaschmir* (*Nourmahal or the Feast of the Roses in Kashmir,* Berlin, 1822) by Gasparo Spontini, was the opera version of his festival play *Lalla Rookh* (1821). Long since forgotten, it lacked unity, Heine says, and poking fun at the din of kettledrums and trumpets in Spontini's *Olympia,* which preceded it ("Spontini intends to write an opera with cannon *obbligato*"), declared the best thing about *Nourmahal* was that "not a shot falls in it."

Moore's poem has been treated as a whole by the first representative of exoticism in music in the grand style, Félicien David.

*Lalla Roukh* (Paris, 1862) by Félicien David, book by Lucas and Carré, is the most unified of all the operas inspired by Moore. It takes the story from the beginning to the happy end where Lalla Rookh, arriving in Kashmir, raises her eyes to the throne where she is to seat herself beside the young King of Bokhara and finds he is the singer Feramorz, whom she learned to love on the road. Musically, Noureddin's (Feramorz') "Ma maîtresse a quitté la tente," and Lalla Rookh's "O nuit d'amour," stand out. David's opera, tremendously popular in its day, was even translated into Persian and its airs sung in the streets of Ispahan.

Another famous composer, yielding to the attraction of Moore's poem, began his opera, practically, where Moore leaves off: *Feramors* (Dresden, 1863) by Anton Rubinstein, book after Moore by Rodenberg. The wedding feast is ready, but Lalla Rookh is sad. She must marry the King of Bokhara, yet loves Feramors, the romantic singer. Musically, the beauties of this act are: a charming Ballet ("Dance of Lights of the Brides of Kashmir"), a muezzin's call to prayer, and the Ballad, "The moonlight beams o'er Persia's sea," in which Feramors avows his love. A secondary love affair (between Fadladin, the Bokharan Vizier and Hafisa, Lalla Rookh's friend) leads Fadladin to surprise Feramors and the princess together (Act II) and the singer is cast into prison. In the concluding act Feramors, escaping from confinement, appears at the marriage feast as his royal self, and Lalla Rookh is clasped to the breast of her crowned singer. The only number of the score which has escaped oblivion is the "Dance of Lights of the Brides of Kashmir," a graceful ballet number still heard on occasion in symphonic concerts.

## 12. *Where Orient and Occident Meet*

*Hashish* (Dresden, 1897) by Oskar von Chelius is a modern Wagnerian score. Paolo an Italian painter (17th century) insists on seeing the harem beauty Hama's face to paint her portrait in the palace of Omar, Bey of Tunis. When the Moslem husband surprises Hama and Paolo in each other's arms, he has three goblets brought: two are harmless, one contains the hashish poison. Hama, Paolo and Omar drink, and Hama falls dead.

In *Namouna* (Paris, 1882), Edouard Lalo's ballet, fine melodies stand out against a rich Oriental harmonic background. In eighteenth century Corfu, a series of childish incidents reconcile the Grand Turk and the Republic of Venice in the persons of the beautiful slave girl Namouna and the Venetian gentleman Ottavio.

*La mascarade des princesses captives* (Brussels, 1924), by Francesco Malipiero. "The score unfolds like some precious fabric of refined colors, scented with fascinating Asiatic perfume." In his castle on the Mediterranean, a Neapolitan nobleman is giving a masquerade, lovely ladies dressed as "captive princesses" stepping a stately dance. A Turkish corsair galley lands its men and they join the revels. The Neapolitans think them fellow masqueraders and greet them joyfully until, as real Turks, they beat the cavaliers and carry off the ladies, now "captive princesses" in fact.

## "DIE ENTFÜHRUNG AUS DEM SERAIL"

### (*The Elopement from the Seraglio*)

WOLFGANG AMADEUS MOZART. Book by Bretzner (Vienna, 1782). A lovely score, rich in tender music. Osmin's "Song of Rage" (Act I) has been called "the first really great German humorous song." Belmont's Air "O, wie ängstlich," Constance's song of vanished bliss, "Traurigkeit," her coloratura air, "Martern aller Arten," and the Turkish "Tattoo" may be stressed.

Constanze, a beautiful Christian slave girl, languishes in the Turkish Pasha Selim's harem. Belmont, Constanze's lover, aided by his ex-valet Pedrillo, now the Pasha's gardener, gains admission to the villa as an architect. Blonda (Constanze's maid) gives Osmin, seraglio overseer, Pedrillo's rival for her favor, a sleeping draught (Act II) which allows Belmont to meet his sweetheart and plan an elopement. At midnight Pedrillo's guitar serenade gives the signal for escape, under Constanze's window; (Act III) but Osmin and his black mutes hurry up and the unfortunate lovers are captured. The Pasha's first thought is the bowstring, but soon his kindly heart relents. He releases the lovers and the opera ends happily with a dramatic ensemble.

*L'italiana in Algeri* (*The Italian Girl in Algiers,* Venice, 1813) by Gioachino Rossini merrily sets to music a Barbary Coast harem intrigue. The Dey of Algiers hopes to clasp a novelty to his heart in pretty Isabella, found floating on a derelict by his corsair captain, after marrying his chief wife, Elvira, to his Italian slave, Lindoro (Isabella's lover); but wily Elvira holds his attention while Isabella and Lindoro escape from slavery. In *Die Ruinen von Athen* (*The Ruins of Athens,* Vienna, 1924), a ballet, a Von Hoffmannsthal libretto, joins Beethoven's "Ruins of Athens" and "Prometheus' music. A Teuton Lord Byron visits Athens under Turkish rule, sees dervishes whirl, janissaries march and Greek girls dance, entering the Acropolis with a "Maid of Athens" on his arm as the curtain falls. *La Circassienne* (Paris, 1861), by François Auber, a sparkling *opéra comique,* presents the savage Russian General Orsakoff, in a Caucasian border fort, madly in love with a fair Circassian girl. Alas, she dies for *she* was Lieutenant Zouboff, who changed his sex to gain the hand of the General's ward, Olga, for *him*self, by promising to marry her guardian as the "Circassian girl."

### 13. *Glimpses of the Oriental Heart*

*Le hulla* (Paris, 1923) by Samuel-Rousseau is a modern Oriental ballet. Taher, rich Ispahanee merchant, repudiates pretty Dilara

on their wedding night, the simple statement being a valid Mohammedan divorce. Regretting his hasty step, he next seeks a *hulla*
(a middleman husband who goes through the form of marriage
for pay, since before a husband can remarry a divorced wife she
must have married again and been divorced) and finds him in penniless Narses, Dilara's former lover. Once married, Narses and
Dilara refuse to divorce, and Taher's hailing them before the king
for judgment results only in the latter's confirming the union of
the happy pair.

## "DJAMILEH"

GEORGES BIZET. Book by Louis Gallet (Paris, 1872). A simple plot has
inspired this charming musical score in which the "Nile Boatmen's Romance" (Act I) hummed with closed lips, and the "Dance of the Egyptian Almees" stand out.

Harun, a dissolute young Turk of Cairo, has wearied of wine, dice,
and women, and the new slave added to his harem each month only
serves to while away an idle hour. Narghile in mouth he listens to
the song of the Nile boatmen and smiles as his steward Spendiano tells
him that the high cost of his living (when he tires of a slave girl Harun
sends her away laden with gifts) will ruin him. Beautiful Djamileh
already is a twice-told tale to Harun, and her master gives her to
Spendiano at his request. But Djamileh adores the young Turk, and
when she sings her hopeless love and he reads her secret in her eyes, he
revokes his gift and grants her freedom. When she refuses it he turns
to gamble with his friends. Evening brings the slave dealer, but when
Harun selects a young *almée* to beguile his boredom, Spendiano (at
Djamileh's request) induces her to change veils with her predecessor.
That night, alone with his new charmer, Harun tears the veil from her
face and beholds Djamileh! When she tells him she would rather be
his slave than be free, genuine love at last awakens in Harun's bored
breast and he clasps her to his heart.

*Emiral* (Rome, 1924) by Barilli tells how, in a vague Oriental
land, Emiral, who ought to love the steady-going tribesman, Ismet,
surrenders her heart to the picturesque bandit Fadil. When Ismet
catches Fadil making love to the girl and kills the romantic robber,
poor Emiral dies of grief. A lyric duet between Fadil and Emiral
has been praised. In *Amour africain* (Paris, 1875), by Paladhile, a
fine air is "L'arabe et son coursier." An art-loving French count
stages a one-act opera at his château in Nice, a young Roman composer, his brother, and the latter's wife singing the rôles. The
ferocious Moors, Zein and Nouman (Act II), struggle madly for
the possession of the slave, Moiana, but just as Nouman has grue-
somely killed both his rival and the girl, the horrified audience at
the château is recalled to reality by the butler's announcement:
"Dinner is served!"

# CHAPTER II

## THE GLORY THAT WAS GREECE

### 1. *In the Beginning*

The myths and legends of ancient Greece begin with the Titans, chief among them Saturn, against whom his son, Zeus, or Jupiter, rebelled, banishing the Titans to Tartarus and inaugurating the reign of the Olympian gods.

*La caduta di giganti* (*The Fall of the Titans*) which Gluck produced in London (1746) led Handel to say his cook knew as much about counterpoint as Gluck did; but *I Titani* (Milan, 1819), by Salvatore Vignano, drew crowds from all Italy at its première. In magnificent mass effects it showed the Age of Gold, the Age of Silver, the Age of Bronze, and the Age of Iron, of violence and murder, with the imprisoned Titans emerging from the bowels of the earth to combat Jupiter, king of the gods, only to be destroyed. The leading idea of *I Titani*—the evils with which the possession of gold curses humanity—is the subject of Wagner's trilogy, *The Dusk of the Gods.*

*Promethée* (Milan, 1813), Beethoven's Vignano ballet, presents in great tableaux the dawn of civilization. When Prometheus, the Titan, brings from heaven the spark which lights the first fire, man realizes his wretchedness, and gratitude is born in his soul. Musically, the most important "Prometheus" is probably Gabriel Fauré's ultramodern score, *Promethée* (Béziers, 1900), in which a "cyclopean" prelude and a beautiful scene, "Pandora's Funeral," stand out.

Jupiter punished Prometheus for stealing the heavenly fire by chaining him to a rock where eagles fed perpetually on his liver; but according to another fable, Jupiter could devise no worse punishment than creating Pandora, the first woman, and bestowing her on Prometheus as a gift. Pandora passed to earth, with a chest of wedding gifts containing blessings and curses. Forbidden to open the box, her curiosity got the better of her, the blessings escaped into thin air and only hope was left at the bottom of the chest. Operatic Pandoras include Dibdin's *Pandora* (London, 1874), Henri Litolff's *Boîte à Pandore* (Paris, 1871), and Alfred

49

Cellier's *Pandora* (Boston, 1881), based on Longfellow's "Masque of Pandora."

*La naissance de la lyre* (*The Birth of the Lyre*, Paris, 1925), by Albert Roussel after a Reinach version of Sophocles' tale, is an opera in whose nobly simple music a ballet of classic beauty and a finale in Rameau's pure and lofty manner stand out. Little Hermes has "rustled" two of Apollo's steers and made him of their horns and entrails the first lyre. Dragged before the god for punishment he plays a tune on his invention and delighted Apollo abandons cattle raising to become a musician, and trades his long-horns for his little brother's lyre. The score has been called the finest work Roussel thus far has written.

## 2. Gleanings from Mythology's Garden

*Apollo und Dafne* (Hamburg, 1708), by Handel, sings of the nymph who escaped Apollo's embrace by changing into a laurel tree; Lulli's *Phaéton* (Paris, 1663), the youth who dared drive Apollo's sun chariot and fell flaming from the skies. Grétry's *Céphale et Procris* (Paris, 1773) tells of the huntsman whose wife, stirring in the bush where she was hid to watch him woo a supposed forest affinity, is pierced by the javelin he flings at the imagined wild beast, and dies happy when her husband says "that odious Breeze" on whom he called to cool his brow was empty air. *Diane et Endymion* (Paris, 1784) by Piccini; Delibes' charming ballet, *Sylvia, ou la nymphe de Diane* (Paris, 1867); and Wellesz' modernist ballet, *Das Wunder der Diana* (*Diana's Miracle,* Vienna, 1919) sing the Greek goddess of the chase. *Merope* (Venice, 1741), best of Jomelli's, "the Italian Gluck's," operas, tells of the girl Neptune's son, Orion, tried to abduct, only to be blinded by her father, a king of Chios.

*Midas* (Paris, 1914) by Maximilian Steinberg, a ballet russe, presents the musical contest between Apollo, god of the lyre, and Pan, god of the shepherd pipe. When King Midas objects to Apollo's receiving the prize, "the orchestra brays" as the god gives him ass's ears. *Le jugement de Midas* (Paris, 1778; revived 1924) by Grétry stages woodchopper Marsyas' contest with Apollo in a Louis XV village. Midas, the village bailli, the judge, prefers Marsyas' "old songs" to Apollo's. The score was Gluck's contribution to the quarrel between Gluckists and Piccinists, Apollo identified with Gluck's reforms, and Marsyas with Piccini's traditional style of opera. Desmarets wrote a *Vénus et Adonis* (Paris, 1697), and Cambert's *Pomone* (Paris, 1669) shows the god Vertumnus winning the wood nymph, Pomona's, heart as an old woman to embrace her as a handsome youth. It is the first opera in which the bassoon appears in the orchestra.

Saint-Saëns' *Déjanire* (Béziers, 1903) is a song of the shirt, the poisoned shirt Hercules' wife, Déjanire, gave him when he left her for pretty Iole, and which caused his death. A "Prayer to Eros" stands out. *Astarté* (Paris, 1901), Xavier Leroux's Wagnerian score, is a hectic version of the same tale. Queen Omphale, worshiper of Astarte, Syrian goddess of love, is the shirt giver, Déjanire, the girl forgotten. Critics have called the work "no less shameless than the goddess," and Hercules' air, "Voici l'instant," an oasis in its musical desert. *Narcisse* (Paris, 1911), by Tscherepnin, a ballet russe, tells how Narcissus, jilting the nymph Echo, is punished by the gods by making him fall in love with his pretty face reflected in a pool, and by drowning in a struggle to embrace himself. In *Medusa* (New York, 1924), by Tschaikovsky, music from the "Symphonie Pathétique" underlies Fokine's ballet russe, which tells of the fair Greek maid whose golden hair was turned into serpents and whose face changed those who saw it to stone because she had offended Minerva, till the hero, Perseus, looking at the *reflection* of her face in his shield, cut off her head. In *Les Erynnes* (Bordeaux, 1920) the Greek furies, "sisters under their skins" to Medusa, pursue criminal mortals in a ballet to Massenet's striking music. Saint-Saëns' opera, *Antigone* (Paris, 1894), sings of a legendary heroine who, sentenced to be buried alive, hangs herself instead. It contains a fine choral "Hymn to Eros." *Œdipus à Colone* (Paris, 1786), by Sacchini, "a score of incomparable beauty," tells how Œdipus, after delivering the Thebans from the Sphinx, marries their queen, Jocasta, and finds he has wed his own mother. After she commits suicide, he tears out both his eyes and wanders off to die of despair. Leoncavallo's *Edipo Re* (*King Œdipus*, Chicago, 1920) is one of his forgotten scores.

## 3. *Centaurs*

The centaurs, part horse, part man, dwelt in the mountains of Thessaly and Arcadia. Drunken and amorous, slaves to their animal passions, they point the moral that "the race is not always to the swift," and the struggle between them and men is supposed to typify that of barbarism and civilization. *Hippodamie* (Paris, 1708), by Compra, shows a graveyard where golden urns, containing the ashes of Hippodamie's fiancés, gleamed beneath cypresses— for her father killed the young men engaged to her when they could not beat him in the chariot race. *Hippodamia* (Prague, 1891) by Zdenko Fibich is a great operatic trilogy blending "Wagnerian spoken song" with the orchestra in modern style. (1) In

*Pelops' Wedding Journey:* Pelops (other legends make Pirithous Hippodamia's husband) did *not* lose his chariot race. He bribed Ornomaus' charioteer Myrtilus, and thus gained his bride. (2) *Tantalus' Reconciliation.* (3) *The Death of Hippodamia.* The wedding feast in honor of Hippodamia's marriage showed that the admittance of the centaurs to intimate human companionship was a mistake. Flushed with wine, certain of the centaurs offered violence to the bride, and a dreadful battle between the semi-equine and wholly human wedding guests ensued which ended in the death of the unfortunate Hippodamia. *Pirithous* (Paris, 1723) by Mouret tells the tale of this unhappy wedding breakfast in pompous, old-fashioned recitative.

## 4. *Fauns and Satyrs*

### "L'APRÈS-MIDI D'UN FAUNE"

#### (*A Faun's Afternoon*)

CLAUDE DEBUSSY. A ballet russe (Paris, 1912; New York, 1915). The music represents a "prelude" to a faun's afternoon, and expresses the "sensuality and grace contained in Mallarmé's poem" by that title. The leading theme, voiced by the flute, lends "an enveloping sweetness and gentleness" to the composition.

The Faun, half goat, half man (the rôle was created by Nijinsky), day-dreams on the stage, till the appearance of bathing nymphs rouses the worst side of his nature, and only a pause of astonishment which allowed the nymph the Faun had seized to escape, seems to prevent a shocking climax. Promptly censored by the police when given in New York, succeeding performances of the ballet were less animalistic. The peculiar charm of Debussy's musical poem has made it a favorite number of the symphonic repertoire. It is "music like an iridescent web of fire and dew" (Lawrence Gilman).

*Pan and the Star* (Peterborough, MacDowell Festival, 1914), by Edward Burlingame Hill, "music rich in inventive figures," is a pantomime version of the death of Pan, whose passing heralded the end of the mythological age. *Cydalise et le chèvrepied* (Paris, 1923), a ballet by Gabriel Pierné, begins in the Park of Versailles (days of Louis XV), where the pretty dancer, Cydalise, is taught love's lesson by a young faun, and ends in her lodging in the château where the faun leaves her as she falls asleep. A "Dance of the Slaves" (Act II) to "violin arpeggios *à la* Corelli" stands out. Dukelsky's ballet russe *Flore et Zéphyre* (Monte Carlo, 1925) makes faunal Boreas suffer for shooting brother Zephyr and abducting his wife.

## 5. *Medea*

### "MÉDÉE"

LUIGI CHERUBINI. Book of Frambéry (Paris, 1797). This score is considered Cherubini's greatest work, "rich in dignity of thought and tragic grandeur of expression," it stands midway between the old classic opera and the romantic opera to come. Two great overtures, Medea's passionate arias, and her duet with Jason stand out.

Dirce, daughter of Creon, King of Corinth (1224 B.C.?) dreads marriage to Jason, hero of the Golden Fleece, for he already is married to the sorceress Medea, mother of his two children. When Medea demands Jason from King Creon, her husband turns away, and the monarch bids her leave the country. Robbed of her little ones (Act II), Medea manages to wheedle Jason into allowing them to spend a last day with her. Then, sending Dirce a poisoned wedding shift and waiting till she hears the dirges mourning her rival's untimely death, the injured wife rushes into the temple, slays her children and emerges brandishing the dripping dagger. While Jason curses her in vain, a chariot drawn by dragons carries her to Athens, in whose king, Ægeus, she is to find a more faithful husband.

## 6. *Six Great Love Stories of Greek Myth and Legend*

The tale of Cupid (Eros) and Psyche, one of the greatest love stories of all time, is the allegory of the human soul (the Greek word *psyche* means both "butterfly" and "soul") prepared and purified by suffering to find true happiness. Losing her lover, Psyche did not regain him until "wings unto her weary heart were given, and she became Love's bride in heaven."

*Eros et Psyché* (Warsaw, 1915) by Ludomir Rozycki, "the Polish Rimsky-Korsakoff," is a huge cycle in which folk themes, used in a modern way, make the old Greek fable express the longing of the human soul for beauty, freedom, and love. Six operas in one, the Psyche of Greek mythology traverses the centuries in various forms, appearing in ancient Arcady, Roman Alexandria, a medieval Spanish cloister, Paris of the French Revolution, and a present-day European capital, seeking her threefold ideal. *Psyché* (Paris, 1857), by Ambroise Thomas, has some charming pages: a "Chorus of Nymphs," and the Air, "O toi qu'on dit plus belle."

*Acis and Galathea* (Canons, 1720), Handel's "masque" to Gay's poem, contains noble airs and choruses. The shepherd, Acis, loved the nymph, Galathea. Crushed by a rock flung by the jealous cyclops, Polyphemus, her lover was turned by the nymph into a crystal spring, bubbling beneath the stone that slew him. *Die schöne Galathea* (*Fair Galathea,* Vienna, 1865) Franz von Suppé's comic opera, and one of his best works, is a humorous variant of the legend of Pygmalion, the sculptor, who made a statue of Galathea and prayed Venus to endow it with life. When Venus grants his prayer, Galathea deceives Pygmalion with Midas, an art fancier, and as he is about to strike her to earth in his rage, she once more turns into a statue to the accompaniment of thunder and lightning. Suppé's score contains a famous vocal waltz.

*Pyramus and Thisbe* (London, 1716, by Leveridge, and Paris, 1726, by Rebel, to mention but two opera settings) is the Greek myth of the Babylonian boy and girl who so loved each other that when their parents forbade marriage (they lived in adjoining houses) they pressed longing lips to the opposite sides of a crack in the wall. They arranged a tryst, but Thisbe, fleeing from a lioness, dropped her veil which the beast seized in blood-dripping jaws. Pyramus finding the veil and thinking Thisbe devoured, plunged his sword into his heart, and Thisbe, finding him, followed his example.

*Philémon et Baucis* (Paris, 1860) by Charles Gounod sings of the Darby and Joan of ancient Phrygia. Outstanding is the Slumber Romance, "Songes heureux." Jove is hospitably received by the ideally married pair. In recognition he restores their lost youth and impressed by Baucis' beauty (Act II) makes love to her. The virtuous young wife promptly begs for the return of age and wrinkles. Jove, abashed, makes Philemon's and Baucis' youth eternal and—a boon to folk rooted in the soil—promises to change them into trees when they weary of mortal life.

*Ero e Leandro* (Warsaw, 1816), by Kupinski; *Ero e Leandro* (Turin, 1879), by Bottesini; *Hero* (Berlin, 1884), by Ernst Frank; and *Ero e Leandro* (Madrid, 1897), by the composer and conductor, Luigi Mancinelli, are opera versions of the tale that inspired Byron's famous poem. A youth of Abydos so loved Hero, priestess of Venus, living in her tower on the Asian side of the Bosphorus, that he swam over every night to keep her company. Taking to the water once too often he was drowned, and Hero cast herself from her tower into the sea rather than live without him.

In *Sapho* (Paris, 1851) by Charles Gounod, the "Scene of Sappho's Suicide," "Héro sur la tour solitaire," and "O ma lyre immortelle!" are the best known airs. It is staged in Lesbos, where Glycerea is Sappho's rival for the love of young Phaon, who turns a cold shoulder on the poetess. Phaon learns that Sappho has found out he is one of a band of conspirators. When the sensitive Lesbian overhears him cursing her among his comrades, she flings herself headlong from the famous promontory into the sea, curing love by death. *Saffo* (Naples, 1840) by Rossini's imitator, Paccini, is considered his masterpiece. A nineteenth century Parisian Sappho may be considered with her Grecian sisters.

## "SAPHO"

JULES MASSENET. Book by Cain and Bernède (Paris, 1897), after Alphonse Daudet's novel, "written for my sons when they are twenty," and showing the sad results of a young man's cultivation of the *demi-monde,* is one of the composer's weaker scores (1884).

Fresh from the farm, Jean Gaussin meets and loves Fanny (Sappho, as the other girls call her), the artist's model, one of the gay frequenters of his friend Caoudal's studio. Sappho—Jean is handsome—lets him think her an innocent young girl. When Jean's parents and his cousin Irene leave him to return home (Act II) Sappho finds the boy suffering from loneliness, and promises to be his.

After a year of happiness together, Caoudal casually reveals Sappho's past—shadowed by lovers and an illegitimate child—to Jean (Act III). The country boy is shocked. He curses Sappho, true to him ever since they met, and she curses her companions for having robbed her of life's one pure love. But the country to which he returns (Act IV) has lost its charm for Jean. When Sappho seeks him out, she is on the point of winning him back with clinging arms, but his parents intervene and sobbing she watches him led away. It is winter in Paris (Act V). Sappho, tearing up old love letters, sees Jean enter her room. He has cast away parents, home, and career to return to her. But the very words of love with which she greets him recall her earlier life, and wearily dropping into a chair Jean falls asleep. Sappho knows the shadows of her past will always blight their happiness, and her noble soul does not shrink from sacrifice. Writing a note of farewell she tiptoes out of Jean's life while he slumbers.

## 7. The Orphic Operas

Perhaps the most moving love story found in ancient Greek mythology is that which has inspired the "Orphic Operas." Among these are Peri's *Eurydice* (Paris, 1600), the second "opera" or drama set to music with vocal solos supported by instruments (Caccini's *Dafne,* Florence, 1597, was the first); Caccini's *Euridice* (1600, performed after Peri's); and Monteverde's noble *Orfeo* (Mantua, 1607), a dramatic and musical advance on its predecessors. Gluck's score is the first really great Orphic opera. In the revival of Monteverde's score in Mantua, 1610, a prima donna, Adriana Basile, for the first time made a producer (The Duke of Mantua) guarantee by contract that her virtue would be free from attack.

## "ORFEO ED EURIDICE"

### (*Orpheus and Euridice*)

CHRISTOPH WILLIBALD VON GLUCK. Book by Calzabigi (Vienna, 1762). This work *founded the modern school of opera*. The part of Orpheus, originally written for a *male soprano,* is now one of the famous *alto* rôles of the repertoire. The immortal air "Che farò senza Euridice," the picturesque "Chorus of Furies," the idyllic Ballet, "Dance of the Happy Sprites," are among its finest pages.

In a grassy vale Orpheus mourns his lost love beside Eurydice's tomb —while shepherds and their lasses bring flowers—and apostrophizing her shade in a haunting melody, declares he will seek her in the shadowland since he cannot live without her.

In dark Tartarus, the Underworld, while the bark of Cerberus is heard, the Furies dance (Ballet) as Orpheus appears. He moves them to pity with the pathetic air: "Gods of death, have mercy!" and they allow him to enter Hades to pursue his quest.

In the Elysian Fields, where the Spirits of the Blest dance on verdant meads beneath sunny skies to bird song and the murmur of brooks (exquisitely expressed in Gluck's music) Orpheus finds his beloved, clasps her in his arms, and to "a farewell chorus of perfect beauty" leads her up to the world above.

Eurydice, as they thread the cavern leading to the upper air, begs him look in her eyes so she may be sure he still loves her. Forgetting the warning given him, Orpheus turns and embraces her and Eurydice once more is reft from him by death. It is then the luckless husband sings his "Che farò senza Euridice." But Eros appears to let him know the gods have taken pity on his grief, and leads him to Love's temple (change of scene), where Eurydice awaits him, and the chorus sings their happy union.

*Orphée aux enfers* (*Orpheus in the Underworld,* Paris, 1858) by Jacques Offenbach, book by Meilhac and Halévy, is the burlesque pendant to Gluck's score. It presents Orpheus as a Theban music teacher, glad his Eurydice has gone to the devil (he is pursuing Chloe, a shepherdess), forced by public opinion to beg Jove to restore her, and delighted to return to the upper world a merry widower, while Eurydice remains below as a bacchante. The mock-melancholy romance "Si j'étais roi de Boétie," the "Bacchanale" (Act II) in which the Olympians dance the cancan and the noble, tender "Death Song" of Eurydice, contrasting with the parody airs, stand out. *Orpheo* (London, 1793), by Haydn; *Orpheus* (Munich, 1800), by Benda; and *Orphée* (Paris, 1887), by Benjamin Godard yield in interest to *Orphée* (Paris, 1916), by Roger Ducasse, a choral ballet russe which substitutes for the happy ending Gluck's public demanded a dramatic climax (Act II). When the wretched poet, losing Eurydice a second time, refuses to join the wine-stimulated revels of the bacchantes, these wild women of Thrace tear him to pieces. Before the last curtain the head, torn from his body, haloed with golden light, is seen floating downstream on his lyre, from whose strings the waters draw plaintive melody. *L'Orfeide* (*The Orpheide*, Paris, 1920) by G. Francesco Malipiero is an ultramodern dramatic trilogy: *La Morte delle maschere* (*The Death of the Masqueraders*), *Sette Canzoni* (*Seven Songs*), and *Orfeo*. The actor-singer is given "music sung in real life in certain situations." In *The Death of the Masqueraders* Orpheus claps the traditional figures of Italian comedy into a cupboard and consigns them to oblivion; and at his invitation "real folk" in the *Seven Songs* sing melodies actually sung in streets, house, and church.

## 8. *Ariadne*

*Ariadne* (Paris, 1906) by Jules Massenet, book by Mendès is Wagnerian in style (the music of the Underworld Scene especially effective), and introduces symbolism into the Greek myth. The hero, Theseus, slays the Minotaur in the Cretan Labyrinth and invites lovely Ariadne to follow him to Athens; but, after landing, Ariadne is furious when she finds Theseus embracing her sister, Phædra. After she has rescued Phædra, who has been killed, from the Underworld, only to have faithless Theseus run off with her, Ariadne listens to the Sirens' song and drowns herself.

### "ARIADNE AUF NAXOS"

#### (*Ariadne in Naxos*)

RICHARD STRAUSS. Book by Hugo von Hoffmannsthal (Stuttgart, 1912; revised version, Vienna, 1916). A parodistic fricassee—it has been called a "hermaphrodite" opera—combining parts of a Molière comedy, *Le bourgeois gentilhomme* (since elided in favor of an introductory scene) and a simultaneous performance of a serious opera, *Ariadne in Naxos* and a comic Intermezzo, "Faithless Zerbinetta and her Four Lovers," a contrast of profane and ideal loves, in an artistically questionable attempt to wed tragedy and burlesque. Zerbinetta's Coloratura Aria is considered one of the most difficult pyrotechnic numbers of the whole vocal repertory, and there is a wonderful vocal quintet.

In the prologue in the home of a wealthy Viennese music lover (eighteenth century) the rehearsal of an *opera seria*, *Ariadne in Naxos*, is in progress. Music master, dancing master, and the young composer of the opera (Strauss in the self-glorified rôle of the misunderstood genius) appear. "The tenor cuffs the hairdresser, Ariadne awaits her

Count, Zerbinetta receives her officer." The stage resounds with chatter and innuendo, as the major-domo brings the command to present opera and intermezzo simultaneously.

The curtain rises on opera in opera. Theseus, like other heroes of Greek legend, fell out of love as easily as in. Lovely Ariadne, daughter of King Minos of Crete, had furnished him a thread, by which he escaped from the labyrinth after slaying the bull-headed monster Minotaur. Sailing for Athens, Theseus took Ariadne with him. But when she fell asleep on the island of Naxos, he, having fallen in love with her sister Phædra, deserted her.

Ariadne fills the empty isle with her lamentations. Naïad, Dryad, and Echo, "when she falls asleep from exhaustion, waken her to wail anew." A pause gives Zerbinetta and her merry companions a chance to cheer up Ariadne with grotesque dance and song. But Theseus alone can console the deserted bride, and Theseus is on the high seas. In despair, Ariadne begs Hermes, messenger of death, to hasten to her. And now Zerbinetta tries to do alone what she could do together with Harlequin, Truffaldino, Scaramuccio, and Brighella. She presents her philosophy of life—the joys of irresponsibility—in the famous aria. It fails to impress despondent Ariadne, but Zerbinetta's four lovers, roused to enthusiasm by her words, pay ardent court to her, and Harlequin, for whom she jilts the others, disappears with his conquest. Now the three nymphs announce the advent of Bacchus. Ariadne expects death: instead love appears. The librettist leaves it open whether it is love, pure and simple, or love in death which Bacchus bestows as he and Ariadne sing their closing duet.

*Bacchus* (Paris, 1909), Massenet's sequel to his *Ariadne,* has Bacchus carry Ariadne to India's coral strand where, his satyrs defeated by an army of holy apes led by the Brahmin, Ramavacon, Ariadne ascends a Hindoo funeral pyre to save her lover and Bacchus induces Jove to slay the Hindoo queen and he cremates her with a lightning bolt. *Fedra* (Milan, 1915), by the Italian ultramodernist, Ildebrando Pizetti, tells the tale of Theseus' cruel wife, Phædra, after a d'Annunzio tragedy. Phædra falls in love with her husband's son and repulsed by him makes Theseus' jealousy the instrument of his death. D'Annunzio (unlike Euripides) makes Phædra the pitiless analyst of her guilty passion over which she triumphs by suicide. The score employs melodic declamation, the orchestra establishes "atmosphere," and the "Prelude" (Act I) and "Threnody" (Act III) stand out.

### 9.  *Alceste*

### "ALCESTE"

CHRISTOPH WILLIBALD GLUCK. Book by Calsabigi (Vienna, 1767). A Greek myth of wifely self-sacrifice. The airs "Divinités du Styx,"

"Non, ce n'est point," and "Grands dieux" are "among the greatest dramatic expressions of the old monumental opera" (Bie).

King Admetos of Pherae is dying in his palace while his people pray for him in the public square. When his wife Alceste leads them to the temple, the oracle says Admetos must perish unless some one die in his place. Alceste offers herself as the victim and is accepted by Apollo. After telling Admetos, despite his passionate plea to let him die, she bids farewell to earth in a touching air (Act II). But Hercules, appearing, snatches her by brute force from Hades (Act III), whose gloomy portals she already has reached, and restores her to her convalescent husband, Apollo blessing the deed.

*Alceste* (Paris, 1674), by Lully, tells the story in pseudo-classic Louis XIV style, but Quinault's libretto makes Hercules rescue Alceste because he is in love with her. One lovely air is "Le héros que j'attends." *Alkestis* (Mannheim, 1924), by Egon Wellesz, book by Von Hoffmannsthal after Euripides (who has Hercules while drunk rescue Alceste to oblige his friend, Admetos) makes Alceste dare death for the ideal of monarchy instead of for love of her husband. *Alkestis* (London, 1924) by Rutland Boughton, a modern music drama with folkwise music of classic beauty, makes Admetos accept Alceste's sacrifice lest his people suffer.

## 10. *The Iliad*

*Paride ed Elena* (Vienna, 1769), by Gluck, makes Paris sing his famous love song, "O del mio dolce ardor," to his lady (Act II), and after a martial ballet in Menelaus' palace (Act III) win her heart with stormy wooing, vanquish her scruples in an even more passionate love scene (Act IV) and induce her to fly with him (Act V), a chorus and ballet attending their taking ship for Troy. *Hélène* (Paris, 1904), by Saint-Saëns, inspired by Gluck, devotes its one act to the flight of the lovers from Sparta, and is a long and passionate duet between them. Venus appears urging Helen to leave her husband, while Pallas dissuades her from so doing.

### "LA BELLE HÉLÈNE"

JACQUES OFFENBACH. Book by Meilhac and Halévy (Paris, 1864). This *opera buffa* score, after *Orphée aux enfers* the composer's most successful Grecian burlesque, has become a classic of its kind.

Before Jove's temple in Sparta, Helen, who does not love her husband, old Menelaus, talks to Calchas, the high priest, of the handsome shepherd Venus has promised as a prize to the fairest of women. When Paris appears disguised as a young sheepman Helen falls in love with him. Helen and Paris (after a fervid love duet) are clasped in each others' arms when King Menelaus surprises them (Act II) and raises a tremendous row, calling on the other kings of Greece for help. At the bathing resort of Nauplia (Act III) Menelaus leaves the decision as to whether Helen has been guilty of misconduct to the chief augur of the goddess Venus. The latter declares Helen must sail with him to Cytherea. But no sooner is she aboard than the supposed priest flings off his disguise and Paris, splendidly attired, stands revealed. In a rage the Greek kings decide upon the Trojan War and the curtain falls to a martial chorus.

### IPHIGENIA IN AULIS

The Greek fleet lay at anchor in the harbor of Aulis, its mariners vainly whistling for a wind. King Agamemnon had slain a stag sacred to Diana, and Calchas—the soothsayer—declared that only if he sacrificed his daughter to the divinity would the wind blow. Distracted between duty and love for his child, who had come to the camp against his wish, Agamemnon listens to the reproaches of Achilles, to whom the maid is betrothed, for he has accused her lover of faithlessness to drive her away. The people clamor for the sacrifice and Achilles vainly leads his Myrmidons to her rescue; a tempest wraps victim and altar in darkness and when it passes Iphigenia appears on a cloud with the goddess Diana, who announces that she shall serve as her priestess elsewhere. While the people praise the goddess the wind fills the sails of the Grecian ships.

*Iphigénie en Aulide* (Paris, 1778) by Christoph Willibald Gluck, book after Racine's play, is rich in music of human interest. Dubarry tried to prevent its production, and Wagner reëdited it. A noble overture (gradual development of a tempest); Iphigenia's F major aria, Agamemnon's dramatic solo scene, and the pathetic closing scene are great musical moments.

Among countless other Iphigenia operas Cherubini's *Ifigenia in Aulide* (Turin, 1788) may be mentioned. Various operas deal with incidents of the struggle between Greeks and Trojans without the walls of Troy. Grétry's *Andromaque* (Paris, 1780) is the tragedy of Hector's wife, who sought to fling herself headlong from the walls when she heard the cruel news of her husband's death.

*Die Kriegsgefangene* (*The Prisqner of War*, Vienna, 1899) by Karl Goldmark, book by Schlicht, presents Briseis, Achilles' concubine, mourning her loveless life; but dismissed by her master, Briseis no sooner has entered the ship awaiting her than Achilles realizes he loves her. Their grand duet of passion is the outstanding musical number of the score.

## "LA PRISE DE TROIE"

### (*The Taking of Troy*)

HECTOR BERLIOZ. Book by the composer (Karlsruhe, 1890). As in the companion score, *Les Troyens à Carthage,* the balance of power rests in the orchestra which achieves the eloquent and picturesque in instrumental combinations. "Berlioz' instruments are as living as his personages are dead. Especially when the spirits of the departed appear, does he stir the depths in characteristic orchestral color" (Bie).

The Trojans in the deserted Greek camp talk of the great wooden horse the departed invaders have built in honor of Pallas when Cassandra appears and prophesies Troy's destruction. Her betrothed Choroëbus begs her to leave the doomed city and on her refusal swears to remain with her. The Trojans sacrifice to the gods beneath the walls of Troy (Act II), but while Priam blesses Astyanax, son of dead Hector, brought by his weeping mother Andromache, Cassandra again prophesies Troy's downfall, only to be told by Æneas that the people have dragged the wooden horse into the town.

Hector's ghost appears to Æneas in his tent (Act III), telling him Troy is doomed and bidding him found a new empire in Italy. Then Pantheus rushes in: Troy is aflame; Greek warriors have crept out of the wooden horse; Æneas must lead the Trojans to battle. In the temple of Cybele, Cassandra tells how Æneas, bravely fighting, has escaped, but that her lover Choroëbus has fallen. As the victorious Greeks rush in she plunges the dagger into her heart, an example followed by her priestesses.

There is a musically important *Cassandra* (Bologna, 1905) by the Italian modernist, Vittorio Gnecchi. The piquant picture of Achilles, the Greek hero, gamboling in skirts with girl companions on the isle of Scyros inspired Cherubini's ballet, *Achille à Scyros* (Paris, 1804) and Arne's opera, *Achilles in Petticoats* (London, 1767). Henri Maréchal's expressive *Déidamie* (Paris, 1893) shows Ulysses luring the supposed maid out of her dresses by a glimpse of a glittering sword, the youthful hero hurrying to the Trojan War despite the pleas of his wife Déidamie. *Achille auf Skyros* (Düsseldorf, 1925), by Egon Wellesz, the Austrian modernist's ballet, tells the same tale. An overture, picturing an Orphic night "filled with Nature's woodland weaving," the music to the scene where Achilles plays ball with the other girls, the "Mirror Dance," Achilles' "Sword Dance," dramatic climax of the score, and the lament of Déidamie as he leaves to join the Greek fleet, stand out.

## 11. *Other Atridæ*

The Atridæ (members of King Agamemnon's family) were a tragic race and have motived works by such opposites as Mozart and Strauss. *Idomeneus* (Munich, 1781), by Mozart, book by Varesco, contains fine choruses and arias. Mozart, like Campra (*Idomenée*, Paris, 1712) shows Electra unhappy in love and in her family life. In Mozart's ballet music a graceful gavotte stands out. Idomeneus, King of Crete, tempest-tossed on his way back from Troy, vows to sacrifice to Neptune the first human being he meets ashore if he escapes. His son, Idamante, meets him at the gangplank. To cheat the sea god his father bids him fly with Electra (come to Crete after her mother's murder) to Argos, marry her and rule the Mycenæan land. But though Idamante slays the sea monster Neptune sends as a terrible reminder of Idomeneus' broken vow, his father prepares the sacrificial knife. As he raises it Ilia (Priam's daughter, Idomeneus' prisoner, and Idamante's true love) rushes up. The lovers' pleas to die for each other melt Neptune's heart, his statue bids them wed, and only Electra, who has lost a husband, cannot share in the general rejoicing.

### "ELEKTRA"

RICHARD STRAUSS. Book by Hugo von Hoffmannsthal (Dresden, 1909). A savage, impetuous score, *Elektra* is a more powerful soul-portrait than *Salome*. Musically the effect of the work lies in the orchestra; but the "Scene of Recognition" between Orestes and his sister Elektra is wonderfully impressive in its quiet beauty.

When Agamemnon returned with the other kings of Greece from Troy, his wife Clytemnestra and her lover Ægisthus foully murdered him in his bath. Around the fountain in the court of the palace of Mycenæ the maids gossip about Elektra. The blows of the ax with which her father was slain reëcho in her soul. The maids gone, she sings her wild lament, which has its climax in the promise that his children will avenge their father and a frenetic dance of blood-thirsty joy. Her sister Chrysosthemis—"Yearning"—now appears. She would leave Mycenæ and seek love, a husband, and the joys of motherhood elsewhere, but Elektra mocks her. Then guilty Clytemnestra, radiant with jewels but ravaged by remorse, is led into the court. Elektra draws a picture of her mother's death at the avenger's hand, and rejoices in her torture. Clytemnestra's servant whispers to her and Chrysosthemis cries "Orestes is dead!" Then Elektra digs up the rusty ax which slew her father. She will avenge him since Orestes is no more. But the stranger who had brought the message steps up to her—he is Orestes himself, who, in order to lull suspicion, has given out the false report. He enters the palace door while Elektra runs to and fro before it like a wild beast. A terrible scream sounds from within—it is Clytemnestra's death cry! (In Lemoyne's *Electre,* Paris, 1782, Orestes taps his mother's head with the ax *on* instead of *off* the stage.) Ægisthus comes up. Elektra holds the torch for him to enter the palace and find his death in turn, then dances in a frenzy of glutted vengeance till she falls senseless.

Various operas deal specifically with Orestes' share in his family tragedy. *Orestes* (Leipzig, 1902), by Felix Weingartner after Æschylus, a trio of Wagnerian scores (*Agamemnon, Das Totenopfer, Die Erinnyen*) with fine pages and moments, has passed from the repertoire. *Agamemnon,* ending with the death cry of the King slain by Clytemnestra, his wife, prepares the matricide to follow. *The Sacrifice* deals with Orestes' murder of his mother and his flight to the temple of Delphi. *The Erynnes* is the tale of Orestes haunted by the Furies till in Athens the goddess Athena declares him innocent of crime, and sends him to rescue his sister, Iphigenia, in Tauris (at which point the legend is continued by Gluck in *Iphigénie en Tauride*).

## "IPHIGÉNIE EN TAURIDE"

### (*Iphigenia in Tauris*)

CHRISTOPH WILLIBALD GLUCK. Book by Guillard (Paris, 1779). Gluck wrote his supreme fusion of musical beauty and dramatic truth at the age of sixty-five. Like Wagner in the case of the sister score, Richard Strauss has prepared a modern version of this one. It is rich in beautiful music: Iphigenia's Airs "O toi, qui prolongéras mes jours," "Malheureuse Iphigénie," "Je t'implore et tremble," and the Hymn to Artemis, "Chaste fille de Latone"; Orestes' "Le calme rentre dans mon coeur"; Pylades' "Unis dès la plus tendre enfance." Orestes' Mad Scene (Act II) has been termed "Gluck's greatest single achievement." The ballet (*Scythian Dances*) exists as a separate number of the ballet repertoire.

In the Tauric Diana's temple (Act I) Iphigenia tells Scythian priestess maids her dream of misfortune visited on her family in distant Mycenæ (Agamemnon's murder by Clytemnestra) and when Thoas, the Scythian king, demands a human sacrifice for the goddess, he is informed that victims have been cast on his shores by the waves. They are Iphigenia's brother Orestes—the matricide, pursued by the Furies— and his friend Pylades. In the temple Orestes' mind gives way as his sister questions him (Act II), but without revealing his name he tells her the horrid tale of the family tragedy. Iphigenia, because Orestes resembles her brother, tries to save him from his doom (Act III), and Pylades agrees to carry a letter to Elektra, hoping to save his friend. The sacrificial knife is raised above Orestes when suddenly

Iphigenia recognizes him (Act IV). As King Thoas insists on his blood-victim, the sister offers to die with her brother, but Pylades entering with a party, rescues both, killing Thoas, and Diana appearing, commands her priestess to return to Greece with her stolen image before which the Scythians celebrated their bloody rites.

*Iphigénie en Tauride* (Paris, 1781) by Niccolò Piccini, book by Ginguène, was a competitive setting by the composer the Du Barry put forward as the representative of Italian musical taste (simply accompanied melody) in the struggle against the reforms (dramatic declamation and fuller orchestral treatment) that Queen Marie-Antoinette's teacher, Gluck, had introduced. It failed on its first night. The beautiful Laguerre, who sang the rôle of Iphigenia, came on the stage hopelessly drunk, and Sophie Arnould (who had created the same title rôle in Gluck's opera), shrieking with laughter, cried: "No, no, she is not Iphigenia in Tauris, she is Iphigenia in Champagne!"

## 12. The Odyssey

In his *Homerische Welt* (*Homeric World*), a great foursome of scores—*Kirke* (1898), *Nausikaa* (1901), *Odysseus Heimkehr* (1896), and *Odysseus Tod* (1903)—August Bungert attempted to challenge comparison with Wagner's *Nibelungen* trilogy and free the world from Wagnerian tyranny. Dresden was to be the Baireuth of a purer, more classic musical gospel. But it soon was evident Bungert was merely "a Meyerbeer in disguise" and, despite grandiose pretentions, his scores (which have fine melodic moments) have passed from the repertoire.

*Ritorno d'Ulisse in patria* (*Ulysses' Home-coming,* Venice, 1641; Paris, 1925), by Monteverde, is a "vast musical sketch in the painter Tintoretto's style," in which the massacre of the suitors (Act II) is the most dramatic page. *Der Bogen des Odysseus* (*Ulysses' Bow*), a transition from the sublime to the ridiculous, is a clever adaptation by Leopold Schmidt (Frankfort, 1913) of music from Offenbach scores to a classic burlesque. *Circe e Calypso* (Turin, 1892), by Buongiorno, is unimportant; and *Circé* (Paris, 1907), lyric drama by Paul and Lucien Hillemacher, is "laboriously insignificant music," but *Circé* (Madrid, 1902), by the Spaniard, Chapi, striving to reconcile Wagnerian forms and Latin tendencies, is a work of serious value.

*Nausicaa* (Monte Carlo, 1919) by Reynaldo Hahn, book by Fauchois, is possibly the composer's best opera. Simple distinction marks its music, and the songs of the heroine and her maidens have lyric charm. Ulysses and Nausicaa, the king's daughter, meeting on the Phæacean strand, Nausicaa's heart goes out to the stranger

for whom in her father's palace hall she sings the victory of
the Greeks over the Trojans. When he takes up her song from
his own memories of the stirring years, all recognize the hero
and press him to stay (Act II). Has not all changed at home
during his long absence? "Not the heart of Penelope!" declares
Pallas Athene, appearing to them, and lovely Nausicaa's tears flow
at the departure of the man she loves.

*Pénélope* (Paris, 1913) by Gustave Fauré, "the most genuinely
natural Hellenic work of our time," focuses on the faithful wife
who, spinning among her maids and hounded by the suitors who
daily carouse in her home, yearns for her husband. Ulysses appears as an old beggar, submits to the abuse of the suitors and
threatens to strangle Eurycle, his old nurse, if she betray his identity. Then (Act II) he reveals himself to his faithful herdsmen,
who joyfully promise to hasten to the palace that evening. There
(Act III) in the great "Scene of the Bow"—the musical and
dramatic climax of the score (though a beautiful orchestral prelude,
Act I, tells Penelope's longing)—the suitors, after vainly trying
to span the hero's great bow, scornfully let the beggar try. And
he, drawing it without effort, slays the fleeing suitors, pursued by
the herdsmen, and takes Penelope in his arms.

## 13. *Vistas from Greek History*

The old Greek fabulist who has so weirdly come into his own
in the moving pictures to-day has been remembered in Konradin
Kreutzer's *Æsop am Hofe des Königs Kroesus* (*Æsop at the
Court of King Crœsus,* Donaueschingen, 1821).

*Le roi Candaule* (Paris, 1920) by Alfred Bruneau, book by
Donnay after Gautier's romance, *L'anneau de Gyges,* is a lyric
score in which Nyssia's revery, "O nuit étrange," and a concluding
duet, "one of the most poignant pages Bruneau has written,"
stand out. King Candaule of Lydia is so enraptured by the loveliness of his wife, Nyssia, that he must share his admiration. He
has Gyges, captain of his guard, gaze on Nyssia in beauty unadorned. Nyssia, daughter of a Persian satrap, discovers the
peeper. Outraged she tells Gyges to choose between slaying his
king and winning her love, or being slain. Gyges makes the
obvious choice. As he stands on the threshold of nuptial bliss,
about to pass into Nyssia's chamber, the dead king's shade appears.
But in ancient days no shade of a departed husband could trouble
two happy lovers in the flesh. Eugene Diaz' *Le roi Candaule*
(Paris, 1865) won a government prize, but is now forgotten.

Anacreon (born 560 B.C.), the Ionian poet who sang of wine
only to choke to death on a grape pit, has been remembered by

Cherubini in *Anacréon ou l'amour fugitif* (Paris, 1803) and by Grétry, *Anacréon chez Polycrate* (Paris, 1797), two airs from which, "Si des tristes cypresses" and "Songe enchanteur," still are sung.

*Andromena* (Basel, 1924), by Pierre Maurice, takes us to an Attic studio, where Phyrrasius, yearning to create an ideal picture of Andromena's anguish while chained to the rock, makes a martyr of his unfortunate slave and model Doris, who loves him. As he puts the finishing touch to his masterpiece he realizes he has murdered her for Art's sake. But when Nicias, Phyrrasius' pupil, tries to rouse the mob against his master, the people kneel, overcome by the beauty of the painting in which Doris seems to live, immortal.

Grétry's *Aspasie* (Paris, 1789) is devoted to Pericles' talented affinity. The death tragedy of the most unhappily married of philosophers has been presented by a modern musical ironist, Erik Satie, in *Socrate* (Paris, 1924), "one of those monuments of cold-storage musical humor belonging in the pantheon of the *Chat Noir.*"

*Phryné* (Paris, 1893) by Saint-Saëns, a classic *opéra comique*, contains a charming air in which a slave describes Phyrné's bed, and a noble aria depicting Aphrodite rising from the foam. Dicephilus is a miser; his nephew, Nicias, a spendthrift. The uncle buys up the nephew's debts and is about to have him arrested when the courtesan Phryné makes her slaves drive off the police and takes the unfortunate boy into her home. When Dicephilus appeals to the Areopagus (town council) Phryné's charms cajole him into forgiving the youth.

## "DIE VÖGEL"

### (*The Birds*)

WALTER BRAUNFELS. (A Lyric Fantasy Play, Munich, 1921.) Book after Aristophanes' (448-385 B.C.) comedy *The Birds*. The modern musical score, rich in melody, has been called "absolute scenic music of symphonic depth." Notable are a romantic "Bird Concert," full of piping, fluttering movement, a delightful Ballet, "Turtledove Wedding," and a "Song of the Nightingale."

Good Counsel and Good Hope, Athenian citizens disillusioned with life, retire to the woods to the society of the birds. Winning the confidence of the wren, the latter introduces them to Hoopoë, king of the birds, and Good Counsel suggests they build a gigantic bird city. Then the odor of human burnt offerings no longer will reach the nostrils of the gods; and the birds, nearer Olympus, may even conquer and rule its inhabitants. Good Hope scorns such ambitions. He prefers to listen to the nightingale sing in the moonlight, dreaming dreams of the beautiful in life and art. While he dreams the bird metropolis rises to the skies in the shape of a huge nest, but Zeus, the Thunderer, sends Prometheus to the bird folk to warn them, and when they scorn his warning, he destroys their city with storm and lightning.

The poor, homeless birds fly to the trees for refuge. Good Counsel, the materialist, returns to the home comforts and fleshpots of Athens; Good Hope goes with him, but clings to his ideals and finds happiness in yearnings only dreams can satisfy.

*Philotis, danseuse de Corinth* (Paris, 1914), by Gaubert, is a ballet, with colorful bacchic and religious dances. Philotis, a *danseuse* no better than she should be, weans the young musician, Lycas, away from Thetes, his betrothed, tries to stab her virtuous rival, and the god Apollo has to drive her away so that the lovers may celebrate their reunion with a wild dance of joy.

Aristotle, who taught Alexander the Great to sleep with a copy of Homer under his pillow, is the hero of the Swedish composer, Ivar Hallström's *Aristoteles* (Stockholm, 1886). Though Johann Georg Conradi, one of the earliest German opera composers in *Diogenes* (Hamburg, 1691), devoted a serious score to the philosopher who lived in a barrel, later musicians have preferred a humorous treatment. In *Diogenes* (Berlin, 1902), by Bogumil Zepler, Diogenes, a bankrupt man about town, takes refuge in his barrel, the better to borrow from strangers. Instead of hunting with a lantern by daylight for an honest man, he aids the courtesan, Laïs, win the heart of the sculptor, Phaon, who refuses to kiss any girl because he is a vegetarian.

*Die Tänzerin* (*The Dancer,* Cologne, 1905) by Arthur Friedheim influenced by Wagner and Liszt, is an operatic version of the beginning of the career of Alexander the Great. Lovely Thaïs, philosophizing with Diogenes in his barrel, loses her heart to Alexander. At a great feast (Act II) her heart reacts upon her muscles, and she cannot dance for the Macedonian. But when he calls the youth of Greece to the conquest of Asia (Act III) she forgets philosophy and flings herself into his arms, while Diogenes sadly returns to his barrel to comfort himself with onions.

Older eighteenth century composers delighted in celebrating Alexander in countless operas, mainly written to texts by Metastasio. We have Alexander in Sidon, Ephesus, Armenia, Susa, Babylon, Persia, and the Indies. Some of these older operas survive in a favorite air; Handel's *Alessandro* (London, 1726), in "Lusinghe più care"; Leonardo Leo's *Alessandro in Persia* (London, 1746), in "Dirti, ben mio"; Piccini's *Alessandro nelle Indie* (Rome, 1758) in "Se il ciel mi divide"; and Sacchini's *Alessandro nelle Indie* (Venice, 1763), a popular "hit" of its day, in "Se mai più saro geloso." Cherubini's *Alessandro nelle Indie* (Mantua,

1784) and the modern score *Persepolis* (Rostock, 1909), by Rudolf Zingel, may also be mentioned.

## "OLYMPIE"

GASPARO SPONTINI. Book by Dieulafoy and Briffault after Voltaire's play (Paris, 1819). This opera contains grandiose vocal movements (Cassandra's Duet with Olympia), melodies, and choruses, yet seems artificial in the quality of its emotions. Some call it Spontini's finest work, others "a spectacle opera full of hollow noise."

In Diana's temple at Ephesus, fifteen years after the death of Alexander the Great, Cassander, King of Macedon, and Antigonus, King of Syria, meet to discuss an alliance. In that city, too, dwells Statyra, Alexander's widow, a temple priestess, with her daughter Olympia, brought up under the name of Amenia. Cassander—who saved the girl's life when her father was slain—leads her to the temple altar to wed her. But Statyra, who is to marry them, as all kneel in prayer, sees Cassander's face. With terrible curses she accuses the Macedonian king as her husband's slayer, and bids hapless Olympia spurn the man she loves. Duty and love struggle in Olympia's breast; but she chooses the path of duty. Antigonus has declared himself ready to avenge Alexander's murder. Defeated in battle by Cassander, however, Antigonus, in his death agony, admits Statyra was mistaken. *He* was the assassin of great Alexander, and Statyra ascends the throne and unites the happy lovers Cassander and Olympia.

*Erostrate* (Baden-Baden, 1862) by Ernest Reyer is devoted to Herostratus, a Grecian nobody whose craving for "publicity" was so great that rather than go down to his grave unsung he seized a torch one October night, in 356 B.C., and wantonly set fire to the Temple of Diana at Ephesus. The ancient world broke out into one cry of horror and despair, but Herostratus was content—his name would go down in history! Méry, who wrote Reyer's book, makes Erostrate commit arson to win the courtesan Athenaïs who, content with what he has done for her sake, leaps with him into the flames. A nocturnal scene between Erostrate and Athenaïs (Act I) and a charming duettino, "Oui, nous irons à Mitylène," stand out.

## "BRISEÏS"

EMMANUEL CHABRIER. Book by Ephraim Mikhaël and Catulle Mendès (Paris, 1899). The tale of the opera goes back to a legend in the "Marvel" of Phlegon of Thralles, and suggested Goethe's *Die Braut von Korinth* and Anatole France's poem "Les noces corinthiennes." Chabrier died before completing his score, but his first act was found to contain the complete story and was given as a three-act lyric drama. Audaciously modern and dissonant, it contains beautiful pages; the

"Sailors' Chorus"; Hylas and Briseïs' love scene, and Briseïs' song, "Là-bas, dans les cités d'Asie."

Near Corinth, Briseïs, who loves the sailor Hylas, lives with her mother Thanastos, afflicted with a mysterious ailment. To marry his sweetheart Hylas must seek distant Asian shores, and gain rich stuffs, ivory and pearls, to win Briseïs' hand. Hylas' galley swims into the moonlit cove, and he comes ashore to bid Briseïs farewell. When he has torn himself from her arms Briseïs is roused from revery by her mother's cries. She had bidden her lover beware of the dissolute Asian cities but the danger which threatens him is in Corinth. For in her agony Thanastos, while Briseïs prays to Apollo, suddenly calls on the God of the Christians to save her; and in answer to her prayer an apostle appears. He raises his cross and says Thanastos shall be saved if Briseïs become the bride of Christ. Vainly the poor girl resists; she cannot refuse her dying mother's plea. The remaining acts present Briseïs' baptism in the sea, her sacred nuptials interrupted by Hylas' arrival; the poor maid's struggle between love and duty; and her driving the dagger into her breast. Before killing herself she promises Hylas she will be true to her vow and come to him. And, a Christian ghost, her spirit leads him to the tomb, where the lovers are united in a grave covered with blossoms.

*Les noces corinthiennes* (*The Corinthian Nuptials,* Paris, 1921), by Henri Büsser, tells the tale after Anatole France's poem. Daphne, a Corinthian girl, torn between love for her betrothed and her conscientious scruples—her Christian mother has vowed her virginity to God—takes poison in order to betray neither heavenly nor earthly bridegroom. Coppola's *La fidanzata di Corinto* (Turin, 1905) is an Italian operatic version of the same sad tale. *Les dieux sont morts* (*The Gods Are Dead,* Paris, 1924) by Charles Tournemire, book by Berteaux, is a series of tableaux "having the immobility of religious frescoes" to music of noble sincerity. Chryseis, a Greek virgin, loved by the shepherd Eugoras, turns Christian. When she curses Zeus, father of the gods, he demands she be sacrificed for blasphemy. Cheerfully Chryseis insists on being buried alive at the foot of the sacred oak. Her lover dies with her and—prophetic of Christianity's advent—the terrified people see a huge shadow cross rise above the martyrs' tomb.

# CHAPTER III

## THE GRANDEUR THAT WAS ROME

### 1. From the Days of the Republic

Rome's earlier days, when hardy heroes of kingdom and republic took their daily dip in the cold waters of the Tiber, emerging ready for heroic deeds, have been celebrated in opera mainly by older composers in scores like Alessandro Scarlatti's *Pompeo* (Naples, 1684), his pupil Giacomelli's best score, *Cesare in Egitto* (Turin, 1735), Vivaldi's *Catone in Utica* (Verona, 1737), Hasse's *Numa Pompilio* (Dresden, 1741), and Graun's—the Graun of the "Seven Last Words"—*Coriolano* (Berlin, 1750). Among Handel's Roman operas are *Flavio* (London, 1723), *Scipione* (London, 1726), and *Giulio Cesare* (London, 1724; revived, 1923, in Göttingen, "the Handel Baireuth"). Mozart's *Il sogno di Scipione* (Salzburg, 1772) and *Lucio Silla* (Munich, 1772), Grétry's *Les mariages samnites* (Paris, 1776) and Cherubini's *Quinto Fabio* (Rome, 1783) also may be mentioned.

### "LA VESTALE"

#### (The Vestal)

GASPARO SPONTINI. Book by De Jouey (Paris, 1807). First performed at the express command of Napoleon I. Licinius' and Cinna's duet, "Quand l'amitié seconde mon courage," the "Vestals' Morning Hymn," and the Head Vestal's Aria, "L'amour est un monstre barbare," stand out (Act I). Chastely sad is Julia's pathetic air as she waits for her lover (Act II), passionate her aria, "Impitoyables dieux"; touching in its simplicity Licinius' cavatina, "Les dieux prendront pitié." In Act III a beautiful "Chorus of Vestals," and a divine air in which Julia expresses her constancy, "Toi que je laisse sur la terre" impress.

The Roman Consul Licinius, victorious in a campaign against the Gauls, returning to Rome for his triumph, finds Julia, his fiancée, has become a vestal virgin. Mad with longing and despair, he manages to obtain the promise of an interview.

It is the night. Julia tends the holy flame of Vesta which never must be extinguished. After the departure of the Head Vestal, who gives Julia the golden rod to stir the altar fire, she unbars the temple's gate for her lover. Alas, as they lament the cruelty of Fate, Julia in Licinius' arms forgets the sacred fire. Suddenly the flame goes out, and Julia falls fainting at the altar's foot. Licinius, about to carry her away, is surprised by the other vestals. News of the sacrilege spreads, the Romans surround the temple, clamoring for the death of the recreant priestess, and Licinius is with difficulty torn from the spot by his friend Cinna. The Pontiff Maximus arrives and covering Julia with a black veil, lays her white one, which she no longer is worthy to wear, upon the altar, and condemns her to the living death.

On the brink of the stone tomb in which she is to be buried alive Julia addresses her last prayer to the gods. Licinius, coming up with his legionaries, declares he alone is guilty, and demands death in Julia's stead. The priests deny his request. At that moment a bolt of lightning strikes Julia's veil on the altar and sets it aflame. The goddess Vesta herself has rekindled her holy fire and forgiven her guilty priestess. While Licinius takes fainting Julia into his arms, the Pontiff Maximus bids the young lovers adore the goddess Venus, and their marriage vows are spoken while games and dances begin in their honor.

*La Vestale* (Milan, 1818), Vignano's most perfect ballet, was a pantomime version of Spontini's opera. A genuine chariot race in antique style and a sacred Bacchanale were among its features, and the tragic grandeur of the climaxing scenes led Stendhal to call the drama "as powerful as the most gripping of Shakespeare's."

In *La Vestale* (Paris, 1841) by Mercadante the vestal virgin Emelia really is buried alive, while her lover kills himself instead of the high priest he means to kill. The Vestal's prayer "Giunia se fine" stands out. *Roma* (Monte Carlo, 1912) by Massenet, book by Cain, takes us to Rome during the Punic Wars, with Hannibal at the gates. Fausta, daughter of the Roman general Fabius Maximus, is the vestal who lets error creep into her heart and arms in the shape of young Lentulus, and whose kindly father presses a dagger on his child to spare her suffocation within her tomb. The "Sacred Dances" (Act III) should be mentioned. *Cordelia* (Petrograd, 1883) by Solovieff, after Sardou's drama *La Haine*, is a Meyerbeerian score whose heroine finds a tragic end amid the struggles of patricians and plebeians in republican Rome. The gladiators, brutal heroes of the "blood and sand" of the Roman arena are invested with the halo of romance in Foroni's *I Gladiatori* (Milan, 1851), Orefice's *I Gladiatori* (Madrid, 1898) and *Spartacus* (Marseilles, 1880) by Monsigu, a musically worthy work. Spartacus, forced to become a gladiator, escapes, but after defeating the Romans, forgets his people in the arms of the courtesan Claudia, and is killed in battle. Plantania's *Spartaco* (Naples, 1891) boasted a great "Roman Orgy," scenically reproducing Couture's famous painting, "The Decadence of the Romans." The "Roman Orgy" is a natural introduction to the operas of the empire.

*Messaline* (Monte Carlo, 1899) by Isidore de Lara, book by Sylvestre and Moraud, is a spectacular score, with a repelling story and "musical ideas poor in quality." In the gardens of the imperial palace (Rome, 40 A.D.) shameless Messaline with her lips closes the mouth of Hares, who sings vile songs about her. Later (Act II), Messaline, on a slumming party, meets his brother, the gladiator Helion, and infatuated with his muscles, lets him rescue her in a drunken row. In the boudoir of a friend, a Roman courtesan (Act III), Messaline and Helion make passionate love when Hares enters, reproaches the empress, and is cast into the Tiber, where fishermen (change of scene) rescue him. In the imperial box at the Circus (Act IV) Helion—who knows his brother was drowned, but not that he has been rescued—determines to slay Messaline. She bares her breast to his sword but he cannot strike. Telling him she fears a man standing near the box he turns, pierces the latter's heart with his blade, and discovers that he has slain his brother.

## 2. *The Neronian Scores*

Composers have delighted to array Nero, premier "bad man" of the Roman empire, in operatic garb. Monteverde's *Incoronazione di Poppea* (Venice, 1624; revised, Paris, 1913, in Vincent d'Indy's "restoration"), tells to beautiful music the tale of Nero's empress who died of the brutal kick he gave her while with child. Kunst's *The Cruelty of Nero* (Moscow, 1703) was a "comedy" opera, given for a state entry of Peter the Great into the city. Handel's *Nero, or Love Attained through Blood and Murder* (Hamburg, 1705), Duni's *Nerone* (Rome, 1735), the *Quo Vadis* of its day; Torchi's *La Morte di Nerone* (Venice, 1792) precede *Nero* (Hamburg, 1879) "the most shining example of Rubinstein's dramatic creative power" (Von Bülow), relating the imperial degenerate's pursuit of lovely Christian Chrysis, her slaying by the mob while Rome burns, and Nero's cowardly suicide. Giovanetti's *Petronio* (Rome, 1924) is a recent Neronian score.

### "QUO VADIS"

#### (*Whither Goest Thou?*)

JEAN NOUGUÈS. Book by Cain, after Sienkiewicz' novel (Nice, 1909; Philadelphia, 1911). An effective spectacular opera by a musical realist, with gripping dramatic and passionate lyric pages. Eunice's and Iris' duet, "Gentle Spring" (Act I), Nero's "Arise, O ardent flame," Lygia's "There is a God" (Act II), the "Funeral March" (Act IV), and Petronius' and Eunice's "Death Duet" (Act V) stand out.

In the palace of Petronius ("Beau Brummel" of Roman society), Eunice and Iris, beautiful slaves, deck Venus' altar with garlands. Petronius enters with Vinicius, and the latter tells of a girl with whom —watching her unseen as she bathed—he has fallen in love. Lygia, the girl in question, is a Roman hostage, daughter of a barbarian king, guarded by Ursus, a giant slave. When Vinicius spoke to her she traced the outline of a fish in the sand and fled. After Vinicius has rejected Petronius' offer of Eunice, the soothsayer Chilon is sent to discover the meaning of the fish symbol, and Eunice passionately kisses the lips of Petronius' statue once the friends have gone.

The revelry in Nero's "Golden House" grates on his empress Poppæa, jealously hiding in the gardens—for Petronius has brought lovely Lygia to the feast! When Poppæa reproaches the *arbiter elegantiarum* he soothes her and she enters the palace, while Vinicius and Lygia seek the shadow of the trees. Vinicius avows his passion, but when Lygia says her God is not his god, desire overcomes him. About to seize her, however, giant Ursus breaks through the hedge and bears her away. Now burning Rome lights the skies, and Nero, appearing with his drunken crew, breaks into exultant song as he beats his lyre. The roar of the enraged mob interrupts him, however, and cowering in terror, Petronius, at Poppæa's request, pacifies the crowd so that the orgy may proceed.

Chilon, questioning Sporus, before whose tavern gladiators drink, denies lodging a virgin in his den, but admits he boards a giant, the gladiator Croton. Demas, a Christian, has seen Chilon idly trace the Christian's pass-sign on the ground, so tells Chilon those he seeks are in his home. Night comes; the Christians gather on Tiber's bank, where the Apostle Peter tells his vision of the Saviour's resurrection. Lygia confesses her love for Vinicius to Peter. But when Chilon sends Croton into Demas's house to abduct the girl, Ursus comes out with the gladiator's dead body balanced on his shoulder. Carelessly flipping it into the Tiber with a twitch of his muscles, he reënters the house while Chilon flees in terror.

In the Colosseum crypt, the Christians wail for daughters violated, children slain, parents tortured. While Peter comforts them, Lygia bids despairing Vinicius farewell, pointing to heaven, as the martyrs march to death with a hymn of triumph. In the arena, Nero announces a piquant struggle. A giant barbarian will fight a savage aurochs, to whose back is bound a Christian maid of ravishing beauty—Lygia! Trumpets sound. Kindly Petronius holds his mantle before Vinicius' face. But Ursus conquers the aurochs and holding out the girl's body to Nero gains his upturned thumb and her life. Then, regretting his mercy, Nero orders the remaining Christians whipped from the crypt to be massacred. Chilon, denouncing the madman, is cast to the lions with torn-out tongue, but the people, sated with blood, curse Nero and shower him with projectiles until, protected by the Prætorians, he flees the Colosseum with Poppæa.

In his villa Petronius refuses longer to rule a society of which Nero is the head. Nor will he follow Vinicius and Lygia to Sicily, where they have gone to love in nature's paradise. Instead, Petronius sends Nero a letter reproaching him with his abominations. Then he and Eunice have their veins opened, and pass into the beyond in agreeable converse with their friends, while soft music sounds, and the moonlight in the garden silvers the spears of the Prætorians sent to seize them.

*Acté* (Barcelona, 1903), a fine modern score by the Spanish composer Joan de Manen, shows Acté, after losing her heart to Nero, converted to Christianity in the Palatine gardens by moonlight (Act I); but Nero, missing her among the dancers (Ballet), learns she has fled his Golden House (Act II), and orders the Prætorians to drag her back (Act III) together with the priest Marcus, who has converted her. On his palace terrace Nero murders Marcus, and when Tigellinus rushes in to say that Rome is burning, the Emperor blames the Christians, and hands over Acté to be torn to pieces by the mob.

## "NERONE"

ARRIGO BOITO. Book by the composer (Milan, 1924). In grandiose spectacular scenes and music of emotional power, Boito has stressed the beauty of celestial love. Asteria, the woman demon, personifies evil; Rubria the good and the pure. Her air, "Sorgi e spera," is mystically tender; and the musical climax of the score is the Finale (Act III), Rubria's vision of love eternal as she dies.

As Simon Magus, the magician, digs a grave among tombs on the Appian Way, Nero appears (hugging to him the urn containing his murdered mother's ashes) and begs the sorcerer to save him from her threatening ghost. Asteria, a Roman girl tormented by a horrid desire for Nero's love, enters, and the emperor flees, thinking her an avenging fury. Simon, when she sings the torments of a passion only Nero can calm, leaves her groveling on the ground.

At dawn comes Rubria (a vestal virgin outraged by Nero) with the apostle Fanuel, to lay flowers on a grave. When the magician proposes to Fanuel that they conquer Rome together, the holy man curses him as Rubria flees and Nero, reappearing as a great procession of legionaries, dancers, and populace passes along the Appian Way, steps forth to be cheered by the crowd.

In Simon's underground temple the sorcerer, veiled in incense, makes black magic before the altar. Nero, entering, sees Asteria's face reflected in a magic mirror. Trembling till her glance overcomes him with desire, he rushes to clasp her in his arms and—her kiss reveals her woman, not Fury! Raging to think she had frightened him, Nero smashes the temple idols with an iron hammer, has Asteria and Simon seized by his guards and mounting the altar, tunes his lyre and bursts into song.

While Fanuel delivers the Sermon on the Mount to the crowd in

Suburra streets, Asteria, escaped from the snake pit, rushes up to warn him that Simon is on his track, and the latter, entering with soldiers, leads off the apostle while his fellow Christians cover him with flowers.

In the Roman Circus, the doomed Christians led by Fanuel enter to the clamor of the mob, and as they cross the arena sands, the building bursts into flame. In the *Spoliarum,* the crypt of the Colosseum, Fanuel and Asteria, torch in hand, find Simon dead and Rubria dying. As Fanuel tells her the Christ tale, Rubria, converted, "expires to the caress of melody." Asteria, swayed by her ruling passion, rushes eagerly to Rubria's side. How did she win Nero's savage heart? But the smiling face of the corpse rebukes her. Bidding dead Rubria sleep in peace Asteria escapes from the crypt as its roof crumbles.

In *Servilia* (Petrograd, 1902), by Rimsky-Korsakoff, a Russian Neronian score, Servilia, a senator's daughter, loves Valerius. When he disappears she turns Christian, renouncing the world and the flesh. He reappears and her terrible inward struggle between pagan passion and Christian vow of chastity causes Servilia's death. Valerius, about to commit suicide, is restrained and instead praises God. A "Hymn to Athena," "Dance of the Mænads," and "Spinning Song" stand out.

### 3. *From the Times of the Later Emperors*

*La clemenza di Tito* (*The Clemency of Titus*), composed for the coronation of Emperor Leopold II as King of Bohemia (Prague, 1791), called by the Empress *una porcheria tedesca,* "a nasty German mess," is Mozart's weakest serious score. Vitellia, daughter of deposed Vitellius, persuades her lover Sextus to conspire against the Emperor Titus and set fire to the Capitol. Titus in disguise escapes burning and his "clemency" consists in pardoning the plotters and *marrying Vitellia.*

In the first year of Titus' reign an eruption of Vesuvius (79 A.D.) destroyed Pompeii and Herculaneum. Various composers have used the panoramic horrors of the eruption as a background for their operas. Those dealing with Pompeii are usually based on Bulwer's novel, *The Last Days of Pompeii,* and among them are: Pabst's *Die letzten Tage von Pompeii* (*The Last Days of Pompeii,* Dresden, 1851); *Die letzten Tage von Pompeii* (Darmstadt, 1853) by Peter Müller, and the Fleming Pierre Bénoit's *Pompeja* (Brussels, 1896).

*Le dernier jour de Pompeii* (Paris, 1869) by Victorin de Joncières, melodically suggestive of Hérold, orchestrally of Wagner, has a finale rising to genuine passion. It tangles the thread of Bulwer's story. Hermes tears blind Nydia from brutal Milon's arms, but the love potion Nydia gives Hermes drives him insane.

# NIGHTS OF OPERA

After his love Ione has been torn from the grove where she awaits him by the priest Ptheas' black mutes, Hermes, accused of her murder, is condemned to death. Vesuvius erupts. When the lava has ceased to run Nydia, Hermes, and Ione are in a boat on the Bay of Naples. Ione and Hermes are asleep; Nydia awake and singing. But song dies in her throat as she recalls her loveless lot and, after a long look at the sleeping object of her passion, she flings herself into the water and drowns.

*La danseuse de Pompeii* (Paris, 1912), an opera-ballet by Jean Nouguès, tells of a Roman youth's infatuation for a Pompeiian dancer. He worships Venus; she Apollo. The jealous gods fall out and the lovers have to die. The music has been called "miraculous . . . uniting poverty and abundance." *Giove a Pompeii* (*Jove in Pompeii*) by Giordano and Franchetti, book by Illica (Rome, 1921), is a cross between operetta and musical comedy. The Pompeiian Fine Arts Director has robbed Jove's altar of offerings and Jove determines to bury Pompeii beneath the lava. But Lalage, an innocent country girl, softens Jove's marble heart with caresses and he lets the Pompeiians escape before their town is destroyed. Good choruses, a contrapuntal finale (Act II), and a Pompeiian Ballet (girls as Tanagra statuettes) stand out.

*Herculanéum* (Paris, 1859) by Félicien David, "despairingly feeble and colorless" (Berlioz), nevertheless contains fine airs: Helion's "Je veux aimer toujours" (Act I), Lilia's "Credo," and interestingly rhythmed ballet music. Olympia, queen of a vague Chaldean land, comes to Herculaneum with her brother, the proconsul Nicanor, to be crowned. A Christian husband and wife, Helios and Lilia, are brought before them and Olympia yearns for Helios and Nicanor for Lilia. Nicanor, killed by lightning while villainously pursuing Lilia, is replaced by Satan, who assumes his form. Helios (a weak character) yields to the temptations Olympia offers, and indulges in the maddest orgies till, conscience awakening, he repents, begs Lilia's forgiveness and as temples fall crashing about them, both die in a religious ecstasy, the ashes of Vesuvius their winding sheet.

*Die Catacomben* (*The Catacombs*) by Ferdinand von Hiller, book by A. Hartmann (Wiesbaden, 1862). Lavinia, a Roman girl of imperial blood (during Trajan's reign, 98-117 A.D.), liberates for love's sake her Greek slave Lucius, who leads Christian services in the catacombs. But when he spurns her earthly passion for Clythia's spiritual affection, Lavinia's blood boils. Denouncing Lucius and Clythia, her satisfaction at seeing them die yields to regret at having caused her lover's death, and she stabs herself. *Et Bryllup i Katakombere* (*The Wedding in the Catacombs*, Copenhagen, 1919) by Georg Holberg is a modern Danish opera on similar lines. Cherubini's *Adriano in Siria* (Leghorn, 1782), devoted to the patron of the handsome farmer lad Antinous, so shocked by the moral decay of Rome that he committed suicide, is a minor score. Zandonai's melodramatic *Melanis* (Milan, 1912) plays in the Rome of the Emperor Commodus (180-192 A.D.) where Marzio, a disappointed politician, finds solace in the arms of the courtesan Melanis till Commodus' favor lets him claim a "good girl's" hand. Cast-off Melanis tearfully strews orange blossoms in the path of the bridal pair, then stabbing herself, bedews the flowers with her heart's blood. *Héliogabale* (Béziers, 1910), Déodat de Séverac's score to Sicard's drama of the degenerate Roman emperor (218-222 A.D.) who, murdered by an outraged people, was appropriately buried in the Cloaca Maxima, Rome's great sewer, is "a grandiose musical reflection of dying paganism" (Mestre).

*Zenobia* (Bremen, 1905) by Louis Adolphe Coerne, book by Stein, a melodious score with fine choruses, shows the Palmyran queen stifling her love for her chancellor Selenos at ambition's call. But when the Emperor Aurelian (270-275 A.D.) captures her the desert queen rejects his love, confesses her passion for Selenos, and stabs herself as he is led to execution. Silas Gamaliel Pratt's *Zenobia* (Chicago, 1883) presents the same heroine. *Aureliano in Palmire* (Milan, 1814) was one of Rossini's failures. *Genesius* (Vienna, 1921) by Felix Weingartner shows the actor Genesius, when his friend Pelagia has been arrested as a Christian by order of the Emperor Diocletian (284-305 A.D.), confessing Christianity himself, to be burned to death with her. *Le martyre de Saint-Sébastien* (Paris, 1911), a mystery (D'Annunzio), music by Claude Debussy, is the tale of the Christian centurion who, brought before Diocletian and refusing to deny his God, was "shot with arrows and struck with clubs" till he expired. In the mystery he dances on glowing coals (the "Dance on the Burning Brazier" has been lauded for the "somber and impressive beauty" of its music) and dies with flowers for a winding sheet, paradise opening in a glory of gold and angel choruses to receive him. *Der Apostat* (Vienna, 1925) by Felix Weingartner, with choral ensembles like those in *Aïda,* the voice handled as an orchestral instrument, subordinates a love story to the struggle between paganism, incarnated in the Emperor Julian the Apostate (331 A.D.), and Christianity, in scenes ranging from Roman Forum to Persian battlefield. *Menandra* (Brunswick, 1925) by Hugo Kaun, book by Jansen, a fifty-nine-minute, three-act opera, tells the love tragedy of Menandra, sentimental blue-stocking, and Helamon, effeminate Greek boy, in Alexandria, in the Emperor Honorius' reign (400 A.D.) amid theatrical battles of brutal early Christians.

### 4. *Romans under the Mistletoe*

## "NORMA"

VINCENZO BELLINI. Book by Felice Romani (Milan, 1831). This Gallicized Medea of druidic groves, whose book Schopenhauer declared unsurpassed in dramatic handling of a tragic theme, is Bellini's greatest work. The noble Aria, "Casta diva," with its broad, classic melody-line still holds its own; while the musically rich Finale of Act II anticipates Verdi.

In the sacred grove, Orovist, chief druid, begs the god's aid to overcome the Romans, while Severus, proconsul in Gaul, and his confidant Flavius listen in the shadows. The Gauls go and Severus tells his mad passion for Adalgisa, a young druidess. Norma, chief druidess, Orovist's daughter, has forsworn her vow of chastity to bear Severus two sons. but his new love makes her image pale. As the Romans depart, Norma comes to declare the god's will. Obediently the druids receive her words: Rome shall perish, but the time is not yet ripe! As the grove falls silent Adalgisa seeks in prayer strength to resist her passion, only to promise, once Severus joins her, to flee with him to Rome. Norma, (change of scene) when Adalgisa confesses her sinful secret, gives her the kiss of sisterhood; but when she asks her lover's name Severus appears, and avows his passion. He meets Norma's reproaches with scorn, and Adalgisa rejects him.

Norma, dagger raised to slay her sleeping babes and self (Act II), shrinks from the horrid deed. Instead, she bids Adalgisa take the children to Severus and become his wife, but noble-hearted Adalgisa offers to lead recreant Severus back to her. Adalgisa's effort is vain. Severus swears to make her his by force. Then Norma calls the Gauls to arms. As they greet her words with enthusiasm Clothilde enters: a Roman has been seized in the hall where the druid priestesses were at prayer. When Severus, lurking in the priestesses' hall to carry off Adalgisa, is brought in to be slain by Norma's sacrificial knife she promises to save him if he will abandon Adalgisa. The proud Roman prefers death, but when Norma tells him the young priestess also will perish in the flames, Severus begs her to spare the girl. But Norma has summoned the druids. She bids them build a funeral pyre for a Roman and a traitorous priestess. "Who is the priestess?" the druids ask. "1 myself," Norma replies. Severus' love is rekindled by Norma's greatness of soul, and the heroic druidess is led to the pyre with her Roman lover, mistress of his heart at the last.

## "MONA"

HORATIO PARKER. Book by Brian Hooker (New York, 1912). An opera whose undramatic character is offset by many pages of serious musical beauty and a poetic text. A scholarly score, it stresses declamation and the contrapuntal chorus, avoiding the straightforwardly melodic.

Mona, last descendant of Boadicea, is to lead her people against the Roman invaders. Gwynn, a political half-breed—his father the Roman governor, his mother a captive Briton—is a pacifist who aims to reconcile the two nations and win Mona's heart. He meets his savage sweetheart in a druid temple; but Mona, though she loves him and he confesses he is but half a Roman, has him taken prisoner. When the Romans defeat the Britons in battle, Gwynn escapes to meet Mona, and once more passionately urges his pacifist plans. Mona turns on him. First wildly denouncing him as a traitor, she slays him just as the Roman governor arrives and recognizes in dead Gwynn his son Quintus. Mona, awakening too late to the fact that her want of faith in Gwynn has destroyed her people's only hope of peace, and the one man whom she truly loved, is led away to captivity.

## "APHRODITE"

CAMILLE ERLANGER. Book by Louis Gramont (Paris, 1906) after Pierre Louy's novel. An operatic chamber of horrors in Egypt at the beginning of the Christian era (50 B.C.) while Messaline and Claudius ruled in Rome. The music is dramatic, colored with "an insincere yet charming Orientalism." Among the best pages are: (Act I), the Preludes, and the Courtesans' Duet with flute *obbligato;* (Act V), the "Prison Scene."

Ladies of light life, sailors, philosophers, flute players, dancers, cultivate the *vie de Bohème* on an Alexandrian wharf. Chimaris, a soothsayer, predicts a bloody future for Demetrius, sculptor of a famous statue of Aphrodite. He ignores her prophecy: Chrysis, a beautiful courtesan, has caught his eye. But if he wishes to win her, says she, he must bring with him the silver mirror of Rhodope (property of wealthy Bacchis), the ivory comb of the high priest's wife, and the goddess Aphrodite's seven-rowed pearl necklace. Thinking lightly of theft, murder, and sacrilege, Demetrius announces an early call.

Demetrius has despoiled Aphrodite of her pearls, and the high priest's wife (murdered in the consecrated grove) of her comb. Remains the mirror. Chrysis enters the temple, and Demetrius, hiding, sees her offer a mirror, comb, and necklace of emeralds to the goddess, which are accepted by the high priest.

At a party in Bacchis' house, Theano dances shamelessly. That she may see herself as others see her Bacchis, amid laughter, sends for Rhodope's mirror. Alas, it has been stolen! Corinna, Bacchis' favorite slave, accused of the theft, is condemned without trial. Her mistress has her crucified but Chrysis is deaf to her cries, charmed to think Demetrius kept his vow. Bacchis and her guests, except Timon, return to the wine cup. Timon closes the eyes of the crucified girl before passing into the dawn.

As Demetrius works in his studio, Chrysis appears from behind a tapestry. He offers her comb, necklace, and mirror, which she puts to use. The mob without now cries "Sacrilege!" and Demetrius is shocked to think he committed crimes at a courtesan's command. After an embrace he says they must part. She swears by the God of Israel (she does not believe in Aphrodite) she will do more for him than he has done for her. So Demetrius orders her to show herself to the mob with the fruits of his crimes, and promises to visit her on the morrow —in jail.

As the people clamor for the criminal's punishment, Chrysis "in a *toilette* drawn solely from Nature's tailoring-shop," climbs the spiral staircase of the tower of Pharos, comb in hair, mirror in hand, Aphrodite's pearls around her neck. A flash of lightning shows her to the mob, and as she sings a song of triumph at the tower's top, many think her the goddess herself. Others, less credulous, have recognized her. She waits while they rush up the stairs to seize her. In the prison (change of scene) the jailor presents the hemlock cup to Chrysis with Queen Berenice's compliments. She wants to put off drinking until Demetrius arrives; but the jailor insists, and dying Chrysis murmurs the love vows she and Demetrius have spoken. The latter, arriving too late, is frightened off by a threatening vision of the goddess Aphrodite. He curses her, remembering Chimaris' prophecy that when two women had died, he would also perish, *after a little!*—and two girls bury Chrysis by moonlight in ground holy to the god Hermanubis.

In *Aphrodite* (Vienna, 1912), by Max Oberleithner, book after Pierre Louy's novel—"Richard Strauss is a Bellini of vocal melody compared to Oberleithner" (Korngold)—Demetrius sculps a statue of Aphrodite with his mistress Queen Berenice as a model. Chrysis gets him to destroy the statue—her rival—and artistlike, his love for her cools. Orgy, crucifixion, crimes, Chrysis' gambols on the lighthouse tower as Aphrodite, her condemnation, and death take place as in Erlanger's score. Demetrius is killed by a rival lover, though the ancients, unlike the moderns, did not kill each other for a light woman's sake.

# CHAPTER IV

## THE CYCLES OF LEGEND

### 1. *The Nibelungen Ring*

Richard Wagner's *Nibelungen Ring,* preceded by a Prologue, *Das Rheingold (The Rhinegold),* comprises *Die Walküre (The Valkyrie), Siegfried* and *Die Götterdämmerung (The Twilight of the Gods).* On a basis of Scandinavian and Germanic legend, these operas present the drama of the death of the ancient gods and the deliverance of man. Fate, ruler of men and gods alike, is ever in the background. In his versions of the Edda and the Teuton myths, Wagner created the *music drama,* a new form of opera, developing the principle that opera melody is an *instrumental type,* its instrument the human throat. The "Ring" operas are musical dramas in which "leading motives" reflect all human emotions. Through text and tone the romantic ideal of redemption runs like a red thread, weaving in and about the two main problems of love and death.

According to Landormy: "In the *Nibelungen Ring* we have *socialistic* ideas (gold and its fatal power a curse); *anarchistic* ideas (condemnation of law and order; opposition of Siegfried, personifying personal liberty, to Wotan, god of contracts); *pagan* ideas (Siegfried following the instincts of nature, living without god, moral code or law); *Christian* ideas (Brunnhilde's redemption of the world by the supreme sacrifice of pity); *optimistic* ideas (the death of egoism and hatred once the law of love rules men); and ideas *pessimistic* (Wotan's renunciation of the wish to live)." "Yet, so beautiful is its music we are tempted to regard the work as one which, finally, achieves relatively clear and definite expression of the diverse ideas it formulates" (Combarieu).

### "DAS RHEINGOLD"

#### (*The Gold of the Rhine*)

RICHARD WAGNER. Festival Play (Munich, 1869). In *Das Rheingold,* the gold of the Rhine Maidens, destined to curse gods and men, is stolen by the dwarf Alberich to forge the ring which gives its possessor dominion over the world. The glorious Opening Scene, in which the Rhine Maidens sing beneath the green waves of the river (which led Wagner's enemies to say he turned the opera stage into an "aquarium"), and the "March to Valhalla" are among the finest numbers.

Alberich the Nibelung sees the Rhine Maidens bathing in the crystal flood and longs to possess them until the sunlight, piercing green depths, kisses awake the golden hoard which the Rhine Maidens guard. Hearing them tell of the boundless power the possessor of the Nibelungen hoard will enjoy, Alberich flings himself upon the gold and disappears with it, vainly pursued by its guardians.

The god Wotan and his wife Fricka resign their daughter Freia, goddess of beauty, to the giants Fafner and Fasolt, in payment for the castle they have built them. But when the giants offer to exchange Freia for the gold of the Nibelungs, Wotan and Loge, god of evil, descend to Nibelheim (change of scene), Alberich's underground kingdom, where Mime, the dwarf's brother, has completed a helmet which makes its wearer invisible. Loge's flatteries lure from Alberich the secret of the helmet, and he and Wotan wrest it from him.

Before Wotan's castle (change of scene), his heart filled with hatred and revenge, Alberich yielding helmet, ring, and gold as the price of freedom, calls down a terrible curse on the ring and the gold. The giants bring back Freia and receive the Nibelungen gold and ring. At once the curse goes into effect: Fafner slays his brother Fasolt for the sake of the treasure. Now the gods can enter the splendid castle bought at so terrible a price. The thunder rolls, the lightning flashes and over a gloriously colored rainbow bridge the gods enter their abode, which Wotan calls Valhalla. Yet as they enter the wailing of the Rhine Maidens, robbed of their hoard, rises to the ears of the gods.

## "DIE WALKÜRE"

### (The Valkyrie)

RICHARD WAGNER. Festival Play (Munich, 1870). In Die Walküre, most popular of the four scores, the tragic love of brother and sister produces the hero of Siegfried. Das Rheingold is elemental; Die Walküre human in its love, hate and tragedy. Its first act is Wagner's most unified musical creation. Outstanding are the "Spring Song," "Siegmund's Love Song," and the famous "Fire Magic," often played in Brassin's piano transcription.

Brünnhilde is Wotan's daughter by Wala, earth's wisest woman, who foretells the twilight of the gods (Die Götterdämmerung) should Alberich regain the ring which Fafner, as a great dragon, guards in a woodland cave. Brünnhilde and her Valkyries (Nordic heaven-maids who speed the brave warrior's soul on the field of battle) gather heroes in Valhalla to fight Alberich's nocturnal hordes, while to gain the ring Wotan descends to earth as Walse, and of his union with an earth woman spring the twins Siegmund and Sieglinde. Siegmund is to become a mighty hero and rob Fasolt of the ring.

Tempest-driven, Siegmund staggers into Hunding's hut and falls exhausted by the hearth. Sieglinde, Hunding's wife, comforts him with mead but when her sinister husband returns, he learns his guest is the Walsung youth he and his clan have been pursuing. He drives him out to await the morrow when they will fight. Gloomily Siegmund broods; he is weaponless till from an ash-tree he sees projecting the sword driven in by Wotan's hand against his hour of need. While Hunding sleeps Siegmund joyfully clasps Sieglinde, and conquering spring, freeing love from winter's fetters, changes the face of nature as Siegmund tears the sword from the ash, and in spite of Sieglinde's confession that she is his long-lost sister, carries her passionately off into the blossoming night.

Amid the rocks where the fight is to take place, Wotan bids Brünnhilde give victory to Siegmund. But Fricka, protectress of wedded love, insists the incestuous lovers be punished, though Wotan explains Siegmund is the hero born to save Valhalla. Wotan has to swear he will not protect his son. As he tells Brünnhilde the story of his vain plans to avert the gods' fate, Siegmund and Sieglinde appear, flying from Hunding's vengeance. While the hero watches over his exhausted mate, Brünnhilde tells him of his approaching death, and that Valhalla awaits him. Yet when he refuses to leave his love and draws sword to slay Sieglinde and himself, Brünnhilde despite Wotan's command, promises him victory. Hunding's horn sounds! Siegmund rushes to the combat. As Hunding's death blow is about to fall, however, Siegmund's sword shivers on Wotan's spear, and Hunding thrusts him through the breast. While Brünnhilde leads Sieglinde off, a scornful wave of Wotan's hand strikes Hunding dead.

Brünnhilde and Sieglinde are on a rocky mountain top, Valkyries riding through the storm clouds of the sky. (The "Ride of the Valkyries" is played as an individual orchestral piece in concert.) Bidding despairing Sieglinde live for the sake of her unborn child, Brünnhilde gives her the fragments of Siegmund's sword, and tells her to seek refuge in the forest, where Fafner guards the ring. Now Brünnhilde must suffer for disobeying the father of the gods, Wotan tells her. Robbed of her divinity, she shall sleep on the mountain, prey of the first man who may find her. But her passionate pleas win for her the magic fire circle, the flaming ring protecting her slumbers so that none but a true hero will win her. With a kiss of farewell Wotan lets her glide on her mossy couch, giving up his dream of supreme power as he does so, and as living flames spring about her he departs, knowing none but a hero will dare the fire.

## "SIEGFRIED"

RICHARD WAGNER. Festival Play (Baireuth, 1876). *Siegfried* is the "Scherzo of the Nibelungen symphony." The forest, with its murmurs, singing birds, familiar or monstrous beasts is, at bottom, the subject of the drama. Siegfried, the young savage, is led from an inferior plane, a life of instinct devoid of moral law, to consciousness of the higher life of the mind, by the power of love. Musically "the winged soulfulness of Siegfried's lovely woodland realm, born of music's self" is most perfectly expressed in the famous "Waldweben" ("Woodland Weaving") of the myriad forest voices; the love duets, and the themes of the "Siegfried Idyl," in the last act stand out. Wagner called this score, "the loveliest of my life's dreams."

In the magic forest wilderness, in the cave of Mime, Alberich's brother, Sieglinde died giving birth to Siegfried. As the boy grows up strong and savage in the dwarf's care, the latter plans to use him as a tool to overcome Fafner, and gain the ring. Mime cannot make a sword to slay Fafner; such a sword none but the fearless can forge; but young Siegfried, amid shouts of joy, welds together the fragments of his father Siegmund's sword, and tests it by splitting the anvil in twain.

Alberich is watching by Fafner's cave at night when Wotan, as a wanderer, wakes the sleeping dragon to warn him of the hero's approach, while Alberich vainly promises Fafner life in exchange for the ring. At dawn Siegfried and Mime appear. Siegfried revels in the charm of the forest, and failing to imitate the song of the birds, sends a merry blast of his horn to the tree tops. Fafner awakes and rolls his hideous length from the cave, but the hero thrusts his sword through the monster's breast. Dying, Fafner warns him against Mime, and the drop of Fafner's blood burning on the hero's finger makes him understand the song of the forest bird, bidding him take hoard, helm, and ring from the cave. Returning with them, treacherous Mime hands Siegfried the poison drink he had prepared while the hero welded his sword; but the bird warns him, and slaying the dwarf he hurries off, the bird leading the way, to find the sleeping bride within her circle of fire.

Wotan tells Erda, the All-Knowing, he hopes for the world's redemption once Siegfried and Brünnhilde have become the parents of a new race. Meeting Siegfried outside the ring of fire, he lets the hero beat down his spear. Sounding his horn Siegfried forces his way through the flames to the top of the hillock and (change of scene) rouses sleeping Brünnhilde with a kiss. At first Brünnhilde, who fell asleep a goddess, resents Siegfried's human passion. Yet she has awakened a mortal woman; she cannot resist the tenderness which overwhelms her, and yields herself to the hero's embrace. Valhalla's stress, the gods, and the world are forgot, for love's star fills her skies.

*Der Wald* (*The Forest,* Dresden, 1901; New York, 1903) by Ethel Smyth, like Wagner's *Die Walküre,* is primarily an opera in which woodland sounds, moods, and voices dominate. The story is a medieval tragedy. Röschen, the woodman's daughter, is about to marry Heinrich, the forester, but Iolanthe, Landgrave Rudolf's mistress, covets the handsome youth. When he rejects her advances she has her henchmen slay him and grief kills Röschen. The voice of the forest is the keynote of the score, however, from the opening scene in a tangled woodland brake to the close. The eternal forest is the background against which "the children of earth fret their brief hour and pass into oblivion." Had the composer succeeded in expressing in its perfection this all-pervasiveness of the forest, "she might have taken her place by the side of Wagner, the only composer of modern times who has handled a philosophical idea of the kind in music with notable success" (Streatfeild). In *La forêt* (*The Forest*), a "musical dream" in two acts, by A. Savard (Paris, 1910), the lovers Nemerosa and Pierre are also musically less important than "the murmuring pines and the hemlocks" which create the mood of their surroundings.

## "GÖTTERDÄMMERUNG"

### (*The Twilight of the Gods*)

RICHARD WAGNER. Festival Play (Baireuth, 1876). In *Die Götterdämmerung*, two innocents, Siegfried and Brünnhilde, atone for Wotan's fault. The curse of the ring lies on Siegfried, but Brünnhilde redeems the world by the sacrifice of unselfish love. "Siegfried's Rhine Journey" (orchestral Interlude), "Siegfried's Funeral March," and Act III stand out. "From the elevation of the last act the whole work appears in its almost supernatural grandeur, like the chain of the Alps, seen from the summit of Mont Blanc" (Saint-Saëns).

It is night. (Prologue.) On Brünnhilde's rock the Norns (Fates) spin the golden thread of world destiny. The wood-ash of which Wotan cut his spear has withered. Its wood lies piled about Valhalla. When the god's raven brings tidings of Siegfried's redeeming deed the wood will burst into flame; the twilight of the gods will fall. Then the Norns' gift of prophecy departs, their golden thread breaks, they vanish. Siegfried and Brünnhilde come from their rocky chamber (Act I). He gives her the fatal ring and mounting her steed Grane, rides off to the Rhine, blowing his horn, ready for deeds of high emprise, while Brünnhilde watches him disappear. (The orchestral Interlude which follows depicts "Siegfried's Rhine Journey.")

In the hall of the Gibichungs sit Gunther, his sister Gutrune, and his half-brother Hagen, Alberich's son, conceived to carry out the dwarf's revenge and regain the ring. In Gunther he rouses desire for Brünnhilde; in Gutrune, desire for Siegfried. Siegfried's horn heard, Hagen welcomes him to the hall. There, as planned by Hagen, Gutrune hands him the draught of oblivion. He drinks and, his true love Brünnhilde forgotten, yearns to possess Gutrune. To gain her he agrees to help Gunther win Brünnhilde as his bride. Hagen watches them set forth with sinister satisfaction. They ride to get the ring for *him!* (The orchestral Interlude carries on this thought and then moves into the Brünnhilde Love Motive.)

On her rocky height Brünnhilde dreams of her absent lover when the Valkyrie Waltraute brings her Wotan's plea to cast the fatal ring into the Rhine, and save gods and men from its curse. But Brünnhilde is now a loving human woman: the gods mean nothing to her, Siegfried everything. She refuses to part with his love token. The magic flames leap up as the hero's horn is heard. Brünnhilde rushes joyously to meet a stranger, Gunther in Siegfried's form, thanks to the magic helm. Siegfried, however, disguised as Gunther, subdues and robs her of the ring. In the night Siegfried follows her into her chamber, and lays his naked sword between them—she is sacred, the bride of his friend!

Before the hall of the Gibichungs at night, Alberich spurs on Hagen in a dream vision to secure the ring. Siegfried appears with dawn, announcing the coming of Gunther and Brünnhilde, and in the hall of the Gibichungs is wedded to Gutrune. But Brünnhilde, accusing him of treachery, declares herself his true wife. Siegfried, the past a blank, swears on Hagen's spear he is innocent. Now Brünnhilde thirsts for vengeance. As Siegfried hastens off with the Gibichung heroes, she convinces Gunther his blood brother has betrayed him. No naked sword lay between Siegfried and herself during the night, she declares. Hagen lures from her the secret that Siegfried is vulnerable in his back; and together with Gunther the hero's death is planned: Hagen's spear shall strike him down from ambush. Then the plotters hypocritically join the gay wedding procession of Siegfried and Gutrune.

Hagen has planned a hunt in a forest valley on the Rhine to carry out his plot. Siegfried, who has strayed from the rest, comes to the river's bank. The Rhine Maidens rise from the stream and beg for the ring. When he refuses it they predict his death. Now come the huntsmen. Hagen drops an antidote to oblivion in the hero's wine, the vision of Brünnhilde rises in his soul, and Siegfried tells how he broke through the magic ring and woke Brünnhilde with his kiss. Then Hagen's spear sinks into Siegfried's back and while the rest surround the dying hero, his slayer strides away. To the solemn "Funeral March" (in whose motives the tragic history of the Valsungs repasses before the listener) Gunther and his vassals escort the hero's corpse through the moonlit forest.

In the Gibichungs' hall (change of scene) Siegfried's widow breaks out into lamentation at sight of his body. Hagen claims the ring and fatally stabs Gunther, who tries to prevent him from taking it. Yet as he clutches at Siegfried's hand, the dead hero raises a threatening arm and Hagen falls back in horror. Now Brünnhilde enters. Out of her grief and despair has come comprehension. Siegfried's unwitting treachery is forgiven. The ring shall be restored to the Rhine Maidens, after passing through the purifying fire of Siegfried's pyre. Thrusting aside weeping Gutrune, she commands Gunther's men to heap the wood. Brünnhilde alone is Siegfried's wife and will follow him to death. The hero's body is placed on the pyre, Brünnhilde draws the ring from his finger, fires the wood and, as the flames leap upward, rides her steed Grane into the towering glow. The Rhine, overflowing its banks, sweeps the hall. Hagen, groping for the ring in the flood, is dragged to the depths by the Rhine Maidens Woglinde and Wellgunde, while Flosshilde exultantly holds up the golden circlet. The red glow of burning Valhalla, where the gods await their doom, lights the horizon. As the shining halls of their heaven, undermined by the lust for gold, crumble into nothingness, a new world on earth, born of a deed of self-sacrificing love, rises from the ashes of the old order which has passed.

*Sigurd* (Paris, 1884) by Ernest Reyer, book by du Locle and Blau, is an opera by a French Wagnerian who uses leading motives, but is no slavish imitator. His score, which "gives new life to old forests of legend," is musically fine and dignified. Its plot, like that of the *Götterdämmerung*, is derived from old Teuton legend. Hilda, the Burgundian King Gunther's sister, loves Sigurd, the French Siegfried. A magic potion wins her his heart and he sets out with Gunther and Hagen for Iceland. To gain Hilda's hand Sigurd forces the magic ring of fire surrounding sleeping Brünnhilde and rescues her for Gunther. When Hilda, in a fit of jealousy, releases Sigurd from his spell, he sees in Brünnhilde the bride the gods meant for him. But before he can taste the joy of his new-found love Hagen treacherously kills him, and the stroke which slays her lover brings death to Brünnhilde, because of the mystic affinity existing between them. *Die Nibelungen* (Berlin, 1854) by Heinrich Dorn was popular before Wagner drove it from the stage with his Trilogy. Siegfried helps Gunther subdue Brunhild, warrior Queen of Iceland, to gain the hand of his sister Kriemhild; the two women quarrel in the rose garden at Worms (Act II); and Brunhild wins Hagen to murder the hero. Siegfried's corpse is brought to Kriemhild (Act III) and she induces her suitor, King Etzel (Attila) to avenge her (Act IV) which he does (Act V), Gunther and his men being slain in Etzel's hall while Kriemhild, her vengeance satisfied, stabbing Hagen, who refuses to reveal the hiding place of the Nibelungen hoard, kills herself to follow Siegfried in death.

In *Baldurs Tod* (*Baldur's Death*, Vienna, 1891) by Cyril Kistler, Wotan's son, dying of evil Loki's spear thrust, announces the twilight of the gods and Christianity's coming. *Gunlod* (Weimar, 1891) by Cornelius, tells of a lovely orphan, captive of the troll Sutting, who eats poison berries to rejoin her lover Wotan in Valhalla. *Das ewige Feuer* (*The Eternal Fire*, Düsseldorf, 1907) by Richard Wetz sings the passing of the Teuton gods. Ariowald, priest of the fire, wishes his daughter Gana to succeed him. Instead, she joins her lover Sigimir in the worship of the God of Love.

*La Burgonde* (*The Burgundian Girl,* Paris, 1898) by Paul Vidal is a brilliant score by a Massenet pupil; outstanding, the "Song of the Sword," and a colorful ballet. Hagen, King of the Franks, Attila, King of the Huns, and Walter of Aquitaine love Hildegunde (Ilda), the Burgundian king's daughter. When she flees with Walter from Attila's wooden castle on the Danube, where captive virgins of all races dance before the king (Act II), he promises Hagen any maid he covets if he bring back the fugitives. Hagen captures them (Act III), but Attila breaks his word when he learns he wants Hildegunde. Hagen is slain releasing Walter, and the latter turns to find Hildegunde fronting him in bridal robes. She has killed Attila with the sacred sword of the Huns. While the Mongols grovel in terror at sight of the blood-dripping holy blade, the lovers escape. Verdi's early *Attila* (Milan, 1864) is notable mainly for its musical picture of a sunrise, "his first step in orchestral tone-painting." In *Herbort und Hilde* (Mannheim, 1902), Von Bausznern's pseudo-Wagnerian opera, the minstrel Herbort wins the heart of Princess Hilde, meant for his master Dietrich. *Mataswintha* (Weimar, 1902) by Xaver Scharwenka, after Dahn's *Kampf um Rom,* is a tragic page from history. Mataswintha, granddaughter of the great Theodoric (Dietrich), is married for reasons of state to the Gothic King Witichis. He, for reasons of heart, is true to his wife Rauthgundis, and when he puts a naked sword between Mataswintha and himself on the nuptial couch, she sets fire to the granaries of the Gothic army, and flings herself into the corn-fed flames.

## GUDRUN

The Middle High German epic *Gudrun,* written soon after the *Nibelungenlied* (13th century) has been called the Odyssey of the latter's Iliad. Herwig, young King of Seeland, loves beautiful Gudrun, child of Hettel and Hilde, but the girl is carried off by Ludwig, King of Normandy, who covets her, and her kinsfolk, pursuing the ravisher, are defeated in a great battle off the Danish coast. For thirteen years Gudrun, captive in the Norman king's castle, performs the meanest household tasks, refusing to wed her abductor. When Herwig, come to rescue her, finds her wringing dirty linen on the seashore, her lovely hands red and roughened, she knows her constancy will be rewarded. The next day the avengers attack Ludwig's castle, put him and his ravishers to the sword and Gudrun, delivered, is clasped in her lover's arms.

*Gudrun* (Leipzig, 1874) by August Reissmann; *Gudrun* (Neustre-

litz, 1882) by August Klughardt; and *Gudrun* (Hanover, 1884) by
Felix Draeseke, lesser Wagnerians, are operas telling the legend.
*Gudrun auf Island* (*Gudrun in Iceland,* Hagen, 1924) by the Danish modernist Paul von Klenau, with the "Scene on the Strand,"
Love Scene, and "Iceland Fisherman's Chorus" outstanding, shows
Gudrun, when Haldor during her lover Kjartan's absence tells
her he has wed abroad, marrying his traducer. Meeting Kjartan
on the strand on a spring night, Gudrun finds Haldor lied. Haldor's father Thorleik, spying on the two, urges his son to avenge
his sullied honor; Gudrun when her husband departs strangles
Thorleik, and hurries to warn her lover, only to see him slain by
Haldor's men when he has killed their leader. In *Islandsaga*
(Munich, 1925), modernist opera by Georg Völlerthun, the love
tragedy yields in importance to the dramatic vigor of the "sea
music" of the score.

*Ullranda* (Plauen, 1910) by Walter Dost is a North Sea tribal
tragedy. Wodmor has beaten his rival Arbogast. Ullranda must
slay the man she loves on the tribal altar. Instead, when the
sword glows white-hot in the altar flame, she strikes down Wodmor, and the tribal elders condemn her to a fate far more terrible than death—to remain a life-long virgin priestess of the
shrine. *Les Barbares* (Paris, 1901) by Saint-Saëns is the unin-
spired tale of a Teuton invasion of France, Marcomir the barbarian
invader luring the Gallic priestess Floria into his arms only to be
stabbed in the back by Livia, whose husband he slew in battle.

## 2. Scandinavian Legends

The legends of ancient Scandinavia have called forth a host
of lesser operas. The Swede Tegner's epic poem after the
*Fridthjof's Saga* tells of the Norse hero who loved Ingeborg,
King Helge's sister, and how her husband, aged King Ring, rather
than stand in their way, nobly slew himself with his own sword
after uniting the lovers. It has inspired *Frithjof* (Berlin, 1871)
by Höpffer; and *Fritjof* (Bremen, 1884; *Ingeborg,* Antwerp,
1910) by Zöllner; *Hiarne* (Berlin, 1891) by Ingeborg von Bron-
sart; and *König Hiarne* (Munich, 1883) by Marschner. *Thorgrim*
(London, 1889) by Cowen, and *Greysteel* (London, Sheffield,
1906) by Gatty, are opera developments of kindred Norse saga
subjects. Operas of the "Viking Age" when, according to the
*Ynglinga Saga,* "he only might with full truth be called a sea-king
who never slept under a sooty rafter and never drank in a chim-
ney-corner," include: *Helges Erwachen* (*Helge's Awakening,*
Schwerin, 1896) by Alfred Lorenz, in which a legendary sea king
returns to punish the viking Hadubrandt who has violated King

Hagen's daughter. In *Vikingerfahrt* (*Viking Foray*, Nuremberg, 1896) by Felix von Woyrsch, Gunnlag, the viking, his wild heart softened by organ music pealing from church, forbears to tear his erstwhile sweetheart from the arms of Christian Ralf—she waited seven years before marrying his rival—and departs without doing harm.

## "GWENDOLINE"

EMMANUEL CHABRIER. Book by Mendès (Paris, 1896). A colorful, dramatic score, influenced by Wagner. Its hero appears as "a kind of pirate Siegfried" in the legend of a Judith who fails in Saxon England. The Overture, "Bridal Song," and Prelude (Tableau 2, Act II) are among the finest musical pages.

Harald, Danish sea king, about to have Armel, Saxon chief, slain for refusing to reveal his treasure, sees golden-haired Gwendoline, Armel's daughter. Harald "has never seen a woman before"; his savage heart grows gentle. Armel agrees Gwendoline shall be Harald's bride, but arranges for his Saxons to murder the unarmed Danes at the wedding feast. Gwendoline, however, has lost her heart to the handsome Harald (Act II). Her sire presses a dagger on her, bidding her murder her husband in their wedding bed, but she flings it away and follows Harald when the cries of his dying followers sound on his ear. On the seashore (change of scene) Harald is stabbed by Armel. Gwendoline, snatching the dagger, sheathes it in her own breast and falls dying on her husband's corpse in the red glare of the Danish rovers' burning ships.

## "INGWELDE"

MAX SCHILLINGS. Book by Sporck (Karlsruhe, 1894). A post-Wagnerian score, whose Second Finale has been called "one of the most powerful among all operas (in Wagner's style) written since Wagner's day." The text is dramatically feeble.

Norse Gandulf of Castle Glangard sees in a vision his sons slain by the sons of the viking Thorstein. Later (change of scene) his dream comes true. To escape death in the burning keep Gandulf's daughter Ingwelde swears to marry Knause, eldest of the Thorstein youths, whom she hates, instead of Gest, her foster brother and lover. In Castle Thorstein, while the other Thorsteins hunt (Act II) Knause is set upon by the Glangard folk and slain; but when his ghost appears to Ingwelde and demands she avenge him, she swears to do so. About to flee with Gest (Act III), however, Bran, Knause's brother, catches Ingwelde on the seashore and slays Gest with his ax, though his love for Ingwelde makes him powerless to harm her. Since life no longer has aught to offer either, they determine to die together. Boarding Knause's burning viking galley, from which his ghost beckons, they sink beneath the waves as it founders.

## "HULDA"

CÉSAR FRANCK. Book by Grandmougin after Björnstjerne-Björnson (Monte-Carlo, 1894). A colorful score, Wagnerian without using leading motives, with a notable allegorical ballet, "The Struggle of Winter and Spring." Streatfeild says: "In the virility of inspiration displayed, *Hulda* strikingly recalls the beauties of Tristan and Isolda."

Two fair women are rivals in the Norroway of viking days. Hulda, carried off by a band of sea rovers, has been thrust into the unloved arms of their chief. Both she and Swanhilde lose their hearts to pale Eiolf, another member of the band. Hulda's charms make him murder her husband at her request; but Eiolf is fickle and Swanhilde's beauty in turn leads him to abandon his first love. Then Hulda, luring Eiolf to a last rendezvous, kills him and flings herself into the sea.

### 3. *Russian Legends*

### "LE SACRE DU PRINTEMPS"

#### (*The Rites of Spring*)

IGOR STRAVINSKY. Hieratic ballet (Paris, 1913). A ritual pantomime of the worship of Yarilo, Slavic god of spring and fertility, in the dim dawn of history (400 B.C.). Complete disregard of tonic centers, development of chromatic alternation in a contrapuntal web of harmonized, not simple melody themes, daring musical pointillism and compelling rhythmic vibration pulsing through broad splashes of tonal color are features of its ultramodern music. It shows primitive man at grips with the inexplicable terrors and cruelties of Nature.

After a prelude, "Adoration of the Earth," on pastoral themes, a "Dance of Adolescents" is followed by the appearance of elders and young girls of the tribe, and a ritual dance in which the act of rape is mimed expresses the desire of the tribe for fruitfulness. "Springtide Rounds" are then followed by the procession of the tribal wise men, and the dance adoration of earth and stars. An instrumental Introduction, "The Sacrifice," precedes the rise of the curtain on a nocturnal plain where moonlight gleams on ghastly poles hung with skulls and bones. The young men dance a mystic round till the young girl, fairest of the tribe, who is to be sacrificed to Yarilo, is brought in to await her fate. Tribesmen garbed as bears glorify her coming death and the victim dances the sacred dance of "The Chosen One." Eloquent of the haunting terrors of the primitive human creature doomed to die before she has tasted life, it ends with a convincing travesty of death in which the girl sinks to the ground, and her corpse is carried off the stage by tribesmen who hold it stiffly above their heads.

*Soleil de nuit* (New York, 1916) by Rimsky-Korsakoff is a Russian game and dance *divertissement* (practically a scene from the composer's opera *Sniegurotschka*) in pagan Russia at a later date. *Mlada* (Petrograd, 1889) by Rimsky-Korsakoff, a fantastic ballet opera, develops a legend of the tenth century Baltic Slavs. Mlada, Jaromir's betrothed, is killed on her wedding eve by a poisoned ring given her by Voislava, daughter of Mstivoi, Prince of Rhetra. Jaromir weds Voislava but, about to embrace her, Mlada's ghost carries him to Mount Triglav, where the gods of Slavic mythology hold revel. Returning to earth Jaromir slays Voislava, immediately seized by Morena the hell goddess, and the goddess Lada blesses his union with Mlada. Fine pages are: Jaromir's "Dream Music" and the spectacular ballet "A Night on Mount Triglav." The famous "Song of India" from this score has been the inspiration of several American popular songs.

*Russlan and Ludmilla* (Petrograd, 1842) by Glinka after Pushkin is considered musically superior to *A Life for the Czar*. A Princess of Kiev, beset by suitors, a Finnish warlock and a Tartar prince, is saved by the Russian knight-errant Russlan, who clasps her in his arms as the curtain falls. The "Ballad of the Wizard Finn" (Act II); "Glorislava's Air" with clarinet *obbligato* (Act III), the "Tatar Air" (Act II) which expresses the "sadness of twilight covering the vast steppes," and the "Oriental Ballet" (Act IV) stand out. Among the *roussalki,* tragic water nymphs of Slavic legend, *The Roussalka* (Petrograd, 1867) by Alexander Dargomijsky is most famous. A young Prince betrays Natasha, a miller's daughter, who drowns herself in the mill pond while her father goes mad. The Prince, meditating gloomily by the pond, meets a *roussalka* child, his daughter. While he hesitates to heed Natasha's call and join her the Mad Miller—with a hideously meaningless laugh Dargomijsky has wonderfully reproduced in music—pushes him into a watery grave. Bie calls the opera "Slavic Marschner," and the great rôle of the score, immortalized by Chaliapin, is that of the Mad Miller. *The Roussalka of the Dnieper* (Petrograd, 1804) by the Italianized Russian Cavos is a more primitive version of the legend—the Russian eclectic Blaramberg's *Roussalka Maiden* (Moscow, 1895) more modern; while Antonin Dvořák's *Rusalka* (Prague, 1900) is a Czech variant, with beautiful pages of "elfin music." Lucien Lambert's *La Roussalka* (Paris, 1911) also may be mentioned, in which a peasant girl, betrayed by her noble lover, drowns herself in "Mother Volga" and then lures her betrayer beneath the waves.

*The Legend of Czar Saltan* (Moscow, 1906) by Rimsky-Korsakoff, after Pushkin, uses the leading motive systematically, and is rich in folk melodies. Czar Saltan hears three sisters discuss him as a husband. Marrying the youngest he is off to the wars. Militrissa's boy born, her wicked sisters send Czar Saltan word she has given birth to a monster. Back comes the command to put mother and monster in a cask and fling it into the sea. On the desert isle to which the cask floats the boy grows up a hero and magician. Calling forth a city from the sea bottom, he is acclaimed Czar by its people, marries a swan princess, and the curtain falls on the reunion of Saltan and his injured wife.

## "SNIEGUROTSCHKA"

### (*The Snow Maiden*)

NICOLAI RIMSKY-KORSAKOFF. Book by Ostrovsky after a Russian folk-tale (Petrograd, 1882). The legend of the Snow Maid, daughter of Frost and Spring, who dies when the first ray of sunlight and love warms her icy heart. The score contains lovely melodies: "Song and Dance of the Birds" (Prologue); the "Song of the Shepherd Lehl"; Prelude (Act III); the Snow Maiden's Death Scene (Act IV). Its music is native, "like the soil and sky of the land."

The Snow Maiden, child of King Frost and Spring, is brought up by peasant foster parents near Berendey. There Lehl, the shepherd lad, darling of the village girls, has no eyes for Sniegurotschka, though for her sake wild young Tartar Mizgyr casts off Kupava, his promised bride. Wronged Kupava demands justice at the Czar's court where blind *guslee* players make sweet melody, but Mizgyr cries: "O Czar, could you but see Sniegurotschka!" When the Czar has looked on her beauty, he knows she is innocent, and promises her hand to the man who can win her heart before the morrow's dawn. While Lehl makes love to Kupava, Sniegurotschka, hastening to her mother, gains the fatal power to love like a mortal. When she again sees Mizgyr human passion stirs in her virgin breast, but that moment a sunbeam pierces the sheltering clouds, and on the brink of love's fulfillment her delicate body melts and she vanishes, leaving Mizgyr to kill himself in despair as the chant to the midnight sun rises on the air.

## "L'OISEAU DE FEU"

### (*The Fire Bird*)

IGOR STRAVINSKY. Fantastic ballet (Paris, 1910; New York, 1916). A nature legend underlies this Muscovite folktale, Kostchei, in older myths personifying Winter and the lovely captive princess, Spring. The score is impressionistic, episodic treatment of situations taking the place of logical thematic development, orchestral tone completing scenic gesture with marvelous unity. Beautiful pages are: the "Fire Bird's Supplication"; the play of the Czarevna's maids with the golden apples; and the brilliant "Dance of Kostchei's Vassals."

Moonbeams silver a forest glade where golden apples hang from a stunted tree. Into it floats the Fire Bird, a vision of flame, caught by Czarevitch Ivan, who releases her when she gives him a golden feather as a talisman in time of need. Now white-robed maidens, captives of Kostchei the Deathless—whose castle rises in the background—enter the glade, shake the apple tree and pursue the rolling fruit. Ivan loses his heart to the beautiful Czarevna, who accepts the apple he offers. But suddenly the maids hasten back to their tower; warning bells resound, and a mad rabble of fantastic figures rushes into the forest. *Kikimoras,* demon spirits, *bolebachki,* grisly phantoms, evil dwarfs, wizards and warlocks surround the daring Czarevitch. Kostchei, ringed by fawning hunchbacks, with a glittering horned crown and fingers clawed like a Chinese mandarin's, draws near with lurking air of menace. In vain the Czarevna begs him to be merciful: there is no heart in his breast. He raised his hand to turn Ivan to stone when the latter waves the feather, the Fire Bird flashes on the scene and Kostchei shrinks back, her golden magic stronger than his black arts. The Fire Bird sweeps the evil horde into a mad dance, casts over them the spell of slumber, and Ivan, plunging his hand into a hollow tree trunk, draws out a steel casket. The sleepers wake, for out of the casket Ivan draws the mystic egg which hides Kostchei's soul. With agonizing gaze the wizard follows the egg Ivan tosses from hand to hand. But when Kostchei leaps forward to grasp it Ivan flings it to the ground. It breaks with a crash of thunder and darkness veils the scene. When shadows clear only Ivan and the Czarevna—sleeping softly beneath the tree, her maidens in the background—remain. As she wakes to his kiss and clings to him in rapture, the Fire Bird is glimpsed winging her way into the regions of faëry.

*Kostchei the Immortal* (Moscow, 1902) by Rimsky-Korsakoff, a "Legend of Autumn," is a symbolic opera. In Rimsky's score the lovely Czarevna is rescued by Ivan and "the autumnal, sin-oppressed kingdom of the wizard lies open to the outside world." But Kostchei dies when the tear of pity which redeems his daughter Kostcheievna from her own jealous rage shatters the crystal globe which holds her father's "life." Effective are: the "Trepak Chorus of Snow Spirits" and the sinister "Slumber Song" the Czarevna sings for Kostchei, wishing his sleep may be that of death. Cavos also wrote an opera, *The Bird of Fire* (Petrograd, 1822) on the same subject.

*Kikimora* (San Sebastian, 1916), a ballet russe, music by Liadoff, tells an old Muscovite fable. When Kikimora, demon spirit of malice and malignity, entered the world in human form the witches locked her up. Kikimora, after a terrific struggle with the great black cat set to guard her, slays the beast with a hatchet, and her freedom secured has been going about the world ever since, sowing evil and stirring up strife.

## "PRINCE IGOR"

ALEXANDER BORODIN. Book by Stassov (Petrograd, 1890), after the Russian *Epic of the Army of Igor*. Notable for fine melodies based on Russian and Tartar folk songs, and straightforward quality of emotional appeal, in this opera stands out Vladimir's "Serenade," a glowing air sung by the hero before the tent of his Tartar mistress.

Prince Igor of Kiev (Prologue) rides against the Tartar Khan Kontchak despite his wife's warnings, entrusting her to the care of his traitor brother-in-law Prince Galitsky, who plans to usurp his throne. Once Igor and his son, Prince Vladimir, are gone (Act I) Galitsky's friends, among them his agents the comic drunkards Eroshka and Skoula, acclaim him their lord. When Yaroslavna, Igor's wife, asks Galitsky for news of her husband, he laughs. Word has come that Igor and Vladimir are captives of the Tartars. In the camp of the victorious Polovtsy horde, however, Vladimir (Act II) has won the heart of the Khan's beautiful daughter, slant-eyed Kontchakovna, and enjoys the wild dances his savage captors perform in his honor at a festal banquet. These dances, the opera ballet, are an independent unit of the Russian Ballet repertoire.

*Dances from Prince Igor* (*Danses Polovtsiennes*: Tartar Ballet, Paris, 1909), according to the French painter Blanche, evoke in color and costume "Persian miniatures, the most madly glowing shawls of Ind, the stained glass windows of Notre-Dame or a garden of geraniums at the close of a stormy day." Surrounding an open space are red Tartar huts from which gray smoke spirals rise. Beyond the river Kalaya the infinite horizon of the steppe "stretches down the centuries to Siberia." Women sing melodies sad as the plain at twilight, and suddenly the warriors of the horde, bow in hand, rush on the stage and begin a frenzied dance. They stamp with barbaric joy. They send flights of invisible arrows toward the skies. The women and girls of the horde have danced in the sensuous manner of the Orient, the gambols of the Tartar youths have foreshadowed the savage realities of their life to come; but the wild dance of the adult warriors, with its concluding charge down to the footlights in a triple row, "seems to bring two epochs of man, the barbaric and the civilized, face to face."

After the dances comes Khan Gsak (Act III) bringing Russian booty and prisoners to the Tartar camp. The horde indulges in a drunken orgy (Borodin's "all too truthful realism" in picturing it has been criticized) and the happy savages pass by the *koumiss* road from revelry to slumber. Igor seizes the opportunity to escape; but when Vladimir with a sigh resigns himself to be true to his better self, lovely Kontchakovna flings herself upon him, and he yields to her clinging arms and remains. Meantime, as Igor's wife mourns her lost husband (Act IV) on the palace terrace, the latter arrives, and the happy townsfolk set the bells of Kiev ringing in honor of their beloved master's return.

### 4. The Musical Morte d'Arthur

The mythic history of Britain, the legend cycle of King Arthur —really a petty prince of South Wales—and his knights, has inspired various scores. The "Merlin" operas deal with the famous enchanter, son of a Christian maid and an incubus or demon.

*Merlin* (Vienna, 1886) by Karl Goldmark, musically reflective rather than inspired, has been called "polarized Wagner." A piquant "Dance of the Will-o'-the-Wisps" and an ensemble, "Sei mir gegrüsst" (Act III) stand out. Merlin, a Christ of darkness, hates his father Satan. When he helps good King Arthur against the pagan Saxons, Satan sends Vivienne to tempt his son. He yields to his love for her, loses his magic power and when the "lady from hell" winds a sacred veil around his head, Merlin's magic garden turns to a desert waste where, bound with red-hot fetters, demons mock him. Merlin (Act II) wins King Arthur's battle against the pagans by promising his soul to Satan but repentent Vivienne ransoms it by dying to save him. *Myrdhin* (Nantes, 1912) by Bourgoult-Ducoudray, a French variant of the legend, makes Myrdhin (Merlin) an inspired bard. Modred, Queen Guinevere's lover, inflames him with tales of Viviane's charms (Act II) and Myrdhin deserts King Arthur to seek the temptress in Broceliande forest. Death-wails from the stricken field tear him from her arms too late to save the day. He returns to sensuous joys, and when his mother banishes Viviane with the holy cross, Myrdhin goes insane! Then, while drunken Saxons revel in their camp, the mad bard cuts the bonds of the British prisoners and as they kill their intoxicated foes, dies seeing paradise open before him. *Merlin* (Berlin, 1887) by Philip Rüfer makes Merlin leave Vivian to guide King Arthur to the Holy Grail. But when he sees the sacred chalice glow golden amid desert sands his devil-father bids him overturn it, that Christ's blood be poured out and the world made subject to Satan. When Merlin refuses, Satan, powerless to touch the Grail himself, slays him. Reissmann's eclectic *Gralspiel* (*Grail Play*, Berlin, 1895), and Davranches' modern French lyric drama *Klingsor* (Nimes, 1914) are dwarfed by Wagner's mighty Grail score.

*The Cairn of Koridwen* (New York, 1917), a dance drama by Charles T. Griffes, has as its story source the legend on which Wagner based his *Tristan*.

Purcell's *King Arthur* (revised, London, 1920) is considered his best score. The Spanish composer Albeniz has an Arthurian trilogy, *King Arthur, Merlin,* and *Guinevere* (1897-1906). *Amor* (Paris, 1898) by Silvio Lazzari wrests from Ked, Queen of the Korrigans (fairies), Arthur's holy crown only to fling it away for her unhallowed kiss. In Chausson's *Le roi Artus* (Karlsruhe, 1900) the beautiful lyric music has analogies with *Tristan,* and Ronald Boughton's *King Arthur* (Glastonbury, 1925) is the most recent Arthurian opera.

Others are: *Lancelot* by R. Hermann (Kassel, 1894), and by Joncières (Paris, 1900); *Elaine* (London, 1892; New York, 1894) by Bemberg (air, "L'amour est pur"); *Lancelot et Elaine* (Munich, 1917), an "elegiac" opera by Walter Courvoisier; *Gwenevere* (London, 1905) and *Enid* (London, 1908) by Vincent Thomas.

## "PARSIFAL"

Richard Wagner. Festival Drama, based on Wolfram von Eschenbach's poem on the legend of the Holy Grail (Baireuth, 1882). Parsifal, "the innocent with the pure heart," unable to rise to the higher plane of the ideal saves guilty Amfortas, the Grail King, once he himself has learned the lesson of human suffering, desire's illusion and sin's vanity. Wagner emphasizes the idea of salvation through sacrifice in terms of Christian mysticism. The Prelude, "Dance of the Flower Maidens," and "Good Friday Music" are jewels of a score which is "a music of transition, in which time becomes space, all that has been turns into a quiet, spreading cathedral where the magic of long-drawn tonal connecting threads" weaves about chiming Grail bells.

The Holy Grail, chalice which caught Christ's blood when he was lifted from the Cross, radiates the magic of the Divine Presence, health, strength and felicity. Angels have entrusted it to the custody of the Grail knights, men pure of heart, who guard it in Monsalvat, the temple castle which rises on a mountain height. Tinturel, first king of the Grail, has been succeeded by his son Amfortas.

The trumpet call to prayer has roused old Gurnemanz and his esquires from woodland slumbers, when knights from the castle announce Amfortas nears to bathe in the lake. Kundry, a seductive witch-woman, gallops up with Arabian balsam for the suffering king, which he takes, sighing for "the pure fool by pity guided" who alone can cure him. Gurnemanz, his esquires expressing doubts of Kundry, presents her as a sinner unknown but repentant, whom black spells hold in bondage. Klingsor, a magician, refused admission among the elect, built a castle filled with girls of seductive beauty, to wean away pure-hearted knights from holiness. Amfortas, setting out with the Sacred Spear (the lance with which Longinus pierced the side of the Christ on the Cross) to set his knights a good example, fell a victim to Kundry's wiles. While he forgot chastity in her arms, Klingsor carried off the spear with ribald laughter, and the king in a vain struggle to regain it was severely wounded in the side. Since then he lives in constant torture. He cannot be cured till a young knight, whose purity is temptation-proof, touch his side with the recovered spear. At this moment a wild swan falls dying to the ground. Parsifal, son of Heart-of-Sorrows, brought up in woodland innocence by the mother from whom he has strayed, appears as the bird's slayer, but breaks his arrows when re-proached by Gurnemanz with the sin of wanton killing in the sacred forest. When Kundry tells him his mother is dead, Gurnemanz leads the grieving youth to Monsalvat, where he witnesses the service of the Grail and sees the golden aura from above irradiate the crystal chalice with supernal light. But when the Grail has been put in its shrine and the king's wound again bleeds, Parsifal, showing no sign that he is the "guiltless one," is pushed out of the castle gate by Gurnemanz.

Parsifal approaches Klingsor's castle, and Kundry shrieks protest when Klingsor orders her to seduce the forest innocent. The latter meanwhile has defeated Klingsor's sin-stained knights, and the sorcerer fearing for himself waves his tower into hidden depths, and bids the magic flower-garden take its place. Parsifal is surrounded by beautiful maidens, lightly scarfed, whom he cannot help but admire, and who invite him to play with them. While the Flower Maidens are decorous, Parsifal enjoys their caresses with innocent delight, and as they become bolder he finds himself confronted by Kundry, lying on a bed of flowers, who talks to the boy of home and mother, and when, deeply affected, he sinks sorrowing at her feet, gives him a long kiss. Parsifal leaps up; his blood surges through his veins; but though filled with a terrible yearning he remains firm, and strengthened by desperate prayer, repulses the temptress. When caresses do not move him Kundry calls on Klingsor. He flings the Sacred Spear at Parsifal, but the steel hangs harmless in the air above the pure youth's head. As he makes the sign of the cross, magic gardens and castle fall in ruins about the swooning Flower Maidens, and Parsifal goes.

Gurnemanz, become a forest hermit with the passing of time, finds Kundry senseless in the brush, revives her and learns a knight in black armor is drawing near. It is Parsifal who, informed it is Good Friday, thrusts the Sacred Spear into the ground and prays. Then he tells Gurnemanz and Kundry that having wandered far he is bringing the Sacred Spear to the Grail Castle. Amfortas still suffers, the Grail never leaves its shrine, and the knights have grown faint-hearted doing good. When Parsifal sinks swooning with remorse, Kundry bathes his feet and wipes them with her hair; and after Gurnemanz has anointed him for the Grail service, the knight baptizes Kundry. Then, while Parsifal admires the loveliness of forest and meadow—due to the "Good Friday Spell"—Gurnemanz brings a Grail knight's tunic and cloak, and they set out for Monsalvat.

There Grail knights march into the sanctuary bearing dead Tinturel's coffin and Amfortas' canopied throne. As the king prays his dead father to intercede for him and begs his knights to kill him with their swords, Parsifal touches his side with the Sacred Spear, proclaiming heaven's absolution. The shrine is opened. The Holy Grail is illumined by golden light from above, while a white dove flutters from the temple dome and hovers above Parsifal's head. Dead Tinturel, recalled to life for a moment, rises in his coffin to bless the knights, Kundry sinks blissfully dying to the ground, and Amfortas and Gurnemanz kneel worshipfully at Parsifal's feet while an angelic chorus adores the Saviour on high.

## "THE TALE OF THE INVISIBLE CITY OF KITZEH AND THE MAID FEVRONIA"

### (*The Russian Parsifal*)

NICOLAI RIMSKY-KORSAKOFF. Book by Bielski (Petrograd, 1907). An opera based on a mystic folk legend of Tatar days, with a "spiritual message akin to that of *Parsifal*," it uses folk melodies influenced by Wagner musically. Evil, contrary to the Occidental conception of *Parsifal*, is regarded as transitory, a prelude to life eternal. Vselovod's air "If I do not love you," and his duet with Fevronia, stand out; the symphonic Cathedral Scene in the Monsalvat of the Slavic paradise "borders on the sublime" (N. C. Bernstein).

In the forest, Fevronia, surrounded by the wild woodland creatures, sings the praise of life amid the flowers. There a strange youth finds and falls in love with her. No sooner have they exchanged rings than horns sound, a company of archers enters the glade, and Fevronia learns her betrothed is Prince Vselovod of Kitzeh.

In Little Kitzeh a *guslee* player sings the Virgin's appearance on Great Kitzeh walls, and foretells the destruction of the city by the Tatars. As Fevronia's bridal procession appears on its way to the great town the vanguard of the horde rushes in, seizes the drunkard Kutermia as a guide and drags off Fevronia who, as the Mongols bear her away, prays the city be made invisible.

From Great Kitzeh's cathedral tower a boy describes Little Kitzeh aflame and the Tatar advance. Vselovod, raging at Fevronia's capture, sallies out and dies like a Christian knight on the stricken field. As the cathedral bells toll of their own accord and the people pray, the boy on the tower calls that a white veil descending from Heaven is hiding the city from the foe. (Change of scene.) Bound to a cart in the Tatar camp Fevronia despairs as two Tatar murzas fight for her possession; but when slumber falls on the horde, she cuts her own and Kutermia's bonds and escapes. At dawn the Tatars rub their eyes. Great Kitzeh's reflection is mirrored in the lake, but the city is invisible.

In the enchanted forest whither she has fled, Fevronia (Kutermia has left her) prays while flowers of gold and silver spring beneath her tread, and the voices of Aklonost and Sirin, birds of paradise, bid her rejoice, since she shall know life everlasting. Suddenly the soul of Vselovod greets her, and tells her that he was slain but is now alive. He gives her the bread of happiness to stay her on the journey before her, and eating and casting the crumbs to the birds, she disappears with him. (Apotheosis.) The people of Kitzeh—for the prayers of the just have carried Kitzeh the Invisible to Paradise itself on the Northern Lights—welcome Vselovod and Fevronia, chanting as they enter the cathedral, "There shall be no more tears, only everlasting peace and joy!"

## "FERVAAL"

### (*The French Parsifal*)

VINCENT D'INDY. In a legendary druidic epoch a Parsifal of the Cévennes sees the world redeemed by love in a twilight of the Cévenol gods. Wagnerian in form, story, and use of leading motive, d'Indy's music is his own (Brussels, 1897). Outstanding are: Fervaal's and Guilhen's Love Scene (Act I); the "Night Music" (Act II), a poetic nature-painting; the Prelude (Act III); and the Finale.

Fervaal, last lord of Cravann (Prologue) raised in a sacred forest by the druid Alfagard, is attacked and wounded traversing the Saracen land. Saved by the lovely Saracen princess Guilhen, his druid vow by which he renounces woman's impure love dies on his lips as he sees her. Cured by her (Act I) the "Son of the Clouds," dreams in her garden when Alfagard calls on him, his "soul and body unstained by love" to save his native land. But Fervaal no longer is a Parsifal: Guilhen has taught him love's lesson and when he tears himself from her embrace to do his duty, she threatens to seek him out with her warriors.

The Cravann chiefs, with midnight ritual make Fervaal their *Brenn* or king, but when Koto, invoked by Alfagard, denounces Fervaal's broken vow, the latter confesses to the Druid and determines to die in battle against the Saracens in atonement.

The battle fought and lost by the mountain men, Fervaal bids Alfagard slay him with the druid knife when Guilhen, lost amid the hills, appears. Fervaal hews down the priest who bars his way with his sword, and clasps his love in his arms. But the daughter of the South has been slain by the cold northern winds and dies against his breast. Then, as red dawn gilds the mountain peaks, Fervaal bearing his beloved climbs toward the cloud-shrouded heights with the triumphal song "Love conquers death!"

## "JUAN GARIN"

### (*The Spanish Parsifal*)

THOMAS BRETÓN. Book after an old Spanish legend (Madrid, 1892). The Spanish *Parsifal* is one of "local association." Monserrat, "the jagged rock," its caves supposed to date from the time the hills were torn asunder at the Crucifixion, is the legendary mountain of the Holy Grail, the home of Parsifal. Fray Garin, however, was too busy redeeming his own sin-stained soul to bother about others. The score, one of Bretón's best, has highly dramatic pages.

Riquela, daughter of Wilfredo II, Count of Barcelona (10th century) was possessed of a demon, and her father took her to Monserrat, tc saintly Fray Garin, that her devil be exorcised. But Beelzebub sug·· gested to Fray Garin that he take advantage of the lovely innocent left in his care after the manner of the flesh. Fray Garin struggled against, temptation only to fall, and his wickedness accomplished, cut Riquela's throat and buried her. Then remorse drove him to Rome. When he had cast himself at the Pope's feet and confessed, the latter bade him creep back to his hermitage nor look at God's pure sky till a child told him he was forgiven. *A gatos andando,* "crawling on hands and feet," he toiled on, till he seemed a wild forest beast, and found by a squire of Wilfredo, was taken to his palace in Barcelona and caged for the amusement of the court. One day a child stopped before the cage and cried: "Arise, Juan Garin, God has forgiven you!" And the wild beast rose and they saw it was a man. He led the way to Monserrat, but at the place where he had buried Riquela they found her alive, only a red mark showing where Juan had cut her throat. Thus did true repentance redeem Fray Garin's sin, and he died in the odor of sanctity.

## "THE PERFECT FOOL"

### (*The English Parsifal*)

GUSTAVE HOLST. Book by the composer (London, 1923). A fantastic, humorous opera, with clever Wagnerian, Donizettian and Verdian musical parodies. Some have called it a parody on *Parsifal;* others, a delightful jest which without irreverent intent shows how a humorous Englishman might picture "the pure fool," the man who would resist a charming woman as—a village idiot. There are many fine musical pages, including some folkwise choruses ("Round of the Girl Water-carriers").

At midnight the Wizard summons the spirits of earth, water, and fire to brew the potion that wins for him who drinks it the love of the princess of the land, so she will choose him for a husband. But at dawn comes a beggar-woman and her loutish son, the Perfect Fool, who settles down to sleep. While the Wizard rehearses his speech to the mother, she slyly wakes her son, bids him drain the draught, and this done refills the cup with spring water from the pail of a passing peasant maid. When the Princess arrives the Wizard empties the cup. A Troubadour tries to win the Princess' heart with a love lay; a Wanderer praises her in mystic terms, but deaf to them, she kneels beside the sleeping Fool. The Wizard knows he has been fooled. He laughs a sinister laugh: the skies darken, towers of flame sweep the countryside, her people beg the Princess to flee; but she cannot bear to leave her beloved. And when the mother wakes her dolt he glances at the Wizard and the latter disappears in a whirlwind of fire. The Princess upbraids her courtiers: a Fool has saved her. "Do you love me?" she asks the oaf and grinning he answers "No!" The Princess is enraptured. She has gained a husband who won her heart, yet whose own is untouched. While the people dance the coronation ceremonies begin. The Perfect Fool, however, about to be united to his lovely bride, yawns, and falls asleep just as the Archbishop places the crown on his head.

### 5.  Don  Quixote

Don Quixote, mad, generous, chivalric fool of Cervantes' great novel, is the hero of numerous operas. One of the oldest is *Don Chissiot della Mancia* (Venice, 1680) by Carlo Sajon, a "drama for music." Sir George Macfarren's *Don Quixote* (London, 1846), De Koven's lighter *Don Quixote* (Boston, 1889), Offenbach's spectacular grand opera *Don Quichotte* (never completed), the spectacular ballet *Don Quixote,* by Pepita, and Jacques-Dalcroze's *Sancho Panza* (Geneva, 1897) are reactions to the theme.

*Don Quijote* (Berlin, 1898) by Kienzl in its music stresses Don Quixote's tragic idealism. Act III has been called "the greatest single act since Wagner." The Don, falling asleep over his romances of chivalry, lives the adventures of Cervantes' novel in a series of tableaux. Then, waking, he casts his books into the fire and, mocked and scorned, death frees him to enter those realms of the ideal where there is neither folly nor deceit.

*Don Quijote* (Munich, 1908), Beer-Walbrunn's tragi-comedy opera (Sextet, Act I; Love Duet, Act III), tells Quixote's adventures with Dulcinea, supposed princess but real washerwoman, and his return home when she has been "disenchanted." *Don Quichotte* (Monte Carlo, 1910) by Massenet deals with various adventures of the hero, but poor Dulcinea is made a courtesan, and when Don Quixote offers her marriage declines because of her profession.

### "EL RETABLO DE MAESE PEDRO"

#### (*Master Pedro's Puppet Show*)

MANUEL DE FALLA. Musical and dramatic adaptation of a chapter of *El Ingenioso Caballero Don Quixote de la Mancha* (Seville, 1920). The ultramodern music—the scene is an Aragonese tavern stable—is archaic Castilian in flavor. Fine dramatic and lyric pages; old dance rhythms, *gaillard* and *seguidilla,* and a clever development of the Spanish "Royal March" stand out. There are quaint oriental effects, mock heroic horn calls, bagpipe imitation, etc.

Master Peter's marionettes are performing by candlelight, in *el retablo* (the stable) an old heroic "romance," *The History of the Rescue of the Princess Melisandra, a Captive of the Moors.* The folk at the inn including Don Quixote and Sancho form the audience; a Boy acts as narrator of the puppet action. *The Rescue of Melisandra* is presented in four tableaux. (1) In Charlemagne's palace, Gayferos, Melisandra's husband, forgetful of his wife in a game of draughts, and twitted by the emperor sets out to free her from the Moors. (2) Melisandra on the balcony of the Alcazar, the Moorish King Marsilio's palace in Zaragoza dreams of Gayferos till a Moor steals a kiss from her, and (3) is bastinadoed in the city square. Next (4) Gayferos is trotting along a Pyrenean path to save his wife. When he draws near (the Boy explains) Melisandra leaps from the tower, is caught in his arms and they gallop off on the Paris road while the bells of the mosques ring the alarm. Don Quixote starts up and cries mosques have no bells. Master Peter quiets him—improbabilities often occur in dramas—but when the Boy describes the Moorish horsemen in pursuit of the fugitives, and says he fears they will be brought back "tied to the tail of their own horse," Don Quixote loses control of himself. With sword drawn, he defies all Moors, and begins to cut the marionettes to pieces to the danger of Master Pedro and the rest present. So doing he sings in praise of peerless Dulcinea, and the curtain falls on his hymn to "knight-errantry" and its glorious champion, himself.

## 6. The Legends of Tristan

### "TRISTAN UND ISOLDE"

RICHARD WAGNER. Book after Gottfried von Strasburg's thirteenth century poem (Munich, 1865). "Never has the poetry and tragedy of love been set to music of such resistless beauty." The underlying thought in *Tristan* is that love has rights superior to all human law, provided it be content to accept death as its final outcome. It is the emotional legacy of Wagner's own passion for Mathilde Wesendonk, a monument to "the fairest of all his dreams." The scene of action is Cornwall, Brittany, and the Breton Sea, in Arthurian days.

Before the Drama. Morold, the Irish king's brother, was slain by Tristan, nephew of King Mark of Cornwall, and his head sent to Isolde, his betrothed, in lieu of tribute. Tristan, wounded in the combat and knowing Isolde's skill in healing, goes to the Irish coast as "Tantris," a wandering minstrel. Isolde tends his wound, but matching a notch in his sword with the steel splinter found in Morold's skull, knows he is her lover's murderer. As she is about to slay him, he looks into her eyes. Love fills her soul; she spares him. In Cornwall Tristan sings Isolde's praises. The nobles suggest King Mark marry her and Tristan sails to Ireland to bring back his uncle's bride. Isolde feels deeply wronged: Tristan, who knows she loves him, has come to woo her for another man. But she sails for Cornwall on his ship.

While a sailor sings, Isolde, on the deck section curtained off for her, grieves. Brangäne, her faithful servant, says Cornwall has been sighted. Invoking destruction on herself, Isolde gasps for air—the curtain hiding the deck is withdrawn, showing sailors, knights, and Tristan, with Kurneval his squire looking at the fleeting waters. Isolde summons Tristan and swears never to wed King Mark, then bids

Brangäne take the poison vial from her casket of drugs. Tristan, willing to die, knowing his love hopeless, shares the goblet's contents with Isolde. But Brangäne has poured a love instead of a death potion into the wine. As the waves of their passion overwhelm the lovers they cling together while the vessel makes its destination.

Hunting horns sound from the nocturnal forest to Isolde's tower above the palace gardens. Isolde signals her lover. They recline on a bank of flowers and murmur their vows. Vainly Brangäne and Kurneval warn them. Then Melot, who has betrayed them, brings King Mark to the scene and the humiliated King reproaches his nephew. As he begs Isolde to follow him Tristan is attacked by Melot and severely wounded. While Kurneval receives his falling body and Isolde flings herself upon it, King Mark restrains Melot.

In the garden of his Breton castle Tristan awaits the vessel bringing Isolde to him. When a shepherd pipe proclaims the glad news, Tristan, wild with sudden joy, rises from his couch and tears away his bandages. Blood pouring from his wounds, he hears Isolde's voice and staggers to meet her. As she clasps him in her arms, he sinks to the ground and with a supreme look of recognition dies at her feet. The clash of arms heralds King Mark's approach. He has come to forgive the errant lovers. Kurneval, not knowing this, is slain by Melot barring the entrance to the castle, killing Melot as he himself is cut down. King Mark kneels sobbing at his nephew's feet, while Isolde, her gaze riveted on Tristan, sings the swan song of the greatest love the world has known, the "Liebestod" ("Love-Death") and dies in Brangäne's arms.

## "PELLÉAS ET MÉLISANDE"

### (The French Tristan)

CLAUDE DEBUSSY. Drama by Maurice Maeterlinck (Paris, 1902). The French impressionist's masterwork. No other opera, perhaps, has such strange, enticing and depressing charm of mood. It is dream music, neutral, shadowy, unreal, with the haunting beauty the decadent so often shows. It prefers color to outline, harmony to melody, for to Debussy music was color expressed in luminous tone vibrations. It opposes a tenuous and kaleidoscopic web of moving tone to the solid architectural reality of Wagner, the elusive to the natural. It is a drama of fatality in love, "a music without formulas, all derived from the soul" (Laloy). "In the love scenes are . . . adorable phrases like long tears falling on crystal, an astonishing music which seems the emotion of the idea in the transparent sheath of the word" (Suarès).

Golo the hunter, son of King Arkel of Allemonde—a mystic medieval land—finds golden-haired Mélisande weeping by a forest spring and induces her to follow him as his bride. All Mélisande knows is that once she wore a crown which now lies at the bottom of a well.

In his castle blind King Arkel and Pelléas, Golo's half brother, welcome the huntsman and his bride, returned because of the signal—a light in the tower window—that King Arkel has forgiven his son for wedding an unknown forest maid.

Mélisande has wandered from the green gloom of the forest to the gray gloom of castle walls, but young Pelléas talks with the wife whose husband forgets her for the chase. He tells her he leaves for a sea voyage the next day but—does not go.

Pelléas and Mélisande sit on a fountain rim in the palace grounds, the girl's hair falling about her like a golden cloud. Toying with her wedding ring, she drops it into the crystal depths. (Change of scene.) As Mélisande ministers to Golo, hurt by a fall from his horse, her husband's deep love leads him to try to console her for her monotonous life. Seizing her hand, however, he sees her ring is gone. Mélisande does not tell the truth. She says she lost the ring in a sea cavern, trying to escape the tide, and Golo bids her hasten with Pelléas to recover it. (Change of scene.) In the sea grotto reëchoing to the waves, Pelléas and Mélisande talk, trying to hide emotions surging within them. A sudden moonbeam lights the darkness, revealing three blind beggars. Mélisande screams, and Pelléas leads her from the cave.

In the castle tower Mélisande combs her golden hair as Pelléas comes to bid her farewell. To music of haunting charm love weaves its spell about them, and Mélisande's hair as she leans from the casement falls about the boy's head. Swept away by his passion Pelléas covers her hair with ardent kisses which, he says, shall travel the golden threads to find her lips. As the white doves of the tower disperse in sudden flight, Golo enters. He only reproves them for their childishness, but leading his brother to the castle vaults (change of scene) halts on the brink of the abyss, tempted to push him over and out of Mélisande's life. He contents himself, however, with warning him to think no more of her and they depart in silence. (Change of scene.) Golo now vainly tries to draw from Yniold, his little son by a previous marriage, information as to the intimacy of his wife and brother, but the innocent child has nothing evil to report.

Golo watching his unhappy young wife in her room gives way to jealous rage and flinging her to her knees drags her across the floor by her hair. (Change of scene.) The lovers meet at dusk by the fountain. They now know they love and sense the twilight shades closing around them. As Golo approaches their lips meet in a kiss and they joy in the knowledge that they must die. Pelléas is thrust through by Golo's sword, Mélisande flees, pursued by her husband.

Mélisande is dying in her castle chamber, not because of the babe she has borne, but of her love. Old Arkel mourns by her bedside. As she wakes and opens her eyes Golo, torn by terrible suspicions, tortures her to tell whether she betrayed him with Pelléas. She denies it, but admits her love for the slain boy and kind old Arkel, pitying the despairing spirit trying to win from earth, hushes his son while Mélisande gently breathes her last. *Pelléas* has been called "the French *Tristan*" because, like Wagner's score, it is a drama of fatality in love. There is no musical bond of union between the works.

## "THE QUEEN OF CORNWALL"

RUTLAND BOUGHTON. Book after Thomas Hardy's poem (London, 1924). An opera version of the Tristan legend, with fine choruses, along the line of folkwise thematic development, a British music drama on a subject the composer regards as being preëminently a British one.

Queen Iseult, King Mark's wife, sails from Brittany at the request of her rival, Iseult of the White Hands, to nurse dying Tristan back to life. Recovering at the news that the Queen of Cornwall is nearing the Breton shore Tristan hurries to Tintagel Castle disguised as a minstrel. Iseult of the White Hands follows him only to see him slain by King Mark in a fit of jealous rage, and the Queen of Cornwall, after killing her husband in her insane fury, flings herself from a cliff.

## 7. *The Legends of Charlemagne*

Around Charlemagne, first Christian Emperor of the West (c. 742-814), cluster fantastic legends of chivalry which have inspired many an opera composer. *Königin Bertha* (*Queen Bertha,* Berlin, 1892) by Kurth tells how Pépin, King of the Franks, left his fiancée Bertha, Charlemagne's mother, in the forest to die, only to have her singing charm him into saving her and punishing her detractors. *Fierrabras* (Vienna, 1861) by Franz Schubert, a heroic-romantic score, its lovely music undramatic, deals with the unsuccessful love of a Moorish prince for Emma, Charlemagne's daughter. Piccini's *Roland* (Paris, 1778), unsuccessful rival of Gluck's *Armide,* contains pages of lovely pastoral and other music; and *Roland à Roncevaux* (Paris, 1863) by Mermet enjoyed brief popularity because Napoleon said to the composer: "I know nothing of music, but yours pleases me!" *Rolands Knappen* (*Roland's Squires,* Leipzig, 1848) by Lortzing tells of three who took their way to King Garcias of Leon after Roncevaux, and finding a magic purse, cap of invisibility, and tablecloth which insured them money, safety, and food, plunged into all sorts of adventures in consequence. *La fille de Roland* (Paris, 1904) by Henri Rabaud, book after Bornier's drama, in which Rabaud "descends from his camel," is a melodious, legendary tale of love, hate, and chivalry in Charlemagne's day. Berthe, Roland's daughter, is the heroine, and Ganelon, son of her father's foe Gerald, the hero.

## "ESCLARMONDE"

JULES MASSENET. Book by Blau and De Gramont (Paris, 1889). Bellaigue has called this romantic "Roland" opera score "at the same time a small French *Tristan* and a *Parsifal.*"

Prologue. Phorcas, Emperor of Byzantium, lays down his crown in favor of his lovely daughter Esclarmonde, who if she would inherit his magic powers must go veiled until she be twenty. Then her hand shall be the prize of the victor of a tourney to be held in the imperial city. Esclarmonde looks over blue Bosphorus waters (Act II) and yearns for Roland of Blois, the knight of her dreams. When news comes King Cleomer means to wed his daughter to Roland, Esclarmonde summons spirits who seize the knight while hunting and bring him to her magic isle. Asleep among the flowers he is awakened by her kiss (Act III) and after exchanging lovers' vows Roland hurries to Blois to relieve King Cleomer, besieged by Saracens, Esclarmonde promising to cheer his nights wherever he may be. The hundred virgins the Saracen king demands as a tribute (Act IV) seem doomed until Roland slays the pagan with a magic sword of Esclarmonde's giving; but when she appears (Roland has confessed to the Bishop of Blois why he will not wed Cleomer's daughter), the Bishop tears off the lovely sorceress' veil, and reproaching Roland for telling, she is carried off by her spirits before indignant monks can seize her.

Phorcas, now a hermit of the Ardennes (Act V), hears tourney time is at hand, but Esclarmonde absent. When she is brought to him he tells her he must die unless she renounces the Christian knight, and Esclarmonde, sending for Roland, tells him she no longer loves him. Seeking death, now life has no more to offer, Roland enters the lists. Acclaimed victor of the tournament (Epilogue) Roland, first refusing the hand of the veiled Byzantine princess, changes his mind when Esclarmonde's features are disclosed and love comes into its own.

## "ARMIDE"

CHRISTOPH WILLIBALD VON GLUCK. Book after Tasso's *Jerusalem Delivered* (Paris, 1777). A Christian knight falls a victim to the magic charms of a pagan enchantress, but renounces unhallowed love at duty's call. The score is considered the composer's masterpiece, and Rinaldo's "Slumber Aria" the gem of the work.

The Glorification of Armide. In her Damascan palace the Saracen princess dreams of the knight Rinaldo (Roland's cousin), blind to her charms. She has promised her uncle, King Hidraoth, to marry Arontes, supposed to have defeated the Crusaders. But his tale of victory is false. He enters Armide's presence wounded by Rinaldo's sword.

The Seduction of Rinaldo. Wandering in the desert, Rinaldo enters the Enchanted Garden Armide's magic has made bloom in the waste. Dagger in hand, she approaches him as he sleeps in a bower of roses. About to avenge Saracen defeats, anger turns to love at sight of him and she clasps him in her arms.

Armide's Scene with the Fury. Back in her palace, Armide regrets her revenge. The fury Hate tells her the Christian hero will escape her if she yield to softer emotions. Yet Armide harkens to the voice of love and dismisses the vengeful spirit.

The Episode of Ubald and the Danish Knight (called "an unnecessary pendant in *cabaret* style"). On Armide and her lover, in the Enchanted Garden, intrude Ubald and a Danish knight, seeking their companion, but cannot wean him from Armide's arms.

Rinaldo's Redemption. Duty forgotten, Rinaldo yields to love in the magic bower. Compelled to tear herself from his arms to attend to magic rites, Armide leaves him to be entertained by a Ballet of Spirits. The knights seize the opportunity. In a polished shield Ubald shows Rinaldo himself as he was and is, and the Crusader grasps his sword. Armide exhausts every art to hold him; but leaving the world of enchantment he returns to the realities of Christian duty. In despair Armide sets fire to her faëry palace and perishes in the flames.

Operas on this subject have been written by Lully, Sacchini, Traetta, Salieri and Righini; and Rossini's *Armida* (Naples, 1817), after Tasso's *Jerusalemmo liberato,* contains some of his best music, notably three passionate love duets between Rinaldo and Armida. *La délivrance de Renaud* (*Rinaldo's Deliverance*), a ballet (Paris, 1619; revised, 1913; music by Guedron, Boesset, and Bataille, adapted by Laloy and Quittard), shows (1) Rinaldo's men seeking him in the forest while his companions release him from Armide's garden, and (2) before Godfrey of Bouillon's tent, princes, barons, and knights in robes of gold brocade dancing a stately round to celebrate the Crusader's return.

## "LE PAVILLON D'ARMIDE"

Nicolas Tscherepnin. Ballet Russe. Book based on Gautier's novelette *Omphale* (Paris, 1909). The music by a Rimsky-Korsakoff pupil has charm and grace. It was the "Coronation Ballet" of King George V (Covent Garden, June 26, 1910.)

De Beaugency, as he posts to his fiancée, is lodged overnight by a sorcerer marquis, in an abandoned pavilion. There a Gobelin tapestry shows the Marquise Madeleine, known at Louis XIV's court as "Armide," the lovely enchantress of Lulli's opera (in Lulli's *Armide et Renaud,* Paris, 1686, the *Passacaglia* of the Spirits stand out).

The clock strikes twelve. Time overturns the hourglass, and the Hours of the Night, youths in gold and silver, dance a Courante, while on the tapestry Armide and her court come to life in magic gardens Tasso sang. Armide mourns absent Rinaldo, but lets infatuated De Beaugency take his place and leads him to her father, King Hydrao, his face—De Beaugency fails to note it—that of the wizard marquis. Then Ethiopian boys, court ladies and cavaliers, buffoons and bacchantes dance in a riot of color and movement. "The Slave of Armide," pearls gleaming on throat, ostrich plumes nodding from turban, dances the despair of a lover rejected. Armide and De Beaugency mingle with the revelers, but as she ties her golden scarf on his breast in a true lovers' knot, Time again turns the hourglass, the figures reënter the tapestry, whose light and color dies and the Hours of the Night disappear in the clock as it strikes one. A shepherd's *pastourelle* wakes De Beaugency. He sees Armide's golden scarf hanging from the clock. It was not a dream! In the door stands his wizard host. When in him De Beaugency recognizes the King Hydrao of the night just past, he is so horrorstruck he falls dead.

## "OBERON"

Carl Maria von Weber. Book by Planche, after Wieland's poem, based on the old French romance of Huon of Bordeaux (London, 1826; New York, 1829). *Der Freischütz* and *Euryanthe* are Weber's dramatic master-scores: *Oberon's* merit is "the musical unlocking of the fairy and elfin world." The Overture is a dramatic tone poem; Puck's "Scene of Invocation" of the ocean spirits and the storm, the musical-dramatic climax. The greatest aria is "Ocean, thou mighty monster" (Act II) for coloratura soprano, establishing "an inner landscape which gave birth to a romantic vision midway between Italian passion and Haydnesque tone-painting" (Bie). Genuine Arabian airs supply the Oriental musical themes.

Oberon, the Fairy King, quarreling with his wife Titania, swears to avoid her arms till he finds human man and maid whose love stands every test. In Huon of Bordeaux—who because he has slain his son is exiled from Charlemagne's court till he pluck the Caliph Haroun's beard in his palace hall—and in the Caliph's daughter Rezia, whom he must kiss, Oberon finds the twain he seeks. In dream visions he shows each to each; then wakes the knight with the gift of a magic horn, to be blown in the hour of need, and sets him down near Bagdad. As Rezia (change of scene) shivers in the harem to think she must marry the Persian Prince Babekan, her slave Fatima brings tidings that Huon is at hand.

Rezia flies into Huon's arms as he enters Haroun's banquet hall, where the wedding feast is in progress. Tweaking the Caliph's beard, he slays Prince Babekan, and as a blast of the magic horn casts slumber's spell on banqueters and guards (his squire Sherasmin wakes Fatima, Rezia's Arabian slave, with a kiss, to provide himself with a sweetheart), flees to the gardens where Oberon, bidding Rezia keep faith with Huon whatever betide, sets the lovers down in Ascalon harbor. (Change of scene.) Now, at Puck's behest, Storm Spirits wreck their ship on a desert isle where pirates drag off Rezia and strike down Huon, who hurries to rescue her. As she, Fatima, and Sherasmin are borne away Oberon bids Puck bear Huon to a blossom-garden where mermaids guard his slumbers (a famous chorus) to wake him at the end of seven days, and take him to the palace of the Emir of Tunis, where he will find his love.

There Huon meets Sherasmin, a gardener slave, and learns Rezia is in the Emir Almansor's harem. Roschana, the Emir's forgotten favorite, deploys her charms to win Huon to murder Almansor and rule Tunis as her lover. But he is true to Rezia, and surprised by the Emir, Huon and Rezia are about to be burned to death when Sherasmin blows the magic horn. The Moslems disperse in terror. Oberon—his vow fulfilled—appears with Titania, and returns the lovers to their home where (change of scene), as Charlemagne enters his throne room to the impressive "Chivalrous March," Huon reports his commands have been fulfilled and is restored to favor.

Sir Michael Costa's ballet *Sir Huon* (London, 1833) was written for the dancer Taglioni. *Amadis de Gaula,* a Spanish romance derived from French romances of chivalry, tells the fantastic adventures of a knight who bears a distant resemblance to Parsifal: Massenet's *Amadis* (Monte Carlo, 1922), containing lovely melodies, which the composer called his "musical testament," and Lulli's *Amidis de Gaule* (Paris, 1684) which lives in the exquisite air, *Bois épais,* have been inspired by it.

# CHAPTER V

## THE MIDDLE AGES

### 1. *Historic and Unhistoric Figures and Backgrounds*

The "Middle Ages" were centuries when men's souls were naïve and the realities of life caught up and fantastically woven into the loom of event by the imagination, devout or profane. The natural and supernatural, real and unreal, material and miraculous, occur side by side or interwoven in opera stories harking back to the Middle Ages.

### "FREDEGUNDIS"

FRANZ SCHMIDT. Book after Dahn (Berlin, 1922). Half Meyerbeerian grand opera, half music drama, the score includes thrilling pages. It turns its heroine, a savage primitive, into a neurotic modern in a tale of mad monstrosities in Merovingian France.

Red-haired Fredegundis, mysterious daughter of the forest (appropriately brought up by a swineherd) found by King Chilperich while hunting and added to his *entourage*, murders Queen Galaswintha, and when Duke Dracola protests, blinds him. Bishop Landerich, her former lover, knows too much of Fredegundis' past, but when she mixes poison in his wine, Chilperich drinks it by mistake and is followed to the grave by their sick child. Fredegundis tries to resurrect him with a witch's dance around his open sarcophagus at night in the square before Rouen Cathedral. Instead of the corpse rising up, the sarcophagus lid claps down, holding Fredegundis by her hair which from red turns silver-white. Why it should be transfigured by a gleam from Heaven when the hysterical sinner in a swift access of repentance dies in Bishop Landerich's arms by the coffin-side is one of opera's mysteries.

*Frédégonde* (Paris, 1895) by Ernest Guiraud, completed by Saint-Saëns, was inspired by the Frankish queen; and *Le roi Chilpéric* (Paris, 1890) by Hervé, creator of the French operetta, turns Fredegundis' husband into a musical figure of fun.

*Diana* (Budapest, 1924) by Eugene Zador—brilliant theatric music—has a French degenerate knight murder his wife's lover and drink his heart's blood with her. She, discovering the nature of her tipple, goes insane and dies. In *Der Vassal von Szigeth* (*The*

*Feudatory of Szigeth,* Vienna, 1889; New York, 1890) by Smareglia, an Italian Wagnerian, Naja (Hungary, 1200), wife of Andor,
oldest son of the Lord of Szigeth, is coveted by his younger brother
Milo. The father abducted his vassal Rolf's wife; Rolf revenges
himself on the sons with a magic potion that drives Naja into
Milo's arms. She confesses to Andor she has fallen, not mentioning
her betrayer's name. He forgives her; but Rolf's poisoned wine
kills her in Andor's arms and he, his suspicions of Milo confirmed, kills him.

### "EURYANTHE"

CARL MARIA VON WEBER. Book by Von Chezy after a medieval French
legend (Vienna, 1823). Theatrically impossible, "terrible Emma with
her ring yearning for innocency's tears upsets the entire opera" (Bie).
The knightly Overture, Euryanthe's "Bell Aria," Adolar's air "Wehen
mir Lüfte Ruh' " stand out in a score containing some of Weber's finest
romantic music.

Cynical Lysiart, Count of Forest, wagers with trustful Adolar, Count
of Nevers, he can prove the latter's sweetheart, Euryanthe of Savoy,
untrue; and while Adolar stakes his estates Lysiart hastes to Euryanthe's castle to win his wager. There Euryanthe has told her false
friend Eglantine Adolar's family secret. His sister Emma poisoned
herself, her ghost must walk till the ring on her finger is "bathed in
the tears of innocence." In the castle garden (Act II) Lysiart rages.
Euryanthe has scorned him. But Eglantine brings him dead Emma's
ring to serve as proof that Euryanthe forgot herself with him, and on
its evidence King Louis bestows Adolar's estates on the Count of Forest.
Adolar leaves court in despair (Act III) dragging Euryanthe with
him; but instead of killing her leaves her to perish in the wilderness
where King Louis, out hunting, hears her tale and promises investigation. When at Lysiart's and Eglantine's wedding Adolar staggers up
in black armor and King Louis says Euryanthe is dead, the bride goes
mad, breaks out in hellish rejoicing, confesses her crime and is killed
by the groom, who then offers Adolar his sword. Too happy to slay
him Adolar is wedded to his true love, while Emma's soul—Euryanthe
has bedewed the ring with the required tears—flies upward.

*Genovefa* (Leipzig, 1850) by Robert Schumann is undramatic,
the lovely lyric "Scene of Genovefa's Desertion" outstanding. It
tells the legend of villain Golo's vain attempt to seduce Genovefa,
wife of the Rhine Count Siegfried, while her husband is fighting
the Saracens. She is driven into the wilderness with her babe at
Siegfried's command; and is restored to his arms when Margareta,
Golo's accomplice, confesses. Offenbach's *Geneviève de Brabant*
(Paris, 1869) caricatures operatic medieval romanticism in a
parody of the tale. *Aucassin et Nicolette* (Paris, 1925) by Paul

le Flem is one of the loveliest of old French romances of chivalry, which strikes the medieval musical note in modernist fashion as a "song-tale."

## "L'AMORE DEI TRE RE"

ITALO MONTEMEZZI. Book by Sem Benelli (Milan, 1913). The music is rhetorically effective, and the Love Scene (Act II) has much passionate beauty. The composer, like Moussorgsky, "knows the mysterious emotion the somber tolling of a distant bell lends the hour of death."

King Archibaldo of Altura (Italy, 10th century), old and blind, hears a strange voice whispering to Fiora, his daughter-in-law, on the castle wall, but its owner escapes him undetected.

Again, after Fiora has waved a farewell to her husband Manfredo from the battlements (Act II), Archibaldo hears the sound of alien lips, kissing the hem of Fiora's garment; and again the unknown escapes. When Fiora admits of a lover (it is Avito, of her own conquered blood royal) but refuses to name him the old King strangles her. Manfredo—he has hurried back when her scarf ceased to wave—shrinks from his father in despairing horror as the old man carries off the lovely corpse. In the castle crypt (Act III) Fiora lies on her bier, while tapers gleam, bells toll and chants of lamentation rise. Avito stoops for a last kiss from her pale lips—and finds his own bitter with the burning poison Archibaldo spread on them. Dying, when Manfredo kneels to kiss his dead wife, Avito cries out against the "desecration." But Manfredo ardently fastens on Fiora's red mouth and garners death. Archibaldo, entering to find the lover his trap has caught, discovers he has slain his son as well.

*Isabeau* (Buenos Aires, 1911) by Mascagni, book by Illica, distorts the simple English Lady Godiva legend to make an Italian librettist's idealistic holiday. Isabeau's father, King Raimondo, makes her ride city streets at noon in a state of nature. Folco, a guileless youth, shocked at the evil thoughts "suggested by the popular attitude," a peeping Tom of purity, fastens a gaze innocent of wrong on the girl as she passes, showers her with flowers and sings her charms from the battlements. Escaping mayhem by the vulgar mob he is imprisoned under sentence of death, though he cries he had gazed on Isabeau as he would at sun, moon, or flowers. Convinced of his purity Isabeau sinks into his arms, but while she speeds to tell her father they love, Folco is murdered by the mob, and Isabeau commits suicide over his body. Such was life, to quote the book, "in those fair, far days, when Legend overspread the world."

*Richardis* (Karlsruhe, 1915) by W. von Walterhausen deals with an Alsatian abbess who (885 A.D.) escapes the wedding ring King Charles the Fat is fain to force on her. *Der Rattenfänger von Hamelin* (*The Ratcatcher of Hamelin,* Leipzig, 1879), by Nessler, tunefully commonplace, is the legend of Hunolf Singulf, the magic piper who, to revenge himself on the townsfolk who had not paid him for ridding their burgh of rats, while their parents were at church lured their children into a mountain which closed after them. In the opera the monetary motive of his piping is complicated by an incoherent love story. *The Legend of the Piper* (Chicago, 1925) by Eleanor Everest Freer, book by Josephine Preston Peabody, is a one-act American score based on the legend of "The Pied Piper of Hamelin," in which "an exquisite tenor solo" stands out. *Hunold der Spielmann* (*Hunold the Minstrel,* San Francisco, 1914), by Hermann Genss is another opera version. *Sanctissimum* (Vienna, 1925) by Kienzl, musically "at times suggestive of the *Rosenkavalier,* at others of Rameau," tells of a fiddler with magic bow whose music sets sculptured cathedral saints whirling with nymphs and gargoyles, who step into their niches as the organ peals a hymn and the sacrilegious fiddler falls dead.

*The Miser Knight* (Moscow, 1900) by Rachmaninoff is a Russian boyar who gloats over bags of gold while he starves his son. The son, realizing his father's sordid avarice has poisoned his youth, kills him. The scene of the miser's death agony as he dies clutching the steel key to his treasure cellar is musically powerful. *Der Dieb des Glücks* (*The Thief of Fortune,* Düsseldorf, 1925) by Bernard Schuster, a warmly lyric modern score, deals with the discomfiture of two greedy heirs when the young knight whose estate they hope to inherit turns up alive and in time to foil their plans and marry his boyhood sweetheart. *Don Sanche* (Paris, 1825) is Liszt's *only* opera, written when he was eleven. A knight adventuring in a medieval forest fights and dies for a fair lady, but is restored to life by the magician Alidor, to be welcomed by his love in the Castle of Love. *Der Meisterdieb* (*The Master Thief,* Weimar, 1889) by Lindner is a Rhenish noble who wins his sweetheart Wallfried's hand by filching from her father, Count Berengar, cattle, personality, and "dearest treasure," the girl herself.

A protagonist of the German fairy-tale opera has written two worthy medieval scores: *Der faule Hans* (*Idle Hans,* Munich, 1885) by Alexander Ritter is a seventh son who idles while his brothers hunt, hawk, and fight. But when the Danes storm his father's keep he leaps into action, and, killing King Harald with the oaken pole to which he was chained for his laziness, marries his beautiful widow. In *Wem die Krone?* (*Whose the Crown?,* Weimar, 1890) by Alexander Ritter three sons of a Teuton queen all love their cousin Richildis. Sent off with a sum of gold, the one who has put it to the best use in a year's time shall gain her hand

and crown. Konrad brings back Oriental silks and gems; Ludwig, weapons; but clever Heinrich who stayed home and gave his money to the poor gets the girl.

## 2. Troubadours, Minnesingers, and Crusaders

"Gaily the troubadour twanged his guitar, as he was hastening home from the war" in many a forgotten opera: Méhul's *Le Prince Troubadour* (Paris, 1813); Sir Alexander Mackenzie's *The Troubadour* (London, 1886) who twanged his strings but dully; and the florid, old-style scores, *Der Troubadour* (Brunswick, 1847) by Alexander Fesca; and *Il Trovatore* (Trieste, 1852) by Francesco Cortesi. One Troubadour leads all the rest.

### "IL TROVATORE"

#### (*The Troubadour*)

Giuseppe Verdi. Book by Salvatore Commerano after Gatterez' Spanish drama (Rome, 1853). *Carmen* is the most popular opera with a gypsy heroine, *Il Trovatore* with a gypsy hero. A commentator says: "The text of *Il Trovatore* is very gloomy and distressing." Tragedy runs the gamut of sorcery, burning at the stake, death by ax, poison, and sword. Though hackneyed, melodies like the famous "Miserere," a church chorus to which the Troubadour and Leonora sing a love duet, the "Stride la vampa" and Azucena's "Slumber Song" are immortal; and the great Finale (Act II), climaxing in Leonora's "O ciel!" is one of Verdi's best ensembles.

The gypsy Azucena's mother was burned at the stake by Count Luna, the elder, who thought she had bewitched his boy. Revenge is the gypsy's creed. Azucena stole Luna's son and brought him up as her own. Trouble begins when young Count Luna and Manrico, the pseudo-gypsy, clash with serenade and sword beneath the window of Leonora, Countess of Sergaste, whom both love. Manrico, the troubadour victor, spares his rival.

Azucena now tells Manrico how, meaning to fling old Luna's son into the flames, she threw in her own by mistake. He, Manrico, is Luna's son. Then she retracts her words; and Manrico, hearing Leonora is taking the veil, rushes off to save her. Young Count Luna has already done this when Manrico, coming up, carries her off from the Count despite his rival's curses, and marries her, but is besieged by Luna in his castle.

Azucena is captured by Luna's soldiers and the Count, finding she is Manrico's mother, orders a burning stake prepared. Manrico, informed by his friend Ruiz, hastens to rescue his mother, only to be captured and condemned to the ax.

Leonora now offers herself to the Count as a ransom for husband and mother-in-law—first taking poison, and dying at Manrico's feet when she announces his deliverance. The Count, however, decides Leonora has not kept her word and Manrico is led to death. After his execution Azucena has the grisly satisfaction of telling Luna that he has murdered his own long-lost and long-sought brother.

## RICHARD THE LION-HEART AND ROBIN HOOD

The textual offspring of Sir Walter Scott's *Ivanhoe* and of the old English legend of "Robin Hood" may here be considered in scores in which Richard the Lion-Heart, crusading king and royal troubadour, plays a more or less important part.

*Richard Cœur de Lion* (*Richard the Lion-Heart*, Paris, 1784) by Grétry, not based on Scott, boasts one famous song, "O Richard, O mon roi." The story is that of Blondel the Troubadour's rescue of his king from the Austrian Archduke Leopold's castle in the summer of 1193. Before the walls the minstrel sings Richard's favorite song and when he joins in the chorus behind iron bars Blondel hurries to Countess Margaret of Flanders, the king's friend, whose knights storm the keep and release him. In Vignano's ballet version of Grétry's *Richard Cœur de Lion* (Vienna, 1794), "the Viennese applauded a procession so well regulated that the iron shoes of the horses struck the stage in perfect rhythm."

*Templer und Jüdin* (*Templar and Jewess,* Leipzig, 1829) by Marschner after Scott is rich in attractive melodies: "Rebecca's Prayer," Bois-Guilbert's Aria, "Saxon Battle Chorus," etc. In Bois-Guilbert's castle, Rebecca threatens to leap from the battlements if the wicked Templar dare his worst. But as Robin Hood's outlaws under the Black Knight (King Richard) sack the keep, the Templar escapes with his prey. His fellow knights think him bewitched and pile fagots for the Hebrew girl. If no champion appear before sundown, she dies. Ivanhoe spurs to the rescue and —God defending the right—Bois-Guilbert falls dead before he is slain. Rebecca joins her father Isaac, and her rescuer marries Rowena, Ivanhoe's Saxon love.

*Ivanhoe* (London) by Sir Arthur Sullivan is after Scott, outstanding songs: "O moon, thy light" (Act I), "Softly, with winged feet" (Act III) and the fine Templars' Chorus, "Fremuere, principes" (Act IV). Bois-Guilbert abducts Rowena and is defeated in the lists of Ashby-la-Tour by Ivanhoe. Richard leads the outlaws of Sherwood forest to the assault of the castle (Act II) and Rebecca, on the brink of her leap, is carried off (Act III) by the Templar. In Torquilstone woods Richard secures Cedric's consent to his daughter Rowena's marriage to Ivanhoe (Act IV) and the latter slaying Bois-Guilbert and rescuing Rebecca, the curtain falls to the chorus, "O love which rules us all!"

Sir Julius Benedict's *Richard Cœur de Lion* (London, 1863); Nicolai's melodious *Il Templario* (Turin, 1840) after *Ivanhoe,* and Balfe's *The Knight of the Leopard,* after Scott's crusader novel *The Talisman,* all sing of the English hero king.

## "ROBIN HOOD"

REGINALD DE KOVEN. Book by Harry K. Smith (Chicago, 1890). A romantic comic opera, it remains the composer's outstanding work, rich in facile, tuneful melodies of which the famous romance "O promise me" is the favorite.

Robert, Earl of Huntington, in the guise of Robin Hood, chief of the outlaw rangers of Sherwood Forest, loses his heart in Nottingham to Lady Marian, disguised as a saucy page. She has heard the Sheriff of Nottingham inform Sir Guy—the claimant he has put forward for the Huntington estates—he means to send the outlaws to the gallows. At the archery match, Robert, when the Sheriff refuses him his rights, becomes an outlaw in earnest. He leaves his sweetheart Marian, telling her he will come back when good King Richard returns from the Crusades and he can make head against his foes.

After a series of humorous and romantic adventures the Sheriff's soldiers—Robin has put him in the stocks—surprise the outlaw and, giving Marian a farewell embrace, he is taken away.

Sir Guy is about to marry Marian when Robin Hood, who has escaped, appears at the head of his merry men and stops the wedding. With Marian in his arms he is about to retreat to the forest when King Richard's herald proclaims a free pardon for Robin Hood and his men. The return of his estates to the lawful Earl of Huntington is foreshadowed in a scene of love triumphant.

*Iolanthe* (Moscow, 1892), Tschaikovsky's last opera, book after Herz' drama *King René's Daughter,* is "a weak echo of the deep emotion of the *Symphonie pathétique*"; but contains fine pages, among them a Mozartian "Flower Chorus" (women's voices), and the Duke's bravura aria. In a hidden valley of Provence (the librettists make it the Vosges Mountains), Iolanthe, daughter of King René, her sight lost as a child when her father's palace burned, has grown up in a paradise of flowers, amid nightingales' songs and fragrance of roses. She does not know she is blind. The Duke of Burgundy and his friend Tristan de Vaudemont chance on the hidden vale where Iolanthe sleeps, guarded by the amulet the learned Moorish physician Ebn Jafia hopes will restore her sight. She wakes, loves the unseen Duke, and intense yearning for the light of her lover's countenance (aided by the Moor's talisman) performs love's miracle and causes her blind eyes to see. The lyric-romantic *Iolanthe* (Cologne, 1890) by W. C. Mühldorfer was a successful opera on the subject; and Julian Edwards' *King René's Daughter* (New York, 1893) is a tragic opera with warmly melodic pages.

*Iolanthe* (London, 1882) by Sir Arthur Sullivan has nothing in common with Tschaikovsky's blind heroine, but carries a fantastic fairy tale into the solemn surroundings of the English House of Lords.

### MINNESINGERS

*Frauenlob* (Dresden, 1892) by Reinhold Becker is a minnesinger love tragedy of Mayence, 1308. Frauenlob has slain the town captain of Mayence and is outlawed. Disguised he returns to town and the dead man's daughter Hildegunde leaps through the fire with him on St. John's Eve. The gypsy Sizyga—Frauenlob's father betrayed her—reveals the knight's identity to Servizio di Bologna, Hildegunde's suitor. Frauenlob begs Hildegunde to fly with him (Act II) but Servizio denounces him as her father's murderer. As he is led to execution the stonemasons of Mayence, who love the minstrel, beg the Emperor to pardon him. The latter bids Hildegunde decide his fate (Act III) and she forgives her father's slayer. At their wedding the goblet of "wine of reconciliation" Servizio hands Frauenlob has been poisoned by Sizyga. The Emperor bids Hildegunde drink—and as she falls dying Frauenlob empties the goblet and dies in turn. Covered with roses the bodies of the minstrel and his bride are borne to the tomb. German minnesinger scores also include *Walther von der Vogelweide* (Vienna, 1896) by Albert Kauders; Edouard Lassen's *Frauenlob* (Weimar, 1860); and *Die Minneburg* (*Love's Castle*) by Arnold Mendelssohn (Mannheim, 1909).

### CRUSADERS

*Magda Maria* (Dessau, 1920) by Von Chelius, book by Treutler after a medieval chronicle of Sant' Agata's Cloister in Apulia, a modern score with fine lyric moments. Manfred, Prince of Montalto, loves Magda Maria, educated in Sant' Agata Convent; but a document read on the day they are to be betrothed proves the girl his half-sister—fruit of an adultery on the part of Manfred's mother, Beatrix, which caused her husband's murder and her lover's death from remorse. , Beatrix atones by suicide; Magda Maria is mortally wounded during the duel in which Manfred slays his mother's accuser. The object of Manfred's unconsciously incestuous passion dies in his arms on All Soul's Day and he, excommunicated, takes the Crusader's Cross to win Heaven's forgiveness in Holy Land.

*Zaïre* (Paris, 1889) by Pierre de la Nux is an eclectic score after a tragedy by Voltaire, also set as an opera by Federici, Lavigna, Bellini, Gandini, Mercadante, Mammi, Carona, Michael Haydn, Winter, and Duke Ernest of Saxe-Coburg. The Saracen Sultan Orosman loves Zaïre, a foundling, and plans to make her his sultana. At her request he frees the crusader knight Lusignan, the girl's father. But a nocturnal meeting between Zaïre and her brother, Lusignan's son, who tries to induce her to flee with him, leads Orosman to think her untrue. He stabs Zaïre, and then, discovering his mistake, himself.

*Castle Agrazant* (Chicago, 1925) by Ralph Lyford is an American opera of the crusades. Richard of Agrazant in Holy Land, Geoffrey of Lisiac abducts his wife Isabeau. A note in her dead baby's cradle informs Richard and he swears revenge. Richard, entering Geoffrey's castle hall (Act II) disguised as a monk, kills him, and Isabeau in the struggle receives her death wound from Geoffrey's dagger. In a moonlit glade (Epilogue) the dying wife is cheered by a vision of the Holy Grail; but Richard realizes he should have stayed home instead of rescuing the Holy Sepulchre, and breaks his sword in despair.

*Flammen* (*Flames,* concert performance, Munich, 1902) by Franz Schreker makes a German crusader instruct an old servant to repeat daily to his wife that, if she is unfaithful to him during his absence, he will die of her kiss of welcome on his return. Bored by reiteration, the wife forgets herself with a minstrel; then drains a flagon of poison on her husband's return to save him from her deadly kiss.

*Olivier le simple* (Brussels, 1922) by Victor Vreuls, a d'Indy pupil, is a modern score, with "pages of haunting beauty." Olivier, a thirteenth century dreamer at variance with his environment, when his father returns from a crusade with Pandosia, a charming Eastern maid, wakes to instant action, and escapes his wearisome home atmosphere by eloping with Pandosia to shores where "the dawn comes up like thunder," deserting friends, family and fiancée.

*Das Rosengärtlein* (Vienna, 1924) by Julius Bittner, a theatrically and musically effective score, has some fine "Arabian Songs." Hadaman von Keunring, a robber knight whose castle overhangs the Danube, has brought with him from Palestine Fatima, a Saracen maid, who loves him devotedly. Is Hadaman content? Seemingly not, for he pursues Witha, daughter of Guntram the ferryman. When the knight bids her (abducted by his men-at-arms) dance unclothed for his amusement, Witha flings herself from the castle's

"Little Rose Garden," a projecting slab of stone, into the river hundreds of feet beneath. The repentant knight is killed with Fatima by the arrows of rebelling peasants led by Leopold the huntsman, Witha's betrothed.

*Schirin und Gertraude* (Dresden, 1920) by Paul Graener, after Hardt's play, develops a historic matrimonial triangle in four acts. For years the Count of Gleichen languished in Saracen captivity while his faithful wife Gertraude awaited his return from Holy Land. At last lovely Schirin, the Saracen emir's daughter who loves him, secures his freedom. He marries her and sets out for home. The Pope grants him a dispensation, for his bigamy is negligible; he has wrested a little heathen soul from darkness. Not to shock Gertraude, von Gleichen appears at the home castle with Schirin disguised as Golem, an Oriental slave boy. But when Gertraude takes a fancy to the handsome lad, the latter is compelled to reveal his, or rather her secret. The good housewife cheerfully accepts the situation and the two women combine to plague their husband and bring what might have been a tragedy to a happy conclusion. *The Meistersinger* has been the composer's model, and his score has depth of feeling and much tonal and lyric beauty to commend it. The Italian Auteri-Manzocchi's *Il Conte di Gleichen* (Milan, 1887), is another opera on the subject.

*Malek-Adel* (Paris, 1837, as *Malvina,* Naples, 1829) by Sir Michael Costa was popular in its day, though a contemporary critic calls it: "Salon music, suggesting the solfeggios of Righini, Crescentini, and Bordogni." Malek-Adel, brother of Saladin, the Saracen sultan, falls in love with Mathilda, sister of Richard the Lion-Heart, but his suit is rejected. Mathilda returns Malek's love while his captive, then, stifling her heart's desire, retires to Mount Carmel convent to forget him in prayer. Malek arriving and demanding to see her is attacked and slain by Christian knights, whose cries of victory lure Mathilda from her cell, and seeing Malek's remains she expires in Archbishop William's arms.

*Tancredi* (Venice, 1813) was Rossini's first great opera success. Orbassan, usurping Duke of Sicily, claims the hand of Amenaide, daughter of Arsir, King of Syracuse. But her heart belongs to Tancred, rightful heir to the Sicilian throne, and when he returns from the Crusades she claims his aid. Condemned to death as a traitor the poor girl is saved by Tancred's timely appearance in disguise. His defeat of Orbassan proves her innocence by the ordeal of battle, and the lovers are united.

*Il Crociato in Egitto* (*The Crusader in Egypt,* Venice, 1824) by Meyerbeer is a Rossinian tale of tangled loves and religions. Elmireno, at Sultan Aaladin of Egypt's court, is really Armand, a recreant crusader-knight. Palmide, the Sultan's daughter—unknown to her father she has presented Armand with a babe as a pledge of her affection—led him to profess Islam. The arrival in Egypt of his uncle Adriano with knights of Rhodes recalls Armand to his Christian self, but Aaladin learns he has been entertaining a Christian unawares and Armand is flung into prison with the Rhodian knights. When the monarch's rebellious guards release the prisoners, he saves the Sultan's life and secures his blessing on his union with Palmide, converted to his own faith. From 1194 to 1489, Cyprus was ruled by a line of Crusader kings, descendants of Guy of Lusignan, titular king of Jerusalem, to whom the Knights Templar sold the island.

## "LA PISANELLA"

### (The Pisan Girl)

ILDEBRANDO PIZETTI. A drama by D'Annunzio (Paris, 1913). The incidental score by the Italian modernist is one of much beauty. On the quay at Famagosta the young king, Sire Ughetto, appears with the queen mother amid knights, barons, attendants, and slaves. A pile of booty rises from the pavement and crowning the heap of golden treasure, spices and silks like a rose, is a young girl of great beauty, almost nude, bound with cords, la Pisanella, the courtesan of Pisa. With this girl the young king falls madly in love and the climax of the play is her slaying by the Queen Mother in the palace hall of Nicosia. As the beautiful Pisan strumpet dances in a sumptuous violet robe, negro slaves, carrying great garlands of roses, silently join in her dance. Drawing nearer and nearer, as they weave their sinister round, they gradually close in on their victim and suffocate her beneath the fragrant flowers they bear. La Pisanella has suffered *La morte parfumée* (*The Perfumed Death*), subtitle of the drama. The Prelude (Act I) and the "Dance of the Perfumed Death" stand out in the score.

*Catharina Cornaro* (Munich, 1841) by Franz Lachner is a romantic version of the history of Catherine, the Venetian girl who, betrothed to Marco Onnero, married in her heart's despite James, the last Lusignan King of Cyprus. Marco, as bride and groom come from the wedding in St. Mark's (Act III), has raised his dagger to kill the King when he recognizes his rescuer from a robber band, and casts it away. When (Act IV) two years later, Marco comes to Cyprus as the Venetian ambassador, the dying King makes him protector of his widow and infant son and, operatically, "Cyprus is lost to Venice"—though historically Catherine, fearing the Turks, resigned her crown and kingdom to Venice in 1489. In a pre-Wagnerian score, musically worthy, *La reine de Chypre* (*The Queen of Cyprus*, Paris, 1841) J. Halévy achieved one of the most brilliant successes of his day. Donizetti also wrote a *Caterina Cornaro* (Naples, 1844).

*Rosamunde* (Vienna, 1823) by Franz Schubert, whose lovely incidental Overture, ballet music and Entr'actes have survived its von Chézy drama, is a tale of a Princess of Cyprus whose lover, a Prince of Candia, gives her evil guardian a poisoned letter the latter meant for the girl, and when he conveniently dies, marries her.

*Solea* (Cologne, 1907) by Isidore de Lara is a modern opera of the taking of Rhodes by the Turks (1522) from the Crusader Order of the Knights of St. John. Rimabombas, a gypsy chief fleeing from pirates, lands in Rhodes with Solea. There Sir Lioncel reveals to the brutalized soul of the tsigane girl the beauty of the ideal in his devotion to the cause of Christ, and rouses in her loathing for the vile conditions of her life. A love rising above animal passion leads her to kill for her hero's sake and when he, before the assault, weakens and begs her to sweeten death with a kiss, she bids him keep their love pure and holy, and they die true to their ideal. The Prelude and Duet (Act III) and Act III, "the musical jewel of the score," stand out in this Debussyan work.

### "LA FAVORITA"

#### (*The Favorite*)

GAETANO DONIZETTI. Book by A. Boyer and G. Waez (Paris, 1840), after the Baculard-Darnaud drama *Le Conte de Comminges*. Leonora is a historic character, mother of Dom Pedro the Cruel of Castile. Considered the best among the composer's tragic operas, it has a mezzo-soprano title rôle. The romance, "Spirto gentile," is the outstanding song.

Ferdinando, a novice in St. James monastery, sees a lovely girl and forgets how to pray. His prior absolves him from his vows. Guided by love Ferdinando discovers his unknown in her island home of St. Leon. There, in her villa set in green gardens, Leonora returns the pure love Ferdinando professes, but hides from him the shameful fact she is mistress (*la favorita*) of King Alfonso XI of Castile. Her illicit relations with the monarch allow her to obtain an officer's commission for her lover, and she sends him off to come back covered with glory and marry her. In the gardens of Seville's Alcazar, which he has wrested from the Moors (Act II) Ferdinando whispers sweet nothings into Leonora's ear, while frowning Alfonso reads the papal bull which bids him cast off his paramour and return to his wife, the queen.

Discovering Leonora loves the new-made Count of Zamora (Act III) the King combines expediency and revenge by bestowing her hand on Ferdinando, and courtiers snicker as they wed. After the ceremony the groom's former prior tells him whom he has married and the wretched youth, flinging sword and chain of honor at the King's feet, seeks the peace of his ancient cloister.

There, his monastic vows spoken, as Ferdinando sings his tenor air (Act IV) *Spirto gentile,* Leonora creeps into his cell, disguised as a novice. Sternly he bids her begone, but she tells how in a letter which never reached him she had revealed her shameful past and thought his silence spelled forgiveness. Deeply moved Ferdinando clasps her. Alas, as he promises to flee with her to some far golden land where they can be happy, she dies in his arms, and drawing the cowl over her disheveled hair, he calls in the monks to pray for the dead.

Felipe Pedrell's operatic trilogy *Los Piraneos* (*The Pyrenees*), book by Balaguer, in *El Conde de Foix* (*The Count de Foix*), *Rayo de Luna* (*The Moon-Ray*), and *La jornada de Panissars* (*The Day of Panissars,* Barcelona, 1902), celebrates in part historic, part mystic wise the ancient glories of crusading Spain. Old Spanish liturgic chants and Catalan and Moorish folk melodies supply the theme material of scores developed along Wagnerian lines, and the composer is considered the founder of the newer school of Spanish music "resting on a basis of national melody."

## "LE CID"

JULES MASSENET. Book by d'Ennery, Gallet and Blau (Paris, 1885), based on Corneille and the Spanish legend of Rodrigo del Bivar (b. 1026), whom the Moors called the *Cid Campeador,* the "Fighting Chief," the famous legendary hero of ancient chivalrous and crusading Spain. Meyerbeerian in style, Massenet's score contains charming ballet music and one of the most popular of all operatic airs, Chimène's song, "Pleurez, pleurez, mes yeux." From the operatic point of view the most effective scene is that in front of Burgos cathedral, "whose organ and bells unite with orchestra and chorus in an ensemble of real grandeur" (Henry T. Finck).

Rodrigo, the Cid, is loved by two women—the Spanish Infanta and Chimène, daughter of the Count de Gormas. When the Count de Gormas insults and defeats Don Diego, the Cid's father, Rodrigo after a terrible soul strife fights with Chimène's father and kills him, though in so doing he knows that he has slain the girl's love for himself and all his chance for earthly happiness.

In *Der Cid* (Weimar, 1805) by Peter Cornelius, a romantic score resembling *Lohengrin,* the story is taken up where Massenet leaves off. Chimène hastens to King Fernando of Spain to demand vengeance on the Cid for her father's death, and is about to slay him with his own sword when (Act II) her love gaining the day, she sends the hero to fight the Moor with the words: "Go, you are forgiven!" He returns a victor (Act III), Chimène's hand his prize. There also is a *Cid* (Utrecht, 1916) by the Dutch composer Waagenar.

*Le tribut de Zamora* (Paris, 1881) by Charles Gounod is an old-style, Meyerbeerian grand opera with an attractive Moorish ballet. Xaima, bride of the soldier Manuel Diaz, torn from his arms on her wedding day, as one of twenty lovely virgins Zamora town must pay the Moorish Caliph of Cordova, after various tragic happenings returns to her husband's arms unharmed by a sojourn within Moslem harem walls. *Los Amantes de Teruel* (*The Lovers of Teruel*, Madrid, 1889) by Tomás Bretón follows Hartzenbusch's drama. Isabel and Marsilla are lovers; but Isabel's father forbids marriage for five years. If Marsilla does not return with the spoils of war when vespers chime on the appointed day, Isabel becomes Roderigo's bride. Marsilla, captured by the emir of Valencia, wins freedom and treasure of gold and gems when he saves the emir's life, but gains the hatred of Zulima, his daughter, whose love he rejects. Disguised as a crusader she hastens to Isabel, tells her Marsilla is unfaithful and Isabel, as vesper bells chime, marries Roderigo. Tied to a tree by Zulima's slaves and released by huntsmen, Marsilla arrives too late. Isabel refuses him even a kiss and he dies of a broken heart, followed to the grave by the bride, who cannot survive his loss.

*Die Almohaden* (Stuttgart, 1860) by Joseph Abert, book by Kroner after Don Juan Pallon y Col's drama *The Bell of Almudaina*. Reminiscent of Wagner and Bizet, it has a fine development of the muezzin's call to prayer, and attractive Oriental ballet music. A tragic tale of the struggle between Moors and Spaniards on the island of Majorca, it is dominated by the "Bells of Almudaina," and ends with the reconciliation of a Spanish governor and a Moorish princess over the bodies of their ill-fated son and daughter, Ismael and Zelima.

*Dom Sébastien* (Paris, 1843) by Donizetti—its failure said to have hastened his mental collapse—has an idiotic story. Dom Sebastian, King of Portugal, leaves Lisbon on a crusade against the Moors of Africa with the lovely slave Zaïda, whose freedom the poet Camoëns secures. On Afric's strand Zaïda, returned to her father, governor of Fez, when the King's army is destroyed by the Moroccans, agrees to marry her hated suitor Abayaldos if Sebastian's life be spared. Next the King arrives in Lisbon and assists incognito at his own magnificent state funeral (the historical warrant of the Portuguese legend of *il rei encuberto,* "the hidden king," the peasants believing some day Sebastian would return to restore Portugal's greatness). Soon after Zaïda, haled before a Christian court, is charged with adultery by her Mohammedan husband, and condemned to death. Camoëns smuggles a rope ladder into her cell. It breaks as the poor girl is gliding down the prison wall and she falls into the sea, Abayaldos, her husband, shooting at her with a musket to make sure that she does not escape. As a contemporary critic asked: "What music, no matter how heavenly, could carry such a tissue of absurdities?" The "Scene of the Inquisition," and the airs, "Seul sur la terre" (Act II) and "O Lisbonne, O ma patrie" (Act III) stand out.

The last romantic period of Moorish rule in Spain called forth Cherubini's *Les Abencerrages* (Paris, 1813), with a fine Overture, telling the tale of the last Moorish King Boabdil's beautiful sultana who, when he thought she had betrayed him with a knight of the family of the Abencerrages, assembled the clan at a feast in the Alhambra and had them massacred by his African guards. Its *première* was interrupted by the first ghastly tidings of Napoleon's Russian disaster. The Lisztian August Conradi's *Musa, der Letzte Maurenfürst* (*Musa, Last Prince of the Moors,* Königsberg, 1855), and Moszkowski's *Boabdil* (Berlin, 1892; New York, 1893), which contains a delightful Moorish ballet, deal with the same subject. In *L'ultimo Abencerrajo* (*The Last Abencerrage,* Barcelona, 1874) by Felipe Pedrell, based on Chateaubriand's elegy on the downfall of Moorish chivalry, *Le Dernier Abencerrage,* Aben-Hamet's beautiful romance "Celesta criatura" and a Mooresque ballet (Zambra, Granadina, Jerezano) stand out. Eighty years after the Moorish conquest Aben-Hamet, last of the Abencerrages, makes a pilgrimage from Tunis to shed a tear for the lost glories of the "Paradise of Granada," his father's home. In the Alhambra he meets Doña Blanca, her family descended from the Cid. Together they traverse palaces and gardens but when he avows his love, and she admits her love for him, she says it never can be realized: he is a Moor, an infidel; she a Christian. They will not renounce their faiths but Aben-Hamet vows to return each year in the hope Blanca may turn to Islam. The third time he returns there is a duel with Lautrec, a suitor for Blanca's hand. The fourth, entering the cathedral, he determines to become a Christian. His own and Blanca's happiness seem assured; but he learns her father slew his father, a defenseless old man, on the threshold of his Granadine palace. His heart torn with agony, Aben-Hamet seeks the African desert, never to return. Blanca passes her days among the ruins of the Alhambra. Though it had broken her heart, she had bade her lover do as honor demanded. The crusade against the Albigense heretics of southern France (1300 A.D.) motived Jules de Swert's opera *Die Albigenser* (Wiesbaden, 1878). Alice marries Amaury the crusader. Returning victorious he finds her bending over Raymond, the Albigense leader, in a grot. When he kills her lover Alice stabs herself over his dead body.

## 3. *In Dante's Century*

### FRANCESCA DA RIMINI

Dante (b. 1265) often had seen handsome, devil-may-care Paolo Malatesta, city captain of Florence, ride through the streets of his native town a few years before he fell by his brother's hand. Paolo was one of the four sons of old Malatesta, Duke of Rimini, and his brothers were Malatestino, Giovanni the Lame, and Pandolfo. Giovanni, ugly, deformed, but a daring soldier, won the hand of beautiful Francesca, daughter of Giovanni da Polenta, Lord of Ravenna. But Paolo, sent to fetch his brother's bride to Rimini, loved her at first sight.

In the grim Malatesta fortress of Rimini, Paolo confessed his love to his brother's wife. In D'Annunzio's drama, based on the old historic Italian legend, she bids her lover fight helmetless and shieldless against the foemen storming the walls. If he win through then it must be Heaven's will that they yield to their passion, and— Paolo comes scatheless through the battle.

Then occurs the touching moment Dante has embalmed in immortal verse. Reading the old tale of the loves of Lancelot and Queen Guinevere together, Francesca and Paolo give way to their passion at the line: "She took him by the chin and slowly kissed his mouth!" They too, like the unhappy Arthurian lovers, are caught in the meshes of a delicious and forbidden love.

But Francesca's beauty has ensnared Malatestino, another brother, and he knowing she hates crippled Giovanni, offers to poison him if she be his. When she refuses he drops hints to the injured husband. The latter, his jealousy aroused, sets out for Pesaro—with intent to return and surprise the guilty ones.

Francesca, her husband gone, dismisses her women and opens the door to Paolo. Suddenly Giovanni's voice is heard. Paolo takes a step toward a trapdoor, to hide, but Giovanni savagely flings himself on him, naked sword in hand. Francesca rushing between them, receives her death blow; and as Paolo supports her in his arms, Giovanni drives the keen blade through his side, then breaks it. Thus the tragedy ends on earth. But Dante carries it to Hell's Second Circle, where Paolo and Francesca, with the other incontinent, are "tormented by most cruel winds under a dark and stormy sky."

Related in action are Ambroise Thomas' *Françoise de Rimini* (Paris, 1882) and Rachmaninoff's *Francesca da Rimini* (Petrograd, 1904). The former has a Prelude "superb in its sombre, lugubrious harmonies . . . and a touching dialogue between the lovers" (Ryer). In the Prologue Dante and Virgil, his guide, stand on the banks of the Styx; and in the end Beatrice, Dante's beloved, appears as an angel to announce their pardon to the sinners. Rachmaninoff's score "in the style of the modern music drama," using the libretto by Modeste Tschaikowsky on which his brother wrote the symphonic poem, also introduces Dante and Virgil. A humming "Chorus of Specters" is an interesting musical feature. Hermann Goetz' *Francesca da Rimini*, completed by Ernst Frank (Mannheim, 1877), counting noble pages, with Diana, a cousin of the Malatestas, introduced to relieve the gloom of the tragedy, *Francesca da Rimini* by Napravnik (Petrograd, 1902), and *Paolo e Francesca* by Mancinelli (Bologna, 1907) have not attracted the attention accorded *Francesca da Rimini* by Zandonai (Turin, 1914) after D'Annunzio, which contains theatrically and musically effective scenes. Max D'Olonne's *Les Amants de Rimini* (Paris, 1915) has a fine love scene between Paolo and Francesca in Act III; and there is a *Francesca* by Létorey (Paris, 1913). Francesco Leoni's *Francesca da Rimini* (Paris, 1914) is a conventional score in which "a voluble verist uses celesta, muted brasses, woodwind and strings without poetry," and Gabriel Pierné has written fine incidental music to Marcel Schwob's drama *Francesca da Rimini*.

*Parisina* (Paris, 1838) by Donizetti, book by Romani, deals with a fifteenth century Malatesta as unfortunate as Francesca, her relative by marriage. Azzo, Duke of Ferrara, has slain his wife Mathilda, thinking her unfaithful, and married lovely young Parisina of the golden hair. At a tourney she bestows first prize on Hugo, and her husband hears her murmur his name in her sleep. Azzo has Hugo killed only to learn he is his own and Mathilda's son. When Parisina sees slain Hugo she falls dead across his corpse. *Parisina* (Milan, 1913) by Mascagni after D'Annunzio tells a different tale with considerable color. Cruel Niccolò, Lord of Ferrara and Este (Romani's Azzo) tries to make friends of his illegitimate son Hugo and the fair, unwilling bride he has married. He sends Hugo in her train on a pilgrimage to Loretto. In a Slavonian attack on the sanctuary, Hugo, wounded, is tended by Parisina, but on their return Zooes, Niccolò's spy, who has peeped through a hole in the ceiling at the lovers' transports, reports to his master. Niccolò catches the pair in *flagrante delicto,* and, condemned to die (Act III), Hugo is beheaded. Parisina, led blindfold to the scaffold, learning that Hugo has preceded her, cries happily: "Now I am glad to die!" In vain Niccolò, his rage past, tears about his palace mad with grief; the son he loved cannot be recalled.

*Gismonda* (Chicago, 1919) by Henri Février after Sardou's

play, is a tale of the time when Athens was a feudal duchy (1204-1311). Zacharia Franco wishes to be duke and has Gregorez, his tool, push the Duchess Gismonda's little son into a tiger pit. The mother offers to marry the man who rescues her child, and the young falconer Almerio promptly does so. Gismonda though she cannot wed Almerio, of peasant blood, promises to spend a night in his hut (Act II). When Zacharia follows her hither Gismonda thrusts a dagger into his heart, and Almario takes the murder on himself. Gismonda then rises above caste prejudice, hands over Gregorez to justice, and marries the falconer with bell, book, and candle.

*Gianni Schicchi* (New York, 1918), by Giacomo Puccini, is the "humor" one-act score of the composer's tryptich. In Dante's Florence (1299) Donati dead, his will leaves his estate to charity. Neighbor Schicchi promises to help the heirs, with a mental reservation. He climbs into Donati's bed and when the doctor arrives imitates the dead man's voice and sends for a lawyer. The new will he dictates and signs, however, leaves everything to him, to the rage of the disappointed relatives who cannot betray him without incriminating themselves. The orchestral score in particular has beautiful pages.

*Die Folkunger* (Dresden, 1874) by Kretschmer is a wearisome imbroglio of thirteenth century Scandinavian intrigues. Magnus Ericson, first Vasa, is finally drawn by the loving arms of Princess Marie, last Volkung, from the monastery he had been compelled to enter and is crowned King of Sweden. A "Coronation March" survives the score.

*Guntram* (Weimar, 1894) by Richard Strauss, musically belonging to "the world of Parsifal," is a redemption drama, vocally "well-nigh unsingable." Guntram's "Renunciation Air" (Act II) stands out. The minstrel Guntram's ideal is the brotherhood of man (Germany, 1300). Rescuing Freihild from drowning, as a reward he begs the lives of five rebels of her cruel husband, Duke Robert. When minnesingers laud Robert, Guntram declares the revolt due to the Duke's tyranny, and when Robert draws sword, the minstrel slays him and is led to prison. Above Guntram's prison cell monks chant about the dead Duke's bier, when Freihild enters to offer him her love; but Guntram feels he must renounce it to expiate a deed of blood not in accord with humanity's highest principles, and withdraws to a hermitage.

The *jus primæ noctis, droit du seigneur* or "right of the feudal overlord," a custom alleged to have existed during medieval times in Europe, gave the overlord the right to the virginity of his vassals' daughters on their wedding night. That there is no trust-worthy evidence of the existence of such a custom in a legalized form has not prevented the opera composer from taking advantage of a theme fruitful in dramatic possibilities.

## "LA JACQUERIE"

### (*The Peasants' Revolt*)

GINO MARINUZZI. Book by Donaudy (Buenos Aires, 1918; Chicago, 1920). The Italian modernist composer-conductor's score has fluent melody and a feeling for dramatic effect.

In their hovel near the medieval town of Noitel, Isaura and Mazurec, peasant lovers, are celebrating their wedding when Viscount Corrado places his naked blade above the lintel of the door. Bride and groom need no explanation; they are versed in the cruel feudal custom of their day. Vainly Mazurec pleads with his lord, and when his father Guillermo attacks his feudal superior he is arrested. In the great castle hall Corrado in turn is celebrating his betrothal (Act II) to lovely Glorianda, and in honor of the event has Guillermo released from prison. Isaura—who has paid her feudal dues—also is returned to her husband, but the outrage has so preyed upon her soul that she dies in delirium in Mazurec's arms.

Mazurec joins rebelling peasants in a successful attack on the castle and Glorianda is thrust into his arms. As he clutches her to him, however, he sees his own cherished Isaura, shudders at the agony she endured, and unable to carry out his fell purpose, he helps Glorianda escape as the hymn of the serfs, "Death to our oppressors!" rises behind them.

*La Jacquerie* (Marseilles, 1894) by Salvatore Agnelli, is another opera dealing with the great French peasant revolt of the Middle Ages. *Die Rauensteiner Hochzeit* (*The Rauenstein Wedding,* Karlsruhe, 1919) by W. von Waltershausen, a milder verist of the Munich (Thuillé) school, is a happy romance turning on the *jus primæ noctis.* Lenz, Lord of Lauenstein, claims the feudal embrace from Wendela, a medieval town girl, bride-to-be of Dietz and, as she is five ducats short of the gold to ransom her from his arms, carries her to his castle, where Lady Marotte, a French adventuress, is turned out with Moorish maid, page, and parrot to make room for her. Wendela is protected by the knight's mother and Lenz falls honestly in love with her. Dietz, about to slay the knight in the forest is suddenly caught up in a mad dance (it is St. Vitus' Day) which allows Wendela to free her lord. As the latter's mother announces the approaching wedding of noble youth and peasant maid to dumbfounded Dietz, Lenz clasps Wendela to him and declares the shameful tribute a thing of the past.

### 4. *When Popes and Emperors Struggled*

The centuries of the struggle between the popes and emperors, the "two swords" of the medieval world, are reflected in older and in more modern operas. *Canossa* (Rome, 1914) by Francesco Malipiero, an unsuccessful modernist opera, takes its title from the castle in the Apennines where the Roman Pope Gregory VII triumphed over the German Emperor Henry IV, waiting barefoot three days, in an outer court, before his enemy would listen to his humble prayer for forgiveness. "*Canossa* does not merit the contempt felt for it today by the composer . . . The Finale in particular is magnificent, a whole people bursting into songs of victory, amid fanfares and carillons" (Prunières).

*Der Waffenschmied* (*The Armorer*, Vienna, 1846) by Albert Lortzing after a play by F. W. Ziegler has an animated Overture, a famous bass aria "Auch ich war ein Jüngling," and a delicate Finale (Act I), the musical climax. In the same general period, it is a tale of true love overcoming difference in rank. Stadinger, armorer of Worms (16th century), is prejudiced against nobles: one of them ran off with his wife. Konrad, Count of Liebnau, turns apprentice in Stadinger's workshop to win the hand as he has the heart of Stadinger's daughter Marie. Learning Konrad is a noble her father threatens Marie with the cloister; but a feigned attack keeps him home as the lovers are married in church (Act II) and he makes the best of it when Liebenau rides up with his new Countess (Act III) and a splendid train.

The fates of the Hohenstaufens, in particular, have been dramatized in operas few of which have won great popularity. Spontini's *Agnes von Hohenstaufen* (Berlin, 1829) is the daughter of the Emperor Henry IV, wife of the first Hohenstaufen Duke of Swabia, who founded the family fortunes. A pompous, spectacular score, in it "an orchestral tempest breaks simultaneously with a vocal quintet and a chorus of nuns." Karl von Perfall's *Junker Heinz* (Munich, 1886) the poor knight, "Sir Harry," who foils the plan of three thieves to abduct the Emperor's Konrad's daughter, using a forged proposal from the Emperor of Byzantium, and is made Duke of Swabia and married to her by his grateful sovereign, is a more romantic version of the event. *Heinrich der Löwe* (*Henry the Lion*, Leipzig, 1877) by Kretschmer tells of a Saxon duke whose wife wins his freedom disguised as a minstrel from the incensed Emperor Barbarossa; and Marschner's romantic *Der Kyffhauserberg* (Vienna, 1816) is based on the legend that Barbarossa sleeps through the centuries in a Thuringian mountain, to sally forth in the Teuton hour of need. Konrad pushes Kuno down a precipice in the Kyffhauser ruins at midnight, and Barbarossa appearing to him in a vision, he departs with golden treasure to claim Hildegarde, for whom he fought, as his bride. Karl Reinecke's *König Manfred* (Leipzig, 1867), undramatic but with fine ballet music, makes Manfred, son of the Hohenstaufen Emperor Frederick II, scorn his wife Helen to tear from her convent the nun Ghismonda to share his guilty love. Excommunicated, Manfred rides to battle while Ghismonda offers Helen wine in which she has dropped poison from a hollow pearl. Manfred—absence makes the heart grow fonder—returns in time to snatch the goblet, but the men-at-arms of Charles of Anjou are at his heels. He rushes off, and when he is brought back a corpse, Helen gladly drains the poisoned wine. *Il re Enzio* (Bologna, 1905) by the Italian modernist Ottorino Resphigi deals with the natural son of the Emperor Frederick II, held a life-long prisoner by the Bolognese. The weaker German eclectic J. J. Abert has written an opera *König Enzio* (Prague, 1852) on the same subject.

### 5. *Miracle Operas*

Miracles occur with reasonable frequency in opera. *Sainte-Odile* (Paris, 1923) by Marcel Bertrand meritoriously sets to music the legend of the patron saint of Alsace, whose father Duke Alberic persecuted her until she miraculously ascended to the skies from the mountain of Hohenburg. *Christelflein (The Elf of Christ*, Dresden, 1917) by Pfitzner, a modern *Singspiel,* is a German miracle-tale of medieval days in which an elf takes pity on a wretched family, pleads their case in Paradise, and they sit down to a roast and wine through the intervention of Child Jesus. Written in simple melodic style, "what is best in the music is the silver sonority of the orchestra." *Der Friedensengel (The Angel of Peace,* Munich, 1915) by Siegfried Wagner turns on whether suicides should rest in consecrated ground (16th century Franconia). Folkwise themes are used in a gloomy tale of wedded love and self-destruction and the composer's theological conclusion, miraculously announced by a chorus of angels, is that those who die by their own hand may rest in hallowed soil.

One of the most ideal figures of operatic miracle is Lohengrin, "The Swan Knight."

### "LOHENGRIN"

RICHARD WAGNER. Romantic opera (Weimar, 1850). The most popular of Wagner operas is an adaptation of Arthurian and Grail legends. The story, in the persons of Elsa and Lohengrin, symbolizes the contrast between worldly and spiritual love. Its moral is that to trust without trying to know is the secret of happiness. Wagner, who wrote it at a time when he was despised and isolated among enemies, identified himself with its hero. Bie sees the work as a struggle between Lohengrin, representing *Music,* and Elsa, *Drama,* in which Music overcomes the old dramatic traditions of the opera form. The action takes place at Antwerp, on the Scheldt, in tenth century Flanders. The Preludes, "Bridal Chorus," the Finale (Act I), Ensemble (Act II), the "Swan Harmonies," Elsa's and Ortrud's Duet are among its beauties.

King Henry the Fowler, trying to enlist Saxon, Thuringian and Brabantine knights to fight the Huns, finds Frederick von Telramund, instigated by his wife Ortrud, insisting Elsa of Brabant murdered her little brother Godfrey. The King, impressed by Elsa's apparent innocence, allows her a champion and at the last moment a knight in silver armor comes up the Scheldt in a boat drawn by a swan. He will fight for Elsa and marry her if she never ask his name or race. Elsa agrees and Lohengrin conquers Frederick and makes him admit his perjury. The knights lead Lohengrin and his betrothed away to feast and rejoice.

Elsa's song of happiness from the balcony in the palace reaches evil Ortrud and fallen Frederick, in beggar's rags, crouching on the minster steps. Ortrud offers to bind the affections of Elsa's unknown lover by magic means, an offer the bride-to-be scorns. The seed of doubt, however, has been sown in her soul. Frederick proclaimed an outlaw, Elsa's bridal procession sets out for the minster; Ortrud tries to precede the bride, saying Lohengrin is unknown. The King coming up, Frederick claims a second ordeal by combat, declaring the knight won the first by sorcery. His request is denied. Elsa defends her nameless champion and together they enter the minster.

Knights and ladies singing a joyful wedding chorus escort the happy pair to their bridal chamber. Elsa is a woman. Her husband has a secret she does not share. What are solemn vows not to ask questions in such case? She tells herself she yearns to share the sorrows of his past; in truth she is devoured by curiosity. She asks the fatal question and her swan-knight listens in sad silence. Before he can answer Frederick bursts in with four accomplices. Elsa hands her husband his sword: the traitor is slain, his tools beg for mercy; Elsa faints. Then the grieving knight bids attendants bear Frederick's body and Elsa herself to the place of judgment, preparatory to going there to reveal his secret.

On the banks of the Scheldt the following morning, King Henry and the nobles approve Frederick's death. The stranger knight now declares that Elsa has asked the question she should have foreborne to ask. That question he will answer publicly. And he reveals himself as Lohengrin, son of Parsifal, and Keeper of the Holy Grail. The moment he has been doubted or his name revealed, he must return to Monsalvat. Too late—now that she has lost her husband—Elsa repents. Lohengrin sorrowfully bids despairing Elsa farewell, saying that had she trusted him one short year he would have remained with her. As he puts into

Elsa's hands gifts for Godfrey, when he returns, his sword, horn and ring, all possessing magic powers, Ortrud triumphantly informs him her evil spells had turned Godfrey into the very swan that draws Lohengrin's boat! Then the Grail Knight performs a miracle of faith. He prays the white Grail dove down from heaven, loosens a gold chain from the swan's neck, and instead of the bird, Godfrey, a fair-haired boy in cloth of silver, rises from the water. While the people kneel reverently, Ortrud drops dead at sight of the youth, rightful lord of Brabant, Lohengrin steps into the now dove-drawn boat, and is carried away from Elsa's pleading arms who, as he vanishes from sight, falls lifeless to the ground.

## "DER ARME HEINRICH"

### (*Poor Henry*)

HANS PFITZNER. Book by Grau (Mayence, 1895). This German music drama has been called "a Tristan shoot." The music is marked by inward depth and sincerity; there are splendidly sensuous pages (Henry's "Farewell to Knightly Adventure") and a nobly exalted one (the Cutting Scene) describing the sacrifice of the pure maid.

In his castle in Swabia (1100), Knight Henry lies ill of an incurable disease, awaiting the return of his servant Dietrich, whom he has sent to a miracle-working monk in Salerno. Dietrich, entering the sick room, delivers the saintly physician's message: "Only a virgin willing to sacrifice her blood for Henry's sake, willing to lie naked on the stone and let her heart be cut in two out of pity, can save the knight's life!" Agnes, Dietrich's daughter, inspired by love, offers herself for the sacrifice to save her lord.

In the Salerno cloister the physician monk is about to lay knife to the dauntless victim's flesh as she lies upon the stone when Henry's nobler self triumphs. He had been ready to let another die that his own wretched life be spared. Now he forbids the sacrifice and claims death so that Agnes may live. As the storm rages about the cloister walls, he tears the knife from the physician's hand, and is miraculously cured of his ailment, while the monk bows before Agnes as before a saint.

In *Die Legende der Heiligen Elizabeth* (*Legend of Saint Elizabeth,* Weimar, 1881, first performance as an opera) by Franz Liszt, the "Children's Rounds," (Prologue) and the "Crusaders' March," one of its themes, an actual melody of the Crusades, stand out. Prologue: Landgrave Hermann of Thuringia receives the little Hungarian princess who is to wed his son Ludwig (Act I). He as her husband has to forbid her sacrifices, she is so charitable, for Charity's sake. Meeting her on the hunt he sees her covered basket (filled with food for the poor) but when he accuses her of carrying bread to the needy and tears the cloth from the basket, it is filled with glowing roses—the "Miracle of the Roses" has taken place. The remaining scenes include the departure of the Landgrave and his knights for the Crusade (Act II), Elizabeth's death, angels escorting her soul to Paradise (Act III), and her canonization in Marburg Cathedral in the presence of emperor, prelates and people.

*La damnation de Blanchefleur* (Monte Carlo, 1920) by Henri Février, book by Lena, is a miracle opera in three acts, outstanding the Oriental Prelude and Blanche's Prayer, "Jésus, Dieu de clémence." Count Thierry, an erstwhile crusader, neglects his wife Blanchefleur to day-dream of the bewitching Saracen courtesan Djamina, whom he knew in Holy Land. When Blanchefleur, longing for his love, is brutally repulsed, she listens to the Devil's offer to lend her Djamina's face and form a single night. He says her kiss as Djamina will make her lose her soul but save Thierry's, though he knows both will lose their souls. Heaven saves innocent Blanchefleur. As their lips meet Thierry's eyes are opened; he repents and their souls, released from the mortal coil, ascend to Paradise as angel choirs sing.

*Sancta Susanna* (*Saint Susannah*, Frankfort, 1922) by Paul Hindemith is a repulsive melodrama of a nun who, obsessed by baser physical urges, atones for her objectionable complexes by being stoned to death. Brilliant modernistic music, Straussian in trend, makes its neurotic pathology vividly dramatic.

*St. Julien l'Hospitalier* (Paris, 1896) by Camille Erlanger after Flaubert has some effective pages and a sonorous symphonic "The Hunt." This hero of hagiology grew up a pitiless Nimrod and a doe whose fawn he slew told him he would kill father and mother. Married to the daughter of the Byzantine emperor, he was in the forest one day when his parents came to the castle. His wife tucked them away in her own bed. Julian coming home, lay down and his hand touching a man's beard, he slew him and his companion. The doe's prophecy had come true. Wild with remorse, Julian became a ferryman in a far land. There because in humility of soul he held in his arms a dying leper, his sins were forgiven. "The roof of his cabin vanished, the skies opened in golden splendor, and Julian rose to heaven to behold his Savior face to face."

## "FEUERSNOT"

### (*Fire Famine*)

RICHARD STRAUSS. Book by Von Wolzogen (Dresden, 1901). In this folk legend of early medieval times, a "Fire Miracle," pagan rather than Christian, is developed. Strauss used his theme—the triumph of

joyous naturalism over the darkness of pessimistic philosophical speculation and intolerance—to score his personal enemies and antagonists in
the Munich world of music with biting irony. The "Old Solstitial
Song," and the programmatic orchestral Interlude, which very literally
paints Dietmund's surrender and love's mid-summer-night triumph stand
out.

The Munich children collecting wood for the Solstice (Beltane) fire
(*Subendfeuer*) stop at the shuttered house of Kunrad, a student who
spends his time over his books. When he sees lovely Dietmund, the
burgomaster's daughter, he tells the children to take all the wood in
the house and rushes out and kisses her. The indignant townsfolk are
calmed by the girl, who plans revenge for the outrage. In his mad
longing (Act II) Kunrad, when Dietmund lures him into a basket by
her house wall by promising to haul him up to her chamber, climbs in
and suspended halfway between ground and window by the vengeful
maid, becomes the laughingstock of the burghers. In a rage he uses
his magic and (Act III) the lights and fires of the town and the love
flame in every breast goes out. Now the repentant townsfolk raise a
great clamor and implore Dietmund to end the "fire famine" by yielding
to Kunrad's passion. Then, love waking in her own breast, the girl
hauls her lover into her chamber, and all the lights and fires of the
town flame up as they embrace.

## "LE JONGLEUR DE NOTRE-DAME"

### (*Our Lady's Juggler*)

JULES MASSENET. Book by Maurice Lena (Monte Carlo, 1902), after
a tale in Anatole France's *Etui de nacre*, retelling the legend of a
medieval miracle play, *Le tombeor de Nostre-Dame*. The leading rôles
(5) are for *men* and, at the creation, Jean, the juggler's part, was sung
by a lyric tenor, as also in Paris and London. In the United States
Mary Garden (1908) established a feminine interpretation of the rôle
as a tradition. Massenet blends human and divine with a reverence and
beauty that makes the score "a kind of little Gallic pendant to *Parsifal*."
The "Drinking Song"; the "Legend of the Sage"—its theme a souvenir
of Massenet's own honeymoon trip, heard in the hills about Naples;
the "Peace of the Cloister" (Act II), and the "Miracle Scene," whose
mystic, musical, and scenic beauty impresses the most hardened, are
notable.

Before Cluny Abbey a monk sells indulgences, boys and girls dance,
peasants buy and sell. Jean the juggler sings an irreverent drinking
song ("Hallelujah of Wine"), and rebuked by the prior, is promised
the Virgin's pardon if he join the brotherhood. Jean, seeing the cook
Boniface's donkey staggering along laden with poultry, sausages, vege-
tables and flasks of wine for the Abbey table, agrees to turn monk.
All the other brethren—there are painter, musician, sculptor, and poet

monks—practice their arts in honor of Our Lady. Poor Jean alone cannot show her his love. And when the cook has sung Jean the "Legend of the Sage"—it saved the Holy Child by hiding Him beneath its leaves when the haughty rose refused—the juggler resolves he will do homage to the Queen of Heaven as best he knows how.

Alone in the Virgin's chapel, the humble juggler piously and devoutly goes through his pitiful bag of tricks before the holy image. But a monk has seen him. The horrified prior and brethren break in as he innocently sings and dances before the Mother of God the profane steps and ditties that delighted the crowd in the market place. The cry of "Anathema!" is raised, but as the infuriated monks are about to seize Jean, Boniface the cook cries: "A miracle!" and points to the statue. The holy image is aureoled in golden light, the Mother of God smiles on the mountebank, and stretches forth her hands in blessing. And while the poor wastrel dies in an ecstasy of joy, the halo descending from the image to glow above his head, angelic choirs chant "Hosanna!"

A lesser German *Juggler* is Stürmer's *Der Tänzer unserer lieben Frau* (*Our Blessed Lady's Tumbler*).

*Le Miracle* (Paris, 1910) by Georges Hüe tells of a captain of mercenaries besieging a Burgundian town (15th century) who promises to depart if Alix, a lovely courtesan, visit his tent. Alix saves the town, but the citizens credit St. Agnes with so doing, and bid sculptor Soys carve her statue. Angry Alix so works on Soys that the statue assumes her face and form. When unveiled it is nude. The bishop cries "Anathema!" The people rage, but Alix laughingly stabs the governor when he tries to deface *her* image. Brought from prison to smash the impious statue (now covered) Alix raises her hammer, is struck herself by Heaven's thunderbolt, and Soys, tearing the cloth from the image, reveals a decently gowned St. Agnes smiling a blessing on the delighted crowd.

*Béatrice* (Monte Carlo, 1914) by André Messager, an expressive score, is "a little sister to Fauré's *Penelope.*" In Palermo (16th century) the nun Beatrice flees her convent with her lover Lorenzo, but the Virgin picks up the mantle she drops and assumes her shape and duties. Lorenzo soon leaves Beatrice for the actress Musidora and the ex-nun, turning courtesan in despair, plies her trade as Ginevra, "so lovely none can resist her, so docile she can resist none." Four years gone, Lorenzo recognizes her with horror, as the inmate of a Sicilian fisherman dive. But when one piscatorial admirer has stabbed another in a rage, Beatrice departs— a mystic voice has called her! Crossing the convent threshold, she beholds the Virgin, clad with her mantle among the nuns, casts herself at her feet, and is absolved, while the Mother of Mercy resumes her place above the altar. *Sister Beatrice* (Moscow, 1912) by Gretchaninoff, containing fine lyric pages, had but a few performances, the Greek Catholic Church holding it "sacrilegious to impersonate the Holy Virgin on the stage."

*Suor Angelica* (New York, 1918) by Giacomo Puccini, book by Illica, is the "sentimental" score of the composer's tryptich, its music veristic in trend. Angelica, a Florentine girl, repenting her sin, has taken the veil. When she asks her stern aunt how her nameless babe fares, the cruel woman tells her it is dead. In despair Angelica kills herself among the flowers, praying the Virgin to forgive her sin. Pitying the hapless mortal mother the Mother of God appears aureoled in golden glory to bear Angelica's soul to the skies. The score is written entirely for female voices.

### "MAREIKE VON NYMWEGEN"

Eugen d'Albert. Book by H. Alberti after Dutch legends (Hamburg, 1923). Tonally effective old Dutch folk themes are a feature of a sixteenth century "Scarlet Letter" story which makes dramatic use of Wagnerian declamation. Notable are: "Heissa, Mareike!" dance air (Act I); the lyric melody "An dem ersten Frühlingstage," and the Ballet Pantomime.

(Prologue.) A beggar lying before the walls of a Maastricht monastery tells his fellows the tale of his life, the contents of the three acts.

Mareike was a girl of light life in sixteenth century Antwerp, in whose house her admirers—among them the singer and lutenist Arnaud—held many a gay carousal. But a band of miracle players appeared in Antwerp to present pious legends. Lucas of Guelders (the beggar) was one of the players, brethren of a wandering holy order, who assumed the sacred rôles. Sworn to poverty and chastity, they renewed their oath before each performance. In Lucas Mareike recognized Lucian, a childhood playmate. When she asked: "Have you shelter for the night, Lucian?" the monk who acted for the glory of God followed her home.

Arnaud, her rejected lover, happened by as Lucas tore himself from Mareike's arms. That day, after the players had renewed their solemn oath, and the miracle play had concluded, Arnaud accused Lucas of perjury—Lucas, who had acted the Savior, sitting in judgment on Luxuria, the personification of wantonness! The curtain falls on the excitement of the crowd who fear that God's wrath will be visited on their city.

Lucas, cast out by the Church for breaking his vows, wanders through the land. Mareike enters the home for repentant Magdalens, blessed by the bishop. But while she finds peace in the shadow of the cloister, Lucas kills his rival Arnaud, delivering his soul to damnation.

The beggar Lucas (Postlude) crouching on the steps of the sacred building, sees the gates open and the Virgin Mary appear in the shape

of Mareike to announce his crime is forgiven. Thus are fulfilled the
bishop's words to the Magdalen: "If on the day your earthly chains
fall, he finds his way to you, drawn by his loving soul, it will be the
Heavenly Father's sign your sin is forgiven you both for love's sake!"

*La légende du Point d'Argentan* (*Legend of the Point d'Argentan Lace,* Paris, 1907; Chicago, 1924) by Félix Fourdrain is
a modern miracle. A wretched lace weaver vows a pilgrimage to
the Virgin's shrine if the life of her sick child (she has no money
for medicine) is spared. A beggar woman (the Mother of God)
whom she entertains unawares, reveals in a dream the secret of an
intricate pattern for whose discovery a large sum is offered. In
her vision angel hands weave the ancient pattern and the Virgin,
haloed in golden light, presents it to her while the curtain falls.
French folk melodies are used with effect and there is a final "Ave
Maria" of archaic beauty.

### 6.  *The Lorelei and Others*

There are many "Loreleis"; *Lorelei* (Munich, 1846) by Ignaz
Lachner, Otto Fiebach's *Lorelei* (Danzig, 1886), the Dane Siboni's
*Lorelei* (Copenhagen, 1859), and the Finn Pacius' *Lorelei* (Helsingfors, 1887). Wallace's *Lurline* (London, 1860) was a success
in its day, but the melodically and dramatically somewhat weak
score by Catalani is the one best known in this country.

#### "LORELEY"

ALFREDO CATALANI. Book of Zandardoni and D'Ormville (as *L'Elda,*
Turin, 1880; as *Loreley,* Turin, 1890; Chicago, 1919). The story is
the legend of the siren whose song lures men to destruction in the Rhine.

Walter, who is betrothed to the Rhinegrave's niece Anna, betrays an
orphan girl. The victim bewails her lost innocence to water nymphs
and spirits of the air. Alberich, king of the gnomes, changes her to
the Lorelei with hair, voice, and comb of gold, so she may gain revenge.
The Lorelei sings Walter, on his way to church (Act II), out of
marrying Anna, who drowns herself in the Rhine. Walter meeting
his late love's funeral procession (Act III) swoons by the river bank
only to be awakened by the Lorelei's luring song. But her vow to
Alberich makes her refuse him her embrace, and Walter in despair leaps
to death in the stream as her song sounds for the last time.

*Lorelei* (Mannheim, 1863) by Max Bruch is *musically* perhaps the finest opera on the subject. Instead of Walter, Otto is
wedding not Anna, but Berta, niece of the Archbishop of Mayence;
the betrayed girl is Leonore, old Hubert the ferryman's daughter.
The text of the opera was originally written by the poet Geibel

for Mendelssohn, whose posthumous *Lorelei* (Vienna, 1881)—
there is a fine orchestral Prelude, picturing a stormy night on the
Rhine—proved dramatically no more successful than Bruch's
setting. A lovely vampire of another sort is a Queen of Georgian
folk tale.

## "THAMAR"

MILI BALAKIREW. Choreographic drama based on a poem by Lermontov
(Paris, 1912). The water music of the Terek "sounds much like the
Rhine" (W. J. Henderson), but orgiastic dance themes ride rhythms of
torrential sweep and "I know of no work more beautiful from the
poetic as well as the musical standpoint" (Calvocaressi).

Queen Thamar's tower casements open on a vista of foaming river
and distant, snowy mountain peaks. Silence broods over the great
chamber, over motionless guards, women, attendants. Suddenly a slave
girl moves, glances through the casement, whispers to another. She
turns to a third, who breathes her message to the Queen and Thamar
stands in the casement, her long scarf fluttering a greeting to the
stranger hurrying down the mountain pass. Guards lead in the victim,
blindfold, and Thamar tears the kerchief from his eyes. Slave girls
dance, wine is poured, and completely enslaved he follows Thamar to
her couch while musicians play. Women lead him off to be clad as a
prince for the coming revels. When the youth reënters Thamar touches
his lips and (after a brief interlude during which they disappear, while
dancers whirl maddeningly) lures him to the far side of the chamber.
Holding him with her glance, one hand fondles his, the other gropes for
the dagger in her girdle. Imperceptibly the guards have closed about
him. One sets the sliding panel in the wall moving in its groove. On
the edge of emptiness the youth leans toward the queen and—with a
sudden bound she thrusts the dagger into his breast! A push from the
guard nearest him and he falls headlong into the Terek, hundreds of
feet below. Noiselessly the deadly panel slides into place. The queen's
women draw off her festal robes; Thamar sinks exhausted on her
couch. Dawn comes through the casements, open on a vista of foaming
river and distant, snowy mountain peaks. Silence broods over the
great chamber, over motionless guards, women, attendants. Suddenly
a slave girl moves, glances through the casement, whispers to another.
She turns to a third, who breathes her message to the queen and
Thamar stands in the casement, her long scarf fluttering a greeting to
the stranger hurrying down the mountain pass.

*Der Vampir* (*The Vampire*, Leipzig, 1828) by Heinrich
Marschner is a romantic opera of a vampire who drinks bride's
blood with tears of self-pity. The "Village Dances" (Act III) and
Malvina's air, "The morning sun of spring," stand out. "Marry
and murder three brides within the year," the Devil tells Lord
Ruthven, the vampire, "or I carry off the soul you sold me!" Ruth-

ven bleeds the first bride, Ianthe, Sir John Berkeley's daughter, in a cave, and Berkeley stabs him over his child's tooth-marked corpse. Edgar Aubry carries Ruthven into the open where the moon-rays cure him. While courting Malvina, Aubry's fiancée (Act II), Ruthven carries off Emmy, the village bailiff's daughter and sucks her blood (Act III). Aubry is powerless to expose the monster——if you tell on a vampire, you become one. But Ruthven about to wed Malvina is exposed as the blood-sucker (Act IV) by Aubry and is slain by Heaven's lightning. Aubry marries the maid widowed before wed.

In *Die Hexe* (*The Witch*, Copenhagen, 1892) by August Enna, Thalea, thinking her lover, Edzard (Munster, 1650) dead, studies the occult. Edzard, returning prefers her sister Almuth to Thalea, who nobly resigns him and, stabbed in the back when a mob gathers to stone her for sorcery, dies blessing the happy pair. *La sorcière* (*The Witch*, Paris, 1912) by Camille Erlanger, after Sardou, with an outstanding Prelude, tells how lovely Moorish Zoyraya leads astray innocent Christian lads of sixteenth century Toledo. Don Enrico is about to marry Doña Juana, and Zoyraya hides in the bride's home on the wedding eve and puts her into a hypnotic trance. She begs Enrico to flee with her (Act II) but an inquisitor intervenes. Enrico kills him and with Zoyraya is dragged before Cardinal Ximenes. To save Enrico, Zoyraya says her magic drove him to commit the crime. Bells toll, the *Dies iræ* sounds, the stake waits (Act III), but doctors' arts and monks' prayers cannot wake Juana. Zoyraya is promised a pardon if she do so; but the mob clamors for a victim. Enrico realizes she cannot escape, so the lovers take poison with their last kiss and die. *El amor brujo* (*Love the Wizard*, Madrid, 1915) by Manuel de Falla is a suite of dance episodes developing an Andalusian tale to folkwise music. Outstanding are the "Ritual Fire Dance" and "Canción del amor doliendo," "Song of Love's Sorrow." The gypsy Candelas loved a gypsy gallant who is dead, but his malicious ghost prevents her happiness with another lover till a gypsy witch flirts with the phantom and lets her kiss a flesh and blood admirer.

*Undine* (Magdeburg, 1845) by Albert Lortzing after Fouqué's romance, shows Sir Hugo jilting Bertalda, the duke's daughter, to marry Undine (changeling from the realm of Kühleborn, king of the water spirits), thinking her fisherman Tobias' child. When she tells him man's faithful love will win her an immortal soul, Hugo swears to be true, but when his wife takes in outcast Bertalda (exposed as the base-born fishergirl) the latter steals Hugo's heart, and Kühleborn takes Undine away. But on Bertalda's wedding night Undine rises from the castle well and draws Hugo from his bride's arms into her own and those of death. The castle is washed away by flooding waters, but Hugo wakes to a new life of love with the water nymph in Kühleborn's subterranean kingdom. *Undine* (Berlin, 1816), E. T. W. Hoffmann's *best* opera, tells the same story in music imitating Gluck and Mozart.

*Die kleine Seejungfrau* (*The Little Mermaiden,* Copenhagen, 1910) by Fini Henriques tells in ballet form Andersen's tale of the mermaiden who assumes mortal shape to win a mortal's love and an immortal soul, though with each step she takes her feet seem cut with sharp knives. *Melusine* (Dresden, 1891), Carl Gramman's romantic Wagnerian opera, is the legend of Count Raymond of Lusignan who married Melusine, the water nymph, promising never to spy on her when she vanishes at the full of the moon. Jealousy turns him into a male Elsa; he sees Melusine in her fish scales. She leaves him, and after wandering long in pilgrim garb, he returns to die in her arms and she lays him away where water lilies grow. The romantic operas *Raimondin* (Munich, 1881) by Karl von Perfall, and Hentschel's *Die Schöne Melusine* (Bremen, 1875) tell the same tale. *La fille du Danube* (Paris, 1836) by Adolphe Adam was a famous Taglioni ballet pantomime. Adam's "melodies . . . have that elegant simplicity the French value as highly as originality." A dumb foundling, found at the Danube's source, grows to maidenhood as "The Flower of the Fields"; but wicked Baron Willibald's attempts on her innocence drive her to fling herself into the river, leaving a bouquet of forget-me-nots on the bank for worthy Rodolphe. He flings himself in after his beloved, but the Danube receives its child and her betrothed like a true parent; and after gay dances with river nymphs "The Daughter of the Danube" and Rodolphe rise from the waves in a glistening seashell, to live happy ever after.

*Silvana* (*The Forest Maiden,* Frankfurt, 1810; Hamburg, 1895) by Carl Maria von Weber, her father slain by the Rhinegrave, her uncle, is brought up as a charcoal burner's daughter in the forest, protected by Dryada, the wood nymph. Gerald, the Rhinegrave's son, sees, loves, and brings her to the castle to wed her; but Dryada, masquerading as a minstrel, rouses the Rhinegrave's rage. Silvana, who defends the singer, is ordered to a dungeon, but when Dryada tells the Rhinegrave she is his dead brother's daughter, Gerald marries her amid rejoicing.

Less amiable than the forest nymphs were the Willis who, torn from their lovers' arms by death on the eve of marriage, haunted the highways to dance to death the chance nocturnal wanderer. "Ogresses of the waltz" (Théophile Gautier), Heine calls them "poor young creatures in whose dead hearts and dead feet still dwells the love for dancing they could not satisfy in life. . . . Mysteriously alluring, these dead Bacchantes are irresistible."

## "GISELLE"

### (*The Willis*)

Adolphe Adam (Paris, 1841; Ballet Russe, Paris, 1910; New York, 1911). A famous ballet of the days of Louis-Philippe, "the Citizen-King," it established the fame of Carlotta Grisi. A mute opera by the lesser Auber, "the blue rays of German moonlight glide mysteriously over the silvery notes of its music" (Théophile Gautier), but a modern critic calls it "one of the most wretched works of a mediocre musician."

Village maiden Giselle, for whom Hilarion the gamekeeper pants, loves handsome Loys, a stranger youth who plucks daisy petals with her while Hilarion eavesdrops on their vows. Suddenly, to the silver call of hunting horns the Prince Regent of Courland arrives and is entertained with humble pride by Giselle in her cottage, together with Bathilde, his daughter. Merry villagers dance but when the Prince greets Loys as Duke Albert of Silesia, Bathilde's betrothed, trustful Giselle, overcome by the terrible shock of her betrayal, goes mad, and after a fantastic exhibition of insanity dies with a despairing glance at her faithless lover who, covering her dead face with kisses, tries to commit suicide.

Spectral moonlight falls on the cross marking Giselle's grave near a black tarn. At midnight the *willis* find conscience-stricken Hilarion (he had dragged Loys' princely cape from his cottage and precipitated the tragedy) grovelling on the grave. Albert, pale with grief, now comes to pray where he thinks his love lies sleeping but while the mad death-dance of the *willis* drives Hilarion to drown in the tarn, Giselle, robed in her winding sheet, saves Albert by bidding him cling to the cross on her grave, where he is found by Bathilde when dawn flushes the skies.

*Le Villi* (*The Witch Dancers*, Milan, 1884) by Giacomo Puccini, book by Fontana, an earlier veristic opera, is a variant of the legend. Black Forest Robert, leaving his village sweetheart Anna and swearing to be true, goes to Vienna to collect an inheritance. He returns broken in health and purse after wild carousals with town sirens. Anna's funeral music greets Robert's ear as he nears the village, and suddenly, amid the snows, the *villi*—at their head Anna who has died of a broken heart—sweep him away in the death-dance (this dance, "La Tregheda," is the ballet), mocking his dying pleas for forgiveness with ironic "Hosannahs!" James Loder's *The Night Dancers* (London, 1846) tells a similar tale which, like Puccini's story, goes back to the Austrian folk legend due to popular belief that brides dying in the bloom of youthful beauty could not be consigned to utter dissolution.

## 7. *Mountain Spirits*

### "HANS HEILING"

HEINRICH MARSCHNER. Book by Phil. E. Devrient (Hanover, 1833). Probably the composer's best opera, Heiling's aria "An jenem Tag" (Act I) and Gertrude's melodramatic song "Des Nachts auf der Heide" (Act II) stand out in its folkwise music.

In the bowels of earth gnomes heap up treasures of gems, gold, and silver but Hans Heiling, their king, casts aside his crown. (Prelude.) As a rich stranger he has met Anna, a country girl, and feeling he cannot live without human love he rises to earth, the portals of his subterranean realm closing behind him.

Anna, in the Harz mountain village, yields to Hans' wooing and promises to marry him. But when he reproves her for dancing with Konrad the huntsman she tells him they are not yet married and comes from a forest tryst with Konrad—which has revealed her heart is his—to reject Hans' splendid bridal jewels, whereupon Hans stabs Konrad and flees.

But the gnome king's heart is broken. In the game of blindman's buff at Konrad and Anna's wedding he rises mysteriously and lets the girl catch him. Vengeance is within his grasp; but when his mother, the earth queen, begs him to forego it, he yields and sinks with her into his subterranean realm while the happy lovers celebrate their deliverance.

*Alpenkönig und Menschenfeind* (*Alpine King and Enemy to Mortals,* Dresden, 1903) by Leo Blech makes Astragalus a kindlier mountain spirit, who uses his power to compel the stiff-necked Tyrolian Rappelkopf to give his daughter in marriage to Hans, her musician lover. *Rübezahl* (Brunswick, 1904) by Hans Sommer has the spirit of the Harz mountains set the townsfolk of Neisse dancing madly to his magic bagpipes in the process of uniting two lovers against their fathers' will.

## 8. *The Plague and the Danses Macabres*

### "DIE GEISSELFAHRT"

#### (*The Flagellants' Procession*)

GERHARD VON KEUSSLER. A modern score, sans leading motives, but using pregnant dramatic declamation and richest orchestral colors. The symphonic Interludes: "Evening Murmurs," "Night of Tempest," "Morning Mood," and "Day of Preparation" stand out.

Swarms of flagellants, mystic religious maniacs, born of the "black death" plague which sweeps the Teuton lands (1349), demand admittance into a South German town and are denied entry by the town council, fearing the plague. Edith, wife of Burgomaster Otfried, in her pity forges a letter from Heaven, ordering the gates opened in the name of Mary, Mother of God. The town counselor Wichtmann, devoured by a guilty passion for Edith, has supported her and the flagellants are admitted on a night of storm and tempest. But when Wichtmann attempts to collect his reward in adultery's coin, Otfried surprises and kills him and innocent Edith takes poison to escape an earth too carnal for her spiritual nature.

*Der Dorfheilige* (*The Village Saint*) by Ernest Maschke after Paul Heyse's novel *Siechentrost,* tells of a martyr of the same period whose sufferings turn him into a practical altruist. Though the "Black Death" rages in their town, weaver Dietmar, his wife Hilda, and daughter Traute are happy till vile Imogena becomes their guest and denounces her hosts falsely to the town authorities as pestiferous. Hilda and Traute, dragged to the lazarhouse, die there, and Dietmar, released, wanders through the country villages as a minstrel, the rustics listening reverently to the fiddle of the "Village Saint." He returns to his home town just as Gerhard Eschenhauer, Imogena's fiancé, sees the abandoned girl hug a stranger in the street. But the divine music of Dietmar's violin soothes Gerhard's despair and he renounces worldly joys to wander with his friend and comfort the afflicted.

Among the *danses macabres* operas—usually exploiting the Holbein engravings which picture emperor, stable boy, pope, strumpet, king, peasant, knight, and serf, caught up in a mad round to their common goal the grave—is Josef Reiter's *Der Totentanz* (*The Dance of Death,* Dessau, 1906); while *Der tod Mon* (*The Dead Man,* Vienna, 1902) by Josef Förster is an effective operatic setting of a "carnival jest" written by Hans Sachs.

### 9. *In the Shadow of Gothic Cathedrals*

Hugo's *Notre-Dame de Paris,* a historical romance of cultural value, reproducing medieval life, personifies in the great Gothic cathedral the soul and spirit of the Gothic Age, and presents the beginning of its conflict with the ideas of the age to follow. In the shadow of Notre-Dame rise Louise-Angélique Bertin's *Esmeralda* (Paris, 1836), in which Quasimodo's "Bell Song," a great "hit" in its day, stands out; Lebeau's *Esmeralda* (Paris, 1857); Dargomijsky's *Esmeralda* (Moscow, 1847), influenced by Meyerbeer; the American William Henry Fry's *Notre-Dame de Paris* (Philadelphia, 1863); the Italian Fabio Campana's *Esmeralda o Nostra*

*Donna di Parigi* (Petrograd, 1869); the Spaniard Felipe Pedrell's *Quasimodo* (Barcelona, 1875); and Manuel Giro's *Nuestra Señora de Paris* (Barcelona, 1897).

## "NOTRE-DAME"

FRANZ SCHMIDT. The Austrian composer's romantic score (Vienna, 1914) contains glowing lyric pages and orchestral Interludes. A son of the Puszta, he gives his Parisian gypsy a Hungarian tambourine. Prelude (Act I); Intermezzo (Act I); Esmeralda's "Dialogue with the Moon," and her great Love Duet with Phœbus are outstanding.

Lovely Esmeralda walks Paris streets, a sacrificial lamb, lascivious hands plucking at her. She saves Gringoire, poet of the pavements, from the beggar mob by taking him for husband in name only. After Phœbus, a captain of the King's Guard, has snatched her from the mob together with Quasimodo, her worshiping adorer, officer and gypsy keep a love tryst, and the husband in name only, stabbing his rival, commits suicide by leaping from a window. Dom Frollo, canon of Notre-Dame, now longs to possess the girl. Repulsed, he has her condemned to death as a witch; but Quasimodo carries her into the cathedral where the hangman cannot seize her. That gentle churchman, Dom Frollo, has the right of sanctuary suspended, and as the hangman drags the unfortunate maid to her doom, Quasimodo, first dropping a huge block of stone on the yelling mob from the tower heights, flings down Dom Frollo after it.

*Esmeralda* (London, 1843) by Goring-Thomas brings Dom Frollo on the scene in an attempt to abduct Esmeralda with Quasimodo's help. Captain Phœbus rescues and falls in love with her, and Dom Frollo, chagrined at her preference of army to church, stabs his military rival and accuses the girl of the crime. When Phœbus, only wounded, again saves her from death, the persistent canon brings his dagger into play, only to kill Quasimodo, who gladly sacrifices himself for Esmeralda's happiness. Goring-Thomas's music is gracefully French in style.

*Etienne Marcel* (Lyons, 1879) by Saint-Saëns is a "Notre-Dame" opera. Beatrice, daughter of Etienne Marcel, city "boss" of Paris (d. 1398) and enemy of the Dauphin Charles of France, loves Charles' squire, Robert. Etienne saves Robert when the mob sacks Charles' palace but regrets it when Beatrice says she loves the youth, who (Act II) tries to induce the girl to flee with him during her father's absence. In the square of Notre-Dame (Act III) where Robert lurks disguised, he is unmasked by Beatrice's father—the choral ensembles and the ballet of this Act are among Saint-Saëns' finest scenic pages—but Etienne is killed (Act IV) when Charles enters the city and dies commending Beatrice to

Robert. Beatrice's romance "O beaux rêves évanouis!" has been called one of Saint-Saëns' happiest inspirations. *The Preceptor or the Loves of Abelard and Heloise* (Dublin, 1739), William Hammond's ballad opera, and Henri Litolff's operetta *Héloise et Abélard* sing a Dom Frollo of fact, a canon of Notre-Dame who betrayed his innocent victim over Latin conjugations after Sunday dinner in her uncle's home.

The Austrian Brüll borrowed from Hugo the name of Esmeralda's "husband" to entitle an opera, *Gringoire* (Munich, 1892), containing one lovely melody, "Die Sonne versank in Purpur." Gringoire, poet of the pavements, is the rival of Olivier, hangman-barber of Louis XI, for the love of Loys, a rich merchant's child. Though first about to die for singing to King Louis a song of his curious orchard "where corpses hang in lieu of fruit," Gringoire puts the wedding ring on Loys' finger. The great medieval poet who grew up in the slums around Notre-Dame is the hero of Membrée's *François Villon* (Paris, 1857) and Noelte's *François Villon* (Karlsruhe, 1920), in which François ends a wretched existence by poison when he finds that of the three women who chiefly ruled his life, he loves only Denise, the last. Gavaert's *Quentin Durward* (Paris, 1858) and MacLean's *Quentin Durward* (London, 1859) bring Scott's love story of King Louis' Scotch archer to its happy ending with his marriage to Isabelle of Croye.

Rheims cathedral, the Gothic minster where the French kings were solemnly anointed with the holy oil, is the church of the "Joan of Arc" operas. The English Wagnerian Raymond Roze's *Joan of Arc* (London, 1923) stresses the Court Scene in which King Charles VII tests the Maid by making her pick him out, disguised, among his courtiers; and the cathedral Coronation Scene. Tschaikowsky's *The Maid of Orleans* (Petrograd, 1881) lives only in the lovely air "Adieu, forêts"; and among others, Verdi's *Giovanna d'Arco* (Milan, 1845) and Rezniček's *Die Jungfrau von Orleans* (Berlin, 1887) after Schiller, may be mentioned. Agnès Sorel, mistress of King Charles VII, who, harking to "voices" profane, not sacred, garnered gold, castles, and jewels on earth instead of martyrdom, canonization, and a mansion in heaven, is remembered in Gyrowetz's graceful *Agnes Sorel* (Vienna, 1808), De Pellaert's *Agnès Sorel* (Brussels, 1823), and César Cui's *The Saracen* (Petrograd, 1899) after Dumas. This last opera combines two love tales, that of Charles and Agnes—"the effeminately tender music" (Rosa Newmarch) of their love scenes standing out—and that of Berthe, wife of the Count de Savernay, whose Saracen slave Jakoub, madly infatuated with her, gladly murders the unloved husband to please his wedded sweetheart. Rossini's *Il viaggio di Reims, ossia l'Albergo del Giglio d'Oro* (*The Jour-*

*ney to Rheims* or *The Inn of the Golden Weathercock,* Paris, 1825) was the "coronation opera" of King Charles X of France (the last French king to be crowned in the famous cathedral) and is a mere occasional score, its best numbers borrowed from the composer's other operas.

## "LA JUIVE"

### (The Jewess)

JACQUES FROMENTAL HALÉVY. Book by Scribe (Paris, 1835). The Gothic cathedral of Constance dominates the action of Halévy's most famous opera, "most of it . . . exceedingly long-winded and dull" (Streatfeild) but revived because Eleazar's tenor rôle contains airs—"Visit us, God of our fathers," "God guides my acts," etc.—of pathetic beauty, though Overture, Ballet, Drinking Chorus, Serenade, Bolero are now antiquated. The humanly pathetic songs (associated in this country with the name of Enrico Caruso) constitute what is really valuable in the score to-day.

In Constance (1414) when the Jew goldsmith Eleazar's irreverent hammering punctuates pious hymns with which the people celebrate Prince Leopold's victory over the Hussites, he and his daughter Recha, torn from their shop and about to be done to death, are saved by Cardinal Brogni. Recha is not Jewish at all. When Brogni burned Eleazar's two boys as heretics, the latter's hideous revenge was to snatch his babe from her father's burning palace and bring it up to worship the God of Isaac under the name of Recha. Is it strange he refuses the hands of friendship offered by Brogni? In knightly armor Leopold has defeated the Hussites. In the smock of the Jewish painter Samuel he has stormed the heart of Recha. After eating Passover bread in her father's home (Act II), he leads his sweetheart to the cathedral steps to watch Emperor Sigismund's entry into town. But—Jewish feet on the steps of God's house in the Middle Ages stood in a slippery place. Mobbed, Leopold's whispered word to an officer, however, wins the lovers an instant release.

Yet when Leopold confesses to Eleazar that, though he loves Recha, he cannot marry her, being a Christian, he barely dodges the dagger the Jew hurls and in the town hall where the Emperor Sigismund feasts (Ballet and Pantomime) with Prince Leopold and his bride Eudoxia, abandoned Recha denounces her betrayer. Death is the portion of a Christian who loves a Jewess. Cardinal Brogni excommunicates Leopold, Recha, and Eleazar, and they are led to prison.

In Recha's cell Eudoxia induces Recha to clear Leopold when she testifies, while Brogni vainly pleads with stony-hearted Eleazar to reveal the hiding place of his long-lost daughter.

In the cathedral square, oil boils in the cauldrons in which Recha and Eleazar are to cross the great divide. For the last time Brogni implores Eleazar to tell him where his daughter may be. Eleazar turns to Recha. Would she care to live in splendor as a Christian? She prefers to die a Jewess with her father, is the reply. Then the savage Jew, waiting till Recha has been pushed over the cauldron's rim cries exultantly, "There is your child!" and plunges happily to his death.

All England made pilgrimage to Canterbury cathedral, the shrine of St. Thomas à Becket, in the poet Chaucer's day, and the journey thither, if not the great English Gothic minster itself, has inspired operas which hark back, one way or another, to Chaucer's *Canterbury Tales*. *The Canterbury Pilgrims* (New York, 1917) by Reginald De Koven, book by Percy Mackaye, a romantically colored American "folk-opera," shows the wife of Bath as the pilgrims jog the road, planning to snare Chaucer for a sixth husband by getting him to wager she cannot secure from the Prioress (whom the poet loves) a certain brooch the latter wears. Alisoun, the wife of Bath, obtains it by a trick and Chaucer is saved from keeping his rash vow only by King Richard II, who says the wife of Bath's sixth husband *must* be a miller. A brave soul dares the venture while Chaucer and the Prioress are reconciled. *The Canterbury Pilgrims* (London, 1884) by Charles Villiers Stanford, book by Gilbert à Becket, an "English *Meistersinger*," using leading motives, orchestral counterpoint, etc., is the tale of Sir Christopher Synge, a Kentish knight who hires a band of ragamuffins to abduct pretty Cicely, taverner Geoffrey's daughter, on her way to the shrine. But Hubert, Geoffrey's apprentice and Cicely's lover, is watching, and (Act II) Dame Margaret, Synge's wife, helping the lovers to escape at Sidenbourne, lets herself be captured as Cicely and, masked, listens to the ardent vows her husband thinks he is pouring into the girl's ears. In view of what Dame Margaret knows, the knight when the lovers are brought before him for trial (Act III) pardons them, and all ends happily with their marriage.

In the shadow of Munster's Gothic-Romanesque cathedral is unrolled the drama of the Anabaptist tailor, Johann of Leyden.

## "LE PROPHÈTE"

### (*The Prophet*)

Giacomo Meyerbeer. Book by Scribe (Paris, 1849). "The score's striving for purely theatric effect and its character's lack of inner verity place it below *Les Huguenots*." The Prophet is a fine old-style tenor rôle (his "Dream" air was a notable Caruso number). Fides' "Ah, mon fils" remains a test song for French altos with operatic aspirations, and the "Coronation March" a model of its type.

The shepherd pipe calls Count Oberthal's vassals to work while Anabaptist preachers call them to revolt. When Fides, John of Leyden's mother, comes to gain permission for Oberthal's serf Berthe to wed her son, the Count, pleased with Berthe's appearance, has the poor girl dragged to his castle.

In John's inn at Leyden the Anabaptists beg him to rule the new Sion (Münster) as God's chosen. After the taverner yields escaped Berthe to her ravisher to save his mother's life, he follows the fanatics, who promise him revenge.

John broods in his tent in the Anabaptist camp before the beleaguered city while his bloodthirsty peasant followers make merry (Ballet) in an ice carnival. When Oberthal is captured John spares him, and even thinks of joining Berthe (she has again escaped) in Münster; but instead of deserting his men he subdues them when they revolt.

Münster taken, however, John—while Fides begs in the streets—is splendidly crowned in the cathedral as "King of Sion." But Fides curses as he blesses the people and, drawing nearer, recognizes in the bloodstained fanatic her own son. He, fearing to be torn apart on Anabaptist swords, denies the ragged beggar woman is his mother, calls her insane, and Fides, trembling for her life, declares she lied.

In his castle, alone with her, the "King" is forgiven by Fides' mother-love; but Berthe who has crept into the palace to blow it up stabs herself when in her whilom lover she recognizes the murderous Anabaptist. Then a ghastly plan matures in John's soul. He calls together the traitors who are plotting to open the city gates to the foe (change of scene) and, while red wine flows, the King of Sion touches off the gunpowder stored in the vaults, and the castle is hurled into the air with its inmates, the revellers' "Drinking Song" mingled with the *De profundis* of Fides and her son.

The cathedral of Seville, known as "The Great," largest of all Gothic cathedrals, of which Théophile Gautier said: "Notre-Dame could walk erect in its middle aisle," is the burial place of Peter the Cruel of Castile and the mistress who motived so many of his crimes. Hilarion Eslava's *Pietro il Crudele* (Madrid, 1843), Reparaz's *Don Pedro el Cruel* (San Juan de Oporto, 1857), Castegnaro's *Don Pedro di Castiglia* (Vicenza, 1888), and Sir Henry Bishop's *Don Pedro* (London, 1828) recall him in opera. Donizetti's *Maria Padilla* (Milan, 1841) contains a fine florid duet for two female voices. The cathedral of Toledo, a magnificent Gothic structure whose monstrance is wrought of the first gold Columbus brought from the New World, dominates the novel by Ibañez that suggested a lyric drama by a distinguished modern French composer. *Dans l'ombre de la cathédrale* (*In the Shadow of the Cathedral*, Paris, 1922) by Georges Hüe presents the subject matter of Ibañez's tale against the picturesque background of Toledo in 1850, in three acts without much dramatic action. There are colorful pages—street scenes, entry of matadors, a liturgic minuet. The story climaxes in the semiconversion of a dying freethinker at the Virgin's altar in the cathedral. Discussions on labor versus capital weigh down a fine score and "lyric controversies in D or A minor between a socialist and a sexton have not much emotional power" (Vuillermoz).

## "LE RÊVE"

### (The Dream)

ALFRED BRUNEAU. Book by Emile Zola (Paris, 1891). Le Rêve, a departure from Zola's naturalist style, is a poetic idyl. It brings us back to this section's starting point, for the cathedral of Zola's score "is erected beside the minster which dominates the emotions and actions of Victor Hugo's Notre-Dame" (J. Korngold). "Ugly and monotonous as much of Le Rêve is, it is alive" (Streatfeild). Bruneau uses Wagnerian formulas and an old French chanson is the melodic jewel of the work.

In the old cathedral town of Beaumont-Eglise, Angélique, adopted child of two lace workers, a "dreamer of dreams," lives in the archaic atmosphere of the missals in which she reads the lives of the saints. Ancient miracles assume life and color in her visions; angelic voices sound on the silence of her little room. Yet Angélique is human and love stirs in her breast at a young man's voice, an artist at work on the cathedral's stained-glass windows. When, in the cloister garden, Félix says he loves her, Angélique is happy. But Félix is the bishop's son. His father wishes him to become a priest and refuses consent to his marriage. Angélique, in the anguish of seeing her hopes wither in the bud, pines till she lies at death's door, when the stern churchman, relenting, restores her with the kiss of reconciliation. Radiant, Angélique is married to her lover in the old cathedral, but crossing its threshold, a smiling bride on her husband's arm, her overwrought heart gives way at his first kiss, and she dies in the excess of her happiness.

## 10. Fifteenth Century Figures

In Flora mirabilis (The Flower of Miracle, Milan, 1886), by Spiro Samara, imaginative music shows Lydia, Duke of Orebro's daughter, rejecting Waldemar "till blossoms deck the snows overnight." It is winter in Sweden but Waldemar, borrowing a magic rose-wand from Adelfjord, whose son died of grief when Lydia repulsed him in the same way, performs the miracle, then (Act II), keeping his oath to Adelfjord, jilts the coquette. Lydia goes insane (Act III), but on Waldemar's return from far lands the rosebush on Wilfrid's grave burgeons with forgiving buds, and Lydia regains her senses in her lover's arms. La jolie fille de Perthe

(*The Fair Maid of Perth*) by Georges Bizet after Scott's novel (Paris, 1867), contains an effective "Danse Bohémienne." It tunefully tells the sufferings of Harry Smith, the armorer, caused by the attentions of the Duke of Rothesay to Catherine, the "Fair Maid," through four acts to a happy ending.

Cherubini's *Lodoïska* (Paris, 1791) established his fame. In wildest Poland savage Durlinsky abducts Lodoïska and in his castle on the Tatar border her lover Floresky turns up, only to be dungeoned. Spurning her captor's infamous advances the girl is to be burned alive with her lover when Tatars in Floresky's service storm the keep and save them. Cherubini's *Faniska* (Vienna, 1806) is practically a variant of the same tale, a Polish wife instead of maid being abducted, and rescued by her husband instead of lover. *Ghismonda* (Dresden, 1895) by Eugen d'Albert, in modern dramatic music, the Love Duet outstanding, tells of the Prince of Salerno's daughter who loves Guiscardo, her father's vassal. Duke Manfredo, her betrothed, stabs Guiscardo after he has torn himself from Ghismonda's arms and the girl has the corpse brought to her, unveils its cherished head, takes poison, and falls dying on the coffin.

*Der Pfeiffertag* (*The Fifers' Festival*, Schwerin, 1899) by Max Schillings, "rooted in Wagner's *Meistersinger*," orchestrally colorful, textually undramatic, uses a medieval Alsatian Fifers' Guild Festival as a foil for a love tale whose hero, Velten, after many misadventures, leaps joyfully from the bier on which he impersonates a corpse to wed his sweetheart Herzland. In *Dalibor* (Prague, 1868), by Bedric Smetana, outstanding the Love Duet "My charming dream" (Act II), Dalibor is captain of the Bohemian king's guard. In a prison cell—the Burgrave murdered his friend, Zdenko, whereupon Dalibor murdered the Burgrave—Milada, the dead man's sister, pleads, and the orphan Yutta plans, for his freedom. Milada, disguised as a page (Act II), brings his violin to him in jail, but the next day (Act III) the king sentences him to death. When Milada (change of scene) hears death bells toll while strings are mute, she leads the hero's friends in an attack on his prison tower, to be brought back dying in his arms.

## 11. *The Devil*

The Devil always has played and always will play a leading rôle in opera. *The Devil's Opera* (London, 1838) by Sir George Macfarren is specifically devoted to him, but so numerous are operatic devils that any attempt to cover the field must represent a compromise. Operatically the Devil is largely a child of the Middle Ages.

## "ROBERT LE DIABLE"

### (*Robert the Devil*)

GIACOMO MEYERBEER. Book by Scribe and Delavigne (Paris, 1831; London, 1832). In spite of a penny-dreadful legendary text, punctuated musically by beats of the great drum, this opera scored a sensational success at its *première* in Paris, and in London, where it was given in two versions, as *The Demon or the Mystic Branch*, and *The Fiend Father or Robert of Normandy* at different houses. An Italianate score (though a work of the composer's third, French, period), the arias "Robert, toi que j'aime" and "Va, va, dit'elle," stand out.

The Devil was father of Robert, son of Normandy's duchess, for Bertram was the Devil in human shape. Banished from Normandy, young Robert strays to Sicily. He decides to joust at the tournament whose prize is the hand of Isabella, the king's daughter, but Bertram induces him to gamble away the shirt of mail on his back. Yet Isabella (Act II) fits him out with new weapons and armor. Then Bertram makes him miss the tournament. Now (Act III) Robert's only hope of winning Isabella's hand is to pluck from his mother's tomb a branch of cypress whose magic powers will let him abduct the girl.

*Ballet of the Phantom Nuns.* "The first serious manifestation of musical romanticism on the French lyric stage," this ballet is often given as an independent *divertissement.* In the Sicilian convent graveyard where Robert's mother lies, dissolute dead nuns who once held profligate orgies there rise in hellish beauty and scanty winding sheets at Bertram's command to tempt his son with unholy dances (bassoons chuckle as the phantoms leave their graves) and when, casting off their cerements, they appear unveiled their blandishments induce Robert to pluck the mystic branch.

In the king's palace the branch puts asleep knights on guard but Isabella's pleas, as he is about to carry her off, soften Robert's heart. He flings away the branch, the knights awake and attack him, and he is saved only by Bertram's intervention.

In Palermo cathedral where Robert has sought refuge, Bertram vainly pleads hell's cause till Robert, learning his supposed friend is his father, is moved by filial piety to go to the Devil—though Isabella waits without to wed him—when the bells chime the midnight hour! With the last stroke Bertram's chance to win his son's soul vanishes. He sinks cursing into the pit and (change of scene) Robert and Isabella are happily wedded.

*La nonne sanglante* (*The Sanguinary Nun,* Paris, 1854) by Charles Gounod, book by Scribe, is a ghost in an eleventh century Bohemian castle who wins a promise from a young noble to kill her murderer, then points out his father as the criminal. A foe assumes the youth's parricide and Baron Luddolf, as his life blood

wells, sees the Specter Nun come to bear his repentant soul to
Heaven. The symphonic Phantom Scene (Act II) and an attractive waltz, "Un jour plus pur" (Act III) stand out. *Grisélidis*
(Paris, 1901; New York, 1910) by Jules Massenet, book by Armand Silvestre and Eugène Moraud, is Boccaccio's tale of the
peasant girl whose faithfulness overcomes the hardest tests. The
Devil's "Forest Incantation" and the "Miracle" music are fine
pages. "Ouvrez-vous sur mon front," Alain's tenor air, is the
outstanding melody.

The Marquis de Saluces, off to the Crusades, wagers the Devil
himself cannot shake his trust in his wife Grisélidis—and the Devil,
with horns, hoofs, and tail, takes up the defiance. He first (the
Marquis' wedding ring his authority) installs a Persian slave
girl in Grisélidis' place, then tempts her with a former lover, Alain
the shepherd. About to yield to him her little son's appearance
saves her and the Devil carries off the boy. He tells her that a
pirate holds her child captive; only if she kisses him will he be
released. Grisélidis hurries to the port town with dagger in sleeve
instead of kiss on lip and meets the Marquis returning from Holy
Land. His faith is rewarded. By a miracle—the story's operatic
climax—a tryptich in the chapel opens, revealing the boy asleep,
haloed with golden light, before the Virgin's image. *Grisélidis*
(Troppau, 1898) by Clemens von Frankenstein is an earlier setting
of the tale.

*The Demon* (Petrograd, 1875) by Anton Rubinstein, after Ler-
mentoff's poem, is considered the composer's best opera. Tamara's
"Ah, how close the night," the ballet, and Tamara and the Demon's
vivid duet stand out. Planning to win the Caucasian Princess
Tamara's love (Act I), a demon drops to earth, rouses savage
Tatars to murder the girl's betrothed, the Prince of Sinodal, as
he dreams of her in his camp; and when deaf to his honeyed wooing she enters a cloister (Act II), proves that perseverance gains
success by winning her lips in that holy place (Act III), only to
be snatched from his hellish triumph by angel legions who carry
Tamara's love-torn soul to Paradise, while the foiled Demon
destroys the convent with a thunderbolt. *Der Dämon* (Frankfort, 1924) by Paul Hindemith is an objectionable dance pantomime by a German modernist, introducing the disorderly house on
the stage in an "allegory" motived by a tale of two girls unable
to withstand the temptations of the flesh.

*Paoletta* (Cincinnati, 1910) by L. Floridia, after a Spanish
legend, a romantic score with fine lyric pages, tells of a Castilian
princess whose beauty wakes desire in the aged Moorish magician
Gomarez's breast. Made young and handsome by the power of
Azazil, the spirit of Evil, he is about to marry innocent Paoletta

when he shrivels into senility beneath the ray of a holy mirror brought from Jerusalem, and Paoletta is clasped in her lover Don Pedro's arms. *Le timbre d'argent* (*The Silver Bell*, Paris, 1877) by Saint-Saëns, to fluent, graceful music, tells how the Viennese painter Conrad turns from his fiancée Hélène to a dancing girl, but finds poverty bars him from favor. Then the Devil appears in a dream, and gives him a silver bell whose tinkle calls forth a rain of gold pieces but—whenever he rings it a dear friend dies. When twice death follows Conrad's ringing of the bell, he casts it from him with a shudder, and waking from his dream and infatuation, marries Hélène.

## "DER FREISCHÜTZ"

### (*The Free Shooter*)

CARL MARIA VON WEBER. Book by Kind, after novel by Apel (Berlin, 1821; New York, 1825). One of the composer's two master works, the other being *Euryanthe*. The story is the medieval legend of a personal devil who induces huntsmen to sell their souls for magic bullets that always hit the mark. The action takes place at the period immediately following the Thirty Years' War. Outstanding are: the Overture (famous opening horn passage strikes the note of romance and mystery maintained throughout the work); Max's lovely melody, "Durch die Wälder, durch die Auen" (Act I); Agathe's Prayer, "Leise, leise"; the ghostly "Devil Music" of the Wolf's Glen Scene (Act II); Agathe's "Cavatina"; the "Bridal Chorus," and the "Hunting Chorus" (Act III).

In a Bohemian village, Cuno, Prince Ottokar's chief huntsman, grieves to see a peasant outshoot Max, the young ranger who loves his daughter, Agathe. When Max despairs, sinister Kaspar hands him his gun and bids him fire at an eagle. Max fires and the bird falls at his feet; for Kaspar's bullets are "free"; he has sold his soul to the Devil to obtain them. If he finds a victim to take his place Kaspar can secure three years' grace. He persuades Max to meet him at midnight in the Wolf's Glen to mold the magic bullets which will give him victory in the morrow's contest.

Max bids Agathe farewell and (change of scene) in the Wolf's Glen the Devil as Samiel, "the black huntsman," amid scenes of supernatural horror, presides over the molding of the magic bullets. Six will strike their mark without fail; the seventh goes where Samiel wills.

In the cottage Agathe's bridesmaids weave her bridal wreath while (change of scene) in the forest Max vainly begs Kaspar for another "free" bullet. All he has left is the bullet that obeys only Samiel's will. At the lists (change of scene) the Prince bids Max bring down a white dove while Kaspar grins to think Samiel's bullet will find the ranger's heart. As Max raises his gun Agathe begs him not to shoot— she is the dove—but his finger has pressed the trigger. Agathe sinks to the ground, yet only in a swoon. Kaspar, however, falls dead from his tree. Samiel's bullet had no power over Max, for he had not come to the Wolf's Glen of his own free will. So Kaspar dies in his stead and Max, confessing all, is forgiven by the Prince. After a year of probation he shall lead his sweetheart to the altar.

*The Devil's Rock* (Prague, 1882) by Smetana, unoperatic but his most original opera, with a picturesque wealth of Bohemian folk tunes ("Dream Music," "Berceuse," etc.) is the tale of a young girl's love for a great lord, Wok of Rosenberg, who prefers her warm affection to a chill monastery cell. The interesting "Devil motive" is brilliantly developed in the orchestra when the tempter appears.

*Der Bärenhäuter* (*Bearpelt*, Berlin, 1900) by Arnold Mendelssohn, with numerous pages of serious beauty and effective "Devil Music," and *Der Bärenhäuter* (Munich, 1899) by Siegfried Wagner, probably his best score, develop a devil legend of the time of the Thirty Years' War. Ruppert, a returned lansquenet, refused by his sweetheart, agrees to serve a year in hell, wrapped in a filthy bear pelt, never washing, hair, beard, and nails untrimmed, to avenge himself on the girl's father who wants to marry her to a noble. When Anna seeks him out in the infernal regions—a pure maid's kiss breaking his compact with the Devil—hell's gates fly open as Anna's lips touch his, bear pelt and filth fall away, and amid the chime of bells the lovers take their way to the village church. In his *Banadietrich* (Karlsruhe, 1910) Siegfried Wagner introduces the foul fiend as the tempter of the hero Dietrich. But when he has induced him to defy God, he repents at his dead wife Swanhilde's prayer, and Satan's hosts, about to seize him, disperse. Halévy's ballet, *La Tentation* (Paris, 1832), shows hell to appropriate music in a "series of grotesque but tiresome tableaux."

*Das höllisch Gold* (*Hell's Gold*, Darmstadt, 1916) by Julius Bittner, an original, genuinely folkwise score, tells the struggle between good and evil in a medieval setting. A peasant's crop has failed, his wife is starving. Ephraim, noble son of the Jew usurer, brings the wife a bag of gold and she gratefully kisses his forehead. Her husband—incited by an old witch—thinks her untrue. As he raises his knife the woman prays the Virgin to attest her innocence, and an arid twig beside the Madonna's image is covered with rosy blossoms. Man and wife praise God. The Devil had planned to buy the man's soul with "the gold of hell." The witch was to bring them together. Foiled of his intended victim, he wrings the witch's neck and carries her to hell. *Der Teufelsweg* (*The Devil Road*, Berlin, 1912) by Waghalter, rich in lovely folkwise female choruses, leads us to the same composer's *Sataniel* (Charlottenburg, 1923), a "fantastic-comic" score with a delightful Quartet (Act II) and attractive lyric pages presenting the devils Sataniel and Furioso attempting the virtue of Marma, a Polish peasant maid only, as devils should, to fail in their nefarious plans.

## "LE DIABLE BOITEUX"

### (*The Limping Devil*)

CASIMIR GIDE. Pantomime Ballet. Book after Le Sage's novel (Paris, 1836). Brilliant, facile music by a composer who rivaled Adam in the Fanny Ellsler ballet of its day. "After she had created the rôle of Florinda she went off to America, among the savages and Yankees, whom she maddened with the rattle of her castagnettes and the undulations of her hips, so that senators drew her carriage and whole citiesful followed her with cheers and brass bands" (Théophile Gautier).

In a series of fantastic pictures of Baroque Spain, Don Cleofas, a student of Alcala, flirts madly with Paquita, the *manola,* a girl of the town, Florinda, a *danseuse,* and Dorothea, a rich young widow. Thanks to the aid of Asmodeus, the Limping Devil, whom he released from a sealed vase, at a great open-air festival on the banks of the Manzanares (Andalusian and *flamenca* dances) he chooses Paquita, the pretty little toiler. Asmodeus, once the wild young collegian is ready to settle down to marriage with a virtuous girl, hands him a silver bell. When Cleofas rings it the Limping Devil will appear to grant his wish. What more could man desire?

*Le diable à quatre* (Paris, 1845) by Adolphe Adam was another famous "devil" ballet of the time.

The greatest of all German devil operas introduces the Evil Principle in the shape of a beautiful "lady from Hell," the goddess Venus who, as Satan's agent, found lost souls for her master in the voluptuous recesses of Thuringia's Hörselberg.

## "TANNHÄUSER"

### (*The Singers' Contest in the Wartburg*)

RICHARD WAGNER. Book by the composer (Dresden, 1845). As in *The Flying Dutchman,* redemption through love is the leading motive of the story, based on Hoffmann's novel, *Der Sängerkrieg,* and a poem by Tieck, developing a thirteenth century legend. The repentant sinner is wrested from the powers of evil—the Devil personified in Venus—by the might of a pure woman's sacrificing love. Its moral is that salvation comes through renunciation. The Overture, the March, "Entry of the Guests into the Wartburg," the brilliant Bacchanale ("Venusberg Music"), Elizabeth's "Prayer," her air, "Dich teure Halle," the "Pilgrims' Chorus," and Wolfram's Romance, "O thou sublime sweet evening star," are high musical moments.

The Venus of ancient Greece dwells as the Devil's emissary in a flowering paradise beneath the Hörselberg, in Thuringia. Tannhäuser, a minstrel knight, after an orgy of sinful pleasure there finds his environment bores him. He longs for mortal joys and sorrows. In vain Venus begs him to stay. He calls on the Blessed Virgin, Venus and her paradise disappear with a clap of thunder, and Tannhäuser is lying on a grassy slope as a shepherd boy pipes a lay. The chant of pilgrims passing Romeward rouses thoughts of penance, interrupted by the appearance of the Landgrave of Thuringia and his knights, who invite him to the Wartburg. Wolfram von Eschenbach mentions saintly Elizabeth, the Landgrave's niece. Elizabeth's name, holding out hope of human love, leads Tannhäuser to go with them.

Into the Wartburg's Hall of Song, scene of famous minstrel tourneys, Wolfram brings repentant Tannhäuser to fall at Elizabeth's feet. Ignorant of Tannhäuser's mythological escapades, the maiden welcomes him. The knightly guests now enter to compete in song: their theme "the power of love," the victor's prize, Elizabeth's hand. Wolfram sings a distant, chaste ideal; Walther, virtue's pure fount; Biterolf, the soldier's chivalrous flame. But Tannhäuser, out of his vast experience, trumps the pale passions of his friends with a mad hymn which, in a moment of self-forgetfulness, turns into a rhapsodic chant in honor of Venus, lovely Devil of the Venusberg. Shocked, the knights, sword in hand, advance on the self-confessed criminal. But Elizabeth pleads for him in the Savior's name and saves the again repentant sinner from his fellow knights; the Landgrave bids him to go to Rome to obtain pardon for his sin. The singing of pilgrim youths on their way to the Eternal City rouses Tannhäuser. "To Rome!" he cries and hastens from the hall.

Elizabeth prays by a rustic cross beneath Wartburg towers (Act III). No news has come from Tannhäuser: pilgrims sing and pass, but not the knight. As she sadly returns to the castle, Wolfram sings his song to the "Evening Star" (the most famous air in the opera) while twilight shades gather. Now Tannhäuser appears, in despair. The Pope has told him his sin is past pardon—unless the dry branch held in the papal hand puts forth leaves and blossoms. Tannhäuser, disgusted, when Venus appears with nymphs and hamadryads, is willing to return to her. A solemn funeral chant sounds, knights in procession bear Elizabeth on her bier. Her last prayer was for Tannhäuser; her last message that she would intercede for him on high. Tannhäuser kneels beside the body and dies with the cry, "Dear Saint, pray for me!" as pilgrims arrive bearing the dry staff which has miraculously blossomed. The dead wood which has burst into bloom shows the repentant sinner has been forgiven, his soul's redemption is assured.

*Tannhäuser* (Darmstadt, 1846) by Karl Mangold compares to Wagner's score as a Japanese dwarf tree to a forest oak; and to many, mere mention of Karl Binder's parody *Tannhäuser* (Vienna, 1857) will seem sacrilege.

Deadlier devils of the operatic species include *La figlia del diavolo* (*The Devil's Daughter*, Naples, 1860) by Leoncavallo's teacher d'Arienzo, damned in its day for "straining after realistic effect"; while Reznicek's *Satanella* (Prague, 1888) and Rozkosny's *Satanella* (Prague, 1898) have failed in our day to win the favor once accorded Michael William Balfe's *Satanella* (London, 1858), book by Harris and Falconer, outstanding song "The Power of Love," in which Count Rupert, a ruined gamester, invokes Satan, and is given the lovely female demon Satanella to serve him, with secret orders on the Devil's part to snare Rupert's soul. But Satanella loses her heart to Rupert, has his bride Leila abducted by Levantine pirates and takes her place at the altar. Rupert recognizing her, drops her hand to rush to Leila's rescue, while Arimanes (Satan) informs Satanella she is doomed unless he obtains Rupert's soul within thirty days. In the Tunisian slave mart Satanella releases Leila after Rupert has signed over his soul, but at the month end when Leila offers her soul to ransom her lover's, the demoness nobly tears up the contract, and when Arimanes comes to collect drives him off with Leila's rosary.

*Nerto* (Paris, 1924) by Ch.-M. Widor after Mistral—the "Devil Music" in Satan's palace, the brilliant popular festival, the Prelude (Act III), and "Nerto's Prayer" stand out—is the tale of Baron Pons who, dying, tells his daughter Nerto he sold her soul to the Devil for gold. Angel voices bid her go to papal Avignon and there (Act II) seized as a witch amid a fête, she is rescued by the Pope's nephew, Rodrigue de Luno. In the convent where the Pope puts her (Act III), refusing Rodrigue's love for his sake, Rodrigue vows his soul to the Devil, pillages the holy place with his men-at-arms, and is carried to hell where (Act IV) the pleasures of Satan's palace pall for lack of Nerto. Yearning takes him to see her before he is hell-bound for eternity; he finds her dying and as midnight chimes the Devil claims their souls. But when Rodrigue draws sword to defend Nerto, Satan vanishes, and Paradise gates open to admit the lovers. *Satan vaincu* (*Satan Overcome*, Nice, 1925) by Alfred Kullman, whose Ballet (Alsatian folk airs) and "St. Blandine's Legend" stand out, turns on Sabine. Alsatian Philip and brutal Teuton Orso love her; the best sculptor will win her hand. Orso smashes Philip's statue of St. Blandine, and his own genial statue of Satan is about to gain the prize when Sabine (none knew she wielded chisel) casts Satan in the shade with *her* statue of St. John, and is free to marry Philip. Old Count Mathias also loved Sabine, but he was no sculptor.

*Satyros* (Weimar, 1923) by Waldemar von Baussnern after

Goethe's *Satyros or the Divinified Forest Devil,* with a fine symphonic Prologue and Idyl (Act II), satirizes cults which preach the worship of nature as sensual nudity. Satyros, the forest devil, curses the good hermit who takes him in, kicks his rosary into the brook, and with sweet flutings lures Psyche and Orsinoe to him in the shade of a well. Fascinated, Psyche falls madly in love with the half-naked devil-youth, and the people turn Nature worshipers and bow to him as god. When he disappears the people disperse and the good hermit thinks Psyche saved when—Satyros' flute calls from the bushes and the maiden flings herself into the nature devil's arms with a happy cry!

## "HISTOIRE D'UN SOLDAT"

### (*The Tale of a Soldier*)

IGOR STRAVINSKY. Book by Ramuz (Lausanne, 1918). A score for actors, narrators, dancers, and musicians in which the verbal, musical, and plastic blend in opposition to Wagnerian principles. The "Royal March," Prelude, "Devil's Curse" and "Chorale"—between each musical pause the soldier whispers to his bride some thrilling naughtiness of his past—stand out. The satiric tale is after a Russian legend.

A Soldier, homeward bound from the wars, is playing his fiddle near a brook when the Devil, as an amiable old man, gets him to exchange the fiddle (symbolizing happiness) for a magic book unlocking earth's treasures. Finding his village sweetheart married and the wealth the book brings him of no solace, he takes the open road to seek his lost happiness. In a town where the king's daughter lies sick he regains his fiddle from the Devil, and by playing it, cures the Princess and marries her. The Devil swears he will have him if ever he crosses the boundaries of the kingdom. Yet homesickness tugs at the Soldier's heartstrings. He sets out for his native village and—the Devil snatches him by the crossroads, his poor wife standing at the milestone with empty arms outstretched! Tango, jazz waltz and other blue rhythms are used with novel instrumental effects to tell the tale.

## "BELFAGOR"

OTTORINO RESPIGHI. Book by Guastalla after a Morselli comedy (Milan, 1923). An ultramodern score which, despite excursions into atonalism, boasts pages of glowing non-Verdian melody. "Musical thoughts, traced as with a silver pencil . . . radiate unexpected power in climaxing moments" (Schaub).

In a medieval Italian town the Archdevil Belfagor picks out for a wife Candida, youngest and prettiest of the drunken druggist Mirocletus' three daughters. She is betrothed to Baldo the sailor, yet her father gladly sells his child for gold to buy drink. But church bells refuse to chime for the unholy nuptials, and on her wedding night Candida runs off with the mariner to whom she is true. Belfagor descends raging into hell but first poisons Baldo's sailor soul with base mistrust of his love and horrid speculation as to how well she and Belfagor were acquainted. When the Madonna intervenes and the church bells, rung by unseen angelic hands, peal out Candida's innocence, the suspicious lover is cured of his doubts and all ends happily.

## 12. *The Faust Operas*

### "FAUST"

CHARLES GOUNOD. Book by Barbier and Carré after Goethe (Paris, 1859). Of all "Faust" operas, Gounod's (known in Germany as *Marguerite*) is the most popular. It does not voice the deeper verities of Goethe's poem, but gives the most acceptable musical expression to a theatrically effective book. A score rich in lyric melody contains Marguerite's "Jewel Song," the Waltz, and the "Soldiers' Chorus," and every great operatic soprano has been associated with the rôle of Marguerite. At the first Hanover performance, perfume sprayed over stage and auditorium lent a touch of questionable realism to the Garden Scene.

Faust, the agnostic, about to drain the poisoned draught in his study, hears Easter carols ring, hesitates—and is lost. Mephistopheles appears, promises the melancholy philosopher youth and love's pleasures, and, seeing Marguerite smiling in the Evil One's magic mirror, Faust cheerfully signs the pact that gives the tempter his soul.

Before the city gates the townsfolk make merry. Valentine leaving with other lansquenets for the wars, is sad: Marguerite, his sister, is left without a protector. But Siebel promises to watch over her and cheers the boy's parting flagon. Now Brander the mercenary sings his god Mammon in the "Song of the Golden Calf," and Mephistopheles predicts his death in battle. Then Mephistopheles toasts Marguerite as a "beauty known to all." Valentine's sword refuses to leave its sheath until the lansquenets stretch out their sword pommels in the form of a cross toward the magician, when his power wanes and he flees. As the soldiers leave, Faust insists on meeting Marguerite and she appears (Mephistopheles has got rid of Siebel), but Faust's offer to escort her home is modestly refused.

Not till Siebel dips his fingers in holy water can he pluck flowers in Marguerite's garden without their wilting, to fasten to his beloved's door. It is love's labor lost: Mephistopheles casts them away as he appears with Faust, substituting a casket of jewels. Marguerite comes home and seats herself at the spinning wheel, the handsome unknown in mind as she sings the ballad of the "King in Thule." Discovering the casket she calls her mother, decks herself with jewels and admires herself in the glass. The hour of seduction nears. While Mephistopheles, returning with Faust, engages her mother's attention, Marguerite walks with him in the garden, sweet with the breath of flowers. For a moment it seems as though girlish innocence will triumph; but Mephistopheles appeals to Faust's baser instincts, shows him the girl confiding her ardent longings to the stars. Carried away, Faust draws her into his arms. . . . "Mephistopheles' fiendish laughter gives their love its hellish benediction."

(In an introductory scene, usually cut, Marguerite is informed that Valentine is returning.) Siebel has not told, yet Valentine suspects, what has occurred during his absence. Entering the house they find Mephistopheles and Faust, and no sooner has the brother drawn his sword in reply to the demon's mocking "Serenade," than he lies dying on the floor, pierced by Faust's blade, cursing his sister, who casts herself despairingly on his body. (Change of scene.) Marguerite is alone: she avoids her brother's slayer and is shunned by her friends. Even in church her prayers are silenced by the voice of conscience. Her reason deserts her, and she drowns the new-born child of her guilty love.

*The Faust Ballet:* Mephistopheles, meanwhile, takes Faust to witches' Walpurgisnight revels in the Harz Mountains, where the loveliest courtesans of the past unveil their beauties and draw him into their wild bacchanale. *Walpurgisnacht,* as the *Faust Ballet* is known when presented as an individual number of the ballet repertoire is not, in the opera, essential to the story. It calls up the vision of ideal beauty sought by Faust and evoked by Mephistopheles in the person of Helen of Troy, to very charming music. The episode, however, has called forth various independent operas, among them the *Walpurgisnacht* (Riga, 1835) by Spohr's pupil Weitzmann.

But in vain the loveliest of the women of the past, magically returned in the flesh, tempt Faust's senses: the shadow of poor, abandoned Marguerite rises reproachfully before him. He insists that Mephistopheles take him to her (change of scene), and finds her tossing in delirium on her prison pallet. Faust urges her to flee with him but she shrinks in terror as Mephistopheles enters, and Faust departs with his demon master. Marguerite, calling on the hosts of heaven, dies while angel choirs sing her salvation (Apotheosis), and Seraphim bear her body to Paradise gardens.

*Le médecin malgré lui (The Physician Despite Himself,* Paris, 1858) by Gounod, a setting of Molière's comedy, is notable mainly because many of its musical themes were later used in *Faust.* In *Le petit Faust* (Paris, 1869), by Hervé, a mad Second Empire travesty of Gounod's original, Faust, an old schoolmaster, falls in love with a high-school Marguerite and is condemned by Mephistopheles to dance for all eternity. Its musical hit is a parody of the *Faust* trio, "Anges purs," rising a whole tone with each verse repeat. Schumann's *Faust* is the outstanding oratorio version.

## "LA DAMNATION DE FAUST"

### (*The Damnation of Faust*)

HECTOR BERLIOZ (Paris, 1846, cantata; Manchester, 1880, opera). Originally a choral work, *Eight Scenes from the Life of Faust,* turned into an opera, the *Damnation* gives Gounod's *musical* characters an *intellectual* presentment. Berlioz evokes them individually in tone, each speaking his or her individual idiom with astonishing fantasy and poignant realism to the accompaniment of gigantic orchestral mass effects. The "Hungarian (Rakoszky) March," the "Ballet of the Sylphs" (Pt. II), and Marguerite's beautiful ballad, "There dwelt a king in Thule" (soprano) stand out.

Faust, wandering through the fields, is unmoved by change of season from winter to spring, by the joy of the peasants, who dance and sing, and by the martial ardor of the Hungarian footmen, who come swinging along to the stirring strains of the national march. He has lost interest in life.

Alone in his study, about to drain a poisoned goblet, the sound of Easter hymns stays his hand, and with the hymn comes Mephistopheles to tempt him. Faust falls. But the wine cellar he visits with his tempter disgusts him, and his dream of a lovely peasant girl Marguerite (in a garden on the Elbe) voices a greater sensual appeal. ("Ballet of the Sylphs.") The sylphs of his vision disappear, and soldiers, avid for the pleasures of the town, and students, singing wine and the love with which youth must be served, march by, strengthening Faust's desires.

Mephistopheles hides Faust in Marguerite's room. Her thoughts on an unknown dream lover, she sings her ballad and hears Mephistopheles' mocking serenade. As will-o'-the-wisps dance in the garden, Faust appears before the startled girl, and forces her to yield herself to him with passionate love-making. They part reluctantly when Mephistopheles warns them the villagers are on the way to warn the girl's mother.

Betrayed, Marguerite despairs in prison while Faust learns from Mephistopheles that his love lies in jail. The demon had given her mother, Marthe, an overdose of sleeping potion, and the daughter is accused of her death. The paper Faust signs gives his soul to the Devil instead (as he thinks) of freeing Marguerite. Then comes the demoniac ride of the Devil and his prey. The voices of women and children shrill in prayer as they pass, blood rains down on them, and the wild course ends in the abyss of eternal damnation. Spirits of the pit (Chorus) exult over Faust's fall; while the soul of Marguerite, saved by faith and repentance (change of scene) is greeted by heavenly choirs. Berlioz's *Faust* has been called a brilliant and flamboyant musical fresco.

## "MEFISTOFILE"

ARRIGO BOITO. Book by the composer (Milan, 1868). Boito's "Faust," *Mefistofile*, stands on a middle plane between Gounod's and Berlioz'. It combines the first and second parts of Goethe's *Faust* in a series of episodes, and as an opera is less dramatic than Berlioz's cantata. The orchestral accompaniment to Margherita's Insanity Scene and Faust's Love Scene, the infernal and celestial choruses are its chief musical beauties, and the rôle of Mephistopheles, sung by Chaliapin, is one of the finest bass rôles in opera.

Mephistopheles appears (Prologue) about to descend to earth to tempt Faust, too wise in his own conceit. Angelic choirs sing in chorus, while cherubim and seraphim cast themselves before the Throne, and the voices of repentant sinners swell heaven's harmonies.

Bells peal gaily in Frankfurt, soldiers and students sing, peasants dance, and cheers ring out as the Elector rides past. To escape a grey friar who clings to him like a shadow, Faust leaves the streets for his study. As he turns from an apostrophe to Nature and opens his Bible, Mephistopheles (the monk) darts from a dark corner with a scream. Dropping his grey gown he stands forth in knightly dress, and promising to do Faust's bidding in exchange for his soul, bears him off on his cloak.

While Mephistopheles dallies with Marta, Margherita's mother, Faust wins the daughter's heart in the garden. After the Evil One and his victim have left (change of scene), they attend the witches' Sabbath on the Brocken. There, on a Grecian river bank Faust meets Helen of Troy, to whom he makes passionate love; and the shade of the World's Desire tells of the fall of Troy while Greek sirens weave voluptuous dances about her fifteenth century lover, picturing Margherita's fate, till Mephistopheles holds up the crystal globe they give him, crying "Behold the earth!" and the fantastic revels end.

Margherita in prison, convicted of the murder of her nameless child, calls on God to forgive her. Insane, she does not understand Faust, who has come to release her, and on the stroke of dawn he leaves at Mephistopheles' summons, as Margherita dies, angelic voices singing her pardon.

Faust (Epilogue), burdened with remorse, refuses Mephistopheles' traveling cloak. In vain the Archfiend surrounds him with voluptuous women in a final assault on his senses. The philosopher opens his Bible: while the lamp holds out to burn, the Scriptures tell him he may be saved. He turns to Heaven, prays and—dies. Celestial roses, covering his body, show that Divine forgiveness has been vouchsafed him. Mephistopheles, foiled, disappears, while angel voices exult in the Archfiend's defeat and Faust's salvation.

*Faust* (Prague, 1816; rewritten 1852) by Ludwig Spohr is based on the old German folk play. A dialogue opera, handling the voices from a violin virtuoso's standpoint, Mephisto's "Die Liebe ist eine zarte

Blüte" and the Ballet ("Witches Sabbath") stand out. Faust betrays two Marguerites, burgher Röschen and high-born Kunigunde, whose husband Hugo he slays after snatching her from his arms. Röschen, finding Faust faithless, drowns herself; and after Kunigunde has tried to stab him Mephisto carries him to hell. Among lesser "Fausts" may be mentioned Pellaert's *Faust* (Ghent, 1834), Zöllner's *Faust* (Cologne, 1887), and Wenzel Müller's quaint *Der Schatten von Fausts Weib* (*The Shadow of Faust's Wife*, Vienna, 1818, while Louise-Angélique Bertin's *Faust* (Paris, 1831) is considered musically the most wretched opera ever written on the subject.

### "DOKTOR FAUSTUS"

FERRUCIO BUSONI. Book by the composer, after the medieval puppet play (Berlin, 1925). A colorful, mystic, ultramodern score, in part atonal, by the late master of "linear polyphony." Outstanding are the "Cortège" and Dances (Ballet) of the Meyerbeerian "Parma Garden Festival," the "Sarabande-Intermezzo" and Faust's "Death Monologue."

In Faust's Gothic study three mysterious Cracow students bring him a magic book. He invokes Satan, and Mephisto amid fire and flame calls up phantoms and enchantments, and a dead child, cast on the stage turns into a bundle of straw out of which steps Helen of Troy. Faust signs the pact. Marguerite (II) does not appear, but Mephisto has her vengeful brother Valentine slain in a church by his fellow soldiers. At the ducal court of Parma (Main Section, I) where Faust, the mighty magician, appears as an honored guest, he seduces the Duchess on her wedding day, abandoning her to a death of despair; but in Wittenberg (II) when the mysterious Polish students demand their book and he no longer has it to return, he feels the hour of fate is nigh. After a Monologue on the snow-covered steps of the minster (Final Scene) he dies with manly repentance, neither damned nor redeemed. From his corpse rises a nude youth who, a blossoming branch in his hand, moves off through the night. Mephisto, finding the cadaver and flinging it over his shoulder, asks mockingly, "Has the fellow had an accident?" The symbolic idea is that Faust's body dies; his soul is immortal, like the eternal struggle between sin and sin's recognition and repentance.

### "PAN TWARDOWSKI"

LUDOMIR RÓŻYCKI. Ballet (Warsaw, 1924). Twardowski is the "Faust" of Polish folklore. Outstanding in the score, combining pantomime with vocal solos and choruses, are the "Polonaise" (Court Scene) and the Market Place Scene where the Devil's magic drives the crowd to mad dances in which the music attains its dramatic climax.

Twardowski, a Polish gentleman (16th century) in quest of the philosopher's stone and of gold making, signs a pact with the Devil and sells his soul in exchange for a luxurious life. But the Devil can claim Twardowski's soul only in Rome. Amusing episodes carry the Polish Faust through all the kingdoms of the earth to Rome on the day when Satan is to claim him. There Twardowski, his thoughts going back to the days when he was a child, sings an old Polish Christmas carol and frightens away the Foul Fiend! He does not escape punishment, however, but is suspended from one of the horns of the moon until the Judgment Day as a horrible example to other sinners.

Giovanni von Zaytz, the first Croatian opera composer, also set the legend of *Pan Twardowsky* (Agram, 1880) as an opera, and *Pan Twardowsky* (Moscow, 1828) by Verstovsky had a "Gypsy Chorus" which insured its temporary popularity.

### 13. *Don Juan*

The original Don Juan Tenorio was a member of the dissolute court of Don Pedro the Cruel, King of Castile (1333-1369). Don Juan legends are found at points as far apart as Iceland and the Azores, for the profligate has no special century nor local habitat. Of the various forms of the legend the one in Mozart's *Don Giovanni* is Da Ponte's retelling of *El burlador de Sevilla* by Tirso de Molina (1630).

*Don Juan oder das steinerne Gastmahl* (*Don Juan or the Stone Banquet*, Vienna, 1761; revived, 1924), Gluck's ballet, a precursor of Mozart's score, was the first *ballet* written on a tragic subject. It tells the Mozartian story in pantomime. In the banquet scene the statue of the Commander does not sit, but beckons Don Juan to follow him to the burial vault, and disappears. There, his vain attempts to move the wretch to remorse are followed by the descent into hell and a closing "Ballet of Furies" (the same the composer used in *Orpheus*, Act II). An allegoric pantomime by Haydn, *Don Juan oder das steinerne Gastmahl*, was given in Leibach, 1804; and here too might be mentioned *La statue du Commandeur* (Paris, 1892) by A. David.

Henry Purcell's setting of Shadwell's *The Libertine* (London, 1693) has preserved some of the latter's indifferent lyrics, and between his time and that of the Spanish composer Carnicer, one of the creators of the Spanish *zarzuela*, who wrote a *Don Juan Tenorio* (Barcelona, 1818), a host of lesser composers—Le Tellier, Righini, Tritto, Gardi, Albertini, Fabrizi, Raimondi, Gazzaniga and others—wrote "Don Juan" operas.

## "DON GIOVANNI"

### (Don Juan)

WOLFGANG AMADEUS MOZART. Libretto by Lorenzo Da Ponte (Prague, 1787). The sublime handling of an old medieval tale—the ghost of a slain man invited to a banquet by his murderer appearing to drag him down to hell—"the swan song of the Rococo period," is accounted the composer's most beautiful score. Modern objection to anticlimax ends the opera with Don Giovanni's disappearance, though a noble closing Sextet is sacrificed with the original expositional end. Outstanding are lovely airs: "Là ci darem," "Deh viene alla finestra" (the mandolin serenade); Zerlina's "Batti, batti" aria, the "Vedrai carino," the simultaneous Minuet and Alemana, and the compelling "Inferno Music" of the close. This opera led Beethoven to reproach Mozart for treating so "scandalous a subject," and to write his own *Fidelio* in honor of wedded faithfulness.

The Don Juan of de Molina's *El burlador de Sevilla y convidado de piedra,* underlies most dramatizations of the hero, and makes him a dissolute Spanish noble (17th century Seville) who wishes to add Donna Anna (betrothed to Don Ottavio), the Comandatore of Seville's daughter, to his list of victims. Creeping into the Comandatore's house to betray his child, her cry for help brings her father to the spot. He is stabbed and killed by Don Giovanni, escapes unrecognized as Don Ottavio, coming up, swears vengeance. The libertine (change of scene) stands in front of his villa talking with his servant Leporello, when Donna Elvira, found, fondled, and forgotten in Burgos, appears to reproach him for his desertion. Turning her over to Leporello, he hurries off and when a peasant wedding party appears, Don Giovanni coaxes Zerlina, the pretty bride, to accompany him to his house (Leporello holding the groom's attention), but Elvira forces him to release his prey. When Donna Anna appears to enlist Don Giovanni's aid in discovering her father's murderer, he places himself at her disposal but Elvira denounces him and to save himself he declares her insane. Donna Anna, however, has recognized the voice of her father's slayer. All the rustic wedding guests are now in Don Giovanni's villa and (change of scene) Elvira, Anna, and Ottavio masked, follow, bent on vengeance. Don Giovanni is gay; champagne flows freely, and while his servants circle about with refreshments three groups of dancers are active in the great hall. But the rake is at his old tricks. He disappears with Zerlina in an adjoining room and soon her cry for help breaks up the dance. When the guests force the door Don Giovanni blames Leporello, and when Ottavio and his companions unmask him, draws his rapier and escapes in the tumult.

Now Don Giovanni's desires turn to Elvira's maid. While he cynically leads Elvira into Leporello's arms in the darkness, he serenades her servant until interrupted by Masetto (Zerlina's husband) and his peasant friends, who come with flails to hold the libertine to account. But he escapes, the beater instead of the beaten, Zerlina tenderly leading her damaged bridegroom away. Now, however, Don Giovanni goes too far. In the churchyard near the Comandatore's equestrian statue he laughs at honor and decency and invites his murdered victim to sup with him. While Leporello trembles, the statue, to Don Giovanni's surprise, accepts the invitation. At supper (change of scene)—after Donna Elvira has vainly tried to turn Don Giovanni from his godless life—music and merriment are at their height when a heavy tread is heard in the corridor. Don Giovanni goes to the door, but the candelabra falls from his hand—the ' Stone Guest confronts him! His fearsome visitant bids him choose between repentance and damnation, but the libertine answers with insolent scorn. Then the statue grasps him with marble hand and while the banquet hall crashes into ruin amid thunders and lightnings, drags him down through the flames to the endless torment of hell.

## "FIDELIO"

LUDWIG VON BEETHOVEN. Book after Bouilly's melodrama (Vienna, 1805)—after which Paër wrote his *Eleanora ossia l'amore conjugale* (*Eleanora or Wedded Love*, Dresden, 1805)—is Beethoven's *only* opera. The subject—a virtuous wife—he deliberately selected to rebuke Mozart for making a godless libertine the hero of *Don Giovanni*. The Overtures, "Fidelio" and "Leonore, No. 3" (played between the acts), Pizarro's "Ha, what a moment," perhaps the most difficult bass aria in opera, Leonore's lovely air, "Come hope," and the Closing Duet (Florestan and Leonore), are among the finest pages.

Florestan, a noble Spanish Benedict, has exposed the misdeeds of Pizarro, governor of a prison near Madrid. Pizarro seizing his foe throws him into a dungeon and says he is dead. Leonore, Florestan's faithful wife, rejects the rumor and suspects its circulator. Disguised as a youth, she obtains employment from Rocco, Pizarro's chief jailer, and so attractive is she that Marcellina, Rocco's daughter, falls in love with her and neglects Jaquino, her country lover. Leonore is encouraging Marcellina's advances to obtain special privileges for her husband when Fernando—prime minister and Florestan's friend—informs Pizarro that he will inspect the prison. Florestan must not be in evidence when he arrives, so Pizarro orders Rocco to kill the supposed criminal. Rocco is willing to dig the grave but not to fill it, and Pizarro agrees to supply its occupant.

Rocco and Fidelio are cleaning out the old cistern to serve as Florestan's tomb when, to the pathetic sound of the counter-basses in the orchestra, Pizarro arrives. As he is about to deal the fatal blow, Leonore, crying that she is the prisoner's wife, stops him. Pizarro, again raising his dagger, finds himself looking into the mouth of a pistol in Leonore's hand! Now trumpets sound. Fernando has arrived. Etiquette demands Pizarro receives him—he must spare Florestan for the nonce, and husband and wife rush into each other's arms. The final scene shows Pizarro's shame and disgrace and Florestan's restoration to dignities and honors.

*Rodelinde* (London, 1725) by Handel develops a plot in which a faithful wife's love for her husband survives the most harrowing test as in *Fidelio*.

*The Stone Guest* (Petrograd, 1872) by Dargomijsky, book after Pushkin, is "pre-Dubussyan rather than post-Wagnerian" (Bie). Realistic mezzo-recitative supplants set numbers, the music fitting the characters "like a skin." Don Juan, returning incognito to Seville after long exile, kills Doña Laura's lover Carlos, and wins her heart, reseduces Doña Anna and kills the Commander (Anna's *husband,* not father, according to Pushkin) and invites the stone statue to the love feast he gives the widow to be duly dragged down to hell by his "Stone Guest."

There is a *Juan de Tenorio* (Petrograd, 1888) by Vietnighoff-Schell and a *Don Juan Tenorio en Napoles* (Barcelona, 1900) by Linan y Vildegain, and it may be said that *Don Juan de Tenoria* and *Don Juan de Marana* practically differ only in name. The twentieth century has witnessed an operatic revival of interest in the hero of Mozart's score. *Chérubin* (Monte Carlo, 1905) by Massenet, after de Croisset's play, makes the Chérubin of Mozart's *Figaro* a seventeen-year-old French Don Juan who, after a hectic affair with l'Ensoleillad, a Spanish dancer, marries good little Nina, his fiancée, just as her disillusioned feet are about to carry her over a convent threshold. Tunefully banal, there is a happy musical allusion to Mozart's *Don Giovanni* "Serenade."

## "L'OMBRA DI DON GIOVANNI"

### (*The Shadow of Don Giovanni*)

FRANCO ALFANO. Book by Ettore Moschio (Milan, 1913). Powerful dramatic music of modern type tells the tale of two souls who pass from sensuous passion to spiritual love.

Weary of seduction among the beauties of Spain, Don Juan Marana returns to his ancestral keep in Cinarca, Corsica, on his way slaying the hope of the Alando family with whom his own has a feud. When the murdered boy's retainers, however, led by his mother, rush into the chapel of Cinarca and find Don Giovanni praying, they think him guiltless and retire.

Yet Vannina d'Alando has recognized her brother's slayer. When she boasts nothing shall stay her vengeance Don Giovanni sees in her a woman to be conquered. He reverts from austere penitent to fascinating lady-killer, "enwrapped in a mysterious atmosphere of light and song," plays the old game of winning hearts and Vannina yields.

At d'Alando's grave on a barren hill his mother, now knowing Don Juan slew her son, incites her people to fire the tower where the murderer dwells alone. Vannina is bound to a crucifix when she opposes, and the rest hurry to their hideous revenge. Released by Orsetta, who secretly loves the handsome seducer, Vannina finds Don Juan and begs him to escape. But, weary of sin, he yearns to find death's answer to love, "creation's great mystery." The lovers, as flames sweep the castle, lost in each other's arms to all but their passion, are trampled underfoot in the onrush of the avengers, "disappearing as though whelmed by a sea of blood."

*Don Juan's letztes Abenteuer* (*Don Juan's Last Adventure*, Leipzig, 1914) by Paul Graener, book by Anthes, a modernist score sonorously orchestrated, has the old reprobate at a festival in the Palazzo Spinelli, Venice, find a new victim in Cornelia, Manzoni's daughter. Passionate vows wring from her a promise to visit him. But (Act II) he finds the hypnotized girl does not care for him; while he, for the first time, loves sincerely. Watchers, suspecting Cornelia's presence, enter (Act III), but when the girl's betrothed, Francesco—for whom Don Juan has sent—hurries in, her cry "Protect me, beloved!" as she clasps his knees breaks Don Juan's heart, and the super-sensualist falls on his own rapier at the feet of the one woman he could not win. *Arlequin* (Paris, 1921) by André Gailhard, book by Magre, in which Micæla's "Death Scene," rich in pathos, stands out in a lyric score, also plays in Venice. After a defile of Don Juan's forgotten conquests, he wins in succession, in a square on a canal, a tavern servant, a duchess in brocades, and a princess. To a green park pavilion the duchess brings her cavalier and the princess her dancer; but Micæla, the poor water-front girl who loves "Harlequin" (Don Juan), when the latter turns up in an archbishop's purple gown, takes in her breast the bullet from a rival's pistol. In the fisher hut where the purple-gowned profligate gives the girl who died for love of him his benediction, he is for the first time troubled with a genuine affection. He dreams, and in his dream passes from life to death. In a cypress grove marble steps lead to a purple door. Guided by an old man, Despair, Don Juan mounts the steps, thrusting aside Youth and Pleasure to gain the mystic portal. Opening, Death appears but vanishes as Micæla, aureoled with golden radiance, draws Don Juan into the garden of love's eternity.

*L'homme à la rose* (*The Man with the Rose*, Paris, 1921) by Reynaldo Hahn, incidental score for Henri Bataille's play, has "music delicate, evocative, light and warmly colored . . . like the characters, it moves in all the silks and velvets of tone." Don Juan, after watching his own funeral in Seville cathedral (the body is that of his love-proxy, Manuelito, slain by an outraged husband) hears himself called "Disgusting old man!" by the young girl he next attempts to seduce. Leaving Seville he settles in a country-town inn. Alas, authentic memoirs he reads to an attractive young widow (to offset a penny-a-liner's scribblings) put her to sleep! The unveiled beauty of a gypsy girl renews belief in his ability to charm but—the strumpet is interested only in the five gold *duros* she demands and, as he slips them into her brown paw, "The Man with the Rose" knows that "Don Juan" is indeed dead. *Der einsame Mann* (*The Lonely Man*, Frankfurt, 1924) by Bruno Hartl is a lyric parody opera dealing with Don Juan's amatory conquests in Venice. *La mille et quatrième* (*The Thousand and Fourth*, Monte Carlo, 1925) by Camille Kufferath, a modernly melodious score, shows Don Juan while waiting for two ladies to keep a rendezvous with him at an inn, trying to make honest Pepita, the serving maid, his "one thousand and fourth" conquest. When the Commander of the old legend appears and insults him, Don Juan, to cut a figure in the girl's eyes, fights a duel with his grisly foe, and, mortally wounded, begs Pepita to let him fancy he had won her heart by a farewell kiss.

## "DON JUAN MARANA"

August Enna. Book by the composer, based on Dante, Molière, Byron, Merimée, and Bojer (Copenhagen, 1925). A colorful modern score, melodically leaning on Wagner and Puccini, in which stand out the Love Duet between Don Juan and Agatha (Act I) and "Satan's Song" (Act III). It is the only opera that makes the libertine's victims receive him with open arms in Paradise.

In Seville, Don Juan after working his wicked will on the nun Agatha, first bride of Christ he has seduced, in the dim, religious light of the cathedral, sinks mortally wounded on the altar steps, and when he sees his coffin borne in ghastly procession along the nave, dies of shock and horror.

At Paradise gates, where the Archangel Michael sits high on golden throne, he turns back the sinner's soul. "Your victims would cry out in terror did they know you were here!" he says. But when Don Juan's betrayed raise a thousand-voiced chorus of intercession to the Great White Throne, begging that he be saved from the weeping and wailing and gnashing of teeth which are his portion, Saint Michael points to a bare rock and says, as Don Juan turns away, "When the stone puts forth blossoms, you may enter in!" Then Agatha, who was a nun, kisses the rock and—a miracle!—its flinty bosom is covered with crimson roses.

In Hell devils are about to put repentant Don Juan to sulphuric torture when hundreds of angelic female figures, the libertine's victims, descend to the realm of darkness on a ladder of golden light, come to rescue him from eternal torment. And while Don Juan kneels and angel choirs sing, they shower him with the fragrant roses which announce he is free to enter Paradise.

*Sang-Po* (Vienna, 1925) by R. Tlascal, book by Burgsun, a modern score based on authentic Chinese themes, is the tale of a Chinese Don Juan, Sang-Po, whose Lu-Lien-Yang, wooed with flute music and oriental pearls, is stabbed in her lover's arms (he escapes through a side door) by her husband. When her seducer's prayer draws Lu-Lien-Yang's soul from the sacred altar flame, he approaches the beloved shade only to be strangled by an invisible fist. Lu-Lien's poetic melodies and an allegorical ballet stand out. *La danse pendant le festin* (*The Dance during the Banquet*, Paris, 1925) by M. F. Gaillard, outstanding the old Spanish romance, "The Cowgirl of Finojosa," and a virile final Fandango, presents an eighteenth century Don Juan, the Prince of Mora, who casts off the singer Catalina for the dancer Hermosa over his wine. Catalina induces Chicot the jester to drop poison into the glass which Hermosa drinks and rejoices to see her fall as though lightning-struck when she drains it.

Byron's *Don Juan*, a London lady-killer of Regency days, has nothing in common with the hero of medieval legend but morals and name. Aside from Pushkin's "Onegin," which Byron's poem is said to have inspired and which Tschaikowsky has set, he is responsible for a major opera by a Bohemian composer.

## "HEDY"

ZDENKO FIBICH. Book after Byron's *Don Juan* (Prague, 1896). The score has been called "a mixture of *Tristan*, *Walküre* and French robber-opera romanticism."

On a lovely isle of Greece, in the first years of the eighteenth century, the breeze ruffles lucent waters beneath blue Levantine skies. Hardy pirates sing as they embark while Lambro, their captain, bids his daughter Haidee receive no guest during his absence. Yet no sooner is he gone than the girl finds Don Juan, whom the waves have cast on the sand, and with the aid of Zoë, her confidant, carries him to a grotto despite her father's command.

There Don Juan loses his heart to the lovely island girl and she to him. Their Love Duet is interrupted by Zoë's news that Lambro is drowned and Haidee gives way to her grief.

Yet youth cannot forever grieve. Pantomime and Ballet celebrate the wedding of Haidee and Don Juan (the girl has made her father's retainers accept her lover) until Lambro appears. Amid cries and confusion (pages worthy of the great classic oratorios as regards the noble order of the choral masses) Don Juan is dragged off in chains, despite Haidee's protests that he is her husband.

By Ægean waters Haidee wanders white sands in despair. The pirates drag on Don Juan in chains and Haidee flings her arms around him. But Lambro appears, thrusts her away, and orders the captive carried to the boat. When the bark holding her lover has vanished Haidee regains consciousness, and plunges the dagger into her breast, while out at sea a young fisherman sings happily as he casts his net.

In *Haydée ou le secret* (Paris, 1847) by Auber, Raphaela's Air (Act II), and the Barcarolle "C'est la corvette," with sailors' humming chorus, stand out. *Volna* (*The Wave*, orchestral numbers performed by Moscow Symphonic Society, 1905) by Paul Blaramberg, a two-act operatic idyl, is a setting of the love episode of Haidee and Don Juan after the sea has cast him "half-senseless" at her feet. A melodious score, it consists of duets, trios, and Greek island dances; its "languorous Levantine atmosphere" reflecting the composer's years in the Crimea.

## 14. *Bluebeard*

All Bluebeard stories, including the famous fairy tale, are based on legends crystallizing about a historic character. Gilles de Rais was a Breton noble, a famous soldier and knight, companion-at-arms of Joan of Arc, lord of wide domains and Gothic castles. Art fancier and music lover he also was a murderer, who celebrated black masses on the bodies of innocent children he tortured to death with sadistic ingenuity. He was strangled, then burned at the stake in Nantes, 1420, for his crimes. Grétry's *Barbe-bleue* (Paris, 1789), Lemaire's *Barbe-bleue* (Paris, 1894), and Rossini's *Le Comte Ory* (Paris, 1828), whose Scribe libretto makes its hero a Picard instead of a Breton monster, are tragic operas. *Barbe-bleue* (Paris, 1886) by Jacques Offenbach is a parody on medieval romanticism, and royalist lickspittling. In a plot with many entanglements—in a happy scene (Act II) Popolani, Bluebeard's alchemist, who has not poisoned his master's wives but given them a sleeping potion, presses a button, and the family tomb opens, disclosing a luxurious apartment in which the present wife's predecessors welcome the latest arrival—it turns out that Bluebeard's six previous marriages are legally invalid, and that Boulotte, his last, is his only true spouse. Contrary to the light-hearted concept of the fun-maker of the Second Empire, more modern opera developments of the legend are serious and symbolical. Aside from the Bohemian Nesvadba's *Blaubart* (Prague, 1844), they include three outstanding modern scores.

## "ARIANE ET BARBE-BLEUE"

### (*Ariadne and Bluebeard*)

PAUL DUKAS. An allegorical French opera (Paris, 1907). Maurice Maeterlinck's libretto makes Ariadne, mystical protagonist of women's rights in Bluebeard's harem, assert her independence and cast off her husband, in a medieval French chateau. The pearls with which the wives too slavish to leave Bluebeard deck themselves stand for tears they will shed in the future. The music is modernist, individual, rich in color ("Jewel Music," etc.) and orchestra and recitative preponderate.

A coach has brought lovely Ariadne to her husband's home, amid rustic warnings that her five predecessors have disappeared. Closing the door on the laments of twenty suitors, Ariadne enters. Bluebeard has given her six silver keys—these she may use—and a gold key whose use is forbidden. Her nurse opens the six doors. Showers of amethysts, sapphires, pearls, emeralds, rubies and diamonds pour out. Ariadne opens the forbidden seventh door—the wailing of women sounds in the darkness!

In a dungeon (Act II) Ariadne discovers the five daughters of Orlamund, Selysette, Ygraine, Mélisande, Bellangère and Alladine. Timid children of tradition, they respond to Ariadne's caresses, and when they confess to a prison routine of tears and prayers, Ariadne says spring glorifies the outer world. Though her lamp goes out, she drags the timid ones over the rocks to a door which floods the cavern with sunshine, and the freed wives greet flowers and trees with cries of delight.

In the castle the five wives adorn themselves with the jewels the nurse has found. Bluebeard is brought in—the peasants have attacked his coach and wounded him—and laid bound at Ariadne's feet. The peasants dismissed, the wives tend him; Ariadne binding his wounds in matter-of-fact fashion, but when he tries to detain her, she refuses to stay. Bluebeard's other wives, more conventional, refuse to leave the monster, so Ariadne the individualist bids them farewell to seek the wider freedom.

## "RITTER BLAUBART"

### (*Knight Bluebeard*)

EMIL NIKOLAUS REZNIČEK. Book by Eulenberg (Berlin, 1918). A score "that runs the gamut of lyric beauty and sadistic savagery" or, as another critic sees it, that "is music equally cheap and shallow." The key to the forbidden chamber becomes a symbol, Bluebeard "a clinical hero," hereditary madman and degenerate, interpreted as a psychoanalytical "subject."

Bluebeard's wife abducted by his best friend, he mistrusts women. When the successors of his first spouse fail to stand the acid test of the key, he murders them, aided by his servant Joshua, blinded as a child to serve as tool but not witness of his crimes. In a vault Bluebeard talks to the heads of his five wives, recalling tender moments of their love-life in common, and cursing himself in a climax of horror. Judith is Bluebeard's last matrimonial venture. As she lies coffined he lays hand on her sister Agnes hoping he has found a woman whose love will redeem him. But Agnes, filled with horror, casts herself into the flames of the castle which Joshua has set afire, and Bluebeard, despairing of life and salvation follows her and dies in "the cleansing flames."

### "KNIGHT BLUEBEARD'S CASTLE"

BELA BARTÓK. Book by Salasz (Budapest, 1921). A one-act score with two characters, Bluebeard and his wife Judith. The other wives enter but are mute. Bluebeard's sad fate is never to know true love, or find a life companion who will trust him. The score, ultra-modern, laconic, and pregnant with serious beauty, has been termed "one of the most significant achievements of modern music."

In Bluebeard's castle, Judith opens locked doors, disclosing a torture chamber, an armory, rooms heaped with gold and jewels, a garden, a vista of distant hills—and a dead, silent pool whose waters are tears. Racks and weapons, gold and gems, flowers and countryside seem tainted with blood. Before the seventh door Judith cries: "Open! Within, bathed in blood, lie the wives you wedded before we met!" But the opened door shows no shambles. Three women step through, and Bluebeard reveres them as the queens of Dawn, Sunshine, and Twilight, whose love has given him riches and power. When Judith envies their beauty, he hangs a dark cloak about her shoulders. "You shall be queen of the Night," he cries, "the glory, sadness, and sweetness of night shall be yours!" Judith answers "Not that, spare me!" but finally yields and follows the others through the seventh door. It closes behind her and Bluebeard standing without sighs, "Alone forever . . . and of all you were the loveliest!"

### 15. *Byzantium*

The Roman Empire of the East—from Justinian (527 A.D.) to the fall of Constantinople (1453 A.D.)—supplies the historic background for some interesting operas. The taking of Constantinople by the Turks and the dispersal of the ancient classic manuscripts throughout Western Europe played a definite part in the ushering in of the Age of the Renaissance which marked the end of the Middle Ages. *Belisario* (Venice, 1836) by Donizetti exploits Justinian's famous general. Crowds acclaim him in Byzantium's streets, but at home his wife Antonia, as wives will, thinks the worst. A dying slave claims Belisarius had him abandon her babe on a savage shore; in revenge Antonia accuses him of high treason. Justinian, letting him free his captive Alamir, hurries the hero to prison. Belisarius blinded and released as harmless, Irene leads him off in search of refuge. Alamir, heading the Alanae host against Byzantium, meets them. An amulet identifies him as the blind man's son and, abandoning his army, he hastens with father and sister to the Greeks. Belisarius leads them to victory, and Antonia having confessed her perjury, he is carried into the palace to die in the odor of heroism. *Théodora* (Paris, 1906) by Xavier Leroux is an opera devoted to Justinian's infamous empress and Antonia's friend, melodramatic and spectacular. In *Byzanz* (Leipzig, 1922) by Paul Graener, book by Anthes, the Byzantine Emperor Alexios is the leading figure in the tale which develops the contrast between pagan and Christian ideals. The culminating dramatic moments of the opera are the compelling "Bacchanale" (Ballet) and Alexios' "Renunciation." Graener, a master of counterpoint, instrumental and vocal, achieves ultramodern effects by the use of "symphonic theme" development.

*Sonnenflammen* (*Sunflames*, Nuremberg, 1920) by Siegfried Wagner, based on German folk melodies, its title motivated by the fact that "Fridolin *singes* himself in Iris' glowing eyes," takes the Frankish knight Fridolin, returning from a pilgrimage to Jerusalem to atone for the murder of his wife's lover, to Byzantium to become Emperor Alexios' rival for the favor of Iris, the court jester's daughter. Condemned to death for encouraging the ruler's murder, fear makes Fridolin become Alexios' court fool, and commit suicide when his father appears to curse his degenerate son. He dies in Iris' arms, whose heart his "brave deed" has captured, while Frankish knights storm the city and end Alexios' reign.

*Le juif errant* (*The Wandering Jew*, Paris, 1852) by Halévy is a Scribe variant of one of the great folk legends of the Middle Ages, localizing Ahasuerus unredeemed amid Byzantine court intrigues. The Wandering Jew, good angel of Irene of Flanders, makes her Empress of Constantinople (1190) and saves the life of her lover Leon, only to see a vision of the Judgment Day and be told to resume his weary round. In this work sax-tubas were for the first time used in the opera orchestra. There is a "Bee Ballet," a scene on Bosphorus' banks where "the trombone's voice is more effective than the singer's," a famous bass song, "De la clémence eternelle," and the "Divine Curse," expressed by an orchestra playing in diatonic progression to which an off-stage military band replies. Victor Kozhunsky also wrote a "Wandering Jew," *Der ewige Jude* (Warsaw, 1842).

*Maometta II* (Naples, 1820; as *Le siège de Corinth*, Paris 1826) by Rossini, a dramatic earlier work, deals with the Byzantine defense of Corinth against the Turkish Sultan (1457), and climaxes in the betrothal of the young hero Neokles to his leader Kleomenes' daughter Pamyra, and the blowing sky-high of the terrible Turk as he leads his hordes to the capture of the women of the town. Mahomet II may have been "blown up" in his harem on occasion, but never in Corinth. "In 1481, the Sultan was thought to be projecting a campaign against the rulers of Syria and Egypt when he died at Gebzah" (Gibbs). Other settings are *Maometta II* (Milan, 1817) by von Winter, and *Maometta II* (Venice, 1892) by Lorenzi-Fabbri.

# CHAPTER VI

## THE RENAISSANCE AND THE REFORMATION

### 1. *The Italian Renaissance*

The Italian Renaissance is an age of cruelty, passion, ecstasy, and grotesque contradiction.  Yet its dark clouds have the silver lining of Art's smile and despite ugliness and cruelty, beauty is its heart's dream.  Among the great cities of the Italian Renaissance Florence, where four generations of Medici princes devoted themselves to the cult of the arts, comes first.  It supplies a splendid, colorful background for some of opera's most thrilling tales.

#### FLORENCE

*I Medici* (Milan, 1893) by Ruggiero Leoncavallo, the only score performed of the trilogy *Crespuculum* (*Twilight*—the twilight of the old, greater Italy) including *I Medici, Girolamo Savonarola* and *Cesare Borgia*.  Though dramatically weak, charming dance music (Act II) and lovely lyric pages; Fioretta's "Monologue," Simonetta's "Death Scene" (Act III) and Fioretta's "Prayer" (Act IV), deserve mention.  Blonde Simonetta rejects the libertine advances of the papal captain Gianbattista da Montesecco, only to yield to Giuliano di Medici's passion in the forest.  From an improvised song and dance festival in the streets (Act II) the consumptive girl is borne home, blood gushing from her mouth, while Giuliano betrays her with her friend Fioretta in the shadows.  Simonetta at her window (Act III) overhears conspirators fix the hour of the Medicis' assassination.  Speeding breathless to Fioretta's house she finds her lover in the arms of her friend and gasps out her life in the cry: "To-morrow, the Medici!"  When the *Sanctus* sounds in Santa Regarata Church Giuliano is struck down by the dagger, but as Fioretta flings herself sobbing on his corpse, Lorenzo bids the Florentines remember he still rules.  Halévy's *Cosme de Médicis* (Paris, 1837), Combi's *Cosimo di Medici* (Padua, 1840), Louis Piccini's *Elisa Valasco* (Rome, 1854), Roberto's *Lorenzino di Medici* (Turin, 1849), and Poniatowski's *Pier di Medici* (Paris, 1860) are other Medici operas.  Ernest Moret's *Lorenzaccio* (Paris,

1924) after de Musset, has been praised as a modern lyric score of genuine sincerity and beauty.

## "MONA LISA"

MAX SCHILLINGS. Book by Beatrice Dovsky (Stuttgart, 1915; New York, 1923). A triangle tragedy in a Renaissance setting, its heroine the original of Da Vinci's "Mona Lisa" portrait of the enigmatic smile. In music "whose echoed song seems to shimmer through mystic stained-glass windows of old" (Bie), the "Scene of the Pearls" stands out.

(Prologue), a lay monk of the Certosa order, Florence, shows two tourists, an elderly husband and young wife, through the historic mansion once the pearl merchant Francesco del Giocondo's home. When he begins the tragic tale of Giocondo's wife, Mona Lisa, the stage darkens, then as the light returns, the story is enacted in its olden setting.

Friends make merry over wine in Giocondo's home, and when an encounter between the Carnival crowd and Savonarola's monks in the streets without has driven lovely Ginevra, scantily draped as the Venus of the gay procession, to take refuge within, Mona Lisa enters. Her jealous husband glooms and curses the baffling smile, whose secret is still a riddle on Vinci's canvas. When Giovanni Salviato arrives, sent by the Pope to buy a great pink pearl, Giocondo opens the double doors of his jewel closet and shows his guests the lustrous gems in the casket he draws up by windlass from its resting place on the bed of the Arno, flowing beneath the house. When his friends go and he is locking up he glimpses Salviato, who has returned—Mona Lisa is his lost love, married off by her parents during his absence from Rome—and after Mona Lisa has promised to fly with him, Giocondo so maneuvers that she hides her lover in the jewel closet. He locks it and after a cruel, sinister scene of pretended love for his wife while Salviato is strangling, flings into the Arno the key for which she begs, clutching her madly to his breast as the curtain falls.

Waking in the gray dawn of Ash Wednesday, Mona Lisa after a moment despairingly beats on the door which hides her dead lover. Then, just as she has snatched the key—it fell into a boat moored beneath the window and not into the stream—from her stepdaughter Dianora, who has found it, Giocondo returns. Cunningly she leaves him uncertain whether Salviato has or has not escaped—showing him the key—and when he unlocks the closet, a demoniac suggestion makes him leap in. Slamming the outer door and locking it on him with a scream of maniac joy, Mona Lisa glories in the knowledge that he will suffer as her Giovanni did.

As her voice dies away (Epilogue) and the scene reverts to reality, the husband reproves his young wife's sigh for the "unfortunate" woman as she leaves money for masses for her soul and the monk, when she drops a spray of white iris at his feet, cries, "Temptress! Mona Lisa!" as the curtain falls.

## "I COMPAGNACCI"

### (*The Bad Fellows*)

PRIMO RICCITELLI. Book by Forzano (Rome, 1923; New York, 1924). Fluent lyric melody is the feature of a colorful score by a pupil of Mascagni. The Love Duet between Anna Maria and Baldo, "Quanto ho sofferto," stands out; the liturgic note is effectively introduced in the Latin chant of the Friars.

In Renaissance Florence (1498) *I Compagnacci* "the bad fellows" or "evil comrades" were the gay youths about town who preferred wine, women and song to the Puritan virtues of Savonarola and the Friars of San Marco. Pope Alexander VI, one in spirit with the younger set of Florence, lays a trap for the reformer monk: a friar minorite and a monk of San Marco shall walk into a great fire, God to judge between them. The plot turns on this ordeal by fire.

Bernardo, a Savonarolist, insists his pretty niece, Anna Maria, marry old Noferi, a gloomy pietist, though she loves Baldo, leader of the *Compagnacci*. Savonarola's "Band of Children"—little ones the reformer has loot Florence homes of worldly books, paintings, masks, lutes, and ribbons for public burning—sent by Bernardo to Anna Maria's room, return with flowers, dresses and Baldo's love letter promising to rescue his sweetheart. But while Bernardo hurries the preparations for the girl's wedding Baldo and his comrades enter the house through the chimney. So sure is Bernardo that Savonarola's champion will walk through the flames that he makes a wager with Baldo. If the monk walks into the flames Baldo's estates go to Bernardo. If the monk does not dare the ordeal, Baldo gains Anna Maria's hand. With breathless anxiety all follow the course of events but in the end no friar dares the flames. They are put out by a sudden burst of rain and while the disappointed crowd howls down all monks, skies clear and golden sunshine smiles on the happy lovers whom the *Compagnacci* shower with flowers.

*Savonarola* (London, 1884) by Charles Villiers Stanford (noble Prologue) tells the tale of Savonarola's love for Clarice, her marriage to another, and his resolve to forego the world—which eventually led to his burning alive at the stake. In *Das Bildnis der Madonna* (*The Madonna's Likeness,* Vienna, 1925) by Marco Frank, book by Ring, "illustrative music," reminiscent of Strauss and Puccini, shows the painter Lorenzo, finding a perfect model for his Madonna (for the altar of Santa Maria del Fiore in Florence) in Beatrice, lovely wife of Captain Ridolfi. But Lorenzo forgets divine striving for earthly passion (Act II) and is surprised by Ridolfi. When the soldier strikes Lorenzo's sword from his hand, Beatrice picks it up and kills her husband, then drowns herself in a well, while Lorenzo finds solace in prayer.

## "EINE FLORENTINISCHE TRAGÖDIE"

### (*A Florentine Tragedy*)

ALEXANDER VON ZEMLINSKY. Book after Oscar Wilde's drama (Vienna, 1917). An impressionistic, polyphonic score, the "Love Scene" and "Spinning Music" standing out.

Simone, a rich merchant, finds Prince Guido of Florence with his wife Bianca. Hatred in his heart, he unrolls a bale of splendid stuffs and when Guido agrees to pay one hundred thousand gold ducats for his silks and brocades, Simone sardonically puts all in his house at the latter's disposal. "Suppose I ask for your white-armed Bianca?" jests the Prince. Simone smiles and, inwardly furious, leads the two to think him unsuspicious. When he sees Guido's lips touch the rim of the glass where Bianca's have rested, however, he hastens into the moonlit garden to hide his rage. Returning he finds the lovers in each others' arms. Rapiers are drawn. Bianca, holding up a torch, pants to Guido "Kill him, kill him!" But Simone's rusty sword strikes Guido's Toledan blade from his hand. Bianca flings down her torch as the enemies draw their daggers, moaning to her lover, "Kill him!" But Simone slays Guido in the darkness. Then Bianca—a Renaissance wife—stares at her husband with admiration. "Why not tell me you were so strong?" she asks. "Why not tell me you were so beautiful?" Simone answers, gathering her in his arms.

*Mandragola* (Charlottenburg, 1914; New York, 1925) by Ignaz Waghalter, book by Eger, based on the Florentine Machiavelli's comedy—a symphonic Prelude (Act III) stands out—expresses, like Strauss in *Feuersnot,* a supposed physician's course of treatment. Pandolfo, old, rich, and married to Beatrice, a young wife, yearns for a son. Doctor Dromis smuggles handsome young Florio into Pandolfo's home as a physician to administer the magic herb *mandragola,* which will achieve the desired result. Beatrice, coy at first, yields to Florio, and all, including Pandolfo, are happy.

## "GUIDO ET GINEVRA OU LA PESTE À FLORENCE"

### (*Guido and Ginevra or the Plague in Florence*)

LUDOVIC HALÉVY. Book by Scribe (Paris, 1838). A melodious older score with fine airs: "Quand renaitra la pale aurore," "written with tears"; "Sa main fermera ma paupière"; and the final trio, "Ma fille, à mon amour ravie."

Ginevra, daughter of Cosimo di Medici, has fainted on touching a poisoned scarf when about to be married to the Duke of Ferrara. Thought to have died of the plague, the requiem mass is said for her and her corpse laid in the cathedral vault. Guido, a young sculptor who loves her and whom she loves, is driven out by the sexton when he enters to pray beside her body. As the midnight chime peals Ginevra wakes from her trance and rises from her bier in her winding sheet. The soldiers sent to guard her tomb flee, thinking her a ghost and she walks the streets of the plague-stricken city inspiring terror wherever she goes till she finds her lover. Even Guido takes her for a phantom, but does not dread the ghost of the one dearest to him on earth (Berlioz calls Guido's song, "Ombre chérie," the loveliest in the score), and when he finds her living flesh and blood his happiness is crowned by Cosimo di Medici who, in his joy at regaining his daughter, lets her marry her humble lover.

*Mathilde* (Paris, 1821-3) by Michele Carafa, Prince of Colobrano, very popular in its day, has the supposedly dead Mathilde, when she leaves her burial vault, driven off by her terrified husband Francesco into her lover Antonio's arms, and the Archbishop of Florence, "a true descendant of the apostles," severs the legally dead woman from her living husband, and marries her to her old sweetheart.

## "LA CENA DELLE BEFFE"

### (*The Jest*)

UMBERTO GIORDANO. Book after Sem Benelli's play (Milan, 1925). The Renaissance Florence of Duke Lorenzo the Magnificent where the mad and merry society of the time gave the name *beffe* to practical jokes and jokers (the title of the opera is literally *The Supper of the Jesters*) is the scene of action. A vividly dramatic action almost turns the music into decorative background, and though the statement that "no principal sings a song so beautiful it is worth remembering for its own sake" (Herbert Hughes) is open to question, the dramatic vitality of the score lends it a breathless interest.

Giannetto, poet and painter, has been from school days butt of the Chiaramentesi brothers, Gabriello and Neri, swaggering captain of mercenaries. Neri, when Giannetto was about to marry pretty Ginevra, bought her of her fishmonger father for fifty ducats to keep as his paramour. When the brothers fling him into the Arno, after tattooing his skin with their dagger points, Giannetto turns, vows revenge, and swears he will "jest" with them for a change. At a supper (the *cena*) in Tornaquinci's house, he bedevils drunken Neri until the latter staggers out to tweak old Ceccherino's nose, as he sits in his wine shop. Then Giannetto sends his servant Fazio in advance of Neri to tell the folk in the wine shop Neri has gone mad, and is headed that way swearing he will turn it into a slaughterhouse. As Neri leaves Giannetto abstracts his housekey.

The following morning Ginevra hears Neri lies bound in the wine shop he has wrecked. But—Neri came home as usual in his green cloak and spent the night with her! On investigation Ginevra finds Giannetto had taken Neri's place. When the escaped Captain, frantic with rage, breaks into the house Giannetto taunts him behind the locked door of Ginevra's room till the Medici's soldiers recapture and hurry him away.

In prison, Neri in his rage bites Giannetto's hand when the latter offers to have him released if he will kiss it. When Giannetto lets in three women whom Neri has cast on the street, Lucrezia forgives her betrayer. Fiametta who wants to put out his eyes with her silver hairpin, is pushed from the room by Lisabetta, who still loves her seducer and leads him from prison when Giannetto finally releases him. The Captain departs, vowing revenge.

As Ginevra talks with her tirewoman in the moonlight, Neri vaults through the window (an effective off-stage "Serenade" is sung by one of Ginevra's admirers in the street) and, threatening her with death if she betray his presence, hides, awaiting Giannetto's coming. A red-cloaked figure—Giannetto wears a red cloak—enters, glides to Ginevra's room, closes the door. Neri, rapier in hand, follows. Then Ginevra rushes screaming from her chamber, after her Neri, gasping, "At last!" But Giannetto, who for that night had yielded his place to Neri's brother Gabriello, stands smiling against the opposite wall. As the climax of his "jest" Giannetto has made Neri kill his own brother—and tells him so. Neri goes mad while Giannetto, overcome with horror, prays.

*Ghitana* (Cologne, 1901) by Max Oberleithner, book by Von Wildenrath—the symphonic Preludes, "Prayer to the Madonna," and Love Scene (Act III) stand out—shows Fra Lippo Lippi (1406-1469), butcher's son, Carmelite monk, and painter (he has cast off his old sweetheart, the Marchesa Ghitana) painting a Madonna in a convent garden, innocent Lucrezia the novice his model. Soon dropping his brush, Fra Lippo's kisses win the girl's consent to flight, but her father finds them locked in each other's arms and the painter is cast into jail. There (Act IV) when he refuses Ghitana's advances, the revengeful Marchioness induces him to drain a glass of poisoned wine. Too late Lucrezia, whose father has promised to let her marry Lippo, hurries in: the painter monk is dead, together with Ghitana, who has shared the poison to die with him. The "Holy Brother Giovanni Angelico of Fiesole" (d. 1455), a monk, who painted saints and angels against backgrounds of golden glory offers a notable contrast to unholy Fra Lippo Lippi.

FIESOLE

## "FRA ANGELICO"

PAUL AND LUCIEN HILLEMACHER. Book by Vaucaire (Paris, 1924). A score of lyric charm which evokes the atmosphere of its archaic time and points the contrast between earthly passion and divine love.

Fra Angelico, painting angels in the blue on convent walls, quiets his child models by singing the "Legend of the Virgin and the Gypsy" (a happy melodic page) in which the gypsy leads the Virgin safely through Bethlehem gates, guarded by Herod's soldiers, the Christ Child hidden in her bag. Then comes Catarina. Once she was an innocent girl, Fra Angelico's playmate catching butterflies. But work as an artists' model in Florence prepared her to become the light-o'-love of Lorenzino Ubaldini, lord of thirty castles, fighting in the war between Pisa and Milan. Fra Angelico refuses to listen to the chronicle of Catarina's love-life, but agrees to pray for her lover. As Catarina carries votive flowers into the church Cecilia, Lorenzino's mother enters. Her son has been slain in battle and she, too, begs Fra Angelico's prayers. Catarina, leaving as Cecilia enters the church, learns the truth. The nuns hasten up at her cry of anguish and she begs to be taken into the fold. Cecilia, her prayers said, comes out of church and, struck by the celestial loveliness of Catarina's transfigured countenance as she stands garbed in the robe of the order asks her to pray for her dead boy, while Fra Angelico, begging the Virgin to guide his brush, begins to limn her face on the convent wall.

### FERRARA

### "LUCREZIA BORGIA"

GAETANO DONIZETTI. Book by Romani ('Milan, 1834), after Victor Hugo's drama, shares with *Lucia* the honor of being the composer's greatest score. Known as *"the* poison opera," some extol the vibrant passion of its melodies ("Paul Veronese in music") while others call its tragedy superficial and deny its songs "the naïve and living charm of Bellini's airs." Favorites among them are: the Prologue, the *Brindisi* (Drinking Song), the Romance "Softly in slumber," and the Cavatina "Haste thee, for vengeance."

From her ducal palace in Ferrara Lucrezia hastens to Venice. There she finds Gennaro, offspring of an early *amour* (brought up a fisher boy he has risen to officer rank in the Venetian service), sleeping on a stone bench before a palace in which he has been reveling. After he has told the masked lady who has roused him the story of his life his friends appear, and Orsini tears off Lucrezia's mask and curses her for a Borgia, since all present have lost a loved one owing to her toxicological skill. When her boy turns from her with loathing his mother faints, for in his case the pitiless poisoner wears her heart on her sleeve.

Gennaro, hastening to Ferrara, tears his mother's coat of arms from the palace gate. Not knowing the offender's identity Lucrezia complains to Duke Alfonso and too late, Gennaro condemned to die, begs he be pardoned. But jealous Alfonso (her fifth husband) himself hands Gennaro the poison cup which he drains. Only the antidote his mother slips him as they walk to the door while she begs him to leave town, preserves his life.

But he has promised to attend Prince Negroni's banquet that night. There Lucrezia has assembled Gennaro's Venetian friends, and prepared the wine. All have quaffed the fatal bowl. Refusing Lucrezia's proffered antidote Gennaro prefers death to such a mother and when Alfonso enters he finds only corpses. Lucrezia, poisoned by remorse, has joined her victims.

In *Le duc de Ferrare* (Paris, 1899) by Georges Marty, a theatric score welding the styles of Wagner and Massenet, a white-haired Duke of Ferrara finds his girl-wife in the arms of his son, and so arranges that the youth, thinking to slay an assassin, kills his love with his own hand.

## PADUA, PISA, BOLOGNA, URBINO, MILAN

*Der Improvisator* (Berlin, 1902) by Eugen d'Albert, book by Kastrepp, is the rhapsodist and singer Cassio Belloni, really Count d'Arco, who (1540) escapes prison to reënter Padua as the newly appointed governor and win the hand of his lady love. *The Garden of Mystery* (New York, 1925) by Charles Wakefield Cadman, book by Nelle Richmond Eberhardt is after Nathaniel Hawthorne's "Rappacini's Daughter." A modernist opera with expressive vocal parts superimposed on an interestingly dissonant symphonic score. Dr. Rappacini of Padua (16th century) delver in Nature's secrets, has reared his daughter Beatrice in a garden of venomous plants. Permeated with their subtle poisons her very breath slays. The student Giovanni falls in love with the charming menace but about to clasp her in his arms she leaps back, remembering her kiss is death. As horrified Giovanni flees, Poison Elementals (Ballet) weave ghastly rounds above dying flowers. Procuring an antidote Giovanni then bids his love drink; but the antidote, while destroying the poison destroys Beatrice and she dies begging Giovanni to leave the Garden of Death and find another love.

## "MONNA VANNA"

HENRI FÉVRIER. Book by Maeterlinck (Paris, 1909). A fine score influenced by Massenet. An earlier setting of the same tale is that by the Hungarian Abranyi, *Monna Vanna* (Budapest, 1907).

Pisa, besieged by the Florentines in the 1490's is about to fall when Prinzivalle, the Florentine captain, says he will raise the siege if Monna Vanna, Guido Colonna's lovely wife, will spend a night in his tent. Guido raises violent objections, but Monna Vanna is ready to make the sacrifice.

Prinzivalle and Monna Vanna were childhood playmates. When she enters his tent he sends food to the starving children of Pisa and then pours out his tale of love. Monna Vanna, unmoved by his eloquence, is too noble to break the vow she made at the altar. Then Prinzivalle learns commissioners sent by Florence are on their way to arrest him for sparing the enemy town. He accepts Monna Vanna's invitation to take refuge in Pisa.

Guido, hearing the cheers of the Pisans as their savior enters, refuses to believe his wife innocent and has Prinzivalle cast into a dungeon. Monna Vanna pretends he has wronged her, and feigning hatred obtains the key to the prison cell from Guido. Then—for the contrast between her husband's petty jealousy and Prinzivalle's generosity of spirit is too great—she opens the prison door in order to pass with her lover into a newer and happier life.

In *La reine Fiamette* (Paris, 1904) by Xavier Leroux, book by Mendès, written with theatric effect in Massenet's style, Cardinal Sforza, in a Renaissance "kingdom of Bologna," is eager to rid himself of "Queen" Fiamette. By saying Fiamette had Danielo's brother slain, he induces young Danielo to promise to ply the dagger. Fiamette's real name is Orlanda, but Danielo learns to love her as "Hélène" in a convent where they foregather and, after golden hours spent in her castle in the hills, hurries to Bologna on the fatal day, and, raising his dagger, realizes he was about to murder the idol of his heart. He is condemned to death, and Fiamette casts away the pearls of her diadem in a vain effort to save him. When she whispers she never killed his brother, Danielo unsuccessfully tries to kill the Cardinal before, at his command, they are eternally united by the same ax. *Duke or Devil* (Manchester, 1909) by Nicholas Gatty, a melodious modern score, tells of a Renaissance Duke of Bologna who, on his way to his city after years of absence, is mistaken for the Devil by ignorant rustics incited by a village priest, and is rescued as he, together with the poor lovers, Pietro and Bianca, who took his part, are about to suffer the ordeal of fire. The curtain falls on the Duke cursing the groveling priest and villagers like the Devil. *Raffaelo di Urbino e la Fornarina* (Barcelona, 1886) by Paolo Mazzi tells the love story of the painter Raphael of Urbino, in which town his boyhood was passed. *Nachts sind alle Katzen grau (At Night All Cats Are Gray,* Zurich, 1925) by Pierre Maurice after Bandello's fifteenth century tale, is a score rich in Italianate melody. Each of two graceless husbands pursues the other's wife till the indignant women, remembering that "At night all cats are gray," pretend each to be the other and shaming their husbands restore them to reason. *Lombardische Schule (The Lombard School,* Nuremberg, 1921) by Leo Kähler tells of an old Renaissance husband who, finding his wife has betrayed him during his absence, gives her lover, a young painter, a day's grace to finish the Madonna for which his wife supplied the model, then kills him.

## MANTUA

### "RIGOLETTO"

GIUSEPPE VERDI. Book by Piave (Venice, 1851), after Victor Hugo's drama, *Le roi s'amuse*. This score (also, known as *La Maledizione, Viscardello, Clara di Pert and Lionello*) precedes *Trovatore* and introduces Verdi's most brilliant creative period. The tale of the court jester who falls into the pit he has dug for his daughter's betrayer (Francis I of France is transformed into a Duke of Mantua) has real human interest. The tenor air "La donna è mobile," sung by the Duke (one of the great Caruso rôles) is a favorite; Gilda's soprano *coloratura* aria the outstanding bravura number; the famous Quartet, with its individual musical characterization, "one of the great art-works of Italian operatic tradition."

Mantua's duke is a Don Juan; his court a place of debauchery. Rigoletto, humpbacked court jester, panders to his master's depravity; suggests that Ceprano, whose wife he loves, be made away with; and insults Monterone, whose daughter the Duke has ruined. Knowing well his Duke, he keeps his own daughter Gilda hidden in a far quarter of town, her existence unknown. As Monterone is led to prison he curses fool and master. (Change of scene.) Gilda leaves her home only to visit a near-by church. Alas, there she meets, loves, and admits to her home a supposed student (the Duke in disguise). The courtiers who have suffered from Rigoletto's jibes, discover the house he visits. Sure its occupant is his mistress they plan to abduct her. Near his home the jester falls in with them. They blindfold him and, thinking Ceprano's wife is being carried off, he holds the ladder while his own child is dragged to the ducal palace!

When next the Duke seeks Gilda he finds an empty house, but when the laughing courtiers tell their tale he hastens to the girl—and gives orders that he be not disturbed. In vain the despairing father kneels before the locked door (he has admitted the girl is his child), pleading madly with his master to forbear. When the door opens and Gilda rushes into his arms, Rigoletto clasps the poor betrayed creature to his breast, vowing vengeance on her deceiver, whom she loves.

Monterone's curse now moves to tragic fulfillment. In vain Rigoletto lets Gilda witness the Duke's ardent attentions to the strumpet Maddalena, the *bravo* Sparafucile's sister, his latest flame. She still loves her seducer. After the Duke's departure Rigoletto pays the ruffian to murder him, having sent his daughter home to prepare for their flight from the city. Gilda, storm-driven, returns to the *bravo's* den for shelter, and hears the sister beg her brother to spare the Duke. Sparafucile refuses: his dagger stroke has been bought and paid for. Suddenly the door opens, and the *bravo*, mistaking Gilda, disguised as a youth—intent on saving her ducal seducer—for his appointed victim, strikes her down. When Rigoletto arrives, his heart swelling with gratified revenge, he is given the body wrapped in a sack. As he drags it from the house to cast into the river, he suddenly hears the Duke's carefree voice raised in a merry song, "La donna è mobile" (*Woman is changeable*), tears open the sack, and recognizes his daughter. When the dying girl's last words have revealed her sacrifice he falls across her body with a cry of agony.

GENOA

## "DIE GEZEICHNETEN"

### (*The Branded*)

FRANZ SCHREKER. Book by the composer (Frankfurt am Main, 1916). The work symbolizes the tragedy of one of Nature's "branded." Cursed with a beauty-loving soul, he lacks the self-reliance to hold the love of a woman who falls victim to another's sensual longings. The pagan splendors of the Renaissance form the scenic background; and the Prelude (Act I) and orgiastic music of the Elysium Scene stand out. The score has been called "an individualist stylistic transference of Debussy and Puccini into German," its ensembles and single movements in traditional forms.

The ugly cripple Alviano has realized his longing for beauty in creating an island paradise, Elysium, in the Bay of Genoa. But the young libertines of Genoa debase the fairy isle born of his ideals, turning it into a Cytherea where, amid flowers and fountains, they celebrate orgies with wives and daughters of Genoa's burghers, snared in seduction's net. Alviano learns the vile uses to which his beautiful isle is put and presents it to the city, though blue-blooded profligates, headed by Vitelozzo Tamare protest. The Podestà of Genoa, accompanied by his daughter Carlotta, visits Alviano to thank him for the proposed gift. A painter, she asks Alviano to let her paint his portrait. Seized with sudden deep affection for the first woman to give him a kind word, he goes to her studio.

In the ducal palace Genoese senators criticize Doge Adorno's tardiness in accepting the gift (Tamare has induced him to delay); but when Tamare, entering with Adorno, reveals the secrets of Elysium's love feasts, liberal-minded Adorno is shocked (change of scene). In Carlotta's studio Alviano realizes supreme happiness. Carlotta admits she loves him! But about to clasp her he pales, confesses she is "a breakable toy," her heart weak, and that she must love delicately. Their chaste embrace is interrupted by the entrance of the Doge to sue for her hand on behalf of Tamare.

Genoa celebrates the city's taking possession of Elysium. Unrestrained license reigns (a tremendous symphonic orgy of sensual pleasure in richest pyrotechnic tone-combinations and colors, climaxing in a "Hymn to the Summer Night"). Amid the masqueraders Carlotta avoids Alviano. The elemental has wakened in the girl: she cannot resist. Eager to yield to Tamare, she follows him to the subterranean grotto. When Alviano is cheered, Doge Adorno accuses him of responsibility for the crimes committed on the isle, and Tamare's name occurring in his denunciation gives Alviano the clue to Carlotta's disappearance (change of scene). Amid faded roses Carlotta, dying, lies on a couch. Alviano curses Tamare but the latter brutally says she preferred death in his embrace to a joyless life of renunciation. Trembling with horror, Alviano stabs him to the heart. Carlotta, roused by his death cry, pushes the hunchback away in disgust. As death's skeleton fingers close on her heart she tenderly calls for Tamare, her beloved, and Alviano, stricken with insanity, staggers babbling from the grotto.

## VENICE AND NAPLES

Venice of the Renaissance, the Venice of blue lagoons and marble palaces, of the Oriental splendors of St. Marks, the Venice of Giorgione and Titian, Bellini and Veronese, is the picturesque stage for many a lesser score, among them Balfe's melodious *Bianca, or the Bravo's Bride* (London, 1860) after Lewis' *Rugantino, the Bravo of Venice,* and the *Daughter of Saint Mark* (London, 1844). More recent is *Albrecht Dürer in Venedig* (Weimar, 1901) by Waldemar von Baussners, book by Bariel. Giorgione's sweetheart Maria, dimpling at Dürer in Venice, rouses the Italian's jealousy. To humiliate the German, Giorgione comes to Dürer's studio with friends, masquerading as Doge and Patriarch of Venice, and suite. No sooner are they arrived than the real Doge and Patriarch come along; but Dürer saves the practical jokers by arranging them in a group as models for a painting he pretends to have in mind, and Giorgione is cured of jealousy. *Albrecht Dürer* (Nuremberg, 1892) by Baselt shows the artist coming to Venice (1505) with wife and niece to prosecute the Italian engraver Raimondi for making copperplates of his paintings, only to give over his suit when the Italian falls in love with his niece and marries her.

## "LA GIOCONDA"

AMILCARE PONCHIELLI. Book by Boito (Milan, 1876), after Victor Hugo's tragedy *Angelo, tyran de Padoue.* Ponchielli, in Italian musical opinion, well-nigh ranks with Verdi, by whom he was influenced. The famous aria, "Cielo e mar," is associated with Caruso's name in this country. The "Ballet of the Hours of the Night and Day" is delightful music of its kind, and the score shows "many favorable examples of Ponchielli's fondness for fanciful melodic designs" (Streatfeild).

Hugo's "Angelo" is a typical Renaissance drama, though Boito's book places the action at a later epoch.

"The Lion's Mouth." Monks, masqueraders and sailors sing (literally) the praises of the Venetian government (17th century) while Barnaba, a spy of the Council of Ten, talks of folk who dance on their graves. Barnaba loves Gioconda, a singing girl; rejected, he plans revenge. Gioconda loves Enzo Grimaldo, a Genoese noble. Alas, Enzo, she discovers, betrays her with Laura, wife of Alvise, a lay inquisitor! Barnaba almost has Gioconda's poor, blind mother, La Cieca, killed as a witch, telling the crowd that Zuane, the boatman, lost the regatta owing to her sorceries. La Cieca, rescued from the mob by the masked Laura, gives her a rosary while Barnaba, arranging a tryst between Laura and Enzo on the latter's ship, sends Laura's husband word she is eloping with the Genoese. The strains of the gay Forlana the Venetians dance while hymns echo from the church, mingle with the sobs of Gioconda, who has overheard Barnaba's plot.

"The Rosary." Enzo sings his aria "Cielo e mar" on the quarterdeck as dawn gilds the waters, and Gioconda, putting out in a boat, boards the vessel and is about to stab Laura praying in the chapel when the latter stops the blade by holding up La Cieca's rosary. As she pushes off with Laura from one side, Alvise's boat nears from the other and Enzo, rushing on deck, sets fire to his ship to destroy all evidence of his meeting with Laura.

"The House of Gold." Alvise, in rich ball dress, drawing a curtain which shows a bier, leaves the poison cup in guilty Laura's hand as Gioconda slips in and persuades her to drink a narcotic instead. The supposed corpse greets Alvise's eyes as he returns. Guests enter: the splendid ball begins (Ballet, "Dance of the Hours," in which the golden hours of day are slain in pantomime by the sable hours of night) but following La Cieca's announcement of Laura's death comes Enzo's denunciation of her husband, who draws aside the curtain and shows the horrified masqueraders the pallid corpse.

"The Orfano Canal." Laura lies unconscious in a ruined *palazzo* on the Orfano Canal, but Gioconda, about to slay her, decides on suicide for, to free imprisoned Enzo, she has promised herself to Barnaba. Enzo enters and, Laura's feeble cry calling him to her side, Gioconda veils her face to shut out their raptures. Helping them escape in a boat, she sings her great "Suicidio" aria; then, seeing Barnaba enter as she stands before a mirror, suddenly stabs herself. Poor Barnaba, ever foiled! Even his shriek into her ear that he has strangled her mother fails. Gioconda cannot hear it; she is dead. With a furious oath Barnaba rushes from the ruins.

*Violanta* (Munich, 1916) by Erich Korngold, book by Hans Müller, is a dramatic, daringly yet effectively harmonized score by the Austrian modernist. Simone Trovai, old city captain of Venice, dwells in a palace on the Giudaca Canal. Don Alfonso, the King of Naples' natural son, has seduced Nerina, sister of

Violanta, Simone's wife, and driven the girl into her grave in shame. Violanta, taking advantage of the Carnival's license and with her husband's consent makes an assignation with the royal libertine in her home. When she sings her song, Simone will fling himself on Alfonso, dagger in hand. The moon rises (Act II) and Alfonso's "Serenade" echoes from the canal. He swings across her balcony. But when he tells Violanta he loathes the life he has led, and longs for the true love she could give, she realizes she loves him. Burning kisses seal the discovery of their bliss, and as Violanta begins to sing in the ecstasy of happiness, Simone rushes in and hears his wife tell Alfonso she loves him. But Violanta's bosom catches the dagger he thrusts at Alfonso and with her dying breath she thanks him for coming in time to save her honor. Other operas that may be mentioned are Thermion's *San Marco* (Venice, 1908), Waagenar's *Doge de Venedie* (Utrecht, 1904), Davico's *Dogaressa* (Monte Carlo, 1920), and Francesco Malipiero's *Sogno d'un tramonto d'autumno* (*An Autumn Afternoon's Dream*), an ultramodernist opera after a D'Annunzio poem, calling up orchestrally "the soul of the dead Venice of the Renaissance as it triumphed in Veronese's paintings," its chief dramatic figure the Dogaressa Grandeniga, and the outstanding musical page the "Scene of the Burning Ships."

*Giovanna II, regina di Napoli* (Milan, 1840), by C. Cocchia, and *Giovanna II, regina di Napoli* (Naples, 1869), by Petrella, are facile, old-style melodious scores throwing the gloss of romance over a foolish and dissolute royal lady who cultivated boyish lovers at the age of forty-five. *Il Giuramento* (*The Oath*, Milan, 1837) by Mercadante, a sentimental opera of the same type, was once very popular. Manfredo, Duke of Syracuse, and his secretary Brunoro both love Elaisa, who prefers Viscardo, Brunoro's friend. Brunoro has the Duke surprise Viscardo with the innocent Duchess Bianca; but though the latter drains a narcotic supplied by Elaisa instead of the poison cup her husband prescribes, she dies of grief on learning Viscardo has slain hapless Elaisa, thinking her at the bottom of their troubles. Viscardo beheaded, Brunoro killed in battle, only the Duke survives the other principals.

### ROME

Renaissance Rome is dominated by the artists, but, though the greatest of sculptor-sonneteers has called forth *Michel-Ange* (Paris, 1802) by Isouard, and *Michel Angelo und Rolla* (Cassel, 1903) by C. Buongiorno, the author of the most famous artistic autobiography known to literature is the opera composer's favorite hero.

## "BENVENUTO CELLINI"

HECTOR BERLIOZ. Book by De Wailly and Barbier (Paris, 1853; first successful production, Weimar, 1855). In Berlioz' score, remarkable for bizarre rhythms and colorful instrumentation, its melodies in part Italianate, "the instruments breathe while the personages are dead."

In the palace of old Balducci, papal treasurer, Cellini, disguised as a monk, is overheard by his rival, Fieramosco, planning elopement with Teresa, Balducci's daughter. As her father enters, Cellini slips out, but his rival of chisel and love song is discovered, Teresa screams for help and Fieramosco flees through a window before an onslaught of women armed with brooms. Among Carnival masqueraders in the square (change of scene) Cellini and Fieramosco, both in white cowls, court Teresa, and Cellini, stabbing Fieramosco's friend Pompeo, again escapes, while the rival sculptor mistaken for him is almost hung by the angry crowd.

In Cellini's studio, Cardinal Salviati declares Cellini's rival shall cast the great statue of Perseus, which the sculptor has delayed completing. When Cellini says he will cast it at once the Cardinal promises him a pardon and Teresa's hand if the casting be done within the hour. All present are pressed into service and, metal lacking for the mold, Cellini flings the gold and silver marvels of his goldsmith's art into the pot to achieve his masterpiece. When the mold is broken and the glorious statue of Perseus is revealed in its perfection, all do homage to the artist and he is awarded Teresa's hand with Balducci's blessing.

There is also a *Benvenuto Cellini* (Vienna, 1847) by Schlösser, a Salieri pupil; *Benvenuto Cellini* (Munich, 1849) by Franz Lachner, and *Benvenuto Cellini* (Paris, 1890) by E. Diaz—a critic said it should have been called *Malvenuto* (*Benvenuto*—welcome; *malvenuto*—unwelcome), telling how Cellini's discarded mistress Pasilea hires two bravos to kill him, how he is jailed for killing them, but when freed by a popular revolt escapes to France with his new sweetheart Delphe de Montsolm. It is the *first opera staging a ballet in jail,* in the shape of charming visions Cellini sees within prison walls. Luigi Rossi's *Cellini a Parigi* (*Cellini in Paris,* Turin, 1845), yields in interest to Saint-Saëns' *Ascanio* (Paris, 1890), book by Gallet, where the sculptor's handsome young pupil, Ascanio is hounded by the furious love of the Duchess d'Étampes, King Francis' mistress, in his master's studio. Cellini, about to aid the boy, falls into a rage when he finds Colombe, whom he loves, is Ascanio's sweetheart. But overcoming himself, he sacrifices his passion for the sake of the lad he cherishes like a father, saves him from the Duchess' claws and sees him safely married to his love. *Die Krähen* (*The Crows,* Munich, 1921) by Walter Courvoisier, a fine modern score, Pomona-Diego's aria, "Es singt sich gut am Abend," outstanding, takes us to a Roman studio festival given to celebrate the end of the plague in the city. To Agnoldo the wood-carver's studio each artist comes bringing his "crow," his sweetheart. Cellini, at odds with his jealous mistress Antea, puts his handsome page Diego into women's clothes and brings him as his "crow." Diego, as "Pomona," plays well his part till the artists' attentions become too strenuous and then, in blushing confusion, whispers to one of the real women that he is in interesting circumstances and must have air. During the resulting confusion the page's true sex is discovered and Antea, who is present, and has been in torture all evening, cured of her jealousy, falls repentant into Cellini's arms.

*Proserpine* (Paris, 1887) by Saint-Saëns, with Act II "containing melodies of charming purity and sweetness," notably in the "Cloister Scene," is the tale of Proserpine, a Roman courtesan, who when young Sabatino will have none of her, and prepares instead to marry Angiola, a convent-bred innocent, is so enraged that, after having Angiola's coach stopped by cutthroats on its way to Rome, and nearly succeeding in getting her carried off, she darts from behind a tapestry in Sabatino's palace (Act IV) to stab Angiola in her lover's arms, but changing her mind buries the dagger in her own breast. *Beatrice Cenci* (Warsaw, 1922) by Ludomir Różycki is a Polish modernist's musical version of the tragic romance of a lovely parricide of late Renaissance Rome. After helping murder a monstrous father whose cruelties included offering incestuous violence to his seventeen-year-old daughter Beatrice, the latter (painted by Guido Reni on the eve of her execution) was beheaded (1598).

## 2. *Valois and Early Bourbon Romances*

*Le pré aux clercs* (*The Scriveners' Meadow,* Paris, 1832) by François Hérold, book after Prosper Merimée's *Chronique du temps de Charles IX*. In the royal palace of the Louvre (1542) Marguerite de Valois has for maid of honor Isabelle, who loves and is loved by the Huguenot, Baron de Mergy, sent by Henry, King of Navarre, to the court of France on a mission. The Count de Comminges, a blustering duelist, favorite of King Charles IX, is de Mergy's rival for Isabelle's favor. Inevitably they quarrel, but when they meet on the famous Paris dueling ground of the day, the *Pré aux Clercs* (the "Scrivener's Meadow"), Comminges, who never yet has failed to slay his adversary, is killed by de Mergy's first thrust, leaving Isabelle free to give her hand to the man of her choice. Curiously effective dramatically is the "Scene of the Barque" in which Comminges' corpse is rowed back across the Seine. The opera has been called Hérold's best score. A vigorous Overture; Mergy's air, "O ma tendre amie"; Isabelle's "Rendez-moi ma patrie" (Act II); and "Jours de mon enfance" (Act III), in fact the entire third act, "a masterpiece intercalated in a masterpiece," stand out.

## "LES HUGUENOTS"

GIACOMO MEYERBEER. Text by Scribe and Deschamps (Paris, 1836). Meyerbeer's greatest opera, which drove Spontini mad with jealousy and made Rossini melancholy, is *the* "St. Bartholomew Massacre" opera. "Count Hannibal" is its best English novel. It was, with "its religious motives, fighting scenes, conspiracies and chants of vengeance" the great hit of its period. Catholicism is "luxuriantly polyphone" and Protestantism "severely monophone" in its music (in Catholic countries the opera was produced as *The Ghibelins of Pisa*). Raoul's "Romance" (tenor) with *obbligato viola d'amore,* the "Page's Song," and Raoul's and Valentine's Love Duet are among Meyerbeer's melodies praised by Wagner.

In the Count de Nevers' (1572) rooms Catholic nobles carouse with their Protestant guest, Raoul de Nangis. Thither comes Valentine St. Bris who loves Raoul, to ask de Nevers to free her from her troth. After he has done so a page gives Raoul a note: it begs him to meet an unknown—his eyes covered with a scarf lest he see her face.

The maids of honor sing sweetly in Marguerite de Valois' garden (the Queen of Navarre herself is a coloratura soprano) and she proposes the marriage of Raoul and Valentine to pledge the reconciliation of Catholics and Protestants. But Raoul (he has seen Valentine in Nevers' rooms) thinks her the latter's mistress, refuses her hand, and only the Queen's presence prevents bloodshed.

The drinking chorus of Protestants and Catholics rises before a Paris inn, and gypsies dance away a quarrel. Valentine, rebetrothed by her father to de Nevers, overhears a plot to kill Raoul when he goes to fight a duel in the *Pré aux Clercs* with the Count. The clash of steel draws gentlemen of both factions to the spot and when Marguerite de Valois' appearance interrupts the struggle Raoul, apprized of Valentine's effort to save him, knows that he has treated her unjustly.

Valentine, wedded to de Nevers, still loves the Huguenot. When he is hidden behind a curtain in her husband's home, he overhears the plan for the St. Bartholomew massacre. When the Catholic nobles leave, after invoking the blessing on their swords, the church bells of St. Germain l'Auxerrois sound the tocsin, and as Valentine swoons, Raoul leaps from the window to alarm his friends.

In the Hôtel de Nesle he bids the Protestants arm. Next (change of scene) he is found in a churchyard by Valentine, who turns Protestant and is married to him by his soldier-servant Marcel only to be separated from her husband in the combat during which the Catholics slaughter the Huguenot women hiding in the church. But soon (change of scene) on a Paris quay, Raoul, mortally wounded, and Valentine supporting him, are united for eternity by a volley from the muskets of soldiers led by her father.

## "LE ROI MALGRÉ LUI"

### (*King Despite Himself*)

EMMANUEL CHABRIER. Book by Burani, Najac and Richepin (Paris, 1887). A romantic comic opera associated with King Henry III, musically so sparkling it earned Chabrier the title of "the laugh in music." An orchestral Fête Polonaise (Act II) and Minka's song, "On dit que notre roi," are among its happy pages.

Henry de Valois, candidate for the crown of Poland (1574), after amusing mischances arising from the fact that he has exchanged identities with his friend de Nangis—nearly slain when conspirators mistake him for Henry—hurries off with a cart driver's ex-sweetheart, to gay Paris he prefers to gloomy Cracow, only to be recaptured by the Polish magnates and crowned "King Against His Will," while de Nangis marries the serf girl pretty Minka, whose heart he has found time to win.

*Le roi de Paris* (*The King of Paris*, Paris, 1901) by Georges Huë, deals in Meyerbeerian style with the struggle of Henry, Duke of Guise, favorite of the Paris mob, against Henry III, King of France, and ends with his assassination at the Valois' command. *Les États de Blois* (Paris, 1837) by Onslow, the story of the Duke's murder at Blois (1588) and Flotow's *La Duchesse de Guise* (Paris, 1840), are musically less important. *La Dame de Montsereau*, (*The Lady of Montsereau*, Paris, 1888) by Gaston Salvayre, after Dumas' famous Valois romance, is another lesser score—as is Paul and Lucien Hillemacher's successful *St. Megrin* (Brussels, 1886). King Henry of Navarre, successor to Henry of Valois and first Bourbon king of France, has motived Méhul's *Le jeune Henri* (Paris, 1797) whose Overture, *"La Chasse"* survives the score, and *Das hölzerne Schwert* (*The Wooden Sword,* Cassel, 1897) by Zöllner, uses attractive Moorish gypsy airs and French folk songs to tell a merry tale of one of Henry IV's soldiers, who pawns his steel blade and wears a wooden sword in his scabbard until, ordered by the monarch to execute a fellow soldier, he escapes punishment by praying that a miracle may turn his sword into wood. *La farce du cuvier* (*The Farce of the Tub,* Brussels, 1912; Paris, 1925) by Gabriel Dupont, is a 16th century burlesque tale, in which a brilliant Overture, charming old French folk songs and a vocal fugue for eight voices stand out, of a hen-pecked husband who gets his wife into a washtub full of warm water and does not release her till she swears he shall be the master.

## "LA BÉARNAISE"

### (The Girl of Béarn)

ANDRÉ MESSAGER. Book by Letièrre and Vanloo (Paris, 1925). A romantic comic opera in which a "Madrigal" and a poetic cradle song, "Fais nono, mon bel enfantou" (Act II), stand out.

Captain Perpignac, a Don Juan of King Henry's court, for leading astray fair Gabrielle is punished by banishment from Paris and a quarantine on "all flirting." In Parma, about to transgress the royal command with the merry widow Bianca, his little cousin Jacquette assumes a male disguise to save him and marries Bianca. Then Jacquette flirting with Pomponio, the Duke of Parma's stupid chamberlain, makes Perpignac realize he truly loves her and he marries Jacquette while Bianca leads Pomponio to the altar.

*Cinq-Mars* (Paris, 1877) by Charles Gounod, a dialogue opera with one fine song, "O nuit silencieuse," tells the tragic tale of the favorite of King Louis XIII who conspired against the all-powerful Cardinal Richelieu and suffered on the block. *Capitaine Fracasse* (Paris, 1878) by Emile Pessard, with charming airs and dance tunes, is an opera version of Gautier's delightful picaresque novel of the same title, which leads an impoverished nobleman from his ruined chateau in the provinces through all sorts of adventures to the heart and hand of an aristocratic heiress. *Les mousquetaires de la reine* (*The Queen's Musketeers*, Paris, 1846) by Halévy, tells of Oliver d'Entragues, an officer of Queen Anne's Musketeers who, condemned to death by Cardinal Richelieu for dueling, nevertheless wins his pardon and the hand of his sweetheart Solange. *Les trois mousquetaires* (Cannes, 1921) by Isidore de Lara, a tuneful, attractive lighter score, is an operatic variant of Dumas' famous novel of the adventures of d'Artagnan and his friends.

## "CYRANO DE BERGERAC"

WALTER DAMROSCH. Text skillfully adapted from Edmond Rostand's drama by W. G. Henderson (New York, 1913). Savinien Cyrano de Bergerac (1620-1655), French dramatist, whose actual exploits in the Guards during the campaigns of 1639-40 made him a true hero of romance, and whose scientific romance *L'histoire comique des états de la lune* supplied a model for Swift, led the stormy life of a man about town and duelist in Paris and died from the effects of a piece of lumber falling on him as he entered his house. The score is a dignified, scholarly endeavor to do justice to its romantic subject.

In the Hôtel de Bourgogne (Paris of Louis XIII), the fat tenor Montfleury is about to sing when Cyrano enters. Driving the tenor from the stage to win a wager, he resents De Guiche's insult to his gigantic nose (his tender point) with a duel, and while his enemy is borne off wounded and all leave, Cyrano delights in lovely Roxane's praise as she passes. But De Guiche waits his egress with a hundred bravos, and Cyrano draws his rapier and, "followed by actors and actresses . . . whirling tambourines, goes forth into the moonlit Paris streets to meet his foes."

In Ragueneau's pastry shop (where Roxane has arranged to meet Cyrano) Roxane begs him to watch over his comrade, Christian de Neuvillette, whom she loves, and resigning his dream of her affection, he gives his promise. When the Gascony "Cadets" swarm in, he draws Christian aside. To further the boy's wooing of literary Roxane he offers to write the *billet-doux* the latter could not frame. Christian joyfully accepts his offer.

De Guiche, in Roxane's moonlit garden, tells her he is off to command the soldiers besieging Arras. Moved by anxiety for Christian she suggests (as a slight to Cyrano) that he leave the Gascony Cadets behind, and he agrees. Cyrano and Christian enter, but the latter unable to do justice to "love" in flowery language, Cyrano brings Roxane to her balcony with his impassioned declaration and wins her kiss—as Christian. A letter from De Guiche brought by a monk, so Roxane falsely declares, contains a command to marry Christian on the spot. While they are wedded, Cyrano detains De Guiche (come to the meeting for which the letter has asked) with a fantastic tale of a trip to the moon. When the wedded pair appear in the doorway De Guiche revenges himself by ordering Christian to join his command.

Christian, in Cyrano's tent before Arras, discovers his friend signs his (Christian's) name to letters addressed to his wife. In his anger he puts one in his breast to deliver it himself when Roxane's coach draws up, and flinging herself into her husband's arms she declares she has come to share his fate. Christian (while his wife walks toward the Cadets in the background) reproaches Cyrano with having written "not my love, but your own," rushes into the mêlée, and is carried back a corpse. Roxane draws Cyrano's letter from Christian's chest as Cyrano, seeking death, mounts the ramparts of Arras. Roxane (change of scene) finds wounded Cyrano on a bench in the convent garden near the battlefield. Praising Christian's love she gives him his own letter but when he pretends to read it aloud, sees he is reciting from memory. Yet, bleeding to death from his reopened wounds, he denies being its author. With a last effort he raises his sword and cries that night when he passes through the jeweled gates of Paradise he will salute the Infinite with that which enters heaven without stain. And to Roxane's question as she stoops to kiss him he replies, as his soul takes flight: "My soldier's snow-white plume!"

*Cyrano de Bergerac* (Montreal, 1899) is a spontaneously tuneful and engaging comic opera score by the late Victor Herbert. *La Rôtisserie de la reine pédauque* (*At the Sign of the Reine Pédauque,* Paris, 1919), by Charles Levadé, a lyric comedy after Anatole France's novel, presents scenes from the novelist's book with the Abbé Coignet as its hero. A modern score, it contains a graceful Gavotte and the Supper Scene at Catherine's is considered the gem of the work. Because of its musical spontaneity Levadé's score has been called the "Cyrano of French music."

### 3. Tudor England

#### "HENRY VIII"

CAMILLE SAINT-SAËNS. A beautifully finished score in traditional style, in which English folk-melodies are artistically used and which boasts a most effective ballet (Paris, 1883). The opera always has been popular in France. The "Danse de la Gipsy," with tympani and cymbals, stands out in the Ballet. The book is by Détroyat and Silvestre.

In Westminster Palace, Gomez, Spanish ambassador, gives Queen Catherine a letter in which Anne Boleyn admits she loves him, when King Henry enters and tells his queen they should be divorced; he then courts Anne to the funeral march of the Duke of Buckingham who has just laid his head on the block, whose music sounds from the street.

In Richmond Park Anne promises to marry Henry if he make her Queen of England. And though Queen Catherine reproves the girl for her godless ambition, and a messenger from Rome forbidding the divorce is ushered in, Henry devotes himself to Anne and the dance, and marries her the next day.

Anne has been crowned Queen of England in Westminster but Catherine, who is dying, has the love letter her rival wrote Gomez, and Anne's head "uneasy rests." A strange note from Catherine rouses Henry's jealousy and he, Anne, and Gomez hasten to dying Catherine intent on securing the incriminating missive. The most powerful scene of the opera, musically and dramatically, now takes place. Henry, jealousy raging in his heart, makes impassioned love to Anne before Catherine's eyes. He hopes that in revenge she will yield Gomez's letter. But Catherine, divorced and deserted, rises to noble heights of sacrifice, knowing she is about to die. With a last effort she casts the love letter into the hearth, sees it flame up, and expires.

*Anna Bolena* (Milan, 1822), Donizetti's first operatic success, lives in the airs, "Ah parea che per encanto," "Nel veder la tua costanza," and tells the tragedy of Henry's queen sentenced to the block for misconduct with five co-respondents, in ear-tickling music of rose-water sweetness. King Edward VI, who followed

Henry, inspired the Anglican Book of Common Prayer, but no operas, though "Bloody Mary" is represented by Gomez' *Maria Tudor* (Milan, 1877). *Merrie England* (London, 1902) by Edward German, a romantic comic score, presents "Good Queen Bess" as a leading figure. Essex, plotting Raleigh's downfall at a Windsor May-day festival, reveals the discoverer of Virginia's love for Bessie Throckmorton. Elizabeth has the unfortunate girl jailed, and seeks out an apothecary to get a dose of poison for her, but the appearance of Herne the Hunter, bugaboo of royal Tudors, gives her pause and the offenders are pardoned. *Elizabetta, regina d'Inghilterra* (Naples, 1815) by Rossini, based on Scott's *Kenilworth,* is an opera of bravura airs, in which Leicester's Duet with Amy Robsart and the Finale stand out. Auber's *Leicester* (Paris, 1823) is a Rossinian imitation, and Costa's ballet, *Kenilworth* (London, 1831), Bruno Oscar Klein's romantic opera *Kenilworth* (Hamburg, 1895), and Isidore de Lara's *Amy Robsart* (London, 1893) sing the tragic fate of the girl wife who, stepping on a hidden trapdoor fell and broke her neck to ensure the peace of mind of Elizabeth's ambitious favorite. Elizabeth Tudor's lovely Stuart cousin also has inspired operas. Among them are *Maria Stuarda* (Naples, 1834) by Donizetti, and the Russian Kashperov's *Maria Stuarda* (Milan, 1859). Though Elizabeth, the great royal figure of the English Renaissance, has inspired no greater operas, the Italianate influence predominates in the Elizabethan dramatists' works and Shakespeare in particular reacted to it.

## The Operatic Shakespeare

Shakespeare himself is the hero of an opera, *Guglielmo Shakespeare* (Parma, 1861) by the Venetian Benvenuto Tommasso, and his *Richard III* (1593) has inspired *Riccardo III* (Milan, 1857) by Meiners, a Donizetti pupil, and Gaston Salvayre's *Richard III* (Petrograd, 1883). The *Comedy of Errors,* first performed in *Gray's Hall Inn,* December, 1594, by "a company of base and lewd fellows" (Did they include Shakespeare himself?) brought forth Sir Henry Bishop's *Comedy of Errors* (London, 1819), "a musical atrocity." The same year produced *Titus Andronicus, The Taming of the Shrew, Love's Labor's Lost* and *Romeo and Juliet.*

*Der Widerspeustigen Zähmung (The Taming of the Shrew)* by Hermann Goetz (Mannheim, 1875), book by Widmann, after Shakespeare, is a lyric rather than a dramatic opera. The air "Es schweige die Klage" (Act IV) is known as a concert solo of the better sort.

Katherine's hatefulness has driven the servants from her home and blocked the happiness of her sister Bianca who cannot marry until Baptista, the Paduan nobleman, has rid himself of his quarrelsome older daughter. Yet Petruchio, a gentleman of Verona, dares sue for her hand, and though Katherine abuses her maid and beats her music master about the head with her lute (Act II), he fixes her wedding day. Petruchio is late at the altar and no sooner have they been made man and wife than he drags her off struggling and fighting. In his villa (Act III) the real "Taming of the Shrew" takes place. Outdoing her at her own game, her husband so completely bullies and bulldozes Katherine that she becomes a most submissive wife, guided only by his wishes. *La mégère apprivoisée* (*The Taming of the Shrew*) by Charles Silver, book by Cain and Adenis (Paris, 1924) after Shakespeare presents the same tale with an especially good characterization of Petruchio as the embodiment of the iron hand without the velvet glove. With a modern touch to its music, the Symphonic Interlude (Act III) and Ballet (Act II) stand out. An earlier French "Taming" is *La mégère apprivoisée* (Paris, 1897) by François Le Rey; the Spaniard Martin y Soler, Mozart's rival (1754-1806), wrote a *La capricciosa Corretta,* and there is *Petruchio* (London, 1895) by Alick McLean. *Love's Labor's Lost* may be said to deserve its title so far as the opera composer is concerned, for it has motivated no outstanding score.

## ROMEO AND JULIET

Based on Italian tales of the fifteenth century, Shakespeare's play of "the star-crossed lovers," is lyric tragedy at its best. It expresses the very spirit of the Elizabethan dramas which "loved the unusual themes, the sweet foreign names, the stories with the symbolic note set in magical places called Milan, Florence, Naples, Venice, Sicily, Verona, Padua, Rome" (R. A. Taylor). Romeo and Juliet are Renaissance lovers, but their human truth and nearness and the perfect climax of their story, makes them "forever young and still to be enjoyed." Among minor operatic settings Georg Benda's (b. 1772) *Singspiel, Romeo und Julia,* was long a favorite, and Daniel Steibelt, a famous eighteenth century piano virtuoso, wrote a *Roméo et Juliette* (Paris, 1793), which celebrated a triumph in his day. *Giulietta e Romeo* (Milan, 1796) Zingarelli's master score, was immensely popular. When the male soprano Crescentini sang its famous air, "Ombra adorata aspetta," tears filled Napoleon's eyes. Niccolo Vaccai's *Giulietta e Romeo* (Milan, 1825) stood out among his sixteen operas, its third act usually being substituted for the third act of Bellini's *I Montecchi e Capuletti* (Venice, 1830) in whose final scene Bellini follows the Dryden innovation (later followed by Gounod), which, contrary to Shakespeare, allows Juliet to awake before Romeo's death in order to sing with him in tender dialogue. *Giulietta e Romeo* (Trieste, 1865) by Marchetti, a brilliant success and the less known, *Les amants de Vérone* (*The Lovers of Verona,* Paris, 1867) by Paul d'Ivry, the conventional *Romeo e Giulietta* (London, 1810) by Guglielmini and *Romeo and Juliet* (London, 1920) by L. W. Barksworth, which has been termed "effective in a popular way," also may be mentioned.

## "ROMEO ET JULIETTE"

FRANÇOIS GOUNOD. Book by Barbier and Carré (Paris, 1867), after Shakespeare. Gounod's *Roméo* ranks after *Faust* among his works. The closing *ritornello* of the scene in Juliet's chamber is colorful and poetic, and other outstanding musical moments are Juliet's "Waltz Song," and the Ballet ("Ball Scene").

After a Prologue (introducing the cast in tableaux) Romeo and his friends appear at the gay masquerade (Act I) in the Capulet mansion. There he sees Juliet and they lose their hearts to each other.

At a pavilion in the Capulet gardens is staged the immortal balcony scene between the lovers (graceful, swaying nocturnal music suggestive of Weber) temporarily interrupted by the appearance of the servants seeking Romeo.

In Friar Laurent's (Lorenzo's) cell, the priest secretly marries the lovers to end the feud between the rival families. Then, in the street before the Capulet house, Tybalt kills Mercutio and Romeo, avenging his friend, slays Tybalt and is banished from Verona.

But Romeo returns from exile and hurries to Juliet's chamber to celebrate their bridal; yet no sooner has he gone than the girl's father tells her she must marry another. It is then the hapless victim of fate takes the sleeping potion from Friar Laurent which casts her into a deathlike trance.

The news of Juliet's death brings Romeo posthaste from Mantua where he had again retired, provided with the poison he has bought, to visit Juliet's tomb. There, convinced he has lost her, he drinks the poison "with a kiss" and Juliet, awakening in time to let him die in her arms, thrusts the dagger into her own heart.

## "GIULIETTA E ROMEO"

RICCARDO ZANDONAI. Book by Rossato (Rome, 1922), after Renaissance novels of Bando, Bandello, and Da Porto from which Shakespeare drew inspiration. The opera has ho Overture and, "neither a complete tragedy of passion nor a complete love idyll with a tragic ending," tells its story in music which, though accused of lacking continuity of inspiration, has Puccinian lyric pages. The symphonic Intermezzo (Romeo's mad ride from Mantua to Verona to find his dead love) and his Love Duet with Juliet (Act III) stand out.

The ball is in progress in the Capulet mansion while in the two street taverns adjoining partisans of the rival clans await the signal for the clash of arms. Tybalt's appearance precipitates a conflict, quelled by the city guards. Then Juliet steps out on the balcony, calls her lover's name and Romeo appears masked and disguised. She lets down the silken ladder and as he climbs it they sing their love together.

In the courtyard Tybalt next accuses Juliet of loving Romeo, bitter foe of their house, and declares he will marry her on the morrow to Count de Lodrone and kill Romeo with his own hand. But the ring of steel on steel is heard; the factions are fighting and Tybalt hurries off to join the fray, as Romeo, hidden in the Capulet home, reappears. While he and Juliet plan flight Tybalt returns and draws sword on the intruder. Romeo runs Tybalt through the body and flees when he falls. Then Juliet's duenna Isabella prepares the potion which is to save her from marriage with a man unloved.

In Mantua Romeo hears the false news of Juliet's death, hurries back to Verona, and the climax of the opera develops in the usual manner.

*Romeo und Julia auf dem Dorfe* (*The Village Romeo and Juliet* (Berlin, 1907; London, 1920) by Frederick Delius, book after Kellar's *Folk of Sedwylla,* is "a kaleidoscopic tissue of tonal imagery . . . in which spiritual values are made manifest." Notable is the symphonic "Walk to the Paradise Gardens." Undramatic, the music is "an impressionistic background" for the stage pictures. Sali, the village Romeo, loves Vrenchen, but their fathers are enemies, and at last, after various vicissitudes, they leave their home hand in hand, and scorning the life of easy loves and baser pleasures the vagabond Dark Fiddler offers them, they prefer to it death, death while love is still pure and beautiful and golden with illusion. Leaving behind them the Dark Fiddler's roisterers they come to a hay barge on the river. "See, our wedding bed awaits us!" cries Sali as they clamber aboard, and he pulls the plug which will sink their bark. A poetic scene describing Vrenchen's vision of a church wedding, "is one of the most spiritual, original, and important operatic scenes of recent years" (Bie).

*I Rantzau* (Florence, 1892) by Mascagni, book by Targioni-Tozetti, after Erckmann-Chatrian, transposes a tale of village Montagues and Capulets to Alsatia. But the love of Louise and George does not end in the tomb, but in the reconciliation of the parents and their consent to the marriage in consequence of Louise's illness. Louise's "Romance" (Act I) and the Closing Scene (Act II) are musically effective. *Die Liebenden von Kandahar* (Breslau, 1907) by Leopold Reichwein carries the tale of Romeo and Juliet to Afghanistan. Moschen and Djemileh, cousins prevented from marrying by their fathers' hatred, flee the parental roof. But the vizier's son, the vizier, and the sultan himself pursue the hapless lovers who, finally, are caught and shot like mad dogs. The Orient is musically depicted as in *Aida* by a good Wagnerian technician and Afghan blunderbuss does duty for poison and dagger.

The year 1595 was productive of Shakespeare's *A Midsummer Night's Dream, Two Gentlemen of Verona* and *King John.*

### A Midsummer Night's Dream

Musically the most outstanding work associated with *A Midsummer Night's Dream* remains Mendelssohn's incidental music for the play. J. C. Smith's opera *The Fairies* (London, 1754) contains a good song, Oberon's "Now until the close of day" (Act II). In *Le songe d'une nuit d'été* (Paris, 1850) by Ambroise Thomas, Falstaff, the fat knight (called "an insult to Shakespeare"), arranges a love tryst with Queen Eizabeth, while Shakespeare himself is haled into the Tudor presence hopelessly drunk, to be taken to Windsor Park, where all sorts of complications ensue. Georges Hüe's *Titania* (Paris, 1903), is a later opera on the subject.

Bishop wrote a *"pasticcio* opera" *Two Gentlemen of Verona* (London, 1821) but *King John* has inspired no opera of importance. The year 1596 aside from *Richard II* produced *The Merchant of Venice.*

### The Merchant of Venice

The tale is well-known of Shylock, the Jew of Venice, who insisted on his pound of flesh; of Antonio, the young merchant who loaned money to his friends without interest; of Bassanio to whom he loaned some money and whose failure to repay Shylock on the appointed hour put him within cutting distance of the Jew's knife; of Portia, the young lawyeress who saved her husband's friend by her eloquence; and of Jessica, Shylock's daughter, who contributed her share to the happy ending by marrying a Christian lover at her father's expense. *Il mercadante di Venezia* (Bologna, 1873) by Pinsuti has dramatic pages, notably in the last act, where Jews singing Hebrew hymns in defiance to those of the Christians are outsung by the latter. In Deffès' *Jessica* (Toulouse, 1898) Antonio's "C'était le soir" (Act I), Portia's charming "Dream Revery," and a Ballet stand out. Flor Alpaerts' *Shylock* (Antwerp, 1914), Taubmann's *Portia* (Frankfort, 1916), and Adrian Beecham's *Merchant of Venice* (London, 1923) yield in musical interest to the Czech composer Josef B. Förster's *Jessica* (Prague, 1905).

*Henry IV* and *Much Ado About Nothing* are the dramatic fruits of Shakespeare's genius during the years 1597 and 1598.

## "BÉATRICE ET BENEDICT"

HECTOR BERLIOZ. Book (Baden-Baden, 1862) after Shakespeare's *Much Ado About Nothing*. The gem of this attractive score is the *Notturno* (Act I), whose tenderness recalls the love scene in the same composer's *Romeo and Juliet* symphony.

Don Pedro, victorious over the Moors, enters Messina but finds warlike Moslems easier to subdue than a determined girl; for Beatrice, Leonato's niece, whom he wishes to marry to Benedict, one of his officers, merely laughs at him. Hero, Leonato's other daughter, is about to marry Claudio, another officer. While musicians rehearse a wedding serenade (a two-part fugue, one voice weeping, the other laughing) Benedict, disgusted with his lady love, takes refuge in the garden. There *his* friends tell him Beatrice loves him devotedly, while *her* friends tell her tales of Benedict's adoration. In the garden, too, Hero sings a tender love song in the moonlight. And now the effect of the persuasions used by their mutual friends on Benedict and Beatrice is shown. Hero's wedding feast is in progress in the governor's palace, guests and musicians disperse in the green garden shades, and Beatrice and Benedict meet. Vows of love are exchanged and soon Hero and Claudio find a second couple ready to sign the marriage contract.

*Much Ado About Nothing* (London, 1901) by Charles Villiers Stanford presents the whole Shakespeare play. Following the festivities in Leonato's house Don John (suppressed in Berlioz' score) plots against Hero's honor and shows Claudio her betrothed, the supposed Hero (Act II) admitting Borachio to her bedchamber. The third scene, in church, follows Shakespeare, and in the fourth (open square in Messina, Hero's tomb to one side) Borachio confesses his villainy and Hero, who is not dead at all, is restored to Claudio's arms. The music "overflows with delicious melody" and is rich in humor, pathos and delicate fancy.

*Beaucoup de bruit pour rien* (*Much Ado About Nothing*, Paris, 1899) by Paul Puget, in which stand out the Prelude, Sicilian Song and Dance (Act I)—Madrigal (Act II)—and Bridal Cortège (Act III), introduces a closing scene not found in Shakespeare. Hero lies on her bier before the cathedral of Messina when Claudio enters and approaches the body, begs forgiveness, and puts on Hero's finger the ring she was to wear. Hero opens her eyes at the touch of his beloved hand and all ends happily.

*Ero* (Cremona, 1900) by C. Podest, and Doeppler's *Viel Lärm um Nichts* (Leipzig, 1896) may be dismissed with mention.

The year 1599 is marked by the production of two plays, *Henry V* and *Julius Cæsar,* the latter not marked by outstanding operatic reactions. The year 1600 gives us *The Merry Wives of Windsor* and *As You Like It.*

## "DIE LUSTIGEN WEIBER VON WINDSOR"

### (*The Merry Wives of Windsor*)

OTTO NICOLAI. Book after Shakespeare by Mosenthal (Berlin, 1849). A comic fantasy opera in which ideals of German and Italian romantic melody are welded with fluent orchestration, tender sincerity and theatrical effect. The arias are not important though Falstaff's "Drinking Song," Mistress Reich's lovely "Ballad" and Fenton's attractive "Romance" stand out. The Overture, with its delightful moonlight and elfin music, and the Dances in the last act call for mention.

The love letters of Sir John Falstaff, the fat knight, to Mistress Fluth and Mistress Reich of Windsor have roused both ladies and they determine to punish the old sinner. Their husbands, as well as Spärlich and Dr. Cajus, suitors for the hand of Reich's daughter Anna, favored by father and mother but unwelcome to the girl who loves poor young Fenton, enter the Reich home and are asked to dinner (change of scene). Meanwhile Mistress Fluth, in her home, listens with secret merriment to the love-making of Falstaff (the bassoon expresses the fat knight's sighs, the flute the snippish answers of his adored) until her husband knocks. Then the fat knight squeezes into the clothes basket full of dirty wash, and while four servants carry it off to dump the contents on the bleaching ground, jealous Fluth scolds and searches the house. When he returns his neighbors berate him and his wife threatens divorce.

In the Garter Inn Falstaff tells Fluth (who has scraped up acquaintance with him under the name of Bach) about his basket adventure, showing him a letter from his wife fixing another meeting (change of scene). In the garden behind the Reich house Fenton's serenade lures Anna out and she swears to be true to him (change of scene). Again Fluth comes home while Falstaff is courting his wife. This time the knight is hid in woman's garb and Fluth, thrusting his sword into the clothes basket, drives his wife's supposed old female cousin out of the house.

In Reich's home the husbands and wives (the former have learned how their wives have been fooling Falstaff) unite to bring his punishment to a climax. Falstaff is to be induced to appear in Windsor Forest as "Herne the Hunter" at midnight. Then, disguised as elves, the others will soundly beat him. Meanwhile Anna (according to father) is to be wed to Spärling, garbed as a green elf, and (according to mother) to Cajus, garbed as a red elf. She gets her elfin suitors fighting and instead is married in the woodland chapel to Fenton (change of scene). As the music calls up the picture of moonlit forest glades, with the glimmer of silver light and the tripping feet of elfin dancers, Falstaff appears. At once gnats, mosquitoes, elves, gnomes and pixies surround him (Ballet) and pinch and cuff and beat him till he pleads for mercy. When this is granted he is invited to the wedding feast and Anna and Fenton present themselves to the dismay of their parents and the other suitors as a newly wedded pair.

*Falstaff* (Milan, 1893) by Verdi, book by Boito, written by the composer at eighty, and considered opera's greatest musical comedy in the grand style since Wagner's *Meistersinger,* presents the story of "The Merry Wives" with deviations in detail from Nicolai's textual version. The many beauties of the work—the Fugal Finale, Act III), the great Nonet, the "Woodland Music," etc.— are the delight of musical gourmands, but the opera has not conquered the favor of the general public.

## "AT THE BOAR'S HEAD"

GUSTAVE HOLST. Book drawn from Shakespeare's *Henry IV,* Parts I and II (London, 1925). Thirty-five Elizabethan folk tunes and dances supply the themes for this "Musical Interlude"; to quote the composer, "the most beautiful tunes in the world, save for half a dozen by Bach." Freely treated, they make a strong, racy musical score, admirably orchestrated. The stirring marching song, "Lord Willoughby" is one of the most brilliant, and "Mr. Isaac's Maggot" one of the loveliest airs in the work.

The scene of action is the Boar's Head Tavern, Eastcheap, where sits Prince Hal when in comes Falstaff, the fat knight, with his comrades Gadshill and Bardolph. They have robbed some travelers on the highway, but the Prince and Poins coming upon them suddenly, without being recognized have driven them off while they were dividing the spoils. Falstaff tells of a terrific fight he waged against fifty enemies, only to be exposed by Prince Henry as a liar: "Falstaff, you carried your guts away as nimbly . . . and roared for mercy as loudly as ever I heard bull-calf!" Alone, Henry discloses his true self: "So, when this loose behavior I throw off and pay the debt I never promised, by how much better than my word I am . . ." and Falstaff returns with news of Owen Glendower's rebellion and the distress cf the King, his father, imitating the monarch in a pompous burlesque while the Prince, answering him, plays the rôle of Falstaff. Next Prince Henry and Poins spy on Falstaff and Doll Tearsheet, the Prince sings to entertain them and, finally, comes Peto. A dozen captains, bareheaded, sweating, are knocking at the taverns, asking for Sir John Falstaff—in order to find the Prince, whose father waits him at Westminster. It is time for Henry to do a man's work in the world. And as the stirring soldier

march "Lord Willoughby" sounds outside the Inn, the Prince takes
sword and cloak and goes. He leaves behind only the fat hulk and
his tawdry woman. Falstaff praises Prince Henry but Pistol, swaggering in with Quickly picks a fight with Doll Tearsheet, only to be
kicked down stairs by Falstaff who, sighing, "Now comes the sweetest
morsel of the night, and we must hence and leave it unpicked!" joins
the pikemen marching to war, Doll Tearsheet tagging after him.

Mercadante's forgotten *La Gioventù di Enrico V* (*The Youth of
Henry V*, Milan, 1834) also deals with wild young Prince Hal,
Falstaff's friend. Papavoine's *La vieux coquet* (Paris, 1770),
*Die lustigen Weiber* (Mannheim, 1794) by Peter Ritter, *Die
Weiber von Windsor und der dicke Hannes* (*The Merry Wives
of Windsor and Fat Jock* (Brunswick, 1796) by Dittersdorf and
Salieri's *Falstaff* (Vienna, 1799) shows how the Falstaff subject
was musically handled one hundred and thirty years ago. Balfe's
comic opera *Falstaff* (London, 1838) preceded Nicolai's, and before
Verdi's came Adam's "musically unconvincing" *Falstaff* (Paris,
1858). *As You Like It* has called forth no major score, though
Bishop wrote an *As You Like It* (London, 1819), and Veracini
*Rosalinda* (London, 1744).

*Hamlet* and *Twelfth Night or What You Will* were written in
the year 1601.

## "HAMLET"

Ambroise Thomas. The book by Carré and Barbier (Paris, 1868),
parodies Shakespeare. "Grandiose rather than grand," the outstanding
number is Ophelia's Mad Scene (Act IV), "dramatically ludicrous" but
musically brilliant and engaging in its "virtuosely subtilized insanity."
Old Scandinavian tunes (Ballade, etc.), the Ghost Scene (Act I), the
grotesque Gravediggers' Duet, and the noble Burial Scene are among
the best pages of a work which "reveals unveiled the radiant illumina-
tion of the decolletée Second Empire" (Bie).

In Helsingfors castle Gertrude (Hamlet's father is only two months'
dead) is wedding Claudius. After a love scene with Ophelia, confided
to him by her father Polonius (change of scene) the ghost of Hamlet's
father appears on the castle battlements and tells his son that Claudius
murdered him to gain his wife and crown. Hamlet swears vengeance
on his father's slayer.

In the castle garden Hamlet orders strolling players to perform a
play but (change of scene) the play he chooses presents the poisoning
of a father. As it ends Hamlet feigns madness and accuses Claudius
of the crime.

Hamlet overhears a conversation between his mother and Polonius,
and learns that Ophelia's father is involved in his father's poisoning.
When Claudius offers him Ophelia's hand he repulses her, reveals his

knowledge of her father's crime and tells his mother he knows her guilty secret. His father's spirit once more appears to him and he hurries off, eager to consummate his revenge.

Innocent Ophelia, rejected by her lover, has gone mad with despair. Life holds no more for her so she drowns herself in the lake.

In the Helsingfors churchyard, Hamlet, fleeing from assassins Claudius has hired, meets Laertes. Their duel is interrupted by Ophelia's funeral cortège. (Berlioz wrote a great symphonic "Marche Funèbre" for this scene.) King Claudius hurrying up Hamlet (his father's ghost urging him on) slays him, and casts himself grief-stricken on Ophelia's bier as the people proclaim him King of Denmark.

Earlier Princes of Denmark include Gasparini's *Amleto* (Venice, 1705), Alessandro Scarlatti's *Amleto* (Rome, 1715), Count Gallenberg's ballet *Amleto* (Milan, 1817), Mercadante's *Amleto* (Milan, 1822), Maretzek's *Hamlet* (Brünn, 1843), Buzzola's *Amleto* (Venice, 1848), and Stadfelt's *Hamlet* (Darmstadt, 1857). In Faccio's *Amleto* (Milan, 1871) the tragic music of the orchestra in the Ghost Scene on the castle ramparts blends effectively with that of the King's band playing in the castle, and Ophelia has a touching "Mad Song." In Hignard's lyric tragedy *Hamlet* (Nantes, 1888), there is beautiful funeral music for Ophelia and some delightful ballet episodes. *Twelfth Night* has called forth a *Was Ihr wollt* (*What You Will*, Berlin, 1872) by Rintel, and a *Viola* (Prague, 1892) by Karl Weiss; and in Taubert's *Cesario* (Berlin, 1874) inspired by *Twelfth Night,* there is fine "Storm" music.

*Troilus and Cressida* and *All's Well That Ends Well* were the plays of the year 1602. *All's Well That Ends Well* has supplied the subject matter for Audran's French operetta *Gilles de Narbonne* (Paris, 1883) and for *Le Saphir* (Paris, 1865), an unsuccessful opera by Félicien David; but it is not until the year 1604, with *Measure for Measure* and *Othello* that we find more famous operatic reactions.

## "OTELLO"

Guiseppe Verdi. Text after Shakespeare by Arrigo Boito (Milan, 1887). The first of the two scores of the rebirth of Verdi's genius (*Falstaff* was the other). In a new individual style, the old system of succeeding operatic numbers was dropped for scene to scene development, and the score's great dramatic moments pass without expression in typical arias. A beautifully orchestrated "Garden Chorus," Otello's and Desdemona's Love Scenes, and the moving Death Scene are among its jewels.

Otello, victor over the Saracens, is acclaimed by the Cypriots in the harbor of Famagusta. At once Iago's demoniac machinations begin.

Plying young Cassio, newly made a captain, with drink, he leads him to toast Desdemona, Otello's wife, and draw sword on Rodrigo. Degrading Cassio to the ranks, Otello makes passionate love to his wife beneath the stars.

Cassio at Iago's suggestions begs Desdemona to intercede for him with her husband, then Iago rouses Otello's jealousy. In the garden, where women, children, and Dalmatian sailors bring her flowers, Desdemona asks her husband's mercy for the offender, but Otello angrily flings to the ground the handkerchief she tries to bind round his forehead to assuage his pain. Iago tells Otello Cassio murmurs Desdemona's name in dreams, and claims to have a handkerchief she gave him. And Iago produces it.

Questioned by her husband, Desdemona says she has lost her handkerchief, and again pleads for Cassio. But the jealous Moor thinks his wife untrue. When a Venetian embassy arrives appointing Cassio in his place, and Desdemona drops a harmless word in the latter's favor to the ambassador Lorenzo, Otello ill-treats his wife in his rage.

Desdemona dons her bridal robe—divining it will be her shroud—and singing the affecting "Song of the Willow Tree," commends her soul to the Virgin, and falls asleep. Long the Moor stands watching her, then wakes her with kisses to tell her she must die. His blind rage will listen to no plea for mercy and he strangles her, her last words protesting her innocence. Otello's cries bring Iago, Lodovico and men at arms into the chamber where Iago's wife, despite her husband's threats, tells how he ruined Desdemona. Yielding up his sword (Iago flees) Otello steps to the bed of his innocent victim and stabs himself with his dagger.

*Otello* (Naples, 1816) by Gioachino Rossini, the great operatic Otello until displaced by Verdi's, follows Shakespeare less closely, and substitutes a letter for the fatal handkerchief. Musically it has fine pages. Desdemona's farewell melody is touching, and the duets between Desdemona and Emilia, Otello and Iago stand out, but it falls short of Verdi's in the Death Scene. Vigano's ballet *Otello,* accompanied by Rossini's music, Stendhal found more affecting than the opera. Verdi's *Otello* has been called "the destroyer of the old Italian aria," as Rossini's has been termed "the destroyer of the traditional *secco recitative*." Bellini's *Zaira* (Parma, 1829), incidentally, is known as "the Persian Othello."

## "DAS LIEBESVERBOT ODER DIE NOVIZE VON PARMA"

### (*The Prohibition to Love or the Novice of Parma*)

RICHARD WAGNER. A development of Shakespeare's *Measure for Measure,* it was Wagner's first attempt at *opéra comique* in the grand style (Magdeburg, 1836; revived of recent years in Germany). Musically influenced by Meyerbeer and Auber, it has a fine Overture and an effective "Salve Regina."

Isabella, a novice, steps from the cloister to beg a stony-hearted governor to pardon her brother. He has been condemned to death because of his love for a girl, forbidden by law, yet blessed by Nature. Isabella's chaste spirit finds such logical defenses for the supposititious crime, and presents them with such warmth that the stern guardian of public morals falls passionately in love with her. He makes her brother's pardon conditional, however, on her yielding to his passion. Then the Shakespearian plot is changed. Indignant Isabella lures the Governor to a rendezvous to reveal his hypocrisy. The people rise in revolt. The Governor, unmasked, is spurned. The brother is saved from the gallows and Isabella, renouncing her vows, gives her hand to the unknown masquerader who has stirred up the revolt and moved her heart.

In the year 1605 Shakespeare produced *Macbeth* and *King Lear*.
*Macbeth* (Munich, 1825) by Chelard, as well as incidental music by composers as far removed as Spohr and Humperdinck, have been inspired by the play. *Macbetto* (Florence, 1847) by Verdi has been called "a miserable perversion of Shakespeare." It foreshadows *Rigoletto* and the witches' scene is turned into a ballet; while "Lady Macbeth trolls a drinking song." The dramatic Sleep-Walking Scene is considered the best in the score. *Macbeth* (Paris, 1911) by Ernest Bloch has been criticized in that "comparative monotony of rhythm and harmony are its musical defects" but praised for its noble choruses. The tragic figures of Macbeth and Lady Macbeth stand out "with voices which have a vast resonance, and the scene of Duncan's murder is gripping musically and dramatically." No less a composer than Debussy has written incidental music to Shakespeare's *King Lear,* but the only score motivated by the play appears to be Kreutzer's *Cordelia* (Donaueschingen, 1819).

For the year 1606 we have *Anthony and Cleopatra* and *Coriolanus;* for 1607, *Timon of Athens;* for 1608, *Pericles;* for 1609, *Cymbeline*. *Cleopatra* has elsewhere been considered (See Index). *Coriolanus* has called forth no important score though there is a *Timon von Athen* (Vienna, 1696) by a good cellist but indifferent composer, the Austrian Emperor Leopold II. Forgetting *Pericles* we may pass to *Cymbeline.*

## "DINAH"

EDMOND MISSA. Book based on Shakespeare's *Cymbeline* (Paris, 1893). Containing attractive musical pages, notably a Masked Ball Scene and a "Chorus of Lords and Courtesans," the title is an arbitrary substitution for the name of Imogen, Cymbeline's daughter.

Transferring the scene of action from Roman Briton to medieval Venice, we find Iachino picking a quarrel with Posthumus, both loving

Dinah (Imogen). Separated as they fight by Philario, Iachino wagers his all that within twenty-four hours he will obtain from Dinah (Imogen) the bracelet Posthumus has given her. Stealing into Dinah's bedroom Iachino steals the bracelet and credulous Posthumus thinks he has lost love and fortune. But truth crushed to earth will rise again. Iachino, mortally wounded by Philario, repents, confesses his deceit with his dying breath and the happy lovers are united.

Despite Missa's opera, the most famous musical reaction to Shakespeare's play still remains Franz Schubert's lovely serenade, "Hark, hark the lark" taken from it.

The year 1610 is that of *A Winter's Tale*. *Hermione* (Berlin, 1872) by Max Bruch, book by Hopffer, is after Shakespeare's *A Winter's Tale*. An undramatic *succès d'estime,* there are notably refined and beautiful melodies in the score.

Leontes, King of Sicily, jealous of his guest Polyxenes, King of Arcadia, bids his cupbearer, Camillo, poison him. When Camillo warns the Arcadian and flees with him, Leontes in his rage casts his wife, Hermione, into prison as an adulteress. Her prison-born daughter, Perdita, disowned by her husband (Tab. II), she proudly leaves her cell to be tried. When Apollo's high priest declares her guiltless (Tab. III) Leontes curses the god only to learn that his son has died of grief, at which news Hermione gives up the ghost. In Arcadia Florizel, Polyxenes' son, falls in love with Perdita, the shepherd girl, and, when his father reproaches him, flees to Sicily with her. In Syracuse Leontes, vainly regretting Hermione, gladly acknowledges Perdita as his child and approves her love match while Hermione (she has been hidden away in the palace of her friend, Irene) appears to the satisfaction of all and the joy of her hasty husband.

*Ein Wintermärchen* (*A Winter's Tale,* Vienna, 1907) by Karl Goldmark, book by Willner after Shakespeare, is the Austrian composer's swan song. The Overture is a fine symphonic poem. There are songs, choruses, dances, and graceful pastoral music (Act II), and the dramatic coming to life of Hermione's statue in Leontes' palace is most impressive. In Goldmark's opera Perdita is alive when the curtain rises. Leontes turns mother and child out; the pastoral loves of Perdita and Florizel develop in Bohemia instead of Arcadia, but (Act II) the lovers duly hie them to Sicily where (Act III) joy reigns as Hermione's statue comes to life, and she forgives Leontes and blesses the lovers. Flotow's *Ein Wintermärchen* (Vienna, 1862) melodious but superficial, and Bernard Zimmermann's *Ein Wintermärchen* (Erfurt, 1900) are other settings. *Perdita* (Leipzig, 1865) by Carlo Barbieri, stresses Hermione's daughter, as does *Perdita* (Prague, 1897) by Josef Nesvera.

The year 1611 is the year of *The Tempest.* The play has a specific American interest because an account of the shipwreck of a vessel of Sir George Somers, while engaged on a Virginia colonization scheme, described in Sylvester Jourdan's *Journal,* is supposed to have furnished Shakespeare with a hint for the plot of his work. Operatic "Tempests," called forth by Shakespearean impetus, have raged in all parts of the globe.

## THE TEMPEST

Prospero, ex-duke of Milan and magician, was cast ashore on an island of the sea whose spirits were ruled by Ariel, and where stupid Caliban, brutish child of Nature, was his slave, and his lovely daughter, Miranda, gladdened his days. Prospero's enemies were shipwrecked on this island, his evil brother, who had cast him out in a boat to perish at sea, the King of Naples, and his followers. Ariel dispersed them while Ferdinando, the King of Naples' son, made love to Miranda with Prospero's approval and won her heart. By toiling for her father he gained his consent to their union and in the end all were reconciled and sailed home for Naples and Milan together.

Whether Purcell composed the music to Dryden's arrangement of *The Tempest* is doubtful, but we have three eighteenth century settings under the name of *Die Geisterinsel* (*The Spirit Isle*) by Peter von Winter (Munich, 1797), by J. F. Reichart (Berlin, 1798), and by Zumsteeg (Stuttgart, 1798), which together with Wenzel Müller's *Der Sturm* (Vienna, 1798) made three German "Tempest" operas for a single year. Among other "Tempests" is Halévy's *La Tempesta* (London, 1850); Napravnik's *Der Sturm* (Prague, 1860); *Der Sturm* by Frank (Hanover, 1887); and *Der Sturm* (Frankfort, 1888) by Urspruch. *La Tempête* (Paris, 1889) is a grand ballet by Ambroise Thomas, in which "Miranda's Slumber Music is a charming orchestral page." Duvernoy's *La Tempête* (Paris, 1880) has a fine duet between Ferdinand and Miranda, "Parle encore." Zdenko Fibich's *Boure* (*The Storm,* Prague, 1895) contains delightful "spirit choruses" and a dramatic Prologue (Storm Music) for orchestra. Kozanly's *Miranda* (Petrograd, 1910), Lattuada's *La Tempesta* (Milan, 1922), book by Rossato, with a fine emotional duet between Ferdinand and Miranda, and Nicholas Gaty's *The Tempest* (London, 1920) also should be mentioned.

Shakespeare wrote no play in 1612, and the *Two Noble Kinsmen* and *Henry VIII,* plays of 1613, do not seem to have called forth any notable operas, the libretto of Saint-Saën's "Henry VIII" not being based on Shakespeare.

## 4. *The Muscovy of Ivan the Terrible*

The sanguinary madman, Ivan the Terrible, was Czar of Muscovy when "Good Queen Bess" reigned in England and Henri III in France, and Ivan's Muscovy is the background of some notable operas.

*The Boyarina Vera Scheloga* (Petrograd, 1898) by Rimsky-Korsakoff is a prologue opera to *La Pskovityanka*. In Scheloga's palace (Pskov, 1555) his wife Vera—he is at war—sings her but not his babe to sleep and tells her sister, Nadescha, the tale of her betrayal by an unknown. Encountering a cavalcade of the Opritchniki, guards of Ivan, on a pilgrimage to Pechirsky Monastery, she fainted with terror, awoke to find herself in a stranger's tent, and her unknown rescuer soon so captivated her that she loathes her husband. When Scheloga comes home and finds the babe, Nadescha claims it, but Scheloga knows better, and returning to the battlefield seeks and finds a soldier's death, leaving little Olga to be cared for by Prince Tomakhov.

*La Pskovityanka* (*The Maid of Pskov*, Petrograd, 1873; rewritten, 1894) by Rimsky-Korsakoff is the "fifteen years after" of the preceding story. Based on a drama by Mey, it contains fine national choruses and Entr'actes, and a colorful Overture. Ivan the Terrible has humbled the pride of Novgorod and washed its street with blood. About to take Pskov, cathedral bells assemble the citizens in the market place (Act II) while Michael Toucha, Olga's lover, vainly bids them resist the tyrant. The town at his mercy Ivan questions Prince Tomakhov regarding the parentage of Olga, and realizes she is the child of his passing fancy for Vera. His savage heart is softened. Instead of having the townsfolk borne apart on the sabres of the Opritchniki, in his yearning for a daughter's love he spares the city in which Olga has grown to maidenhood. The last scene of the opera, one of convincing anguish, shows Olga—the monster's last hope of redemption through human love—snatched from his arms by inexorable death. In France this opera is known as *Ivan le Terrible;* and there is also an *Ivan le Terrible* (Paris, 1911) by Raoul Gunsbourg.

*The Opritchnik* (*The Guardsman*, Petrograd, 1892) by Tschaikowsky, with occasional intensely emotional pages, tells of young Morosoff, who becomes an opritchnik, one of Ivan the Terrible's savage guardsmen, vowed to celibacy, and breaks his vow to marry lovely Natalia. At the wedding banquet Ivan sends for the bride to dishonor her, the young husband resists, and the Czar forces his mother to watch the headsman hold up her boy's decapitated head in the square before her home. *The Bold Merchant Kala-shnikov* (Petrograd, 1880) by Anton Rubinstein after Lermontov's poem, with a fine dramatic scene in which Ivan listens to Alena's prayer for mercy, and "When I go into the garden" as an outstanding song, is the story of the opritchnik Kiribeivitch who, mad for pretty Alena, the merchant Kalashnikov's wife, carries her off in Moscow streets while on her way to vespers. The "bold merchant" objecting, is cast into prison, but the virtuous wife's pleas move the Czar's savage heart and (though Kalashnikov sings his doubts as to what may have happened to her while he was in jail in the opera's most powerful scene) she is allowed to bring her husband the good news of his release and her own. *Prince Serebrany* (Petrograd, 1892) by G. A. Kazachenko, a successful score influenced by Rimsky-Korsakoff, book after Alexander Tolstoi's historical novel, relates the fortunes of a young Russian prince who loves Helena, loveliest of Moscow's women, wedded to the old boyar Morosoff. When Morosoff has been beheaded for telling the mad Czar the truth, Prince Serebrany hopes to gain his heart's desire. But the lovely widow tells him the blood of Morosoff flows between them and Serebrany rides off to seek death in battle against the wild Siberian tribes. *The Bride of the Czar* (Petrograd, 1899) by Rimsky-Korsakoff, after Mey's drama, the composer's most popular opera (in France *La Fiancée du Tsar*) is colorfully melodious. Martha, daughter of rich Sobakin, Novgorod merchant, is betrothed to the boyar Lykov. But the opritchnik Gryaznoy, devoured by a mad passion, begs a love potion of the court physician, while as Martha comes from church (Act II) Ivan glimpses her loveliness and determines to make her his bride. Lykov, Gryaznoy, and Sobakin are at table (Act III) and Gryaznoy has just poured the potion into a cup he offers Martha when boyars in splendid court dress enter to tell the wretched girl the Czar has chosen her for a wife. In the Kremlin (Act IV) Martha lies sick (Liuba, Gryaznoy's cast-off mistress substituted poison for the love potion) when the opritchnik tells her Lykov, the only man she loves, has been beheaded at Ivan's command for trying to poison her. Martha goes mad. The opritchnik, when Liuba has confessed her deed, kills her and is led to execution with Martha's pathetic cry, "Come back to-morrow, my Ivan (she thinks he is Ivan Lykov in her madness), ringing in his ears.

## "BORIS GODOUNOV"

MODEST MOUSSORGSKY. Text after Pushkin's drama (Petrograd, 1874; the only version now heard is the one reorchestrated by Rimsky-Korsakoff, 1896). Above the series of disconnected scenes making up the

score, rises the tremendous dramatic figure of Boris, typifying the soul
of the Russian people with masterly musical naturalism. Moussorgsky's (and Chaliapin's) Boris is a transcended Macbeth, clutching at
life and dignity while the abyss of his own digging widens beneath
his feet. The choruses voice the cry of a downtrodden people, bitter
in thwarted desire (Church and Coronation Choruses), or titanic in
mirth (Tavern Scene, Act II). Waarlam's picturesquely great Ballad,
Xenia's Plaint, Marina's Polonaise and her love scene with Demetrius,
are pendants to Boris' tremendous Aria (Act II), overpowering in its
passion.

In the courtyard of the Novodievitch (Prologue), Boris—Czar
Feodor has died—ostensibly refuses the crown the people offer him
under the spur of henchmen's whips and pilgrims' venal prophecies:
(Scene 2, American version.) In Tschudov Convent, Pimen the
chronicler inflames the novice Gregory (afterward the False Demetrius),
with his tale of how Boris has murdered the Czarevitch, and the youth
elects to become the instrument of divine retribution on the usurper.

In the Square of the Kremlin Boris' splendid coronation processional
passes with bell chime and pageantry to the cathedral, while the populace, encouraged by the boyars, acclaim him. In a Lithuanian inn (Act
II, Scene 1, American version) Gregory, with bibulous, ballad-singing
monks, enters to ask the way to the border, leaping from the window
when the Czar's spies come to take him.

Xenia, Boris' daughter, in the women's wing of the Kremlin palace,
is wailing for her bridegroom who has died (her nurse trying to comfort her with the "Song of the Flea") when Boris enters, devoured
with remorse for his murder of Demetrius. When Count Shouisky
reports a False Demetrius has risen in Lithuania (though he himself
has seen the murdered boy in his coffin) the Czar breaks down. A
mechanical clock chimes, one of his own son Feodor's toys, and while
the accusing clangor of the coronation bells rings through his brain,
Boris' guilty conscience evokes the vision of his hapless victim, till
he writhes on the floor in despair. (The scene is the most harrowing
in the opera.)

In Sandomir Castle, Polish girls pay homage to lovely Marina,
daughter of the Voivode. Her ambition covets the Muscovite crown,
and Demetrius shall place it on her white brow! Gladly she promises
the Jesuit Rangoni to win the Russian people to the Roman faith
through the Czar whose heart she controls. Later in the castle gardens (in the American version this scene ends Act III), where a gay
Polonaise is danced, Polish magnates interrupt Marina's and Demetrius'
passionate love duet, promising to make the adventurer Czar.

In Kromy forest the starving people beat a boyar, torture an idiot,
and cheer Demetrius as he rides by in the light of flaring torches on
his way to Moscow and the throne. (This scene, voicing the very soul
of the Russian people, with the chorus in the rôle of the "star,"
Moussorgsky planned to make the final one of the opera but the last
act, as usually given, ends with Boris' tragic death.) In the great

reception hall of the Kremlin, while assembled boyars condemn the False Demetrius to death Boris, half insane with the torture of his guilty conscience, appears and breaks down with a terrible cry. Pimen's message (a shepherd has miracuously regained his sight after praying on dead Feodor's grave) kills his last hope. He consigns the empire to his son and dies in agony trying to say: "I still am the Czar!" while his soul passes on to the chant of monks and the toll of bells.

## "DIMITRI"

VICTORIN DE JONCIÈRES. Book by Bornier and Silvestre (Paris, 1890). A melodious Italianate score which completes Moussorgsky's tale with colorful ballet music, warmly emotional airs (Marina's "Pales étoiles," Act I), and dramatic ones (Dimitri's passionate invocation, "Moscou, la ville sainte").

Boris Godounov, clutching at the empire slipping from his grasp, has vainly tried to induce the widow of Ivan the Terrible to declare Dimitri (The False Demetrius) an impostor, only to see her acknowledge Dimitri as her son. The youth enters Moscow in triumph, while bells peal and the people acclaim him. But Count de Lusace, who revealed to Dimitri the lofty destiny awaiting him, wishes him to marry Vanda, the King of Poland's niece, for reasons of his own. When instead, Dimitri prepares to have his love, Marina, daughter of the Voivode of Sandomir, crowned Czarina, rejected Vanda swears revenge. Her loveliness makes de Lusace the tool of her fell design. On the threshold of the cathedral where the jeweled crown of Ivan is to be placed on Dimitri's head, he is suddenly downed by a musket shot fired by de Lusace and dies without knowing whether he is the true or the "false" Demetrius.

Antonin Dvořák's *Dimitrje* (Prague, 1882), another version of the tale of Demetrius, despite fine ensembles and choruses is quite untheatric.

## "A LIFE FOR THE CZAR"

MICHAEL IVANOVITCH GLINKA (Petrograd, 1836). After the False Dimitrii (there were several) had ceased troubling, the Russian boyars elected a boy czar, Michael Feodorovitch Romanoff (1613-1645)—the first of the dynasty that disappeared in the Russian Revolution of 1917 —to the vacant throne. Glinka's opera is woven around a plot against the young Czar's life. It is rich in beautiful folk tunes, whose themes are developed with the best of taste and proportion. The young Czar Michael's exalted aria, "Dawn, thou art come!" and the splendid closing scene in the Red Square of the Kremlin, where a tremendous chant of triumph ringing out to the peal of all the Kremlin's bells "seems to sum up the whole character of the Russian people," stand out.

Ivan Soussanin, a loyal moujik, is celebrating his daughter Antonida's marriage with Sobinin, a soldier back from the wars. But (Act II) the revels of Polish magnates are disturbed by a messenger; their men are in retreat, the Russians have chosen a Czar. Soon Polish soldiers burst into Ivan's *izba* (hut). He shall guide them to Moscow, so they may capture the Czar. While preparing to lead them astray, Ivan's whisper bids his son Vanya warn his sovereign. When Sobinin arrives, Antonida, uncheered by her companions' nuptial songs, sends him in pursuit of the foe with his men. In Act IV (Scene 1) Sobinin's followers hunt the enemy, while Soussanin (Scene 2) leads the Poles into a swampy woods, away from Kostroma monastery where Michael Romanoff has taken refuge. At dawn Soussanin (Scene 3) avows his heroic deceit only to be borne apart on Polish sabers. Joyous Muscovites chant the "Slavsya" chorus (Epilogue) in honor of the Czar on his way to be crowned in the Kremlin, as he makes an impressive pause on the threshold of the cathedral to salute the peasant hero's corpse.

## 5. *Austria erit in orbe ultima*

When the Emperor Mathias (1612-1619) had the motto *Austria* (by which he meant the house of Hapsburg) *erit in orbe ultima,* "Austria will endure forever," stamped on gold and silver plate, medals, books, liveries, housings, and all that was his, he could not foresee the irony of history, though operatically, perhaps, the motto, so far as the Hapsburgs are concerned, holds good for an opera or two by one of the greatest Italian composers, Verdi. The family fortunes were founded by Rudolf of Hapsburg (d. 1291), first to suppress the robber knights of his day. Robber knights are remembered in Leo Sachs' worthy *Les Bourgraves* (Paris, 1924), a setting of Victor Hugo's gloomy play; and Karl Goldmark's *Götz von Berlichingen* (Budapest, 1902), presenting five scenes from the life of a famous robber baron after Goethe. Rudolf's descendant, the chivalrous Emperor Maximilian (1493-1519), brother-in-law of "bluff King Hal" of England, inspired Brüll's *Der Landfriede* (*The Truce of God,* Berlin, 1875), in which, about to punish his foster son for leaguing with a robber baron to abduct Katherina, a decent Augsburg burgher girl, he relents when she avails herself of an old custom and saves the boy's life by claiming his hand in marriage. In *Theuerdank* (Munich, 1897) by Ludwig Thuille, Max disguised as that minstrel, intervenes to unite two hapless lovers. German lansquenet life from Maximilian's day onward has supplied many a fine, picturesque operatic background. *Der Dusle und das Bäbeli* (Munich, 1903) by Karl von Kaskel, a colorful lyric "folkopera," outstanding the "Lansquenet March" (Act I), "Drinking Song" (Act II), and Bäbeli's lovely air, "Gut' Nacht due Sonnenschein" (Act III) has the blond peasant lad, Dusle, enlist among Frundsberg's lansquenets despite his sweetheart Bäbeli's pleas

In the camp before Pavia, where she follows him, he kills the brutal sergeant, Brunone, defending her honor, and when Bäbeli's tears win him a chance to die in battle instead of by hempen noose he improves it by capturing the French King Francis, and gaining a full pardon with Bäbeli for his bride. *Das Nothemd* (*The Shirt of Need*, Dessau, 1913) by Woikowski-Biedaus climaxes in a similar duel, and contains fine old lansquenet songs. *Die rote Gred* (*Red Gred*) by Julius Bittner in a rich polyphone development of Austrian folk themes tells of a strumpet whose loves are for a day and who, become the bone of contention between two friends, Hans, the burgomaster's son, and Heinz, the town captain, turns from Hans (when her lovers fight) in a way which changes Heinz's liking to loathing, so that he lets her go her way to end as a harlot of the lansquenet camps.

*Juana la Loca* (*Joan the Mad*, Madrid, 1890) by Serrano y Ruiz and *Giovanna la Pazza* (Brussels, 1852) by Emanuel Muzio, Verdi's pupil, are operas based on the story of the insane mother of Emperor Charles V. Child of Ferdinand and Isabella, Joan was queer from the cradle. She idolized the Austrian Archduke Philip who married her, but Philip forgot Joan with a charming Portuguese lady, and his wife poisoned him, and went mad with remorse. For years, at night, through darkness and storm, she hurried in grisly fantastic procession over the highways and byways of Spain. In advance rode gold-bribed mercenaries, carrying pitch-dripping torches. Behind a crystal coffin, swinging between poles lashed to four mules, rode the mad queen, oblivious to all but the corpse which faced her while torches flared and the riders swore when their horses stumbled. It is not strange that the Spanish peasant who chanced to meet the grisly train at night crossed himself in horror.

It is in *Ernani* (Act III) that Charles V, mad Joan's son, makes his dramatic entrance into Charlemagne's funeral vault, amid the roar of distant cannon, preceded by torch-bearing soldiers, and followed by the Electors of the Holy Roman Empire carrying the regalia in a blaze of jewels, armor, and banners.

## "ERNANI"

GIUSEPPI VERDI. Book by Piave (Venice, 1844) after Victor Hugo's drama *Hernani*. First produced as *Il Proscritto*. The outstanding score of Verdi's first period, sanguinary, sensational, vigorous to vulgarity in the styles of Meyerbeer and Rossini, yet burning with passion and patriotism. Coincident with the revolt of Italy against Austrian rule, its ardent choruses, such as "Si ridesti il leon di Castiglia" (Act III), raised the patriotic enthusiasm of Italian audiences to fever pitch. When Victor Hugo saw what the librettist had done to his drama, he flew into a rage, and for years opposed performances of the opera. Outstanding musical numbers are Elvira's Air, "Ernani involami," one of Verdi's loveliest melodies, Silva's "Infelice" (Act I), the King's "Oh, de verd'anni miei" (Act III), and Ernani and Elvira's passionate Love Duet, "Ah, morir potesi adesso."

In his Aragonian mountain haunt, Ernani, outlawed son of the Duke of Segovia and captain of a robber band, is gloomy because Elvira, his heart's love, is to marry Don Ruy Gomez da Silva, an aged grandee. To cheer their leader the faithful fellows promise to abduct her (change of scene). Elvira in her room, scorning Don Ruy's wedding gifts, calls in song on Ernani to save her. On her intrudes Don Carlos (Charles V), King of Spain, in disguise and uses force to compel the love Elvira refuses. But—the secret panel opens—from it steps Ernani, who offers to fight both the King and Don Ruy (who has entered) and whispers to Elvira, as he leaves, to make ready to flee.

Later Ernani enters Don Ruy's palace as a pilgrim, as Elvira, believing him dead, is about to stab herself. Surprised by Don Ruy, Ernani refuses to fight the grandee till Elvira is freed from the King's clutches and the enemies uniting to secure her release, the noble bandit swears to die by his own hand whenever Don Ruy sounds his hunting horn, once their object gained.

Meditating within Charlemagne's tomb in the funeral vaults of Aix-la-Chapelle, Don Carlos is to be slain by Ernani, Silva, and others whose plotting he overhears outside the tomb. But when he strikes the bronze door of the tomb his followers seize them. All are condemned to die, but Elvira's pleas save Ernani's life and the changeable monarch even betroths the lovers.

No sooner are they married and safe in Ernani's ancestral keep, than, announced by a fatal, thrilling hunting horn call, Don Ruy enters and without a word offers Ernani dagger and poison cup. Ernani, stabbing himself to the heart, dies in Elvira's arms ("Music cease, go out, ye lights!") while Don Ruy gloats over the corpse.

In one of his most genial scores Richard Wagner has embodied the spirit of Teuton life in the day of Maximilian and Charles V, and the historic Hans Sachs, the shoemaker poet, "adds to the heroism of his own personal sacrifice the solemnity of the religious chant in which, with the voice of the people, he glorifies Luther and the Reformation" (Alfred Bruneau). For the great event in the intellectual life of the real Hans Sachs was the coming of the Reformation. In 1523 he wrote his poem "The Nightingale of Wittenberg" in Luther's honor, and though Wagner's drama is primarily a heart story, a simple, lovely tale of everyday life, the spirit of the Reformation lives and breathes in its pages. A human comedy whose sentiment is true to all ages, it identifies itself with the Reformation from the very rise of the curtain on the interior of Saint Catherine's Church in Nuremberg, where the faithful sing their Lutheran chorales.

## "DIE MEISTERSINGER VON NÜRNBERG"

### (*The Mastersingers of Nuremberg*)

RICHARD WAGNER. Book by the composer (Munich, 1868), after Hoffmann's novel *Der Sängerkrieg*. Wagner's only comic opera, staging the unceasing struggle between genius and pedantry, its story is at the same time a comedy of manners and a drama of passion in sixteenth century Nuremberg. The magnificent polyphonic Prelude, which epitomizes the drama in the development of its three main themes, Walter's "By silent hearth" (Act I), the contrapuntal Donnybrook (Act II), the Reformation Hymn, the incomparable Quintet, and Walter's "Prize Song," are among the great pages.

A young Franconian knight, Walter von Stolzing—who reads the poems of others in his lonely castle in wintertime and writes his own in the greening springtide forests—falls in love and scrapes acquaintance with Eva, daughter of the wealthy Nuremberg goldsmith, Pogner, in St. Catherine's Church. When Walter learns Eva's hand in marriage goes to the winner in the morrow's Mastersinger contest he determines to break a vocal lance. David (apprentice of Hans Sachs, the popular cobbler) tries to teach Walter the endless pedantic rules governing singing as the Mastersingers practice it. Walter the next day sings his trial song—all of love and spring—but Beckmesser, the stupid, jealous, and malicious "official marker," covers his slate with Walter's violations of the rules. Though Hans Sachs sees the beauty of his heartfelt and untutored song, Walter is refused admission to the guild, and rushes from the hall in despair.

After David gives indignant Magdalena, Eva's maid, the news of Walter's defeat, and fights jeering fellow apprentices, Hans Sachs sits down in front of the cobbler shop. There Eva discloses that she loves Walter, and Sachs, though he loves the girl, determines to help his rival. Now Beckmesser sings beneath Eva's window, but Sachs insists on scanning the music with a hammer blow for every error. The noise wakens the neighbors. David thinks Beckmesser is serenading Magdalena and uses his cudgel on him. Townsfolk and apprentices pour into the street and fight, but Hans Sachs stops Eva and Walter as they try to elope under cover of the confusion. He sends Eva home and takes Walter into his own house, while with the mellow sound of the watchman's horn the crowd disappears from the moonlit street.

To Sachs, brooding over the folly of man, comes Walter who has dreamed of a wonderful song. He sings it and at Sachs' request jots down the words on a bit of paper. Beckmesser, crawling in after Sachs and Walter have left, finds the paper, and is caught in the act of stealing. Sachs, however, tells him he can keep the poem. When Eva comes in Walter sings her a stanza of his dream song, and the arrival of David and Magdalena motives the famous Quintet. On the banks of the Pegnitz river the Nuremberg guilds and their families watch the Mastersingers move in procession to the platform. Sachs calls on Beckmesser to sing, and the pedant makes a pitiful botch of fitting Walter's new words to his old tune. Laughed from the platform, his place is taken by Walter, whose singing of the "Prize Song," the love melody to Eva, wins the laurel crown and his sweetheart's hand in marriage. Sachs, who has shown that Art's future lies in the happy union of the traditional and the inspired, is acclaimed by all.

*Hans Sachs* (Leipzig, 1840) by Albert Lortzing, book after Deinherdstein. This sentimental Hans Sachs, an ancestor of Nessler's trumpeter, scorned by the goldsmith, Steffen, whose daughter, Kunigund, he loves, leaves Nuremberg for Emperor Maximilian's court. Görg, his apprentice, loses a poem of his master's which, found and brought to Maximilian, leads him to Nuremberg to honor the writer. There the Augsburg counselor, Eoban Hesse, who claims to be the author of the poem, is proved a liar, and Sachs, returning at the psychological moment, is covered with honors and marries his Kunigund. Gyrowetz' eighteenth century *Hans Sachs* was still given in Leipzig as late as 1834.

## "DON CARLOS"

GIUSEPPE VERDI. Book by Méry and Du Locle (Paris, 1867), after Schiller's drama. A score of Verdi's middle period, with music varying in value, but many noble pages. The "Aïda" mass effects are forecast by the massed choruses of the Finale, funeral marches of the heretics condemned to be burned, the disarming of Don Carlos, etc. The outstanding figure of the drama is the gloomy Philip II, whom Chaliapin's inspired portrayal shows in every phase of his character, and elevates to a figure of tragic grandeur equal to Boris. History has dismissed as a fable the supposition that the real Carlos, a degenerate moron, was judicially done to death by his father.

In Fontainebleau forest (1560) Don Carlos, King Philip's son, declares his love for Elizabeth of Valois, soon to become his stepmother. Before he leaves for Flanders to banish Elizabeth from his mind, the lovers again forget duty in each other's arms.

In the gardens of the King's palace in Madrid, Carlos meets the masked Princess of Eboli and thinking her the Queen, makes love to her. When, her mask removed, she finds herself scorned, jealousy moves her to the betrayal of Don Carlos' illicit passion (change of scene). Merrily chime the bells of Nuestra Señora d'Antocha. Heretics are to be burned in the square, in the presence of King and Court. Don Carlos, pleading for the victims of the *auto-da-fé*, is led away, and the funeral pile is lit to the glad chant of the inquisitors.

In the royal library the Princess of Eboli has revealed to Philip his son's guilty love and the Grand Inquisitor his criminal heresy, while (change of scene) in Don Carlos' prison cell a bullet, clerically inspired, strikes dead his friend the Marquis of Posa.

Don Carlos, released from prison, hurries to the Cloister of San Just, to bid his stepmother a last fond farewell. While Elizabeth exhorts him to forget his heart's sorrow in doing good to the Flemings who have rebelled, the King surprising them, delivers his son to the Grand Inquisitor to be chastened in the cleansing flames.

With Verdi's *Don Carlos* might be mentioned Sir Michael Costa's *Don Carlos* (London, 1844); Marchetti's *Don Juan d'Austria* (Turin, 1880)—King Philip's half brother whom he is thought to have poisoned—Orefice's *Egmont* (Naples, 1878); and Gregor's *La Dernière Nuit du Comte Egmont* (*Count Egmont's Last Night,* Brussels, 1851). Count Egmont was one of the unfortunate Dutch nobles who rebelled against Philip II and was executed, his tragic fate calling forth one of Beethoven's finest overtures.

If, operatically, *Die Meistersinger* is the score most eloquently expressing the spirit of the Reformation, the musical soul of the Counter Reformation, whose chief instrument was Philip II of Spain, and whose successors together with the Austrian Hapsburgs, carried on the struggle, has been embodied in a great religious opera of recent years. Like *Die Meistersinger,* Pfitzner's *Palestrina* has a human story. Yet while it is the drama of a great musician's soul struggle, its "Angel Mass" is a crystallization in music of the inner soul of the new spirit which had come over the Church of Tradition, those reforms from within whose practical execution the Council of Trent decreed. In painting, the Counter Reformation expressed itself with greater luxuriance. Not only did Guido Reni paint tenderly appealing saints, weeping because of their abandoned altars; the naturalists Caravaggio and Ribera painted pictures of terror, saints martyred, speared, and flayed, looking down reproachfully on the recreant, from black skies. In opera, however, the traditional church is most truly expressed in *Palestrina's* ethereal music and in a modern master's ideal development of its spirit. Pfitzner's *Palestrina* carries the soul to God in music which describes the creation of the mass in ultramodern harmony, harking back to Palestrina's own style. In "the intoxicating glory of the angelic mass . . . dwells in word and tone a tender melancholy archaism, unique in our literature" (Bie).

## "PALESTRINA"

HANS PFITZNER. An ultramodern "musical legend," whose keynote is heavenward inspiration (Munich, 1917). Legend declares that Pope

Pius IV (1536) was so moved by Palestrina's "Missa Papae Marcelli" that he rescinded his sweeping condemnation of all church music more worldly than the Gregorian plain chant. Angels were supposed to have inspired the tones of the famous mass, so that church music might be saved. From this point of departure the composer has extended his work to embody in *Palestrina* the eternal tragedy of the artist's relation to the world. Pfitzner has been called a romanticist rooted in the Wagnerian music drama; his *Palestrina* the "most matured fruit of Wagnerism." In his music, mood is stronger than dramatism, and he is controlled in effect where Wagner is glowingly sensuous and passionate. The Prelude establishes the musical atmosphere of the great composer, aging in solitude.

In Palestrina's study, Cardinal Borromeo tells him that the Emperor Ferdinand and himself, before the Council of Trent confirms the edict doing away with figurated music, have stipulated Palestrina be given a chance to save it with a mass. He refuses, but when they leave, the voices of the great masters of the past, resounding in the darkened room, recall him to the duty genius owes the world. Conscience wakens the urge to create and—as the shade of his loved wife Lucrezia plunges him in ecstasy, angel voices sing in jubilant chorus. Feverishly the master notes down the divine music and, the mass written, falls into the slumber of exhaustion. (The original development of a melodic quote from the actual "Missa Papae Marcelli" has been called one of the most genial inspirations of the whole operatic stage.) With the matin chimes of the Roman church bells Ighino enters to gather the sleeping master's' manuscript pages, joyous to think his father is once more active.

The scenes at the Council of Trent (1545-1563) where bishops and prelates of opposing parties, Italian, French, Spanish, German, work themselves up to a pitch of excitement in their political wrangles and discussions—Pfitzner is the first composer to set a Parliament to music —make a little opera in themselves. It ends with the servants of the princes of the Church attacking each other with their knives and being forced to return to reason by a salvo of musketry.

In Palestrina's study, the aged musician looks out on Rome through the open window. The mass, at that moment, is being sung before Pope and cardinals. Cheers of the populace break the silence. Singers of the Sistine Chapel rush into the room: the master's work has won a triumph; the Pope himself is coming to thank him, and reinstall him as director of the Sistine Chapel. While Ighino hurries into the street where the people are acclaiming his father Palestrina, alone, turns gratefully to Lucrezia's picture. His hands glide over the organ keys and "on music's tones his soul rises to those heights of genius removed from earthly suffering." An earlier and forgotten score is *Palestrina* (Ratisbon, 1886) by Rheinberger's pupil, Melchior Sachs.

America was discovered when Ferdinand and Isabella were "kings" of Spain; the epoch of Charles V is that of the conquest of Mexico and Peru, that of Philip II and Elizabeth the beginning of the age of colonization. And it is time, now that the masses of Palestrina are sung in the cathedrals which rise in the Spanish cities of South America, to turn from the Old World, and consider the New World as revealed in opera.

# CHAPTER VII

## THE NEW WORLD OPERA STORIES

### 1. *The Isles of the Spanish Main*

If we take the Discovery as the starting point of a series of New World Opera Stories we find—after paying homage to Norse claims by mention of Gerard Tonning's fine *Leif Ericcson* (Seattle, 1910)—that it has called forth no *great* opera. There is Fabrici's *Il Colombo* (Rome, 1787), Morlacchi's (Genoa, 1828), Luigi Ricci's (Parma, 1829), Sangiorge's (Parma, 1840), the double-bass Giovanni Bottesini's *Cristoforo Colombo* (Havana, 1847), Barbieri's (Berlin, 1848), Mela's (Verona, 1857), Bignani's (Genoa, 1883), Llanos' (Naples, 1892), Carnicer's *El Colon* (Barcelona, 1818), and the American Silas Gamaliel Pratt's *The Triumph of Columbus* (concert form, New York, 1892). Columbus' final point of departure on his journey suggests mention of *Nisidia, ou les Amazons des Açores* (Paris, 1848) by François Bénoist, an episode of the conquest of the islands by the Portuguese.

### "CRISTOFORO COLOMBO"

ALBERTO FRANCHETTI. Book by Illica (Genoa, 1892). "The most contemporaneous Columbus opera," its music, Meyerbeerian in its pomp and pretentiousness, has been accused of lacking individuality.

In the courtyard of a Salamancan convent Roldano incites the mob against Columbus, while within the Council of Castile rejects his proposal as insane. As Columbus emerges the mob hoots. But Queen Isabella appears on the threshold, and with inspired gesture hands him her golden crown. (Symbolizing the pledging of the crown jewels to pay for his expedition.)

Aboard the caravel *Santa Maria,* as the sailors, incited by Roldano, rush toward the Admiral, shouting "Down with the Genoese!" the outlook's cry of "Land!" resounds, emphasized by cannon-shots from the *Pinta.* The mutiny is over.

In Xaragua, near Columbus' camp, Roldano has killed the Indian Queen Anacoana's husband. The widow feigns love for the murderer to gain revenge; her amorous approaches supported by a colorful ballet of feather-plumed Indian girls. But Anacoana is betrayed by her daughter Iguamota, who loves the Spaniard Guevara. Roldano's intrigues succeed. By King Ferdinand's order Columbus is seized. Roldano stabs Anacoana, who will not lend herself to his plans, and Iguamota, foiling her lover's efforts to save her, joins her mother in death. The curtain falls on Columbus in chains.

Epilogue (1506). In Medina del Campo, Columbus and Guevara meditate in the crypt of the dead kings of Castile. When Guevara leaves in search of Isabella, Columbus questions young girls who enter with wreaths of flowers. They tell him good Queen Isabella lies buried where he stands. Overcome, Columbus' reason leaves him. After a delirious apostrophe he breaks down at the queen's tomb, where Guevara finds him on his return.

It was on the island of San Salvador, the Guanahani of the Indians, that Columbus first trod the soil of the New World. The next larger island to be discovered on this, Columbus' first voyage, was the island of Cuba, and Cuba, once "the ever faithful isle," still "the Pearl of the Antilles," has found a distinguished native composer to develop her graceful native *danzones* in a dramatic score.

## "LA DOREYA"

EDUARDO SANCHEZ FUENTES. Cuban ideological legend. Book by Hilarion Cabrisas (Havana, 1918). This opera by the most distinguished of contemporary Cuban composers was suggested by the discovery (1913) of the first *canayes de muertos* (pre-Columbian Indian burial mounds) on the island. Sanchez Fuentes in his musical score has made effective and convincingly moving use of authentic Siboney Indian airs, dating from the time when the island was still known as *Coaibai*, before the Spanish conquerors gave it its present name. Outstanding are: the "Canto real" (Royal Chant), the lyric solos of Doreya, and the picturesque Indian Ballet, "Danza Epitalamica," with its preceding "Votive Hymn."

On the banks of the Arimao, in the primitive tropical forest, a Siboney Indian tribe dwells patriarchally beneath the palms, ruled by Analay, the *cacique*. For ages the savage Caribs have been their only enemies. But a new foe has sought them out: the conquering Spaniard. The curtain rises on Manfredo, a *conquistador*, as he steps from canoe to shore and summons lovely Doreya, the *cacique's* daughter, with the call of a nocturnal bird. Only a few days before he had saved her from the brutal, constraining arms of Yarayo, a tribal warrior, who had assaulted her; and now she is his passionately devoted slave. But the approach of Damuji, the tribal *behique* or high priest, with a chorus of sun worshipers, drives the Siboney princess' Spanish lover to flight. Doreya steals off in turn, and fearing Yarayo's persecutions, hastens after Manfredo. Meanwhile the sacred tribal dances begin (Ballet) interrupted by an Indian who tells Analay his daughter is fleeing with a white man. Furious, the Siboney warriors with wild cries take up the pursuit. Yarayo, a Carib by birth, a Siboney only by favor of the *cacique,* meets some of his own savage tribesmen by stealth, and bids them follow the *cacique* in secret. Analay leads them to a *caney* (graveyard) where Naya, Doreya's confidant, refuses to betray the lovers' hiding place, though Yarayo, bids Analay promise their pardon. Yarayo's Caribs, however, soon drag the fugitives before Analay, who curses his daughter, while the *behique* superintends the building of the funeral pyre on which Manfredo is to burn, a victim to the sun god. In vain Doreya begs her father to be merciful. Manfredo, however, while the Siboneys listen with growing excitement, tells of the assault made on the *cacique's* daughter by Yarayo. Blind with rage, the Carib fits arrow to bow and before the Spaniard can utter his name, discharges it. Doreya, to save Manfredo, casts herself in the way of the dart, which pierces her breast. While Manfredo bursts his bonds to clasp Doreya's body to him in despair, the Siboneys drag Yarayo to the funeral pyre to burn in his stead.

*La Esclava* (*The Slave,* Havana, 1921) by J. Mauri, book by Tomas Julia, is a folkwise opera with Cuba at a later period of Spanish rule as its scene of action, in which folk themes and rhythms are used in a modern style in the presentation of a tragic tale of a presumably white heroine who discovers that slave blood flows in her veins. A symphonic Intermezzo, Mathilde's "Romanza" and a choral "Himno à la Muerte" ("Hymn to Death") are outstanding pages.

It was during his first voyage that Columbus also discovered the island variously known as Hispaniola, Haiti or San Domingo. The fact is commemorated in the Mexican Morales' *Cristoforo Colombo a San Domingo* (Mexico City, 1892). In connection with it we have Donizetti's *Il furioso all' isola di Santo Domingo* (*The Madman on the Island of San Domingo,* Rome, 1833), a mad romance of a cursing, stone-throwing maniac for love's sake, in which the song "Raggio d'amore" once was popular. The part of San Domingo known as Haiti has called forth a score by a distinguished modern German composer.

## "DIE JASSABRAUT"

### (*The Jassa Bride*)

ALBERT MATTAUSCH (Magdeburg, 1923). Book by Bethge, after Kleist's *Die Verlobung in Santo Domingo.* The stirring, dramatic music is in the style of the Italian verists.

Congo Hoango, a bloodthirsty old negro of Haiti, murders his French master in the great revolt of the blacks (1803) and turns the latter's home near Port-au-Prince into a death trap for fugitive whites. Toni, a young charming "yellow girl," a Marseilles merchant's by-blow, quiets the victims' suspicions with smiles and caresses. Babekane, her fanatic mother, summons the assassins. Gustave de Ried, a young French officer, knocks at the door of the murder house at midnight. Admitted, he reveals that with a little party, hidden in the woods, he plans to gain Port-au-Prince. When Toni fetches water to Gustave he yields to a sudden passion for the young mestiza. It is returned. In her supreme surrender Toni, when Gustave promises to take her to Europe as his bride and gives her his dead betrothed's golden cross, wordlessly vows eternal fealty, planning to save him. Alas, Congo Hoango returns with his black cutthroats! To save her lover for the nonce, by turning suspicion from herself, Toni binds him to his couch. Gustave thinks she has betrayed him. His friends arrive, for whom Toni has sent, and the blacks are overpowered but Toni enters Gustave's room only to be stretched dying on the ground by his pistol-bullet. When the dying girl sighs "You should have trusted me!" Gustave puts a bullet through his brain.

On his second voyage (1493) Columbus discovered Guadalupe and opera composers have followed in his wake: Battista with *Il Corsaro della Guadalupe* (Naples, 1853), Petrella in his *Pirati Spagnuoli* (Naples, 1856), and Offenbach in his *La Créole* (Paris, 1875), the tale of Dora, a lovely Creole of Guadalupe (there is an attractive "Chanson Créole") who wins a French naval officer's heart at the expense of an aristocratic rival. The island of Juan Fernandez, discovered in 1563 by the Spanish navigator who left behind him the goats whose offspring were hunted by Alexander Selkirk, the original Robinson Crusoe, has been remembered in connection with the last-named classic of world fiction, in Valentino Fioravanti's *Robinson nella isola deserta* (*Robinson in the Desert Isle*, Naples, 1825). Dalyrac's *Azémia ou le nouveau Robinson* (Paris, 1789) is the tale of Azemia, daughter of an English pseudo-Crusoe living on a Pacific isle who, after various adventures in which a Spanish sea captain figures as the villain, and savages, English and Spanish sailors as a chorus, finds happiness in the love of Prosper, another island white.

*Robinson Crusoe* (Paris, 1867) by Jacques Offenbach, book by Cormon and Cremieux, carries Crusoe from his Bristol home to "the mouth of the Orinoco river" only in Act III. No Frenchman of the Second Empire could imagine a Robinson utterly deprived of female companionship, so a certain Susanne is cast ashore with him, who sings "Enfants des pampas" to the man with the goatskin cap under the cocoa palm. The score contains piquant melodies and a taking Entr'acte, "Marche des Sauvages."

## "THOMAS L'AGNELET"

Léon Jongen. Book by Claude Farrière after his buccaneer novel *Thomas l'Agnelet, gentilhomme de fortune* (Brussels, 1924). A successful score in which "music conservatively meritorious" interprets a dramatic tale, it is the most recent buccaneer opera.

The Norman sailor Thomas l'Agnelet (the Lambkin) of St. Malo— the scenes are laid in the Norman port town and aboard the buccaneer's ship—sails for the Spanish Main on a St. Malo "corsair frigate" and becomes a pirate of the tropic waterways. When he returns to his home port with the beautiful and depraved Andalusian Juana, prize of his sacking of Ciudad-Real, whose abject slave he has become, ignoring his former sweetheart Anne-Marie, retribution overtakes him. Thomas had defied King Louis' orders against piracy, and, condemned by the Royal Commissioners, finds he cannot die too quickly. When Juana, abandoned comrade of his wild life, sends him her curse as he stands on the scaffold, together with the mocking news the child she is about to bear is not his own, Thomas leaps to death from the platform with such violence that the taut rope snaps off his head. (This, of course, does *not* happen on the stage.)

*Le Flibustier* (Paris, 1894) by César Cui, book after a Richepin play, contains some noble "sea music," Breton folk dances, and a picturesque "Chanson Bretonne." Janik, returning to his native village after years of buccaneering adventure, is mistaken by old Legoez, Pierre's grandfather, for Pierre. Fearing to kill the old man, none of the family dare tell him the truth, and not until Janik has won the love of the real Pierre's fiancée Jacquenn does the latter appear with Mexican gold garnered on the seas. After some violent scenes Janik is cast out. But Pierre's better nature tells him he is not to blame; he forgives his double for the wrong unintentionally done him and unites the lovers. The Pole Dobrzynski's *Mombar, le Flibustier* (Warsaw, 1861) may also be mentioned.

### 2. Central and South America

From Cuba to the Central American mainland was but a step, as Cortez discovered, and the conquest of the golden Aztec empire probably first took tangible operatic form in one of Purcell's "Semi-operas," to Dryden's *The Indian Emperor* (London, 1665). *The Indian Queen* (London, 1695), one of the same composer's most dramatic scores, to Dryden's verse melodramatically pictured the love tragedy of Queen Zempoalla (arrayed in a real Aztec feather dress) with battles, sacrifices, spirits singing in the air, the god of dreams rising through a trap, etc. The ballad, "I attempt from love's sickness to fly," is still sung. The German Graun (1701-1759) wrote *Montezuma*, Sir Henry Bishop *Cortez* (London, 1823), and there is *L'eroina della Messico* (*The Heroine of Mexico*) among Luigi Ricci's thirty scores. The fine chorus "Hark, 'tis the Indian drum" in Bishop's score survives. The Italian Zingarelli wrote *Montezuma* (Naples, 1781), but among older operas of the Mexican conquest Spontini's tragic grand opera is the most famous.

## "FERDINANDO CORTEZ"

GASPARO SPONTINI. Book by de Jouey and Esmenard (Paris, 1809). A famous "political" opera favored by Napoleon I because he hoped it would flatter the vanity of the Spaniards he was trying to conquer. A cavalry charge was a feature of the first night, attended by Napoleon and the kings of Saxony and Westphalia. The music, despite fine choruses, now seems antiquated.

Cortez' camp by the sea. The Spanish soldiers clamor for home. Cortez quells the revolt and sends an embassy to Montezuma to obtain the release of his brother Alvar, a Mexican prisoner. The arrival of an Aztec embassy motivates a "Mexican Ballet," followed by a military drill. Cortez burns his ships to deprive his men of all hope of escape as the climax of the act. [Ruperto Chapi's *Las naves de Cortez* (*The Ships of Cortes*, Madrid, 1874), dramatic opera scene, may be mentioned in this connection.]

Amazilly, an Aztec princess, Montezuma's niece, has abandoned home and family for love of the Spanish leader. When Morales, seeing Cortez neglects his captive brother, urges him to lead his soldiers to the rescue Amazilly flings herself into the great lake of Mexico and swims home to hasten his release.

As Alvar is to be sacrificed to "the god of evil," dripping Amazilly presents herself as a burnt offering in Alvar's place. The high priest is willing but Telasco, Amazilly's brother, objects. During the dispute Cortez forces the temple gates, rescues his mistress from the flames, and Spaniards and Aztecs sing: "O day of glory and of hope!"

Native Mexican composers' operas on Aztec legends include Ancieto Ortega's *Guatimozin* (1867), Ricardo Castro's *Atizamba* (1900), Carlos Saintanego's *Netzhuacoyotl*. *Huemac* (Buenos Aires, 1916) by Pascual de Rogates is a meritorious score based on the adventures of Huemac, a Chichemechan priest who (600 A.D.) led the five tribes of his people from Huehuetlapallan to the valley of Mexico. Francesco Rogers Fanciulli's *Malinche or The Day of Sacrifice* (MS.) is based on Lew Wallace's novel, *The Fair God*. Americans, Frederick Grant Gleason, *Montezuma* (MS.), John Humphreys Stewart, *Montezuma* (San Francisco,

1903) and George Colburn, *The Masque of Montezuma* (1913) have essayed the Aztec subject.

## "AZORA"

### (*The Daughter of Montezuma*)

HENRY HADLEY. American tragic opera (New York, 1917). Book by David Stevens, its tale developed in a poetic libretto, it has fine lyric airs: Duet of Xalca and Azora, Papantzin's "I dreamed that death" (Act I), the Temple Scene (Act II), the effective Finale (Act III), and symphonic Preludes (3), and Dances.

Xalca, Prince of Tlascala, loves Azora, his conquerer Montezuma's daughter. She returns his love. At the sun god's feast, Canek, the High Priest (Ramatzin, the Aztec general, has whispered that the Tlascalan loves his fiancée) warns Xalca to give up hope of Azora's hand. As a result he and Azora vow to be true to each other. In the sacrificial ceremonies, Montezuma misses Azora. His sister Papantzin admits she advised the girl to miss the repulsive service—human hearts torn from victims' breasts and held dripping to the sun. Montezuma rebukes her, but Papantzin announces "the coming of Christ's warriors and the triumph of the Cross over superstition." An army of Tarascans approach. The victims are hustled to the altar and Xalca sent to defeat the foe. Any favor he asks shall be his if he return a victor.

As Azora prays for her love in Totec's temple, Canek tells her he is dead and Ramatzin begs her to marry him. When she refuses he grows so brutal Canek interferes. Ramatzin then begs Montezuma to announce his betrothal but Azora says she will wed Xalca though the Aztec monarch intimates Xalca will not live long. At this moment Xalca enters the temple victorious. He suggests a sacrifice and Montezuma agrees—with Xalca in mind. When the prince claims Azora's hand as his reward, the emperor's fury bursts all bounds. Amid jubilant shouts of soldiers without the temple, ignorant of their leader's fate, Xalca and Azora are told their "red jewels"—a poetic term for the human heart—will be torn from their breasts the next day.

In the Cavern of Sacrifice Papantzin tries to convert Azora to Christianity as Canek declares Montezuma will spare her life if she marry Ramatzin, but the girl prefers death with the Tlascalan to life with the Aztec. The prisoners are led to their doom. When the sunlight touches the altar, Canek will open their breasts with obsidian knife, and Canek's knife is raised when his arm grows rigid as Cortez, followed by soldiers and priests bearing banners and a cross, appears as the god out of the machine. The shaft of sunlight falls on the Cross and Canek faints, dropping his knife. While Montezuma and his subjects call frantically on Totec, "the overpowering manifestation of the Christian faith is invincible, and the scene closes with the triumphant strains of *Gloria in Excelsis Deo*."

From the Mexican to the Peruvian conquest is a natural transition. Rameau's heroic ballet *Les Indes galants* (Paris, 1735) introduced "the Incas of Peru" to picturesque music. Next came Caudeille's lyric tragedy, *Pizarre* (Paris, 1785). In the same year were produced Méhul's unsuccessful *Cora* (Paris, 1791), the tale of an unfortunate Peruvian girl who, though betrothed to the sun god, loved a Spaniard with tragic consequences; and Cimârosa's *La virgine del sole* (Petrograd, 1791) whose fluid melody rivals that of Mozart. Lortzing's *Die Schatzkammer des Inka* (*The Inca's Treasure Chamber*) never was performed, and Alessandro Rolla is remembered as Paganini's teacher rather than the composer of *Pizarro o la conquista del Peru* (Milan, 1807). Sir Henry Bishop's ballad opera *The Virgin of the Sun* (London, 1812), based on Kotzebue's melodramatic play *Die Spanier in Peru,* was a success in its day, as was Wenzel Müller's *Die Prinzessin von Kakambo* (Vienna, 1814) also after Kotzebue, and his Mexican *Vitzilipututzli* (Vienna, 1817).

*Das Unterbrochene Opferfest* (*The Interrupted Sacrifice,* Vienna, 1796) by Peter von Winter, a German tragic opera whose music was a "triumph of tears," was an earlier historical grand opera. Fate makes an Englishman general of a Peruvian Inca. Condemned to burn on the stake through jealousy, he is saved by elaborate intrigues in which figure sweethearts, friends, foes and priests.

*Ollanta* (Lima, 1901) by José Valle-Riestra—the fine "Hymn to the Sun" has been published in the United States—is a setting of the Quichua drama of the same name, once performed before the Incas in the great public square of Cuzco. The chieftain Ollanto loves beautiful Cusi Coyllar, daughter of the Inca Pachacutec. He rescues her when she is imprisoned by her angry father, but is overcome in battle by the new Inca, the Emperor Yupanqui, Pachacutec's son, to whose generosity the lovers owe their final happiness. As in his opera *Athualpa,* also based on Peruvian folk tunes, Valle-Riestra uses old Inca melodies (*jaravis*) and the Quichua national flute, the *quena.* Modern reactions to the Peruvian theme are *Die Inkasöhne* (*The Sons of the Inca,* Darmstadt, 1855) by Wilhelm de Haan, and *Assarpai* by Ferdinan Hummel (Gotha, 1898), book after Wildenbruch by Dora Dunker. Alonso, a Spanish officer, draws innocent Assarpai, the Inca Athualpa's daughter, to his breast in a hidden Peruvian valley, though her dumb attendant, Odahia, mutely warns. Captured by Pizarro, the stake on which she is to burn because her father will not surrender already ablaze, dumb Odahia's unexpected scream as Alonzo's bridal procession passes—he is marrying Pizarro's daughter Inez—startles the groom. He leaps from his bride's side into the flames, and dies together with Assarpai.

*The Virgins of the Sun* (New York, 1922) by Julius Mattfield, a distinctive post-Debussyan ballet score, with an outstanding "Temple Dance," presents a Peruvian myth. A mortal, straying into the sun god's garden wakes human love in the chaste celestial hearts of the deity's daughters who, realizing too late they have erred, cast their lover from a precipice to conceal their fault. The fading light of day, however, reveals their peccadillo to their father and they perish, blighted by his curse. *La Monja Alferez* (*The Nun Ensign*, Madrid, 1875) by Marques, is based on the picaresque adventures of the Basque novice Catalina de Erauso (b. 1585) who deserted her convent disguised as a man and led the wild life of a Spanish soldier of fortune in the "kingdoms of Peru and Chili," as ready to spill *Chuncho* blood in battle as Spanish blood in the *duello*. Legend has it she fell by the sword on the road to Vera Cruz when the convoy of mules she had in charge was attacked by bandits. Eleodoro Ortiz de Zarate's *La Fioraria de Lugano* (Santiago, Chile, 1895) has been called "the first native Chilean opera."

## "LE CARROSSE DU SAINT-SACREMENT"

### (*The Coach of the Holy Sacrament*)

Lord Berners. Book after Mérimée's comedy (*Théâtre de Clara Gazul,* Monte Carlo, 1923). Music ultramodern in trend, with the "Parrot's Song," a notable bit of Spanish color, an outstanding air.

Don Andreas de Ribera, viceroy of Peru, cursing his gout, listens to his secretary Martinez recount spicy details of Lima gossip about La Périchole, the popular actress and his own mistress, and when he hears of the pearl necklace she flung the toreador Ramon at the last bullfight he drives the secretary furiously from the room as his charmer is announced. La Périchole's caresses soon calm his rage and—he lets her have his new gilded state coach, just come from Spain, to drive to church. La Périchole is not content to upset the blue-blooded *grandes dames* of Lima figuratively. She so manages that she literally upsets the coach of the Marchioness of Altamirano on her way to the cathedral; and soon that lady's lawyer, Tomas d'Esquival, complains to the viceroy that unless La Périchole is punished she will appeal to the King in Madrid. At this juncture the actress enters—hand in hand with the Bishop of Lima. She has played a trump card. "I could not bear to see venerable priests risk sun-stroke rushing through Lima streets to administer the Holy Sacrament to some dying sinner, fearing to arrive too late, so, inspired by the Blessed Virgin, I have dedicated this splendid coach to the service of God." Her indictment quashed, all praise the clever actress, telling her the "Coach of the Holy Sacrament" will one day be her Elijah's chariot and bear her straight to heaven.

*La Périchole* (Paris, 1869), Offenbach's famous operetta, outstanding its "Letter Song," "O mon cher amant," makes La Périchole a pretty street singer whom Don Andreas—with the worst motives, for a Spanish viceroy's mistress must be married, so etiquette decrees—weds her to her gutter lover, Piquillo; but moved by the wedded sweethearts' pleas, gives up his designs on the girl, and dismisses the pair laden with gifts.

*The Desert Flower* (London, 1863), William Wallace's ballad opera in the style of Balfe, idealizes the New Guinea Papuans in the same tale Saint-Georges paraphrased for Halévy's *Jaguarita l'Indienne* (Paris, 1865), the latter's brilliant "bird song," "Charmant colibri," with flute *obbligato,* still being sung in concert. A confused action in Dutch colonial Surinam shows *lovely* Jaguarita (Oarita)—books of travel prove operatic fancy contrary to Papuan reality—queen of the head-hunting Anacotas, losing her dusky heart to a young Dutch officer and marrying him with Indian rites. Ballet dances in tropic forests are features of both scores. Surinam, too, is the scene of the tragic loves of the fair (?) Imoinda and *Orinokoo, the Royal Slave,* Southerne's drama (London, 1695) which Purcell set to music.

The best known South American opera by a native composer on a native subject is by the Brazilian Gomes (1839-1896). His *Condor* (Rio de Janeiro, 1891) was unsuccessful; but *O Guaraney* was successfully performed in Italy.

## "O GUARANEY"

Antonio Carlos Gomes. Brazilian tragic opera. Book by Antonio Scalvini after José de Alencar's Brazilian novel (Milan, 1870). Dedicated to Dom Pedro II, Emperor of Brazil. A score in which Guarani and Aimoreo Indian themes lend color to a tale of days when Brazil was a Portuguese colony. The Romance, "C'era una volta un principe," and the great "Bacchanale Indiano" stand out musically.

Huntsmen before the castle of Don Antonio de Mariz, governor of Brazil for the King of Portugal, inform him one of them accidentally has slain an Aimoreo Indian maid. Her tribe will resent it. To offset this news Peri, chief of the Guaranies enters and vows friendship. Cecilia, Don Antonio's daughter, now appears and at her father's command—submits to the embrace of Gonzales, a Spanish adventurer. Then, alone with Peri, she begs the chief to aid her, lest forced into a loveless marriage she die like a flower torn from its stem.

In a Brazilian jungle cave Peri sings his love for Cecilia, hiding when the traitors, Gonzales, Ruy Benito and Alonso, enter and plan an Indian revolt to gain the silver mine whose secret Don Antonio possesses. Peri confronts Gonzales after his companions have left, but spares his life when he swears to leave the country. In her bower, where moonlight falls softly on vases of flowers, Cecilia drinks in the beauty of the night. She sings of a prince ("C'era una volta") who does not know how to love until the chance glimpse of a beggar maid sets his heart aflame, and calls on Peri to come to her. Instead, Gonzales leaps into the room, but as he is about to drag her off an arrow hisses through the window, wounding him. He discharges his pistol, signal for the uprising, and from one side enters Don Antonio with torch-bearing colonists, from the other the rebellious adventurers. All fall back when Peri denounces Gonzales, and join in cursing the miscreant. Now a messenger bursts in: hostile Indians are swarming about the castle! All hasten to defend it.

In the Aimoreo camp captured Cecilia sits beneath a tropical tree. The Indians sing the combat, and how their *maracaes* (thigh bones of enemies slain in battle) wrought havoc among the Portuguese. The *cacique,* in tapir-hide mantle, a red-feather plume rising from his head, enters. Cecilia should die, but the *cacique* has fallen in love with her: she shall be his queen instead. Peri, brought in a prisoner (he had come to kill the Aimoreo chief), is told he will be the roast at the tribal banquet to celebrate the victory. A *Bacchanale Indiano* precedes the feast. While knives are sharpened for the cannibal orgy, Indian girls and warriors dance. The lovers are alone for a moment. Neither the son of the *selvas* nor the daughter of the Portuguese noble tremble. Each yearns to die for the other. The *cacique,* returning, invokes the sun god but as he is about to dispatch his victims the irruption of Don Antonio with Portuguese soldiers saves them.

In the subterranean vaults of the castle Gonzales and his fellows again conspire while Aimoreos rage without. Don Antonio and Cecilia, trapped, despair, but Peri knows the secret passage leading from cellar to hill outside. Don Antonio, preferring to die, gives Peri permission to save Cecilia. But wait—he is a pagan! Peri will not let a few Indian gods stand in the way of love's dream. "I renounce the idols of the Guaranies!" he cries and Don Antonio, baptizing him on the spot, tears his weeping daughter from his breast and entrusts her to the noble Indian. Gonzales appears as the lovers flee. When they do not stop he hurls his torch into a powder barrel, but, as the smoke of the explosion clears, Cecilia, on a hill beyond the Aimoreo camp, clasped in Peri's arms, points to the heavens. Love has come into its own!

*La perle du Brésil (The Pearl of Brazil,* Paris, 1851) by Félicien David, book by J. Gabriel and Sylvain-Etienne, is a weaker *Africaine* with a Brazilian Indian girl instead of a Madagascan queen for its heroine. The soprano coloratura aria "Charmant oiseau," a graceful bird-imitation song with flute *obbligato,* survives the score. As a souvenir of a Brazilian voyage, an elderly Portuguese admiral is bringing back a lovely Indian maiden, Zora, with intent to marry her in Lisbon. But Zora does not believe none but the brave deserve the fair: she prefers young lieutenant Lorenz to his aged admiral. The latter is about to take advantage of his rating to avenge himself when a providential tempest arises, the storm bursting just as the old sea dog has revealed to his entire crew "the sweet secret of his love." The vessel shipwrecked on the Brazilian shore, savages hurry up to slay the castaways. But Zora invokes the Great Spirit: her wild compatriots kneel. The admiral—what else can he do?—blesses the happy lovers' union, and sailors and savages sing their wedding hymn.

*Brésilia,* a ballet by F. Taglioni, pleased Parisians of the 1830's with bevies of Brazilian savages scantily draped in blue, in the tale of an Amazon queen's daughter (Mlle. Taglioni) who writes love letters on plantain leaves, and a lover killed with arrows for daring to aspire to her heart.

Recent scores by Brazilian composers include: Francisco Braga's *Jupyra,* and Francesco Mignone's *The Diamond Contractor,* its story woven around the historic eighteenth century exploitation of the Brazilian diamond mines. In the Argentine, where native Indian, Spanish, and African folk themes are available, Pablo Berutti's *La Pampa,* Felipe Boreo's *Tucuman* and his one-act opera *Raquela* (Buenos Aires, 1923), presenting folk songs and dances of the pampas, may be mentioned. *Don Juan de Garay* (Buenos Aires, 1900) by Riccardo Bonicioli is a lyric drama whose hero is the founder of the city in which it was first performed. *La magnífica* (*The magnificent One*) by Timothy Mather Spelman, book by Leolyn Louise Everett, a dramatic one-act tragedy by an American composer, is a love drama, enacted in an atmosphere of conspiracy and corruption in a South American capital in 1800.

### 3. *The American Indian in Opera*

The American Indian had been seized upon as an operatic subject long before Natoma did her "Dagger Dance." Nelson Barker's *The Indian Princess or la belle sauvage* (Philadelphia, 1808) was one of Poia's forerunners, and Sobelewski's *Mohega or the Flower of the Forest* (Milwaukee, 1859) walked her "Sunset Trail" long before *Alglala* was conceived. In Europe, too, the American Indian enjoyed a certain popularity in opera and ballet. We have Piccini's *L'americano ingentilito* (*The Civilized Indian,* Vienna, 1770), and Gabrielli's *L'americano in fiera* (*The Indian at the Fair,* Naples, 1838), Franz Genée's opera *Die letzten Mohicaner* (*The Last of the Mohicans,* Vienna, 1878), and a grand ballet are after James Fenimore Cooper's novel. *Les Mohicans* (Paris, 1837) by Adolphe Adam, a ballet in two acts, presented charming Alice, noble Cora, unfortunate Munro, the delightful Uncas and his majestic father Chingachgook, the Great Serpent, and Natty Bumpo, the famous Leatherstocking himself in scenes familiar to the reader. Of the music a contemporary critic said: "It would have been a pity to devote a *valuable* score to the grotesque gambols of a mob of Mohegan braves."

*Hiawatha* (London, 1924), Coleridge-Taylor's cantata as a spectacle *opera,* with a striking ballet, incidental dances interpolated by H. Coleridge-Taylor, the composer's son, gave Longfellow's Indian epic its first operatic presentation. Though there is a *Pocahontas* (Minneapolis, 1911) by Willard Patton, and a pageant opera *Waushakum* (Framingham, Mass., 1917) by Edith Rowena Noyes, the operatic Indian of the present usually is not a "forest Indian," but is a child of the West. *Tammany or the Indian Chief* (New York, 1794) by James Hewitt, book by Mrs. Hatton, is the *first American Indian* opera. The most interesting number, musically, is the air "The sun sets in night," based on the "Alkmoonok," or "Death Song of the Cherokee Indians," anticipating later American composers in their use of native material. In a historically fantastic story, Tammany, the noble Indian chief, loves dusky Manana. Columbus, among his followers, has some objectionable characters, however, for Ferdinand carries off the forest maid. When "her shrill cries through the dark woods resound" Tammany comes to the rescue; but in the end evil Ferdinand prevails and Tammany and his beloved squaw are burned in their wigwam by the Spaniards while a chorus of Indian priests sings their dirge. (For detailed consideration of this subject *Early Opera in America* by O. G. Sonneck is authoritative.)

## "NARCISSA"

MARY CARR MOORE. Book by Sarah Pratt Carr (Seattle, 1912; San Francisco, 1925). A score in which Indian themes are used with effect in a "missionary opera" (early 19th century) when American girls were leaving homes and lovers in the East to "carry the Gospel to the perishing souls" of the Western aboriginal.

Marcus Whitman and his bride Narcissa take the Oregon Trail to carry the gospel to the Indian tribes. At the Hudson Bay Company post, Fort Vancouver, they are welcomed by the factor, McLaughlin, and royally entertained in his great baronial hall, "lit with a thousand perfumed candles."

Settling down to work, Marcus and Narcissa are supported by Chief Yellow Serpent and win many converts, Narcissa singing her way into the savage Salishan heart.

Delaware Tom, half-breed Dartmouth graduate, incites part of the tribe to rebel against the missionaries and their teachings, but Narcissa, "the golden singing bird," weaves her soothing spell around the inflamed redskin souls and violence for the time being is averted. Then Marcus finds Congress preparing to sell the whole Oregon country to Great Britain and makes his famous historic overland journey to Washington (1842-1843) to save it for the United States. He is successful; but on his return the Indian uprising breaks out. The door of the mission house is battered down, and Marcus and Narcissa, "the golden singing bird," are killed, while above the death wail of Indian women echoes Yellow Serpent's oath of vengeance on the tribesmen who have taken part in the massacre.

*The Sunset Trail* (Denver, 1925) by Charles Wakefield Cadman, "operatic cantata," book by Moyle, employs Western Indian themes (outstanding: "Come, ye warriors," "Awake the morn has come," choruses; Wildflower's "Ah, my beloved") in a love episode between Red Feather and Wildflower, its background exciting scenes attending the removal of a Western Indian tribe to its reservation by the United States troopers.

## "POIA"

ARTHUR NEVIN. Book by Randolph Hartley (Berlin, 1910). A musicianly score using Wagnerian procedure in the treatment of actual Indian tribal melodies gathered by the composer among Blackfoot tepees. There are outstanding lyric pages and a colorful "Ballet of the Seasons."

Poia, nicknamed "The Scarred Face," is a dreamer in the wigwams of the Rock Mountain Blackfeet (named after their black moccasins). He loves Natoya, who prefers handsome, evil-minded young Sumatsi and says that she will listen to Poia's love-making when he can show an unblemished face. Poia's love for Natoya drives him to seek the Sun God in his forbidden woodland shrine to remove his scar.

Wandering in the snowy primeval forest Natosi, the Sun God, suddenly stands before Poia in a blaze of glory, with the four seasons, Mota, Nepu, Moka, and Stuyi, the Day Star, and the Moon. The offended deity is about to reprove the mortal who has dared seek him out in his forest sanctuary when Kokum, the Moon, cries that an eagle is attacking her son, Episua, the Morning Star. Poia's arrow slays the bird. In his gratitude Natosi grants his plea and ("Ballet of the Seasons") the dreamer's face is covered with the blanket while the solemn ceremony takes place.

Poia rises scarless to return to his people as Natosi's prophet, bearing the magic love flute, the Sun God's gift, whose music will win Natoya's heart. When its pleading brings Natoya to his arms, Sumatsi rushes at the prophet knife in hand. Natoya flings herself in his way, and the blade sinks to its hilt in her breast; but when Sumatsi raises the knife to thrust into Poia's back as he kneels over the dying girl, Natosi strikes him dead with a ray of burning light. Then Poia, taking Natoya's body in his arms, leaves the wigwams of his tribe to go with her to the Sun God's realm, never to return.

*Daoma* (MS.) by Charles Wakefield Cadman, book by Nelle Richmond Eberhart, is a romantic Indian opera of the Omahas ("Those who go before the wind") before the coming of the White Man, in which actual tribal melodies are used with lyric and dramatic effect to tell the tale of Nemaha, a young brave who, devoured by a mad passion for Daoma, niece of chief Obeska, betrays his successful rival, her lover Aedeta (after she has shown her preference for him in the antilope-hoof game) to the Pawnees in battle. His treachery revealed by Aedeta, who escapes when about to be sacrificed to the Morning Star, he has to step forth stripped according to Indian custom, and drive his dagger into his heart in the rôle of his own executioner.

## "ALGLALA"

### (*A Romance of the Mesa*)

FRANCESCO B. DE LEONE. Book by Cecil Fanning (Akron, Ohio, 1924; New York, 1925). Alglala takes us to the "Painted Desert," the mesa land now Arizona, among the Chippewas, in 1850. The Indian musical note is strongly struck in a colorful score of lyric beauty, in which stand out the initial "Ode to the Great Father" (Choral Ballet), Prelude (Scene 1), Interlude, Alglala's "Bird Song," "Prayer to the Moon," "Narrative," and "Fire Song," Ozawa-Animiki's Air, and the love scenes between Ralph and Alglala, climaxing in "Over the mesa."

Alglala, "Little-Good-for-Nothing," daughter of the Chippewa chief Namegos by a girl ravished in a tribal raid from Iroquois tepees, while her father chants the passing of his race, grieves because she must stop her ears to a lover's flute. But the young brave Ozawa-Animiki, "Yellow Thunder," coming on her as she sings in the moonlight, tells her his wigwam needs her silver smile; and she lets him fold her for a moment in the betrothal blanket, before breaking his hold to run into her tepee and draw down the deerskin over its entrance. Coming out after "Yellow Thunder" has gone, Alglala dreamily prays Ra-wen-ni-yo, Iroquois god of love, to teach her love's ways when Ralph, a white youth nearly dead of exhaustion, staggers in. Alglala stills his thirst and in the magic moonlight which floods the rolling mesa land they bare their souls to each other. He is a fugitive from a Western mining camp, falsely accused of shooting a man over the gold of a saloon gaming table, and fleeing to save his life has well-nigh died on the desert trail. She tells him of her life and hopes, and before they know it, Ra-wen-ni-yo has welded their hearts. Ozawa's love flute sounds in the distance, but clasped in each other's arms, white boy and Indian girl do not hear it.

But in the morning, after Namegos has threatened to have the white fugitive slain—he suspects his daughter loves him—Ozawa surprises them. He reminds Alglala he has held her under the blanket, and scornfully pushes Ralph aside. The rivals struggle and Alglala seeing Ralph, weakened by starvation and thirst, give ground, fells Ozawa with her woman's ax. As she begins to dance the Death Dance, Ralph bids her remember her ways now are white and Alglala, carelessly dropping her white blanket over Ozawa's body, leaves the canyon rim with her lover. Then comes Namegos followed by Chippewa braves. He lifts the blanket edge and pointing to the nearest crimson butte cries, "Beyond the spring! . . . Kiil both!" As the Indians run stealthily forward, the curtain falls to a burst of barbaric music as the old chief, huddled before his tepee, sings the death chant for his child about to die.

## "SHANEWIS"

### (The Robin Woman)

CHARLES WAKEFIELD CADMAN. Book by Nelle Richmond Eberhart (New York, 1918). "The Song of the Robin Woman" is the outstanding individual number of a lyric score which develops Oklahoma Indian thematic material.

Amy, Mrs. Everton's daughter, has returned from Europe, and a fashionable soirée at the wealthy society woman's home marks the event. Shanewis, an Indian girl protégé of the hostess does credit to her vocal studies by singing in native costume. Lionel Rhodes, Amy's fiancé, infatuated with her dark-eyed beauty, proposes to her. But Shanewis informs him her acceptance depends on the consent of her people on the Oklahoma reservation. Amy does not know Lionel is unfaithful to her, nor Shanewis that he is Amy's fiancé.

At the Indian reservation (ceremonial dances), Lionel tries to persuade Shanewis to marry him. Her Indian suitor, Philip Harjo, has given her a relic—the poisoned arrow another Indian maid used to slay a false white lover. Suddenly Mrs. Everton and Amy appear, the latter to win back her recreant love. When poor Shanewis learns Lionel has made love to her while engaged to another girl she rejects him and curses the white race, but does not use her poisoned arrow. Philip Harjo, however, snatches it up, draws his bow, and Lionel shot through the heart dies while Shanewis cries: "He is mine in death!"

## 4. These United States

Operatically the United States is well represented in music. In the South, Louisiana supplies local color and musical suggestion for an act in settings of operas based on Abbé Prévost's *Manon*. Massenet does not venture out of France in his *Manon* (for the fourth "Louisiana" act of Puccini's *Manon Lescaut,* see p. 364), and the operas of the same name by Balfe and Kleinmichel call for no further consideration. In the Louisiana act in Auber's *Manon* (Paris, 1856) Auber kills Manon's dramatic plausibility by trying to whitewash her character, but offers a characteristic "Negro Dance," and a dramatic instrumental portrayal of Manon's death and Des Grieux's grief. Halévy, too, wrote a *Manon Lescaut* (Paris, 1830), a "grand ballet." A ballet scenario, its scene New Orleans under Spanish rule, has allowed a fine orchestral poem by an American composer to make its bow on the dramatic stage. *The Dance in Place Congo* (New York, 1918) by Henry F. Gilbert, book by Ottakar Bartik. The work's chief interest is musical, an article by George F. Cable (*Century Magazine,* 1866) inspiring the symphonic poem to which the ballet action was adapted. It develops a triangular tragedy of passion, jealousy, and revenge in dance and pantomime with Aurore, a quadroon girl, as the prize for which Numa, the unfortunate, and Remon, the fortunate lover, struggle. "Place Congo" in New Orleans was a public square beyond Rampart Street, "where the palisaded wall of the town used to run in Spanish days," shaded by oak and sycamore trees. A universal rendezvous, to it came "rich man and military officer, all who went to make up the ruling class, and also butcher, baker, raftsman, sailor, quadroon, painted girl and negro slaves." On the turf dancing floor, surrounded by a circle of squatting musicians, the negroes, mostly field hands, danced their wild African dances, the *bamboula,* the *counjaille, calinda, chacta,* and *congo,* "not pleasant to describe." The Congo Square dancing was suppressed in 1843, "the rags and seminakedness, the *bamboula* drum and dance, and almost the banjo are gone; but the darky melodies and lovers' apostrophes still live on."

Passing to the English colonies of the Atlantic seaboard we find a famous opera which might never have had an "American subject" had not European political conditions made one obligatory.

### "UN BALLO IN MASCHERA"

#### (*The Masked Ball*)

GIUSEPPE VERDI. Book by Somma, based on Scribe (Rome, 1859). (The work is also known as *Amelia.*) When the composer first submitted his score for performance in Naples (1854) the police objected to a king's murder on the stage. The murder of a governor of Boston, by the Boston "nobility," however, was not objected to in Italy. From an American point of view, it is one of the most entertaining opera stories ever written. Originally in five acts, now condensed into three, it is the loveliest score of Verdi's transition period. Amelia's Solo Scene, the tender Love Duet, the Mazurka-Minuet, a death-dance melody, "which surrounds Richard's parting from Amelia with gracious irony," the Trio (Act II), Ulrica's Scene (Act I), "on a par with the noblest of Mozart and the best of Rossini" (Bie); the Barcarole, Amelia's "Prayer," and in the Finale, Masked Ball and Death "contrapuntally united in a torrential flow," are among its great pages.

Count Richard, one of Boston's governors toward the end of the seventeenth century, surrounded by citizens in the mansion house who express their love for him, is cursed by negro conspirators without. Renato, his secretary, watches over his safety; the governor in return makes love to his wife, Amelia. In black Ulrica's hut Amelia confesses her sinful love for Richard, and the witch bids her pluck a graveyard herb at midnight for a cure. Richard, there to glimpse the future, overhears her confession, and is told death awaits him, and that his slayer will be the first man who clasps his hand that day. Renato appears, shakes hands with him, and when Ulrica utters a warning, Richard laughs and gives her a canceled order of banishment. The grateful witch joins in the chorus which the adoring Bostonians raise to their governor.

It is midnight. Amelia is looking for the magic herb in the graveyard. Thither comes Boston's governor, but their passionate love scene is interrupted by Renato. He has come to save the governor from negro enemies. Renato does not recognize veiled Amelia and (exchanging cloaks with Richard), promises to escort her safely to town. The black conspirators appear: Richard is gone. Exasperated, they attack his friend. Amelia rushing between the swords, lets fall her veil—and Renato beholds his wife! Can he be blamed for swearing to avenge his supposed wrongs (in reality, Amelia is innocent) and promising to meet the conspirators in his own home the following morning?

Renato has determined to slay Richard, instead of Amelia. While she, unknowing he has changed his mind, takes farewell of her little son, the conspirators arrive. Lots are drawn and Renato is chosen to commit the bloody deed as Oscar, the gubernatorial page, arrives with an invitation to a masked ball at the governor's "palace." The conspirators provide themselves with a password, "Death!" and choose blue dominoes with trimmings of red—the color of blood!—as their costume. . . . The ballroom is thronged with the masked gentry of Boston. Amelia intercepts the governor, begs him to fly, but Richard's New England conscience has awakened. He gently tells her that he has conquered his evil passion, and intends to send her off to England in the next ship that sails. His good resolution comes too late. Renato, to whom page Oscar has innocently betrayed Richard's disguise, wields his dagger. When the guests try to seize the assassin, the noble governor waves them aside and with dying breath tells his contrite friend Amelia was innocent. Blessing Boston and pardoning Renato, he expires!

*Gustave III ou le bal masqué* (*Gustavus III or the Masked Ball,* Paris, 1833) by François Auber tells a bloody page from Swedish history—the assassination of King Gustavus by Anarström at a masquerade ball in Stockholm Palace, March 17, 1792. It is musically unimportant, only the rôle of the page having individual color. Its Scribe story, with slight changes, supplied that of Verdi's *Ballo in Maschera. Le maître généreux ou les esclaves par amour* (*The Generous Merchant or Love's Slaves,* Paris, 1795) by Paisiello tells how Mr. Dull, a rich Boston merchant of Colonial days, frees two white slaves in a sudden access of generosity, and two American scores also show the New England conscience influencing the action.

## "THE SCARLET LETTER"

WALTER DAMROSCH. Book by George Parsons Lathrop after Hawthorne's *Scarlet Letter* (New York, 1896). Johanna Gadski created the rôle of Hester, in this dignified musical setting of Hawthorne's great romance.

The well-known tale of the Puritan lovers Hester and Arthur, their sin, suffering, and expiation is presented in three acts. Led from Boston prison with the Scarlet Letter affixed to her breast, Hester, pilloried amid the jeers of the righteous, refuses to speak the name of the man who misled her, while the Reverend Arthur Dimmesdale, her unsuspected betrayer, is forced to plead with her to reveal it. When he has gone she faints in the arms of Chillingworth, her husband, as the Doxology sounds from within the church.

Chillingworth, meeting Arthur on his way to Hester's forest hut, tells him to talk to her and mutters, "Let her deal with the man as she will, the black flower blossom as it may!" Wretched Arthur tells Hester of the unseen Scarlet Letter blazoned on his own flesh, and shows it to her. When she reveals that Chillingworth is her husband, and agrees to flee with Arthur to a distant land, he tears the Scarlet Letter from her breast, the darkness of their despair lit for a moment by a star of golden hope.

In Boston Harbor Hester finds Chillingworth has taken passage on the ship by which she meant to fly with Arthur, and waits for her with a devilish smile across the market place. But his plan of battening on the souls' anguish of the lovers is foiled. When Governor Bellingham enters, escorted by the Ancient and Honorable Artillery Company, followed by the worthies of the colony, the Reverend Arthur Dimmesdale among them, the black-gowned sinner calls Hester to him. They mount the pillory hand in hand and there, defying Chillingworth, Arthur confesses his sin and tearing away his shirt, shows the blood-red mark on his skin. As the amazed crowd sings the justice of God and her dying lover tells her he is bound for that far golden land of which they had dreamed, Hester draws from her bosom a little vial of poison and drains it, so that Arthur need not make his voyage alone.

### "THE WITCH OF SALEM"

CHARLES WAKEFIELD CADMAN. Book by Nelle Richmond Eberhart (Chicago, 1925-6). Irish folk songs, pirate tunes, Puritan hymns and Indian melodies are effectively exploited in a colorful score.

From the same period (Salem Village, Massachusetts, 1692) is the story of a hapless victim of the religious hysteria of the time. Irish Sheila Meloy, come to Salem as Willoughby's ward, had been kissed at Mayo's Pool in the old country by her Irish cousin Arnold Talbot. Talbot has forgotten the kiss, and, when Sheila meets him under the Willoughby rooftree, loves Claris, Willoughby's daughter. Around the Willoughby hearth Salem girls discuss "witches" and Elizabeth, Claris' sister, innocently wonders whether the blood-red mark on Claris' breast is the Devil's seal. Willoughby and Arnold enter to say witches must be done away but Claris rebukes their superstition. Then (the others gone) Arnold and Claris tell their love and Claris after a moonlight "Prayer" (a charming lyric moment of the score) goes upstairs.

Arnold, returning, finds Sheila waiting. When he rejects her love, furious with jealousy she conceives the idea of denouncing Claris as a witch, induces her friend Anne to accuse the girl, and in the presence of a crowd of neighbors tears open Claris' gown and—the red mark disclosed—she is led to prison.

In the open, the gallows in the distance, Arnold tells a strange dream of seeing Claris sign the Devil's book in a haunted forest. Then, preceded by the folk of Salem and a band of pirates from the Madagascan coast, Claris appears in a cart on her way to be hung. As her lover lays hand on the wheel to leap in beside her Sheila and Tibuda, the old servant who has abetted her, rush up to confess that they have lied, that Claris is innocent. Reluctantly Arnold yields to Sheila's prayer to kiss her "as one might kiss the dead," and gathers Claris to his breast as Sheila is dragged off on the road to Salem and the gallows.

John Van Brokhoeven has written *A Colonial Wedding* (Cincinnati, 1905), and the Puritan subject has been developed in various operettas, among them Edgar Stillman Kelley's *Puritania* (Boston, 1892), book by MacLellan, and the popular *Priscilla, the Pilgrim's Proxy* (Boston, 1889) by Surrette, book by D. Coleridge. Aside from Bristow's *Rip Van Winkle* (New York, 1855), with tuneful, old-fashioned music, Max Maretzek's *Legend of Sleepy Hollow* (New York, 1879), and Franco Leoni's *Rip Van Winkle* (London, 1897), Reginald De Koven utilized Washington Irving's legend to revive operatically a Dutch community in the Catskills, circa 1750.

## "RIP VAN WINKLE"

REGINALD DE KOVEN. Book by Percy Mackaye, based on Washington Irving's legend (Chicago, 1920). The "Wedding Scene" at the "General Washington Inn," graceful Entr'actes, and tuneful airs and choruses are features of the score.

Rip, about to marry pretty Katrina in the Catskill Mountain village forgets his wedding to go fishing with Peterkee, the bride's little sister, to whom he tells the legend of Hendrik Hudson's reappearance on the scene of his exploits every twenty years. Suddenly the ghost of the navigator appears and challenges Rip to a midnight game of ninepins in the mountains. Rip takes the magic flask the phantom offers him, and accepts the challenge.

In a Catskill Mountain glen Rip plays a ghostly game of bowls with Hudson and his crew, and drains a draught from the magic flask which puts him to sleep.

He wakes twenty years later, old and gray. Katrina has married and is the mother of a family. When Rip turns up in the village to claim his bride, all mock the white-haired lover. But Peterkee hands him the magic flask, which she has kept, and Rip drinking once more grows young. Then—Hendrik Hudson and his crew among the wedding guests—he marries Peterkee.

The Mohawk Trail from upper New York to romantic French Canada leads us to *Le Huron* (Paris, 1768) by Grétry after Voltaire's charming story, *L'ingénu,* on which its book is based. The *ingénu,* or "child of nature," is an innocent white boy raised in a Huron Indian wigwam who lands in France. Finding a sweetheart, his savage innocence brings him into conflict with the manners and customs of the civilized world. In Paris his incarceration in the Bastille and his release by his sweetheart, who has come to Paris to save him and can do so only by the sacrifice of her honor, because of which she dies of grief, make the tale an eloquent picture of the morals of the latter part of the reign of Louis XIV. In *Le Huron* (Paris, 1921) by Louis Dauphin, a young gallant disguised as a Huron to win a fair marquise's heart, acts cave-man love so brutally that she is glad to see him lay aside his primitive "make-up" and resume his silks and madrigals. In a charming duet, "On aime aussi chez nous" (*We love in our land, too*), muted horns ironically invoke the American savage.

## "EVANGELINE"

XAVIER LEROUX. Book by de Gramont and Alexandre after Longfellow (Brussels, 1895). A refined, distinctive opera, which sings Longfellow's Acadian legend in pages of flowing lyric music. A poetic Prologue, expressing the voices of "the forest primeval," establishes the mood of the score.

In Grand-Pré, where the Acadians dwell in their houses of oak and the meadows stretch to the sea Evangeline and Gabriel murmur love vows beneath the stars. Their happiness is not to endure (change of scene). The arrival of the English fleet (1755) to transport the wretched Acadians from their homes, the dread proclamation of their banishment and, in the village church, the parting of Evangeline and Gabriel—"Far asunder on separate coasts the Acadians landed"—concludes the act.

In Louisiana, on the lakes of the Achafalaya, where the air is sweet with magnolia blossoms, Evangeline seeks Gabriel, whom she hears has become a *voyageur* of the Louisiana lowlands. And, in his swift boat, "its prow turned to the land of the bison and beaver," Gabriel passed Evangeline unseen and unseeing, as she rests on the opposite bank, hid by a screen of palmetto, though she hears his voice in her dream, and wakes as the sound of his paddle dies in the distance.

In Penn's city, vain her year long search, Evangeline has become a Sister of Mercy, Gabriel's image in her heart still clothed in "beauty of love and youth, as last she beheld him." Devotion to others is the lesson life has taught her and at last, in the almshouse, she finds Gabriel dying of the pestilence which ravages the city. In a tender scene of love he recognizes her and strives to whisper her name as she kisses his dying lips, while the light of his eyes sinks "as when a lamp is blown out by a gust of wind at a casement." Once more the murmuring pines and the hemlocks of the "forest primeval" sing the song of throbbing hearts at rest to the mournful and misty Atlantic, which "in accents disconsolate answers the wail of the forest."

*The Disappointment or the Force of Credulity* (Philadelphia, 1767), a ballad opera, book by Andrew Barton, musically nil as regards its tunes, introduces "Yankee Doodle" ("Probably the earliest reference to the tune in American literature," O. G. Sonneck). In a Philadelphia tavern, Hum, Parchment, Quadrant, and Rattletrap, to see to what lengths greed for gold will carry men, invent a map showing where Teach, alias "Captain Blackbeard," hid his treasure. A succession of humorous scenes end with Washball and Raccoon, the practical jokers' chief dupes, finding the chest of pirate gold filled with stones, while the "humorists" run laughing from the stage. "Until James Ralph is positively proven not to have been born in America, *The Disappointment* will have to be considered the *first American opera*" (*Early American Operas,* O. G. Sonneck). Shield's *Poor Soldier* (Dublin, 1783; New York, 1786), a favorite ballad opera of the American public, "from George Washington to the humblest gallery god," dealt with the adventures of a gallant Continental.

## "LA SPIA"

### (*The Spy*)

LUIGI ARDITI. Book by Manetta, after James Fenimore Cooper's *The Spy* (New York, 1856). The work, a success in its day, is a Bellinian score; the air, "Come un śuave balsamo," its best lyric number. The Father of his Country, as the librettist explains, is not brought on the stage in person from a feeling of reverence and respect.

The story develops the essentials of Cooper's romance of the Westchester County Continental spy, Harvey Birch, who, disguised as a peddler, brought information of the enemy's movements to the one man who knew his secret, General George Washington. Birch's saving of Edith Wharton, fiancée of Major Dunwoodie of the Virginia Dragoons from the flames of her burning house, is one of the opera's most thrilling scenes, and it concludes with the triumphant exposé of Birch's patriotic activities by the reading of a letter from Washington declaring him the faithful servant of his country, to the chorus of "Hail Columbia," with rattle of drum and blare of trumpet.

Here might be mentioned Angelo Villani's *La spia ossia il mercaiuolo americano* (*The Spy or the American Pedlar,* Turin, 1850), Robert Goldbeck's *Saratoga* and *Newport* (1888) and Julian Edwards' tragic opera, *The Patriot* (Boston, 1907).

*L'éclair* (Paris, 1835) by Halévy is an *opéra comique* with a Finale (Act I) in grand opera style, outstanding the air, "Quand de la nuit." Henrietta, on a "plantation" near Boston (1797, last year of George Washington's first term as President), loves nature. Her gay widowed sister, Madame Darbel, prefers the madding crowd. Enter George, to whom a wealthy English uncle has left a fortune—on condition he marry one of his cousins in three weeks. Delivering his message he falls asleep and awakened by a thunderstorm, sees Henrietta enter with Lionel, an officer she saved from drowning when his boat was struck by lightning, but whom the bolt has blinded.

Madame Darbel sings (Entrance Song). Lionel sings his sad fate. Henrietta sings her love for him, and he joins in her song. Then the surgeon operates on blinded Lionel and he sings his recovered sight. Alas, to Henrietta's despair, he thinks Madame Darbel his rescuing angel!

Henrietta, fleeing sadly to Boston, returns thinking her sister and Lionel betrothed. The latter, however, has realized his mistake, and all is joy as Lionel and Henrietta wed, and the marriage of Madame Darbel to George keeps the fortune in the family.

## "THE WHITE BIRD"

ERNEST CARTER. Book by Brian Hooker (Chicago, 1924). The composer's gift of thematic invention is shown in moving melody and skillful orchestration.

Reginald Warren is deer hunting (1804-05) on his vast preserves in upper New York. Reginald is deformed. His wife Elinor loves her husband's handsome forester Basil, who returns her passion, but both honorably conceal their love. Jealous Warren has guessed his wife's secret and taunts her with it. When Basil, at Elinor's request, drives off an officious steward, Wardwell, who annoys her, the latter carries his tale to Warren, while the honorable lovers, now their love is revealed, decide to part. Warren, however, believes Wardwell's tale of Elinor's guilt. His revenge is diabolic. Basil sees Elinor's white scarf flutter in the mist, Warren, knowing it is his wife, tells Basil it is "the white bird," the gull which has been flying about their camp. Basil shoots, kills Elinor, then discovering what Warren has done, he strangles him with his bare hands.

Leaving the East with mention of *The Forest Rose or the American Farmers* (New York, 1825) by Samuel Woodworth, who wrote "The Old Oaken Bucket," we find that picturesque Spanish California, the California of royal Spanish grants, of great rancherias and silver-chiming mission bells has motived two American scores.

## "NATOMA"

VICTOR HERBERT. Book by Joseph D. Redding (Philadelphia, 1911). To an 1820 Californian background the composer has written an effective, colorful American grand opera score, one of whose best instrumental numbers is the spirited "Dagger Dance," while among lyric pages the passionate Love Scene between Paul and Barbara (Act I), and Natoma's "Indian Lullaby" (Act III) stand out.

On a California hacienda, Don Francisco with friends and servants awaits his daughter Barbara, returning from a convent school. In vain Natoma, a lovely Indian girl, last of her race, tells Paul Merrill, a young American naval lieutenant, Don Francesco's guest, the story of her life. She cannot prevent his falling in love with Barbara on sight. Both Merrill and Alvarado make love to Barbara. When it is clear she loves the American, Alvarado determines to abduct his cousin. The curtain falls on a passionate love scene between Paul and Barbara in the moonlight.

Before Santa Barbara Mission there is color, movement, music. The *fiesta* is in progress, soldiers flirt with pretty girls, *vaqueros* crack whips, mandolins and guitars ring out. Mission bells chime as Paul comes from the ship with the sailors of the *Liberty* brig. The dancing begins and when Barbara has refused to dance the *Pañuelo*, the handkerchief dance, with Alvarado his half-breed henchman Castro challenges any girl to dance the wild Dagger Dance with him. Natoma accepts the challenge and while the attention of all is drawn to the dancers Alvarado throws his serape about Barbara's head, hoping to carry her off unnoticed. It is then that Natoma with a feigned thrust at Castro slips past him and buries her dagger in Alvarado's heart. In the tumult Paul and his sailors protect the girl from the crowd until Father Peralta, the priest, grants her the Church's protection.

On the altar steps of the Mission Natoma mourns her hopeless love. She is done with the world, its joys and sorrows; and when the priest speaks to her of the Blessed Virgin's love she begs to be taken in as a bride of Christ. When all come in to mass she passes through the ranks of kneeling nuns, stops to slip her amulet into Barbara's hand, and as the hymn "Te lucis ante omnium" rings out the gate of the convent garden closes behind her.

## "THE SACRIFICE"

FREDERICK FIELD CONVERSE. Book by G. E. Barton (Boston, 1911). Music of genuine quality tells a tale of the struggle between the United States and Mexico in California, 1846.

Bernal, a Mexican officer who has to visit his sweetheart Chonita by stealth because the Americans occupy the village, grinds his teeth with jealous rage to see her encourage the American, Captain Burton, though she does so only for expediency's sake. Bernal wounded, Chonita hides him in the mission occupied by the American. He reveals himself in a delirious attempt to assassinate Burton and is seized and condemned to death as a spy. Chonita, who flung herself in the way of her lover's blade to save Burton, begs Bernal be allowed to visit her, and the American captain, seeing his love hopeless, wins the death he seeks by reckless exposure as the Mexicans storm the mission. The reunited lovers mark their appreciation of Burton's sacrifice by praying for his soul at his grave.

## "THE GIRL OF THE GOLDEN WEST"

### (*La Fanciulla del West*)

GIACOMO PUCCINI. Book by Zangarini and Civinini (New York, 1910), after David Belasco's famed "Gold Rush" melodrama, *The Girl of the Golden West. The Girl* is usually held to be Puccini's weakest score. It has been much criticized as being vulgarly sensational, and does not, in fact, attain the genuine inspiration and beauty of *Madame Butterfly*.

In the "Polkadot" saloon (California mining camp during the gold fever of '49) Minnie, its orphan proprietress, rejects Jack Rance's advances at the revolver's point. Dick Johnson (Ramerrez), leader of a robber band enters; Minnie is attracted to him. When she invites him to visit her cabin Johnson gives up his idea of robbing the saloon and as Castro (a captured member of the band), having seen his chief's horse, leads his would-be lynchers off in search of him, Johnson promising to visit Minnie walks out.

Dick in Minnie's cabin (room and loft), she makes him hide when Rance and others enter to tell her that Johnson and Ramerrez are the same man. When Dick admits he is the outlaw after they go, Minnie drives him out into the blizzard, only to help him to the loft when he staggers back wounded by a pistol shot. Blood dripping through the ill-joined timbers of the loft floor betrays Johnson's presence to Rance and in a game of draw poker—staking Johnson's life against her marriage to the sheriff—Minnie cheats and wins.

Johnson, healed of his wounds, has left Minnie's cabin only to be caught. His solo, "Ch'ella mi creda libero e lontano," "Let her think I am free and far away," which he sings with the rope around his neck, has been called the one really inspired number of the score. Minnie dashing up on horseback as he is about to be "swung off," holds Rance and the crowd at bay with her revolver, and so eloquently pleads her lover's cause that they turn him loose despite the sheriff's rage, and he rides off with his sweetheart to begin life anew.

The Mormons have inspired only scores of a more frivolous nature, such as Brandl's operetta, *Die Mormonen* (Vienna, 1879) and the American composer Dudley Buck's *Deseret* (New York, 1880), book by Crofutt. It should have presented piquant contrasts in tune and action but critics, while they called its music too churchly in tone, spoke of its "repulsive theme . . . offensive to the moral sense"; and said "Twenty unlawful wives to one man instead of a single lawful one excite disgust."

Ante-bellum days in the South have supplied the time and locale for *Uncle Tom's Cabin* (Philadelphia, 1882) by Caryl Florio, handling the familiar story in music which has its merits; while *La capanna dello zio Tom* (Milan, c. 1875) by Paolo Giorza is an Italian version of the tale. *Koanga* (epilogue performed, London, 1922) by Frederick Delius, book by Keary, after Cable's novel *The Grandissimes* (1880) is an opera whose story deals with Creole life in Louisiana in the early nineteenth century.

### "A DAUGHTER OF THE FOREST"

ARTHUR NEVIN. Book by Randolph Hartley (Chicago, 1918). A score which, without definite "period" established, suggests the time of action as that of the Civil War, comprises three "Pictures," and three characters, Girl, Father, and Lover.

A Girl is reared in the woods (the Daughter of the Forest) by her Father and taught to "follow her instincts." The hero meets and loves her in the twilight, their embrace broken by the roll of the distant drum calling him to battle.

In the woodland cabin the Girl asks her Father whether motherhood is a disgrace. He replies it is when "unblessed by the Church." When her Lover returns on furlough she begs him to marry her, but her Father "not knowing all," hurries the boy back to his regiment "where his duty lies" before he can do so.

The Girl's lifeless form lies beside a forest stream. She has killed herself. Her Lover, come back to marry her too late, thinks of killing himself as well. The Father, however, intervenes. He blames himself for not going more into detail while educating his child along nature lines—"the truth I told her was but half the truth"—and bids her Lover seek a nobler death in battle.

*The Lovers' Knot* (Chicago, 1916) by Simon Buchalter, book by Cora Bennett Stevenson, develops a slight tale in an American milieu. In Norfolk, Virginia, 1870, shortly after the Civil War (his father killed in battle after trying to rescue Beatrice's father) Walter, returned from wandering abroad, finds Beatrice's brother Edward wooing Sylvia. His own polite attentions to Sylvia rouse Edward's jealousy, but the girls bring about the declaration of love each desires by a simple trick. Beatrice allows Walter to see Sylvia, disguised as a man, making passionate love to her and realizes the happy climax which makes four hearts beat as two. The Chinatown of old San Francisco (1906) before it was destroyed by fire and earthquake evokes an interesting operatic development.

## "L'ORACOLO"

### (*The Oracle*)

FRANCO LEONI. Book by Zanoni, after Fernald's play *The Cat and the Cherub* (London, 1905). An effective, modern Italian score, its scene of action the old "Chinatown" of San Francisco before the great fire of 1906. There is attractive local Chinese color in the score, and a "temple-bell" Intermezzo.

Chem-Fen, an opium joint keeper, is infatuated with pretty Ah-Yoe, the rich merchant Hoo-Tsin's daughter; but young San Luy has won the almond-eyed beauty's heart, serenading her from the street. When Chem-Fen hears the astrologer Win-Shee, San Luy's father, tell Hoo-Tsin the oracle predicts ill luck for Hoo-Chee, his little son, the dive keeper kidnaps the merchant's baby boy. The frantic father promises Ah-Yoe's hand to whoever will restore his child, and San Luy, suspecting Chem-Fen, traces the missing boy to his cellar. But Chem-Fen unseen, kills him with a hatchet and pushes the boy down a trapdoor. When poor Ah-Yoe learns of her lover's death she goes mad, and Win-Shee, the dead youth's father, determines to take a hand in the grewsome game.

It is the night after the Chinese New Year.  Win-Shee, lurking about Chem-Fen's cellar door, hears the kidnaped boy cry and releases him. Then, luring the villain to a bench outside his den, he strangles him with his own cue.  To avoid arrest—though he has only done justice on a scoundrel—he props up the corpse, chatting with it as a bluecoat strolls on without suspicion.

The American immigrant theme in opera harks back to the eighteenth century when Piccini, in his *I Napolitani in America* (Naples, 1774), touched on it; but the incoming alien's hopes and disappointments, his suffering and pathos in America in the twentieth century have been expressed in a distinctive score (MS.) by a distinguished American composer.

### "THE IMMIGRANTS"

Frederick S. Converse (MS.).  Book Percy Mackaye's lyric drama of the same name.  It is an opera modern in style, employing the dramatic recitative or arioso, interspersed with frankly melodic moments. The chorus plays a part and the orchestra comments situations and moods in characteristic fashion.  The leading motive is used but not to the extent of monotony; and since the music is distinctively "twentieth century," it is a "jazz opera" in the sense that "jazz" is occasionally employed as a valid "American musical idiom."

In the first act Scammon, rascally American immigrant agent, comes to a little Italian hill town where orange and almond trees flower and peasants are holding a *fiesta,* to fill his steerage cabins at thirty dollars a head.  His donkey-drawn float with its Statue of Liberty, his scattered handbills and speeches glorifying America, the land of milk and honey, bring recruits, among them Maria and Giovanni, the latter just out of jail, where he was put for nonpayment of taxes.

New York Harbor.  The Statue of Liberty looms through the fog, but on the steerage deck of the liner, Scammon (who wants to possess Maria) has Giovanni listed for return to Naples.  He has been in prison; only for nonpayment of taxes, it is true, yet the law will not let him land.  Maria alone, should be Scammon's easy prey.  Giovanni is dragged away, struggling, after Maria has repulsed Scammon, while the immigrants, as the skyscrapers rise above the waters, cry: "New York! The city! Towers—towers of the new world!"

In an East Side slum, on a stifling midsummer night, the dwellers of the Italian mountain town droop and languish.  Turned into wretched industrials of the sweatshop, amid filth and refuse, they long for the vineyards of their home hills, the fountain in the village square.  Scammon has not yet had his will of Maria and cannot understand why. His offer to set up the girl and her sister Lisetta in an apartment with lift and call boy has been refused.  When Scammon tells Maria Giovanni is dead and renewing his offer pulls a roll of greenbacks from his pocket, she stabs him, only a moment later—to see Giovanni (who, helped by Noël, the artist, their good angel, has passed the barrier) before her. She tells of Scammon and as she flings his bills on the ground, he staggers to his feet and is killed by Giovanni. Police whistles shrill, Maria and Giovanni are led off by patrolmen amid tumult and scuffling. Noël looks after the unfortunates and cries: "O Liberty, when will you cease to destroy the souls that seek you?"

## "A LIGHT FROM ST. AGNES"

W. Franke Harling. Book by Minnie Maddern Fiske (Chicago, 1925). Old Creole folk airs and typical New Orleans tunes interwoven with modal chant, have a "jazz" backbone of rhythm which lends actuality to a melodic score depicting a bayou tragedy of "jazz" life in the closing year of the nineteenth century. A redemption opera in a modern setting, veristic, with effective musical climaxes, it has been called an American "jazz opera" in the sense that Strauss' *Rosenkavalier* is a Viennese waltz opera." The Overture, the Serenade, "Memories of Mardi-Gras," and the Final Scene stand out.

During the last years of the nineteenth century, Agnes Deveraux came to the Louisiana bayou village of Bon Hilaire, and tried by precept and example to raise its "Cadians" from the slough of tawdry pleasure in which they wallowed. And on a hill above the *paroisse* she built a chapel and convent dedicated to her namesake, St. Agnes. But the villagers laughed at her teachings and when she lay on her bier ragtime melody rose in gusts from the saloon at Champfleury across the marshes, where the rowdies celebrated her passing, while nuns chanted *De profundis* in the chapel. Toinette, pitiful and lovely, is a "jazz baby" of the Louisiana marsh hamlet. Into her hut at the foot of the hill drifts a crowd of village boys to take her to the saloon celebration. But Toinette, refusing to go, drives them away. Then comes Père Bertrand, the priest. He hands the sullen girl a crucifix Agnes has sent and repeats the dead woman's tender plea to give up her "jazz life." As he turns to go Toinette's drunken lover Michel lurches in, mouthing insults. Toinette manages to get the priest out, and Michel while he rolls the dice, hiccoughs he has seen a diamond cross on the dead woman's breast in the chapel. If he steals it he and Toinette can go to New Orleans and "live." She warns him the nuns will wake, ring the bell, and give the alarm. Michel says he will cut the rope, but Toinette cajoling his knife from him, runs out, declaring she will cut the bell rope herself, and the bell peals the alarm! Michel meets her on the threshold, murder in his eye. Holding up the crucifix, she tells him a new life has sprung from her dead love for him. Cursing, he tears the knife from her and stabs her. As she sinks dying on her cot a Chorus of Spirit Voices calls, and "The Light from St. Agnes," the dawn rays reflected from the chapel window, haloes her face with a golden glory. Michel, after washing the blood from his hands in the sink, lurches out.

*Krazy Kat* (New York, 1921) by John Alden Carpenter, a "jazz pantomime," a "cartoon classic," based on the cartoons of George Herriman, is a clever musical burlesque of syncopation and "jazz," in which such numbers as "The Catnip Blues" and the concluding fox trot stand out. Krazy Kat, "the world's greatest optimist, Don Quixote and Parsifal rolled into one," is discovered sleeping to a "snore theme." Bill Postem puts up a poster and Krazy Kat waking, investigates a mysterious bundle and parodies Debussy's "Faun" in a passionate, sexless dance in the Spanish dancer's costumes he draws from it, interrupted by the appearance of a mysterious stranger (Ignatz in disguise) who at the conclusion of the fox trot reveals his true self by flinging a brick at the dancer, who once more falls asleep as Officer Pup strolls past.

### "SOONER OR LATER"

EMERSON WHITHORNE. Book by Irene Lewisohn (New York, 1925). A Dance Satire on the Progress of Civilization which pictures "in music, movement, and color a fantastic 'slant' on three states of existence."

(1) A tribal ritual, working up (chamber orchestra and voices) to a frenzy, primal in emotion but sophisticated in expression. (2) An epitome of the machine age in a metropolis, with puppets in a never ending round of toil, satirizing the futility of the mechanical grind; a burlesque of a typical "Follies" show, girls in cloth of gold swaying syncopatically as musical comedy peasants dance Broadway folk tunes; a negroid pony ballet dancing a White Way version of the jungle frenzy. (3) Life as a geometric pattern in the Crystal Age of the future. Magnetic tuning forks rhythm the work of toiling figures seen in silhouette, instead of time clocks and factory whistles. In the theater of the future the "show" begins; a Synthetic Melodrama, a revival of the old "twentieth century melodrama," in a confusion of lights and noises. The musical score, brilliantly written, is original and effective in its contrast of styles and clever satire, not the least being the detached and dehumanized crystalline music of the geometricized life of the future.

*Skyscraper* (MS.) by John Alden Carpenter. A ballet originally composed for Paris production under the name of *Le chant des gratte-ciels* (*The Song of the Skyscrapers*), the work has no story or scenario in the usual sense and no literary intention beyond the desire to produce a musical-choregraphical abstraction of contemporary American work and play. "I have tried to realize in terms of music the vigorous rhythms and sonorities of industry coupled with the official contemporary 'play' noises, which are, of course, 'jazz'" (John A. Carpenter).

# CHAPTER VIII

## BETWEEN THE AGES

Certain opera types do not seem to warrant inclusion within a period scheme, and have been considered separately under the above head. The sea is a "timeless" entirety, the idea of "period" does not apply to it; hence we have "The Operas of the Sea." "The Frozen North" includes scores in which the picturesque features of a "geographic" grouping seemed to justify segregation. The nomad instinct is an atavism, a life instinct of the ages before history. True nomads are apart from "period" and with them the pseudo-nomads have been included under the group "Gypsies." The struggle between religion and instinct in human nature since Christianity's advent is a matter of psychosis, not of period, and has been summed up operatically under "Sacred and Profane Love." Like the nomad, the peasant, whether of the first or the twentieth century, is only externally colored by his period environment. "World history is the history of the *city* dweller . . . the Renaissance style is developed only by the Renaissance *city*, the Baroque style only by the Baroque *city* . . ." (Spengler); and in opera, as in other forms of art expression, the pastoral and rural lie outside the period scheme and have been considered in "The Operatic Children of Nature." In "The Verist's Rosary" operas exploit the criminal passions of the urban underworld as well as those of the naturalistic peasant who lives too close to the soil. The fairy tale, a "timeless" imaginative inheritance, has been considered in "Fairy Operas." The "Symbolic Operas," finally, practically a nineteenth and twentieth century development, include scores uninfluenced by the ordinary facts of time and space, records of unseen emotions, adventures of the soul, the diaphanous, nebulous and mystic, the philosophic and metaphysical.

### 1. *Operas of the Sea*

#### PROFESSIONAL SEAMEN

Beginning with *Alcyone* (Paris, 1706) by Marais and La Motte, with a famous Sailor Chorus and Tempest Scene (Act IV), we find among those who "go down to the sea in ships"

professionally *Der Lotse* (*The Pilot*) by Max Brauer (Karlsruhe, 1895; revived, Lucerne, 1923), a melodious score in the manner of Gade. The pilot Hialmar, tempted by a south-coast
Norwegian meerwoman, drowns himself rather than yield to
her wooing when he hears his wife Iduna calling from shore.
*The Boatswain's Mate* (London, 1923) by Ethyl Smith, book
after W. W. Jacobs, "not tunely enough for its comic opera subject," is a brief score humorously handling an English port
town's water front love jealousies. In *Der Seekadett* (*The Naval
Cadet*, Berlin, 1877) by Genée, Parisian Franchette, coming to
Lisbon (1702) finds her old flame Lambert secretly wedded to the
Queen of Portugal. Disguised as a cadet, she drinks with graceless sailor lads in a naval academy before she secures the hand ot
a Pernambuco millionaire. *Eddystone* (Prague, 1889) by the
Wagner tenor Wallnöfer dramatizes the famous lighthouse. Lord
Winstanley, its builder, finds he loves Kitty, Tom the keeper's
wife. Tom hears him telling her so (Act II) but when, in the
dark tower, Kitty realizes she is clinging to Tom instead of Winstanley, she leaps from the window into the sea, and lightning
striking the lighthouse buries husband and lover beneath its ruins.
Passing from lighthouse keepers, we find a navigator the hero of
one of the most famous of sea operas.

## "L'AFRICAINE"

Giacomo Meyerbeer. Book by Scribe (Paris, 1865). Vasco da Gama
(c. 1590) appears as the bone of contention between a Portuguese lady
and a Madagascan queen. Musically more consistent than *Les Huguenots*, the melodies of *L'Africaine* (outstanding the Adamastor ballad,
"Adieu, terre native," "D'ici je vois la mer," "Fille des rois," and the
glowing "O paradis sorti de l'onde") "have a dignity and serenity rarely
present in the scores of Meyerbeer's French period."

Lovely Inez sheds tears in the king's palace in Lisbon. Her sailor
lover, Vasco da Gama, is said to have perished at sea, and she is
threatened with marriage to unloved Don Pedro. No sooner has she
left the royal presence than the supposedly drowned navigator appears.
His eloquence, maps, and charts lead younger members of the Council
to favor giving him a ship for another trial. But the Grand Inquisitor
is horrified a layman should discover lands not mentioned in Holy
Writ, hence not existing. Vasco insults the priest and is led to prison,
while in the confusion his rival, Don Pedro, steals a chart pointing the
way to India's coral strand.
Tossing in a frail canoe on the high seas Vasco had picked up two
savages, Selika and Nelusko, who share his prison cell and stir its
monotony with human passion. Selika secretly loves the sailor and

sings him to sleep ("Here in my lap") while Nelusko, who loves Selika, boils inwardly and whets the dagger for his rival. But the latter thinks only of his next voyage. To him Selika is no more than a native guide. Meanwhile Pedro has made good use of the stolen map. *He* is to head the new expedition, and Inez has promised to wed him if Vasco is released. When the two appear in his cell the sailor, ignorant of her sacrifice, thinks Inez has betrayed him.

On the deck of Pedro's galleon, Alvar vainly warns him against his steersman Nelusko (whose "Storm Ballad" is the great baritone air of the score) but even when Vasco da Gama, who suddenly steps from the ocean's nowhere to the deck of the galleon, repeats the warning, Pedro pays no heed. Vasco is bound and about to be shot when Nelusko finds the hidden reef he sought. As the ship grounds, his fellow savages pour into the wreck from their canoes and massacre all save Inez and Vasco, spared at Selika's command.

The Brahma-worshiping Madagascans rejoice at Queen Selika's home-coming (Ballet) to her native spice groves; but the high priest makes her swear the strangers shall die. Selika, knowing Vasco does not love her, says he is her husband to save him, and Nelusko loves Selika so greatly that he swears it is true. Vasco, moved by Selika's devotion, agrees to remain with her on the island. Yet sailors change their minds. While the Brahminic marriage ceremony is in progress Vasco hears Inez' voice. Leaving his bride at the altar he rushes off, clasps Inez in his arms and attempts to flee with her.

Easily recaptured, the fugitives are brought before the savage queen and find her noble to the end. Nelusko is ordered to put the lovers aboard a ship which will take them safely home. Then Selika, in the manzanillo grove, looking out on the far blue sea, inhales the fragrant poison of the manzanillo blossoms and dies, an invisible chorus promising her happiness in love's immortal realms.

*Le navigateur des Indes Orientales* (Prague, 1792) by Masek and *Vasco da Gama* (Berlin, 1801) by Himmel were popular in their day.

Professionals of the sea include pirates and corsairs. *La Corsara* (Naples, 1772) by Piccini; *Il Corsaro* (Rome, 1831) by Paccini; by Verdi (Trieste, 1845); *The Corsair* (London, 1801) by Arnold; by Blewett (London, 1812); by Deffel (London, 1873); *The Corsairs* (Copenhagen, 1835) by J. P. E. Hartmann, and Leslie Stuart's comic opera *Captain Kidd* (London, 1910) were written at the sign of "The Skull and Crossbones." *Il Pirata* (Milan, 1827) by Bellini, book by Romani, contains Rubini's famous air, "Nel furor della tempesta." Gaultier, losing rank and fortune, becomes a pirate captain while his sweetheart Imogene marries Ernest, Duke of Calabria, to save her father's life. Storm-tossed ashore, Gaultier discovers this, kills Ernest in a duel, and when he is condemned to be beheaded, Imogene goes mad.

## "ZAMPA, OU LA FIANCÉE DE MARBRE"

### (Zampa, or the Marble Bride)

FERDINAND HÉROLD. Book by Mélesville (Paris, 1831). Musically influenced by Weber, the score's outstanding numbers are: the dramatic Overture; Scene of the Statue (Act I); "Prayer of the Fisherman's Children," and Zampa's Air, "Douce jouvencelle" (Act II).

Zampa, the pirate chief, landing with his ruffians at Castle Lugano on the Sicilian gulf (16th century), forces shrinking Camille, about to wed Alphonse, to promise to marry him instead, lest a terrible fate befall her father. In the midst of a drunken orgy with his corsair crew, Zampa (singing the famous air, "Que la vague écumant") mockingly slips a betrothal ring on the hand of a marble statue of Alice, a poor young thing he had earlier betrayed. When he tries to take back the ring, however, the statue crooks its finger and refuses to release it. Annoyed but undaunted Zampa continues his preparations (Act II) and though Alphonse dares him with drawn sword, the wedding takes place. In the evening Zampa tries to assert his conjugal rights, Camille flees from him, and the pursuing pirate finds himself suddenly confronted by the vengeful marble statue which draws him down into the depths of the sea as Camille and Alphonse fall into each other's arms.

Picturesque pirate ballets were Paris favorites during the first half of the nineteenth century, among them Adam's Le corsaire (Paris, 1856), his L'écumeur de la mer (The Rover of the Seas, Paris, 1840), and Gide's ballet pantomime L'île des pirates (The Pirate Isle, Paris, 1835). The scourge of the seas captures a young bride. Her lover, with a flotilla of boats, attacks the rover's floating citadel, whose cannon belch flame, and folds his love to his breast on the bodies of the slain. Most pirate operas and ballets are based on Lord Byron's poem, "The Corsair." Sullivan's delightful Pirates of Penzance (London, 1880) "pour the pirate sherry" but no blood to happy melodies that tell how Frèderic, apprenticed to learn their trade, is readmitted within the social pale when with his companions, all "noblemen who had gone wrong," he gives up crime for marriage and respectability.

### THE FLEET AT SEA

Aside from vessels already mentioned, opera's "fleet at sea" includes others of heavier and lighter tonnage. Il Nave (The Ship, Genoa, 1899) by Arturo Vanbriauch is wearisomely symbolic and tiresome. Mast, sails, captain, crew and cabin boy are "symbolic characters" and act accordingly. Il Nave (The Ship, Milan, 1918; Chicago, 1919) by Italo Montemezzi, based on D'Annunzio's drama, is a modern symbolic score, in which stands out Basiliola's brilliant orchestral "Dance of Seduction" (Prologue). The Graticii brothers, Marco, the Tribune, and Sergio, Bishop of Venice (8th century), have blinded Basiliola's four brothers, political rivals. When they enter St. Mark's square Basiliola captivates them with a dance of genial wantonness, the first step in her plan of revenge. She soon holds both brothers captive on the leash of passion (Act I) by her charm, and a holy hermit vainly warns them to cast her off. In St. Mark's cathedral (Act II), unveiling and dancing in that sacred place (Ildebrando Pizetti has written a passionate "Dance of the Seven Candelabra" in his incidental music to D'Annunzio's drama) she so inflames the mob that it is beaten back with difficulty, and (the next step in her plan of revenge) she makes Marco slay his brother, Bishop Sergio, for her sake. But fratricide cools Marco's ardor. He forgets passion for patriotism, and as Venice's great war galley, the *Totus Mundi* (*Whole World*) puts out of the harbor for battle (Act III), Basiliola goes along, nailed to the prow, an agonizing human figurehead.

*Il nave rosso* (*The Red Ship,* revised version, Milan, 1921) by Armando Sepilli is a verist opera, its passion plot salted with Calabrian sea breezes. Eduardo Sanchez de Fuentes' *Il Naufrago* (*The Shipwreck,* Havana, 1901), a romantic score, tells a tale of love and shipwreck on the Cantabrian coast. Flotow's *Le naufrage de la Méduse* (*The Shipwreck of the Medusa,* Paris, 1839; as *Die Matrosen* (*The Sailors*), Hamburg, 1845), and Reissiger's *Schiffbruch der Medusa* (Dresden, 1846) tell the same tale. Maurice, bos'n's mate of the *Medusa,* has to sail before he can marry Aline, who loves the A. B. Urbain. The latter is put in the brig for snatching Maurice's bridal bouquet and, the equator passed (Ballet), the ship is wrecked. On the life raft dying Maurice, whom Urbain gives the last swallow of water, turns over to him his rights to Aline, and Urbain makes the home harbor just in time to tear his love from the arms of an old miser to whom her father is marrying her. *Matelots* (*Sailors*), ballet by Georges Auric (Paris, 1925), based on popular songs, has a sailor test a "salt-water girl's" fidelity by asking her into a bar in disguise, clasping her in loving arms when she refuses.

### "H. M. S. 'PINAFORE'"

Sir Arthur Sullivan. Book by W. S. Gilbert (London, 1878). Sullivan's first great popular success. "There is a smack of the sea in music and libretto alike" of this nautical burlesque staged on the *Pinafore's* deck in Portsmouth, with "Dear Little Buttercup" an outstanding song.

British tars sing their welcome to Captain Corcoran, and Admiral Sir Joseph Porter appears. He wants to marry Josephine, Corcoran's daughter, but she loves Ralph, a simple Victorian "gob." After the Admiral has sung how he reached his swivel chair by polishing the brasswork, Ralph confesses his fondness to Josephine. When she tells him how hopeless their case is, he threatens to shoot himself. Then the girl, rushing into his arms, promises to go ashore with him that night and marry him.

After Captain Corcoran has sung his serenade on the bridge, sailor Dick Deadeye betrays the intended flight of Ralph and Josephine, and the Admiral, foaming with rage, orders Ralph into irons. It is then that Little Buttercup tells Sir Joseph how two babes were once given into her keeping, how revenge led her to shuffle them so that low-born Corcoran rose to be a "four-striper" while blue-blooded Ralph remained a simple sailor. Shocked, Sir Joseph at once orders the two men to exchange ratings and while Captain Ralph Backstraw receives the hand of lovely Josephine, sailor Corcoran marries Little Buttercup.

## TRAGEDIES OF THE SEA COASTS

### "L'APPEL DE LA MER"

HENRI RABAUD. Book after J. M. Synge's *The Riders of the Sea* (Paris, 1924). A lyric drama evoking the fatality ruling the lives of those who respond to the call of the sea. The pulse of the tides, the ground swell's ominous note surge in the impressive music of the score, which sings those who "have gone the seaward way."

Old Maurya has had a husband and five sons reft from her by the sea. In the hope that the body of Michael, the fifth victim, may be cast ashore, the mother has a coffin made ready, but the boy's body is not brought in by the tide. Instead, Maurya's last and youngest is swept away and drowned. It is when *his corpse* is cast up on the sands that hope forever leaves the old woman's breast. The resignation of her anguish is expressed in her words: "Michael has a clean burial in the far north, by the grace of Almighty God. Bartley will have a fine coffin of white boards and a deep grave surely. No man at all can be living forever, and we must be satisfied."

*The Wreckers* (Leipzig, 1906) by Ethyl Smith offers "sea music" of dramatic power in a fine modern score. The Methodist fisherfolk of the Cornish coast (18th century), encouraged by their minister, light false flares which lure doomed vessels to shipwreck on the rocks and bring them the spoils of the dead. Thurza, the minister's faithless wife (she betrays him with a young fisherman), has the decency to protest and make her lover light a true beacon to warn ships of the death trap. Her clerical husband and the villagers discover her "treachery," truss up the lovers and leave them to drown in a sea cave submerged at high tide.

*Graziella* (Paris, 1925) by J. Mazellier, book by Cain after Lamartine, makes effective use of Neapolitan folk songs and saltarellos. The Procidan fisherman Andrea's boat is wrecked. His passenger, a Parisian poet, buys him a new one, thus meeting, loving, and promising marriage to his sister Graziella. His mother's illness calls him away. When he does not return the girl dies of a broken heart. *Les pêcheurs de Catane* (*The Fishers of Catania,* Paris, 1860) by Maillart makes a Catanian fishing village the musical background for the tale of a salt-water girl who, for love of a gentleman, dies of a broken heart.

*Die Bruid der Zee* (*The Bride of the Sea,* Antwerp, 1901) by Jan Blockx, a fine modern score, (Love Scene, Act I; Flemish folk song, "There were two kings' children," stand out) tells of Kerlien, a Flemish fishing village girl who, keeping faith with her drowned lover, is driven mad by her parents' threats when she refuses to marry another suitor. *Albatros* (*The Albatross,* Milan, 1905) by Pacchiarotti, book after Coleridge's poem *The Ancient Mariner,* has a fine symphonic Prelude. Erik bids Nilvana farewell on a North Sea isle to go on a cruise. She awaits his return in vain till the albatross, wounded by her lover's bolt, around its neck the charm she had given him, falls dying at her feet. Then, knowing Erik lies fathoms deep, Nilvana leaps from a cliff to death in the waves.

*L'étranger* (*The Stranger,* Brussels, 1895) by Vincent d'Indy, noble, symbolic music, the old sailor's *De profundis* and the climaxing Sacrifice Scene stand out. A philanthropic old "Stranger" finds his kindness misunderstood by the folk of a wretched Breton fishing village. When Vita, a girl betrothed to André, the customs officer, breaks her engagement because of the Stranger, village opinion brands her a coquette. Her love, however, is justified by events. A wrecked ship signals in the offing. Vita, "seized by an overwhelming impulse of self-sacrifice" helps the Stranger launch a boat to rescue the doomed crew, and both meet death in the angry waves.

*Kermaria* (Paris, 1897) by Camille Erlanger, book by Gheusi, has a noble Prologue, picturesque "Marche Chouanne" (scene of action 18th century Vendée) and a Symphonic Intermezzo "filled with the poesy of the maritime coast." In the Prologue a monk who has sinned in the flesh, about to cast himself into the sea, is stayed by a divine voice saying his redemption will be wrought in the ruined château of Kermaria; two pure lovers shall redeem the fault of two impure. Tiphaine, a Breton sea-farm girl, sings Yvon, the wounded Republican sergeant whom she has taken in and nursed, the legend of Kermaria, haunted by the Blue Lady who watches over true lovers, the organ of whose roofless chapel, played by invisible hands, sends music of tender solace over the countryside. Yvon, troubled in mind by his wound, rushes for the ruin in an ecstasy, followed by Tiphaine. Seeing the girl, he thinks her the Blue Lady and clasps her in a spiritual embrace as Yan, the girl's rejected Chouan lover, arrives to murder him. The sudden peal of the haunted organ makes Yan's musket fall from his hand, as a mounting hymn of gratitude and glory announces the monk's fault has been forgiven him.

*Stella Maris* (*Star of the Sea*, Düsseldorf, 1910) by Alfred Kaiser, a verist opera, makes effective use of Breton folk themes and dances. Marga, waiting long for her sailor lover Yanik to return (a fine symphonic Prelude describes her yearning) marries Sylvain. When Yanik returns to curse her she promises to yield to him once, if he will leave the village forever; and when she confesses to Sylvain, he nobly forgives her sin. Marga's "Star" is the Mother of God; the sea the Evil Principle which brings back Yanik to snatch his moment of illicit joy.

*La Glu* (*The Snarer*, Brussels, 1911) by Gabriel Dupont is a verist opera with strong dramatic pages. "La Glu," a Paris *cocotte* companioning an elderly Count in his Breton coast villa, kills leisure hours debauching Pierre, an innocent fisher lad. After Pierre flings a vase of flowers at his mother when she tries to coax him from the siren's arms, La Glu's temporary absence makes him realize his errors, and he celebrates his betrothal with pretty Naic, his village sweetheart. When La Glu reappears and again toys with Pierre's emotions, his sturdy Breton mother kills the gay Parisienne with an ax.

*Les Pêcheurs de Saint-Jean* (*The Fishermen of St. Jean*, Paris, 1905) by Ch.-M. Widor, presents "Scenes from Maritime Life," with Wagnerian and Rossinian inflections, in which the Love Scene, "Quand la nuit" (Act I), and Anne-Marie's prayer, "Vierge Marie, Dame des flots," stand out. Through three acts the lovers, Anne-Marie and pilot Jacques of the Breton fishing village of St. Jean de Luz, are separated by the girl's father. But though Jacques tries to knife the old man while intoxicated, in the end he rescues him in a raging tempest, following which Breton wedding bells chime.

*Liebesketten* (*Love Chains*, Vienna, 1912) by Eugen d'Albert, book after Guimera's drama *Filla del Mar*. Breton folk songs help tell a tragedy in which verist boat hook takes the place of knife. Wild, passionate Sadika, cast up by the sea, adopted by innkeeper Noël, serves as a pretext for guilty visits pilot Martin pays Marion, Noël's wife. When the innocent girl takes the fancy of the fishing village Don Juan, he swears to be true to her; but when Sadika catches him visiting Marion one night (Act II), and accuses the latter, Noël seizes his hatchet and she says Martin came to see *her*. The innkeeper then drives both women into the street where with Caterina (Act III), another of the pilot's cast-off loves, they quarrel for his possession, while the men curse till Noël's deadly blow at Martin with the boat hook is caught by Sadika, who sacrifices herself, and her body is cast back into the sea whence it came.

In *Irrlicht* (*Will-o'-the-Wisp*, Dresden, 1894) by Karl Gramman, a verist tragedy of the Norman coast, Captain Tournon's daughter Gervaise takes no joy in the launching of her father's new boat. Her mind is on the stranger who found—and forgot her—in Paris. As her betrayer's yacht, the *Will-o'-the-Wisp*, struggles in a storm, a telegram comes that her babe is dying. Gervaise thinks only of the child's father. When her village lover André refuses, she herself launches a boat only to see the yacht plunge beneath the waves. Drawn from the sea by André, Gervaise empties a pocket vial of poison and dies.

*Der Liebeskampf* (*The Love Battle*, Dresden, 1892) by Meyer-Helmund has a "simple" plot and crass verist music. Maritana, a coastwise Corsican girl, loves sailor Pietro, who puts out to sea leaving her a child, pledge of his affection. Three years pass, Pietro's ship reported missing, Maritana weds innkeeper Arrigo, who has saved her and her love child from starvation. Returning Pietro, when Maritana refuses to fly with him, insults her husband's niece at her wedding, and as other Corsicans fling themselves on him with knives he flings himself into the sea, promising to meet Maritana in heaven. *L'Ouragan* (*The Hurricane*, Paris, 1901) by Alfred Bruneau, its music "finely imagined," is a Breton fisher-folk opera, showing jealousy and crime dissolved in sacrifice and friendship, and introducing the fantastic "Singing Tree" at whose sight "wounded creatures become invisible, free to express their tenderness, tears and joy."

SUPERNATURAL OPERAS OF THE SEA

## "DER FLIEGENDE HOLLÄNDER"

### (*The Flying Dutchman*)

RICHARD WAGNER. Romantic opera. Book by the composer (Dresden, 1843). The legend of the world-wearied wanderer, as old as Homer, combined with the seventeenth century belief that the ghosts of ship-wrecked vessels haunt the seas, and with Heine's motive of a sinner's redemption through a woman's faithful love, is Wagner's story. The composer said that in the words and music of "Senta's Ballad" he had concentrated "the thematic germs of the whole score." The Overture is a picturesque seascape, and striking is the "chain of choruses" (Act III) between the girls and sailors. An eighteenth century Norwegian fishing village supplies the scene of action.

While the storm rages off the Norse coast, Daland's ship has hove to in the cove. He waits for fair weather to go ashore to his daughter Senta. Captain and crew are below, the boy at the wheel asleep when —with blood-red sails, black masts and spectral crew—the phantom ship, the *Flying Dutchman,* drops anchor besides the Norwegian fishing bark. Seven years have passed since the Dutchman has set foot on land. Again he has his chance to find a woman who, sacrificing herself, will free him from his curse. As the Dutchman despairs and, aboard Daland's ship, to which he has been rowed, longs for the Day of Judgment, Daland mentions Senta's name. He is willing to sell his daughter for the gold which fills the phantom ship, and the wind having shifted, the two are rowed ashore.

In Daland's home Senta is spinning (singing her famous ballad, the "Spinning Song"). But her thoughts are with the Dutchman whose picture hangs on the wall; on his vow by all the devils of hell to double the Cape of Good Hope though he sail till Doomsday, and of God's curse which makes him roam the seas till he finds a woman who will die to save him. Senta prays heaven to pity the unfortunate man. The huntsman Eric, Senta's lover, rebukes and leaves her, only to clear the way for the Dutchman himself, who comes in with Daland. When her father leaves the room the wanderer asks Senta to marry him. He is the hero of her dreams, she is his hope of salvation; they love each other at sight. Rejoicing at the prospect of lifting the curse, they plight their vows happily in Daland's presence.

In the bay lie the two vessels. Lights and festivity reign on Daland's ship; from the phantom craft rises a weird sepulchral chant, while blue flames hover on spars and masts. Eric, coming from the house with Senta, falls at the girl's feet and pleads passionately with her to give up the stranger. Senta refuses; she loves none but the Dutchman. The latter has seen Eric kneeling at Senta's feet. He thinks her untrue and rushes aboard his ship, despairing that his curse ever will be raised. Yet as the wind fills the blood-red sails and the phantom ship is about to disappear, Senta proves the greatness of her love. Running to the near-by cliff, she casts herself into the waves, and, as they close about her, the curse is lifted. The phantom ship disappears beneath the water and Senta and the Dutchman, rising to the surface clasped in each other's arms, are transfigured by celestial radiance from the bosom of the sea.

*Frutta di mare* (*Fruit of the Sea,* Basel, 1918) by Hans Huber is a fine fantastic musical score by a Swiss composer. Rejecting the advances of two fauns, Herto the mermaid longs for human love and comes ashore as a peasant girl. But Sir Kurt, the handsome knight who is her love's young dream deserts her for a rich old hag with money. When she makes the waves cast up corals and pearls on the sand, young patrician girls of the near-by town try to have her seized as a witch; and when she takes refuge in the cloister, the monks sing godless songs over their wine and the prior, to whom she flees from their importunities, curses her as a temptress. Disillusioned with human love, the mermaid slips back into clean ocean waves as the two fauns fight for her.

## "THE SEAL WOMAN"

GRANVILLE BANTOCK. Book by Mrs. Kennedy-Fraser (Birmingham, 1924). An English tragic opera built up on Hebridean folk tunes, its story based on a legend of the Outer Hebrides. "The Seal Woman's Croon," the "Eriskay Love Lilt," and the "Spinning Song" are notable among its lovely, haunting melodies.

On a lone Hebridean isle of basalt, the Isleman, a young fisherman, a dreamer of dreams, waits to meet the Seal Woman, the beautiful maid who has the gift of "skin changing," and whom he has seen and loves. When she appears with her "Seal Sister," the Islander passionately confesses his love. The Seal Woman's heart is torn between longing for him and her wild sea life. When he seizes her magic seal robe and refuses to return it, she agrees to follow him ashore.

Seven years pass and ever the sea's call comes more insistently to the Seal Woman, though she struggles to ignore it. One day her child Morag enters the hut with the magic furs he has found hidden in the peat stack. The Seal Woman can resist no longer. Tearing them from the boy in a frenzy she wraps them around her and with a last passionate embrace plunges into the waves. As she disappears the Isleman, come too late upon the scene, sadly bends over the boy, now his all.

*Vineta* (Breslau, 1895) by Reinold Herman is a distinctive musical score. On Baltic shores (1530) the necromancer Albertus lures knight Magnus, whose wife he loves, beneath the waves by calling up a vision of the buried city of Vineta. There Magnus is about to wed the lovely Phœnician Princess Sareptha when his wife in a boat on the water's surface says the Lord's prayer, and at once finds him on a rock before the castle. The legend also has called forth *Vineta* (Mannheim, 1864) by R. Wuerst, and *Vineta* (Leipzig, 1895) by A. Könnemann.

## "LE ROI D'YS"

### (The King of Ys)

EDOUARD LALO. Book by Blau after a Breton legend (Paris, 1898). The composer's one important opera, with echoes of Meyerbeer and Gounod in its music, has beautiful lyric pages (Rozenn's air: "Vainly

I spoke of absence without end"; Margared's "Oh, Mylio, if the struggle be near"; Rozenn's Wedding Scene) but tells a story of unrelieved gloom.

In Ys, a royal city on the Breton Sea, the King's daughters Margared and Rozenn both love the warrior Mylio, in days gone by. Mylio loves only Rozenn. Margared, the Pearl of Brittany, is betrothed by her father to Prince Karnac for political reasons; and shortly after she has been led away to be robed for marriage with him, Mylio, whom she loves but who loves her not, returns. At the news Margared refuses to wed Karnac, and when Karnac challenges the Breton king to mortal combat, Mylio picks up his gauntlet.

Looking from the palace window, Margared sings her heart's terrible conflict. Her sister Rozenn's tender parting from Mylio leads her to cry wildly that she hopes he never returns from battle. Rozenn, thinking her mad, in vain tries to calm her: Margared rushes off cursing Rozenn and St. Corentin, patron saint of Brittany. When Mylio returns victorious to Ys, Margared, filled with hatred, steals to defeated Karnac. Would he conquer Ys? she asks. He would. So the wretched girl promises to open the dyke gates which hold back the waters of the sea from the town.

Rozenn has been wedded to Mylio according to charming folk customs of ancient Brittany. Now appear Margared and Karnac to do their fell work. As the wedding procession returns from the chapel, Margared, distraught, warns them the sea gates are down, and the crowd fills the square as the floods spread through the town.

On a hill near the sea the people of Ys kneel in prayer as the waves cover the city. Margared admits her guilt as the waters rise and suddenly, eager to atone for the wrong she has done, runs to a jutting rock and casts herself into the raging flood. The vision of St. Corentin appears in a golden glory to accept her sacrifice as the waves retire and all are saved.

## "SADKO"

NICOLAS RIMSKY-KORSAKOFF. Russian legendary opera (opera-byliny, Moscow, 1897). In extended form the tale related by the fantastic dance poem *Sadko* (Paris, 1911; New York, 1916), Russian Ballet, the music of the latter, however, being the composer's symphonic poem by the same name. In the opera the "Sea Queen's Slumber Song," Sadko's aria (Scene 5), and the exotic Vangarian (Scandinavian), Indian (Hindoo), and Venetian (a gondolier) songs stand out in a score which combines the lyric and the declamatory in a national Russian work.

Sadko, wandering *guslee*-player of Novogorod, plays himself into the good graces of Volkhova, daughter of the sea king Czar Morskoi, waxes rich and powerful and dwells in a palace of white stone. Putting to sea with a fleet he sails for home, his holds filled with "casks and buckets of red gold, pure silver and fair, round pearls." Suddenly his ship will not move and Sadko with his "little harp of maple-wood, its strings of pure gold," has to descend to the ocean bottom to make music for Czar Morskoi. In the great undersea hall whose waving walls of seaweed give glimpses of far purple seascapes, where the hulks of wrecked ships are robed in anemones and golden sunlight filters greenly through the waters, Sadko sweeps the strings and strikes up a dance whose rhythm the sea king and his court cannot resist. As it sounds ever more madly the swaying dancers vainly call on the minstrel to stop. They cannot breathe and the upper waters of the sea, stirred by the mad whirl of the lower deeps, tear down houses along the shore and strew the waves with wreckage. At last, as Czar Morskoi sinks dead, his daughter snatches up the *guslee* from Sadko's hand, and the waves grow calm as the princess of the seas ascends with her lover to the surface, to be borne ashore and live happily ever after in Sadko's "palace of white stone where all things are heavenly."

## 2. *The Frozen North*

### RUSSIAN VISTAS

### "PIQUE-DAME"

#### (*The Queen of Spades*)

PETER TSCHAIKOWSKY. Book by Modeste Tschaikowsky after Pushkin's story (Petrograd, 1890; New York, 1910). The latter is changed to secure a love interest, making Herman love Lisa, for Pushkin knew gamblers do not love. The eighteenth century Petrograd hero is a romantic gambler; the tale has "a psychological problem stronger . . . a dramatic appeal more direct (Rosa Newmarch) than the composer's *Eugen Onegin.*" The music has the thrill of the supernatural and among charming folkwise pages is the "Pastoral Comedy" (Act II).

Herman, poor Hussar lieutenant and inveterate gambler, meets Lisa, granddaughter of an old Countess, once "the belle of St. Petersburg" who now lives only for cards. She owes her nickname, "The Queen of Spades," to the secret of a three-card combination which always wins. Herman has learned to love Lisa, but though his love is returned she is engaged to rich Prince Yeletsky; the penniless officer's only hope is to win enough gold to obtain her hand. If he can discover her grandmother's secret their happiness is assured, and Lisa gives him the key to the Countess' room so that he can wring it from her.

Herman hides in the Countess' bedroom but when he suddenly appears to extort the secret with a pistol, the old woman dies of fright without telling the names of the three winning cards. Escaping half mad with remorse Herman is haunted by the dead woman's shade, which whispers the names of the cards he wishes to know.

In vain Lisa, on the Neva's bank, tries to dissuade him from using the knowledge gained in so ghastly a way. When he insists she drowns herself. The night of the old woman's burial Herman puts his ghostly "tip" to the test in the gaming house. Twice he wins; gold is piled before him. The third time he stakes all he has won and, instead of the ace, turns up—the Queen of Spades! As he does so the old Countess' specter faces him across the table with a malicious smile and, mad with terror and disappointment, Herman stabs himself.

*Nadeshda* (London, 1885) by Arthur Goring-Thomas, book by Sturgis, with a quaint Russian folkwise Ballet and the charming air, "My heart is weary," plays on Princess Natalie's estate near Moscow (1760). The serf Ossip, Wladimir, older, and Iwan, younger son of the Princess, love Nadeshda, the serf girl. Wladimir meets her in her forest hut and confesses his love. When his mother accuses the girl of dishonoring her house, Wladimir declares he will marry her that day. When Wladimir leaves to make preparations, Iwan, alone with the desirable serf, attempts her honor and when Ossip knifes him the Princess, learning why he was killed, approves Wladimir's and Nadeshda's marriage.

## "EUGEN ONEGIN"

Peter Tschaikowsky. Book by Modeste Tschaikowsky and Shilovsky after a Pushkin drama (Moscow, 1879). Onegin is a soul brother of Byron's Don Juan, a Russian Werther, "a Muscovite masquerading in the cloak of Childe Harold." The score, tenderly atmospheric, deals with human beings who "would not give love that which was love's, while it would have made for happiness, only to admit it when youth, friendship and faith had vanished." Italianate, sentimental, charmingly melancholy, colorful choruses and dances, Lensky's air for tenor (Auer has transcribed it for violin), and Tatania's soprano Letter Scene stand out.

Onegin, dissolute man about town, a "Corinthian" of early nineteenth century Petrograd instead of Regency London, is called to the countryside to take possession of an estate left him. There the poet Lenski presents him to Madame Larina and her daughters, Olga, a creature of surface emotions, and Tatania, who dreams over books her mother read when a girl, the thrilling adventures of Lovelace, the wicked hero of Richardson's novels. In Onegin Tatania sees *her* Lovelace and reveals her sentimental girlish soul to him in a tender love letter. Onegin is touched, but knows too well his cynical, soul-debasing course of life has unfitted him to be an innocent girl's husband. He frankly refuses her love, and Tatania, her dream shattered, still cherishes him as her heart's ideal.

Onegin, however, finds the country stupid, and to annoy Lenski begins a violent flirtation with Olga, the latter's fiancée, at Tatania's birthday ball. It leads to a duel; Lensky challenges Onegin and the latter, without intention, kills the poet on the bank of a near-by stream and leaves the country filled with remorse.

Years later he is in Petrograd, at a splendid ball in the Greminsky palace and seeing the girl he knew as Tatania now a woman of the world, the Princess Gremin, he falls violently in love with her. Tatania still loves him but places duty to her husband above the claims of her heart, and so tells her adorer. And Onegin, broken-hearted, leaves his Russian Pamela with a Byronic reflection on the emptiness of life.

## "PETROUSHKA"

IGOR STRAVINSKY. Russian Ballet (Paris, 1911). The "grotesque scenes" composed by Michael Fokine. Realistic modern music and Russian folk-tune themes emphasize the sinister development of a tragedy of puppet passion, jealousy, and murder. The vigorous "Down St. Peter's Road" (song of the post drivers of Tver); the Ballerina's waltz (trumpet and bassoon duo), and the elegiac piccolo solo depicting Petroushka's anguish stand out in a colorful score. One of the great creations of the Russian dancer Nijinsky, the latter told the writer the ballet had an underlying symbolic meaning: Petroushka represents the soul of the Russian people; the Charlatan, the autocratic power of Czarism. The moujik, dreading a brutal government with the fear of the oppressed, seeks to break the chains of bondage only to fall beneath the sword of the Moor (the Cossack), while the Charlatan, deriding his agony, shows the world it is wasting pity on a sawdust man. Petroushka's concluding ghostly menace has since been realized in sanguinary fact.

Admiralty Square (Petrograd, 1830) with a Shrovetide fair in progress on a sunshiny winter day. Nursemaids, droshky drivers, a peep-show man, Cossacks, women and children, police agents, men about town, grooms, soldiers laugh and chatter while two hurdy-gurdy men (convincing hand-organ tunes sound in harmonious discord) play for dancers. An old Charlatan with quaint flute *roulades* draws attention to his puppet show. Its curtain rises: a Ballerina, in red pantalets, a Moor, in a uniform, and poor Petroushka, in motley dance imitating mechanical dolls, for the old Charlatan, a magician, has found them souls. Suddenly all three make their way through the crowd and dance at the front of the stage.

The walls of Petroushka's marionette cell are of black, dotted with hopeless stars. Petroushka has more soul than his companions, hence a capacity for suffering beyond theirs. In despair he curses his slavery. With the Ballerina a gleam of hope enters his cell, but frightened by his fantastic exultation, she leaves.

The Moor in his cell plays idiotically with a cocoanut, then worships it. The Ballerina now enters and in a graceful toe dance circles round her affinity—for their puppet souls feel a kinship that rejects Petroushka's finer psychic nature. The marionette's waltz ends in a pose which casts the Ballerina across the Moor's knees. Unhappy Petroushka enters in search of the Ballerina. His rival casts him out and as the Ballerina reseats herself on his knees darkness envelops the scene.

Merriment has reached its climax at the fair. *Dvorniks* (droshky drivers) and nursemaids dance Russian folk dances; a showman with a bear crosses the stage; a drunken merchant, accompanied by lithe gypsy girls, flings bank notes to the crowd and, as darkness falls, masqueraders rush in and throw the crowd into commotion. The curtains of the marionettes' booth become strangely agitated. Suddenly they part: Petroushka, the Moor, and the Ballerina dart out, the Moor slays Petroushka with a blow of his saber and disappears after his inamorata, while the excited crowd watches Petroushka's dying agonies. The Charlatan, confronted by the corpse, roughly seizes Petroushka and shaking him, shows the spectators they have been wasting pity on a puppet. The crowd begins to disperse. The Charlatan, dragging the marionette toward his puppet theatre, sees the ghost of murdered Petroushka, blue and livid, suddenly rise at the top of the booth, with threatening gestures. His top hat falling from his head, unable to face the wraith, the guilty Magician flees panic-stricken from the stage.

*Kata Kabanova* (Brünn, 1922) by Leo Janaček, book by Cervonik, after Ostrowski's drama, *The Storm*. An arraignment by a Czech composer of the traditional patriarchal system of Czarist Russia's small town and country life, its curse the absolute authority vested in male or female head of the family. The great musical number is the Love Scene between Kata and her lover. In Kalinov on the Volga (1860) the rich widow, Marfa Kaban, a family tyrant, rules her son Tichon with iron hand, driving her daughter-in-law Kata to despair. A blind "yearning for love" forces Kata into the arms of a cultured Russian worldling from Petrograd, whose uncle rules him as Marfa does Kata. A summer night—Tichon is absent—brings their madness to a head. A thunderstorm ("God's judgment"), however, leads hysterically religious Kata to confess her sin to her husband and, conscience still reproaching her, to drown herself in the Volga, with a parting vision of her lover to cheer her leap into dark waters.

### "FEDORA"

Umberto Giordano. Book after Sardou's play (Milan, 1898). Considered less vital, musically, than the composer's *Andrea Chénier,* the score is a drama of Russian horrors in older nineteenth century imperial days. The music is pictorial, both in light moments (Waltz in the Society Scene, Act II) and in the tense, dramatically emotional ones. "Oh, eyes clear with truth" and "The darkness is falling" (Death Scene) are outstanding airs.

As Fedora Romazov, fiancée of dissolute Count Vladimir Andrejevitch, a titled police spy, is sitting in the drawing-room of his home in Petrograd, rapturously kissing his photograph, *troika* bells announce his coming. But—he is brought in mortally wounded. It is thought Nihilists have assassinated him and Fedora resolves to devote her life to discovering the murderer.

Circumstances alter cases. In Paris, at a reception in Fedora's home, she finds Count Loris Ispanov destroyed Vladimir because he had seduced his wife. Fedora pities then loves Loris and renounces her vengeance.

In a mountain villa Loris and Fedora should be happy but Fedora has no ears for bird song or the Angelus. Before she met Loris, in her thorough-going vengeance she had caused the deaths of his mother and brother. This weighs on her mind. At last, when Loris is about to learn the truth from his friend Borov, the wretched girl drops poison from a hollow in her crucifix into a cup of tea, drinks, confesses, and dies in Loris' forgiving arms, while a mountain lad (off stage) sings: "My mountain maid returns no more!"

*Mavra* (Paris, 1922) by Igor Stravinsky, scene in a *bourgeois* Russian nineteenth century interior, after Pushkin, rehabilitates with a touch of sarcasm the grand opera air dear to the nineteenth century composer. Parasha and her hussar lover sing a duet at windows across the street till the girl's mother—her cook has died —sends her to find a new one. She returns with Mavra, but no sooner has her mother gone than Parasha and Mavra fall into each other's arms; for Mavra is the hussar in girl's clothes. The mother returns unexpectedly to find Mavra shaving "herself." Suffocating with indignation she calls in the neighbors, and Mavra flees to despairing cries of "Basil, Basil!" from poor Parasha. *Chout* (*The Buffoon*) by Serge Prokofieff, a Russian Ballet, is an ultramodern Russian composer's development of a folk tale of the Archangel region, the adventures of a buffoon disguised as a cook serving as the thread for amusing satirical dance variations.

## "RISURREZIONE"

FRANCESCO ALFANO. Book by Hanan after Count Tolstoi's novel (Turin, 1904). One of the Italian modernist's youthful works, influenced by Giordano, with powerful dramatic pages (Finale, Act III), but little local Russian musical color.

The opera dramatizes scenes from the work: Katjuscha's betrayal (Tab. I); the scene in which she awaits the advent of her betrayer, Prince Dmitri—she is with child—in the railroad station (Tab. II); her discovery by Dmitri, in prison, a loose woman accused of murder (Tab. III), and the wayside Siberian convict camp (Tab. IV) where wretched Katjuscha refuses pardon and wedding ring Dmitri brings, and rather than degrade the one true love of her heart marries her fellow convict Simonson.

*Anna Karenina* (Budapest, 1915) by Jeno Hubay is based on Tolstoi's novel-study of later nineteenth century Russian life. The score illustrates musically the tragedy of Anna Karenina, a woman of the world married to a dull old man, and Count Wronsky, officer in a Guard regiment, young, impassioned and unprincipled, who offers her "the rich wine of life at a draught." Deserting husband and child, she drains the cup to its poisoned dregs, and when Wronsky's devotion wanes cuts the hopeless knot of life by killing herself.

*L'aube rouge* (*The Red Dawn*, Rouen, 1912) by Camille Erlanger, book by M. Marcon, is the conflict between love's claims and the duty of assassination expressed in a veristic score. "Your Nihilist lover Serge has died in Siberia," General Lavaroff tells his daughter. "Why not marry Ruys, the French surgeon?" But at the wedding supper Serge carries Olga off to Nihilist headquarters in the Paris *Quartier Latin*. The advent of a Russian diplomat provides a target for bombs the conspirators have made; Serge is to do the throwing. When he hesitates out of love for Olga, his comrades shoot him. Awaking in the hospital he finds his rival's, Dr. Ruys', operation has saved him. Resolved to do his duty he casts his bomb and is blown up. The shock drives Olga insane.

*Der Heilige Morgen* (*The Holy Morn*, Schwerin, 1918) by Platen, shows an evil Russian governor driving two hapless lovers to die in the frozen Ruthenian forests while dead Oliana's mother invokes "the Holy Dawn," when the people will overthrow the Czar's throne. *Rasputin* (MS.) by Umberto Giordano, book by Forzano, dramatizes the religious charlatan who dominated the late Czar Nicolas II and his Czarina. The book is credited with "audacity and power without precedent in opera." *Quand la cloche sonnera* (*When the Bell Tolls*, Paris, 1922) by Alfred Bachelet, is a Russian town tragedy of the German offensive of 1914. Manoutschka is to meet her soldier lover Vania on the Niemen bridge, to follow his retreating regiment. Her father Akimitch, ex-soldier, under secret orders, is to toll the town bell when the Germans advance, a signal to blow up the bridge. Manoutschka learns of the order too late to warn Vania. At her father's appeal to her patriotism she yields the bell-tower key she had snatched, and the roar of the explosion which scatters her lover over the landscape drowns her agonized sob: "For . . . my . . . country's . . . sake!" *Stefan* (Mayence, 1925) by Ebbe Hamerich, book by Nygaard, with effective Russian folk songs and marches, is the first operatic setting of the Russia of 1917. Stefan, in love with Naja, a moujik's daughter, brutally repulsed by her father, becomes a Soviet *commissar*. Betrayed by a Russian political "Carmen" and condemned to death, he hides in Naja's home. When Leo enters at the head of *cheka* soldiers, Stefan shoots Naja, behind whom Leo leaps; and about to be crucified by his captors his last words vision reunion with his beloved. *Vera Finger* (Leningrad, 1925) by Fieroff is an episode of Russian Nihilism based on secret archives of Schlüsselberg fortress, its heroine a Nihilist girl persecuted during the Czarist *régime*.

## BLOOD AND SNOW

## "THE SNOW BIRD"

THEODORE STERNS. Book by composer (Chicago, 1923). A colorful, modern "symphonic" opera, thematically original, in which a poetic Ballet and effective lyric pages stand out.

A Tartar girl, rescued in time from infamy aboard a Chinese "love-junk" by her father, finds him dead when the storm casts their boat ashore on the Siberian coast. The old hermit who discovers her wraps her in a white sealskin and names her Snow Bird. In his rock cave the wearied little maid dreams (Dance Pantomime of the Little Dream Gods). She sees the Little Dream Gods, playing with the Northern Lights, watch a glimmering iceberg become stranded on the shore, with Love and Hate imprisoned in its crystal shell. When the Little Dream Gods send Childhood with her flower wreath to release them, Hate tears Love from Childhood and dashes the poor little Dream God on the fanged rocks.

As Snow Bird wakens in the inner cave, three Mongol chiefs and an archer stalk into the outer cave seeking their lost Prince. He fled the black *izbas* of the horde, thinking he had slain his father in a fit of rage. And when Snow Bird steps forth in the moonlight holding the jeweled amulet the hermit gave her the Siberians recognize their Prince's jewel. Thinking the young girl a witch, the archer's feathered arrow quivers in her bosom as the hermit enters, tearing off his disguise. He kneels beside the dying girl, his heart torn with love and anguish, but the Little Dream Gods are calling her. Untouched by passion, the Snow Bird's little white soul takes flight, and sadly leaving her in her cavern tomb, the Tartar Prince departs as from a shrine.

*Beniowski ou les exiles de Kamchatka* (*Beniowski or the Kamchatkan Exiles*, Paris, 1800)) by Boieldieu, is an old "convict" opera. Beniowski, Polish political prisoner, escapes with his love, the Russian governor's daughter, after fleeing from precipice to precipice, with the aid of a Russian convict leader who first tries to kill him. A Convict Chorus (the musical gem of the score) in an icy cave, a battle, a bear hunt, and burning of Kamchatka fort helped make it a success in its day. Now it is forgotten as is Donizetti's *Otto mesi in due ore o gli esilati in Siberi* (*Eight Months in Two Hours or the Siberian Exiles*, Naples, 1827), and Rubinstein's *The Siberian Hunters* (Petrograd, 1853).

## "SIBERIA"

UMBERTO GIORDANO. Book by Civinni (Milan, 1903). Never commonplace, *Siberia*, a gloomy tale of crime and retribution in Czarist Russia, strikes the note of pathos with firmer and surer hand than any other score the composer has written. Bie calls it "too intellectual for Italy, too musical for the intellectual."

In his Petrograd palace Prince Alexis, vainly waiting for his mistress, Stephana, falls asleep, waking to learn Stephana's couch has not been occupied that night, as Stephana slipping through the garden gate at dawn, ignores the queries of Gleby, Alexis' spy. Vassili, a young sergeant, now enters the palace to report to Walitzin, his captain, about to leave with the Prince. When Stephana enters the room he recognizes a lovely unknown seen in the street who has captured his pure young heart. Prince Alexis, suspicious, returns and inquires who Vassili may be. When Stephana declares him her lover, the Prince insults him, Vassili draws sword on his superior officer and a court-martial condemns him to Siberia.

At a convict station on the Siberian border Stephana, showing her permit, approaches No. 117 (Vassili) and in an impassioned duet the lovers tell their affection and suffering. In the end Stephana joins the convicts to share Vassili's fate, and the march to their frozen exile is resumed. Easter in the Siberian prison town, with the log-cabin love nest of the convict lovers showing in the rear. Walitzin, the governor, makes advances which Stephana rejects. Gleby (under orders from Prince Alexis) tells Vassili Stephana has been unfaithful to him; but she proves his charge false. Then the prisoners flee but—a shot rings out—Stephana is mortally wounded and Vassili captured. Walitzin, touched by her prayer to free her lover complies with it, and Stephana dies happily in her sergeant-convict's arms.

*Peter Sukoff* (Nuremberg, 1922) by Waldemar Wendland, book after Wohlbrück's novel, uses Siberian folk songs for local color in a fine score in which "Mitjushka, come to me" (Act I), the Wedding Chorus (Act II), and the Bath House Scene (Act III) stand out. Peter Sukoff, dissolute owner of Siberian gold mines, his one redeeming feature his love for his mother, catches Njuta, a girl gold panner, hiding golden grains to help her flee toil's dull round with Mitja, the foreman, her lover. Struck by her beauty Peter marries her against her will instead of punishing her and when Mitja breaks in on the drunken wedding feast, makes him sing a wedding song for his amusement. Njuta sees Mitja, promises to meet him in the Bath House to flee with him, and Peter, overhearing, determines to blow up the Bath House with the guilty pair. But his old mother so movingly shows Njuta her wrong that she determines to abide by her duty. Peter's mother, going to the Bath House to tell Mitja Njuta will not come, is blown sky-high by her son, who presses the electric button in the mansion. After he has drowned his sorrow in vodka with his illegitimate son Alexander, Peter staggers to the scene. Finding he has unwittingly slain his mother, the one he loved best on earth, he commits suicide by flinging himself into the flaming ruins.

## SVEALAND

*Linnée ou les mines de Suède* (*Linnæus or the Mines of Sweden,* Paris, 1808) by Dourlen is a botanical opera. Linnæus, Swedish naturalist, who first classified plants, has the right (conferred by a grateful government) of occasionally freeing a criminal; and instead of plucking a new plant from the soil, drags a youth condemned to life labor in the chill Swedish salt mines from his thirsty prison. The plot, to quote a contemporary critic, was "one capable of freezing the warmest musical imagination."

## FROM GREENLAND'S ICY MOUNTAINS

### "KADDARA"

HAKON BORRESEN. Book after *Pictures from Greenland Folk Life* by C. M. Norman-Hansen (Copenhagen, 1921). A score which shows love flaming hotly amid Greenland's icy mountains. Individual, though often Wagnerian in harmonization, piquant primitive rhythms, tribal tunes, dances and "cries" lend the tale picturesque exotic quality.

Ujarak (Ouriak), a young Eskimo "catch-man" (the name given whale hunters of the frozen seas), returns minus a catch, and out of sorts at his bad luck from the hunt. The women of the tribe flaunt and jeer him for his want of success and his wife Kaddara insults her husband and refuses to let him come into his home. In despair at his humiliation Ujarak flings himself into his *kajak* (canoe) and paddles away.

In the open sea he harpoons a whale and tows his booty to the Widows' Strand—barren, for no grass grows for the Greenland widow. Tribal custom decrees she must live apart, eking out a starvation existence with her children along wind-swept cliffs above the ocean shore. The approach of Ujarak's *kajak* towing the monstrous promise of many meals fills the widows with excitement. Tulewatte, an old experienced widow, implores her daughter Anouna, a bewitching girl, to captivate the *kajak* man and compel him, by means of the magic bite in the shoulder to become her slave. Ujarak lands, generously gives his catch to the starving women and Anouna asks him to dance with her the "Dance of the Whale's Capture," in which the opera climaxes musically. Ujarak begins the curious aboriginal dance by tearing his shirt from his body with a sweeping gesture and, nude to the waist, carries out its primitive movements, "in part like a fish moving its fins, in part yearningly erotic." At a given moment he seizes Anouna in his sinewy arms, swings her high in the air and disappears with her in a cleft among the rocks.

The society of Anouna and the company of the widows merry over their blubber, however, cannot dim Ujarak's longing visions of Kaddara, and he determines to escape. In vain Anouna calls in the *angekok,* the magician, in vain she pleads with him, Ujarak flees to the village where he has left his heart.

On the roof of her hut Kaddara, who long since has regretted her anger and longs for her Ujarak's return, sings to her papoose ("Lullaby") when in answer to her unspoken prayer as she gazes into the radiant Polar night (or, rather, day) the whale hunters appear. They bear the body of unconscious Ujarak, found on the ice. In Kaddara's arms he wakes again to life and love, and the Aurora Borealis blesses their wedded happiness reborn.

## In the Shade of Mount Hekla

### "LE PAYS"

#### (*The Homeland*)

J. Guy Ropartz. Book by Charles le Goffic (Nancy, 1912). A score by a modernist composer who uses thematic exposition by leading motive to develop original musical ideas. The "human" love music in the tale is less vital than that expressing the Breton's love for his "stern and rock-bound coast" which (Act III) often has remarkable beauty and eloquence.

The Breton fisherman Tual, shipwrecked on the coast of Iceland, falls in love with Koethe, daughter of the Iceland fisher Yorgen, who has found and nursed him, and marrying her has sworn to be true on the *Hrafuaga*. The *Hrafuaga* or "Valley of the Ravens" is an immense morass frozen solid during winter, but a treacherous bog which swallows up any human being who ventures to cross it once the melting of the snows has been announced by the croaking of the ravens who inhabit it. The long northern winter drags on and the Breton finds that stronger than his love for Koethe is homesickness for his native land. Even his wife's news that a child is under way cannot drive thought of the Pardon of Pamipol, his native village, from his mind. The white blossoms of the pear trees in old Brittany call. He cannot resist the home appeal and abandons wife and family to return to his "God's country." To do so he must cross the still frozen *Hrafuaga,* but no sooner is he well advanced on the ice than the hideous croaking of the ravens announces its melting, and Tual is drawn into the abyss before the eyes of Koethe, who already has forgiven him.

### 3. *Gypsies*

### "CARMEN"

GEORGES BIZET. Book by Henri Meilhac and Ludovic Halévy (probably best libretto of the Scribe type) founded on Prosper Merimée's novel (Paris, 1875). Pallades' conclusion, reading Merimée's novel, "Woman is bitter: She has but two good hours: one in bed, the other in death," typifies the treacherous gypsy Carmen. Nietzsche calls Bizet's score "the opera of operas." Though its scene is Seville, in 1820, and its music Spanish in flavor, it has never been popular in Spain. The Habanera, "L'Amour est un oiseau rebelle," the Seguidilla "Sur les remparts de Séville" (Act I), the gypsy dance song in the inn, "Les tringles des sistres m'avais jetée," the famous "Toreador's Song" (Act II), the "Card Trio," Micaela's romance, "Je dis que rien ne m'épouvante" (a lovely number, Act III), the ballet (Act IV), are high moments in a score whose music reveals adventure, love, fate, "all the great things which make up the secret and the strength of life."

Looking for her lover, Micaela, the country maid to whom Don José, corporal of dragoons, is engaged, enters a square in Seville. The relief arrives (military music and "Street Boys' Song") after she has gone, and José is told she has been seeking him. He thinks of her while the cigarette girls—their leader captivating Carmen—pour from the factory opposite. When soldiers, crowding around her, ask her to choose a lover she sings (Habanera) with the indifferent José in mind: "If you do not love me, I'll love you and if I love you, beware!" and flings the flowers she wears to José with a provocative look and shrug. Micaela next delivers a kiss and letter from his mother (urging him to marry her) to her soldier. But now there is uproar in the factory. Carmen has stabbed another girl; José brings her out a prisoner. Pretending love, she so works on him he loosens the rope tying her hands, and she makes her escape.

In Lillia Pastia's tavern on Seville ramparts are Carmen, Frasquita and Mercedes (gypsy songs and dances). Jealous Morales, angry at Carmen's indifference, taunts her with loving José, sentenced to two months in the guardhouse for her escape. She laughs at the idea, and when the famous bullfighter Escamillo enters, devotes herself to him, enraging Morales, till both men leave. The tavern closed for the night, the innkeeper admits two smugglers. The other girls leave with them, but Carmen remains to meet José, and persuades him to join the lawless band. He comes, confesses his love, and Carmen so bewitches him he ignores the trumpet call to duty. Yet when she asks him to betray his soldier honor and join the smugglers he refuses. Fate then knocks at the door in the shape of Morales. When he orders José to leave, the latter disobeys and draws his sword. Smugglers and gypsies rush in to prevent a fight, but the die is cast. José knows his army days are over and joins the band.

José, on guard in the smugglers' mountain camp, is rallied by Carmen on his gloom. He tells her his thoughts are with an old woman who prays for her son in whom she believes, and the heartless gypsy mocks him, suggesting he abandon his uncongenial life. He protests his passion, then finding her unmoved, threatens to kill her. Death comes as fate decrees, is her answer, and she joins Frasquita and Mercedes, who are telling fortunes. The cards, no matter how she deals, predict she and her lover will die. The girls go to help the smugglers distract the attention of the guards and Micaela comes in. Before she can reveal herself a shot rings out; Escamillo enters seeking the gypsy girl. José (whose shot has not wounded him), wild with jealousy, challenges him. The advent of Carmen prevents a struggle, and Escamillo leaves, offering to meet José anyhere, at any time, and inviting all to the next bullfight in Seville. Micaela now tells José his mother lies on her deathbed and implores him to go to her. Unwilling to leave Carmen, he first refuses, then goes, vowing to return.

Carmen, now his love, beside him, the bullfighter in a gala procession of officials and *toreros,* enters the square where the people await their idol. About to enter the ring, Escamillo bids Carmen farewell, both vowing undying love. She ignores Frasquita and Mercedes, who warn her José may seek her. He appears—the man she has morally and physically destroyed—a dramatic contrast to his triumphant rival. Ruined, cheated, an outcast because of his love, he cannot forget it. He implores Carmen to be kind to him. But Escamillo's name sounds in the arena amid wild applause; Carmen's every thought is there. She repulses José with biting scorn, with such open joy in her passion for the bullfighter that, when Escamillo's name is again thundered forth by the unseen crowd José stabs her to the heart. As the crowd pours from the arena, Escamillo, seeking Carmen, at their head, José flings himself despairingly upon the dead body of the woman he adored.

*Carmencita* (Prague, 1908) by Paul Zochovlich, an unsuccessful operetta whose heroine is supposed to be a daughter of "Carmen," and many another operatic gypsy before and after Bizet's Spanish girl, have emphasized the fact there is but one *Carmen.* These scores include: *Cyganie* (Warsaw, 1822) by Mirecki, a pupil of Hummel; *The Gypsy's Warning* (London, 1836) by Sir Julius Benedict; Taubert's *Der Zigeuner* (Berlin, 1834); Ambroise Thomas' ballet, *La Gipsy* (Paris, 1839); J. N. Fuchs' *Zingara* (Brünn, 1892); Alexander Schaefer's *Tsygany* (Petrograd, 1901); Zöllner's *Zigeuner* (Stuttgart, 1912); and the Swedish ballet *Iberia* (Paris, 1920), Ibañez' music, which pictures the Port of Cadiz, gypsies in Granada, and Corpus Christi Day in Seville.

Often the operatic gypsy is not "to the manor born," but a babe ravished from lordly castle and brought up by Romany camp fire.

## "THE BOHEMIAN GIRL"

MICHAEL WILLIAM BALFE. Book by Alfred Bunn (London, 1843). A favorite old-fashioned score in which a raggle-taggle gypsy girl turns out to be a haughty noble's long-lost daughter. The famous air "I dreamt I dwelt in marble halls" is sweetly sentimental, one of the melodies which leads Streatfeild to say: "the score lives solely by reason of the insipid tunefulness of one or two airs." The scene of action is in and about Pressburg, Hungary, in the eighteenth century.

Thaddeus, a noble Pole, rushes on the scene as Count Arnheim is raising the flag of a now defunct empire over his sovereign's statue and, realizing he is in enemy territory, hastens off to join a gypsy band led by Devilshoof. While with them he saves Arline, Arnheim's daughter, from a bear, the child receiving the slight flesh wound necessary to identify her in Act III. When the grateful father begs him join in the toast to the Austrian emperor at the banquet in Thaddeus' honor, the latter flings his wine glass at the statue while Devilshoof abducts little Arline, kicking away a tree bridging an abyss to prevent pursuit.

Twelve years pass, the twelve years during which Thaddeus has watched over Arline's slumbers in the gypsy queen's tent, waiting for her to grow from infancy to girlhood, to tell his love and find she returns his honest passion. But the gypsy queen, who also loves the handsome Pole, treacherously hangs about Arline's neck a medallion stolen from Florestan, Count Arnheim's nephew. He, trying to steal a kiss from her in Pressburg at the fair, sees it, has her arrested and brought in to her father, who sits singing before his lost daughter's picture with tears in his eyes. As terrified Arline tries to stab herself the scar of Act I is revealed, speaks for itself, and Arnheim catches his girl to his heart.

About to meet the local gentry (she has refused Florestan), Arline thinks of happy days with Thaddeus in the Romany tents. As she draws her old gypsy dress from a closet Thaddeus appears at the window. Trying to coax her back to the open road he lingers too long, and as guests draw near hides in Arline's closet. Enter the vengeful gypsy queen. The Count rages when she cries that a man is hidden in his daughter's chamber and Thaddeus emerges. But when he learns Thaddeus' blood runs blue as his own, he awards him Arline's hand with a sigh of relief. A happy closing incident is the gypsy queen's death. Ordering a gypsy to shoot Thaddeus, Devilshoof so turns the gun that she herself is shot.

*Preciosa* (Berlin, 1921), a play by P. A. Wolff, is still given in Germany because of Weber's *incidental music*. A blue-blooded babe robbed from a baroque Spanish cradle is brought up in a

gypsy camp and falls in love with a huntsman who is a noble
in disguise. After much tripping hither and thither on the part
of all concerned, Preciosa's noble birth is revealed and she marries
her lover. The eleven musical numbers, beginning with the Overture, and including the "Gypsy March," Preciosa's three Spanish
dances, and her touching song, "Einsam bin ich, nicht alleine,"
comprise some of the finest gypsy music known to the dramatic
stage. *La reine Topaze* (Paris, 1856) by Victor Massé (the air
of the "Carnival of Venice" with the Paganini variations, Act II,
stands out) is the tale of Topaze, daughter of Venetian patricians,
robbed from the cradle by gypsies and brought up to become their
queen, who loves Captain Raphael, a gallant soldier. The secret
of her noble birth revealed, he is glad to marry her.

## "MIGNON"

Ambroise Thomas. Book by Barbier and Michel Carré after Goethe's
*Wilhelm Meister* (Paris, 1866). The book is little like Goethe's
original, Wilhelm, the Teuton *bourgeois* being turned into a Parisian
man of fashion. Here, too, a supposititious gypsy maid works her way
through distressing adventures to a lover's hand and a father's heart.
The ecstatic, dreamy air, "Connais-tu le pays" ("Knowest thou the
land?"), in Act I, is the most famous aria; while the brilliant vocal
Polonaise, the Waltz, "Je suis Titania," and the Gavotte, "Me voici
dans son boudoir" (Act II), are outstanding pages. Eighteenth century
Germany and Italy are the background for the action.

Lothario, a mad singer seeking a long-lost daughter, enters a German
tavern courtyard. There gypsies spread a rug but Giarno, their chief,
cannot make seventeen-year-old Mignon dance the egg dance. His
whip is raised when Wilhelm Meister, a student, draws pistol and
purse and buys the waif. Loving Wilhelm with a love he never suspects Mignon (modestly attired as a page, lest she awaken injurious
suspicions) follows her rescuer when he departs with Filena, the actress,
and other members of a traveling troupe, to fill an engagement as the
company "poet" in the castle of Frederick's uncle (Frederick is one of
Filena's admirers).

In the castle Mignon soon realizes Wilhelm loves Filena. Slipping
into her old gypsy skirt she goes out to drown herself in the park lake
and there meets Lothario. When she tells him her sad tale and in a
flash of rage at Filena, asks why heaven does not destroy the castle
with lightning, the amiable mad man hurries off to make good heaven's
omission. Soon the castle is in flames, the inmates hasten out. Filena,
seeing Mignon, says a bouquet Wilhelm has given her is still in the
conservatory. Blossoms touched by Wilhelm's hand to perish in the
flames? Unthinkable!—to Mignon, at any rate. She rushes into the
burning building to rescue them, and is herself rescued by Wilhelm,

who lays her on a mossy bank, the withered flowers clutched in her hand.

In Italy—where Lothario, Mignon, and Wilhelm Meister are occupying the Cipriani castle—old Lothario suddenly regains his reason. He remembers the castle is his, that he is Count Cipriani, and identifies Mignon as his little Sperata, whose loss drove him insane. While father and daughter are clasped in each others' arms Wilhelm hastens up (he has heard Filena, whom he now loathes, is on her way to him) and makes the embrace a triple one, pending the chiming of wedding bells for Mignon and himself.

*Mignonette* (Paris, 1896) by George Street, a Bizet pupil, is a three-act opera parody of *Mignon.* In *Maritana* (London, 1845) by William Wallace, an opera of the type of *The Bohemian Girl* (with "Scenes that are brightest" and "There is a flower" as its favorite melodies) King Charles of Spain takes a fancy to Maritana, a gypsy street singer. Spanish etiquette demands the king's mistress be married or a widow. Don César de Bazan, jailed under sentence of death for a duel fought to defend Lazarillo, a street Arab, is promised by Don José, prime minister, bullet instead of rope if he marry a veiled lady (Maritana) before his execution. The marriage takes place, but Lazarillo provides the firing squad with blank cartridges and Don César, feigning death, escapes. In the royal villa (Act III) where King Charles is pressing Maritana hotly, Don César rescues his wife, kills Don José —who has been similarly pressing the queen—and, royal rage turned to gratitude, is made governor of Valencia. *Don César de Bazan* (Paris, 1872) by Massenet tells practically the same tale in a Gounodian score, in which stand out the March Interlude (Act II), Entr'acte Sevillana, and Lazarille's Arietta. A successful Russian setting is Lishin's *Don César de Bazan* (Kiev, 1888).

*Aleko* (Petrograd, 1893) by Rachmaninoff, book after Pushkin's *The Gypsies,* is the tale of a Petrograd club man, weary of the conventional society round, who weds a gypsy girl, Zemfira, for happiness, and kills her when he finds her untrue. Montagu-Nathan thinks the music is influenced by Mascagni's *Cavalleria;* the composer says it was "written on the old-fashioned Italian model." *Kinder der Heide* (*Children of the Plains,* Vienna, 1861) by Rubinstein, after Beck's *Yanko,* a wild sequence of loves and murders on the Ukrainian plain, ends with Isbana, a gypsy girl, stabbing herself when Wauja, an excitable hostler (loving Maria, whose lover he slew) is deaf to her passion pleas. *Manru* (Dresden, 1901) by Ignaz Paderewski, introducing Polish gypsy airs and dances, tells how Ulana, a Galician village girl, marries Manru, the gypsy. Driven from home by the cries of their baby, he takes up with Asa, a gypsy girl, and when Ulana drowns herself

in despair is pushed into the same lake to die by Asa's lover Oros.
*Le Cobzar* (Monte Carlo, 1909) by Gabriella Ferrari has Stan,
Roumanian *cobzar* (gypsy guitarist) forget his love Jana for a
gypsy girl. When Jana marries innkeeper Pradea who beats her,
Stan drops his gypsy wench and finds Jana loves him though
married. The scorned gypsy tells Pradea, Stan kills her, Pradea
tries to prevent his escape, and Jana knifes her husband. But
she and Stan are happy. What is a life sentence in the Roumanian
salt mines if they can serve it together? *Gli zingani* (London,
1912) by Leoncavallo shows gypsy Filena stealing from camp to
meet Radir, a stranger, 'neath the stars. Caught, Radir says he
wants to be a gypsy and is taken into the tribe. But Tamar, a
gypsy poet who loves Filena, sings dismally at her wedding to
Radir and (Act II) when the newly wed pair have sought the
bridal tent, drenches it with oil and applies the torch. *Le Gardien*
(Nice, 1924) by Molinetti, a veristic score, tells how Luroux of
the wild bulls of the Camargue, saves his fellow *gardien* Perran
in the arena, but not himself from his sudden passion for gypsy
Zimella. Forgetting his "good girl" Michelette, he bears off the
gypsy on horseback, but when the girl's Romany lover Paino
reclaims her from Luroux, the latter, "sending a supreme thought"
to Michelette, drowns himself in the Rhone. *Miarka* (Paris, 1905;
revised 1925) by Alexandre Georges, book after Richepin's novel
*La fille a l'ourse*, has a poetic score, Miarka's "L'eau qui court"
and the contralto "Hymne des Morts" outstanding. Gypsy blood
runs in village Miarka's maiden veins. She repulses Gleude who
loves her, sets fire to her cottage and takes to the road with her
grandmother, La Vougne, for the sake of her gypsy dreams.
When the grandmother dies soon after they have set out, Gleude,
that Miarka may be happy, brings the Romany king and his tribe
to the girl and sees them disappear over the Champagne plains,
love's future bright before them.

## "LA VIDA BREVE"

### (*A Brief Life*)

MANUEL DE FALLA. Book by Carlos Fernandez-Shaw (Nice, 1913).
A lyric drama which symbolizes the fleeting nature of human life and
love, and which "combines the exterior seductions of verism with an
absence of its blemishes." Its *flamenca* melodies and dances have the
direct appeal of folk music. Salud's airs, "Vivan los que rien! Mueran
los que lloran!" ("Let those live who laugh! Let those die who
weep!"), "Paco! Paco! Non!" her duet with her lover (Scene 5),
and the whole of the brilliant final choral Dance Scene with its gripping
close stand out.

In the Albaicin, gypsy quarter of present-day Granada, in a house whose door opens on the street, Salud, the gypsy girl, enters as merry laughter of young girls, cries of street vendors and the chime of church bells mingle with clank of steel in the forge close at hand. Her love for Paco is so great, the young girl tells her grandmother, it makes her sad, and to the rhythm of clanging forge hammers, she sings the song of the flower born at dawn to die at eve. Then Paco her lover comes and protests undying devotion to the girl beneath him in caste, who has given him her heart. As he pours out his passionate avowals, Salud's uncle, Sarvaor, a fierce old gypsy, enters and is about to kill Paco, when the grandmother intervenes. Sarvaor has discovered that Paco is about to marry Carmela, a wealthy girl of his own class. Little Salud has been basely betrayed! Sarvaor then enters his forge, unable to tell Salud the news that will break her heart, while night closes down on the lovers, who hold each other fondly embraced. (A symphonic Intermezzo paints the soft Grenadine night, a night of sighs and flower fragrance, echoing snatches of joyous song and merry laughter (choral, off stage) which rises like a shower of golden fireworks into the skies, until gradually all dies into silence.)

In the home of Carmela and Manuel, her brother, large windows opening on the street show the brilliant festival scene of Carmela's betrothal to Paco, with guitar playing, singing and dancing. The *ole,* Andalusian folk dance, introduced chorally, is brilliantly taken up by the dancers alone. While they dance within, Salud, in the street, as her grandmother and uncle come up, sings into a window the song the blacksmith sang at his forge (Act I) "Evil betides the women born 'neath a luckless star!" When she adds "come no more to the Albaicin! . . . she is dead! . . . the very stones would rise beneath your feet!" guilty Paco hears, starts and trembles. Salud and her uncle turn to the door of the house.

Within, the guests, men and women of the well-to-do middle class take their ease. When the gypsies enter Manuel asks what they want, but his guests, thinking them come to dance for their amusement, acclaim them. Then, while the women in Manila shawls with bright flowers in their hair, and the men in evening clothes listen in amazement, Salud tells how Paco has ruined and left her, though the air of her room still echoes to his words of love. When he cries "She lies! Drive her out!" Salud takes a step toward him. With the one word "Paco!" spoken with infinite tenderness, she puts her hand to her heart and falls dead, while her grandmother and uncle curse "the Judas" who has betrayed her, as a murmur of horror sweeps the courtyard.

### 4. *Sacred and Profane Love*

#### "THAÏS"

Jules Massenet. Book by Gallet (Paris, 1894), after Anatole France's novel. Massenet's score is the outstanding operatic contrast of sacred and profane love. It pictures the struggle between Christian asceticism and pagan sensuality, "of a sinner who became a saint and a saint who became a sinner . . . a courtesan who turned from the god of love to the love of God" (Henry T. Finck). The symphonic "Méditation," its music symbolizing the conversion of the sinner Thaïs, is the most popular number of the atmospheric score, much played as a violin solo. Athanaël's "Voilà donc la terrible cité," and Thaïs' Death Scene yield to the duet in the desert between cenobite and courtesan, the musical high moment of the work. An "exquisite mixture of earthly and heavenly love" sounds in the music which accompanies the words "Baigne d'eau tes mains et tes lèvres."

Athanaël, hermit monk of the Egyptian desert, burns with indignation at shocking tales of the dissolute lives of the idle rich of Alexandria, where the lovely courtesan Thaïs rules the revels of sin. A dream vision of the shameless one, scantily clad, acclaimed as the goddess of love by the multitude, haunts him. He feels a call and turning his back on his cell hurries to the great city to convert the impure beauty.

Nicias, a loose-living millionaire and former friend of Athanaël, is entertaining Thaïs, his mistress of the moment, with a festival in his palace. Nicias good-naturedly fits out the zealous cenobite with proper clothes and introduces him to Thaïs, who tries to tempt the solemn stranger by casting off her robes when he preaches contempt of the flesh.

But when he seeks her out in her own home and pleads with her, withstanding all her blandishments, she realizes beauty passes, that death is the goal of all earthly things. She begins to dread the hereafter, and leaving her friends to their wine, she passes out into the moonlit night to wake Athanaël, sleeping outside the house, and says she will follow wherever he lead. Then, flinging a burning torch into her palace, she departs with the monk as it flames up behind her, the mob scrambling for the gold pieces scattered by Nicias to favor their flight.

In the desert Athanaël, who has been harshly driving Thaïs on, repents and tearfully kisses her feet when she falls prostrate with fatigue. But in vain, after he has delivered her to the good nuns who dwell in the oasis, does he strive to forget her.

Back in his cell he is haunted, he confesses to Palemon, his abbot, by impure and enticing visions. The abbot advises holy meditation, but visions of a smiling, alluring Thaïs rise before Athanaël's eyes, instead of prayers to his lips. In the process of weaning her from earthly to heavenly love he himself has turned from love sacred to love profane. Calling her name in an agony of passion, he carries his burden of suffering out into the desert, where the simoom blows. There another vision, a ghastly one of Thaïs dying, startles him.

Hurrying to the convent in the oasis he finds Thaïs lying on her deathbed, about to breathe her last. Alas, while she sings of purification and paradise in a dying ecstasy, Athanaël begs her to live to gratify his own uncontrollable passion! But her thoughts cannot be recalled to the things of earth. She dies as a saint, calling on God, while he sinks down beside her in despair, imploring her in a frenzy to live— for him!

*Antonio* (Milan, 1900) by Cesare Galeotti paints St. Anthony's struggle in the desert against haunting visions of voluptuous women. *Ekkehardt* (Berlin, 1898) by J. J. Abert, is the tenth century monk who loved Duchess Hadwig of Swabia but felt death, incurred fighting the pagan Huns, redeemed his fault. *Ekkehard* (Brünn, 1925) by Josef Wizina, a neo-Straussian score, is based on Scheffel's novel, like its predecessor. *Frieden* (*Peace,* Mayence, 1907) by Heydrich, is what a monk who seduces the wife of a knight, his benefactor, finds in cloister cell when his paramour poisons herself. *Der Asket* (*The Ascetic,* Leipzig, 1893) by Karl Schröder, tells how Manuel enters a monastery (18th century Spain) to forget lovely Isabella, devil in female form. When she appears with a hunting party passing the cloister he rushes out, breaking the neck of the prior, who tries to stop him, and, when a messenger from Rome rides up with absolution for past sins, drowns himself in the river with his temptress. In *Die Beichte* (*The Confession,* Berlin, 1900) by Ferdinand Hummel, the hermit Jacinto (Portugal, 1800) confesses his sin to the man whose wife he betrayed, now monk Manoel, and receives his forgiveness and absolution. In Emil Kaiser's colorful *Das Hexenlied* (*The Witch Song,* Berlin, 1894), Hadwiga, taking refuge in a Benedictine monastery (14th century Germany), is surprised in a passionate moment with the monk Menardus, who falls dead while she is led to the stake with a song on her lips. *Il cuor delle fanciulle* (*Maidens' Hearts,* Dresden, 1902) by Buongiorno, a verist score, shows Alba, opera singer at an eighteenth century Italian court, who, torn between her struggle against musical rivals and her love for the young priest Marino, dies in his arms as he cries: "These are the first kisses my lips have known!" *Il Viadante* (*The Prophet,* Mannheim, 1906) by Enrico Bossi, is a lyric drama of a wandering prophet who preaches love and the forgiveness of sins. Living with a slave and two young girls in a cave, the slave suspects the holy man of sinful love for one of the girls and denouncing him to a mob, the latter promptly burns him alive. *Frasquita* (Memel, 1910) a veristic score with notable Prelude and dramatic duets, by Miersch-Rieclus, presents Frasquita listening to Hidalgo's love vows (20th century Spain) while they dance. Jealous Ravanola tells Hidalgo Frasquita is betraying him with the priest in the confessional while, on the contrary, the girl has been so hard pressed by the sinful man of God she has had to kill him. When Hidalgo visits his love in the murderer's cell she proves she was true and, about to fly with him, is shot by a guard through the bars.

## "PEPITA JIMÉNEZ"

J. ALBENIZ. Book after Juan Valera's novel by Monez-Coutts (Barcelona, 1896). The score whose piquant folk melodies and rhythms underline Valera's tale of the victory of human love over a religious vocational inhibition, is probably the composer's best known opera.

In an Andalusian village Don Pedro loves the pretty widow Pepita Jiménez. Pepita loves his son Don Luis, and the father withdraws his suit. Yet Don Luis is to take holy orders and is to be ordained a priest. When the girl asks her confessor's advice he tells her to renounce her lover. Don Luis has promised to bid the girl a last farewell, but while she waits, hearing a young officer speak lightly of her in the street, he challenges him and fights a duel for her sake.

Pepita, grieving because of Don Luis nonarrival, hurried joyfully into the room when he appears. The young candidate for the priesthood is still firm in his resolve to dedicate himself to the Church when Pepita's cry, "You wish me to die and die I gladly will!" makes him change his mind, and Church and priesthood forgot, he clasps her in his arms.

## "JOCELYN"

BENJAMIN GODARD. Book by Silvestre and Capoul (Brussels, 1888). The composer's lyric score has passed from the repertoire, but survives in a melody which is one of the most generally popular of any French opera, the famous "Berceuse" or Lullaby, "Cachés dans cet asile," a delicate, graceful air played in its violin transcription as often as sung. The Prayer, "Seigneur, ayez pitié," is another happy lyric page.

While terrorists of the French Revolution persecute the priests of Dauphigny, Jocelyn, a young seminarist, takes refuge in a hidden valley, his retreat known only to the shepherds of the countryside. There, too, comes Laurence, a young girl of noble family, disguised as a boy, and her father. Jocelyn conceals them in his hiding place, the Eagle's Cave. But troubling emotions fill his breast when, Laurence having fainted, he finds she is a girl, and in that idyllic valley, the young Priest-to-be yields to a love which is returned.

In Grenoble the aged bishop, about to be guillotined, commends Laurence to Jocelyn's *spiritual* care. Torn with anguish the young priest swears he will renounce his vows. But Laurence, withdrawing from his arms, bids him remember he is a man of God, and he departs to take up the duties of his priestly estate. Laurence, too, leaves the valley, but though she lives in the gay world she is not of it. Jocelyn rebels against fate, however, hastens to Paris to find her, but beneath her balcony is recalled to his duty by the chime of the Angelus, and resigns himself to what must be. When Laurence dies, victim of a love pure and unappeased, on Corpus Christi Day Jocelyn, not knowing who claims his aid, is called to give her absolution, and she expires expressing the hope they may be reunited in Heaven.

*Ramuntcho* (Milan, 1921) by Stefan Donaudy, book after Pierre Loti's novel. Though the Basque village church bells which chime in Loti's romance ring in Donaudy's score, it has been called "a dramatic work with musical illustrations rather than an opera." It is a tale of a girl who holds the vow which makes her a bride of Christ higher than the promptings of earthly love.

Ramuntcho, Pyrenean village boy and smuggler, is illegitimate. His mother Franchita's love for him is the purifying flame of her existence. But Graziosa, Ramuntcho's sweetheart, has a mother whose virtue cannot overlook the poor boy's tarnished name. Returning after three years' service in the French army with the *médaille militaire,* Ramuntcho finds his mother dying and Graziosa, who loves him, driven into a convent as a result of her mother's persecution. In despair Ramuntcho, aided by Graziosa's brother, visits her in the convent to urge her to flee with him to Uruguay, where a wealthy uncle has offered to push his fortunes. But Graziosa, heart-broken and near yielding to her lover's importunities, remembers that she has put away all the joys of earth, and refuses to break her vows. Ramuntcho, despairing, has to leave her to take up a life devoid of hope in South America.

*The Holy Mount* (Dessau, 1914) by Christian Sinding, book by Dora Duncker, is modern in spirit. A mystic Prologue, Dion's "Childhood Song," Daphnis' "Entrance Song," and her Love Duet with Dion stand out. The scene of action is the Greek monastery of St. Gregory on Mount Athos. Phocas (1800) killed his wife's brother and father thinking them Turks, and found it wise to leave her. Handing over his infant son Dion to Abbot Philemon of Mount Athos, he made the priest promise to bring the lad up in ignorance of women. One evening Daphnis, a young girl, enters the cloister garden, her companion the elderly Wanderer (Dion's mother in disguise). Dion feels stir emotions he does not understand; but the young things soon become friends and Daphnis teaches the monk to kiss. Not till Angelus bells chime reproachfully does Dion realize his sin and tearing himself from Daphnis' lips, rush off only (Act II) to find her sobbing over him as he lies in the monastery court on a stretcher, while his mother doffs her disguise to the monks' horror. Since the cloister walls do not come tumbling down, the abbot sends out tidings of the miracle, marries Dion to Daphnis, and they depart singing the praise of love.

## "LA FAUTE DE L'ABBÉ MOURET"

ALFRED BRUNEAU. Book after Émile Zola's novel of the same title
(Paris, 1907). A melodramatic score employing dramatic declamation.
An Overture built up on a liturgic theme and glowing, sensuous pic-
tures of the Garden of Paradou (Acts II, IV) stand out.

The Abbé Mouret, a young parish priest sent to a little Provençale
village near the ruined château of Paradou and its enormous gardens,
which neglect and passing years have turned into a natural wilderness,
a place of rioting blossom, green shades and sun-kissed prairies, forgets
his vows of chastity under the influence of the innocent wooing of
Albine (daughter of Jeanbernat, the village atheist and bad man), a
child of Nature.   Amid trees and flowers the young priest no longer
remembers he has renounced the world (Acts II, III) until, through a
gap in the green garden wall he sees the steeple of his abandoned
church, and is recalled to his duty as Chaplain Archangias suddenly
stands before him as he starts from Albine's twining arms.   When
the stern priest exhorts him to leave the girl, the Devil's tool, he allows
himself to be led off without a word, while Albine in despair calls his
name in vain.   When he returns to the altar the girl, only knowing
she has lost her lover, begins to pine.   Sadly Jeanbernat seeks out the
priest and begs him to visit his daughter.   The Abbé Mouret does not
answer.   And when Albine, pale and broken, stands before him and
reminds him how he swore to be true to her, crying, "You are mine!"
he turns away with the reply, "I belong to God!"   Albine, conscious of
no wrongdoing, dies of a broken heart among the fragrant, glowing
flowers which adorned their transports and the Abbé Mouret, all priest,
calmly recites the De profundis over the poor girl who loved him with
so boundless an affection.

Abbé Mouret (Berlin, 1910) by Max Oberleithner, book by
Adalbert von Goldschmidt after Zola, contains effective orchestral
Intermezzos as well as folkwise melodies introduced to vary the
polyphonic structure.   Abbé Mouret, an early opera by Georg
Vollerthun, book by Klenau, transfers the action of the story,
objectionable to the Roman Catholic Church, to India, although
the interesting modern score (Act II outstanding), rich in lyric
and orchestral beauties, is entirely without oriental color.   In Noël
(Christmas, Paris, 1912) by Camille Erlanger, book by La Rose,
Madeleine—the child of her shame in her arms—faints in the
Christmas snow on the threshold of the parish church, whence
sound the chimes of midnight mass and caroling voices of children.   Entering the church (she has been turned from the door
of decent Jacques, who loved her before her fall), she lays her
babe in the Christ Child's manger in the Virgin's Chapel (Act II),
commending it to the Mother of God after Jacques and Blanche,

his fiancée, depart. In a hospital bed (Act III) Madeleine, delirious, sings the carol, "Flower of the Thorn," as Jacques and Blanche, newly married, enter. Jacques, recognizing his peccant love, says he would have married her had she made it possible, and the poor girl sinks back dead as Blanche, taking the child, cries: "He shall be as our own! We will call him Noël!"

## "DER EVANGELIMANN"

### (The Evangelist)

WILHELM KIENZL. Book by the composer after a true tale recorded by a Vienna police official (Berlin, 1895). The music of the score is rich in lyric pathos and (Act II) introduces a charming old Lanner waltz.

The actuary Matthias Freudhoffer (St. Othmar's Benedictine Monastery, Lower Austria, 1820) loves pretty Martha, the steward Engel's niece, and so does his envious brother Johannes. The latter maligns Matthias and he is turned out by his uncle. But Martha scorns the liar and when Johannes hears the girl swear to be faithful to Matthias, he sets fire to the monastery in the madness of his jealous rage, denounces his brother as the incendiary, and the latter is seized and sent to prison.

Thirty years after, Magdalena, Martha's friend and sick Johannes' nurse, meets an Evangelist in the courtyard of her patient's house and in him recognizes Matthias. For twenty years, innocent of any crime, he languished in prison. When freed he learned that Martha had killed herself in despair, and he, jailbird and outcast, unable to find work, turned Evangelist. In the Vienna streets and courts he sang the praise of God, taught the children their catechism and lived on alms.

In Johannes' sick room the sinner's conscience troubles him; the wrong done his brother gives him no rest. As he lies suffering he hears the Evangelist's voice in the other room and begs Magdalena to bring him in. Not recognizing his injured brother, Johannes confesses his crime to him and Matthias, after a moment of revolt as he reviews his ruined life, makes himself known to his brother and forgives him that he may die in peace.

*Dichter und Welt* (*The Poet and the World*, Weimar, 1897) by W. von Baussnern, book by Petre. A Chorus of Spirits (Prologue) praises those who turn from the earthly to the divine. Hermann von Suso (14th century religious mystic) thinking he loves Irmina with purely spiritual fervor, resigns her to his friend, the knight Wolfbrecht, only to find he is not dead to the desire of the senses. He curses Irmina bitterly in his hermitage, but when the sufferings of the peasants, assailed by the Black Death, turn his activities into nobler channels (Act III), his peace of mind regained, he blesses his friends.   An Epilogue sings the glory of those who overcome themselves.

In connection with Sacred and Profane Love the titles of the following operas may also be mentioned: *Le Cloître* (*The Cloister*), lyric drama by Maurice Lévy after Verhaeren's play (Lyons, 1925); *Il Santo* (*The Saint*) by Ubaldo Pacchiarotti (Turin, 1913); *La Carmelite* (Paris, 1902) by Reynaldo Hahn; August Conradi's *Die Sixtinische Madonna* (Berlin, 1864); and *Die Hochzeit des Mönchs* (Dessau, 1886; as *Astorre*, 1888) by August Klughardt, musically influenced by Liszt, after Meyer's novelette.

### 5.  *Operatic Children of Nature*

Longus, Greek sophist and romancer (200 B.C.), in *Daphnis and Chloe* wrote the first human-interest novel, an unpretentious tale of "tender sighs among the sheep," whose literary descendants include Saint-Pierre's *Paul and Virginia,* Goethe's *Hermann and Dorothea,* Longfellow's *Evangeline,* and many another.   In opera the countryside with its gentle shepherds and melting village swains has inspired much beautiful music.   Somewhere, of course, between the artless, innocent rustics of romantic opera and the bestial peasants of veristic opera akin to those of Zola's *La Terre* (neither having anything in common with the American farmer) lies the true countryman.   But discussion of the unreality of realistic operas and the naturalism of idealistic ones is not within the scope of the present volume.   Gentler children of the soil are here presented as they appear in scores devoted to them; for the peasant in the raw the reader is referred to "The Verist's Rosary."

#### PASTORALS AND IDYLS, TRAGIC AND OTHERWISE

#### "DAPHNIS ET CHLOÉ"

MAURICE RAVEL.  Dance symphony with choral accompaniment.  Book by Michael Fokine (Paris, 1912).  An impressionistic score with interesting "nature imitations," notably a "Nocturne," solo flute with music-box accompaniment, evoking the wailing of the wind.

Shepherds and shepherdesses in classic undress trip it on Grecian meadows in dances sacred and profane, while Daphnis and Chloe, lovers, try to rouse each other's jealousy.  A sudden onrush of Tyrian pirates from the nearby ocean strand disturbs the revelers.  Lovely Chloe is carried off by the marauders and Daphnis, returning to rescue her, finds only the little sandal she dropped.  Clutching it, he sinks fainting to the ground.

In the red glare of torches the pirates hurry back and forth on the seashore laden with their spoils, while Chloe dances for Bryaxis, the pirate chief. Her graceful movements rouse his dormant passion. Already he has seized her, the ultimate outrage looms, when kindly Pan, protector of shepherds and shepherdesses, sends fauns and satyrs to the rescue, who drive the terrified pirates before them.

Back in green meadows Daphnis recovers when Chloe returns, and in the joy of reunion they pantomime the love-making of Pan and the nymph Syrinx with so much feeling that they pass from acting to earnest. Falling into each other's arms, as rustic companions flock about them, they are married at the altar of the nymphs, and the ballet concludes with a general dance of joy.

*Daphnis et Chloé* (Paris, 1899) by Charles Maréchal, a musically worthy score, inflates the tale of Daphnis and Chloe's life in wood and field, among bees, birds, goats, and lambs, the corsair episode and the wedding into a three-act opera.

*Daphnis et Chloé* (Paris, 1860) by Jacques Offenbach, is an operetta parody. Young bacchantes, attracted by reports of Daphnis' charms, hasten from all parts of Greece to find him, but seek in vain. Chloe confesses her love, but while she hurries off Daphnis appears and, falling asleep, is wakened by the bacchantes, who all make love to him. Faithful to Chloe, he repulses their attentions, and they are about to force the draught of forgetfulness down his throat when Pan snatches away the cup. Then the rustic god—Daphnis is absent—initiates Chloe into the arts of love, and when the shepherd returns she falls happily into his arms.

*Le devin du village* (*The Village Soothsayer*) by Jean-Jacques Rousseau, first given at Fontainebleau, 1752, King Louis XV in the audience, put the village on opera's sentimental map, preaching simplicity and the return to nature. The shepherdess Colette begs the village soothsayer to help her regain the affection of faithless Colin. Reading from a magic book he tells her to cultivate a new admirer and, sure enough, jealousy brings Colin back to her arms. In *Les amours de Bastien et Bastienne* (Paris, 1753) Madame Favart borrowed Rousseau's plot for a simple ballad opera in which the village soothsayer enters "singing to the bagpipe" and—musically the most charming setting—Mozart used it for his *Bastien und Bastienne* (Vienna, 1768). Other variants are: *Annette et Lubin* (Paris, 1800) by Martini; *Rose et Colas* (Paris, 1764) by Monsigny, Vanderbroeck's *Colin et Colette* (Paris, 1789) and Burney's *The Cunning Man* (London, 1766). Introduced by *Le devin du village,* all sorts of sentimental rustics swarmed on the operatic stage. Grétry's *Colinette à la cour* (Paris, 1755) takes the innocent country girl to the royal court; and Dalyrac's *Nina ou la folle par amour* (Paris, 1786) introduces her to the aristocratic villain. Nina is opera's *first mad girl,* and Paesiello also wrote a *Nina* (Naples, 1787). The many rustics of opera defy enumeration. Some are genuine "village types," redolent of new-mown hay, others only eighteenth century urbanites masquerading as children of Nature.

## IN THE HILLS OF SAVOY

### "LINDA DA CHAMOUNIX"

GAETANO DONIZETTI. Book by Proch after Rossi (Vienna, 1842). One of the tender, pathetic scores the composer wrote to rival Bellini's successes. The famous air, "O luce di quest'anima" ("Oh, guiding star of love") is probably the favorite single number, and the hurdy-gurdy is used to accompany the score's Savoyan airs.

When the Marquis de Boisfleury (1760) combines intense admiration for Linda, daughter of Antonio, the poor Savoyard farmer, with a promise to renew the lease on the old homestead, it hints the eighteenth century woodpile has a black inhabitant. Antonio thinks so, for he sends Linda to Paris to forestall disgrace.

In Paris Linda lives in lodgings provided by Arthur de Sirval, the rich Countess de Sirval's nephew, whom she knew on the farm as a poor painter. Villainous de Boisfleury has traced the country girl to the city, however, and enters her rooms to offer her dishonorable wealth. No sooner has he been repulsed than Arthur comes—he and Linda had planned to marry—to say his aunt insists he marry another. Next comes her father. He glances at the costly furniture in Linda's apartment, jumps to a wrong conclusion, and leaves her with his curse. When Pierrotto, a poor but unintelligent Savoyard, enters to inform her Arthur's wedding is in progress at the Hôtel de Sirval Linda's mind gives way.

The action shifts back to the countryside. Savoyard street musicians are leaving Paris for Chamounix' dells and dingles. Following them comes insane Linda, led by Pierrotto. After them, later, comes Arthur. On the farm the fair maniac first does not recognize her lover when he tells her he has won his aunt's consent to their union. When the truth pierces her darkened brain, however, Linda swoons, and, waking from her coma in her right mind, the curtain falls on the happy tears of all concerned.

*Lisbeth* (Brussels, 1797), Grétry's "operatic swan song," book after Florian's *Claudine,* is another Chamounix girl. Derson hastens off to help the Americans gain their independence, forgetting that Lisbeth, the country innocent he has seduced, is about to give birth to a child. When he returns repentant, Lisbeth's father Simon—who had seized his musket to blow from sight little Nannette, token of his daughter's overtrustful affection—blesses their union. *Les deux journées* (Paris, 1800; as "The Water Carrier," London, 1801) by Cherubini, "Un bien fait n'est perdu" a favorite air, tells of Michel, the noble Savoyard water carrier, who brings Count Armand safely out of Paris—where Cardinal Mazarin's soldiers are hunting him—in his water butt and (Act III) turns up with a royal pardon in the village where his whilom benefactor is about to be seized, thus saving him a second time.

### SWITZERLAND

## "LA SONNAMBULA"

### (*The Sleepwalker*)

VINCENZO BELLINI. Book by Romani (Paris, Milan, 1831). The score with its tender, graceful melodies ("Prend l'anel ti dono"; "Vi ravviso"; "Ah, non credea"; "Ah, non giunge") and its pathetic Finale, is considered the composer's happiest idyllic work.

Swiss villagers make merry (c. 1800) for Amina, Teresa's, the mill owner's foster child, is about to marry Elvino though Lisa, the innkeeper, has cast sheeps' eyes at the sturdy Alpine lad. As the groom sings "Prend l'anel" ("Take the ring!") Rodolpho, lord of the castle, who, weary of the joys of a military life, has returned incognito to revisit the scene of his boyhood days, drives up to crack of whip in his post chaise. His routined eye glows at sight of Amina but Elvino, though he censures his beloved for encouraging Rodolpho's glance as he enters the inn, leaves her with a kiss.

Lisa, leading Rodolpho to his room, drops her kerchief and retires after some coquettish passages. Turning, her guest with much surprise sees Amina coming through the window, clad only in a white shift. The unhappy girl is a sleepwalker! Rodolpho, a perfect gentleman, as she sinks on his bed puts out the candle and leaves the room, lest his presence embarrass her, and in a moment, led by Lisa who has seen all, the rustics pour in. About to withdraw when they see a girl on the officer's counterpane, hateful Lisa holds high a taper and clutching Elvino's arm, points to the bed. Amina wakes. Her innocent confusion is mistaken for guilty shame and in an expressive duet, "D'un pensiero," indignant Elvino casts her off.

Vainly when next the lovers meet, kindly Rodolpho explains that Amina is a somnambulist—Elvino does not know the word, and tears his ring from her hand to use it to wed Lisa. But later, at the crucial moment Rodolpho cries "See!" Amina, still in her shift, sleeping as she walks, passes from her window in the old mill over the black waters of the mill pond below. A rotting plank breaks beneath her tread, her lamp slips from her hand, but Providence watches over her and she gains the bank. Waking as Elvino restores the ring to the finger from which he robbed it, waiting to lead her to church, she appropriately sings the brilliant coloratura gem of the opera "Ah, non giunge!" ("The rapture now o'er me stealing").

Cherubini's *Elisa ou le mont Saint-Bernard* (Paris, 1794) has a first act once called "the most pathetic known to the vocal stage"; and *Die Schweizerfamilie* (*The Swiss Family,* Vienna, 1807) by Weigl has touching melodies which brought tears to sentimental eyes. Count Wallstein's life saved by a Swiss peasant, he establishes him on his estate, but Emmeline pines, though the Count had an exact imitation of her father's châlet built to cheat her supposed homesickness. Not till Jacob Freiburg, blowing his Alpine shepherd pipe, appears is the true cause of Emmeline's grieving revealed. As they fly into each other's arms amid parental blessings their fellow-rustics leave their toil to praise Heaven they are united. *Le châlet* (Paris, 1834) by Adam, best known opera version of Goethe's *Jery und Bartely*—others are *Jery und Barthely* by Winter (1790), Kreutzer (1809), and Julian Ries (Berlin, 1840)—is the tale of a Swiss sergeant, home from the wars, who bullies a reluctant sister into marrying a timid farmer lad whom, once he has been thrust upon her, she finds she loves. The romance, "Dans ce modeste et simple asile," stands out. In *La Wally* (Turin, 1892) by Alfredo Catalani, book by Illica, its "Edelweiss Song" the favorite air, Swiss Wally's suitors Gellner and Hagenbach quarrel and her father turns her out for refusing to marry the former. A year later (Act II) when Hagenbach, meeting the girl by chance, jilts Afra for her sake, Gellner makes Wally believe Hagenbach false. Promising to wed Gellner if he kills the other man Gellner (Act III) botches the job; but though repentant Wally drags her lover from the abyss into which he was cast, an avalanche (Act IV) sweeps him from her side as they are picking flowers, and she leaps into it to join him in death.

### Plain Tales from Other Hills

*Le val d'Andorre* (*The Vale of Andorra,* Paris, 1848) by Jacques Halévy, book by Saint-Georges, has three airs once popular, the "Chamois Hunter's Song," "May Romance" (Act I), and Stephan's Romance (Act III). In the mountain republic of Andorra dwelt "the pet of the valley," young Stephan the chamois hunter. Georgette and Theresa, wealthy farmer women, seek to share his heart, but he loves Rose de Mai, Theresa's serving maid. Stephen conscripted, Rose de Mai takes money from Theresa's desk to buy off her lover, is tried and condemned to death—punishment for theft in eighteenth century Andorra. When it appears Rose is Theresa's child, the mother declares she lied and her daughter is free to sink into the chamois hunter's arms.

## "LA DAME BLANCHE"

### (*The White Lady*)

FRANÇOIS-ADRIEN BOIELDIEU. Book by Scribe after Scott's *The Monastery* (Paris, 1825). A Scotch romance of 1759. The harpist Labarre, who had .traveled in Scotland, gave Boieldieu some of his best chorus themes; the harp is effectively used when the "White Lady" enters, and among charming airs George's "Viens, gentille dame" (Act II) may be mentioned.

The English Lieutenant George Brown (really Edwin Avenel, heir to title and estates, but brought up in England by the steward Gaveston's orders in ignorance of his origin) happens in as Avenel tenants celebrate the baptism of Dickson's child, in time to play godfather to it. He hears the legend of the "White Lady of Avenel" whose kindly ghost haunts the castle rascal Gaveston has offered at auction, meaning to buy it in himself. Gaveston's pretty ward Anna is the ghost, but when she summons her friend farmer Dickson to the castle he fears to go, and George takes his place.

Anna appearing as the "White Lady," thinking George is Dickson, begs him to foil Gaveston's plot and buy the castle to save it for Avenel's true heir. The ghost's soft hand rouses tender emotions in George's breast as he clasps it, and he vows to help her.

At the auction George outbids Gaveston and the castle is knocked down to him for 300,000 pounds (though George has no money) and wandering through the baronial halls George hears the old bardic chant of the Avenels, familiar to his childhood and joins in the refrain.

While Gaveston waits for the adventurer to be humiliated as Justice McIrton demands the money Anna appears with the golden treasure hidden in the "White Lady's" statue in the keep. Documents she presents show George is the rightful heir of Avenel, and raging Gaveston, tearing the veil from the "White Lady's" face, recognizes his ward whose union to Edwin (George no longer) brings the tale to a happy close.

Bardic chant echoes also in Méhul's *Ossian* (*The Bardes,* Paris, 1804) and in his *Uthal* (Paris, 1806) based on MacPherson's melancholy "Fingal," bardic operas of which Napoleon at St. Helena said that in them "he heard the winds and waves." *The Two Sisters* (Cambridge, 1922) by Cyril Rootham tells of Scotch Ellen, who drowns her younger sister, preferred by her own lover, her crime discovered when an old bard strings his harp with the murdered girl's hair and it sings its accusation. Josef Hoolbrooke's *The Children of Don* (Vienna, 1923), untheatrical, but with fine lyric and dramatic pages, is a fantastic legendary tale of bardic days centering about Don, a Celtic goddess whose children, after much blood is shed, ascend the throne rightfully theirs.

## "LES DRAGONS DE VILLARS"

### (*Villars' Dragoons or the Hermit's Bell*)

LOUIS AIMÉ MAILLART. Book by Lockroy and Cormon (Paris, 1856). One of the best French comic operas, based on the historic fact that the Marshal de Villars' dragoons were sent to the Cévennes mountains in 1704 to suppress a revolt. The Overture is popular and in the grateful rôle of Rose (soprano) the aria, "Il m'aime" (Act III), stands out.

Dragoon trumpets drive girls of a Cévennes village into hiding. Sergeant Belamy is to lead his men to St. Gratian's grotto, where he suspects Huguenot refugees are hiding. When malicious Rose, the goat girl, has betrayed the hiding place of farmer Thibaut's wine and wife, Georgette, the wife, lets the soldier make love to her, and tells him the tale of St. Gratian's hermitage. After two hundred years its bell still keeps village wives true to vows by ringing violently of itself when others than husbands kiss them. While his dragoons dance with the rustic maids, who have come from hiding, Belamy vows he will put the legend to the test, and Georgette agrees to meet him at the chapel.

Near it Sylvain, Rose's lover, waits to lead the Huguenots across the French border by a hidden pass. As they exchange fond vows Georgette's red lips are just pointed to meet the sergeant's mustachioed ones when—the hermit's bell rings as Thibaut hurries up! As Georgette flees the dragoon soothes the suspicious husband, returns to investigate the mystery, sees the Huguenots setting out guided by Rose as Sylvain returns to the village, and his dragoons ride that night to intercept them.

Thibaut, jumping to false conclusions, tells Sylvain the bell rang because Belamy kissed Rose and that she betrayed the fugitives. When Rose's wedding bells ring the groom thrusts her off as a traitor, only to clasp her to him when Georgette produces a note from the fugitives, saying that thanks to Rose they are safely in Savoy. Belamy, entering wild with rage at the escape of his prey, is laughed to scorn for going skirt instead of Huguenot hunting, and all ends merrily.

In *Des Adlers Horst* (*The Eagle's Eyrie,* Berlin, 1833) by Franz Glaeser, Marie, a Silesian mountain village innkeeper's daughter, stands between love for Forester Richard, whose bastard babe she has borne, and duty to Anton, eager to wed her despite her lapse. Rose's babe carried off by an eagle, its father's hand trembles as he raises his gun. But lightning drops a tree across an abyss: the mother runs to the eagle's eyrie, snatches her child and returns as Richard shoots the bird, the villagers cheering while the parents embrace preliminary to a formal union.

## Villages of France

*Les Quatre Journées* (*The Four Days,* Paris, 1917) by Alfred Bruneau, rich in sincere and eloquent Nature music (Love Duet, Act I; Death of Abbé Lazare), is a modern French pastoral. First day. It is spring in Provence. Jean and Babette, peasant lad and lass, meet, love, and their union is blessed by Abbé Lazare, Jean's uncle. Second day. Summer: Jean—the World War has come and he is a soldier—rescues a wounded Alsatian on the battlefield and they sing freedom and peace triumphant. Third day. Autumn: on Jean's farm the Abbé dies amid the children born of the devoted couple. Fourth day. Winter: the flood sweeps away all the household save Jean, Franz, the rescued Alsatian who works for him, and his little daughter. The Lord giveth and the Lord taketh away.

## "LE PARDON DE PLOËRMEL"

### (*Dinorah*)

Giacomo Meyerbeer. Book by Barbier and Carré (Paris, 1859). Also known as *Dinorah*. The composer's one pastoral opera, attractive reapers and huntsman choruses standing out.

When Hoël and Dinorah are on their way to church to be married, lightning destroys Dinorah's cottage. Hoël abandons his bride in despair (to go off gold hunting among the *korriganes,* the gnomes of Brittany) and Dinorah goes mad and wanders through the hills with a faithful goat in search of her vanished lover. After she has danced and sung the charming "Shadow Song," lyric jewel of the score, in the moonlight, Dinorah, crossing a tree which spans a gorge, is swept away by a sudden flood. Hoël, hunting treasure near by, rescues her (Act III), and she opens her eyes to regain her reason in his arms as wedding bells prepare to chime. "Meyerbeer wanted to write a pastoral opera; instead of pastoral it sounds pasteurized" (Gustav Kobbé).

## "MIREILLE"

Charles Gounod. Book by Barbier and Carré after Mistral's Provençal poem (Paris, 1864). A score charming in its rustic, folkwise Provençal color. The Overture, the graceful *valse-ariette,* "Hirondelle légère," and the Duet, "O Magali, ma bien-aimée," are favorite numbers.

Under flowering mulberries, other village girls tease Mireille, who blushingly admits her love for Vincent, the poor basket maker, and when he comes responds to his vows. There is festivity in Arles (Act II) where peasants and townsfolk dance the *farandole.* Comes Ourrias, the wild herdsman, asking Mireille's hand. Refused, he vows revenge on Vincent, though Ramon, Mireille's father, has rejected the plea of Ambroise, Vincent's father, who sued for his boy. Despondent Mireille (Vincent has been wounded by Ourrias) makes a pilgrimage (Act III) to the Church of Sainte-Marie, where (Act IV) she falls unconscious into Vincent's arms during the processional—but does not recognize her lover. Yet the solemn chants recall her wandering senses: opening her eyes she knows Vincent and the gates of Paradise open wide as her repentant father withdraws his opposition to Mireille's choice.

## "CLOCHES DE CORNEVILLE"

### (*Chimes of Normandy*)

JEAN-ROBERT PLANQUETTE. Book by Clairville and Gabet (Paris, 1877). Light, flowing melodies, and the graceful "bell music" of this *opéra comique* score, its action laid in the days of Louis XIV, has made it a perennial favorite.

The villagers of Corneville (Norman coast), celebrating the return of the old Marquis de Villeroi to his estates, discuss Serpolette, feminine "cut-up" among the fisher maids, and curse miser Gaspard for his cruelty to his niece Germaine. He wants her to marry an old sheriff; she loves handsome Jean, the brave fisher lad who saved her from drowning. On Villeroi's arrival, Germaine and Jean enter his service to foil Gaspard's plans.

The Villeroi château is being overhauled. Gaspard has spread the tale it is haunted. Why? Because he keeps his gold in the cellars. Discovered gloating over it, he is driven insane by the shock. He dashes into the night a gibbering maniac.

While the mad miser rambles about the village, the Marquis de Villeroi feasts the fisher folk. Jean, too thrifty to keep on loving Germaine when the miser's papers seem to show Serpolette is his heiress, makes love to Serpolette. Germaine does not repine. She has won the Marquis' heart in humble servant guise. Gaspard, in a lucid moment, proves Germaine is truly his heiress and thrifty Jean must content himself with Serpolette while the "Chimes of Normandy" ring out for Germaine's wedding to the Marquis de Villeroi.

*Les noces de Jeanette* (Paris, 1853) by Victor Massé, the composer's best score, is a tale of village loves. Jeannette's "Romance" and the "Nightingale Aria," an effective *coloratura* parade piece, stand out. Bells are ringing, candles gleam, the wedding contract lies on the table when Jean decides bachelor freedom is preferable to wedded slavery, and leaving Jeanette in her bridal gown, rushes off to the village tavern where fat Marguerite, blonde Marie, black Jacqueline, and Fanchette with the mole welcome him. Outraged Jeanette plans revenge (Act II) but when intoxicated Jean signs the wedding contract and, sober, realizes his own unworthiness, the good girl forgives him and sews up the tears in his torn wedding jacket as a preliminary to stepping with him before the altar. Massé's *Les Saisons* (Paris, 1856) with its pretty air, "Nous n'irons plus au bois," tells of the wedding of Simone and Pierre, planned during harvest, broken off at vintage time, taken up again in winter, and carried out in spring.

## "LE POSTILLON DE LONGJUMEAU"

### (*The Postilion of Longjumeau*)

ADOLPHE ADAM. Text by De Leuven and Brunswick (Paris, 1836). The famous "Postilion's Song," Madeleine's Rondo, "Mon petit mari," and the Trio, "Pendu, pendu" (Act III), stand out.

Chapelou's song of joy—postilion of Longjumeau, he has just married charming Madeleine—is interrupted by the Marquis de Corcy. The noble's carriage (swiftly repaired by envious smith Bijou, to take the groom from his own wedding feast) has broken down, but the Marquis, intendant of the Paris Opéra (1756) blesses the accident. He has discovered a tenor in Chapelou. A brilliant offer makes the postilion realize his first duty is his career, so he leaves his wife to follow music's call.

Six years have passed. Chapelou—now St. Phar—has become a great singer, and forgotten what Madeleine looks like. She comes to Paris as Madame de Latour, and wins the tenor's heart and a promise of marriage. But St. Phar shrinks from bigamy. He induces the singer Bourdon to play the priest; but Madeleine goes him one better by engaging a real cleric.

In Madeleine's villa, de Corcy (whose amatory plans St. Phar has often crossed) gives the tenor and his friend a fright by disclosing the fact that his base plan is known, and producing the police to hale him to jail. At the last minute Madeleine, however, puts him out of his misery and happiness reigns.

*Les voitures versées ou le séducteur en voyage (The Emptied Carriages or the Traveling Lovelace,* Paris, 1820) by François Boieldieu, regarded as "the best of Boieldieu's Franco-Russian scores" is another "coach" opera. The gem of the score is the soprano and bass duet, "Au clair de la lune," with delightful variations. The master of a château on the road to Paris, forced to live in the country, dreams only of the delights of the capital. He "treats" his roadbed so that passing carriages must break down and their various occupants stop to enliven his monotony. There Florville, a young Parisian, the "traveling Lovelace," attempts to take advantage of an innocent country girl, his host's niece, but is befooled by a malicious widow who smooths out the misunderstanding between the pretty provincial and her lover, and sends Florville off with a flea in his ear.

*Le cœur du moulin* (*The Heart of the Mill*, Paris, 1909) by Déodat de Séverac is rich in colorful rustic music ("melodious Debussy"). Jacques, returning to his native village at vintage time finds the old mill wheel singing the same song, but Marie, his sweetheart, has married his friend Pierre. Pierre greets him like a brother, but Jacques, so great is his love for Marie, tells his parents he will run off with her. When his father shows him no happiness is founded on the misfortunes of others Jacques, resigned to his fate, leaves to return no more.

## Not "Shepherds All"

*Das Nachtlager von Granada* (*The Night's Encampment,* Vienna, 1834) by Konradin Kreutzer, book after Kind's play. Save for a "Bolero," the graceful antiquated music has no Spanish local color, though Gabriele's aria, "Da mir alles nun entrissen," equals some of Weber's best. Poor Gabriele! Uncle Ambrosio frowns on her love for Gomez—the Spanish sheep country, 1550—and insists she marry Vasco. Gomez must beg the Prince Regent, hunting in the hills, to speak a word in their favor. A young huntsman appears with her lost dove. Promising to speak for Gomez to the Prince his master, he is seized by Vasco and Pedro. But gold flung the shepherds wins promise of a night's lodging in a ruined Moorish castle. Gabriele rouses him (Act II), warning him of danger. He seizes his gun—it has been unloaded. Sword in hand the huntsman —the Prince Regent himself—awaits his assailants. When Gomez enters with the Prince's men and shepherds, Vasco the assassin is dead, and while the Prince forgives Pedro, Ambrosio unites the lovers.

*María del Carmen* (Madrid, 1898), by Enrique Granados, a score rich in local color, tells the loves of a Murcian village boy and girl whose difficulties end when another lover sacrifices himself for the girl's sake. *Maia* (Rome, 1910) by Leoncavallo, a folk score with effective folk songs and dances (the Camargue, France, 1809) tells a village tragedy in a sheep country. Maia, faith in her soldier lover Renaud shaken by the jealous lies of the shepherd Torias, flings herself between the rivals when they draw knives and is accidentally slain.

*Das lustige Füchslein* (*The Merry Little Fox,* Brünn, 1925) by Janáček, whose music, brilliantly orchestrated, is described as "a phrase-mosaic of no deeper emotional content," and whose climax is a drunken scene between a forester and a schoolmaster, comments the tale of a fox which, not content with the society of its own kind, seeks the society of men and gets shot. *Le Renard* (*The Fox*, Paris, 1922) by Igor Stravinsky, Ballet Russe, is a dance burlesque: a Cock, a Goat, a Cat, and a Fox combine the dancing of Russian folk dances to modernist syncopated music with an action in which the Fox twice dupes the Cock only to be killed by the Goat and Cat. *Le loup et l'agneau* (*The Wolf and the Lamb*, Paris, 1921) by Louis Urgel, a pantomime ballet, modernizes a La Fontaine fable in dance. A "wolf" with prodigious biceps, after half an hour's choregraphic coaxing, carries off the timid shepherdess who plays the "lamb." The music is attractive, notably a "sobbing Adagio for 'cello."

## Where Mill Wheels Clack

### "DER CORREGIDOR"

#### (*The Corregidor*)

Hugo Wolf. Text by R. Mayreder-Obermeyer (Mannheim, 1896) after Alarcon's novel *El Sombrero de tres picos* (The Three-Cornered Hat). Wolf's *Corregidor*, a masterpiece of contrapuntal skill, has been called "the *Meistersinger* translated into Spanish." Rich in inspired melody, it is absolutely untheatric. The Prelude and Frasquita's "In dem Schatten meine Locken" (Act I) are among its jewels.

When Frasquita upsets old hunchbacked Don Eugenio di Zuñiga, the Corregidor, from a bench to the ground as he annoys her with his attentions, while her husband, Lucas the miller, laughs in the arbor where she has hidden him, the wearer of "the three-cornered hat" (headgear of officials in old Spain) departs vowing vengeance.

Tonnelo, the Corregidor's summoner, bids Lucas appear before that magistrate, and he leaves Frasquita alone. Don Eugenio pops up, dripping wet (he fell in the mill pond), and when he tries to gain his ends at the pistol's point, faints when the indignant woman seizes her husband's musket. Put to bed by his servant Repela, he sends the latter after Frasquita (he thinks she is off to report his misconduct to her husband) to bring her back. Lucas, meanwhile, returns from town, discovering his summons was a hoax.

Peeping through the keyhole at the mill he sees Zuñiga in his bed, jumps to the conclusion Frasquita is faithless, and hurries back to town to visit his rival's wife, reputed handsome. Zuñiga, rising, cannot find his clothes and puts on those of the miller. Mistaken for Lucas, he is beaten by the Alcalde's men, come to take the miller, and then with Frasquita, hurries to town.

When he tries to enter his home the Corregidor receives another beating; but as Lucas already has been cudgeled for trying to intrude on Doña Mercedes de Zuñiga, honors are equal, and the Corregidor resolving to confine his love-making to his own fireside, Lucas and Frasquita, reconciled, returned happily to the mill.

*El corregidor y la molinera* (*The Corregidor and the Miller's Wife* (Madrid, 1919), by Manuel de la Falla, as *El sombrero de tres picos* (*The Three-Cornered Hat*, Paris, 1920), tells the same tale in a brilliant pantomime ballet, the Overture, the Adalusian-Moorish "Miller's Dance," Grape Scene, music and *jota* and *vito* dances standing out.

*La molinara* (*The Miller Maid*) by Paisiello, survives in the melody "Non cor più non mi sento," which Rode transcribed for violin. *Giralda* (*The New Psyche*, Paris, 1850) by Adolphe Adam, whose Act II with trio, quintet, and Giralda's "Romance" is the best, turns on the efforts of a King of Spain to seduce charming Giralda, miller Gines' bride. After amusing contretemps in a dark bedroom, the royal libertine is foiled and the rustic lovers united. *Die Mühle im Wispertal* (*The Mill in Wispertal*, Berlin 1889) by W. Freudenberg, tells how Louise, adopted daughter of Mother Waltraud of the mill, later proved to be of noble birth (though with bar sinister) puts four lovers to work as mill-hands and chooses Reinold, Mother Waltraud's son, who has won an officer's commission and a title in the Austrian Emperor's service (1715), for a husband. Reissiger's *Die Felsenmühle von Eta-lières* (*The Mill on the Etalières Rocks*, Dresden, 1829) is re-membered because of its Overture. *The Miller and His Child* (Graz, 1907) by Bela von Ujj, a tuneful Hungarian folk opera, tells the sad fate of Marie, Miller Reinhold's daughter, who dies because a village superstition and her father's hard-heartedness separate her from her lover, her last moments in a blossoming garden soothed by the sound of Konrad's flute, her joy in happier days. *Der Müller von Sans-Souci* (*The Miller of Sans-Souci*, Frankfort, 1896) by Otto Urbach, is based on the historic anecdote of the sturdy miller who refused to sell his land so that Frederick the Great could round out his gardens at his famous palace retreat.

## German Operatic Village Life

*Barfüssle* (*Little Barefoot*, Vienna, 1903) by Richard Heu-berger, book after Auerbach, a Black Forest village idyl making happy use of folk tunes, carries the uneven course of serving maid Amrei's (Little Barefoot's) loves to a happy ending in marriage to her soldier lover Johannes. *Hermann und Dorothea* (Dessau, 1882) by Gustav Rössler and *Hermann und Dorothea* (Berlin, 1899) by Jean Urich, set Goethe's simple poem of village life in which he mirrored some of the most pregnant ideas of his day.

*Das goldene Kreuz* (*The Golden Cross*) by Ignaz Brüll, book by Mosenthal (Berlin, 1875), tells how Thérèse, about to wed Colas in a village near Mélun (1812), drops her bouquet of rosemary as the groom is conscripted for the army. Christine, the bride's sister, offers her golden cross to the man who will bring it and Colas safely back and the Marquis Gontran de l'Ancre (Act II) jumps at the opportunity. Gontran gets back with wounded Colas (Act III) minus the cross, but Sargent Bombardon who also escaped freezing to death during the retreat of the *grande armée* from Moscow, appears with it and Christine and Gontran are married. A world success in its day, Christine's F minor "Romance" (Act I) stands out and music if not locale is German.

In *Die beiden Schützen* (*The Two Marksmen*, Leipzig, 1837) by Lortzing, a "pseudo-Italian score influenced by Auber," Wilhelm and Gustav, young grenadiers, return after ten years to their native village, and after contretemps based on exchanged identities, lead each other's sisters to the altar. *Das steinerne Herz* (*The Stone Heart*, Prague, 1888) by Ignaz Brüll, shows Peter Munck, charcoal burner, selling his heart to Dutchman Michel, demon spirit of the Black Forest, to gain gold to win Lisbeth's hand by paying her father's debts. But Lisbeth, once married, drops dead from shock and Peter, tricking the demon, exchanges the heart of stone the latter gave him for his own living one, and clasps resuscitated Lisbeth happily to his breast. *Das War Ich* (*That Was I*, Dresden, 1902) by Leo Blech, book by Batka, shows farmer Paul refusing cousin Röschen's hand to his son Peter, because he likes to give her wheelbarrow rides and snatch stolen kisses. But when German village gossip of the 1830's arises, Paul quickly turns to wife Martha again and Peter, meeting each query anent kisses with the statement "That was I," marries his sweetheart with a grateful father's blessing. *Der Dorfbarbier* (*The Village Barber*, Vienna, 1796), by J. Schenk, a favorite "song-play," shows how Süschen marries her Josef despite her adopted father Lux, the village barber; and Dittersdorf's *Doktor und Apotheker* (*Doctor and Druggist*, Vienna, 1786) also ends in a happy marriage between Gotthold and Leonore, respectively children of a country town doctor and druggist, after the parents have put all sorts of obstacles in their way. Joseph Haydn's *Lo Speciale* (*The Apothecary*, composed 1796, performed Dresden, 1895), is Sempronio, a village apothecary, eager to wed his ward Griletta, pursued by Volpino who (disguised as a Turkish pasha, pretending he comes to appoint Sempronio the Sultan's apothecary) tries to carry her off, but is unmasked by her true love Mengino, who gains her hand. In *Der Schwur* (*The Oath*, Munich, 1892) by Reich, Brigitta, Meran cowgirl, learning her lover Andrä is her brother, takes poison.

## FROM THE ITALIAN COUNTRYSIDE

### "L'ELISIRE D'AMORE"

*(The Elixir of Love)*

GAETANO DONIZETTI. Book by Romani (Milan, 1832). A musically sparkling Italian *opera buffa,* its scene a Tuscan village, end of the eighteenth century. A delightful Finale, "a ravishing 'Whispering Chorus'" for women's voices, and the celebrated "Una furtiva lagrima" stand out.

Nemorino, a country lad, shyly woos Adina, wealthy young village beauty, but she repulses him and favors Sergeant Belcore, so Nemorino buys a bottle of the Elixir of Love from the quack doctor Dulcamara. The bottle contains a heady wine, and its effect is to make Nemorino treat Adina so coldly that, piqued, she determines to capture his heart. To do so she agrees to marry the sergeant and the wedding feast is prepared when Nemorino, sober, and in despair, enlists as a soldier.

Then Adina refuses to sign the wedding contract and proves her love by purchasing Nemorino's release from military duty, and their reconciliation and marriage follow.

*Le philtre* (Paris, 1831) by François Auber tells the same tale, giving the characters other names. The air, "Je suis sergeant" and the duet—barcarole, "Je suis riche, vous êtes belle," were favorites in their day. *La jarre* (Paris, 1924) by Alfredo Casella is a Sicilian pastoral dance farce with brilliant Rossinian music by the Italian modernist. A great oil jar has been broken on a Sicilian olive farm. A hunchbacked potter creeps through the hole to repair it, but cannot get out because of his hump. Merry rustics dance madly about the jar till the farmer has it rolled into a ditch where it breaks and the delivered hunchback is borne off in triumph.

### CORSICAN BRETHREN

The Corsicans, daggers ever drawn in the family feud, always have voiced an attraction to the opera composer. Among lesser operatic Corsicans are *The Corsican Bride* (New York, 1861) by Frederick Mollenhauer, *Die Korsen* (Weimar, 1866) by Karl Götze, *Korsische Hochzeit* (*Corsican Wedding,* Wiesbaden, 1904) by Heinrich Spangenberg, *Vendetta* (Cologne, 1906) by Emilio Pizzi, a pupil of Ponchielli, and Nouguès' realistic *La Vendetta* (Marseilles, 1912).

## "COLOMBA"

HENRI BÜSSER. Book after Prosper Merimée (Nice, 1921). Büsser's music has the "adorable defect of being songful yet not commonplace."

Colonel della Rebbia has been assassinated by Corsican brothers, the Barricini. His daughter, Colomba, swears vengeance, her brother Orso to be its instrument. But Orso, educated in France, is out of sympathy with the old-fashioned Corsican vendetta. He prefers to appeal to the courts and Lydia Nervil, the English girl he loves, encourages him to do so. Colomba, child of tradition, despairs, but finally manages to stir up a quarrel between Orso and the Barracini boys, and the former shoots the latter in the Corsican brushwood "in self-defense." Colomba is happy, her father is avenged; Orso, first a refugee in the hills, later exonerated by the courts, marries lovely Miss Nervil. Colomba, though, dies of a gunshot wound received while diverting soldiers from her brother's hiding place in the mountains.

Sir Alexander Mackenzie's *Colomba* (London, 1883) tells the same story and uses old Corsican folk tunes effectively in the score. *Schemo* (Paris, 1914) by Alfred Bachelet, book by Charles Meré, is a savage tale of the tragic loves of a Corsican peasant girl and a shepherd poet, persecuted by superstitious peasants. Bachelet's music, Wagnerian in spirit, is richly lyric. In scenes of tenderness, ferocity, spring, joy, jealousy, and supreme sacrifice, blood, voluptuousness and death are dispensed in musically moving proportions. *L'Ancêtre* (*The Ancestress*, Monte Carlo, 1906) by Saint-Saëns, book by De Lassus. In First Empire Corsica the Fabiani and Nera families bury the feud hatchet, except grandmother Nunciata, the Fabiani "ancestress." Vanna Fabiani and Marguerite, her foster sister, love Tebaldo Nera: he loves Marguerite but shoots Leandri Fabiani in "self-defense" while Marguerite plucks roses with him in mind. Convinced by Tebaldo's plea, the hermit Raphael marries the rose-picker and the feudist; but when the "Ancestress" sees Vanna drop her gun instead of putting a bullet into Tebaldo she picks it up, and—hits Vanna, who dies in a swineherd's arms to save the man she loves. The music contains charming love passages between Tebaldo and Marguerite and is beautifully orchestrated. *Ludovic* (Paris, 1833) by Halévy, is a young Corsican peasant so passionately attached to his mistress, a Roman tenant farmer, that he *shoots* his way into her heart, for when she is about to marry another he fires at her in despairing rage and when she is recovering from her wound, she is so impressed by his wooing that she marries him.

## "LES TROIS MASQUES"

### (*The Three Masqueraders*)

Isidore de Lara. Book after Charles Meré's play (Marseilles, 1912; Paris, 1924). A colorful orchestration and music in which lyric charm and dramatic power alternate distinguish the score. A "Corsican Lullaby" and the beautiful Finale (Act IV) stand out.

Paolo, a Prati of Ajaccio (early 19th century) who loves Viola Verscotelli cannot marry her because his father refuses to let him wed his social inferior. The three Verscotelli boys, Viola's brothers, regard Paolo as her betrayer and swear revenge. On a Shrove Tuesday Viola and Paolo lose each other in the street crowded with merrymakers and masqueraders. Not long after three masqueraders enter Paolo's home. They are drunken and merry, the reveler in the middle so intoxicated that his friends drag him along. Corsican hospitality forbids Paolo's father to eject his guests, but he pays no attention to their antics as they plump their companion into a chair and dance around him. The old man is worried about his son, who has not yet come home. Soon two masqueraders leave, forgetting their friend huddled in his chair. Old Prati tries to rouse the drunken man and, as the mask falls from his face, recognizes his son Paolo. The Verscotelli boys have stabbed and carried him to his home to die beneath his father's unseeing eyes, their carnival merriment a dance of satisfied revenge.

*Il re Teodoro* (Naples, 1784; as *Le roi Théodore* in Paris) by Giovanni Paisiello, is a merry not a tragic Corsican brother, the historically famous German adventurer who made himself King of Corsica (1736) and died in a debtor's prison in London. Paisiello presents him in Venice where, penniless, he is courting the daughter of the innkeeper with whom he lodges. Corine, dazzled by the idea of becoming a queen, is about to marry Theodore when he is arrested for debts in Leghorn, Genoa, Rome, Paris, London, Hamburg, and Madrid and saved only by the intervention of the Turkish ex-Sultan Achmet, who pawns his jewels to pay them. With a sigh Theodore forgets his Corsican crown to settle down to love in a Venetian cottage.

### Czecho-Slovakian Pastoral Operas

## "THE BARTERED BRIDE"

### (*Prodaná Nevěsta*)

Bedrich Smetana. Bohemian comedy opera. Libretto by Karla Sabina (Prague, 1866). True love in a Slavonic village comes into its own by a trick played on parents and marriage broker. Beautiful Bohemian folk and dance melodies are an outstanding feature of the score; and the heroine's air "Alone at last" (Act III) is a touching melody.

Jenik loves rich Krusina's daughter Mařenka, whose father, won by the praises Kezal the marriage broker lavishes on Vasek, Micha's half-witted son by a second wife, insists she marry him. (Jenik, too, is Micha's son by his first wife, driven from home by his stepmother, but this Mařenka, Krusina, and Kezal do not know). While her father goes to hunt up Micha and arrange the marriage, Kezal seeks Jenik.

In the village inn Vasek comes in drunk, and Mařenka follows, making him promise he will refuse to marry her. Meanwhile Jenik is laughing up his sleeve. Kezal has bought his claim to Mařenka's hand for two hundred ducats, Jenik selling it on condition Mařenka marry "Micha's son."

When Vasek's mother comes to lead her son to Krusina's home to be married he has fallen head over heels in love with Esmeralda, the tight-rope walker of an itinerant circus troupe, while Kezal, showing Mařenka Jenik's "quit-claim" rouses her indignation so that she is ready to marry Vasek. But when Jenik arrives and proves that he is "Micha's son," hence never sold his right to Mařenka, he gains her hand with his father's blessing, and the money obtained from the marriage broker with which to start housekeeping.

*The Kiss* (*Hubička*, Prague, 1876), by Smetana, book after Svetla's novel, is a poetic idyl of rustic life depicted in music of national color. The betrothal kiss Mařenka refuses the young widower Hanno (from exaggerated respect for his first wife) he angrily culls a hundredfold from easy-going tavern lips; but, his rage overcome, later meets repentant Mařenka in the woods where "The Kiss," cause of their trouble, is at last exchanged.

Dvořák's *The Peasant a Rogue* (Prague, 1878), book by Vesely, village songs and dances in the "Folk Festival" (Act II) outstanding, is an undramatic variant of *Figaro*. The heroine Regina, a farmer girl pursued by a Czech baron (three "Susannas" appear at a time, in window, garden, and hayloft), is ultimately united to her sturdy peasant lover Gottlieb. Her father the "rogue," is always intent on gain. Beautiful Bohemian folk music may also be found in Dvořák's *King and Charcoal Burner* (Prague, 1874), *The Blockhead* (Prague, 1878), and *The Devil and Wild Kate* (Prague, 1899), the tale of a rough and ready peasant girl who gets the better of the devil. Smetana's *The Secret* (Prague, 1878), considered musically more mature than *The Bartered Bride*, and *The Two Widows* (Prague, 1874), an opera in the style of Auber on a French subject, were unsuccessful; though the former, like Blodek's *The Well* (Prague, 1867), Karavoric's *The Dogs' Heads* (Prague, 1898), a tale of the bloody suppression of the Chodek peasant revolt, and *On the Old Bleaching-Ground*,

Klicka's *The Fair Miller Maid,* and Josef B. Förster's dramatic village tragedy *Eva* (Prague, 1897) are rich in lovely music illustrating rural life in Bohemia and Moravia.

## VARIOUS PASTORAL SUBJECTS

*Shamus O'Brien* (Breslau, 1907) by Charles Villiers Stanford, a romantic score using Irish melodies and rhythms, tells how the hero, pride of his native village, a rebel against English authority (end of 18th century), is caught to be hung, but aided by a brave priest escapes beneath a hail of bullets which kill the spy who betrayed him. Bagpipe dances and jigs, happy love songs and an offstage "Coronach" are among the musical features. *Eine Hochzeit in Bosnien (A Bosnian Wedding)* by Josef Bayer is a ballet whose flowing melodies and piquant rhythms are based on the folk tunes of the Bosnian hill folk. *The Deserted Village* (London, 1880) by the Irish composer John William Glover is a score built up on the famous Goldsmith poem.

## "BODAS DE ORO"

### (*The Golden Wedding*)

AUGUSTE MAURAGE. Book by Armand Crabbé, English version by Dr. Theodore Baker (Madrid, 1923). A one-act "lyric idyl," scene a Flemish fishing port, in 1890. The score is graceful and poetic; a Prelude introducing the old Flemish folk tune, "L'automne, après l'averse," recurs (Tab. 2) as the outstanding baritone song with chorus. The tender ballad "L'autre matin la douce fée," an old Flemish folk air, should be mentioned, as well as the brief, colorful orchestral Interludes.

About the cottage table sit Jan, Ventje, his wife, and Jan's partner Albert. It is the festival of the Virgin, patron saint of the fishermen, and while echoes of song drift through the window the three old people within celebrate the Golden Wedding of Ventje and Jan. But when the men have lighted their pipes their talk of old times takes shape as a dream picture (change of scene) and the happenings of fifty years before are visualized on the stage.

Angelus bells ring as Ventje, a young girl of sixteen enters to lay her bouquet of field flowers before the Virgin's shrine, affixed to a tree. Albert hastens up, begs Ventje to be his and when she refuses catches her up only to release her when her lover Jan comes up and flings him to the ground. After Jan has reassured his trembling sweetheart they go off, not knowing Albert follows them, knife in his hand. But Albert, about to pass the Virgin's shrine, sees it suddenly illumined with a glory of golden light. Seized with swift remorse he drops his knife, and prays before the holy image, then disappears in the moonlight.

Again the three old folk are in their cottage. The picture from the past has vanished but Jan, overcome by his memories, clasps Albert, his loyal friend, to him, and when he has gone, falls asleep over his pipe in his armchair. Ventje draws her own chair close to his and, her head on his shoulder, closes her eyes as the village clock strikes ten and a ray of moonlight falls on her silver hair.

*Si j'étais roi* (*If I Were King,* Paris, 1852) by Adolph Adam, musically "deceitfully piquant and stupidly frivolous" (Pierre Lalo) tells how in East Indian Goa (1520) Zephoris, a net dragger in a native village, sees his wish to be "king for a day" granted with happiest results for all concerned. There is a "Bayadère Ballet"; Zélide's "Indian Air" and Zéphoris' "J'ignore son nom" are attractive melodies. In *Der Dorflump* (*The Village Ne'er-do-well,* Berlin, 1902) by Jeno Hubay, an undramatic Hungarian "folk opera," larded with folk melodies, Sandor, the titular hero, shoots an old sweetheart because she marries, and leaves little Boriska, his next love, to flirt with a strumpet; but when Boriska leaps into the river, he rescues her, and promises to return to marry her when he has "made good."

*Guernica* (Paris, 1895) by Paul Vidal, book by Gailhard and Ghensi, a musically distinctive score with an effective duet, "Dans ce pays aux larges fleurs," plays in the Basque country. Nella, a country girl, betrothed to the Spanish Captain Mariano, sees her brother shot by her fiancé while trying to induce him to leave the rebel Carlists, and gives up the man she loves to enter a convent.

*The Fair at Sorotshinsk* (Moscow, 1914) by Moussorgsky, book after Gogol's fantastic tale, is a vast musical tableau of Ukrainian country life in dance and song. The farmer boy Grytyko gets her father's consent to marry Paraska at the fair. But Paraska's stepmother induces the girl's father to rescind his promise, and not till a cunning gypsy's tricks have frightened the old man out of his wits are the Ukrainian village lovers safely joined by the tie that binds. Outstanding are: Grytyko's "Song of Longing"; Paraska's touching "Complaint"; the "Devil Music" which accompanies horrible tales of the foul fiend; and the magnificent *hopak* at the conclusion of the work.

In *Halka* (Vilna, 1854) by Stanislav Moniusko, "the first thoroughly national Polish opera," Pan Janusz is preparing to wed Sophie, a landowner's daughter. From Jontek, the peasant lad who loves her hopelessly, village maiden Halka learns she is betrayed and (after singing a lovely *cantilena* in G Minor) tries to enter Janusz' castle by moonlight, only to be cast out by the servants (Act II). After chanting her despair (Act III) she caps Pan Janusz's wedding with a horrid climax by killing herself in the bride's presence (Act IV). Outstanding are: the Polonaise and "Blue Mazurka" (Act I), and the Peasant Ballet (Act III). *The Raftsman* (Philadelphia, 1925) is a short river idyl by the same composer with graceful Polish folkwise melodies.

## IDYLS OF THE TROPICS

*Elisca ou l'habitante de Madagascar* (*Elisca or the Madagascan*, Paris, 1799; 1812 as *Elisca ou l'amour maternelle*) by Grétry, "the Raphael of French music," tells how little Madagascans born during a certain month are immolated by the cruel Ombis on the altar of Niang, god of evil. A devoted Arab mother, Elisca, aided by a faithful negro and a white planter, saves her babe and others; and after alarums and excursions in which Madagascans of the Lion Tribe, French soldiers, negroes, etc., are involved, the curtain falls on a pirogue laden with Madagascan pickaninnies, brands saved from the burning, waving banana and palm leaves, heaving into sight while French soldiers give three rousing cheers.

*Le code noir* (*The Black Law*, Paris, 1842) by Clapisson, shows life in Martinique when no color line was drawn in the affections. Zambra, a *caffresse*, mistress of a white planter of the town of Grenada, escapes from slavery with her babe. Years afterward, she is recaptured. Her son, despite the fact he has become an officer in the French service, according to the "Black Law" is a slave. Both are about to be sold as such when the planter appearing on the scene, frees his *caffresse* and son, Donation, and the latter marries his mulatto sweetheart Zoe. Though the story has "an unpleasant color complex," the music includes charming numbers, notably a negro Bamboula.

In *La Creola* (*The Creole*, Bologna, 1878) by Gaetano Coronaro Mirza, a black slave girl, jealous of Raoul, the planter (Isle de Bourbon, 18th century) because he loves Eva, a charming Creole, pushes Eva into the water with the cry "Die!" Then winding around her forehead a wreath of poison flowers Mirza in turn dies in agony.

## "PAUL ET VIRGINIE"

VICTOR MASSÉ. Book by Barbier and Carré after Saint-Pierre's romance (Paris, 1876). The old-time romantic music includes graceful numbers: the "Banana Leaf Duet" ("O joy, O delight"), Bamboula, and Entr'acte (Act I); Virginia's Romance, "Through the forest at night" (Act II), Paul's "In vain on this shore," and the Choral Finale (Act III).

Paul and Virginia run laughing into the cottage under the same banana leaf, pelted by the tropic storm, and his mother plans to send her boy to India, there to outgrow his mute love for Virginia beneath the banyan tree before it is spoken. As the children crouched at her feet sing the affection of the pure at heart, Melea, a fugitive slave, enters. When Virginia goes to her cruel master's plantation to intercede for her, St. Croix, the Legree of Martinique, drinking rum as his hands dance and sing the bamboula to clashing coconut shells, alarms Paul into hurrying off the girl as the negroes sing more loudly to drown lashed Melea's cries. (A charming Intermezzo depicting the forest's serenity contrasts with this horrid scene).

Virginia, in fine clothes and jewels—Paul does not know his little comrade of the banana leaf—is on the eve of departure for France, and listens in silence to Paul's reproaches for leaving him till his mother's revelation that he is base-born gives the unhappy boy something else to think of as he goes. Virginia, sleeping in a hammock, lulled by Melea's voice—she has bought the girl—sees St. Croix's house go up in flames lit by revolting slaves in her dream, and wakes to board the ship which will carry her to France.

Mad with longing, yet cheered by Virginia's letter breathing love and loneliness, Paul stands on the seashore. A vision shows him Virginia dancing the minuet in a Paris *salon,* and when she seats herself at the harp her voice comes to him across the weary miles and his own joins in her song while St. Croix nears only to be repulsed. But no sooner has he told black Domingo his glorious dream than a great ship is dashed on the rocks by the tropic hurricane, and wrecked. Paul hears Virginia calling him and then—her body is washed ashore at his feet, her features smiling in unvanquished sweetness and serenity, and with a cry of despair he flings himself on the lovely corpse.

Lesueur's *Paul et Virginie* (Paris, 1784) and Kreutzer's *Paul et Virginie* (Paris, 1791) preceded Massé's opera, followed by the Spaniard José Rogel's *Pablo y Virginia* (Madrid, between 1890-1900) and Rabaud's incidental score for Nepoty's drama *Paul et Virginie,* more than mere theatric music, whose classic "Funeral March" expresses guileless Virginia's virginal soul with tender pathos. Italo Montemezzi's *Paolo e Virginia* (ann. 1925), book by Simoni and Adam, contains pages of exquisite nature music; and the French musical ironist Eric Satie has also written a *Paul et Virginie* (MS.).

*Le Spahi* (Monte Carlo, 1897) by Lucien Lambert, a colorful lyric drama after Loti's novel, presents Jean Peyral, the Spahi, in St. Louis, Senegal, bewailing the infidelity of the white courtesan Cora to her servant, the negress Fatou-gaye. Flinging himself on the sand (Act II), Jean wakes to find Fatou-gaye has put up a shelter to protect him from the sun. Touched by her affection he yields to it (Ballet, grand festival, voluptuous songs, nature dances of the blacks to celebrate spring's coming). In a camp in a forest clearing (Act III) Jean dreams of the Cévennes, his old mother, his fiancée; but Fatou-gaye has stolen the money he meant to send home. In a scene of tears and remorse she wins his pardon before the Spahis march to battle. It is night. Jean, falling as a last shot is fired, dies in Fatou-gaye's black arms, and she, strangling her babe, takes poison and joins him in death. *L'île du rêve* (*The Isle of Dreams*, Paris, 1896) by Reynaldo Hahn, book after Loti's *Mariage de Loti*. The score, subtitled *Idylle polynésienne*, cloudy and poetically musical, is really a duet in three tableaux, in which the melody "Les fleurs de nos pays se fanent" stands out. The tale is that of the love of the pretty Tahitien Mahenu (the Rarahu of Loti's novel) and the young naval officer Georges de Kerven (Loti), with incidental interruptions: the silly old Chinaman's amorous pursuit of the girl and the gloomy prophecies of mad Teria, once the "port love" of Georges' dead brother. When Georges' ship is ordered away he tries to hide his coming departure from Mahenu, but she learns of it and falls senseless as the cruiser's smoke fades on the horizon.

## 6.  *The Verist's Rosary*

Earlier veristic operas (Verdi's middle period, etc.) may be found elsewhere in this volume. The rosary of veristic opera-pearls here strung includes works reflecting the brutal naturalism which dramatizes in music sensual passion, homicidal jealousy, murder, incest, robbery, and secret crime as expressed by village primitives or urban degenerates.

### ITALY

### "CAVALLERIA RUSTICANA"

#### (*Rustic Chivalry*)

PIETRO MASCAGNI. Book after Vergas's folk play (Rome, 1890), by Torgioni-Tozzetti and G. Menasci. The best known and, with the exception of *I Pagliacci*, the most successful and popular of all veristic operas, it struck the keynote of its type (with insertion of triplet-figure in melodic phrases to lend greater swing; violent dynamic contrasts; and piquant introduction of notes alien to the harmony) and its music underlies the dramatic situations with telling strokes. The Prelude establishes Santuzza's tragic fate; and its best known numbers are: the famous symphonic Intermezzo dividing the work into two parts; the glowing Siciliana (a south Italian folk tune), and the terribly hackneyed "Ave Maria."

It is Easter morning in a Sicilian village, yet the heart of Santuzza, a young peasant girl, knows no Easter peace, for Turiddu (before the curtain rises his voice is heard serenading handsome Lola, Alfio's wife) has robbed her of her honor. Then the deceiver left her to court co-quettish Lola whose lover he had been, but who jilted him to marry the carter. The Easter message sounds from the church door, where Santuzza waits to beg her betrayer to make her an honest woman. He laughs at her passionate prayers and when Lola appears (to the accompaniment of a frivolous waltz tune) flings her aside so brutally that she rolls down the church steps as he follows Lola into church to hear Easter Mass. At that moment unsuspecting Alfio comes by. Santuzza reveals the story of his shame and his vow of vengeance makes her realize too late what she has done. (In effective contrast to the tragic catastrophe brewing, the Intermezzo Sinfonico depicts the idyllic peace of the sunny Easter morning.) Mass is over, gaily the drinking chorus rings out in Mother Lucia's inn. Alfio mingles somberly with the others. When he refuses the wine Turiddu offers, Turiddu senses he knows all. A bite in Alfio's right ear shows the betrayer is ready for the duel with knives. With a tearful farewell from his mother, to whom he commends hapless Santuzza, he rushes off. The tense moments of waiting end when the peasants announce Turiddu's death. Alfio's honor is avenged.

Direct operatic offspring of the tragic Sicilian are: *Clara d'Arta* (Milan, 1899) by Bendetti-Busky, which has the questionable honor of being the worst *Cavalleria* imitation; *Celeste* (Brescia, 1901) by Orsini; Domenico Monleone's *Cavalleria rusticana* (Amsterdam, 1907; as *La giostra dei falcatore,* Florence, 1914); *Der Stärkere* (*The Stronger,* Budapest, 1924) by Siegmund Vincze, book by Stefan Gezy, a Hungarian *Cavalleria* with the customary triangle in which the husband gains the upper hand and instead of knifing the lover flings him down a precipice; and *Cavalleria Berolina* (Berlin, 1891), Bogumil Zepler's musical farce-parody of Mascagni's score. *Il Misterio* (*The Passion Play,* Venice, 1921) by Monleone, copies Mascagni in a tragedy of "rustic honor," where the girl's father kills her betrayer; and *Festa a marina* (Venice, 1893) by Gellio Coronaro, is a slavish imitation of *Cavalleria* with identical arrangement of musical effects, save substitution of an attractive ballet for the Intermezzo. Sara, Tonio's faithless wife, loves Cicillo. Her husband (like Alfio) discovers it and instead of his rival (as in *Cavalleria*) slays his wife, who dies uttering gurgling sounds as she falls with cut throat.

## "I PAGLIACCI"

### (*The Comedians*)

RUGGIERO LEONCAVALLO. Also known as *Il Bajazzo* (*The Clown*). Book, founded on an actual incident, by the composer (Milan, 1892). What *Cavalleria's* veristic twin may lack in originality it makes up for in superior technique and instrumentation, melodic power and an ad-

mirable libretto. The outstanding numbers (often heard on the concert
stage) are: Tonio's "Veste la giubba," one of Caruso's most electrifying
songs; Canio's Song (Act I); and Nedda's "Bird Song" (soprano).
The "Comedy Music" (Act II) is piquant.

Before the curtain rises Tonio prepares the audience for the performance to be given with his Prologue song, "A Word," which explains the
play is from life, declares actors are human beings with passions like
their own, and that the author has tried to express them.

Wandering players enter a Calabrian village to blare of trumpets,
cries of children and curiosity seekers, and Canio, manager of the
troupe, announces a performance that evening. He descends from the
chariot, but when Tonio helps down Nedda, Canio's wife, he gets a box
on the ear, to which he replies with a muttered curse. It is not a happy
theatrical family. Canio adores his wife (who betrays him with Silvio,
a young villager) and is passionately jealous of her. When bystanders,
however, who have noticed the incident utter dubious jests, he shows
how deeply he resents suspicion of his wife's faithfulness.

While the vesper bells call the villagers to church, Canio and Beppo
drink in the tavern, while Nedda ("Bird Song") expresses her yearning for the golden freedom which would let her follow the urge of her
heart. Her song lures Tonio, the misshapen clown, to her, and when
his impudent suit for favor from his master's wife is chastised by a
blow of the whip, he threatens to betray her illicit love affair. Now
Silvio comes to persuade Nedda to give over the player's chariot and
flee with him that night. She agrees. But they have been overheard.
Tonio and Canio (whom he has brought along) interrupt the lovers
only in time to see an unknown leap the wall. While Tonio boasts his
ignoble revenge, Beppo protects Nedda from Canio's dagger. But the
villagers are hurrying to the performance. His heart torn with rage
and despair Canio must play the buffoon and rouse laughter with tears
in his eyes. He is not a man (as he explains in the moving song "Ridi,
pagliacci") but a toy to amuse the mob.

Preceded by the Intermezzo which echoes the warning of the Prologue—that the author is telling a true tale—the comedians begin the
"Comedy of Columbine" on their strollers' stage. Curiously enough,
its incidents parallel the tragedy of the players' real lives. Columbine
(Nedda) signs to Harlequin (Beppo) that he may visit her. And Taddeo's clownish advances end in his being driven off by Harlequin. But
no sooner do the lovers sit down together than he announces Columbine's husband, the Clown, who has discovered a man in the house. The
allusions of the play are bitter realities to Canio, and losing self-
control he fills the audience with horror in what they think his superb
acting of the injured husband's part. Nedda plays her part in an agony
of terror and suddenly—the play passes from comedy to tragedy! Canio
demands her lover's name. When she refuses it he stabs her. Calling
on Silvio as she dies, he hurries to her aid only to be struck down in
turn, while the murderer calls out with sinister calm to the excited
auditors: "The play is over!"

In De Camondo's *Le Clown* (Paris, 1906), an effective realistic score, the clown of an ambulant French circus is seen kissing Zepherine whom he bores, by Auguste, her lover. The latter cuts the rope on which the clown swings and he falls to his death, his last moments sweetened by the fact that, held in Zepherine's pitying arms, he once more can tell the girl who does not love him he loves her.

*Mala vita* (*A Life of Ill Fame,* Rome, 1892; Milan, 1897, as *Il voto, The Vow*) by Giordano, is musically not exceptional. Vito, a sick young dyer who vows to rescue and marry a prostitute if he recover does both; but when a former sweetheart, now a married woman, comes his way he forgets his Cristina who, her faith in mankind ruined by her hoped-for savior's lapse, returns to her old home, the house of ill fame, to fall dying on its threshold, purified by suffering from all earthly contacts. *A Santa Lucia* (Berlin, 1892) by Antonio Tasca, book by Golisciani, another drama of Neapolitan low life, tears passion to tatters in melodious tunes. Cicillo, oyster man Totonno's son, has given Maria an engagement ring and Rosella a babe, which he promises to legitimize by marrying its mother when his navy enlistment runs out. While he is serving his "hitch" Maria taunts Rosella into drawing a knife on her, causing Rosella to go to jail, whence Totonno (who loves her) bails her out (Act II). Maria tells the returning sailor boy vile tales of Rosella and his father, and he curses both. Rosella, her love and innocence doubted, flings herself into the bay. Cicillo dives and drags her out—too late. She dies in his arms, whispering, "It is not true, it is not true!" *A Basso Porto* (*In the Lower Harbor,* Cologne, 1894) by Niccolò Spinelli, book by Checchi, uses the same milieu. Luigino flaunts his mother and jeers at his sister's Camorrist lover Cicillo in a water-front dive. Cicillo, when Luigino tries to stab him, and Sesella refuses to run off with him, decides to put the boy in a convict cell and the girl on the streets. But after he has had Luigino flung out of Pascale's den as a traitor to the Camorra, Maria confesses to her daughter that she was Cicillo's mistress, and reveals him as the Camorrist traitor. When Cicillo refuses to flee for her son's sake, Maria stabs him.

## "I GIOJELLI DELLA MADONNA"

### (*The Jewels of the Madonna*)

ERMANNO WOLF-FERRARI. Book by C. Zangarini and E. Goloschiani (Berlin, 1911). These three acts of Neapolitan underworld life have been summarized as: "a transposition of *Aphrodite* to a *poissard* environment." A brutal, realistic plot is wedded to colorful music. The delicate Serenade, "silk-spun," the touching harmonies of the mother's blessing, the wild rhythms of the "Apache Dance," and the moving Postlude are notable.

As the Madonna's processional passes through a Naples slum, Maliella, dress and hair disordered, flies out of the house, avid for the freedom of the streets. Inviting the idle youths of the purlieus to kiss her, a chase ensues. But good-looking Rafaele (gang leader of the Camorrists) catching her, she stabs with her hatpin instead of giving her lips. Her savagery inflames Rafaele the more. He kisses his wound, swears to possess her and—while hymns to the Virgin sound—ardently voices his profane passion and thrusts a flower into her bosom. As the sacred image passes he cries he will risk damnation for her sake, and steal the jewels of the Madonna to hang around her neck. The gangsters laugh at the girl's horrified shriek and Gennaro (who loves her) coming up to intervene, is sent about his business. Yet, despite superstition, Maliella picks up Rafaele's discarded flower, and runs into the house with it between her lips.

In her garden Maliella (Carmela, who has adopted her as a foundling, having left) inveighs against the drear sameness of life to Gennaro. Bidding her farewell, the latter draws her close and incoherently bares his devouring passion. Maliella, slipping from his arms, taunts him with her love for Rafaele, and the latter's offer to commit sacrilege for her sake. As she scornfully leaves him, Gennaro's passion-darkened mind snatches at the robbery of the jewels as his only hope. While he goes off for false keys and files, Rafaele lures Maliella to the garden gate with a serenade, to vanish at his rival's approach. Gennaro has consummated his crime. To the cry his ghastly face draws from Maliella, he answers: "For you!" The jeweled necklace, the pearls, the diamonds, the emeralds, stolen from the Mother of God, flash and glitter in the moonlight. While Gennaro babbles mystically of the Virgin's forgiveness Maliella winds them around her head, neck and wrists. Then, as if in a dream, seeing Rafaele in the man before her, she lets him have his will.

Before the dregs of Naples, in a Camorrist dive, Rafaele boasts he will be the first to possess Maliella. And while the underworld, to the music of a mechanical piano, begins a wild Apache dance soon degenerating into an orgy Maliella bursts in, a scarlet shawl round her shoulders. From her incoherent lips Rafaele forces her hideous secret, sends gangsters to fetch Gennaro, and then learns that the latter has preceded him in the girl's favor. Maddened by his followers' derisive howls, he brutally flings her to the ground, the flashing gems scattering over the floor as she falls. When Gennaro rushes in, glad to have found her, Maliella, spurning the jewels, curses him bitterly for losing her Rafaele's love. While the storm wind blows out one by one the candles which light the dive, she flings out into the night to drown herself in the bay, the superstitious gangsters scattering in terror as church bells ring out the sacrilege to the sleeping city. Crazed Gennaro's eye now lights on a wall fresco of the Virgin. Crawling to it he reverently lays the jewels at its feet and, as the armed mob with pitchforks raised bursts furiously in to kill him stabs himself, dying with his head pillowed on Maliella's red shawl.

*Zanetto* (Pesaro, 1896) by Mascagni, book after *Le Passant* by François Coppée, is a one-act *bozetto* (sketch) with a choral Overture without words, sung before rise of the curtain. Sylvia, despite wide experience no better than she should be, confronted with Zanetto's stormy wooing finds she never has known "true" love. Stifling her nascent passion, however, she dismisses Zanetto inviolate, her tortured heart finding relief in a flood of tears. *Tilda* (Florence, 1892) by Cilea supplies musical opportunities (there is a catchy "Saltarello") in connection with the coming and going of thieves, detectives, women of light life, and virtuous brides. *Hochzeitmorgen* (*The Wedding Morn*, Hamburg, 1893) by Karl von Kaskel, realistically effective music, tells an Italian frontier town tragedy. Paolo, the smuggler, loves Giovana, whose mother keeps the inn. She loves Pietro Moralto, the Bersaglieri captain. Paolo jailed, Giovana begs her lover to free him—they were childhood playmates—and when he refuses to stain his military honor she does so. Grateful Paolo at once so besets her she has to ring the alarm bell, and next morning, as her wedding procession is moving to church, Paolo rushes at Pietro and—buries his dagger in the breast of Giovana, who catches the stroke. *Jana* (Milan, 1905) by Renato Virgilio lends the Sardinian landscape a verist tinge. The landowner Esisie Mammu's farm hands go on strike. Vainly Jana begs her husband Gaddu not to go out; their child is starving. Portu, a former admirer, arriving in town (Gaddu is off haranguing fellow strikers), finds Jana unconscious in the street, helps her home and leaves his purse. Gaddu, informed by gossip his innocent wife is faithless, shoots her, but, her character cleared, flings himself at her feet imploring pardon. Her dying glance seeks Portu and the Sardinian Othello, stricken to the heart, falls dead of jealous shock.

*Der Brautgang* (Mayence, 1892) by Bruno Oelsner, a score with effective lyric pages shows Bianca, an Italian village beauty, jilting the soldier Sebaldo, to marry rich Scandozza. As Bianca's wedding procession nears the church Sebaldo shoots her sister Serafina by mistake. As he remorsefully kneels beside the dying girl, Bianca comes up, and when Sebaldo curses her as her sister's real murderess, the sensitive bride stabs herself.

*Margarita* (Antwerp, 1923) by Timmermann, book by Van Roy, takes us to Italy during the building of the Mont Cenis railway tunnel. Two workmen, Marci and Pietro, love Margarita, a village girl, out of whose preference for Marco develops a web of murder and madness ending with both lovers lying mortally wounded and Margarita about to go insane. The unequal score has occasional brilliant pages.

*Nacht* (*Night*, Berne, 1900) by Bogumil Zepler, in which psychic moods are convincingly handled in music, shows blind Captain Andrea in despair in his villa on the Italian Riviera. A painter, Francesco, loves Magda, his wife: she returns his love. A letter from Francesco to Magda his new chambermaid reads betrays their intended flight. When the blind man tries to stop it Francesco shoots him, and with his last gasp he forgives the woman who betrayed him.

*Il Macigno* (*The Boulder*, Milan, 1917) by De Sabata is musically successful (chorus ensembles) in rendering mob passions. The villagers of Torrana and Gayella are Apennine Montagues and Capulets. When the Gayellese burn a Torrana crucifix, both villages prepare to fight with scythes. Driada, the Torrana beauty, loves Ibetto the Gayellese, so Martano, the girl's rejected lover, plans a unique revenge. Gayella lies at the foot of the hill; Torrana at the top. While the church bells below ring out Driada's wedding chimes, Martano pushes over the tremendous boulder which overhangs the village, destroying it. Driada and Ibetto, mortally wounded, have time only to exchange a last word of love.

*La Figlia di Jorio* (Milan, 1906) by Franchetti is a score "veristic without being musically brutal." Innocent Mila, "Jorio's Daughter," driven into the Abruzzi peasant Lazaro's home by a vile band of mowers—her father is reputed a wizard—wins the heart of Aligi, Lazaro's son, about to be married. In a mountain cave, before the Virgin's image, Aligi and Mila avow their love, but the boy's father, whose worst instincts Mila has roused, pursues her and, beating his son like a dog, has him bound by shepherds. Returning to wreak his will on the girl, Lazaro is killed with an ax by Aligi, who has freed himself. Out of love for Aligi Mila accuses herself of the murder and before her lover can prevent is burned by the raging mob, a sun ray falling on her face haloing it with golden glory.

*Der Eiserne Heiland* (*The Iron Savior*, Vienna, 1917) by Max Oberleithner has a climax of horror. In the Dolomites (1860) the German village smith, Andreas Reutter, has married an Italian wife, Annina. Annina longs for her southern home. Riccardo, ambulant musician, comes to the village and the gentle rustics set on him crying, "Kill the dog!" Annina, her husband, and the village priest save the wounded man, who is nursed in Andreas' home and becomes the wife's lover. Andreas, working on his statue, "The Iron Savior," sees Riccardo kiss Annina, and sending a bullet after him, flings Annina over his shoulder and strides off into the night. Dawn reveals the mad smith on a Dolomite glacier peak, his faithless wife nailed to a huge wooden cross. As the villagers draw near carrying his "Iron Savior," the maniac shouts: "See, a new god has risen!" falling lifeless as Riccardo buries a dagger in his back.

## SPAIN

*Manuel Menendez* (Prague, 1905) by Lorenzo Filiasi projects verism back to 1600 in Seville, in a theatric score with effective solos. The poet Manuel Menendez loves Ferma, the flower girl. When she refuses his escort on a walk he writes above her door that her favors may be bought; and, when Ferma forbids him the house, chops off his lying hand and bleeds to death. *La Cabrera* (*The Goat Girl*, Milan, 1904) by Gabriel Dupont, sings verist Spain in neo-French harmony, outstanding the Spanish "Folk Dance" (Tab. 2). The goat girl loves Pedrito, but while he is serving a navy enlistment forgets herself with Cheppa, another boy. The sailor, her fault betrayed by living evidence on his return, repulses La Cabrera, who flees with her babe to the mountains. Chastising Cheppa and drowning his grief in the inn, Pedrito meets the girl coming back, her child choked by the raw mountain air; but when he clasps her in forgiving arms the goat girl's sudden death prevents the peal of belated wedding bells. *La Dolores* (Madrid, 1895) by Tomas Bretón uses the Aragonese jota (Act I) and other folk themes with effect. Dolores, a Calatayud barmaid, betrayed by Melchior, the barber, hears him strum his guitar while he sings before a gay crowd that she is common property. Lazaro, Gaspara the innkeeper's son, an incipient priest, loves Dolores and, knowing Melchior will visit her that night, she first bids him come to her room (Act II) then forbids his coming, fearing he may be hurt. Lazaro bursts into her room while Melchior is torturing and insulting her; they fight, falling out of the window, and when Dolores tries to take the blame for the barber's death Lazaro cries: "Melchior made you vile and so I killed him!"

## "TIEFLAND"

### (*Marta of the Lowlands*)

EUGEN D'ALBERT. Book by Rudolf Lothar, after Guimera's drama *Terra baixa,* its material drawn from the morass of Hispanic rustic realism (Prague, 1903). Probably the most notable German verist music drama,

having an ethical apposition to its naturalistic horrors. Clever theatrical music, with beautiful pages (the yearning clarinet motive of the
shepherd boy in the Prologue; Pedro's love plaints, the romantic
"Legend of the Wolf"; the transcendant closing melody) happily express the dramatic action.

An orchestral Introduction pictures the peace of the snow-capped
Pyrenees where (Prologue) Pedro the herd boy, a child of Nature,
plays his shepherd pipe and dreams of a woman's love (a vision seen
in his slumbers), while guarding his master Sebastiano's flock. Now
Sebastiano comes from the Lowlands, the Catalonian plain, with him
old Tomaso, the village elder, and—a girl, Marta. Bought by Sebastiano from a passing vagabond, ,he has debauched her. He must make
a rich marriage to pay his debts, yet his unbridled sensuality refuses
to relinquish its victim. Pedro, the unsophisticated shepherd boy, shall
marry Marta and he will secretly enjoy her favors as before. Marta's
soul revolts, but Pedro sees in her the maid the Virgin promised in his
dream. He agrees to become Sebastiano's miller in the Lowlands and
descends happily into the valley.
The tale of Marta's shame, innocently betrayed by little Nuri, makes
mill hands and villagers laugh the witless husband to scorn and Sebastiano's answer to the girl's final plea to forego the marriage is to
announce his visit to the bridal chamber that night. After the wedding, the young couple alone, Pedro's honest tenderness (he presses a
silver dollar, his most valuable possession, into his young wife's hand,
and tells her how it was given him for slaying a wolf, the terror of
his herd) makes Marta realize he is clean of heart. A light flashes in
her bedroom, but, daring Sebastiano's wrath she remains in the mill,
Pedro crouching at her feet, happy to be with the woman he loves.
The light in the bedroom, her strange actions, arouse Pedro's suspicions. He returns from the village aware of Marta's shame but not
knowing her betrayer. Marta—love for the honest youth has flamed up
in her heart—since she cannot hope to win him, tries to make him kill
her. But when he wounds her with his dagger he realizes how greatly he
cares for her. In reply to her passionate confession of love he bids
her follow him to the hills where the air blows clean. There her fault
shall be forgotten. But Sebastiano confronts them, brutally commands
Marta to dance for him, and when she denounces him to Pedro as her
betrayer, the shepherd is flung out of the house. Then Sebastiano learns
his plan for marrying the rich widow has come to naught. Maddened
he tears Marta to him, and at her cry for help, as she struggles to
avoid his kisses, Pedro leaps through the window. Casting himself on
Sebastiano he strangles him, like the wolf in the hills, and flinging the
corpse aside, while the horror-stricken onlookers recognize the judgment of heaven, he draws Marta to him, and they turn from the Lowlands to the pure air of their beloved hills.

*La Catalane* (*The Catalan Girl,* Paris, 1907) by Ferdinand
Le Borne tells the story of *Tiefland* in a French opera, which con-

tains some colorful Spanish dances. *Hand und Herz* (*Hand and Heart*, Dresden, 1925) by Kurt Striegler, a theatrically effective score in the *style* of *Tiefland,* presents a jailbird husband returning to claim his wife from the decent man she has innocently married. He is murdered by the second husband, who commits suicide when he learns his wife has drowned herself.

*Conchita* (Milan, 1911) by Riccardo Zandonai after Pierre Louy's *La femme et le pantin,* an effective veristic score, offers "low-life" scenes in a cigar factory, dance hall, and street in Seville. When rich Mateo visits the cigar factory, Conchita recognizes in him a man who saved her from a policeman's too pressing attentions. She invites him home. There (Act II) her mother leaves them to go marketing; the girl flies into a rage when Mateo slips her money, and leaves home. In the dance hall when Mateo finds her doing *risqué* dances (Act III) she promises to settle down in a little house he owns. She has agreed to let him in at midnight but she taunts him from the window instead of opening the door, and he staggers off. Then the girl comes to his home (Act IV) to say she hoped he would kill himself for love of her. When he seizes her she tries to stab him. Then Mateo beats her, brutally, thoroughly, mercilessly and Conchita—now she knows he truly loves her!—nestles in his arms radiantly happy, declaring she has loved him all the time.

*La Jota* (Paris, 1911) by Raoul Laparra has a first act of somber, passionate intensity and a second "more noisy than profound." The Spanish *jota,* the folk waltz, runs like a red passion-thread through the score. Zumarragua, Basque lover of Aragonese Soledad, leaving Anso, a Pyrenean town (1835) to join the Carlists, dances a farewell *jota* with the girl, whose beauty rouses the evil desires of Mosen Jago, the village priest, who after desperate struggles overcomes his passion by prayer. Amid rattle of musketry (Act II) the Carlists hem in the defenders of Anso around the altar of the village church, Juan sees Soledad encouraging the Federalists to resist, but, amid flying bullets, they cling against the altar, singing the *jota* to which they danced their farewell. Morsen Jago curses the lovers, then, as the Carlists nail him to the cross, dies in anguish of body and soul.

## "LA HABANERA"

RAOUL LAPARRA. Book by Petit and Boisvent (Paris, 1908). A French verist's drama whose music "dispenses with the facile sentimentality cultivated by the Ítalian verists." From the beginning to the end of the score the "Habanera" passes from the voices to orchestra and back again as the work's essential element, the musical materialization of Ramon's fear and remorse.

When drunken peasants have lurched out of a small Spanish town's tavern, Ramon glooms over his brother Pedro's approaching marriage to Pilar, for whom he burns. When she enters in rustic bridal costume, soon followed by Pedro with whom she is to dance the Habanera, Ramon talks of his unknown sweetheart and when she runs out, forces Pedro into a quarrel and, as he turns to escape, buries his knife in his back. The dying man realizes his brother has slain him; his last words are a promise to return for him in a year's time. The bride, finding the body, swoons and Ramon, returning as though unawares raises his bloodstained hand and swears to avenge his brother.

It is the anniversary of the murder. The old father mourns his unavenged boy. When three blind men enter to play for a dance, a fourth, unseen save by Ramon comes with them. It is Pedro, bearing a guitar as they do. And through Pilar's loving glances and the music of the Habanera as they dance Ramon hears Pedro's words: "Tell Pilar the truth before you desecrate my grave"—they were to lay flowers on it—"to-morrow or I draw her into the tomb with me." Ramon stops dancing in despair. (An Entr'acte fixes the atmosphere for the tragedy's climax by depicting Ramon's night of horror.)

In the churchyard Pilar scatters flowers on Pedro's grave but Ramon cannot make his confession. As the sun sinks in crimson he hears Pedro's voice humming the Habanera, starts and—sees Pilar lying across the grave. He screams his confession into her ear: she does not stir. Night falls like a pall, the wind blows out the candles flickering on the graves. Vainly Ramon shakes Pilar: she is dead. Ramon's mind gives way. He flings back his mantle, plays a few measures of the fateful Habanera on his guitar and rushes into the darkness, cemetery gates clashing to after him.

*La Navarraise* (*The Girl of Navarre,* London, 1894) by Massenet, book after Claretie's *La Cigarette,* written for Emma Calvé, has a charming Duet (Act I) and a poetic orchestral "Nocturne" in a verist score shrouded in powder smoke and rhythmed by roll of drums. Near Bilbao, General Garrido looms amid fugitive soldiers (Carlist War, 1874) but grows cheerful when Anita offers to murder Zucarragas, the Carlist chief, for the two thousand *duros* she must have if her lover, the soldier Araquil, is to wed her. In his tent she stabs the guerilla leader as jealous Araquil, who has followed her, is struck by a bullet. But bells tolling for the Carlist assure him his suspicions were unjust, and he dies happy while Anita, after vainly trying to stab herself, goes mad. Massenet's *Espada* (Monte Carlo, 1908), a picturesque ballet, is the tragedy of a *posada* dancer whose lover, a handsome bullfighter, is killed in the arena. She must dance for the inn's customers instead of hastening to him and she dies when his body is brought in as she dances. *Die Rose von Pontavedra* (Vienna, 1894) by Josef Förster, in which a duet, "Weshalb erscheint dein Aug' so trüb," stands out, shows Portuguese Pedro playing the guitar of seduction 'neath the window of Rosita the innkeeper's daughter. The traditional quick curtain as he climbs her balcony announces the worst for the girl, whose mother is on a pilgrimage to St. Jaime de Compostella. José, the girl's sailor fiancé, returns and—does naught. Her mother returns and forbids Rosita's marriage to Pedro. Then Dolores, the wife Pedro never has mentioned, appears, and her revelation that she stands on the brink of bigamy rouses Rosita to the dagger thrust which sends the Portuguese into the beyond.

## FRANCE

Before "verism" came into opera, a score such as Hérold's *L'Illusion* (Paris, 1829) in whose musically fine climax the heroine commits suicide by flinging herself into an abyss, might have stirred an audience. The climax of Litoff's *Les Templiers* (Brussels, 1886) when in the Paris of 1307 all the Knights Templars of France are burned on one tremendous pyre, even René, the hero, flung into the flames when King Philip learns he loves his daughter Isabelle, may have thrilled earlier opera goers; but modern verism calls for horrors more subtle or more brutal. In *La fille de la terre* (*The Daughter of the Soil,* Monte Carlo, 1921) by Déodat de Séverac, with fine choruses and noble Prologue, a Languedoc country girl running off with a smooth-tongued city wooer, is stopped and her abductor killed by her father's heir, son of his tenant. Here the veristic note is simply struck, for as the Daughter of the Soil loses her mind her father merely has her lover's cadaver flung off the farm. *La plus forte* (*The Strongest,* Paris, 1924) by Xavier Leroux, book by Richepin, is a brutal tale to "music of distinct charm" (?). Julie, Pierre's second wife, weary of playing second fiddle to plough and hoe, is thrilled when two woodchoppers fight as to which shall have her; but as she keeps a tryst with Jean, the victor, her old husband reveals that the boy is his child by his first marriage. Julie, horrified to find she has betrayed her husband with her stepson, leaps into a mountain torrent while the men return to the farm. *La Mauviette* (*Little Mauve,* Havre, 1924) by Paul Gautier to expressive music shows Fleuriot, the rich farmer, casting his servant, La Mauve, whom he has betrayed, out of the house, spurning her when she returns with La Mauviette and begs to be taken in. He is murdered in a fit of rage by the indignant mother. *Naïs-Micoulin* (Paris, 1907) by Alfred Bruneau, outstanding the dramatic Duet between Naïs and Frédéric, shows the two lovers, their twilight embrace about to be severed by Nicolin's hatchet (he is Naïs' father), saved by Toine le Gibbeux (hunchback) a "heart simple and sublime." Later, when inconstant Frédéric goes adventuring scabrously with the girl's father, Toine digs a deep pit, the sinners drop into it (Frédéric pushed in by exasperated Naïs) break their necks, and Toine takes into his arms the girl he later will marry. Such is verism in the Provence.

## "LA LÉPREUSE"

### (*The Leper Girl*)

SYLVIO LAZZARI. Book by Bataille (Paris, 1912; revived 1925). A ghastly subject "does not diminish the artistic value of the work," its music evoking with moving exactitude medieval Breton customs, and the curse attaching to lepers. The score has distinct originality, and is rich in pages of genuine emotion and picturesque Breton color.

Ervoak, a Breton peasant lad, loves Aliette, a leper woman's daughter; but his parents refuse to accept the poor girl tainted with her horrid malady, as their daughter-in-law. The wretched lovers, thinking to win Heaven's aid, make a pilgrimage together to the "Pardon" at Folgast, Aliette warding off Ervoak's kisses lest he become infected.

When they return, Tili, an old village witch, rouses Aliette's jealousy by her lies and when she has induced the credulous boy to pretend love for another the better to soften Aliette's heart toward him, the leper girl, seizing a glass of wine, first drinks and then offers the glass to Ervoak, whose lips touch the rim where her own have sipped.

Ervoak now infected, the priest comes to take the two lepers to the desert place where they will be kept, men and women apart. The anguish of separation is more than the hapless Breton lovers can endure, however, and they commit suicide rather than live their living death deprived of each other's society.

*Sirocco* (Darmstadt, 1921) by Eugen d'Albert has a "moving picture action" clad in the coarse garb of Italian verism. Petroff's Love Scene (Act II) and the Strangling Scene are musical and melodramatic high points. The call of the wild leads a Russian prince, alias Dupont, to enlist in the Foreign Legion, and join the rest of the battalion in the worship of La Roquine, cabaret singer and mistress of the regiment, nicknamed "Sirocco," because she drives men mad and destroys them. When his fiancée, Natascha, appears and tells Dupont his mother is dead and his release purchased, he seeks out La Roquine who informs him that a mother knelt to her to beg her to give up her boy, some Russian prince, and she—kicked her. The legionary strangles the strumpet, but his morphomaniac comrade, de Montigny, says (and thinks) he murdered her and kills himself; and when Dupont's friend, Petroff, holds him blameless, he leaves Africa for Petro-grad with Natascha.

## GERMANY

## "DER POLNISCHE JUDE"

### (*The Polish Jew*)

KARL WEISS. Book after Erckmann-Chatrian by Léon and Batka (Prague, 1901). A richly melodic, colorful score using Slavic dance and song themes, which enjoys deserved popularity. The French composer, Camille Erlanger, has set the same tale in his *Le juif polonais* (Paris, 1900).

In an Alsatian village inn (winter, 1833) Schmitt, the forester, is telling a circle, including the rich burgomaster Mathis, whose girl Annette is about to marry Brehm, a *gendarme* officer, his strange experience during a winter fifteen years ago that day. The inn was filled with guests, the storm howled without, when suddenly sleigh bells sounded, and in came a Polish Jew who asked shelter and went his ways the following morning. A few hours later the Jew's horse, running loose, was caught. On the highway lay a bloodstained cap, but no trace of the man's murderer ever was found. As all listen sleigh bells jingle, the inn door flies open and in walks a Polish Jew, saying "The peace of God be with you!" Mathis, respected for his charity, was the murderer of the Polish Jew who had come into the inn fifteen years ago that night; his fortune founded on the gold he robbed. The ghastly coincidence of storm, sleigh bells, entrance of the Jew and his greeting thus repeated on day and hour, makes him swoon with terror.

In bed in the upper room where he has been laid, Mathis has a dream. He is in a court of justice. Standing before the judge he first denies, then confesses his crime; and the judge condemns him to be hanged by the neck until he is dead. As the hangman and his assistants come forward to seize him Mathis cries out in despair and awakes, but does not escape the sentence pronounced by the phantom judge on the testimony of his victim's ghost, for he is found dead in his bed in the morning.

## FROM OTHER LANDS

## "LE SAUTERIOT"

### (*The Grasshopper*)

SYLVIO LAZZARI. , Book by Roche and Perrier after Keyserling's drama *Sacre de Printemps* (Chicago, 1918). An opera on a Lithuanian subject by a Tyrolese of Italian descent, most of whose works have been given in Paris. A musically effective score with dramatic pages.

Orti, the little Lithuanian, nicknamed "The Grasshopper," stands by the bedside of dying Anna (wife of peasant Mikkel, whose natural daughter Orti is) as the curtain rises. In Orti's hand is medicine, three drops an alleviant, ten drops certain death. Trine, Anna's old mother, tells the Lett legend of the mother whose prayer that death might take her in her babe's place was granted, and Orti, despised household drudge whom nobody loves, wishes she might die. The Grasshopper is secretly in love with Indrik, but the only girl he has eyes for is Madda, Mikkel's young sister.

At the village festival Indrik, who has quarreled with Madda and been cast off, fights with Josef, Madda's new swain, and as knives flash Orti rushes forward in time to seize Josef's hand and prevent his fatal thrust. The heroine of the festival, Indrik makes love to her. A few days later, however, he goes back to Madda, and the poor little Grasshopper, with nothing left to live for, remembers Anna's medicine and takes ten drops.

*Die schwarze Kashka* (*Black Kashka*, Breslau, 1895) by Georg Jarno, book by Blüthner, is an emotional modern score. The Moravian peasant girl, Kashka, refuses gold the Pomeranian villager, Stortbeck, offers her when he learns her child is his son Peter's babe, and when Peter marries the girl, his father turns him out. Kashka's jealousy (Act II) makes their life wretched. When his father accuses Kashka of infidelity, Peter seizes a stake and wounds Stefan, innocently suspected. Then, thinking he has killed him, he takes an agonized farewell of his wife, both crying that all their troubles come from excess of love. Peter rows across the lake in a terrible storm and his boat disappears. Kashka goes mad. Kissing her little one farewell, she walks into the water and drowns.

## "JENUFA"

Leos Janaček. Book by Gabriele Preiss after her drama of Moravian peasant life, *Jeji Pastorkyna* (Prague, 1916). A modern verist score preferring dramatic declamation to melody, with national dance rhythms underlining the action's tragic moments. "Apparently . . . in these middle European countries . . . you shave yourself to a Krakoviak, cut a man's throat to a Mazurka and bury him to a Czardas" (Newmann). Bie praises highly the thoroughly Slavonian soul and color of the score.

The widow Burya owns the village mill. Her handsome, drunken grandson, Stewa, loves Jenufa, with "cheeks smooth as a satin appleskin," who is anxious to have him marry her, lest she be disgraced. Old Burya's step-grandson Laca also loves Jenufa. After Stewa has staggered away to sleep—he has been drinking and dancing at the tavern, where he escaped being drawn for army duty—Laca tries to steal a kiss from Jenufa. When she refuses him her lips he slashes her across the cheek with his knife in a jealous rage.

The sexton's widow is Burya's daughter-in-law and Jenufa's mother. Stewa has not made Jenufa an honest woman and, hidden in her mother's cottage the wretched girl has borne Stewa's boy. The widow prays God it may be taken, yet sends for Stewa. He comes, looks at sleeping mother and babe—and refuses to right his wrong. He is about to marry Karolka, daughter of the village judge. Then Laca comes. His love is test-proof. Though he winces at the thought of acknowledging Stewa's child, he rejoices to think his affection will make his poor sweetheart happy. But the girl's mother, noticing his shudder of repulsion, tells him the child is dead. Laca gone, while Jenufa still sleeps, the sexton's widow takes the little innocent and, lest it reveal her daughter's disgrace and prevent her marriage to Laca, drowns it under the ice. Jenufa, waking and groping for her babe, is told it died of fever and her mother's story of Laca's tenderness moving her, she agrees to wed him.

In her home, where the wedding guests, including Stewa and his fiancée Karolka are gathered, the sexton's widow is about to bless her daughter when the villagers' shouts announce the discovery of the murdered babe. They threaten Jenufa, whom they accuse of the crime. As the mother confesses she has done the deed for her daughter's sake, and is led away, Karolka turns with loathing from Stewa and casts him off; while Laca, whose love endures through shame and disgrace, comforts the unhappy girl who realizes at last that she has "found that greater love on which God Himself looks down with favor."

*Scaramouche* (Copenhagen, 1922) by Jean Sibelius, book by Knudsen, is a fantastic pantomime set to mystic, rhythmically piquant music. Though his wife, Biondina, is a passionate dancer, Leilon has a weak heart. One night Scaramouche, a wild fiddler, joins the guests and plays music so diabolically sensuous that Leilon stops the dance and flings him out. Blondina, fascinated, follows him to the forest in the moonlight and does not return until the next morning. Having soothed Leilon's anxieties, she is arranging her hair when in the mirror she sees Scaramouche's pale face. He has come to urge her to flee with him. When he refuses to leave her, Blondina stabs him and hides his body behind a tapestry. A broad stream of blood, however, flows out on the polished floor; Blondina slips in it, falls and dies as Leilon, his heart giving way, himself falls dead on her corpse.

*La Griffe* (*The Claw*, Paris, 1923) by Felix Fourdrain, book by Sartène, in whose music dramatic vigor and lyric tenderness alternate, takes us to Servia. The old wine grower Marovitzis is paralyzed. He cannot move but hears Milena, his son's young wife, curse her brutal, fifty-year-old husband who abuses her. Milena loves and is about to flee with a young painter. The steep cellar stair is broken but her husband does not know it. He takes the fatal step into space. His wife watches him break his neck in murderous silence, old Marovitzis writhing in awful struggles to make his paralyzed vocal cords send forth a cry of warning. When his daughter-in-law steps near him, however, the old man manages to clutch her, and in a last prodigious cramp strangles her with his "claw."

*La Martire* (*The Martyr,* Naples, 1894) by Spiro Samara, book by Illica. A verist "scenic novel" with dramatic pages of music introduces a Servian Tristan different from his Wagnerian namesake. In Sulima on the Danube, Tristan Petrovitch, head stevedore, when his wife Natalia tells him little Anka, their child, lies dying, tears the gold watch from her waist and hurries to give it to Nina, the cabaret singer for whom he buys wine. Coming home only to knock Natalia senseless (Act II) Tristan laughs gayly on learning little Anka is dead; but when Michael, the sailor, is about to beat him up, Natalia, recovering from her faint, intervenes. Later (Act III), Michael begs Natalia to flee with him and she promises to do so after the funeral. She changes her mind, however, for Tristan, coming home wildly intoxicated, finds she has accomplished her verist "Liebestod," closing door and window and lighting the charcoal burner.

*Aspasia* (*The Palikar Woman,* Sondershausen, 1892) by Karl Schröder is a tale of the Greek War of Independence (1835), the heroine taking her uncle's, the *palikar* Apostolos, bullet in her breast to save Bavarian Konradin who is marrying Destima. *Evanthia* (Gotha, 1893) by Paul Umlauft, a verist score of the same period, shows the *palikar* Miles Standish, Euthymios, making Dimitrios his John Alden and Evanthia, the Hellenic Priscilla, marrying Euythimios whom she does not love. When he discovers the girl loves his friend, Euthymios rushes off to meet a Turkish bullet and is brought back to bless the lovers with his dying breath. *Mara* (Berlin, 1893) by Ferdinand Hummel is a verist tragedy of the Circassian hills. Mara's husband, Eddin, has shot her father in self-defense and, hiding in a hollow tree, hears his brother-in-law Djul threaten to cut the throat of his baby boy, Dmitri, unless Mara reveal his hiding place. Crawling out, Eddin is about to be pushed from the precipice to dash on jagged rocks hundreds of feet below, when his faithful wife shoots him to save him from the more horrid fate. As she buries her face in her hands, little Dmitri, who wants to play with her, runs from the hut and tries to pull down Mara's fingers with the merry cry "Cuckoo!" Musically negligible, *Mara* offers an exceptionally ingenious pyramiding of veristic horror upon horror in situation.

## 7. Fairy Operas

### "HÄNSEL UND GRETEL"

ENGELBERT HUMPERDINCK. Book by Adelheid Wette (Weimar, 1893). "A genuine Christmas gift for the musical world" (Eisenmann). The first great success among post-Wagnerian operas, and a striking contrast to the brutal veristic scores. Its naïve German folk tunes have been beautifully worked out in contrapuntal style, around the action of one of the most charming German fairy tales. Notable are: the Prelude, a noble orchestral review of the main themes; the songs "Suse, liebe Suse" (Act I), "Ein Männleih steht im Walde," the touching "Abendgebet" (Evening Hymn), Act II; the "Witch Dance" and the "Knusper Walzer" (Act III).

The hungry children Hänsel and Gretel, broom making in their hut, find a pot of milk and dance around it, neglecting their work. When their mother comes home and angrily chases them, the milk is upset and she drives the little ones out to the forest to pick berries. Back comes her husband from town. He has sold his brooms to advantage. But where are the children? In the forest? The anxious parents hurry out. Perhaps they have strayed to the Ilsenstein, where the wicked witch lives in the cottage into which she lures innocent children and bakes them into gingerbread in her oven.

In the forest (Orchestral Interlude pictures the "Witch's Ride") Gretel is winding a flower wreath under a tree when Hänsel comes running up, his basket full of strawberries. The children eat them, but when they set out for home twilight shadows fill the woods and will-o'-the-wisps and misty shapes frighten them, till the Sandman comes and lulls them to sleep, and as they drowsily sing their "Evening Hymn" angels descend to watch over them.

The Dewman wakes the little sleepers and as they rub their eyes they see the Witch's gingerbread hut and begin to nibble at it. Up comes the old hag and bans them with her magic wand: Hänsel is put in a pen to be fattened with apples and raisins, while Gretel must help the Witch. The oven is red hot and the Witch rides triumphantly around her hut when Gretel, who has overheard the magic spell, repeats it, gets the Witch in front of the oven (she has already released Hänsel) and then she and her brother quickly push her in and close the door. The Witch must burn and that is the end of her. As the children hug each other in their joy, the oven falls apart with a tremendous crash and all the gingerbread boys and girls who make up the palings of the fence around the Witch's cottage turn into living children once more and rejoice in their release. Father and mother appear to embrace their little ones, and the curtain falls on the hymn of praise to the Heavenly Father for His help in time of need, in which all join.

*Marienkind* (*Mary's Child*, Dresden, 1902) by Eduard Behm is akin to Humperdinck's *Hänsel und Gretel* in spirit and naïve melodic charm. The Angel Gabriel, entertained in the guise of an old beggar on Christmas Night in the poor woodcutter's hut, carries little Mary to heaven with him. But Gabriel hurries the woodcutter's little daughter out of heaven when she denies having opened its forbidden thirteenth door, and not till, as the king's dumb wife, is she to suffer death by flame for having let a demon steal her babe (Gabriel took it), does she admit she lied and, praised by Gabriel, sink joyfully into her husband's arms.

## CINDERELLA, THE SLEEPING BEAUTY, AND OTHER FAIRY-TALE FAVORITES

The Cinderella story, common to all nations and known to every one, has been told in opera an infinite number of times. *Cendrillon* (Paris, 1810) by Isouard, "the Greuze of music," preceded Rossini's *Cenerentola* (Rome, 1817) in which Cinderella's father is a comic figure, the duet he sings with Dandini still regarded as a masterpiece of musical humor. *Aschenbrödel* (Zurich, 1879) by Schulz-Beuthen, develops Wagnerian leading themes symphonically instead of melodically, music paralleling action. Incidental personages take the place of the unkind stepmother and instead of shoeing her sisters with a red-hot slipper Cinderella forgives them. A "Lentil Song" with dove-twitter accompaniment deserves mention. Other German "Sleeping Beauty" operas include *Aschenbrödel* by Langer (Mannheim 1878), and by Leo Blech (Prague, 1905). Wolf-Ferrari's *Cenerentola* (Venice, 1900; as *Aschenbrödel* (Bremen, 1902), not an operatic success, musically "is on a plane with Humperdinck's *Hänsel und Gretel*" (H. Teibner). *Cendrillon* (Paris, 1899) by Jules Massenet, a pleasing score with a charming Gavotte, transports the Cinderella story to a Louis XIII period atmosphere, and tells it with tender love scenes, comic interludes, and graceful dances. *Cœur de rubis* (*The Ruby's Heart*, Nice, 1922) by Gabriel Grovlez to a book by Montoya, is a graceful modernist score with a Cinderella heroine.

Among ballets *La belle au bois dormant* (*The Sleeping Beauty*, Petrograd, 1890) by Tschaikowsky follows Perrault's fairy tale, and the Entr'acte Symphonique (describing Princess Aurore's hundred-year slumber on her bed of unfading roses) is charming. There are *Dornröschen* operas by Langer (Mannheim, 1873) and Hofer (Nuremberg, 1918). Humperdinck's *Dornröschen* (Frankfort, 1902), an opera, with sun, moon, stars, asteroids, and other incidentals introduced for spectacular effect, has beautiful musical pages: the "Flower Song" (Act I), symphonic ballad, "A hundred years later" (Act II), and "Ballet of the Stars" (Act II). *Le petit chaperon rouge* (*Little Red Riding Hood*,

Paris, 1818), by François Boieldieu, book by Théaulon, dedicated to King Louis XVIII, is a sophisticated version of the nursery tale in which Nanette's enemy is a human wolf of noble birth named Rodolphe, and the tale ends happily when he is robbed of the charm which makes her love him. More recent is *Le chaperon rouge* (Paris, 1900) by François Thomé. *Old King Cole* (Cambridge, 1923) has been set by Vaughn Williams, using old English country dances in modern orchestration; and there is *Hans Däumling* (*Hop-o'-My-Thumb*, Brunswick, 1911) and *Zwerg Nase* (*Dwarf Nose*, Brunswick, 1912) by Max Clarus. Hérold's *La clochette* (Paris, 1818) transposed the tale of Aladdin and the Wonderful Lamp, making the former Azolin and the latter a bell. "Few scores contain so many numbers excellent as regards workmanship and inspiration" (Arthur Pougin). *Il gatto dagli stivali* (*The Cat and Boots*, Milan, 1924) by Giuseppe Mariani is a modern opera which tells the tale of "The Marquis of Carabas."

## OPERAS ON "COMBINED FAIRY MOTIVES"

Fairy-tale operas or ballets which combine different motives are frequent. One is *Ma Mère l'Oye* (*Mother Goose*, Paris, 1912) ballet, by Maurice Ravel. The music, orchestrated from the composer's *Cinq pièces enfantines* for four hands, with rare and precious play of tonal hues, "makes dream people seem real in an atmosphere of childish legend." Princess Florine has hurt herself playing with an old woman's spindle and falling asleep, the old woman—Mother Goose in disguise—brings heroes and heroines of nursery fairy books into her dreams: Beauty and the Beast, Tom Thumb, Laideronette, the Empress of the Pagodas, and finally Prince Charming, to lead her to enchanted gardens of Fairyland. *La boîte à joujoux* (*The Box of Toys*, Paris, 1913) by Claude Debussy is a ballet similar in type; and *Dolly* (Paris, 1913) by Gabriel Fauré, a ballet, tells of the spoiled little girl who lives in a tiny cottage set in a Noah's ark landscape, and coming into its garden plays with clowns, listens to a stroller's serenade, dances with a dancer and finally drops her other friends to go off with a ferocious Spanish pirate, all these goings-on scandalizing a black rabbit wearing coquettish pantaloons of white lace, which lives in the garden. *Der holzgeschnitzte Prinz* (*The Prince Carved of Wood*, Hellerau, 1923) by Béla Bartók, fairy dance pantomime, is the tale of the willful Princess who preferred to dance with the Prince Carved of Wood instead of the really true Prince, though the latter sacrifices crown, mantle and golden curls for her. But mad dancing is too much for the Wooden Prince, who gets broken, and the good Fairy brings the true Prince and Princess together. It has been called "a masterpiece of modernist music," the "Dance of the Trees," the "Dance of the Waves" and the "Fourth Dance, compellingly beautiful" standing out.

*La forêt bleue* (*The Blue Forest*) by François Aubert, book by Chenevière (Geneva, 1912; Boston, 1913) combines motives from "Red Riding Hood," "Hop-o-my-Thumb," and "The Sleeping Beauty" in a modern score in which the "woodland mood" is especially well established by the music. The story carries the other characters into the forest after an opening scene in which Prince Charming sees the Princess in a fairy village and falls in love with her, and ends with the waking kiss in her castle and the chime of wedding bells.

*Die versunkene Glocke* (*The Sunken Bell*, Berlin, 1899) by Heinrich Zöllner after Hauptmann's drama, a melodious score, is the tale of Heinrich, bell founder in a Harz village, who, enchanted by an elf, Rautendelein, abandons wife and child to follow her (Act II) and leaves her when his dreams reveal his child bearing a pitcher filled with his wife's tears (Act III), as the elf descends into a well to yield herself to Nickelmann, an Elemental (Act IV). But Heinrich's wife has drowned herself in despair, and her dead hand touching the sunken church bell stolen by a forest demon, sends Rautendelein back to her lover to give him the kiss of death (Act V). Outstanding are the orchestral Preludes (Acts I, V); and the closing "Dawn Chorus" with angel voices and bell chimes.

### Operatic Fairy Tales by Hans Andersen

Hans Andersen's "The Swineherd and the Princess" is one of the most delightful of Scandinavian fairy tales. Ivar Hallström's opera *Per Swinaherde* (Stockholm, 1887) is a setting rich in Swedish folk color; *Le Porcher* (*The Swineherd*, Paris, 1924) Swedish Ballet, a Ferraud orchestration of Swedish folk tunes to accompany a pantomime version of the story.

### "THE TRAVELING COMPANION"

Charles Villiers Stanford. Book by Sir Henry Newbolt (Liverpool, 1925). An adaptation of the Hans Andersen fairy tale in a romantic musical score, outstanding the Incantation Scene and the Wizard Scene.

In a church—it is midnight—a dead man lies awaiting burial. John entering the church to seek shelter from the storm, is followed by two robbers. About to despoil the corpse—they claim the dead man was their debtor—John ransoms it. Then (change of scene) the townsfolk tell John of the beautiful Princess who will marry the man who guesses her riddle but who, if he fail, joins the other skeletons dangling from the walls of the royal garden.

John takes to the road and arrived at the royal palace is given twenty-four hours to answer the question the Princess has asked—to tell the thought in her mind. But the mysterious Traveling Companion who has joined John tells him all will be well.

When the Princess (Incantation Scene) rides on the whirlwind to the Wizard's cavern and bids him tell her something on which to fix her mind he tells her to think of his head. But the Traveling Companion has ridden the tempest with the Princess, unknown to her. As she flies back to the palace he steps forward, and one blow of his sword sweeps off the Wizard's head.

The next day when the Princess asks her question John draws the Wizard's gory head from beneath his cloak and holds it up. He has solved the riddle and released the Princess from slavery to the sorcerer. And the Traveling Companion—none other than the dead man whom John had befriended—takes his departure to whence he came, his debt of gratitude repaid.

Waldemar Wendland's *Das kluge Felleisen* (*The Wise Knapsack,* Magdeburg, 1909) is an operatic version of "Big Klaus and Little Klaus." *Le petit elfe ferme l'œil* (*Little Elf Shut-Eye,* Paris, 1924) ballet-pantomime, music by Florent Schmitt, calls up the fantastic dreams—a wounded stork, evil black cavalier, writing lesson, Chinese fairy tale, doll wedding—of Andersen's story in a brilliant orchestral score. *Le jardin du paradis* (*The Garden of Paradise,* Paris, 1923) by Alfred Bruneau, dramatically obscure, is Andersen's fairy tale exploded by de Flers and Caillavet into a four-act opera libretto by means of a literary "puffed wheat" process. The story—there are noble pages of music—presents in vast detail how Prince Assur, despairing of his betrothed's faithfulness, enters Paradise to punish Mother Eve, originator of all human wickedness, only to be subdued by the eternal feminine, and return to the maid he had unjustly suspected. August Enna's ballet *The Shepherdess and the Chimney Sweep* (Copenhagen, 1901) and his intimate melodious opera, *The Little Match Girl* (Copenhagen, 1897), are Andersen fairy tales; and in his *Yolka* (*The Christmas Tree,* Moscow, 1913) the Russian decadent Rebikoff has set the same tragic subject—a little match-girl, freezing to death in the snow, admiring the glittering Christmas tree through the pane of the rich merchant's house—to weird harmonies. Among other musically important Andersen operas may be mentioned Ehrenberg's *Anneliese* (Düsseldorf, 1922), dealing with the awakening of mother love in a girl's heart; Mraczek's *Der gläserne Pantoffel* (*The Glass Slipper,* Brünn, 1902), and

Leoni's *Ib and Little Christina* (London, 1901). The Austrian ultramodernist Felix Petyrek's *Die arme Mutter und der Tod* (*The Poor Mother and Death* (Münster, 1925) is a setting of one of the loveliest, most pathetic of all Andersen fairy tales.

## Two Gozzi Fiabe

### "CRISPINO E LA COMARE"

#### (*The Cobbler and the Fairy*)

Luigi and Federico Ricic. Book by Piave after Carlo Gozzi's *fiaba* (Venice, 1850). One of the Venetian story teller's happy combinations of farce and fairy tale. The opera is reckoned among the best of post-Rossinian *opere buffe*. Annetta's ballad-vending song "Pretty Stories" (Act I) ; the Cavern Scene, and Annetta's concluding "So glad a moment I have never known," stand out.

Crispino the cobbler (17th century Venice) and his wife Annetta are in despair. Their miserly landlord, Don Asdrubale, is about to evict them for nonpayment of rent. When Annetta enters the café where Asdrubale is drinking coffee, none buy her ballad sheets, and he demands his rent, but—Annetta is pretty—hints he will not insist on it if she be kind. When she tells poor Crispino he rushes off to drown himself in a well, but a fairy rises from its black depths and tells him not to despair. He must give himself out for a famous doctor and any patient at whose bedside she does not appear will be cured. Off go Crispino and Annetta rejoicing.

Crispino's shingle excites the derision of his neighbors, especially Mirabolano, the apothecary, but when Crispino cures a wounded stonecutter doctors cannot help, they change their tune.

Crispino's success goes to his head. He builds a stately mansion on the Grand Canal, ignores old friends and illtreats Annetta, driving her out of the house. Then he berates the Fairy to whom he owes his good fortune. She touches him and sinking beneath the earth he finds himself in a vast subterranean cavern. There stand images of Time and Judgment and the Fairy wears a death's head. She points to a row of candles, some burning brightly, some about to go out, and tells the cobbler his candle flame will soon flicker, but that Annetta will live long and happily to spend his money. Repentant and alarmed, Crispino begs to be allowed to see his dear wife and children once more, and wakes to find himself at home where Annetta sings her joy at his return.

*Die Feen* (Münich, 1888) by Richard Wagner after Gozzi's *fiaba,* "La donna serpente" ("The Snake Lady") is an early score influenced by Weber and Lachner. The fairy Ada can become mortal only if her lover Arindal, King of Tramond, stand a test— no matter how repulsive she seem he must never lose faith in her. Gozzi turns the fairy into a snake and the lover by kissing her wins her for his wife. Wagner turns the fairy into a stone which melts and becomes human under the influence of Arindal's passionate song (Act III). The experiences Arindal undergoes in his efforts to win his love drive him mad, but like Lucia and Ophelia "the madder he gets the better he sings," and after a brilliant aria he recovers his reason with his sweetheart and, turned into a fairy himself, enters fairyland to live happily ever after. *Le lac des cygnes* (*The Swan Lake,* Moscow, 1876), by Tschaikowsky, a ballet with charming instrumental waltzes, is the tale of an enchanted swan maiden, poor Odette, whose plaintive cries when she circles castle towers as her lover Prince Siegfried is about to wed Odillia, sorcerer Rothbart's daughter, who has impersonated her, stop the ceremony, but do not prevent Siegfried from being drowned in the magic lake where she joins him in death. *Le lac des fées* (*The Fairies' Lake,* Paris, 1839) by François Auber, spectacular grand opera is Scribe's version of a Musäus' fairy tale. A student steals a fairy's veil as she bathes in a lake and marries her, but when he goes mad in a debtor's prison his wife induces the Fairy Queen to rescue him so that they may live happy ever after.

Auber's *Le cheval de bronze* (*The Bronze Horse, Paris,* 1835), one of his best scores, a Chinese fairy opera in which the song, "Là-bas, sur ce rocher sauvage," may be mentioned, translates Stella, the Grand Mogul's daughter, too shy for earth, to the paradise groves of the planet Venus. There Prince Yang-Yang flies to her on the magic bronze horse but those who visit Venus may not tell what happens to them, and the Prince joins other flyers (the mandarin Tsing-Tsing and Yanko, the Chinese country boy, both of whom love Peki, the tea-house keeper's daughter) as a wooden image before the pagoda. Finally Peki makes the trip, keeping her own counsel, and disenchants the tattlers, and pagoda gongs chime for Yanko and herself, Stella and the Prince.

*Casse-Noisette* (*The Nutcracker,* Petrograd, 1892) by Tschaikowsky, is a ballet version of Hoffman's fantastic tale of events in a burgomaster's home on Christmas Eve. His daughter Marie's toys come to life, she befriends the Nutcracker, set upon by the others, and the grateful toy man carries her off to the Sugar-Plum Fairy in the kingdom of sweets. Of the seven dances (a favorite orchestral suite) the "Waltz of the Flowers" is a favorite.

## 8. *Symbolic Operas*

Whether or no, as some authorities, either in jest or earnest contend, the future of metaphysics lies in the symbolic opera and ballet, and Bergson's philosophy is best expounded in music drama and dance, does not come within the scope of the present volume.

*Azraël* (Reggio d'Emilia, 1888) by Franchetti, its libretto termed "a metaphysical monstrosity," its music lacking Puccini's melodic charm, is a tale of two angels. Nefta stays in Heaven while Azraël goes to Hell; then both repair to earth to meet. Handsome Azraël, in the course of incredible adventures, refuses the love of Lidora, witch queen of Brabant, but involves himself with the gypsy queen, Loretta. His soul mate, Nefta (she passes as Sister Clothilde on earth), sees that the better gains the upper hand of the worse in Azraël, however, and Heaven opens for the angelic affinities as the walls of the convent in which they stand crumble. *Das Glück* (*Fortune*, Vienna, 1898) by Rudolf Prochazka, shows Fortune, whom all pursue, hid by hermit Winfried in his cell. After he has told knight, soldier, merchant, and poet she has passed on, happy Fortune makes flowers grow and birds sing, and offers Winfried release from earth's ills if he kiss her. Old Winfried struggles against temptation but seeing the temptress asleep kisses her, and is released from earth's ills—for he is dead. Sadly dropping a rose on him Fortune wanders on to endure man's pursuit. *Lobetanz* (Mannheim, 1898) by Ludwig Thuillé, book by Bierbaum, in which the shuddery "Hangman's Ballad" stands out, tells of a sick Princess whose mysterious malady, cured by the vagrant minstrel Lobetanz's fiddle as he stands on the gallows, may be said to symbolize music's curative powers. *Gugeline* (Bremen, 1901) by the same composer has been called "a weaker *Lobetanz*. *Ilsebill* (Karlsruhe, 1903) by Friederich Klose, a modernist dramatic symphony rather than opera, book by Von Hoffmannsthal, uses the North Sea folk tale of the fisherman's wife who induced a rescued magic flounder to make her count, duke, king, emperor and pope, but when she asked to be made God Almighty returned her to her odorous hut, to symbolize those whom greed for power hurls back into obscurity when they seek to rival God.

*Die Rose vom Liebesgarten* (*The Rose of Love's Garden*, Elberfeld, 1901) by Hans Pfitzner, a romantic redemption opera, symbolizes the gaining of Love's paradise by the soul suffering has transfigured. The pictures of the Edenic world are "expressed in music of well-nigh supernatural clarity and beauty." Siegnot is given the sword as guardian of the Garden by the Virgin of the Star as nature awakes to blossom. But he forgets his trust to pursue the forest nymph, Minneleide, who (Act II) repulses him, preferring power to love, though captured by the Night Wanderer he is wounded in her defense. In the evil Night Wanderer's underground cavern Siegnot pulls down its supporting columns, and in a death of atonement escapes his foe; while Minneleide, protected by the mystic rose her lover gave her, accompanies his body to the Garden's gate. There the Star Virgin, bearing the Sun Child in her arms, calls them both in to share the life eternal. *Le festin de l'araignée* (*The Spider's Banquet,* Paris, 1912) by Albert Roussel, a ballet pantomime, stages the insect world to impressionistic music in the symbolic tale of the Spider and the Fly (Butterfly). The Ants have dragged off a fallen rose petal when the Butterfly enters, entangles herself in the web and is killed. The ballet ends with the "Funeral of the Ephemerid," after its brief life on earth has been reviewed.

### "THE PIPE OF DESIRE"

FREDERICK SHEPHERD CONVERSE. Poem by George Edward Barton (Boston, 1906; New York, 1910). A score of notable originality whose beautiful lyric pages poetically symbolize the truth that those who die for love's sake have not died in vain.

As Nature awakes in the forest, Iolan, the country boy, wandering in the woods meets the Old One, the Elf King, and mocks the powers of his magic pipe—the pipe with which Lilith lured Adam to her arms in Eden Garden. Iolan weds Naoia on the morrow, and in his joy, though the Old One tells him it is death for a mortal to discover its secret, he puts the Pipe of Desire to his lips and plays. Before him, borne on music's tide rise visions of wealth and joy, roses twine around his cottage, Naoia smiles her greeting from the threshold where their children play. He calls on his beloved to come to him. Alas, she appears with garments torn and bleeding face—to die in his arms, for the curse of the forbidden music has overtaken her! Iolan blasphemes but the Old One takes the pipe and the country boy's soul passes to a burst of wild, joyous sound, for those who die for love leave behind a life achieved.

### "DER FERNE KLANG"

#### (*The Distant Sound*)

FRANZ SCHREKER. This opera (Frankfort on the Main, 1912), symbolizing the human soul's yearning for a visionary ideal, shares with *Der Schatzgräber* the reputation of being the composer's most genially conceived score. The world of the real and the unreal are dramatically contrasted in its music, in which the "Nocturne," an orchestral Intermezzo "depicting Fritz's soul state with visionary beauty" (Act III) is a notable page.

Fritz bids Grete adieu, renouncing love for music. The stake in a bowling game, Grete is lost by her drunken father to an innkeeper, from whom she flees only to follow an old procuress. Grete (Act II) now is an inmate of a Venetian disorderly house, though "enshrined in her heart, like a sacred relic," is the memory of her first love. One evening she offers herself as a prize to him whose narrative most moves her and her companions. The winner is Fritz, who is shocked to recognize his first love and repulses her. Her self-respect destroyed, the poor girl's "last remaining purity" leaves her. (Climaxing symphony of worldly enjoyment with gypsy orchestra, Italian mandolinists, off-stage choruses, gondoliers' cries, laughter and merriment.) Fritz (Act III), still hunting the "Distant Sound" writes an opera, *The Harp*. It is hissed. Brooding in an all-night theater restaurant, the composer, a moribund failure, realizes he has ruined his life for the sake of a vague ideal when, dying in Grete's arms, the "Distant Sound" for the first time echoes in his ear in enchanting perfection—" 'The Harp' sings the music of the spheres!"

## "DIE KÖNIGSKINDER"

### (*The Royal Children*)

ENGELBERT HUMPERDINCK. Book by Rosmer (New York, 1910). In this opera the composer has drawn on the wealth of German folk melody, but the music comments a deeper symbolic meaning. Outstanding are: the Prelude, introducing the *Königskinder* motive; the Goose Girl's "Prayer"; and the noble orchestral Prelude (Act III), a great lament for the tragic fate of the royal children, for all humanity's children royal in soul, whose ideals and dreams of beauty are destroyed by the power of the drab commonplace of everyday.

Before the witch hut in the Hellawald, the Goose Girl dreams, surrounded by her geese. The old witch has brought her up but the girl's instinctive goodness rebels against kneading a magic death loaf at her foster mother's command. The King's Son enters, loves her at sight, and offers her his crown, for he has wandered out into the world to find a queen, and senses the Goose Girl has a royal heart for all her rags. She yields to his love but, about to flee with him, the Witch's spell holds her back. The King's Son curses her cowardice. Not until a star falls from the skies and the magic lily stalks growing before the hut blooms, will he return to her. Burghers of Hellabrün (their music typifies the everyday) arrive, following the return of the Witch, to ask who will reign in their city. He shall be king, she answers, who rides through the gate when the bells ring the midday hour on the city's festival day. And, as the Goose Girl prays, the golden star falls from heaven and the petals of the magic flower unfold!

In a meadow before Hellabrün the burghers await their king, among them the King's Son. As a serving man at an inn, true to the innocent Goose Girl, he has repulsed the brazen inn maid. The bells chime the hour of noon. At the eleventh stroke the watchmen open the gates. There stands the Goose Girl with her geese, her crown of flowers in her golden hair. Followed by the Minstrel, while the crowd stands speechless, she steps up to the King's Son, who falls at her feet, and acclaims her Queen. But the burghers with rude scorn drive their king and queen out of town though a broommaker's child cries: "They truly *are* the king and the queen!"

It is winter. (A beautiful symphonic Prologue, "Ruined—Perished," precedes the action.) The lost royal children, whom cold and hunger have driven from the cave where they had sought refuge, draw near the Witch's hut. The Minstrel dwells there since the Witch was burned at the stake. Weak and worn, but loving each other the more tenderly, the unhappy pair approach the hut, and the King's Son enters. There woodchopper and broommaker await the return of the Minstrel, searching for the lost ones. To save his love from starvation the King's Son offers his golden crown and—they give him the Witch's death loaf. He carries it out to his love; they share it, and death comes to them gently on the wings of slumber, the drifting snow their winding sheet. Thus the Minstrel and the innocent children of Hellabrün, the only believers in their royalty, find the lovers. And in the golden twilight, with songs of sorrow, they bear to their last rest those the world's blindness and unkindness destroyed.

## "L'OISEAU BLEU"

### (*The Blue Bird*)

ALBERT WOLFF. Book by Maeterlinck (New York, 1919). A French lyric score which comments a most poetic symbolic tale with graceful and fluent music.

Tyltyl and Mytyl, the woodcutter's children, wake from Christmas Eve dreams to obey the Fairy Berylune's command to seek the Blue Bird of Happiness for a neighbor's sick daughter. The diamond in the cap the Fairy gives Tyltyl draws the Hours from the clock to dance, the Souls of Bread, Sugar, Water, Fire, and Light appear, and Cat and Dog speak. When Tyltyl's father knocks the Souls flit through the window with the children as the parents enter to find their babes (as they think) fast asleep.

In Memory Land the children visit with Grandfather and Grandmother, and little dead brothers and sisters; but find the only bird there is black.

In the Palace of Night Tyltyl opens the caverns that hold the plagues and ills; and behind Destiny's forbidden door discovers a garden of beautiful birds. Alas, they die as the children touch them and in the forest beyond the garden, the Spirit of the Oak tries to slay them for seeking the Blue Bird!

In the Palace of Happiness, feasting Luxuries flee to the Cave of Misery when exposed to the ray of Tyltyl's jewel-stone, while the children meet the Happinesses and Joys.

Even the Cemetery from a place of midnight horrors turns peaceful, lovely and serene in the radiance of Tyltyl's gem.

Then, in the Kingdom of the Future, Tyltyl and Mytyl see old Father

Time sending down myriads of unborn babes to earth in fluttering robes of blue, and as Light calls out that she has caught the Blue Bird, the scene changes.

The children are back before their own door.  As the clock strikes one Light, Bread, and the other Souls leave Tyltyl and Mytyl who enter their home without the Blue Bird.

It is Christmas morning and their mother wakes the sleeping children, shaking her head as she listens to the confused tale of their adventures.  But their neighbor Mrs. Beringot's daughter is ill.  Will Tyltyl let her have his bird, the real live bird they own, not the fairy bird they did not find?  A little later the sick girl comes in, well and happy, bird cage in her hand.  As the children play with the bird it escapes, and Tyltyl addresses the audience:  "If any of you should find our Blue Bird, pray give him back to us for we shall need him in order to be happy later on," he says.

*L'oiseau bleu* (Paris, 1894) by Arthur Coquard is also a symbolic fairy drama.

## "DAS SPIELWERK UND DIE PRINZESSIN"

### (*The Bell Chime, and the Princess*)

FRANZ SCHREKER.  An operatic mystery symbolizing the struggle between love and sensuality in impressionistic music, often of dramatic power (Frankfort and Vienna, 1913; revived Munich, 1920).  "A coloristic sea of sound," the Prelude, and music of the "Scene of the Orgy" stand out.

Master Florian has made a magic bell chime whose silver voices ring only in an atmosphere free from animal lust.  But in the castle above the town the Princess has driven away Florian's son (men build a coffin in Florian's cottage for the dying boy, who has returned) after leading Florian's wife and Wolf, his helper, to betray husband and master. The Princess misuses the bell chime at drunken feasts.  Its clear tones veiled, its buzzing still excites the passions of shameless revelers.  Then the Princess decides on an orgy in the town, and the people rage drunkenly through the streets, while she tears off her garments and dances before them.  She promises to yield herself to Wolf, who yearns to possess her, if he will destroy the bell chime; but coming from the coffin of Florian's son, she encounters "an unspoiled child of nature" in the shape of a wandering journeyman.  He offers to cure the sickness which weighs her soul, and drawing forth a magic flute, plays— and the bell chime begins to sound.  When it rings in crystal purity at the height of the Princess's mad orgy, Wolf in vain destroys it.  Princess and journeyman, united in "pure and understanding affection," ascend the path to the castle in the rosy sunset, for a night of celestial love without a morrow.

## "DER SCHATZGRÄBER"

### (*The Treasure Digger*)

FRANZ SCHREKER. In all Schreker's operas sex and animal impulse struggle with the ideal. Here a magic lute discloses hidden treasure (the necklace bestowing youth and beauty), the longed-for ideal; while woman, following a baser urge, opposes its realization. The scene of action is a medieval Teutonic kingdom of legend. *Der Schatzgräber* has been called Schreker's best work (Frankfort on the Main, 1920). The "Treasure Theme" (Act I), "Cradle Song," orchestral Interlude (Act III), a glowing picture of a night of love, and the tone-painting of the "Heavenly Vision" stand out.

The Queen's emerald necklace (youth and health) has been stolen (Prologue). When the King's fool advises recourse to Elis, a wandering minstrel whose magic lute reveals hidden treasure, the King promises him "a woman," for under the motley beats a yearning heart.

Els, a forest inn servant, has had her love slave, Albi, murder three suitors for the necklace's sake. She has sent him to slay a fourth when Elis enters and tells her how the music of his lute led him to a dead man and a necklace of jewels in the forest and gives the latter to Els. As Albi rushed in crying "Murder!" all rush out. Els—ready to sacrifice her virtue for the minstrel—flings her arms about Elis' neck, and breaks down as the bailiff seizes him for murder.

Elis is saved on the gallows by the Fool, and rides to court promising to find the jewel thief by means of his lute. Els knows discovery threatens, has Albi steal the lute, and decides to surrender the necklace voluntarily to Elis and save them both.

Luteless Elis, entering Els's chamber by moonlight, swears never to seek to discover the mystery surrounding the necklace which she gives him; and she yields to him, crying, "Love me, even in the hour you find you do not trust me!"

When the bailiff enters as the minstrel is being fêted at a royal banquet and—Albi has confessed under torture—accuses Els of the crime, this is just what Elis does not do. Then the Fool, claiming Els was the woman due him, leads her into banishment when Elis disowns her.

Els, wearing away of a broken heart (Epilogue) nursed by the Fool, dies with Elis (who has "found himself") to console her last moments with a radiant vision of paradise attained.

*Fairyland* (Los Angeles, 1915) by Horatio Parker, book by Brian Hooker, is a scholarly score with a medieval background to lend color to symbolic meaning. After mystic and mysterious adventures, King Auburn and Rosamond meet at the stake, where the latter is to be burned as recreant to her vows, and when she touches Auburn with pity's hand, faggots fail, chains drop off, and while nuns (Church) and soldiers (State) flee, the people turn into fairies and the lovers mount the throne of Fairyland (the Ideal). *The Immortal Hour* (Glastonbury, 1916) by Rutland Boughton, book after Fiona Macleod's play, a modern symbolic score, is by an outstanding exponent of the newer British music drama. Dalua, Lord of the Hidden Way, lets Eochaid, young King of Irin, and Etain, lost Princess of the Shee, the fairy folk, wed. When Midir, Etain's lover from the hidden Land of Heart's Desire, breaks in on the lovers' "Immortal Hour" of felicity, Eochaid cries out in despair as he leads Etain away. Dalua lays his hand on the King's brow and says, "Naught is left but the Dream of Death." Eochaid (the earthly) must yield when Etain (the soul) is called home.

*Arlecchino* (Zurich, 1918) by Ferrucio Busoni parodies the bathos of older operas in a series of heavy comic episodes, ending with Arlecchino, supposed to typify depths of hidden thought, crying out to his fellow actors, "You are all comedians!" *Micarême* (Wiesbaden, 1920) by J. Brandt-Buys, is "a glorification of the Carnival spirit in music." *L'avviatore Dru* (Lugo, 1920) by Pratello, sets a futuristic aviation libretto to Mascagnian music. *Graziella* (Kiel, 1921) by Mattausch, a modern music drama with a fine Prelude (Act III), tells how after Ubaldo's "malicious animal magnetism" has led Graziella to betray her husband, she does her seducer to death in a horrid way when his evil influence wanes. *Die Hochzeit des Faun* (*The Faun's Wedding*, Wiesbaden, 1921) by Bernard Sekles, is a burlesque modern dream play, "tonally subtle." In confused action amid forest glades aswarm with nymphs and fauns, a Bostonian falls asleep when wooed by the "lady faun," Quillauna, and nymph Lyra, her lover Silvio punished for infidelity in a land of free love, weds him amid dadaistic cries. For the opera's symbolic program the reader is referred to Morr's libretto. It may enlighten him.

### "THE LOVES OF THREE ORANGES"

SERGE PROKOFIEFF. Book (Chicago, 1922) after Carlo Gozzi's *L'amor delle tre melarancie*. A dissonant, impressionistic score of dramatic power has outstanding pages: the "Royal March"; "Marche à la Cantonade"; the Prince's "Laughing Song" which covers the whole *tessitura* of his voice; and the Prince's and Princess's duet in the desert "Thank you, dear Prince."

In his palace where the King of Trifle rules, his son the Prince, poisoned by a hateful aunt, lies ill. The only thing that will cure him is a hearty laugh which the court tries in vain to call forth. At last, the sight of the somersault the ugly witch, Fata Morgana, turns as she is cast out of the palace produces the curing laugh; but Fata Morgana lays a curse on the Prince: he will have to fall in love with three oranges and shall know no happiness till his love is returned.

Setting out with his servant Truffaldino, the Prince finds in the desert the three oranges of his quest. Each contains an enchanted Princess but two have died within their rinds for lack of water and only the third, Nicoletta, survives. With her the Prince returns to court, and though she first is turned into a rat, the tale ends with old Fata Morgana sinking through a trap into hell flames, while the Prince and Nicoletta live happily ever after. The ultramodern work has been called "the most amusing burlesque opera of the day."

*Echo* (Chicago, 1922) by Frank Patterson, an American symbolic opera, sings man's victory over evil. Acanthia, shipwrecked on the isle of the Echo Folk (Destructive Lusts), as she tries to escape with the Wanderer repulses Yfel (Base Desire), who has scantily draped charmers dance to tempt her companion, and dashes from Cunnan's (Evil Counsel's) hand the inebriating cup ere she flees with her rescuer in a boat to an orchestral Finale. *Zwingsburg (The Bastile)*, Ernst Krenek's "scenic cantata" (Berlin, 1924) uses dramatic modern dissonance to symbolize the mass, yearning for escape from serfdom. The mob attacks the "Bastille," scenic embodiment of Fate's compulsion, whipped up by the organgrinder's bitter tune of daily slavery, to be flung back defeated and to relapse into servitude. *Erwartung (Expectation,* Prague, 1924) by Arnold Schöenberg, a mimodrama, to atonal music of powerful tension develops the psychosis of a woman mourning her dead lover's body before a rival's castle, in lamentation lasting thirty minutes through three changes of forest scenery. *Irrelohe (Flame of Madness,* Cologne, 1924) by Franz Schreker, synchronizes voices and orchestra in a partly atonal, dissonant score with symbolic action. The Irrelohes (18th century Bavaria) are cursed with hereditary satyriasis. Villager Peter exists because Count Heinrich's father met his mother in a mad moment. When Eva, Peter's fiancée, offers herself to the Count he, overcoming his inhibitions, says they must be wed in church and they are. When they come out Peter flings himself on his half-brother, is strangled by the latter, and as Irrelohe Castle flames (incendiaries have been busy) Eva cries "Out of blood, ashes, and flame rises pure love, triumphant over sinful lust!"

## "WOZZEK"

Alban Berg. Book after Büchner's drama (Frankfurt, 1924). An Austrian ultramodernist's operatic reaction to symbolism, described as "a descendant of Schreker's *Ferne Klang.*" In fifteen scenes, each a definite musical composite (Act I—Suite; Act II—Symphony; Act

III—Variations, Inventions) the voice moves from speech to declamation and thence to song (lyrically Marie's "Cradle Song" stands out); both in orchestra and vocal parts "psychological and musical *strettos* of effect are synchronized"; and the vocal demands are such that "a singer needs a year's rehearsing" to sing his part.

Wozzek, the hero, is the ordinary "man in the street"—symbolizing the poor, weak, and despised in the hands of those who wield the power. His wife Marie, sensual and obstinate, is weaned away from poor Wozzek by the animalistic drum major, who jeers at the wretched husband till the idea of murdering Marie takes root in his soul. After he has done so Wozzek commits suicide, and the curtain falls on his orphaned child playing merrily over the dead bodies.

*Der Sprung über den Schatten* (The Leap Over the Shadow), by Ernst Krenek (Frankfort, 1924), an ultramodern score in contrapuntal style, introduces jazz fox trots in a masked ball scene, and satirizes the "blues." Its symbolic idea is that "No one can jump over his own shadow," that is, go beyond his own limitations. A mystical soulmonger makes the people with whom he comes in contact dance as he pulls the strings, to find in the end his human puppets are more clever than he is.

*Arlequin* (*The Harlequin*, Paris, 1925) by Max d'Olonne, a score with effective lyric pages, symbolizes the death of dreams brought in contact with life's realities. Christine, Princess of a Happy Isle of Fancy, falls in love with a clever actor, son of humble folk on Capri, and elopes with him. Thence, when his own townsfolk mock his efforts as an artist, he takes his wife back to the Happy Isle, where she dies of her shattered dreams, and he drearily mounts the throne his father-in-law insists he occupy, disillusioned with love and life.

## "L'ENFANT ET LES SORTILÈGES"

### (*The Child and the Enchantments*)

Maurice Ravel. Book by Colette (Monte Carlo, 1925). A ballet opera which symbolizes the griefs and joys of childhood in a poetic lyric fantasy. Dance and song are associated throughout the score, rich in delicate, ingeniously rhythmed melodies. Aside from the dances the shepherd "Scene of Lament," based on an old French air, the Duet between the Child and the Princess, and the burlesque "Scene of the Figures" stand out.

Surrounded by neglected school books, the Child is reproved by his mother for laziness and left in disgrace. The door shut the Child flies into a rage, strikes the tame squirrel, chases the cat, tears up his copybooks, pulls down the tapestries with nursery figures of shepherds and shepherdesses, and says: "I am free and very naughty!" But when he drops into the armchair, it shakes him out, and dances a minuet with a Louis XV shepherdess—the figures stepped out of the tapestry when the Child tore it down—thanking heaven it is rid of the brat. Then the grandfather's clock, whose pendulum the Child has torn out, reproaches him sadly, and recalls the happy hours it used to strike. Next the British teapot talks "kitchen English" to a china cup on the floor and they dance a fox trot. The Child takes refuge by the hearth but the fire darts out and threatens (Gigue) while the ashes try to choke him. Frightened and lonely, he hears the Watteau shepherdesses lamenting their "blue dog" and their "dear green lambs" which the naughty boy destroyed. And while he sits on the floor, crying big, round tears, comes the Princess of the fairy tales, who gently reproaches him for his cruelty, and shows him her torn and tattered book. After a passionate Duet she leaves her little lover vainly trying to find the torn pages of his book of fairy tales among the tatters of his arithmetic. Out steps a little old man, Arithmetic, followed by columns of grinning figures, which dance madly about the terrified Child.

At last a big black cat and a white cat lure the Child into the moonlit garden, filled with the voices of frogs and insects of the night. There the Child hopes to taste the joy of independence, but the dragon flies abuse him because he stuck a pin through one of their sisters; the bats (Round of the Bats), because he has killed one of them; and after a dance interlude by the Dragon Flies (American Waltz) and a Frog Interlude, the squirrel the Child wounded scolds him from a tree. Next all the creatures decide to punish the Child and surround him threateningly—only to fall to fighting among themselves. In the struggle the squirrel falls wounded and the Child, full of pity, bandages its paw with a ribbon. The creatures cry in surprise, "Why, he's binding up the squirrel's wound!" and seeing the Child has become his better self, they solemnly escort him to the house and when he calls "Mother" the curtain falls.

*Die Frau im Stein* (*The Woman in the Rock*, Stuttgart, 1925) by James Simon, a "drama for music" by Lauckner, stylistically-unmodern, but melodious, interprets the Greek Ariadne legend symbolically. Theseus slays the Minotaur (raises a people to a higher cultural plane), but aboard ship prefers Phædra's merry laughter (pleasures of the everyday) to Ariadne's dark charm (serious beauty of the Ideal). Ariadne, abandoned in Naxos, wails till the flinty rock takes her into its cold bosom. *Traumliebe* (*Dream Love*, Weimar, 1925) by Hubert Pataky, is a "score which expresses passion's most delicate psychic shadings"—Werner's *buffo* "Drinking Song" stands out—in a grisly somnambulistic tale. Painter Harald has a "dream girl" whose picture he cannot limn, for he sees her face only in dreams. After a party with his friend, Richard, and the latter's young wife, Ingerolde—his studio and their apartment in the next building are connected by a frail bridge hundreds of feet above a stone pavement—Harald falls asleep. In his dream his unknown love leads him to a trysting place beneath a linden tree in the moonlight: he clasps her as Richard, waking, looks out on the bridge and cries "Traitors!" and—Harald sees he holds his friend's wife in his arms. Startled by the husband's voice, the somnambulists lose their balance and fall to their death.

*Mira* (Essen, 1925) by Kurt Oberhoff, a polyphonic dramatic score using guide themes as "tonal symbols," the "Song of the Harp" outstanding, introduces the Christ in a "timeless" drama symbolizing the soul's redemption through love. In a camp before Jerusalem gates, one Leper, hope of living again in his children lost, suffers above the rest. His "Song of the Harp" all strings but one snapped in the desert, sings his yearning. Mira, lured by his song, first pities, then loves him. When a Wanderer (Jesus) promises to cure, he scoffs, then rages when he learns what he has lost, and nobly rejecting Mira's embrace, love—in the higher psychic sense—effects his cure. *Die Môra* (Düsseldorf, 1925) by Ernest Viebig, a quarter-tone colored score, rich "in ethically barren songs of blood," sings an old husband who voluntarily kills himself when his young wife's lover is too cowardly to pour his poison. The "Môra," demon spirit of a haunted weir, symbolizes the erotic frenzy which leads to murder. *Traumspiel* (*Dream Play*, Bochum, 1925) by Julius Weissmann, an opera after Strindberg's drama, with fine symphonic Preludes and lovely pages characterizing the "Child of Heaven," is undramatic. God Indra's daughter descends to earth to redeem mankind, and a series of fantastic dream pictures of her human suffering ends with her meeting the Christ in Fingal's Cave, and the Poet's Vision of Him walking the waves as he hands the "Child of Heaven," returning to Paradise, Man's plaints in the form of a petition.

## "THE ALCHEMIST"

CYRIL SCOTT. Book by the composer (Essen, 1925). "A Parable in Three Scenes with Music," with a picturesque medieval setting, its underlying symbolic meaning (the writer is indebted to the composer for the explanation) is "that many persons spend their lives acquiring possessions and never take the necessary time to enjoy them, since the great 'elemental' desire ever goads them on to acquire *more*." An opera combining modernity in music with pronounced melodiousness. "Beautifully orchestrated, it is the greatest 'corker,' to conduct since *Elektra*" (Albert Coates).

A Youth seeks out the Sage in his cottage, and heedless of his pretty daughter sitting at her spinning wheel, begs for the magic spell which will grant him his heart's desire, "shining gold and jewels brighter than the moon." The Sage gives him the scroll whose incantation will force the Elemental to do his bidding for an hour, warning him all gold has its alloy.

At a rude forest altar, the Elemental appears in obedience to the magic words and successively, at the Youth's wish, coffers of golden coin, caskets of gems, a palace, dancing girls and guards, royal robes and crown, are conjured forth. But—he must wish unceasingly, for if he stop wishing during the hour the Elemental is at his command, the spirit will devour all it has called out of the nowhere. The Youth's invention runs dry. He demands a jester, and at his suggestion a rain of flowers, a ring of dancing gnomes and a huge dog materialize, and then—the jester disappears. Relentlessly the Elemental hurries him and at last, amid the fluttering wings of a flock of birds he asks for, the Youth rushes off in terror as the spirit moves toward him and casts himself on the heaped-up treasures.

Back at the feet of the Sage, the Youth sees the light as the latter gives the Elemental a little dog, and bids him straighten out its tail, which the spirit labors vainly to do. The secret of happiness—which the Youth sought in gold—lies within the soul, the Sage tells him; and the Youth begs to be accepted as his pupil, to learn the alchemy of the soul's transformation which opens Heaven on earth before death comes.

# CHAPTER IX

## THE BAROQUE

### 1. *Germany*

*Blanik* (Prague, 1881) by Zdenko Fibich, an opera whose passionate Love Duet is outstanding, tells the conversion of the hero Rudenz, henchman of the foreign invader during the Thirty Years' War, into a Bohemian Tell when the ancestress of his race leads him into the magic hall in Blanik mountain, where the old heroes of the Czechs slumber. Luigi Denza's *Wallenstein* (Naples, 1876) is an unsuccessful musical portrait of the great imperialist general. *Oberst Lumpus* (*Colonel Good-For-Naught,* Wiesbaden, 1892) by Theobald Rehbaum, a clever *opéra comique,* tells how a German musketeer captures a cask of French gold doubloons at Herbsthausen (Thirty Years' War), deserts, buys coach and four, hires servants and lives riotously in Munich as "Colonel Lumpus" till his general turning up, he wins back his forfeited life at dice and marries the innkeeper's daughter. *Der Schelm von Bergen* (*The Knave of Bergen,* by Behm (Dresden, 1899), Ernst (Zwickau, 1885), and Sahlender (Heidelberg, 1895), after Heine's legend of the hangman of Bergen, tell of the social outcast who so yearned for equal rights that he danced with the Duchess at a masked ball in Düsseldorf. Forced to unmask, he was recognized and about to be slain by the courtiers when the Duke, admiring his daring, knighted him and led out his wife, Barbara, on the floor.

*Der Trompeter von Säkkingen* (*The Trumpeter of Säkkingen*)· by Victor Nessler, book after Scheffel (Leipzig, 1884), is a commonplace hypersentimental score with a song, "Es war so schön gewesen," known wherever cornet is blown. Werner, a trumpeter in the days of the Thirty Years' War, saves a countess and her daughter, Marie, from rebel peasants but when (Act II) he makes love to the girl, is told to pack, which he does after playing "God guard thee, love, it was too fair a dream" while Marie faints. But saving Baron Schönau's castle from clodhopper assailants, and proving that blue not red blood runs in his veins, he is married to his sweetheart. E. Kaiser's *Der Trompeter von*

347

*Säkkingen* (Olmütz, 1882) a worthier musical setting (which also applies to Bernard Scholz's *Der Trompeter von Säkkingen,* Wiesbaden, 1877), has Werner meet Marguerite, the Baron's daughter, in Rome, where he has graduated from trumpeter to choirmaster of the Sistine Chapel. Werner resigns his position to marry the girl after the Pope has made him Marquis of Camposanto, and her father consents to the union, not because of the title, but because Werner "has elevated German music and art." Franz Beier's *Der Posaunist von Speikingen* (Cassel, 1899) is a successful parody of Nessler's score.

*Ännchen von Tharau* (Hamburg, 1878) by Heinrich Hoffmann, a folkwise opera, its song "hit" of the same title repeated *ad nauseam* through the score, is the pretty girl beloved by a young student and an old professor of theology, old Simon nobly sacrificing his own hopes and rescuing young Johannes from life in the army during the Thirty Years' War to make the young girl happy. *Das Glockenspiel (The Bell Chime,* Dresden, 1913) by J. Brandt-Buys, a melodious modern score, shows a newly-wed peasant boy and girl (time of Thirty Years' War) hiding in a monastery bell tower. He is hiding from Wallenstein's recruiting sergeants; she is hiding from the monks. The bells of the tower chime for the first time in centuries when, her boy husband absent, the girl, besieged by monastic admirers, rings them in her hour of need; but Cupid saves her and brings all to a happy conclusion. *Dr. Eisenbart (Doctor Ironbeard,* Mannheim, 1922) by W. von Waltershausen, dramatic, with effective use of folk themes, has Eisenbart, a learned doctor, called to a baroque residential castle to help the Princess Florinda secure a son and heir. Florinda, a boyhood sweetheart of the doctor, wishes him to use extra-medical and personal means to attain this end and Eisenbart, thinking his wife has deceived him, is first inclined to yield, then, his better self getting the upper hand, he is jailed, to be pardoned on the scaffold when cannon roar out the birth of a baby prince due to some other practitioner's offices, and he can return happily to his wife Kate.

## 2. France

The reign of Louis XIV, greatest of all baroque monarchs, especially its earlier and middle portion, sums up the period in France. *Le roi l'a dit* (*'Tis the King's Command*) by Léo Delibes, book by Godinet (Paris, 1873), is a comedy of manners rich in graceful melodies. The Marquis de Moncontour is lucky: he catches Madame de Maintenon's escaped parrot and is presented to Louis XIV, the Sun King. Confused, he admits of a son when he has only four daughters, and when Louis commands he be presented, has to drill his farm boy, Bénoit, lover of his daughter's maid, Javotte, to play the part. Bénoit quickly becomes a model young noble of the day, sets fire to the convent in which Montacour's daughters live and demands one of them for a wife. But when Bénoit is wounded in a duel, the Marquis tells King Louis he is dead, and Bénoit recovering to find himself a farm hand once more, is glad to settle down quietly with Javotte. *Die Heirat wider Willen* (*The Compulsory Marriage*, Berlin, 1895) by Humperdinck, book after Dumas' play, with melodic pages of genuine sentiment, and August Chapuis' *Les Demoiselles de Saint-Cyr* (Monaco, 1921) a graceful lyric score, both tell the same tale. The nobles, Montfort and Duval, compromise Hedwig and Louise, young girls of blue blood, by secret meetings in Saint-Cyr Park. Put to eating dry bread in the Bastille till they marry the girls, they do so, but desert their wives to fly to Madrid, where Montfort's friend, the Duke of Anjou, reigns as King of Spain. Their girl wives follow, and after Montfort has rescued Hedwig from his royal friend's too pressing attentions, the husbands find they love the wives thrust upon them and hurry happily back to Paris.

## "LA CHANSON DE FORTUNIO"

### (*Fortunio's Song*)

JACQUES OFFENBACH. Book by Crémieux and Halévy (Paris, 1861). The score has been called "one of the most charming and stylistically unified works of musical literature."

In the Paris of Louis XIV, Fortunio, the advocate, in his younger days, wrote a song no woman's heart could withstand. But marriage and middle age turned the young sentimentalist into a matter-of-fact domestic tyrant, neglectful of wife and abusive of clerks. Then one of the latter found the forgotten song under a pile of legal papers, passed it along and all Fortunio's clerks soon were joyfully singing it to their sweethearts, for it had kept its magic power. Fortunio, when he found his clerk Valentine using his own song to make successful love to his master's wife, yielded to its forgotten magic, sang it to her himself, and took her into his forgiving arms while his clerks sang the air in chorus. The operetta was one of Offenbach's greatest successes. The famous song which gives the work its title, set to the words of the Requiem Mass, was sung at the composer's burial service in the Madeleine church, Paris.

*Jean de Paris* (Paris, 1812) by Boieldieu, in which the Seneschal's *buffo* air, "Qu'à mes ordres," stands out, is the tale of the French Dauphin who not wishing to marry the Navarrese Princess selected for him on sight unseen, meets her as plain "John of Paris" in a Pyrenean inn and there falls in love with her. *La Vallière* (Kiel, 1922) by Oberleithner retells to engaging music King Louis' love affair with gentle Louise, whom his fickle heart so soon forgot; and *Raymond* (*The Queen's Secret*, Paris, 1851) by Ambroise Thomas, a gloomy opera, its Overture occasionally heard, is the tale of the Man in the Iron Mask. *La Marquise de Brinvilliers* (Paris, 1831), an operatic curiosity, written by *nine* composers, Auber, Batton, Berton, Blengini, Boieldieu, Carafa, Cherubini, Hérold, and Paër, dramatizes the historic poisoner of Louis XIV's day, whose trial involved the noblest families of France in a revolting criminal scandal.

### 3. *England*

Baroque England is the Stuart England of King Charles I, King Charles II, King James I and, by extension, of good Queen Anne. *L'uomo che ride* (*The Man Who Laughs*, Milan, 1920) by Arrigo Pedrollo, book after Victor Hugo's famous novel, is a dramatic score of the period, its outstanding pages the "Invective in the House of Lords" and a Death Scene. Philpot's *Nigel* (Birmingham, 1910) is a melodious opera whose tale is one of the day of Roundheads and Cavaliers.

### "I PURITANI"

#### (*The Puritans*)

VINCENZO BELLINI. Book by Pepoli after Sir Walter Scott (Paris, 1835). The composer's last score, to his worst libretto, contains some of his best sentimental melodies: Arthur's "A te, o cara," Elvira's Polonaise, "Son vergin vezzosa" (Act I), her Mad Scene, "Qui la voce sua soave," and "Vien diletto" (Act II), and her pathetic "A una fonte afflitto" (Act III).

Lord Walton holds Plymouth Castle for Cromwell, but lets Lord Arthur Talbot, the Cavalier lover of his niece Elvira, enter in to marry the girl. Instead, Arthur, who places loyalty above love, improves the chance and rescues from captivity Queen Henrietta, widow of Charles I, condemned to death by Cromwell (?). His Puritan rival, Sir Richard Forth, seeing Henrietta wrapped in Elvira's veil lets them pass. Poor Elvira, who has seen Arthur flitting with a veiled lady, thinks him untrue and goes mad. She devotes herself (Act II) to singing those tender Italian *cantilene* of which Bellini was a master until Arthur, chancing to meet her (Act III), wins her back to sanity with the true tale of what had happened. Captured by the Puritans rather than leave his love, Arthur is to be shot at sunrise, when the arrival of a pardon permanently restores the reason Elvira again lost when he was condemned to death.

Sir George Macfarren paid his respects to "Old Rowley" in his *King Charles II* (London, 1849); and in Brüll's *Königin Mariette* (Munich, 1883) the plot of an attractive musical score turns on Mariette Durand's, the Calais dressmaker's impersonation of Queen Catherine of Braganza, Charles II's Portuguese wife, to let her join him safely in Scotland (1660). With Charles's triumphal entry into London, "Queen Mariette" is rewarded, and her French sailor lover Edmond's suspicions set at rest. *A Scene in Time of Plague* (Moscow, 1901) by César Cui after Pushkin, shows young Lord Walsingham drinking madly by candlelight while death carts rumble through black London streets in the days of the Great Plague. Outstanding is the song of Mary, his mistress, "Time was," Scotch in character and pathos. In *Robins Ende* (*Robin's End*, Mannheim, 1909) by Eduard Künneke, a Cornish Squire who married Catherine, a London milliner, discovers King Charles in his innocent helpmeet's closet. About to shoot his liege (he scoffs at Charles' claim to kingship), he releases him when he signs Robin's patent as Duke of Cornwall. When soldiers arrive and lead him, not to the scaffold, but to his estate, it is squire Robinson's end as "Robin," his beginning as Duke of Cornwall. *A Tale of Alsatia* (London, 1925) by Vincent Thomas, a graceful lighter score, book by Cornforth and Ingram, recreates the famous thieves quarter in a London "'picaresque' which has affinities with *The Beggar's Opera*," in the days of King James I.

## "LUCIA DI LAMMERMOOR"

GAETANO DONIZETTI. Book after Scott's novel, *The Bride of Lammermoor*, by Cammerano (Naples, 1835). Musically *Lucia di Lammermoor* is considered Donizetti's masterwork, though *Lucrezia* is more brilliant and dramatic. The Mad Scene (Act III), a brilliant *scena* with recitatives and flute *obbligato*, remains one of the coloratura soprano's great display arias. From a musical standpoint the "Sextet" is the finest number of the score; and in its music the individual parts each reflect the character of the singer as revealed by the action.

Lord Henry Ashton rages at his sister Lucia (park of Lammermoor castle, 1700) when he finds she loves Edgar of Ravenswood, mortal enemy of their house; but Lucia meeting Edgar later in the park—he is off to France on a political mission—the lovers plight an eternal troth. A forged letter prepared by Henry makes Lucia believes Edgar untrue. She marries Lord Arthur Bucklaw and, the ink scarce dry on the marriage contract, Edgar enters, concludes Lucia has betrayed him, and flinging her ring at her feet as he wildly curses her and her house, rushes out, while Henry follows to challenge him to the duel.

Edgar, last of his line, broods among the tombs of the Ravenswoods, planning to spit himself on Henry's sword on the morrow.

Suddenly, as all sleep in Lammermoor castle, shrieks sound. Lucia's mind has given way, and she has murdered her husband in the bridal bed. Appearing among the disheveled wedding guests she sings her "Mad Scene" and falls dying with its last note. Edgar, in the church-yard, hears the castle bell toll the death chime, learns Lucia is dead, and plunging his dagger into his heart, falls lifeless among the tombs.

Mazzucato's melodious *La Fiadanza di Lammermoor* (*The Bride of Lammermoor,* Padua, 1834), was cast in the shade by Donizetti's score.

### "MARTHA"

FRIEDRICH VON FLOTOW. Book after Saint-Georges (Hamburg, 1844; Paris, 1843, as a ballet, *Lady Harriet*). Melodious airs in French *opéra comique* style and folk songs, including "The Last Rose of Summer," which Patti immortalized, as well as the "Spinning Quartet" (Act II) lend it charm.

Lady Harriet Durham and her friend Nancy, weary of life at Queen Anne's court, yearn for rustic simplicity and hire out as Martha (Harriet) and Julia (Nancy) to two young farmers, Lionel and Plunkett, at Richmond Fair. Their employers fall in love with their help (Act II). Lionel steals Martha's rose as he shows her how to spin, and pro-poses when she sings "The Last Rose of Summer." Plunkett courts Julia. But blue blood cannot mingle with red. The girls deny their hearts, refuse the calloused hands of honest toil and disappear at night with cousin Tristram's aid, leaving their lovers disconsolate. When (Act III) Lionel sees Martha among the Queen's attendants at a royal hunting party and flings himself at her feet, she has him jailed for insolence and insanity, and he is dragged off singing "Ah, may heaven to you grant pardon!" But Plunkett (Act IV) carries Lionel's ring—sole heritage of a mysterious father who left the boy to be brought up on the Plunkett farm—to Queen Anne. She recognizes it as that of the dead Earl of Derby, and Lionel regains his sequestered estates and title. Now he scorns Harriet. Yet when she again comes to him humbly dressed as Martha, at Richmond Fair, his heart melts. Clasp-ing her, as Plunkett does Julia, the quartet sing "The Last Rose of Summer" forecasting wedded bliss to come.

### 4. *Spain*

### "IL BARBIERE DI SIVIGLIA"

#### (*The Barber of Seville*)

GIOACHINO ANTONIO ROSSINI. Book by Sterbini after Beaumarchais' comedy, *Le barbier de Séville* (Rome, 1816; New York, 1825). (Among the audience at the New York *première* were James Fenimore Cooper, Fitz-Greene Halleck, the poet, and Joseph Bonaparte, ex-king of Spain, then living in Bordentown, N. J.) Perhaps the best operatic example of Italian musical humor, it destroyed the vogue Paisiello's *Barbiere di Siviglia* (Paris, 1776) had enjoyed. Its music has flowing melody, merry mood, unity of invention and situation; even Rosina's colorature arias appear natural, and not a concession to virtuoso technique. Among the famous airs are: Figaro's "Ecco ridente" Serenade; the "Largo al factotum" and "Una voce poco." The scene of action is seventeenth century Seville.

Rosina is Doctor Bartolo's lovely ward, jealously guarded by him, since he plans to marry her. Count Almaviva, who has fallen madly in love with her is about to give up all hope of meeting her, after serenading her at her window, when Figaro the barber, poet, romancer, intriguer, and terror of husbands, at home with razor, pharmacist's syringe, and guitar, smuggles the Count into the house as a billeted soldier, but no sooner have the Count (as Lindoro, a poor youth) and Rosina exchanged notes than he is discovered and ejected. A second invasion, in which Almaviva appears for the singing master Basilio, supposed to be ill, is more successful and while Figaro shaves Doctor Bartolo, to prevent his watching the new singing master, the latter gives Rosina her lesson (*The Singing Lesson*). Rossini left it to the prima donna to choose an air to sing in the "lesson" *ad libitum,* like the *ad libitum* cadenza in a violin concerto. "Di tanti palpiti" from Rossini's *Tancredi* was favored for a time, and Grisi sang a violin piece vocalized, Rode's "Air with Variations." The "Laughing Song" from Auber's *Manon,* Arditi's "Il bacio" waltz, the "Bolero" from Verdi's *Vêpres siciliennes* (Patti); Proch's "Air with Variations," Strauss's "Voce di Primavera" waltz, and "Ah, non giunge" from *Sonnambula* (Sembrich); Arditi's "Se saran rose" waltz and the "Mad Scene" from *Lucia* (Melba); and the Queen of the Night's air, "The vengeance of hell is in my heart," from *Die Zauberflöte,* and "Charmant oiseau" from David's *Perle du Brésil* (Galli-Curci) are among these "lesson arias"; a song like "The Last Rose of Summer," or "Home, Sweet Home," being used as an encore).

Basilio, the real singing teacher, now makes his appearance; but Figaro gets rid of him by means of a well filled purse. Taking advantage of the opportunity, the Count arranges to elope with Rosina. Bartolo (to whom "Lindoro" gave Rosina's letter as an excuse to see her) shows the girl the letter she wrote her lover. Thinking herself scorned, Rosina confesses the proposed elopement and Bartolo hurries off for a notary to marry them. But Figaro and Almaviva entering, the latter kisses away Rosina's doubts and Bartolo's notary arriving before Bartolo, they are married out of hand. When the Doctor enters —too late—Almaviva turns Rosita's fortune over to him and, his rage appeased, he blesses the lovers as the curtain falls.

## "LE NOZZE DI FIGARO"

### (*The Marriage of Figaro*)

WOLFGANG AMADEUS MOZART. The "model" German comic opera. Book by Da Ponte, after Beaumarchais' comedy (as *Die Hochzeit des Figaro*, Vienna, 1786; *Le mariage de Figaro*, Paris, 1793). The story is the sequel to that of *The Barber of Seville*. The play was a continuation of the author's attacks on aristocratic license, governmental autocracy and existing political institutions. The Austrian Emperor Josef II forbade the performance of the opera until assured all "that might give offence in a Court theatre" has been removed. The score is rich in lovely melodies, among them the "Voi che sapete" aria, the airs "Non so più," "Non più andrai," and the famous "Zephyr Air," "Che soave zeffiretto. "The dominant characteristic of the music is that wise and tender sympathy with the follies and frailties of mankind which moves us with a deeper pathos than the most terrific tragedy ever penned" (Streatfeild, *The Opera*). The time is the Baroque Age, the scene, Aguas Frescas, three miles from Seville.

Countess Almaviva (Rosina of "The Barber") discusses with Figaro the fact that her maid and Figaro's fiancée, pretty Susanna, has caught the Count's roving eye. The Count already has dismissed page Cherubino for finding him flirting with Barberina, the gardener's daughter, but when peasant lads and lasses come to thank him for resigning his *jus primæ noctis*, he forgives Cherubino and takes him back. When the Countess hears from Susanna that her husband has begged the girl to meet him in the garden (Act II) they dress blushing Cherubino in girls' clothes to keep the assignation and shame the philanderer; while the Count is delighted to put off Figaro's wedding to Susanna because of the appearance of old Marcellina, from whom Figaro borrowed money, promising to marry her if it were not returned. But Figaro turns out to be Marcellina's illegitimate son (Act III) and after peasant boys serenade the Countess and peasant girls bring her flowers, the Count invites all to supper (jolly rococo March, Chorus, and Fandango). Figaro, however, has seen his master slip Susanna a note. In the castle garden (Act III) Figaro, whose jealousy has led him there to spy on Susanna, finds Barberina, whom Cherubino had promised to meet, while Cherubino, thinking the Countess (disguised as her maid) is Susanna, tries to steal a kiss and Almaviva turning up as the page slips away, gets a box on the ears meant for him. He gives his supposed Susanna a ring and Figaro, when the real Susanna calls him, thinks her the Countess, woos her tenderly and is soundly thumped by his fiancée who, however, at once forgives him. The Countess having slipped away, Almaviva thinks Figaro is kneeling at his wife's feet and while Susanna slips into a summerhouse, seizes his valet and calls for servants and lights. But when he discovers Cherubino, Barberina, and Susanna in the Countess's clothes in the summer house, he refuses to pardon the lovers till his wife arrives to show him how cleverly he was fooled. Then, like the great gentleman he is, he begs the Countess to forgive him, and the properly assorted pairs move to the château for "The Marriage of Figaro."

*La fille de Figaro* (*Figaro's Daughter,* Paris, 1914) by Xavier Leroux is survived by her more vigorous father.

*La forza del destino* (*The Power of Fate*) by Giuseppe Verdi, book by Piave, after De Rivas' drama *Don Alvaro o la fuerza del sino* (Petrograd, 1862), a transition opera to the richer harmony of *Aïda,* has Leonora's Prayer, "Madre pietosa," as its outstanding melody. In Seville, Don Alvaro, eloping with Leonora, the Marquis of Calatrava's daughter, accidentally shoots the girl's father who surprises them and who dies cursing his child. While Don Carlos seeks his sire's slayer (Act II) Leonora establishes herself as a male hermit, Father Raphael, near a monastery. In Italy where Don Carlos has become Don Alvaro's (now Don Federigo's) closest army friend, Don Alvaro mortally wounded, he reads his letters and the hideous truth disclosed, challenges Alvaro to a duel as soon as he can fight. Alvaro runs him through and thinking him dead, becomes a monk in the monastery near Leonora's hermitage. Near Father Raphael's grot, Don Carlos, who was not slain, resumes the duel (Act III) and is mortally wounded. Lenora, rushing out with flying cowl at Alvaro's cry, is stabbed to the heart by her dying brother as she bends over him and Alvaro dashes himself to death from a precipice as monks enter appropriately singing the *Miserere.*

*Diana de Solange* (Coburg, 1858) by Duke Ernest of Saxe-Coburg, tells a Portuguese baroque palace intrigue whose assassinated heroine dies in her lover's arms. *Donna Diana* (Berlin, 1886) by Heinrich Hoffmann, melodiously sings the Count of · Barcelona's daughter who won Don Cesar de Urgel's heart by affecting a coldness she did not feel; and *Donna Diana* (Prague, · 1894) by Reznicek, is a modern version of the story with an Overture and the heroine's Spanish-Peruvian "Love Song" outstanding. *Das Unmöglichste von Allen* (*The Most Impossible of All Things,* Karlsruhe, 1897) by Anton Urspruch tells Lope de Vega's tale of the proving of the Spanish queen's saying that the most impossible of all things is successfully to guard a woman in love, in Mozartian music with the dramatic scene instead of the aria as a unit. *Donna Kobold* (Vienna, 1916) by Weingartner, in the manner of Auber, is interesting as an attempt to present the polyphony of two different rooms simultaneously on the stage.

*Der Zwerg* (*The Dwarf,* Vienna, 1923) by Alexander von Zemlinsky after Wilde's *The Birthday of the Infanta,* is the tale of the deformed, sensitive dwarf, sport of a spoiled Infanta's whims in the baroque court of King Philip IV. When the Dwarf's tragic, reverent love is mercilessly mocked by the cruel child, he kills himself. Charming dance movements, notably a tragic Bolero, stand out. Schreker's *Der Geburtstag der Infantin* (Vienna, 1923), John Alden Carpenter's *The Birthday of the Infanta* (New York, 1924), and Bernard Sekles' *Der Zwerg und die Infantin* (Frankfurt, 1907) tell the same tale in pantomime ballets. *Tragabaldas* (Hamburg, 1907) by Eugen d'Albert, book by Lothar, its scene Cadiz, "in days when men wore silk cloaks and rapiers," makes lovely Donna Laura pretend her cowardly cousin Tragabaldas her husband to find out if Don Ottavio really loves her, and a series of comic situations ends with Laura and Ottavio falling into each others' arms while Tragabaldas is kicked out.

## "DON GIL VON DEN GRÜNEN HOSEN"

### (*Don Giles of the Green Breeches*)

WALTER BRAUNFELS. Book after Tirso de Molina's play *Don Gil de las calzas verdes* (Munich, 1925). A musical comedy opera by one of Germany's outstanding modern composers, influenced by Pfitzner and Strauss, with a notable Prelude and piquantly colored Dance Intermezzo ("Bohemian dance music such as Smetana loved"), the score racy with Spanish musical rhythms.

Juana's lover, Don Manuel, has deserted her. Passing herself off as a certain Don Gil (disguised in green breeches) the abandoned sweetheart manages by a series of desperate intrigues to prevent her lover's marriage to Inez, a rich merchant's daughter whom he is courting. Her difficulties increase when Inez and her cousin Clara fall in love with the dashing *caballero,* unaware her breeches are not justified in fact, but in the end Juana secures her Manuel and both are happy.

*Die Höhle von Salamanka* (*The Cave of Salamanca,* Dresden, 1924) by Bernard Paumgartner, its slight humorous plot based on a play by Juan Ruiz de Alarcon, a reminiscence of its author's student days (1604-1608) in the Spanish university town, has been criticized as "thin and musically impotent." *Las Meninas* (*The Maids of Honor*) Gabriel Fauré's "Pavane" supplies the music, is a Ballet Russe dance picture, after Velasquez's paintings, of the court of King Philip IV of Spain, first given in San Sebastian, 1916. *Ruy Blas* (Milan, 1869) by Filippo Marchetti, book after Hugo's tragedy, a melodious score with dramatic scenes in Verdi's earlier manner, is the tale of Don Sallustio, prime minister who, his advances rejected by the Queen of Spain, Doña

Maria de Neuburg, achieves a unique revenge. His valet Ruy Blas worships the Queen from afar. Don Sallustio enters him at court as a young noble. He is young, handsome; the Queen's heart inclines to him. Through her he wins wealth, is made Prime Minister and Duke of Garofa and then—his master reveals to the Queen that she has stooped to love a lackey! When the proud woman turns from him Ruy Blas kills himself.

## 5. *Italy*

### "BIANCA"

HENRY HADLEY. Book by Grant Stewart after a Goldoni comedy (New York, 1918). A vivid, musical score, one act, among whose colorful pages are: Bianca's Entrance Song, "Nay, do not rise"; Fabricio and Bianca's Duet, "Against my will"; Bianca's Air, "Now why did I not think of that?" and the final Ensemble.

At the inn near Florence of which Bianca is mistress, Count della Terramonte and Marquis d'Amalfi, rivals for her favor, dice for a flagon of wine. Enter the Cavaliere del Ruggio, a woman hater who orders Bianca about like a kitchen-maid. When Fabricio, who 'loves her, resents it, however, she drives him away. Del Ruggio does not know Bianca has made up her mind to win him until, pretending to burn herself with a hot iron, he touches her hand—and finds it cold. Denouncing her trick, he leaves. Count and Marquis, thinking him the favored man and that he will soon return, decide to leave the inn as well. But their jealousy leads them to draw sword on each other. Bianca cannot stop the duelists but Fabricio, knocking their rapiers out of their hands with the ironing board, takes Bianca—full of admiration for his bravery—into his arms, and the curtain falls on the chorus the noblemen and inn servants raise in praise of love and chivalry.

### "ALESSANDRO STRADELLA"

FRIEDRICH VON FLOTOW. Book after the French by W. Friederich (Hamburg, 1844). The real Stradella (? 1645-1682), dissolute music teacher and composer, wrote seventeenth century operas, *Il Floridoro* the best, while betraying sisters, wives, and mistresses of others. He did not write the *Pieta signore,* whose composer may have been Rossini. The historic fact remains that his life often was attempted by those he wronged. The "Serenade" (Act I), Tarantelle of Fishermen of Capri and Ischia (Ballet) and "Hymn to the Virgin" (Act III) stand out.

Stradella, after serenading Leonora by moonlight on Venice lagoons, carries her off despite the threats of her guardian Bassi, who had planned to wed her. Married in a Romagna village by an aged priest (Bell Chorus), Bassi's assassins, seeking their victim (Act II), are so overcome when at the wedding banquet Stradella sings Salvator Rosa's "Romance," that tears drop from their eyes and daggers from their hands. At the festival of the Madonna, Bassi and his two bravos seek their victim where he sings alone in church (Act III) but, come to slay, remain to pray when they hear him render the "Virgin's Hymn," and Stradella forgives them and is led off in triumph to sing at the festival. *Stradella* (Paris, 1837) by Niedermeyer, makes the tale climax with Stradella's return to Venice where arrested as Bassi (now Doge of Venice) is about to wed the Adriatic, he sings so wildly well that the people insist he be freed. In the scene with the bravi Stradella sings "a paraphrase of the *Dies Iræ.*"

Giuseppe Simco's *Alessandro Stradella* (Lugo, 1863) is another opera on the subject.

### 6. *Russia and the North*

In Russia the personalities of Peter the Great, Catherine I, of Elizabeth and Catherine II have suggested various operas, but Adolphe Adam's *Pierre et Catherine* (Paris, 1829), Auber's *Lestoque* (Paris, 1834), and others yield in importance to Moussorgsky's great opera.

### "KHOVANTCHINA"

MODEST MOUSSORGSKY. A "folkwise music drama in five acts," book by Stassov (Petrograd, 1885). A stirring picture from Russian history it follows historically Glinka's *A Life for the Czar.* The symphonic Prelude ("Dawn in Moscow") with its bell chimes; Tschaklovity's wonderful aria, praying God to protect Russia (Act II), the "Persian Slave Girls' Dance" (Act III) and the Death Chant of the "Old Believers," are among the noblest musical pages.

In the Red Square of the Kremlin, Prince Ivan Khovantsky, captain of the Strelitzi Guard of Peter the Great and leader of the reactionary "Old Believers," opposed to the Czar's new ideas, urges his men to resist the Czar's boyars and soldiers; and Dosistheus, religious head of the Old Believers, saves Marfa, Prince Andreas' cast-off love, from a beating, and the German Lutheran girl, Emma, whom he pursues, from worse; while in Prince Galitzin's home (Act II) the boyar Tschaklovity brings news that Peter has ordered the rebellion put down with an iron hand. In the Moscow quarter of the Strelitzi, where Marfa sings her betrayal and Tschaklovity his glorious patriotic air (Act III), a scrivener rushes in with news that the Strelitzi have been beaten, and Prince Ivan Khovantsky, appearing at a window, bids the people give up resistance. In Khovantsky's country palace Persian slave girls dance and singing girls sing. He rises from the board to accompany Tschaklovity to the Czarevna's council (Act IV), thinking himself forgiven, but is stabbed by assassins on the threshold of the palace while his servants flee. In Moscow, meanwhile, cavalry on shaggy ponies escort the captured Strelitzi, carrying blocks and axes for their own execution, only to be told they are pardoned and free to return to their wives and children. (Vignano's ballet *I Strelitsi*, Padua, 1809, offered a gripping picture of the sanguinary suppression of the revolt.) In the forest the Old Believers, among them Prince Andrea Khovantsky and Marfa (Emma has escaped to marry her lover), clad in white robes mount a great pile of flaming wood to die the "Red Death," but above their glory hymn, led by Dosistheus sound the trumpets of Peter's soldiers, ringing out the old and singing in the new.

*Mazeppa* (Petrograd, Moscow, 1882) by Tschaikowsky, book after Pushkin's *Poltava*, an opera of unrelieved gloom which won the composer the name of "the Tourgenieff of music" contains his finest declamation, Kotchubey's "Monologue," and a macabre "Slumber Song." The wily Cossack Hetman who dared plot against Peter the Great is presented as a Don Juan of the steppes. Maria (whom he has coaxed from Andrew, her young Cossack lover) goes insane after she discovers Mazeppa has had her father killed and, "a Russian Ophelia," wanders to her old home. There, when Mazeppa gives Andrew his death wound, she gathers him into her arms and, in her madness not knowing her lover, croons him into the death sleep with a tender lullaby. *Mazeppa* (Bordeaux, 1925) by Emile Nerini, book by Montoya, presents Mazeppa from an idealized Polish angle, a hero who conquers a kingdom, loses his own heart and is carried off in a wild gallopade of death across the steppes. "Mazeppa's Ride" is a number of dramatic power. The score, by a pupil of Massenet, has melodic charm and is not ultramodern, using Russian folk songs and (Ballet, Act III) Urkrainian airs with effect.

*Czar und Zimmermann* (*Czar and Carpenter*, Leipzig, 1837) by Lortzing, outstanding Peter's baritone air, "Once played I with scepter," is a comedy of mistaken identity. Peter Romanoff, learning shipbuilding on Saardam wharves, is pursued for political reasons by the English and French ambassadors, and Van Bett, the burgomaster (his niece Marie beloved of Peter Ivanoff, a Russian refugee, bribed to point out the imperial Peter), is about to arrest both at a banquet (Act II) when General Lefort arrives to recall Romanoff to Russia. As Van Bett pays homage to the false Czar the true one is revealed on the quarter-deck of the ship taking him home, and Ivan the Less, unfolding a note left by his greater namesake, finds a pardon and permission to marry Marie.

*L'étoile du nord* (*The Star of the North*, Paris, 1854) by Meyerbeer, book by Scribe, shows Peter winning the heart of Catherine, the sutler girl of Vyborg, who loses her reason (Act II) when she sees him drinking with strumpets in the Russian camp, and regains it (Act III) when he plays on his flute the air—"Là, là chérie," made famous on two continents by Jenny Lind—she loved when he courted her, and tells her she is Czarina of Russia. *Das Feldlager in Schlesien* (*The Camp in Silesia,* Berlin, 1843) was turned into the preceding opera by substituting for Scribe's tale one of the escape of Frederick the Great—another flute player—from capture by Croats, and by Russianizing the Prussian grenadier choruses and cavalry marches. In *Santa Chiara* (Gotha, 1854) by Duke Ernest of Saxe-Gotha, Alexis, Peter's son, rages when his wife, Charlotte, refuses his mistress as maid of honor, and orders his physician to give her a dose of poison. But he administers a narcotic and while her coffin stands in the chapel Charlotte is in Naples (Act II) where Saint-Auban, a Russian officer who loves her, arrests a mysterious stranger who has annoyed his sweetheart and finds he is her husband. The latter intelligently stabs himself and makes the world safe for the lovers.

*Der Gefangene der Zarin* (*The Czarina's Prisoner,* Dresden, 1910) by Karl von Kaskel, a distinctive score, outstanding the "Blessing of Swords" and Love Scene (Act II), shows Empress Elizabeth of Russia (1750) mistaking Lieutenant Sascha Romanuski for a rebel Duke of Courland and condemning him to Siberia. But a passionate love scene between soldier and sovereign leaves him captain of her guard where, still "the Czarina's prisoner," he will also be the support of her heart and throne. *The Captain's Daughter* (Petrograd, 1910) by César Cui, after Pushkin, develops a love tragedy of the peasant rebellion of the brigand Pougatscheff, self-styled "Czar Peter III," subdued by Catherine II. Michael Ivanoff's *Potemkin's Feast* (Moscow, 1888) and Ugo Afferni's *Potemkin an der Donau* (*Potemkin on the Danube,* Annaberg, 1897) deal with the Empress Catherine II's triumphal progress through the Crimea, where Potemkin raised whole towns of "false fronts" to please his imperial mistress.

*Christmas Eve Revels* (Petrograd, 1895) by Rimsky-Korsakoff, after Gogol, outstanding the symphonic Prologue (describing the Nativity), is a kind of Russian miracle play. Solokha, an old Cossack witch, plans with the Devil to prevent her son Vakoula, the smith, from marrying Choub's lovely daughter, Roxana. But when, after various complications, the girl says she will marry him if he brings her the Empress's golden slippers, the Devil carries him through the air to the imperial palace, where his Cossack dancing so pleases the Empress Catherine that she gives him her golden slippers on learning of his dilemma and he returns triumphantly to marry Oxana. *Le caprice d'Oxane* (Moscow, 1887; as *Vakoula*, Petrograd, 1870) by Tschaikowsky, rich in poetic melodies, tells the same tale. *Der Bettelstudent* (*The Beggar Student*, Vienna, 1881) by Karl Millöcker, with outstanding waltz song, "Ich hab' sie ja nur auf die Schulter geküsst," is the tale of two Polish students who, in the comic opera Poland of King Augustus the Strong (1704), by wit and courage displayed in various contingencies, win hearts and hands of two noble Polish girls.

*Elga* (Düsseldorf, 1910) by the Bohemian Lyvovsky, and *Elga* (Mannheim, 1916) by the Hungarian Lendvai, Puccini's pupil, after Grillparzer's *Kloster von Sandomir,* tell of Polish Count Starzenski who, surprising his wife Elga in the arms of her former lover Oginski, kills him in a duel and wipes the blot from his escutcheon by forcing Elga to perish with him in the flames of his castle. In *Pan Voyevode* (Petrograd, 1904) by Rimsky-Korsakoff, with fine Cossack and Polish Dances, Incantation Scene, and Swan Scene, a Polish Voyevode (Governor) seeing blue-blooded, orphan Maria out hunting, tears her from her lover, Chaplinsky, and prepares to wed her by force. While the Voyevode's ex-love, the widow Yadviga, prepares poison for the girl, Marie sings her melancholy "Song of the Swan" at the bridal feast. In vain Chaplinsky and his friends rush in; they are overpowered by the Voyevode's guards, led away prisoner, and the feast resumed (Act III) but the Voyevode drinks the poison Yadviga had poured into Maria's cup, and the curtain falls on the lovers' reunion.

### 7.  Baroque Masters of the Brush

Some great baroque painters have inspired operas: *La route d'émeraude* (*The Emerald Way*) by Auguste de Boeck, book after de Molder's novel (Ghent, 1921), presents Rembrandt, "the Shakespeare of Art," in a musical score based on Flemish folk melodies; outstanding Dirk's ballad, "Elle avait la beauté du diable," and Francesca's aria, "Vous avez deviné" (Act III). *Cornelius Schütt* (Prague, 1893) by Antonio Smareglia, book by Illica, romantically paints the Flemish painter (1597-1654) who married two wealthy wives in succession. Sentimental music tells how Cornelius jilts his fiancée Gertrude for Elizabeth, but tiring of love in a cottage, returns to the fleshpots of Antwerp and finds he has lost his inspiration. Sitting with drooping brush in a church nave he hears Elizabeth's voice and hastes to her with open arms but she is a nun, dead to the world, so Cornelius flies to his canvas, limns a Madonna having Elizabeth's features, and drops dead with the last stroke of the brush.

*El Greco* (Paris, 1920) by Inghelbrecht presents the great Spanish painter's (d. 1614) masterpiece, "The Burial of Count Orgaz," as a living picture on the stage in the form of a Swedish ballet, building around it the pantomime tale of a Toledan blasphemer whose brother is stricken by lightning, while he is saved by a maid whose pleas restore his faith.

*Der Sicilianer* (*The Sicilian,* Zurich, 1924) by Karl Heinrich David is a tale after Molière's *Le sicilien ou l'amour peintre.* In his Moresque palace in a Silician town, miserly old Don Pedro jealously guards his lovely Greek slave Isidora. Adraste, a French noble, taking advantage of his skill with the brush, obtains admission to the *palazzo* to paint Isidora's portrait and instead (amid comic adventures) abducts the happy girl. Delicate and effective music is the keynote of the score.

*La chanteuse voilée* (*The Veiled Singer,* Paris, 1852) by Victor Massé, a score abounding in Spanish romances and boleros, with a cornet solo Overture, is a tale of Velasquez (1599-1660) who made dogs bark and horses move in his paintings. Velasquez has married his serving maid and every evening a veiled lady slips from his home and sings in the public square of Seville to earn a few pence for her debt-ridden husband and master.

There is a *Van Dyck* (Brussels, 1845) by Willent-Bordogni, and various operatic portraits of the gloomy Neapolitan, Salvator Rosa. He created the "romantic landscape" and, writer and musician as well as painter, in one of his "Satires" inveighed against the indecency of painting "sprawling, half-naked saints of both sexes." Opera has remembered the savage wielder of a romantic brush in Rastrelli's *Salvator Rosa* (Dresden, 1832), Sobelewski's *Salvator Rosa* (Königsberg, 1848), and *Signor Formica* (Vienna, 1892) by Eduard Schütt.

# CHAPTER X

## THE ROCOCO

### 1. *France*

Lulli and Rameau were the great musicians of the baroque and rococo but, as has been said, "the delicate tinkling of Rameau's music, like the patter of pearls on a silver dish, is too short of breath." Ever since Rameau's time composers have tried to express the spirit of the age when living was cultivated as a fine art with more human feeling, passion, and breadth in their scores, and have largely succeeded in so doing.

Operas whose scene of action is eighteenth century France are numerous. *Le perruquier de la Régence* (Paris, 1838) by Ambroise Thomas sends a fashionable wigmaker of Regency Paris as envoy extraordinary to Petrograd. There Peter the Great has taken the wigmaker's adopted daughter (child of an exiled Russian noble) and the *perruquier* diplomat brings about her marriage to her lover, the Marquis de Forlanges, who won her heart as Firmin, the lawyer's clerk. *Madeleine* (New York, 1914) by Victor Herbert, book by Grant Stewart, is the Paris Opera *diva* who, when her lovers, the Chevalier de Mauprat and the painter Didier, refuse in turn to dine with her on New Year's night (1760), props her mother's picture up opposite her plate, and has the guest dearest to her heart bear her company. *L'amoureuse leçon* (Paris, 1913), Alfred Bruneau's ballet, is Mendès' story of two lovers who have fled from the château's candle-lit ballroom to the green glades of the park. There the Spirit of Love evokes the beaus and belles of Watteau's *fêtes champêtres* who offer their old-time dances as the key to "Love's Lesson." *Fêtes galantes* (Paris, 1914) by Claude Debussy, using the composer's Verlaine song settings, beginning with "En sourdine" shows, in a lyric ballet, a young lover calling up the shades of vanished lovers in a Watteau dream park in a vain effort to communicate his own divine frenzy to a shallow girl. *Les petits riens* (*Trifles*, Paris, 1778) by Mozart was a ballet with Love in a cage delivered by Cupids, and shepherds and shepherdesses playing blindman's buff to charming gavottes. Many different stories have since been adapted to Mozart's charming ballet music; the most recent *Die grüne Flöte* (*The Green Flute,* Vienna, 1923) by von Hoffmansthal. *La fille mal gardée* (Paris, 1828) by Hérold, a rococo romance of shepherd loves, is another of many musically graceful ballets with a rococo setting. Manon, the heroine of the Abbé Prévost's famous novel, has motived the most famous French rococo opera.

## "MANON LESCAUT"

GIACOMO PUCCINI. Book after the *Histoire de Manon Lescaut et du Chevalier des Grieux,* by the Abbé Prévost, his tale "the lovers' book of hours and the romanticists' breviary" (Milan, 1893). Manon's "professional inclination" and temperament make her a grateful subject for musical treatment. Puccini gives the most effective theatric scenes: the coach abduction (Amiens); her episode with de Ravoir (Paris); her meeting with Des Grieux when she is to be deported to America (Havre); and her pathetic death on a Louisiana highway. He tells his tale in elegant conversational manner, rising to real emotion in the tragic death scene, one long, sorrowful duet between the lovers.

Manon, descending from the coach with her brother Lescaut before the inn at Amiens, sets the heart of the student Des Grieux afire. She promises to meet him. Géronte de Ravoir, royal treasurer-general, covets the lovely girl. His coach is in readiness to abduct her while her brother is gambling in the inn, but when Manon appears Des Grieux, carries her off in the old *roué's* equipage to Paris.

In Paris, Des Grieux's pockets soon empty, Manon makes no bones about settling down as Géronte's mistress. He is old and tiresome but she revels in gold, jewels and pretty dresses. (A charming rococo bit, light graceful song and dance, is the "Minuet of Manon's friends.") Returning unexpectedly he finds her with Des Grieux (the passionate Love Duet, "Vieni colle tue braccie") and though she regrets her luxuries, she tells him she prefers Des Grieux's companionship. Warned by her brother that the malicious financier (who has pretended approval of their affection) plans revenge, the girl snatches up her jewels, only to be dragged to jail as a thief, though she drops the jewels at Géronte's feet.

On the Havre quay (an orchestral intermezzo depicts the trip to Havre), the *filles de joie,* the loose women of Paris gathered for deportation to Louisiana, are embarked under guard. Des Grieux's and Lescaut's attempt to free poor Manon foiled, rather than be parted from the pale girl who walks to the ship's side amid the jeers of the crowd, Des Grieux begs to be allowed to work his passage to be near her, and the pitying captain grants his plea.

A gray sky above a vast plain near New Orleans, is the setting for the tale's tragic end. Drooping with fatigue Manon stops. When Des Grieux hurries off to seek water for her she thinks herself abandoned. He returns and she dies, the pathetic lovers declaring their affection for each other in a masterly duet which strikes the true tragic note. Des Grieux, as Manon's spirit passes in his arms, despite his frantic pleas for her not to leave him, sinks fainting on her dead body.

*Manon* (Paris, 1884) by Jules Massenet. Book by Meilhac and Gillé. Puccini's score may be called dramatically more effective; Massenet's is superior psychologically, and gives a better idea of the heroine's "struggle with love and life." The fine Seminary Scene, in which Massenet mingles strains sacred and profane, Manon's song, "Je suis encore tout étourdie," and the "Cours de la Reine" Scene (Act III, in Paris) combine eighteenth century charm and grace with genuine passion.

As with Puccini the opera begins with Des Grieux's flight to Paris in the post chaise (Act I). In Act II, however, Des Grieux is carried off by his father's command from the apartment he shares with his sweetheart. Though rich de Bretigny's mistress (Act III), Manon gives over the pleasures of Paris to follow her heart, and though Des Grieux calls on heaven to help him resist temptation, she abducts him from St. Sulpice Seminary (change of scene) where he is a novice. In a Paris gaming house (Act IV) where Manon takes Des Grieux to make money quickly, Guillot, his losing antagonist, accuses him of cheating. The police arrest Des Grieux and Manon, "his accomplice." In Act V (usually given as Act IV, Scene 2) Manon is on her way to Havre, to be deported to America with other women of loose life. Des Grieux's plot to rescue her having failed, he bribes a guard to let him see her for a few minutes by the roadside. Worn out by fatigue and heartbreak, she dies in his arms on the lonely road to Havre instead of in a Louisianian meadow.

*Le portrait de Manon* (Paris, 1894) by Jules Massenet, book by Boyer, a slight, graceful score evoked by the popularity of the composer's *Manon,* shows the portrait of his lost beloved, the consolation of Des Grieux's years of mourning intervene (Aurore, whom Des Grieux's nephew, Jean, loves against his uncle's will, is dressed to resemble the portrait) to make two lovers happy. (For other operatic *Manons* see *New World Opera Stories.*)

## "ADRIANA LECOUVREUR"

FRANCESCO CILÈA. Book after Scribe's play (Milan, 1902). A score whose music is at times reminiscent of the later Verdi. Outstanding is Adrienne's Death Scene, the solo "Poor little flowers," and the duet, "Ah, nobler far than any queen."

In the foyer of the *Comédie Française* (1730) Adrienne Lecouvreur, about to appear in a Racine tragedy, gives an unknown lover a bunch of violets and accepts an invitation to supper from the Prince de Bouillon, who promises the Count de Saxe will be there. At the villa Adrienne recognizes in the Count de Saxe her unknown lover (Act II), who asks her to help him avoid the Princess who pursues him; and the actress holds the great lady in a dark room in discussion of their mutual love for Count Maurice till the Princess slips away as her husband enters to lead his guests to supper. In the Princess' *salon* her husband takes from her the white poison the Abbé de Choiseul has erroneously offered her for face powder (Act III). When Adrienne enters, the Princess, to make sure she is her rival, tells her Maurice has been wounded in a duel and the actress faints. Maurice appears, tells his adventures trying to make himself Duke of Courland, and a Ballet ("The Judgment of Paris") is performed. When the Princess asks Adrienne to recite, the latter delivers a speech from *Phèdre* full of insulting references to her rival and goes, leaving Maurice behind. In her home (Act IV) her maid brings her a casket—in it the faded violets she once gave Maurice. When Maurice arrives and begs Adrienne to marry him, her mind begins to wander—the Princess had steeped the innocent violets in the deadly poison the Abbé had shown her—and crying, "Save me, I do not wish to die!" she dies in her lover's arms who, when the others mourn, says, "Dead? No, for glory cannot die!"

The lovely actress who actually sold her plate and jewels to finance Maurice de Saxe's ill-starred Courland adventure also has inspired an *Adriana Lecouvreur* (Milan, 1857) by Tommasso; and an *Adriana Lecouvreur* (Rome, 1907) by Settacili.

*Sophie* (Paris, 1924) by Levadé (Quintet, Act I; Corentin's Romance, Act III) tells how Sophie Arnould, French actress and singer, famous for her wit and *diablerie*, shut up in a convent by her mother, manages to escape with her country lover Corentin, only to be caught by royal command to become a *fille d'opéra*, an "opera girl." *Ninon de l'Enclos* (Bordeaux, 1921) by Louis Maingueneau, to "music with moving charm of lyric phrase" tells a tragic incident from the life of the famous French beauty of easy virtue who seemed a lovely young girl in her *nineties*. Her son by the Count de Villarceaux, raised on the farm, not knowing Ninon is his mother comes to town and, since it is the thing to do, falls in love with her. When she reveals to him the secret of his birth and declares she cannot love him, he commits suicide. There is also *Ninon de l'Enclos* (Paris, 1895) by Edmond Messa, Massenet's pupil. Together with these "opera portraits" of the France of Louis XV, might be mentioned Emmanuel Moor's *Pompadour* (Cologne, 1902); Millocker's *Gräfin du Barry* (Vienna, 1879) and Camussi's *Du Barry* (Milan, 1912). *Cartouche* (Berlin, 1868) by Heinrich Hoffmann deals with the historic French bandit who (1720) about to wed a marquise who has handed him her jewels thinking him her relative Germain, escapes because the police who have surrounded him make the same mistake. Other operas on French rococo themes are: *Der Vicomte de Létorières* (Hamburg, 1899) by Bogumil Zepler, with charming airs and dances in rococo style, and Massenet's *Panurge* (Paris, 1913).

## 2. *Italy*

### THE GOLDONI COMEDIES

The comedies of Carlo Goldoni (1707-1793) mirror eighteenth century Venice and Italy in general (his satirical comedies, which attacked the Venetian nobility, had their scene of action carefully laid in some other Italian town) in all its rococo charm. They call up the city of the lagoons with its bridges, *piazze*, bell towers, cafés, canals, and gondolas, and the life of its colorful period, its manners and morals to perfection, and this appeal has called forth operas of peculiar charm and grace. For a more comprehensive survey the reader is referred to *Venise au dix-huitième siècle* by Philippe Monier.

### "LE DONNE CURIOSE"

#### (*The Inquisitive Women*)

ERMANNO WOLF-FERRARI. Book by Sugana after Goldoni's comedy (Munich, 1903). Delicate, Mozartian music, naïve melodies, fashioned with the most modern art. Outstanding Rosaura's "Song of Longing," with *ritornello,* and the Love Scene (Act II).

"Women Not Admitted" reads the sign over the door of the eighteenth century Venetian social club, *for men only,* which—gossip credits the clubmen with all sorts of goings-on—rouses members' wives to wrath. This feeling is in the background as Pantalone, "club host" of the dinner to be celebrated, orders his servant Arlecchino (supposed woman hater but really Colombina's lover) to make ready the feast. The scene changes to Ottavio's house, where Beatrice and Eleonora quizz Arlecchino and Ottavio in vain to discover the club secrets. Rosaura is more successful with her lover Florindo, and wrings from him the password "Amicizia!"—which admits those who speak it to the Club. . In Lelio's home his wife finds a letter in her husband's pocket (Act II) ; new keys have been made for the club door. Now all the women try to steal the husbands' keys, and aided by Colombina succeed in so doing, Rosaura even inducing love-sick Florindo to give her his. But when the women reach the street in which the clubhouse stands (Act III) they fail to get in till they capture Arlecchino and use his key. Once in, peering through the thick glass door which separates banquet hall from antechamber, they are surprised to see the men harmlessly busy eating a good dinner and, discovered and forgiven, join them happily at the table.

*Die Vier Grobiane* (*The Four Oafs*, Munich, 1906) by Ermanno Wolf-Ferrari after Goldoni's comedy *I quatri rusteghi*, the "Oafs' Council of War" (Act III) has been praised, shows masked Filipeto entering the home of Lucrezia, whom he is to marry, in order to be able to run away if he does not like her looks. Discovered by Lucrezia's father, Lunardo, and his three friends (the "Four Oafs") Lunardo in his indignation swears there shall be no wedding; but the girl and her betrothed, having seen each other now insist on it and Lucrezia manages to soothe her father's rage and win his consent to their union. *Gli amanti sposi* (*The Wedded Lovers*, Venice, 1925) by Ermanno Wolf-Ferrari, book by Forzano, the "Song of the Garter" (Act I) and Quintet (Act III) outstanding, finds the Marchioness when her husband, whom she thinks hates her, leaves her, coquetting with seven lovers. Purposely losing her garter, the Marchioness (secretly hoping her husband may find it) promises to be kind to the admirer who restores it, and so manages that her husband returns it and a "blue band of happiness," it motives their glad reunion.

*Les femmes de bonne humeur* (*The Good-Natured Ladies*, London, 1918), Russian Ballet, is a pantomime version of Goldoni's *Le donne di buon umore*, the music clavecin sonatas by Domenico Scarlatti, Goldoni's contemporary; Respighi's *Scherzo veneziano* (Rome, 1920) a ballet picture of Goldoni's Venice, outstanding a *forlana*. *Pulcinella* (Paris, 1920) is a Russian Ballet whose Stravinsky orchestration "throws into relief the old Italian master Pergolesi's music by underlining it in a modern way." *Pupazzi* (Paris, 1907) is Florent Schmitt's ballet, in which personages of the eighteenth century Italian comedy dance. *Le astuzie femminili* (*Women's Artifices*, London, 1920), Russian Ballet, is an eighteenth century Italian comedy with modernized Cimarosa music in pantomime form. *Il convento veneziano* (Rome, 1925) by Alfredo Casella, a choregraphic comedy, pictures Goldoni's Venice, crowded with masqueraders, monks, gondoliers, patricians, artisans, and the exiled Grand Turk in person.

Francesco Malipiero's *Tre Commedie Goldoniane* (*Three Goldoni Comedies*, Milan, 1925) is a modernist's musical journey through streets, alleys, palaces, and canals of eighteenth century Venice as reflected by Goldoni. (1) *La bottega del cafè* (*The Coffee House*) is followed by (2) *Sior Todero Brontolon*, a tone picture of the old miser who hides his sugar and coffee and scolds his valet for using too much kindling wood; while (3) *Les que-relles de Chioggia* (*The Squabbles of Chioggia*—Venice's sea quarter) or to use Goldoni's title, *Le Baruffe Chiozotte,* reproduces the squabbles, joys and merrymakings of the *batellanti,* the fisher folk of the water front.

Giannetti's opera *Don Marzio* (Venice, 1903) is based on Goldoni's comedy describing an old misanthrope; and Pier di Pietro's *Magia* (Rome, 1924), is a graceful picture of Venetian life (1797), in which a hussar pretends to be a musician to gain the good graces of fair Norina, wife of the merchant Pandolfo. Johann Strauss's *Eine Nacht in Venedig* (*A Night in Venice,* Vienna, 1883) turns on the vain efforts of a skirt-hunting Duke of Urbino to abduct charming Barbara, a Venetian senator's faithful wife (1750), and contains an effective Venetian Carnival Scene.

## CASANOVA AND CAGLIOSTRO

The Venetian Casanova, blood relative to Lovelace, Valmond and Byron's Don Juan, a frivolous romanesque epicurean, is the typical eighteenth century adventurer in love's byways, while Cagliostro, also adored by the ladies, is its most representative charlatan, who dabbled in every form of chicanery, from political intrigue to love philters. Both have inspired operas.

*Casanova* (Leipzig, 1841) by Lortzig, outstanding the charming Venetian "Evening Chorus" and its hero's air "Off and away to seek my love," has been revived as *Der Mazurka-Oberst* (*The Mazurka-Colonel,* Vienna, 1925), in a textual and musical revise by Jacoby and Spangenberg. In Artur Küsterer's *Casanova* (Stuttgart, 1921) the hero corresponds from a prison cell with a fair unknown, slips out to meet her at a village fair and, finding she is the wife of the commandant of his prison fortress, returns to jail to avoid compromising her. *Casanova* (Warsaw, 1923) by Ludomir Różycki, book by Krzewinski, a *buffa* opera, presents three episodes from the adventurer's life. In "On the Bosphorus" Turkish melodic exoticism is contrasted with Italian *bel canto,* outstanding the "Serenade at Sea." In "At the Court of Stanislas Augustus," the "Airs Antiques," and in "The Carnival of Venice," the "Gamester's Chorus" may be instanced. Casanova is pictured writing these episodes of his *Mémoires* in the retreat of his old age, and closing his manuscript his heart stops beating and the pen falls from his dead hand. *Abenteuer des Casanova* (*Casanova's Adventures,* Dresden, 1924) by Volkmar Andrae, book by Lion, a modern score influenced by Strauss and Puccini, comments with theatrically effective music scenes from its hero's career: his mistress rescues him from the Venetian Inquisition; he plays the gallant in a Paris millinery shop, rejects the love of a prima donna who has stabbed her admirer for his sake, and finally betrays the innocent daughter of a Potsdam drill sergeant.

*Cagliostro* (Berlin, 1913) by Könnecke, a serio-comic opera with fine musical pages, has a weak book, but *Cagliostro* (Gotha, 1924) by Otto Wartlisch, a fantastic score, has powerful musical as well as effective theatric scenes. Akiba, the Evil Principle, as Cagliostro is about to become a monk, tells him he can gain untold power and wealth if he use Lorenza, a virgin, as a medium. Cagliostro gives his desire to change Lorenza's pure estate the shape of the devil-dervish Zizimi and imprisons it in a grandfather's clock. When Lorenza demands to be loved as a woman should, he indignantly repulses and casts her off. Later, arrested in Paris, in connection with the "Affair of the Queen's Necklace," he calls on Lorenza and she comes to him. Alas, while Cagliostro's back is turned Zizimi slips from his clock-prison and strangles his master, who dies in Lorenza's arms looking forward to eternal happiness with her in Paradise. Adolphe Adam's comedy opera *Cagliostro* (Paris, 1844) and Johann Strauss's *Cagliostro in Wien* (Vienna, 1875) make the famous charlatan cut a less tragic figure.

### Other Eighteenth Century Italian Tales

*La serva padrona* (*The Maid as Mistress,* Naples, 1731) by Pergolesi, book by Nelli, the first genuine "comic opera," *opéra bouffe,* is a three principal score with solo arias and a final duet, "music of crystal clarity, melody of sweetly charming movement," which tells how bachelor Pandolfo, content to have his maidservant Serpina look after him, never thinks of marrying her. Ingenious Serpina induces Scapin to play the rôle of sea captain, suing for her hand, and rouses Pandolfo's jealousy to the point where marriage turns the maid into the mistress of the house. The composer of *La serva padrona* is unkindly remembered in Tasca's opera *Pergolesi* (Berlin, 1898) where he plays a villain's part in a fictitious episode happening in the Naples Conservatory in which he taught.

*Il matrimonio segreto* (*The Secret Marriage,* Vienna, 1792) by Cimarosa, book by Bertati, like *La serva padrona,* an ideal *opera buffa,* sings hidden love while "flowery melodies in the orchestra, borne on Neapolitan breezes, sweeten the situations." Outstanding are Paolino's "whisper" aria, "Priache spunti," and the final duet. Lawyer Paolino is secretly married to Carolina, daughter of rich Geronimo, but when his friend, the Count, meets the girl and sues for her hand, not only does Geronimo promise it, but Paolino is shocked to see his elderly sister Fidalama cast sheep's eyes at him. The unhappy married lovers deciding to flee as a last resource (Act II), are discovered, but all ends happily, though at first Geronimo rages. Mozart's *La finta giardiniera* (*The Gardener from Love*, Munich, 1775) is an earlier score, a rococo comedy of errors ending with the happy mating of four lovers; and his *La finta semplice* (*The Feigned Innocent*, Karlsruhe, 1921), written when he was twelve, but never performed in public, another slighter work in a rococo setting. *Le maître de chapelle* (Paris, 1821; New York, 1923; as *Il maestro di cappella*) by Paër is an amusing *buffa* score whose action tells the story of Barnaba, the music master who wrote an opera, *Cleopatra,* and, imitating flute, horn, and drum, tried to teach his pretty cook Gertrude to sing it and make love to the hatrack as Marc Antonio, in a sparkling musical parody of the Italian *opera seria* of the time.

*I dispettosi amanti* (*A Lover's Quarrel*, Philadelphia, 1912) by Attilio Parelli, book by Comitti, a slight, graceful score tells a tale of two lovers, Don Florindo and Rosaura, really at odds but pretending affection for fear news of their break will cause the girl's sick mother to die. Finally, they pass from acted to actual love and all ends happily. *Der lustige Krieg* (*The Merry War*) by Johann Strauss, after *The Bat* and *The Gypsy Baron* his most popular score, makes a war between Carrara and Genoa (1750), where the Carraran officers are *women,* the excuse for a sentimental military background against which tangled love trails run to a happy conclusion. *Madame l'Archiduc* (Paris, 1874; revised, 1921) by Jacques Offenbach tells how a fantastic Duchess of Parma abdicates in favor of an inn maid and her stable-boy lover when they give themselves out as a Count and Countess banished from their estates; but "Madame the Archduchess" has to return to her tavern with her mate once the trick is discovered.

## "DON PASQUALE"

GAETANO DONIZETTI. Book (Paris, 1843) after Anelli's old Italian opera, *Ser Marc' Antonio* by Guannarano. It has been called Donizetti's best opera. Norina's is a difficult cololoture rôle, and the Quartet, Finale (Act II), and the Serenade (Act III) are the jewels of the score.

When Ernesto refuses to marry his uncle Pasquale's choice—eighteenth century Rome—the latter decides to punish him by marrying himself and disinheriting him. His physician Malatesta's innocent, convent-bred sister is the wife the doctor (Ernesto's friend) prescribes. He induces the young widow Norina (Ernesto's sweetheart, whom he has told of his uncle's unkind plan) to play the part of his sister.

Once she has won the old man's heart as Sophrona, Norina's coquetry and caprice will make Pasquale repent. The widow acts the convent innocent to perfection and the mock wedding takes place (Act II). But once infatuated Don Pasquale has turned over his fortune to Norina, she plays ducks and drakes with it, prefers the theatre to her husband's company on her wedding night, and shows herself an accomplished shrew. An intercepted love letter fixing a rendezvous in his own garden determines the unhappy old man to surprise his guilty wife with her lover and hale them to court. Ernesto and Norina do not *act* the part of lovers in the garden (Act III). But Pasquale's attempt (in Malatesta's company) to surprise them, fails. Ernesto flits, undiscovered, and instead of turning his devilish wife out, her husband is showered with bitter reproaches. Malatesta easily persuades Pasquale to let Ernesto marry whom he will; perhaps Ernesto's wife will drive out his own. Pasquale's rage, when he finds that his Sophrona and Ernesto's Norina are the same yields to joy in his recovered liberty, and he ends by blessing the happy couple.

*Così Fan Tutte* or *La Scuola Degli Amanti* (*'Tis Thus They All Do* or *The School for Lovers,* Vienna, 1790) by Wolfgang Amadeus Mozart, book by Da Ponte. An idealization of feminine faithfulness in a comedy of intrigue. Some charming lyric numbers in the elegiac vein characterize a score which *Le nozze di Figaro* has overshadowed. (Artistic violations are: the adaptation of its music to a Shakespeare comedy, Paris, 1863, as *Les peines d'amour;* and that by Scheidemantle, Vienna, 1909, as *Dame Kobold,* a comic opera to a Calderon de la Barca play.) An old cynic, Alfonso (Onofrio) eighteenth century Naples—wagers with two young officers, Ferrando (Fernando) and Guglielmo (Alvar) that their sweethearts Fiordeligi (Rosaura) and Dorabella (Isabella) will not stand the acid test of faithfulness. After a touching farewell they return disguised as Albanians and make love to each other's fiancées. The ladies yield and (according to the version used) either are shamed by the production of marriage contracts or, their yielding is a mere pretext since they had discovered the trick, and shame their lovers. A final scene of reconciliation is common to both versions, whether the scene of action be Naples or Cadiz.

*Il Campanello* (Naples, 1836; Berlin, 1923, in a new version by Dr. W. Kleefeld, as *Die Nachtglocke, The Night Bell*) book by composer, Gaetano Donizetti. Attractive *opera buffa,* with colorature ariettes, duets, and ensemble numbers in French-Italian vaudeville style. The ringing of the "night bell" is cleverly stylized in the Introduction. Hannibal, an elderly Neapolitan doctor and apothecary (Naples, 1800) marries young and pretty Serafina, for the sake of her dowry. Enrico, the bride's cousin and lover, plans revenge. Whenever Hannibal prepares to enjoy his marital rights, Enrico rings the "night bell," disguised respectively as an Englishman suffering from indigestion, a tenor with throat trouble, and an old female hypochondriac, to claim medical aid. Three times Hannibal appears *ante portas,* and loses Serafina's dowry owing to the expiration of the legal term before the consummation of the marriage.

*Don Procopio* (Monte Carlo, 1906) by Georges Bizet, book by Colin after an eighteenth century Italian comedy. An early score, which suggests a "posthumous opera by the Rossini of the 'Barber.' " Outstanding are a serenade duet (Act II), a humorous trio, Ernesto's charming cavatina, "Vraiment elle est belle," and Bettina's colorature air, "En vain l'on croit nous désunir." Procopio, old and rich, is to marry young Bettina, who loves Odoardo, a handsome officer. When Bettina appeals to her brother Ernesto with tears in her eyes to stop the marriage, he paints so unfavorable a picture of his sister's deficiencies that the old man withdraws, and when he runs away rather than fight the duel Ernesto—pretending indignation at his sister's jilting—insists upon, Don Andronico, the old miser's disgusted friend, lets Bettina marry her soldier boy.

*L'amore medico* (*Dr. Cupid*) by Ermanno Wolf-Ferrari, book by Golischiani, transfers Molière's comedy, *Le médecin malgré lui,* to an Italian rococo setting (Dresden, 1913; New York, 1914). Delicate music lacking in deep feeling, it is one of the composer's less successful scores. Selfish Arnolfo's daughter Lucinda (baby talk, clothes, and toys his devices to keep her from growing up and marrying) falls ill, and he calls in four doctors. Clitando, a young gallant whose clandestine serenade has earned a windowcast rose, comes when his colleagues give up the case and, a specialist in heart trouble, tricks Arnolfo into approving the marriage which cures the ailing maiden.

*Der Violinmacher von Cremona* (*The Violin Maker of Cremona,* Budapest, 1893) by Jeno Hubay, book by Coppée and Beauclair, is a tuneful and successful score. Cremona's Town Council (1750) offers a gold chain for the best violin. Taddeo Ferrari, master builder, adds the promise of his daughter's hand to the pupil of his who wins the prize. Deformed Filippo, madly in love with Giannina, Ferrari's daughter—who loves Sandro—generously exchanges the wonderful instrument he has made with his rival's, so that the latter may win. Sandro, not knowing it, secretly changes the instruments back again, thinking to best Filippo; but when Filippo gets the prize he nobly yields the chain and Giannina's hand to the man whom she loves, after Sandro has confessed his fault.

### 3. *Germany*

The French rococo in its artistic, social, and other aspects is exemplified by the reign of Louis XV. As regards arts, manners, and morals the little German rococo courts imitated the example "Louis, the Well-Beloved" set them in Marly and Versailles. Opera composers have chosen the German rococo subject in various cases, and an interesting group of operas deals specifically with music and musicians. Some introduce well-known historical figures.

*Friedemann Bach* (Rome, 1901) by Fazio is a clever score to which the titular hero's own compositions lend archaic flavor. The story travesties truth, the successful première of Friedemann's opera killing him with joy instead of its failure killing him with grief. *Il Piccolo Haydn* (*Little Haydn*, Como, 1893) by Gaetano Cippoloni is a sweetish musical portrait of an infant prodigy, alternately archaic and neo-Italian in style. Porpora, writing his *Armida* (1750) in Vienna, has been unable to invent the vocal "hit" of the score, though Count Kaunitz clamors for the music. Enter "Little Haydn," who confesses he has secretly composed the number, sings it amid applause, and is laurel-crowned by Porpora's hand. *Ein Abenteuer Händels* (*An Adventure of Handel,* Schwerin, 1874) by Carl Reinecke uses Handel's famous harpsichord air with variations, "The Harmonious Blacksmith," as the hub of a happy tale of the loves of Kathleen and Charlie 'neath village smithy oaks.

*Mozart and Salieri* (Moscow, 1898) by Rimsky-Korsakoff after Pushkin, dramatic scene rather than opera, music in eighteenth century style—"Mozart himself seems playing when he sits down at the piano and performs an *Allegretto* and *Grave*"—presents the historically discredited legend that Mozart was poisoned by Salieri. At a restaurant Salieri assures Mozart that Beaumarchais never poisoned a rival (as rumor says) since genius would not stoop to murder. Then he slips poison into Mozart's champagne, the latter falls from the piano stool and dies while trying to play his "Requiem," and Salieri realizes with despair that his own act has convicted *him* of not being a genius, most awful thought any musician could entertain. *Der Schauspieldirector* (*The Impresario,* Schönbrunn, 1786) by Mozart, an opera *pasticcio* performed at a court dinner for the Emperor Josef II, turned on the trying of the voices of would-be opera singers by the impresario Frank. *Mozart und Schikaneder* (Berlin, 1861), a modernized version by Taubert, introduces Mozart and Schikaneder composing *The Magic Flute,* and Genée's version, *Der Kapellmeister* (Berlin, 1896) has Mozart appear at Potsdam (1789) instead of Schönbrunn. *Mozart* (Vienna, 1923) is a tuneful operetta by Hans Duhan.

*Auf Hohen Befehl* (*By August Command*) by Carl Reinecke book after Riehl's *Ovid at Court* (Hamburg, 1886), outstanding the charmingly varied folk song "Kein Feuer, keine Kohle," tells of a feud between two singers at a little German rococo court such as Thackeray satirizes, the hero in a dual personality rôle, and ends with the happy union of two lovers, son and daughter of the feudists. *Flauto Solo* (Prague, 1905) by Eugen d'Albert, book by Von Wolzogen, combines rococo minuet, Tyrolian waltz and operetta tunes with Italian *bel canto* aria. The tale is a musical anecdote of Frederick the Great. Prince Ferdinand (Frederick) orders Pepusch, German composer, to play his "Swines' Canon" for six bassoons so his Italian singer, Emanuele, may deride it. Pepusch arranges Emanuele's Italian opera aria for flute as a "suckling" part to his canon and makes Ferdinand play it, confounding contemners of German music and gaining the hand of Peppina (a supposed Italian prima donna, really a Tyrolian girl) who was to have sung Emanuele's aria.

*Der Ring des Polycrates* (Vienna, 1916) by Erich Wolfgang Korngold, after a Tewele comedy, shows Wilhelm Arndt, music director at a German court (1797), welcoming friend Vogel, his wife Laura's old sweetheart, come to visit them. Vogel has just read Schiller's *Ring des Polycrates* and makes Wilhelm believe he is *too* happy and, like the Sicilian tyrant, owes the gods a sacrifice. Not until Wilhelm reads Laura's diary and Laura Schiller's poem do they realize why Vogel has set them quarreling, and drive the trouble maker from the house. *Cæcilie* (Vienna, 1920) by Oberleithner, the composer's finest folkwise score, makes its titular heroine, wife of old Erasmus, Prince of Cobentzl, the heroine of an opera by the dying young court composer, Hans Lobesang, which has been gathering dust in the court archives for a year. The opera given, its composer madly in love with the Princess, dies before he can enjoy his triumph, but Saint Cæcilie appears to him on his deathbed in the likeness of his love and crowns him with the crown of immortality.

*Der Musikant* (*The Musician*, Vienna, 1910) by Julius Bittner, charmingly contrasts Italian rococo artificiality in music with sincere German folk song. The German musician Wolfgang (1780) in despair when the singer Violetta, whom he loves, follows ambition's call to Paris, is about to commit suicide when the violinist Friedericke wins his heart and he decides to live for her. *Das Hofconcert* (*The Court Concert*, Charlottenburg, 1922) by Paul Scheinpflug, half opera, half operetta, outstanding Feodor's Air and the "Court Ladies Quartet," stages an eighteenth century

German court whose Duchess loves music much but singers more. To secure his position, Feodor, a tenor, pretends his wife Helen is his sister and while the Duchess makes love to him the Court Marshal and young Prince Bernhard pursue his wife till Bubi, their child, breaks up a sentimental court concert by disclosing the true relationship existing between Feodor and Helen, and they leave in the post chaise as the bass Untersteiger, the new bachelor "star," arrives.

## "WERTHER"

JULES MASSENET. Book by Blau, Milliet, and Hartmann after Goethe's novel *The Sorrows of Werther* (Vienna, 1892; New York, 1894). Massenet is said to have set *Werther* because friends begged him for once to present a virtuous woman on the stage instead of a courtesan. A score with tender emotional pages, its dramatic climax is the duet between Werther and Charlotte, "Ah, pourvu que je vois ces yeux toujours ouverts!"

Charlotte, cutting bread and butter for the children, lets Werther, whom she has learned to love during her fiancé Albert's six months' absence, take her to the ball and kiss her there. Taking Charlotte home, Werther tells her mother he loves the girl and—her father announces Albert's return. Werther leaves with wrung soul, assuring Charlotte that if she keeps her promise to Albert he will die. In vain, after Charlotte and Albert are married (Act II) does Werther try to cultivate Charlotte's sister Sophie as love's consolation prize. He neglects her at the dance and Albert and Charlotte find her in tears. On Christmas Day he suddenly appears in Charlotte's home (Act III). The harpsichord, the books they used to read evoke tender memories. Charlotte weakens and Werther, in Goethe's words, "covers her stuttering lips with furious kisses." But her innate virtue triumphs. Pushing Werther from her Charlotte hastens into another room and locks the door. When Albert returns a servant gives him Werther's note: "I am going on a long journey. Lend me your pistols." Charlotte hands them to the servant and soon, filled with a horrid presentiment, hurries after him. Werther has shot himself on Christmas Night. Rushing into his room, Charlotte flings herself upon him and cheers his last moments by confessing she always has loved him. Children singing Christmas carols in the snow without lend a seasonal touch to the pathetic swan song of Werther's passion.

*Luisa Miller* (Naples, 1849; New York, 1886) by Giuseppe Verdi, after Schiller's *Kabale und Liebe* (*Intrigue and Love*) musics the bourgeois tragedy which mirrors the evil effects of rococo license at the Würtemberg Court in 1784. Rodolfo, Count Walter's son, persists in refusing to marry the Duchess of Ostheim, his father's choice, because he loves Luisa, daughter of the old soldier Müller. But Luisa, to rescue her father from Count Walter's prison (Act II) writes a letter saying she cared only for Rodolfo's rank and wealth and will fly with Wurm, the Count's evil steward. Rodolfo, shown the letter, agrees to marry the Duchess while planning to kill Luisa and himself. When in her home Luisa admits she wrote the letter (Act III) he poisons the cup from which both drink. Then Luisa, feeling death absolves her from her oath of secrecy, reveals the truth to her lover and both pass away before the eyes of their horror-stricken parents. Luisa's brilliant "Lo vidi" aria (Act I) and her pathetic "The tomb is a couch decked with roses" (Act III) stand out. Cammerano, Verdi's librettist, calls the three acts: "Love," "Intrigue," and "Poison." *Ferdinand und Louise* (Vienna, 1917) by Zajčzek-Blankenau is another setting of the tale, outstanding Luisa's "Madrigal" and the tragic final scene.

In *I Masdanieri* (London, 1847) after Schiller's *Die Räuber* (*The Robbers*), one of the eighteenth century's most vital dramas, Verdi wrote what has been called one of the nineteenth century's poorest operas. Mercadante's *I briganti* (*The Robbers,* Paris, 1836), after Schiller, though its "robbers are sprinkled with rose water," triumphed with Grisi while Verdi's setting failed in spite of Jenny Lind. *Die Abreise* (*The Departure*) by Eugen d'Albert, book by Count Sporck (Frankfort, 1898), a musically grateful rococo comedy, has Gilsen delay departure from his château, not trusting his wife and his friend Trott if left together. Trott, taking advantage of a coolness between Gilsen and his wife Louise, tries in every way to speed the husband's going, but at the last moment the pair are reconciled and Trott takes his departure instead of Gilsen. .*Herzog Wildfang* (Munich, 1901) by Siegfried Wagner, in which the composer "tortuously attempts the folkwise," shows the wild young ruler of a rococo duchy (1750), led by a false counselor to shoot at a peasant deputation, wounding the girl Osterlind, and abdicating when her father demands redress, to let the people make the counselor duke. As a peddler Wildfang then vainly tries to win Osterlind's heart (Act II) and when she publicly jilts him for her peasant lover Reinhart, returned from the wars (Act III), the Duke consoles himself by reoccupying his throne. Ernst Theodor Wilhelm Hoffmann (1776-1822), master novelist of the German romantic movement, a mad, fantastic spirit, painted, conducted, and, besides his "Strange Tales" wrote eleven operas, his best *Undine* (Berlin, 1816) a setting of Fouqué's romantic fairy tale (for story see p. 140). Among the "Strange Tales" by Hoffmann which have called forth opera settings one stands out.

## "LES CONTES D'HOFFMANN"

### (*Hoffmann's Strange Tales*)

JACQUES OFFENBACH. Book by Barbier after Hoffmann's *Novellen* (Vienna, 1881). (The *Ringtheater* in Vienna burned down with deplorable loss of life during the *première,* which for many years led the score to be regarded as a "hoodoo" and prevented its performance.) The opera is a cycle of individual acts, grouped about a leading figure, E. T. A. Hoffmann, the narrator and also lover of the singer Stella, a heartless courtesan and prima donna with whom Hoffmann's rival Lindorf—incorporating the Evil Principle in Hoffmann's life—cuts him out. Stella appears only momentarily in the Postlude, but her characteristics are incorporated in Olympia, Giulietta and Antonia. The "Students' Drinking Chorus," the famous "Barcarole," Olympia's Waltz, and Antonia's Romance are the melodic jewels of the delightful score.

An invisible chorus of Wine and Beer Spirits precedes the entry of Town Counselor Lindorf into the Luther Wine Cellar in Nuremberg (Prelude) where he bribes Hoffmann's servant to give him the singer Stella's *billet-doux* addressed to the poet Hoffmann. It contains the key to her boudoir and promises a meeting after the opera. Hoffmann and the students who have been listening to Stella in Mozart's *Don Giovanni* enter during the intermission after the first act. They sing and drink, but Hoffmann, over a bowl of fiery punch, watches Lindorf and tells his friends the tale of his "love madness," three episodes, beginning with that of Olympia, which takes shape on the stage.

At a soirée in Spallanzani the physicist's home, Hoffman falls madly in love with his supposed daughter Olympia, really a mechanical doll who sings and dances with consummate art. Her automatic acceptance of his love vows fills Hoffmann with joy, but when, breathless from the mad dance with her, he falls on a sofa and breaks the "glasses of optimism," gift of Coppelius (Lindorf in diabolic disguise), he sees her as she is; and Coppelius, raging that the poet has discovered the truth, smashes the doll despite Spallanzani's outcries, the guests jeering at wretched Hoffmann as he sees his idol lying in fragments.

In the courtesan Giulietta's palace in Venice, Hoffmann has abandoned ideal for sensual love. Dapertutto (Lindorf in another diabolic incarnation) is the strumpet's master. He incites her jealous lover Schlemihl to pick a quarrel with Hoffmann, and guiding the latter's rapier, makes him slay his rival. His useless murder—Giulietta's tender song ("Barcarole") echoes from Venice waters as another admirer carries her off in his gondola—shows Hoffmann he has nearly lost his soul to the Devil, after weighing it with blood for a worthless woman's sake.

In Crespel's home his daughter Antonia pours out her heart in a "Love Romance." Her father and her lover Hoffmann have begged her to give over singing, for with a wonderful voice she has inherited her mother's consumption; and after Doctor Miracle (Lindorf in his third demoniac disguise) has treated her with an elixir she promises Hoffmann never to sing again. But her lover and father gone, Doctor Miracle returns as the ghost of her dead mother, and with pleas not to give up her heritage of wealth and fame lures Antonia to sing her love song again and—die. Rushing in, Hoffmann hears her last sigh only to be accused of her murder by Crespel. Hoffmann's tale is done (Postlude). Overcome by wine and emotion, the poet's head drops on the table. The Muse, who has dried the tears born of his wild passions, appears to him in an aura of golden light, and promises his dreams in the future shall be of her alone. And as Stella stands in the doorway—the performance of *Don Giovanni* is over—Hoffmann does not see her. It is Lindorf's hour, yet when he hurries to take the actress to her lodgings her glance clings to Hoffmann.

*Die Brautwahl* (*The Choice of the Bride*, Hamburg, 1912) by Ferruccio Busoni, book after E. T. A. Hoffmann's tale, considered the composer's best opera, stages a demoniac vision in Berlin of 1820. Albertine has to choose one of three suitors, a pedantic Counselor, a Jewish man about town and a sentimental painter. The Jew Manasse (Evil Principle) and the goldsmith Leonard (Good Principle) try to influence her decision, determined as in *The Merchant of Venice*, by a jewel casket; Leonard (the Good) prevails and the painter secures Albertine as his bride. In the ultramodern music, the Scene of Manasse's Curse, one in which radishes are turned into gold ducats, and a ghostly "Midnight Dance" stand out.

*Prinzessin Brambilla* (Stuttgart, 1909), a lyric score by Walter Braunfels, is a setting of another fantastic tale by Hoffmann.

*Coppélia ou la fille aux yeux d'émail* (*Coppelia or the Girl with the Enamel Eyes*, Paris, 1870) by Léo Delibes, a grand ballet, after A. T. E. Hoffmann's tale *Der Sandmann*, one of "those scores which gave ballet music greater color, rhythmic variety, movement and richer orchestration" (Alfred Bruneau), makes villager Franz, forgetting his sweetheart Swanhilda, fall in love with Coppelia, the lovely automaton made by Dr. Coppelius; but Swanhilda takes the doll's place in the shop and as the old magician plies Franz (who has confessed his love for Coppelia) with wine, so that the lad's soul may pass into the automaton, Swanhilda pretends to come to life, to Coppelius' delight which yields to sorrow when she undeceives repentant Franz and they run off together. The Russian Ballet version makes Coppelius, his fondest illusions destroyed, fall dead of a broken heart, "lifting the story to a higher plane of dignity by showing respect for human striving toward an ideal, no matter how fantastic." *La Poupée de Nurembourg* (*The Nuremberg Doll*, Paris, 1852) by Adolphe Adam, a French *opéra comique*, tells how Cornelius' life-size doll has been made in the hope she will turn Galathea and wed his son Benjamin. But his niece Berta acts the doll's part in such wise that her uncle destroys his automaton and lets Berta marry her lover Henri. *La Poupée* (*The Doll*) by Edmond Audran is another lighter score in which a charming girl takes an automaton's place, and Lancelot, who buys Alesia as a great big beautiful doll, is delighted to find her flesh and blood and the owner of a feeling heart. *La Boutique Fantasque* (*The Fantastic Toyshop*, London, 1919), is a toyshop ballet of dancing dolls, music by Rossini (Tarantelle, Cancan, etc.), orchestrated by the Italian modernist Respighi.

*Herbergs Prinses* (*The Tavern Princess*, Antwerp, 1896; New York, 1900) by Jan Blockx, book by Laye, is the Flemish composer's outstanding score. Flemish folk-song themes are used and the Guitar Serenade, "Rita, sun of ravished hearts," Rita's "Ring out, O carillon" (Act I), the colorful "Kermesse Scene" (Act II) and Rita's "Birdling Song" (Act III) are favorite numbers. In Brussels under Austrian rule (1750), Rita, the taverner's daughter who winds the wild boys of the town around her little finger, returns from church followed by a crowd of poets, painters, and musicians, and, making drink free to all comers in the inn, leads the respectable, decent Merlyn to kiss her amid the plaudits of the crowd. Merlyn turns from Puritanism to profligacy (Act II) and spends his mother's money carousing with Rita, the act climaxing in the Kermesse Scene, in which they pass down the main street in a chariot of flowers. But Rabo, one of Rita's rejected lovers, stabs Merlyn in a tavern brawl he has purposely incited, and while the dying boy looks wildly for Rita (who has veiled her face with belated remorse) his mother and sister curse her as a gay throng enters the inn shouting that Merlyn's poem has won the prize.

## "DER ROSENKAVALIER"

RICHARD STRAUSS. A "Comedy for Music." Book by Hugo von Hoffmannsthal (Dresden, 1911). A love comedy of Vienna in the picturesque days of the Empress Maria Theresia. Piquant stage situations and colorful music have made it a favorite, though the chief waltz melody, covering fifty pages of the score, has been called "coffee-house music of finest workmanship." "Strauss sings more in his *Rosenkavalier* than in previous operas . . . yet his greatest power is shown in the orchestral tone . . ." (Julius Korngold).

Octavian, a seventeen-year-old Austrian youth of noble birth, after a night spent with the Princess von Werdenberg, is breakfasting with her in her bedroom. The Field Marshal Prince von Werdenberg is hunting in Croatia. When the Princess's rustic cousin, Ochs von

Lerchenau, is announced, Octavian slips into a soubrette's dress and becomes Mariandl, a waiting-maid. A country Don Juan, Von Lerchenau has come to his betrothal to Sofie, daughter of newly ennobled von Faninal. His cousin the Princess must find him a "Cavalier of the Rose," a gentleman who, according to custom, will present the silver betrothal rose to his fiancée as his proxy. She suggests young Lord Octavian—with whom, in the rôle of Mariandl, the old satyr has begun a flirtation—and then those waiting in the antechamber for an audience with the Princess are admitted. In a burlesque interlude a notary, the Princess *chef,* a dressmaker, a scholar, an animal-merchant, three orphan girls of noble family, a flute player, and an Italian singer crowd about the great lady while the hairdresser attends to her coiffure and an Italian adventurer, Valzacchi and his companion Annina, present their budget of gossip. Then all retire and the Princess is left to her melancholy thoughts. She is growing older. How long before boys of good family will stop coming to her home when the Field Marshal is hunting in Croatia? Octavian, who has returned in cavalry uniform, cannot cheer her up. When she tells him he soon will leave her for some fresh young beauty, he hurries away in a pet, and she sends her negro page after him with the silver rose.

When Octavian enters the Faninal home with the silver rose, Sofie's beauty robs him of speech. After Von Lerchenau's lascivious advances to the convent-bred innocent, and a repulsive Intermezzo in which the Von Lerchenau lackeys attack the Faninal female servants, the two young things, left alone—it is a case of love at sight—cling together in a kiss, interrupted by Valzacchi and Annina who have been spying and whose shouts bring back Von Lerchenau. Octavian wounds the Baron, trying to force a duel, while Faninal curses and servants scream; but the country lover forgets his troubles when Annina slips him a note from the supposed Mariandl and he hurries off to meet her.

In a private chamber in an inn Mariandl (Octavian) drives the amorous Baron mad with rage and fear with a series of practical jokes (carried out by Valzacchi and Annina, now in his employ) and climaxing with Annina's rushing in with ten children, claiming Von Lerchenau is the husband who abandoned her. When the police commissioner arrives Von Lerchenau says Mariandl is Sofie, his bride, and refuses to recognize Faninal (secretly sent for) who is shocked at the lie and the scandal. As the Princess von Werdenberg enters, Octavian, who has dropped his disguise, appears, and resigned to the fact that youth will be served, she drives off Von Lerchenau. Faninal conducts the Princess to her coach and Sofie and Octavian fly into each other's arms. The curtain falls on a little negro page, who trips in after the lovers have gone, looking for the handkerchief the happy young girl has dropped in the ecstasy of her bliss. (In the inn scene Lerchenau says Marianol is his bride because supping in Vienna (1750) with a woman of light life was a crime, the Empress Maria Theresia's special "moral police" being employed to spy on and punish offenders against the moral law.)

## 4. *Spain*

## "L'HEURE ESPAGNOLE"

### (*The Spanish Hour*)

MAURICE RAVEL. Book by Franc-Nohain (Paris, 1911). A witty one-act comedy which, as the auditor may react to its modernist music, is: (1) "a scientifically cacophonic symphony"; (2) "a salacious vaudeville of mediocre originality"; (3) "a musical dainty of marvelous flavor."

In eighteenth century Toledo, muscular Ramiro, the muleteer, enters old Torquemada's clock shop and its owner, delighted to see him, since he must be off to regulate the town clock, begs him to tend shop for him during his absence. Concepción, Torquemada's young wife—the embarassed muleteer shows he is more at home with mules than with women—when her lover Gonsalvo arrives unseen by him, hides him in a grandfather's clock and gets the stable Hercules to carry it upstairs. He also carries up with perfect ease, Inigo, the banker, similarly hidden. But the ease with which the muleteer juggles grandfathers' clocks thus weighted attracts Concepción. She beckons blushing Ramiro and they disappear into another room. Torquemada, returning, finds the poor forgotten lovers moping sadly in their clocks, releases them with a philosophic sigh and, as his wife and Ramiro reappear, joins in the jolly Quintet which concludes the work.

*Die Drei Pintos* (*The Three Pintos,* Leipzig, 1888) by Carl Maria von Weber, posthumous opera completed by Gustav Mahler, shows a loutish Spanish squire, Pinto de Fonseca, bound for Madrid to marry Don Pantaleone's daughter. Don Gaston, a Salamanca student, steals his identification papers, which in turn are stolen from him by Don Gomez, Clarissa's true lover, who, thanks to the deception, is the "Pinto" who marries her before the other arrives. Outstanding is a "Duo" (Clarissa and Gomez) and a vocal "Seguidilla." *Don Ranudo* (Zurich, 1919) by Othmar Schoeck, book after Holberg's play, a melodious modernist comedy opera, is the tale of Don Ranudo, Spanish grandee (1750), so insanely proud of his blue blood that he refuses his daughter Maria to Count Gonzal who has two quarterings less in his coat of arms than himself. The lovers trick him and marry, and, since Don Ranudo has not a penny to his name, the fact that he solemnly disinherits his child makes no difference. *Der Goldschmied von Toledo* (*The Goldsmith of Toledo,* Mannheim, 1919) by Jacques Offenbach after one of Hoffmann's "Strange Tales," is a post-humous score with effective airs and ensembles, completed by Stern and Zamara. Malaveda, famous Toledan goldsmith, is the unknown midnight assassin who, unable to withstand his insane lust for rare gems he has sold, slays his customers to regain them at the foot of St. Sebastian's statue, in a lonely lane, whither he passes from a panel door in his workshop through a secret underground passage. Retribution comes when thinking he buries his dagger in the back of the Marquesa Dolores, to regain a lustrous pearl necklace, he finds he has murdered his own daughter Magdalena.

*Carlo Broschi* (*The Devil's Part,* Paris, 1843) by François Auber, book by Scribe—"Ferme ta paupière" one of the charming airs in a score which "reveals some of the most subtle sides of Auber's operatic production"—has for its hero the famous male soprano Farinelli. Carlo puts his sister, Casilda, a milliner, in a convent, to save her from naughty clerical persecutors (Act I), and when her lover Raphael, in despair because she has vanished, appeals to the Devil—we are at the Spanish Court—to help him (Act II) Carlo plays the part in such wise that the priests, who have drawn Casilda from her covert in hopes of making her the king's mistress, are foiled, and the disappointed monarch unites the happy lovers (Act III), Carlo's plea that he devote himself to his royal wife touching his heart. Other operas with the same hero include Tomas Bretón's *Farinelli* (Madrid, 1903) and Zumpe's *Farinelli* (Hamburg, 1889) in which the male soprano is the husband of a nun he has abducted from a convent and, as in Auber's score, is rewarded for reconciling the king and queen of Spain.

## "GOYESCAS"

### (*The Rival Lovers*)

ENRIQUE GRANADOS. Book by Periquet (New York, 1916). A tuneful score built up on piano compositions by the composer, a fine concerted Fandango outstanding, rich in local Spanish musical color, presents scenes suggested by the famous painter Goya's pictures of Spanish life, in the first year of the nineteenth century.

Rosario, a court lady, stops her sedan chair in a Madrid public square, where *majos* and *majas* flirt and youths toss the *pelele,* the strawman, in a blanket, as Paquito, the toreador, darling of the *majas* (girls of the lower class) comes up with a flourish to remind the lovely aristocrat of a *baile de candil,* a candlelight ball of the baser sort she once attended, and to beg her to honor another with her presence. Paquito's Pepa drives up in her dogcart, overhears and grows jealous, as does Don Fernando, captain in the Spanish Guards, Rosario's lover, who tells the bullfighter haughtily that he will escort her to the ball. At the ball (Act II) Paquito, goaded by Pepa, and Fernando, the sneering soldier, quarrel and after a challenge has been passed the captain leaves with his lady. In Rosario's garden (Act III) Fernando tears himself from her and disappears in the shadows. Rosario soon hears a cry, and vanishes to reappear supporting her wounded lover, who dies in her arms on the stone bench to which she guides him.

*Les diamants de la couronne* (*The Crown Diamonds*, Paris, 1841) by François Auber, book by Scribe and Saint-Georges, outstanding the Bolero Duet, the air "Ah, je veux briser ma chaîne" and the vocal Quintet (Act III), is a fantastic tale of a Queen of Portugal who enlists the aid of counterfeiters to help her carry the crown jewels across the frontier in a coffin to sell them to "save the state," and as "Theophila" falls in love with Don Enrique her prime minister's nephew, whose betrothed, to his great joy, forgets him while he wanders (Act II) to yield to the love-making of Sebastian, his friend; while the Queen meeting Enrique in Lisbon, no longer in her low estate (Act III), marries him out of hand. A counterfeiter is the hero of Auber's opera *Le serment* (*The Oath*, Paris, 1832), one of his lesser scores. *Die Banditen* (*The Bandits*, Paris, 1869) by Jacques Offenbach is a *buffa* score in which the Spanish bandit Falsacappa and his daughter Fiorella lay hand on millions in gold by the impersonation of the Princess of Granada, come to meet the Prince of Braganza, to be pardoned in the end (Fiorella saved the Prince's life as he was straying in the woods) the bandit chief being appointed chief of police in accordance with the rule of setting a thief to catch a thief.

## 5. *Georgian England*

George I was King of England when Handel became director of the new Royal Academy of Music for the production of Italian operas in London. Among the operas he produced there from 1720-1741 the following may be mentioned because of their frequent revival on twentieth century German stages. *Radamisto* (1720), whose soprano air "Ombra cara," Handel considered his best melody; *Floridante* (1721); *Ottone* (London, 1721; Göttingen, 1921), a story of how the Greek Emperor's daughter Theophano, who never has seen her betrothed, the German Emperor Otto, is saved at the last moment from an impostor who pretends to be her intended husband, by the latter's advent in Rome, delayed owing to his capture by pirates; *Giulio Cesare* (London, 1724; Hanover, 1923), "its airs known to every parrot in London" when it was first produced; *Tamerlano* (1724) elsewhere described; *Rodelinda* (London, 1725; Göttingen, 1920) with a noble "Mad Air," "Diese Zweifel"; and the lovely Siciliana, "Hirtenknaben, die Hüter der Triften"; *Scipione, Alessandrone* (1726); *Admeto,*

*Riccardo Primo* (1727), the year King George II ascended the throne; *Siroe, Tolemeo* (1728), the year the Royal Academy failed. Handel was supported by King George, while the English aristocracy, opposed to the Hanoverian king, the powerful Marlborough family in particular, put forward the Italian Buononcini and the two composers had to fight their patrons' battles in music. Added to this were the disputes about the merits of the rival *prime donne,* Cuzzoni (whom Handel once threatened to throw out of the window) and Faustina. Duchesses cut each other at Windsor, and gentlemen fought duels because they could not agree concerning them; but when the two ladies themselves fought it out on the stage with fists, clawing each other's hair, the public patience was exhausted. Dean Swift, leader of the patriotic "English" opera party, sounded the death knell of Italian opera for the time when Gay's famous *Beggar's Opera,* whose music in part travestied the highflown style of the Italian operas so wittily and entertainingly that they were killed with ridicule, was produced.

## "THE BEGGAR'S OPERA"

JOHN GAY. The English poet wrote his own book, and Dr. Pepusch put together his score out of the "ballads," the popular songs of London, of his day. It was the first "Ballad Opera," the first opera which dealt with the Apaches and "flash Molls" of its own period, evoked the atmosphere of their hidden dens, used thieves' slang and, with the exception of the Overture (composed by Pepusch) set them to music in folksong and folk-dance tunes (69), though the "Brigand's Chorus" (Act II) is a direct take-off of an air in Handel's *Rinaldo.* It fathered whole flocks of similar "ballad operas." More than a caricature of Sir Robert Walpole, Gay satirized the high society of his time in the score, showing the corruption and immorality of the governing class in the persons of the thieves and highwaymen who trod the boards. The opera "made Rich—the producer—gay and Gay rich." Gibbon the historian said it would improve the morals of any highwayman. Given in London, in 1728 (first time in New York in 1750) its frequent twentieth century revival in both cities still makes it a living score of the repertoire. (It was given in Paris, 1922, as *L'opéra du mendiant*).

After Gay (disguised as a Beggar) tells his aims in a Prologue, Peachum, a thief-taker, and Filch, a thief, decide that honesty is as rare among the highly placed as among the lowly, "because, like great statesmen, we encourage those who betray their friends." (Jonathan Wilde, the famous thief-taker who supplied the gallows with thirty-five highwaymen, twenty-two housebreakers and ten assorted criminals, is the historic original of Peachum.) As Peachum consults his "black list"—he trafficks with Justice, to which he sells his thieves—his wife informs him their daughter Polly has married Macheath, the highwayman, adored by every lady of low life in town. The father is harrowed to think Polly's usefulness as a stool pigeon is ended, and when Polly overhears him planning to deliver her husband for blood money, she warns Macheath who goes into hiding.

In the tavern where he has taken refuge, Peachum's "flash Molls" beguile Macheath until constables seize him; and in Newgate, Lucy, an earlier wife from whom he had secured no divorce when marrying Polly, reproaches him for having deserted her. When Polly enters, Macheath pretends not to know what she means by calling him "husband" and caressing him, and when Polly is removed by her father, the highwayman induces Lucy to steal Lockit's keys and let him out.

Lockit and Peachum both swear to recapture him, however, and this time he is discovered in Mrs. Coaxer's house. In jail both Lucy and Polly insist that he recognize one or the other as his lawful wife; but Macheath hangs back until the Beggar and the Player decide he shall be freed, "to comply with the taste of the town." Then the highwayman chooses Polly as his legitimate spouse and all ends happily, though Polly's admirable mother mourns: "If she had only an intrigue with the fellow," she tells Peachum, "why, the best families have excused and huddled up a frailty of the sort. 'Tis marriage, husband, that makes it a blemish!"

Among the remaining operas Handel wrote, beginning with the year 1734, *Serse* (London, 1738; Göttingen, 1924) has called forth the famous "Largo." The tale is one of Xerxes, King of Persia, a lover of Nature, standing in his palace garden beneath a spreading plantain tree. Overcome by the peace and loveliness of his surroundings he sings to the tree the "Largo," beginning "Frondi tenere"—that noble melody transcribed for well-nigh every instrument—only to have a court lady, a pretty worldling, poke fun at the lover who sings his adoration to leafy tree instead of lovely woman. The peace of the palace gardens is gone. King Xerxes flies into a rage, and his brother Arsamenes, the sisters Romilda and Atalanta, Queen Amastris, her father Ariodant, all quarrel violently until at last calm is restored. In the opera the happy fantastic humor of this mad scene—its underlying meaning that Cupid can upset the dignity of even the most philosophic of kings—makes the famous "Largo" all the more effective.

The Rebellion of 1745, the rising of the Highland clans on behalf of "Bonnie Prince Charlie," the Young Pretender—whose defeat prompted Handel's *Judas Maccabæus,* the "conquering hero" of its celebrated chorus being the Duke of Cumberland—has wakened certain operatic echoes, and is represented, among others by Flotow's *Rob Roy* (Paris, 1836); De Koven's *Rob Roy* (Detroit, 1894); Jean Urich's *Flora Macdonald* (Bologna, 1885); and Franz von Holstein's a historic-romantic opera *Die Hochländer* (*The Highlanders,* Mannheim, 1876).

## Tom Jones

Fielding's great novel, *Tom Jones or the History of a Foundling* (1748), "written with the sincere purpose of recommending goodness and innocence," has motived various operatic settings, which present the two-volume tale in the scenes best utilizing its dramatic and musical opportunities. Philidor's *Tom Jones* (Paris, 1765; London, 1785), book by Linley, is a tearful *bourgeois* emotional comedy; Planquette's *Tom Jones* (London, 1889), an operetta stressing the humorous sides of the original; but the most engaging setting of the theme is probably Edward German's opera *Tom Jones* (London, 1907) whose happy musical invention shows its subject voiced a real appeal.

George III already was king when Goldsmith's famous pastoral novel appeared. It has found a light and graceful musical version in Liza Lehmann's *The Vicar of Wakefield* (Manchester, 1907); and Sir George Macfarren has set *She Stoops to Conquer* (London, 1864). The poor, gifted seventeen-year-old poet who drank arsenic in his Brook Street garret when starvation stared him in the face, has been idealized in Leoncavallo's *Tommasso Chatterton* (Rome, 1896); and Frances Sheridan's farce *The Critic* (1779), has called forth an entertaining musical caricature. *The Critic or an Opera Rehearsed* (London, 1916), is Sheridan's play set to a sparkling score by Charles Villiers Stanford, musically an entertaining caricature of the older Italian opera in which such numbers as the "Choral Prayers to Mars" and "Auld Lang Syne" stand out. The King's highway has been remembered in Henry David Leslie's *Romance of Bold Dick Turpin* (London, 1857).

Byron's day was that of Beau Brummel's "fat friend" George, Prince of Wales, afterward King George IV, and Byron is the hero of the Chilean composer Luigi Stefano Giarda's opera *Lord Byron* (Santiago de Chili, 1910). The Greek revolt against Turkish tyranny for which Byron fought with sword and pen, dying at Missolonghi, had awakened universal sympathy both in England and in France. In the latter country it called forth Hérold's dramatic setting of Ozannaux' *Le dernier jour de Missolonghi* (Paris, 1826) and *Le maçon* (*Mason and Locksmith*, Paris, 1825) by François Auber, book by Scribe and Delavigne, with the outstanding air, "Du courage, à l'ouvrage," and the unique "Quarrel Duet" (Act III), considered Auber's best comic score. The rôles of the Turks and the Greek girl voice the hatred for the Moslems and the enthusiasm for the Greek struggle for liberty current in Paris in 1825. Henriette, just married to Roger the mason and, according to custom, first to arrive at their new home, waits in vain for her husband. Roger has been taken blindfold to the Turkish embassy, to do a job of bricklaying for Abdullah Pasha; Irma, a lovely Greek innocent in Abdullah's hands, has attempted flight with De Merinville, a young officer and the mason's friend. When Roger finds he is to brick them up alive in the cellar to please the cruel Turk (Act II), he sings while bricklaying to let them know they will be saved. Next morning Henriette (a rumor reached her that Roger spent the night in a Turkish harem) reproaches him when he appears. But Roger, just come from the rescue of the captives of his trowel by the Paris police, removes her doubts and all ends happily.

### WILLIAM RATCLIFF

In 1822 a German poet, Heine, wrote a drama on a Scotch subject, "time, the present" which, among others, has motived operas by Italian, Russian, and French composers. William Ratcliff has twice murdered the bridegrooms of Maria MacGregor, daughter of a Scotch laird, for, rejected by the girl, he cannot bear to see her marry another. Twice he has entered her bridal chamber to show her hands stained respectively with the blood of Macdonald, Earl of Ais, and of Lord Duncan, disappearing with a hideous laugh. But Lord Douglas, Maria's third fiancé, is made of sterner stuff. When William tries to kill, he overcomes him, but spares his life. His generosity is rewarded by Ratcliff's attempt to abduct the unfortunate girl. When her cries bring her father hurrying into the room, he kills the old laird, and drags his helpless prey into an adjoining cabinet. Lord Douglas hurries after the dastard too late, for William has shot Maria and himself. Insane Margaret, Maria's old nurse, chuckles as, raising the curtain of the cabinet, she reveals the dead bodies.

In *Guglielmo Ratcliffe* (Milan, 1895) by Mascagni, a veristic score, the Prayer, "Padre nostro," may be mentioned. *William Ratcliffe* (Nice, 1906) by Xavier Leroux, is a declamatory score using expressive leading themes in Wagnerian style; and there is a *Guglielmo Ratcliffe* (Bologna, 1889) by Emilio Pizzi. César Cui's *William Ratcliffe* (Moscow, 1900) with light, piquant songs in the dance rhythms Auber used, rises to a genuine glow of passion in the Love Duet (Act III) between William and Mary.

# CHAPTER XI

## THE FRENCH REVOLUTION AND THE EMPIRE

### 1. *Earlier Operas of Freedom*

#### ITALY

#### "RIENZI"

#### (*The Last of the Tribunes*)

RICHARD WAGNER. Rienzi, who rescues the medieval Romans from aristocratic tyranny, is betrayed by the people he has freed. Influenced by Meyerbeer's, Auber's, and Rossini's "historical operas," Wagner's earlier score (Dresden, 1842), has a fine Overture and some beautiful melodies, including the famous Rienzi's "Prayer."

Irene, Cola di Rienzi's sister, is dragged from her brother's house by Paolo Orsini, the prize for which he battles with his enemies, the Colonna, in the streets of Rome. Rienzi, his sister rescued, determines to abolish the tyranny of the nobles. In the Capitol he sternly reproves them (Act II) and they swear vengeance. Warned by Adriano Colonna, Rienzi's shirt of mail worn beneath his cloak saves him from Orsini's dagger. He pardons the offender. Supported by the people of Rome, Rienzi takes the field (Act III) against the nobles and defeats them, returning to Rome, the last of the Tribunes, to wield supreme power. But Steffano Colonna, Adriano's father, has been killed in the battle, and Adriano curses his friend Rienzi's ambition, accusing him of turning Irene against him. Rienzi's death is resolved upon in a gathering before the Lateran Church in Rome. (Act IV.) Adriano's dagger shall deal the deadly stroke and Cardinal Raimondo lays the ban of the Church on the Tribune at a solemn high mass. To the Capitol comes Adriano, imploring Irene to flee. She refuses to leave her brother and (change of scene) the conspirators in the square before the Capitol flinging firebrands, Irene and Rienzi are trapped in the burning palace. When Adriano seeks to save Irene the roof crashes down, burying all three beneath the ruins.

Other Rienzi operas include: Achille Peri's *Rienzi* (Milan, 1862); the Russian Kashperov's *Rienzi* (Florence, 1863); and *Cola di Rienzi* (Venice, 1880) by Luigi Ricci, Jr. Verdi's *I Lombardi alla prima Crociata* (*The Lombards of the First Crusade,*

389

Milan, 1842); as *Jerusalem,* Paris, 847, and *Giselda,* Constantinople, 1851, with text changes) like other earlier Verdi operas,
is one the Italian people regarded as an "opera of freedom,"
Giralda's "Prayer" being taken to voice the aspirations of the
Milanese to cast off Austrian tyranny. The same applies to Verdi's
*La battaglia di Legnano* (Rome, 1849) in which the German
Emperor Frederick Barbarossa was the political villain, personifying the Austrian power, and the concluding scene "Death for
the Fatherland," the patriotic "hit."

In *Giovanna di Guzman* (Paris, 1855; New York, 1859) by
Verdi, also known as *Les vêpres Siciliennes,* book by Scribe, akin
in style to Meyerbeer's *Huguenots,* Verdi "sang the deliverance of
Italy from the Austrian yoke, in the guise of narrating the massacre of the French invaders of Sicily at vespers in Palermo on
Faster Monday" (1282). The outstanding number is the bolero
(Act V) though Hélène has a noble cavatina, "Courage!" (Act I).
Henry, son of Simon de Montfort, French Viceroy of Sicily, is
in a dilemma. Nature bids him spare his father, honor says he
must die if the conspiracy against French tyranny (Henry is one
of the conspirators) is to succeed. The Sicilian Duchess Hélène
who ioves Simon's son, has been told by Jean de Procida, the
patriot leader, that the hour she marries Henry—who has listened
to Nature's voice—will be the hour of his death. In vain she
refuses to marry her lover, the curtain falls on the mob about
to kill Simon, Henry, and Hélène.

## "LA MUETTE DE PORTICI"

### (*The Dumb Girl of Portici*)

FRANÇOIS AUBER. Book by Scribe (Paris, 1828). The historic Masaniello (Tommaso Aniello) led a successful popular revolt against the
Spanish viceroy of Naples, De Arcos (1647), but after he had seized
the government, fell into acute melancholia and his insanity regarded
by the people as a sign of Divine displeasure, De Arcos had him shot.
B. Keiser, *Masaniello Furioso* (Hamburg, 1706) and M. E. Carafa's
*Masaniello* (Paris, 1827) already had celebrated the revolutionary hero,
and to avoid confusion with Carafa's score Auber changed his title
*Masaniello* to *La Muette de Portici.* The Duet, "Amour sacré de la
pâtrie," sung by Nourrit in Brussels in 1830, caused the outbreak of the
revolution which freed Belgium from Dutch rule (the Belgian Gregoir's
opera *De Belgen en 1848,* Brussels, 1851, should here be mentioned).
It also was the rallying song of the German students in the revolutionary
troubles of 1848. *La Muette* is Auber's greatest musical triumph. Fenella, the heroine, is dumb (a dance and pantomime rôle) and speaks
through the orchestra. The glowing southern color of the Barcarole,
Tarantella, and Spanish dances was largely imitated by Auber's con-

temporaries; and comedy and pathos, "dancing madness and masked revolution" are genially welded in a grand opera of Meyerbeerian pomp, its outstanding themes presented in an effective Overture.

The Neapolitans cheer Alfonso, the viceroy's son, on his way to church to wed Elvira, a Spanish princess, but the still small voice of conscience reproaches him for having betrayed Fenella, a dumb but attractive fisher girl. Returning from church, Fenella (she has escaped those guarding her in a secluded place to prevent scandal) rushes up to kind-hearted Elvira and with eloquent fingers tells the tale of her betrayal by Alfonso, disappearing in the excitement her speaking pantomime has called forth. On Portici's strand (Act II) where merry fishermen sing as they cast their nets, Masaniello (Fenella's brother) mourns her disappearance, then bursts into the Barcarole which rouses the people against their Spanish oppressors. After Fenella arrives and fingers reveal what tongue cannot tell, Masaniello calls the Neapolitans to arms. Alfonso has been pardoned by Elvira, but when Selva, captain of the guard, tries to capture Fenella in the market place to bring her to the palace, with the best of intentions, the revolt breaks out. Blood runs in the gutters and powder smoke fills the air, Masaniello overcomes the Spaniards and Naples is his. But he is too merciful to suit his fellow conspirators and (Act IV) they secretly poison him when Fenella, love for her betrayer having induced her to hide Elvira and Alfonso in his fisher hut, he protects them from the daggers of his friends. Masaniello's poison now has driven him insane and he falls in the struggle against the fresh troops Alfonso has led into the city (Act IV). Fenella, poor thing, has a choice of suicides, according to the version used. She may fling herself from the palace terrace into the Bay of Naples or leap into a torrent of burning lava cast up by an irruption of Vesuvius, while the people pray the sacrifice of her life may placate the angry volcano.

*Giovanni Gallurese* (Turin, 1905; New York, 1925) by Italo Montemezzi, book by d'Angelantonio, tells the tale of a Sardinian Tell "to attractive music wedded to an outmoded plot" (Oscar Thompson). Sardinian folk tunes to the *launedda*, triple shepherd's pipe; and dances, "Danze Montanare," to accordion accompaniment, stand out, as does the Love Duet (Act I). In seventeenth century Sardinia, Giovanni Gallurese, outlaw patriot, saves Maria, the mountain girl, from Spanish outrage but when the Spanish prisoner Rivegas tells her falsely that Giovanni is a criminal, credulous Maria flees from her savior in horror. When Sardinian exiles testify to Giovanni's patriotism and nobility, however, she hastens back to his arms (Act III) only to see him blown from her embrace by a musket shot discharged by the villain Rivegas. But he is foiled in his dastard attempt to abduct the girl by the hero, who like Roland at Roncevaux winds his horn as he dies, and brings his men to the scene in time to allow Maria to fling herself sobbing on his dead body. *Matteo Falcone* (Hanover, 1898) by Theodore Gerlach—outstanding a brilliant "Tarantelle"—is a Corsican father. The Corsican patriot Sanpiero betrayed his daughter Beatrice, so Fortunato, her boy brother, betrays Sanpiero's hiding place to the Genoese. But Matteo forces his son to leap from a cliff to wipe out the dishonor done the Corsican code of hospitality by Sanpiero's betrayal, and after his wife has died of shock and he has buried both, meets Sanpiero on his way to execution. Then, as the patriot in a last interview is being pardoned by Beatrice for the wrong done her, Matteo stabs him to avenge his daughter's honor before he is hung by the Genoese. Zöllner also wrote a *Matteo Falcone* (New York, 1894). *Poliuto* (Paris, 1849, as *Les Martyres*) by Donizetti after a Corneille tragedy, is less interesting as a tale of early Christian martyrdom than as an example of tyranny applied to art. The Naples police forbade its performance (1838) because Nourrit, the French tenor cast for the title rôle, was reputed a *carbonero* (Charcoal burner)—the "Reds" of that day being black —and when Nourrit told the King of Naples Poliuto was a saint, the latter said "Leave the saints in the calendar and do not bring them on the stage!" *Polyeucte* (Paris, 1878) is a rather dull opera by Gounod on the same subject. Sir Frederick Cowen's operetta *Garibaldi* (London, 1874) and Marenco's ballet *Lo sbarco di Garibaldi a Marsala* (*Garibaldi's Landing at Marsala,* Genoa, 1841) bring the hero of United Italy on the stage.

### SWITZERLAND

### "GUILLAUME TELL"

#### (*William Tell*)

GIOACHINO ROSSINI. Book by Jouy and Bis after Schiller (Paris, 1829). The music in the romantic style of the grand French opera rises to noble dramatic heights. The famous Overture comprises four sections: the "Cello Idyl," the "Storm," the "Alpine Dance" and the "Great March," four individual musical dramatic pictures fine in invention, temperament, and expression. Other outstanding numbers are: the "Fisher Barcarole"; splendid choruses ("Wedding Procession," "Hunting" and "Sharpshooters'" Choruses); "Tyrolienne" (Act II); the "Tell Aria" (with cello); the "Prayer" and the "Ranz des Vaches." *Tell* was Rossini's last opera.

It is May Day on the Vierwaldstätter Lake. The village brides old Melchthal is blessing do not include his son Arnold's chosen, for he secretly loves Princess Mathilde of Hapsburg, whose life he saved. But village dances break up in confusion as Leuchtold rushes in. He has slain an Austrian soldier who tried to outrage his child, and though storm clouds gather, Tell rows him over the lake to save him from his pursuers, who seize old Melchthal and carry him off to die in Leuchtold's stead. In the woods (Act II), Arnold passionately singing his love for Mathilde, lets song die in his throat when Tell tells him the Austrians have murdered his father. That night on Mount Rutli he joins the chiefs of the Swiss cantons in an oath to free Switzerland from the oppressor. While Arnold bids Mathilde farewell (Act III) to set about avenging his father, Gessler in Altorf market place (change of scene) has topped a tall pole with the hat, symbol of Hapsburg overlordship, to which all passersby must do reverence. Tell passing with his son Gemmy, refuses to do so. Told he may save his boy's life by shooting an apple from his head, he accomplishes the feat, and telling Gessler his second arrow was meant for his tyrant breast had he slain his son, he is led to prison, while in Melchthal's hut Arnold invokes his father's spirit (Act IV) and rouses the Swiss. Mathilde (change of scene) restores Gemmy to his weeping mother, and as signal fires of revolt flame from the hills, Gessler's bark, containing the tyrant and his prisoner, is seen drifting shoreward over the stormy lake. Suddenly, with a daring leap Tell springs to land, thrusting the bark far back into the water with his foot. As his arrow finds Gessler's heart, the patriots, rushing up from every side, join in a hymn to freedom while Mathilde nestles in Arnold's arms.

*The Archers or the Mountaineers of Switzerland* (New York, 1796) by Benjamin Carr, book by Dunlop, was a ballad opera with Tell in the rôle of an "active politician." Grétry's *Guillaume Tell* (Paris, 1791) was revived after the first performance of Rossini's score. *Hofer, the Tell of the Tyrol* (London, 1830) by Sir Henry Bishop is Rossini's *Tell* with a new text to evade copyright. Louis Lacombe's *Winkelried* (Geneva, 1892) sings a Swiss patriot of Tell's day; J. Reiter has written a *Wilhelm Tell* (Vienna, 1917); and the Tyrol patriot of Napoleonic days is sung in Friedrich Emil Kaiser's *Andreas Hofer* (Reichenberg, 1886).

## GERMANY

*Arminius* (Dresden, 1877) by Heinrich Hoffmann, book by Dahn, deals with the German folk hero of old Roman days who destroyed the legions of Augustus in the Teutoberger Forest (9th century). After Fulvia, a Roman lady, has tried in vain to lure Arminius from his wife Thusnelda, she appears in the midst of the famous battle (Act IV) and when the hero prevents her from stabbing her lawfully wedded rival, buries the dagger in her own breast while the Teutons sing their recovered liberty.

*Die Hermannsschlacht* (Munich, 1835) by Chélard, Zingarelli's pupil, is considered his best score.

## "TILL EULENSPIEGEL"

RICHARD STRAUSS. Satiric-dramatic ballet by Waslav Nijinsky (New York, 1916). Till Eulenspiegel or Ulenspiegel, born in Kneitlingern, Brunswick, toward the end of the thirteenth century, a contemner of constituted authority, "the evil conscience of his times," expresses the spirit of liberty during the Middle Ages incarnated in a merry peasant rascal. The ballet was adapted to the music of Strauss's symphonic poem, in free rondo form, *Eulenspiegels lustige Streiche,* a picturesque, unified and brilliant score.

In the market place of a medieval German town, shadowed by its Gothic minster, Till, in the rôle of a tragic buffoon, mocks in turn burgher, knight, and learned clerk, representatives of class and prerogative in the "Holy Roman Empire" of his day. As a buffoon, he plays practical jokes on baker, confectioner, apple woman and merchant. As a knight he flirts with lovely *châtelaines* of neighboring castles. As man of science, he mocks the pedants who, fascinated by his pseudo-learned jargon trail after him in a ludicrous game of "follow my leader." Till's upsetting revolutionary activities lead to his arrest. To beat of drum he is haled before the town counsellors and when he flaunts them he is condemned to the gallows. The hangman appears, Till is swung aloft (a trill of the flutes depicts his loss of breath) and dangles from the gallows while the people gape below. Suddenly Till's spirit flashes down, electrifying the huddled town folk. They realize that he typifies the revolt of the oppressed against abuse of power and place, and that he will live forever in their hearts. For the irreverent wit which makes superstition, malice, and tyranny ridiculous is beyond hangman's power to destroy.

*Thyl Eulenspiegel* (Brussels, 1900; new version, 1920) by Jan Blockx, book by Cain and Solvay, after Charles De Coster's novel, a local application of the legend, makes Thyl the incarnation of Netherland patriotism in the sixteenth century struggle against Spanish oppression. The score contains music of elemental power, in folkwise style. Outstanding are "Thyl's Entry" (Act I); the Kermesse Scene, with the Flemish folk song "Daar ging een pater langs het land" ("There was a monk went by the way"); the Love Duet (Act II); and the scene between Nèle and Vargas, against the chant of the condemned on their way to the stake (Act III). Thyl flings a Spanish soldier into the river. About to be arrested (Act II) he secures from Vargas, a Spanish officer who interrupts his wedding to Nèle, not knowing who he is, the reward for his own capture, and uses it to foment rebellion. Then bidding his love farewell (Duet) while a chorus of the dead call on him to avenge them on the tyrant, he goes to dare his fate. While Vargas insults Nèle in his cabinet (Act III), Thyl leaps in and rescues her, but (change of scene) captured and about to be marched to death, the irruption of the people saves him and his comrades. The Spaniards take their captives' places on the burning pyre, and the opera ends with an apostrophe to Flemish freedom. Two other modern composers of importance have devoted operas to Till: Emil Reznicek, *Till Eulenspiegel* (Berlin, 1902), and Walter Braunfels, *Till Eulenspiegel* (Stuttgart, 1913).

*Der Bergesee* (*The Mountain Lake,* Vienna, 1911), by Julius Bittner, with fine revolutionary choruses, deals with a sixteenth century revolt of tax-oppressed peasants of Salzburg. The lansquenet, Jörg, deserts his colors for the sake of the peasant girl Gundula. With the rebels he descends from the hills into the plain to battle and Gundula, despairing of seeing him again, opens the flood-gates of the mountain lake which sweeps down the valley drowning all, including the girl herself. The German "liberty opera" of the eighteenth century is Mozart's *Magic Flute,* though its "political" program was supplied by the librettist, and Mozart wrote it purely as an art work and not as a plea for freedom.

## "DIE ZAUBERFLÖTE"

WOLFGANG AMADEUS MOZART. Book by Emmanuel Schikaneder (Vienna, 1791). Schikaneder originally had planned a book for a great fairy opera—Mozart's score came near being known as *Lulu*—and though in one sense of the word it remained a fairy opera, on the other hand the ideals of eighteenth century Freemasonry, born of the French Revolution and developed in Georgian England, ideals of liberty, tolerance, and internationalism, became part and parcel of the text. "Gathered from a hundred and one corners, the text of *The Magic Flute* is a pyramid of noble, strange, and mysterious ideas, rooted in the world concept of distant, exotic cultures (Schürig). The Emperor Joseph II, idealized in *The Magic Flute* as Tamino, the liberal prince, was the same who first was inclined to forbid the performance of Mozart's *Marriage of Figaro* because of its attacks on aristocratic privilege. Mozart's music is timeless. It has survived its political program and endures as one of the most human of all operas ever written. The colorature arias of the Queen of the Night; the Overture; the "Priests' Chorus," "O Isis und Osiris"; the Invocation; the air, "Bei Männern welche Liebe fühlen," are among its loveliest pages. It is sung in Italian as *Il flauto magico.*

Tamino, a young and virtuous prince (the future Emperor Joseph II, friend of the Masons) after an adventure with a serpent in a forest, meets Papageno (typifying the light-hearted Viennese) and the Queen of the Night (the bigoted and reactionary Austrian Empress Maria Theresia) who begs Tamino to rescue her lovely daughter Pamina (the Austrian people) from the clutches of old Sarastro, high priest of Isis (grand master of the Masonic lodges) for Sarastro has removed the girl from her mother's influence. Tamino promises to undertake the quest. He receives a golden flute and Papageno a silver bell to defend them from danger, and they set forth, guided by three angel boys.

A room in Sarastro's palace (Act II, when the opera is given in a three-act version) shows dusky Monostatos (Monasticism and Clerical Intolerance) dragging in terrified Pamina. Papageno, in bird plumage, appears and frightens him off. Meanwhile (change of scene), Tamino tries to enter the temple of Isis, where a priest explains that Sarastro is the opposite to a villain. Yet when Papageno appears with Pamina, all three decide to escape. Monostatos stops them and though Sarastro punishes the blackamoor for making love to the princess he is not yet ready to free Pamina; instead he leads Tamino and Papageno into the temple to undergo an ordeal.

The priests of Isis (Masons) decide if Tamino passes the test he shall have Pamina. The prince keeps silence during temptation and the scene shifts to a garden. Here Clericalism (Monostatos) gloats over the sleeping Austrian people (Pamina) until Imperial Bigotry (Queen of the Night) appears to press into Pamina's hand a dagger with which to slay Freemasonry (Sarastro). Happily Pamina has no intention of so doing.

Reverting to the hall of ordeal, Papageno cannot hold his tongue; but Tamino manages to resist even Pamina's questions, and she thinks his love for her has grown cold.

With a heart as hard as the pyramids, to which the scene now shifts (sometimes Act III begins with this scene) Sarastro parts the lovers; while bestowing pretty Papagena on Papageno as a bride. From the pyramids the scene changes to the open country, where the angel boys find it hard to restrain despairing Tamino, who thinks Pamina unfaithful, from committing suicide. Yet his trials are coming to an end. In a rocky cavern where a stream flows and a fire burns, Tamino and Pamina undergo a final Isisian or Masonic ordeal of water and flame, and pass it successfully by means of the Magic Flute. In the concluding scene Freemasonry (Sarastro) blesses the tie between the liberal young Emperor (Tamino) and his People (Pamina) and uniting their hands in marriage bids them be happy together.

*Das Labyrinth* (Vienna, 1794) by Peter von Winter is an attempt to give *The Magic Flute* a sequel opera, but the old Pepita ballet, *The Magic Flute*, music by Riccardo Drigo, is the tale of a rococo country girl's narrow escape from becoming an elderly admirer's darling.

Frederick the Great who, measured by the standards of his time, was a liberal monarch, is remembered in operas which make the most of the musical opportunities afforded by the picturesque military background of his day. Among them are *Ziethenhusaren* (Breslau, 1869) and *Serenissimus* (Berlin, 1903) by Bernard Scholz; *Des Grossen Königs Rekrut* (Brunswick, 1889) by Max Clarus; *Fredericus Rex* (Berlin, 1901) by Paul Geissler; and *La Barberina* (Crefeld, 1912) by Otto Neitzel, its performance forbidden—it deals with an episode between Frederick and an Italian dancer for whom he is supposed to have had a fondness—because it staged a Prussian king "not dead over two hundred years."

*Theodor Körner* (Cassel, 1918) by Alfred Kaiser, Weissheimer (Munich, 1872), and Donaudy (Hamburg, 1902) sing the hero of the German struggle for freedom in 1813 and Humperdinck's *Die Marketenderin* (*The Vivandière*, Cologne, 1914), a patriotic Blücher opera whose heroine prefers a private in the ranks to the field marshal, is an inferior musical reaction to patriotic emotion excited by the World War. *Der Roland von Berlin* (Berlin, 1904) by Ruggiero Leoncavallo after Alexis' "patriotic" novel, was the opera ex-Emperor William II of Germany commissioned the Italian composer to write as a Hohenzollern glorification of the person of his ancestor, the Elector Friedrich of Brandenburg. In Berlin (1442) the famous statue of the Roland of Berlin is the emblem of civic liberty. The burgomaster tells the young weaver Henning that not until the statue of Roland leaves its pedestal shall he marry his daughter Elsbeth; but though the young lover enters the town in triumph with the victorious knights of the Elector Friedrich, and the latter has the statue cast down, it is too late for Henning since, slain in the fighting, he is carried in a corpse.

*Patrie* (*Fatherland*, Paris, 1886; as *Vaterland*, Hamburg, 1889) by Emile Paladhile after Sardou's drama, an effective score along Meyerbeerian lines, outstanding Rysoor's air, "C'est ici le berceau de notre liberté," the Conjuration Scene, and the Apostrophe, "Pauvre victime obscure," was revived in Paris during the World War because the Spanish occupation of Holland by the soldiers of King Philip II seemed to offer an analogy to the German occupation of Belgium. When Rysoor, a Dutch patriot, tells his wife Dolores he will kill her lover (not knowing him to be his friend Karloo), she betrays to the Duke of Alva that Jonas, the Brussels bell ringer, will sound the signal for revolt. When he does so and the patriot conspirators are surrounded and captured by the Spaniards, Rysoor makes Karloo swear to avenge their death on the woman who betrayed them. Karloo, entering Dolores' chamber as avenger, not lover, makes her witness the execution of his fellow conspirators, poniards her and then flings himself from the window to dash out his brains on the stone pavement below.

### 2. Operas of the French Revolution

Old Jean Jacques Rousseau, French philosopher, novelist, and musician, was among the men of letters who prepared the advent of the French Revolution. *Les Charmettes* (Paris, 1925) by Armand Bolsène, book by Jules Méry, after an incident in Rousseau's *Confessions,* tells how the philosopher, host of Madame de Warens in his château of Les Charmettes is happy in her love. A beggar happens by, is taken in, cared for, and clothed. Rousseau, called away, returns after a month to find the tramp master of *his* home and *his* mistress's heart. Disillusioned with love, Rousseau leaves never to return. Graceful lyric music underlines the tale. *La Marseillaise* (Paris, 1901) by Lucien Lambert, is a one-act score written around the French Revolution's greatest song and presents Rouget de l'Isle-Adam singing the immortal melody for the first time to the applause of the crowd in Dietrich's tavern.

### "DER KUHREIGEN"

#### (*Ranz des Vaches*)

WILHELM KIENZL. Book by Batka after rococo novelette by Bartsch (Vienna, 1911; New York, 1913). Kienzl's music drama *The Cow-Call,* is based on the fact that the Swiss Guards (Paris, 1792) were forbidden to sing the "Kuhreigen" or "Ranz des vaches" since homesickness for their Alpine hills so overcame them they deserted. The music has charm and color. Outstanding is the "Ranz des vaches" itself; the "rhythmic musical fireworks of the French Revolution Scene"; and the dramatic Finale with its thrill of horror.

In the barracks of the Swiss Guard at Versailles the soldier Primus Thallus sings the forbidden song, "At Strassburg on the bastion," which introduces the "Ranz des vaches" and next morning at the palace (Act II) Marquis Massimelle, captain of the Swiss Guard, presents his death sentence to King Louis XVI for signature. The kind-hearted king refers the matter of Thallus' life or death to Massimelle's young wife, the Marquise Blanchefleur, who, delighted to have a real Swiss to play the shepherd in her court *pastorale,* saves him. Then the lovely young aristocrat is seized with a passing fancy for the handsome soldier; but she is the idol of his pure dreams; he cannot stoop to love her lightly as she would have him do and, disappointed, she dismisses him. When the Revolution sweeps France (Act III), Massimelle's Paris *hôtel* is sacked, he is led to prison, and Blanchefleur, hiding in a secret passage, is saved from outrage only by the advent of Thallus, now a captain in the Revolutionary army. Following her to prison he pleads with her to marry him and escape the knife. He pictures their happiness in the

Swiss hills; but Blanchefleur, spoiled darling of a splendid court, cannot imagine herself calling the cattle home. Yet to show her appreciation of her faithful lover she grants him a dance, and as her name is called in the roll of those who are to lay their necks on the block of the guillotine she frees herself gently from his arm and dances off to death to the music of the Mozartian minuet they have been stepping.

*Thérèse* (Monte Carlo, 1907) by Jules Massenet, book by Claretie, a palpitant dramatic score with drumbeat, crowd cries, "Marseillaise," and charming lyric moments, notably the duet "Oublier, t'oublier" (minuet with clavecin accompaniment between Thérèse and Armand) and Thérèse's air, "Si je ne t'aimais pas," is the tale of the Girondin Thorel whose royalist friend, Armand de Clerval, whom he hides in his château (once Armand's) while the latter is on his way to join the royalists in the Vendée, makes love to Thorel's wife and plans to abduct her. But Thérèse learns her husband has been arrested and is on his way to the scaffold. She rejects her tempter and crying from her window, "Long live the King!" is dragged off by the howling mob to share the death of the man she really loves while Armand escapes. *Les Girondins* (*The Girondists*, Lyon, 1905) by Fernand Le Borne, a worthy score, makes Laurence, Duclos the Girondin's mistress, after the traitor Varley has had him jailed and offers to release him if the girl will be his, pistol the villain, snatch the order of release and hurry to jail. Finding Duclos prefers to join his fellow Girondists in death, she remains to share his fate.

## "ANDREA CHENIER"

Umberto Giordano. Book by Illica (Milan, 1896; New York, 1896). The score has been summed up as music of "cool, intelligent moods, contrasting with grateful outbreaks of song, interesting combinations of piano concertos with love duets and piquant orchestral details" (Bie).

After the poet Andrea Chénier has improvised a poem condemning the loveless treatment of poor by rich in the Countess de Coignay's Paris *hôtel* at the request of the Countess' daughter, Madeleine, who hates the artificial life she leads, starving wretches of the Paris gutters, the Countess' servant Gerard their spokesman, crowd into the ballroom with pathetic pleas, but are hustled out by the lackeys. In the Café Hottot—the Revolution an accomplished fact—Chénier receives a note from the fair unknown he loves (Act II) and is followed on his way to her by Gerard, now a Revolutionary officer. The unknown is Madeleine; and her two lovers crossing swords, Gerard, wounded, bids his rival hurry her off, and when he is found by his friends, pretends not to have recognized his antagonist. Before the Revolutionary Tribunal Gerard appeals for money for France (Act III) and women thrust their jewels on him to the tune of "La Carmagnole." Andrea in prison, Madeleine offers Gerard to sacrifice her honor for his life, but when he pleads for his rival the crowd cries *A la lanterne!* and Chénier is led away. In St. Lazare prison (Act IV) as Andrea is writing his last poem, Madeleine is shown in. She has bribed the jailor to substitute her name for another on the death list, and they await the call to the guillotine happy in the thought that their heads will fall together into the basket. *Die Revolutionshochzeit* (*The Revolutionary Wedding*, Leipzig, 1919), by Eugen d'Albert after Sofie Michaelis' drama, a "brutally theatric" score, melodramatic pages alternating with charming rococo melodies, shows Alaine de l'Estoile and Ernest de Tressailes, just married in her château, seized by the revolutionists (1793) and condemned to death as aristocrats. Marc-Antoine, the Republican commander, madly in love with Alaine, accepts her offer of herself in exchange for her husband's escape, and when the girl wife realizes her plebeian lover's generosity means his own death, she flings herself freely into his arms and as he faces the firing squad at dawn for losing his prisoner, casts herself before him as the volley rings out and dies by the same bullet.

## "IL PICCOLO MARAT"

### (*Little Marat*)

PIETRO MASCAGNI. Book by Forzano (Rome, 1921). A melodramatic verist score with clever musical characterizations, outstanding Marat's "Song to his Mother," called "a jewel in Mascagni's purest lyric style" (Act I) ; the orchestral Intermezzo, and the Love Episode in Puccini's style (Act II).

In Nantes during the time of the Terror, Orso, the butcher (the historic Carrier) the revolutionary chief, has his victims shot, guillotined, or drowned wholesale, putting them in flat-bottomed boats with trapdoor bottoms, the famous *noyades* of Nantes. To this city of horror comes a French nobleman who pretends to be a Jacobin of reddest dye in order to rescue his mother from prison and who plays his part so well that he is nicknamed "Little Marat." In Orso's home, Little Marat meets and falls desperately in love with Maliella, the monster's pure and beautiful young niece, and the flight of the lovers with Little Marat's mother, aided by a ship's carpenter, who from coward turns hero, is the climax of the work. The Overture, dramatic choruses and musically and theatrically effective crowd scenes, notably that in which (Act I) the men, women and children of Nantes are confronted by Orso's soldiers in a passionate interweaving of choral and orchestral tone, built on four connected themes, are a feature of the score.

*Maria de Bréval* (Trieste, 1925) by Alberto Randegger, book by Macchi, tells a similar tale of a French aristocrat who turns *sans-culotte* in order to save the life of one dear to him, and offers the same contrast between lyric sentiment and mob passion. The "Madrigal" and "Grotesque Contradance" (Act I), symphonic Intermezzo (Act II), the Quarrel Scene ensemble, and Finale (Act III) stand out in a colorful work orchestrated in modern fashion.

*La Vivandière* (Paris, 1875), by Benjamin Godard, a tuneful *opéra comique*, shows Georges, induced by pretty Marion, the *vivandière,* to enlist in the Republican army (1794). He is disowned by his noble father, and the girl, though court-martialed for letting his aristocratic parent escape from captivity, is pardoned to marry her lover. Kempter's *Sans-culottes* (Zurich, 1900); *Die Göttin der Vernunft* (*The Goddess of Reason,* Vienna, 1897), a revolutionary operetta by Johann Strauss, *Der Jacobiner* (Graz, 1890) by Zois, and *Die scharlachrote Blume* (*The Scarlet Pimpernel*) by the Norwegian Schjelderup are among scores inspired by the French Revolution. *La Vendée* (Lyons, 1897) by Gabriel Pierné, paints the war between the "Whites" (Royalists) and "Blues" (Republicans) in sanguinary colors as the background for a tragic love tale, outstanding Vendean folk songs and the air "Ah, mon coeur" (Act I). *Charlotte Corday* (Paris, 1901) by Alexander Georges—the symphonic musical picture of the *Palais Royal* outstanding in the score—shows Marat carried in triumph about the Peacock Tavern in Paris (Prologue) while Charlotte Corday in Caën determines to kill him. Buying the dagger in the *Palais Royal* Gardens in Paris (Act II), she seeks out the monster, drives it home as he lies in his bath (Act III) and, captured and tried, the curtain falls as the executioner seizes her hair on the scaffold.

### 3. *Directory and Consulate*

Within the period of the French Directory fall various operas, including the famous *La fille de Madame Angot* (*Madame Angot's Daughter*) by Charles Lecocq, book by Girardin, Clairville, and Koning (Brussels, 1872), outstanding Clairette's air "I owe you thanks," Pomponnette's romance, "Behold, she is so innocent," and the Final Chorus and Dance. It is the story of pretty Clairette, Madame Angot's daughter, who loves the poet, Ange Pitou and, preferring jail to marriage with the hairdresser Pomponnette, sings a satiric ballad about Mlle. Lange, the actress, Director Barras' mistress, and is arrested. Good-natured Lange, finding Clairette a girlhood friend (Act II), has her released and Pomponnette jailed on a false charge, but finds out (at a meeting of conspirators which is explained away as Clairette's wedding party to the raiding police by Lange) that Clairette loves her own lover. When Clairette discovers Ange Pitou really loves the fascinating actress (Act III) she resigns herself to wedding her faithful hair-dresser and all ends happily. Hippolyte Mirande's *Une Fête Directoire* (Lyons, 1895) is an attractive period ballet; and *Misé Brun* (Stuttgart, 1908) by Pierre Maurice, Massenet's pupil, a melodious lyric drama of the Provence (1800) where the robber Gaspard de Besse, blameless lover of Misé (Madame) Brun, the goldsmith's wife, is captured defending her from the attack of the libertine Marquis de Nieuselle, and she dies at her lover's feet as he mounts the scaffold. Operatic echoes of Napoleon's Egyptian campaign (1798) are not missing.

*Zélis et Valcour ou Bonaparte au Caire* (Fontainebleau, 1809) by Michel Oginski, a quaint old-time score, shows the Mameluke Pasha Abuboukir surprising lovely Arab Zélis, an inmate of his harem, in the arms of Valcour, a French prisoner, and condemning the lovers to death. General Bonaparte, the Mamelukes defeated, irrupts in time to stay their separation by the saber and all ends in a festival in his honor. Ludwig Schytte's operetta *Der Mameluk* (Vienna, 1903) with songs and choruses of finished workmanship, should also be mentioned here.

Most representative is Bogumil Zepler's *Monsieur Bonaparte* (Strasburg, 1913) book by Hochfeld, an *opéra comique* of high quality, akin in style to Nicolai and Smetana, whose unequal score has charming lyric pages. Bonaparte, in camp before Cairo, ar-ranges to call on the Cairo merchant, Selim, for gold to pay his soldiers. François Tailleur, army tailor, finds the note his niece Hedija wrote Bonaparte appointing a rendezvous, impersonates the General and (Act II) wins Hadija's heart in a uniform given him to repair. But, surprising her uncle having the gold Bona-parte needs carried off, he sternly orders five hundred thousand gold pieces instead of four hundred thousand sent to the French camp. Then, confessing his true identity to Hadija, who proves she loves him for his own sake, Bonaparte's sudden appearance and discovery of his double leads to François' arrest. The Battle of the Pyramids has been fought and won. To Bonaparte come Selim (to get a receipt for his gold) and Hadija (to intercede for her lover). Bonaparte, learning the truth, makes the happy tailor a lieutenant and marries him to dusky Hadija "over the drumhead" in approved army style.

### "LA TOSCA"

GIACOMO PUCCINI. Book after Sardou's play, by Illica and Giacosa (Rome, 1900). *Tosca* followed *La Bohème* as a world success. A verist drama of swift, violent passions, "a tragic operetta" (Hugo Riemann), "calculated for crowds impatient of enjoyment and indif-

ferent to the quality of their emotions" (Paul Landormy), "its electric
vigor . . . the truly impressive manner in which Puccini is able to in-
tensify and underscore the more dramatic moments in the action" (Lawrence Gilman), and the dramatic prima donna titular rôle (immortalized
by Sarah Bernhardt in the play) have made it one of the most popular
operas of the repertoire. "A repellent text, bloody in subject and treatment . . . a music of bells, choruses, concerts, disguised dances, ecstatic
phrases, butcher-work in the guise of amiability, smiling murder . . . a
dozen scattered beauties in the Love Duet and the two great Arias sacrificed to the Moloch of the 'movies'," is Oscar Bie's summing up. The
Rome of *Tosca* is that of Pope Pius VII. The thunder of the cannon
of Marengo (echoing in Mario's impassioned apostrophe of Scarpia)
was supposed to herald a new reign of liberty Napoleon, now First
Consul, was to give the Papal States.

In the Church of Sant' Andrea, Mario Cavaradossi, the painter, working on a blonde Madonna—his mistress, Tosca the singer, is dark—finds
his friend Angelotti, escaped political prisoner pursued by the agents of
Baron Scarpia, papal chief of police, and sends him off to hide in his
country villa. Tosca, entering, sees the Madonna's features are those of
the Marchioness Attavanti and Mario's fervent vows do not quite soothe
her jealous rage. Scarpia, his suspicions aroused and a sudden passion
for the girl seizing him, plans her lover's death while he joins in a
*Te Deum* for the supposed Austrian victory at Marengo. (Cavaradossi's aria "Recondita armonia" stands out in this act.) Tosca comes
from a concert at the palace of Queen Caroline of Naples to Scarpia's
bureau in the Farnese Palace (Act II) and Mario's groans, heard in an
adjoining torture chamber, make her reveal Angelotti's hiding place.
When the painter has been led away after passionately scoring the government and singing Napoleon's victory at Marengo, Scarpia reveals
his soul's black depths. Peeling an apple, he tells the girl that if she
yield to him Mario shall be shot—with blank cartridges. Tosca, distracted, sings the famous "Vissi d'arte e d'amore" which, as the listener
reacts, is either "the most beautiful air in the repertoire of modern
Italian opera" (Gustav Kobbé) or "the old-fashioned Italian aria of
unsavory fame . . . merely couched in more modern terms . . . a piece
of arrant musical vulgarity" (Lawrence Gilman). Tosca agrees to
Scarpia's infamous proposal to save her lover's life, and as he writes
the passes to see them over the papal border, she stealthily takes the
knife on the table and when he rushes to seize her in lustful arms
stabs him so that he dies without a cry, suffocated by his own blood.
Putting candles at the head of the corpse and her crucifix on its breast,
Tosca steals out as drums roll.

On Sant' Angelo battlements dawn glows, a shepherd boy sings in the
distance, and the bells of Rome chime the hour of early mass. Mario,
waiting for death in his casement, sings "E lucevan le stelle"; and when
Tosca brings him the glad tidings, faces the firing squad laughing and
—falls dead when it fires! Scarpia had lied and in death has avenged

himself. Tosca, leaping from her lover's body as Spoletto, followed by soldiers, rushes to seize her, thrusts him back, jumps to the parapet, and, plunging to her death in the turgid Tiber below, escapes her earthly judges. *Paganini* (Vienna, 1925) by Lehar, an operetta, makes him the hero of a love episode with Napoleon's sister, Princess Elise, at her court in Lucca (1809).

### 4. *The Empire*

Napoleon, in 1804, crowned himself "Emperor of the French." As such he inspired various operas musically unimportant but historically interesting, among them *Le triomphe de Trajan* (Paris, 1807) by Lesueur, which paid homage to the French Emperor in the name of the Roman one, celebrating the reëntry of the Imperial Guard into the city; and *Andromena* (Warsaw, 1807) by Oginski, heard by the Emperor during his Polish campaign and rewarded with a gift of 500 gold *napoléons,* which allegorically showed Andromena (Poland) rescued by Perseus (Bonaparte). Passing to more modern works, *Der Stier von Oliviera* (*The Bull of Oliviera*) by Eugen d'Albert, book after Batka's drama (Leipzig, 1918), a verist score in which Napoleon has a "speaking part," takes us to Spain (1808-1809). There General Guillaume, quartered in the castle of the Spanish Marquis de Barrios, listens with his officers to his host's daughter Juana describe a bullfight, to hold their attention while her father (the French have killed the townsfolk's best fighting bull) rouses them against the foreigners. But Guillaume hears the shots and puts down the revolt and when (the entire family condemned to death) Juana pleads for her youngest brother, he makes his pardon conditional on her marrying him. The General is old and one-eyed, Juana's former betrothed, Pablo de Palos, is young and handsome. Pablo, a guest at the castle, the wife's coquetries drive her husband wild. Catching them flirting he forces Pablo to play a game of bowls, the loser to forfeit an eye and—Pablo loses. But Juana thinks she can best "the Bull of Oliviera," and tempts him to commit treason. Napoleon already on his way to the castle where the Spaniards are to trap him, however, the old soldier's honor revolts, and despite tears and pleas he kills his wife. When the Emperor arrives and Guillaume silently points to the corpse after giving him his sword and begging him to depart, Napoleon, as he reenters his traveling coach, guessing the situation restores it, knowing the veteran means to die in his stead. The year 1811 saw the Empire at the zenith of its power and glory, still radiant with the light of the sun of Austerlitz.

## "MADAME SANS-GÊNE"

### (*Madame Free-and-Easy*)

UMBERTO GIORDANO. Book by Simoni after Sardou's play (New York, 1915.) Musically *Andrea Chénier* and *Siberia* are regarded as superior to *Madame Sans-Gêne*, but the underlying play is sparkling and attractive. The charming duet between Lefebvre and Catherine (Act II); the clever introduction of the "Marseillaise" (Act I) and the dramatic Closing Scene before the merry fanfare of hunting horns (off stage) which ends the opera, stand out. It is probably the only grand opera which introduces Napoleon, *who could not sing,* as a baritone.

In Catherine Huebscher's laundry in Paris (1792), to the echo of street fighting, Fouché scores the poverty-stricken Corsican lieutenant, Bonaparte, who does not pay for his wash. When Count Neipperg, a wounded Austrian, staggers in Catherine hides him in her bedroom. Lefebvre, French sergeant, Catherine's betrothed, comes in, tells of the taking of the Tuileries and pushing past his sweetheart when she tries to keep him from entering her room returns to say the fugitive is dead. When she remains indifferent, his jealousy disappearing, he clasps her in his arms, to break from her embrace as the "Marseillaise" sounds and drums call to arms without. Nineteen years later (1811) at the Château de Compiègne, Lefebvre is Marshal of France and Duke of Danzig, and Napoleon is Emperor. But Catherine, now Duchess of Danzig, so scandalizes the Court with her breaches of etiquette that he tells Lefebvre to divorce her (Act II). The Love Duet in which Lefebvre discusses it with his wife is a charming melodic number. After a scene in which she pokes irreverent fun at Napoleon's sister, the Queen of Naples, reminding her that her husband once was a waiter in a country inn, Napoleon sends for her. Ushered into Napoleon's cabinet (Act III) however, when he brings up divorce and attacks her manners at Court, she tells of the wound she received on the battlefield and pulls out an unpaid laundry bill he never had settled when he was an obscure lieutenant. Napoleon forgives her, and as she is leaving Count Neipperg is brought in. He has been caught lurking near the Empress Marie-Louise's apartment and Napoleon, raging, tears the medals from his breast and is about to strike him when officers rush in and he is led off to be shot at sunrise. Catherine, deploring the Emperor's fatal resolve (Act IV), induces him to put the Empress's love and loyalty to the test. Changing her voice to imitate that of the latter's Matron of Honor, she whispers at the door that Neipperg has arrived. A letter is passed out. Napoleon breaks the seal and reads— a request addressed to Marie-Louise's father to recall the Count since he annoys her. Ordering Neipperg's sword restored, Napoleon tells Lefebvre to thank heaven he has such a wife, and departs for the hunt announced by horns off stage.

*The Duchess of Dantzig* (London, 1903) by Ivan Caryll is a tuneful romantic comic opera setting of Sardou's play.

*Hugh the Drover* (London, 1925) by Vaughan Williams, book by Harold Child, a genuine folk opera, uses English folk songs with skill and effect, outstanding the "May Day Carol," the traditional "Drinking Song" and the beautiful solo airs in which Hugh and Mary sing their love. In the England of 1812, dreading a Napoleonic invasion, John the Butcher, in Cottswold town, betrothed to the Constable of Cottswold's daughter Mary, is thrusting unwelcome attentions on her at the local fair (flower, mussel, and toy vendors' street cries, ballad songsters, morris dances, and rustic choruses) when Hugh the Drover turns up and he and Mary love at sight. When to prove who is "the best man in England" is suggested, Hugh agrees to fight John, with Mary's hand as the prize instead of a purse of twenty pounds; but no sooner has Hugh thrashed him than the Constable hales him to jail as a "French spy." The next morning (Act II) Mary joins her lover in the stocks and the sergeant in command of a squad of "lobsterbacks" which enters town, recognizing an old friend in Hugh, frees him to take the King's shilling and Mary marches off with him (a vocal ensemble before their departure is one of the loveliest pages of the score), to a new life of love and freedom, her father interposing in vain.

*Germania* (Milan, 1902; New York, 1910) by Alberto Franchetti, book by Illica, is a drama of the German struggle for freedom against Napoleonic tyranny in 1813. Ricke's air, "I tremble at the threat of coming sorrow" (Act I) and the symphonic Epilogue describing in music the retreat of Napoleon's sullen, defeated host from the battlefield of Leipzig, stand out. Carl Worms, a patriot miller, has beguiled leisure moments not devoted to rousing his native land against Napoleon, to seducing Ricke, daughter of the printer Palm and betrothed to the poet Frederick Loewe, his friend. After she has told Carl she must confess her guilty secret he dissuades her; but seven years later (Act II) when Carl appears in the Black Forest hut where Frederick and his wife live, her little sister Jane innocently discloses the relations formerly existing between Ricke and her husband's friend, and while the wretched wife flees, Frederick decides to live thenceforth only for his country. After Queen Louise of Prussia has prevented a duel between wronged Frederick and his enemy (Act III) by an appeal to his patriotism in the cellar where the Königsberg *Luisenbund* of patriotic conspirators gathers, a symphonic Intermezzo describes the great Battle of Leipzig. (Epilogue). As Napoleon rides by in the background amid his defeated legions, Ricke finds Worms already dead and Frederick dying. He curses, then forgives her betrayer, and falling dead with the cry "Free . . . Germania . . . Free!" Ricke lies down to await death beside him. Certain operas merely use the Empire setting, musically, and scenically, for the sake of color.

## "LA FILLE DU RÉGIMENT"

### (*The Daughter of the Regiment*)

GAETANO DONIZETTI. Book by Saint-Georges and Bayard (Paris, 1840). A piquant French *opéra comique*, with "change of country and palace interiors, prayer, farewell, romance, singing lesson, character songs, a Tyrolienne" and animated military rhythms. Marie's "Grenadier Song" with cadenza; the "Drumstick Duet," the favorite "Song of the Regiment," Marie's melancholy farewell song, "When I was left," and the concluding "Salute to France" (Act II) stand out.

In the Tyrolian hills is camped the 21st regiment of the line. Marie, the pretty *vivandière* found by Sergeant Sulpice and adopted on the battlefield as "the Daughter of the Regiment," is among them. When Tonio, a mountain lad, saves Marie from falling over a precipice, he cannot save himself (nor wishes to) from falling in love with her but— she must wed a grenadier. Tonio enlists only to see his sweetheart, identified as the Marchioness de Maggiorivogleo's niece, swept off to the latter's castle. Poor Marie (Act II) weary of lessons in music, dancing, and deportment, is ready in despair to marry the ducal son of Craquitorpi when—the drums beat, the grenadiers appear and Marie scandalizes noble guests who have gathered for her wedding, by rushing into Tonio's arms. He is now an officer, and while soldiers cheer the Marchioness blesses the "Daughter of the Regiment" as she weds her happy lover.

In *Gina* (Naples, 1899) by Francesco Cilèa, a Breton village idyl with a recruiting chorus and military song background, one village boy, to win the heart of another lad's sister, joins the recruits for the Russian campaign of 1812, both returning safely to their sweethearts. Uberto and Lilla's "Scene of Farewell" (Act II) stands out. *Sakhara* (Frankfurt, 1924) by Simon Bucharoff (Buchalter), book by Isabel Buckingham, a Meyerbeerian grand opera with processions, orgies, and ballet (Act II), climaxes in "the heroine's sacrificial death in a flower-adorned chamber to sweet violin song." A French nobleman's mistress bears him two children and, leaving him Sebastian, vanishes with the girl, Sakhara. The abandoned lover turns abbot of a monastery in despair while Sakhara, her mother dead, is trained by a brutal impresario for the stage. In Paris Sebastian sees and falls madly in love with his sister who, when the impresario (he himself has designs on her) tries to get him murdered, kills the villain. When the children's abbot-father tells Sakhara her lover is her brother, the wretched girl stabs herself lest the gruesome tidings cause him suffering.

### WATERLOO AND AFTER

*Le soir de Waterloo* (Paris, 1910) by Nerini, is a score in which the downfall of the Empire is visioned in a passing glimpse. Nouguès' *L'Aiglon* (*The Eaglet,* Rouen, 1912) after Rostand's famous drama of Napoleon's young son "The Eaglet," brought up in Vienna as an Austrian Duke of Reichstadt, is a melodramatic score, musically less important than a German post-Napoleonic score.

*Die Bettlerin vom Pont des Arts* (*The Beggar of the Pont des Arts*) by Karl von Kaskel, book by Ludwig, after Hauff (Cassel, 1899). Musical mood-pictures influenced by Italian verism, with dramatic Overture, melodious "Song of the Kiss (Act II), and graceful rococo pantomime music. (Prologue.) Josefa, a young beggar girl sings on a Paris bridge, the Pont des Arts (1823), while gay masqueraders pass. Compassionate Froeben gives her money to buy medicine for her sick mother, and the charming mendicant tells how her father, who left to fight for Napoleon in Spain, never returned home. It is love at first sight. A kiss, a ring, a vow are exchanged, but honor and duty intervene—the girl disappears in the crowd. In a Stuttgart hotel (Act II) Don Pedro, an old Spanish officer, vainly seeks wife and child. Meeting Froeben in a picture gallery they recognize in the same picture, one his child, the other the beggar of the Pont des Arts. In vain Froeben seeks to stifle romantic longings for her by a visit to his friend Faldern's Rhineland estate. There he finds (Act III) the beggar girl installed as his friend's wife. His innocent farewell to Josefa, surprised by Faldern, leads to a duel. Don Pedro, still seeking his family, intrudes at the psychological moment and saves wounded Froeben by killing his host. Froeben, thinking himself Faldern's slayer (Act IV), hesitates to marry Josefa, though she loves him. But her father (they are staying at Countess Landskron's Rhenish castle) relieves his scruples, and the lovers join hands in the final chorus: "Love is over all!"

*Oberst Chabert* (*Colonel Chabert,* Vienna, 1912), by W. von Waltershausen is a melodramatic score mingling veristic procedure and the ensemble of the older opera. The "Marseillaise" is introduced and Chabert's "Monologue," the vocal Quintet (Act II), and Finale (Act III) stand out. Colonel Chabert is the hero of a novel by Balzac, "the literary Napoleon who loved to glorify the military one" (Paul Bourget). Colonel Chabert, Enoch Arden of the Napoleonic epoch, is wounded, thought dead, and cast into a mass grave in the bloody battle of Eylau. Waking in a hell of dead bodies, the living dead man digs his way out, and for years disappears in hospitals and madhouses of Germany. At last, disfigured, unrecognizable, he returns to France, and finds his wife has married Count Ferraud. In vain the broken old soldier, decried as an impostor, tries to gain his rights. His wife personifies the heartless egotism of the Restoration, when souls were rotted with gold. Count Ferraud, convinced of the truth of Chabert's claims, when his wife refuses to swear that he is an impostor, wishes to resign wife, children, and estate but in vain. Finally Chabert gives up and kills himself (Act II) and his sacrifice regains his wife's love which she seals by poisoning herself over his body. (Balzac's original, truer to human nature, shows the poor wretch creeping away to end his days in Bicêtre, an old men's home, while Countess Ferraud lives on, rich and socially triumphant.)

## "I CAVALIERI DI EKEBÙ"

### (*The Pensioners of Ekeby*)

RICCARDO ZANDONAI. Book by Rossato, after Selma Lagerlöf's *The Story of Gösta Berling* (Milan, 1925). The lonely province of Värmland, Sweden, at the beginning of the nineteenth century is the scene. A unique expression of Swedish psychology, it falls within the period of the First Empire. Little Rustler, "the pensioner," led the van of the Swedish army when it marched into Germany in 1813, and all the broken-down gentlemen who made up the Round Table at Ekeby had fought in the Napoleonic wars. The score is an atmospheric musical mosaic (in Act I the snowy immensity of the desolate Swedish plains is perfectly expressed); and the orgiastic "Chorus of the Pensioners" (Act II), which returns in the last act combined with the programmatic accompaniment of hammers beating on the forge, has been called the gem of the score.

In the manor house of Ekeby, the "Commandante," rich widow of Major Samzelius, rules her Round Table, of twelve "pensioners," broken-down gentlemen, veterans of the wars, who loathe honest work. With them she makes merry, to the sound of song, fiddle, and hunting horn, with dances, feasts, cards, and banquets where brandy flows like water. Gösta Berling, a minister unfrocked for drunkenness, loves Anna Stjarnhök, daughter of Sintram who plays the rôle of the tempting devil on earth. Cast off by the girl, Gösta resolves to die. In a roadside inn he meets the "Commandante" and tells her his tale. She tells him her own sad story and persuades him to join the pensioners at Ekeby.

Anna, turned out of doors by her father because of Gösta, also comes to Ekeby. There young girl visitors prepare to give a comedy. Anna and Gösta are to sing a love dialogue, but Anna refuses. Then Gösta, to prove his love, thrusts his hand into the flame of the hearth and the comedy goes on before the eyes of the astounded audience, Gösta speaking with such eloquence that Anna, conquered, returns his kisses, and her father Sintram, come to curse her, is thrust out of the house.

On Christmas night the pensioners drink in the great hall when Sintram, disguised as the Devil, publicly reveals the "Commandante's" past, telling how she betrayed her husband with Altringer, and how the Major repudiated his wife. When Sintram declares the "Commandante" has promised the Devil a soul a year, the pensioners tempted by the riches of Ekeby drive the "Commandante" from her home.

Anna returns repentantly to her parents' home; but brutally driven away, is compelled to share with Gösta whatever fate may have in store.

Then evil and wretchedness reign in Ekeby. The pensioners carouse, the iron mines are neglected, the foundries shut down, the fields lie fallow, and Sintram rejoices, while Anna is forgotten by Gösta for the brandy bottle. But evil cannot endure. In the end the pensioners' consciences awake; Gösta turns from drink to doing good. When the "Commandante" is brought back to her mansion house to die the souls of the wastrels are filled with remorse. At her dying exhortation to find the right measure in work, joy, and love, all compete as to which shall make sacrifices. The forge fires blaze again, work in the fields is resumed, and while the pensioners intone their hymn of rejoicing as sledge hammers ring, Gösta and Anna bid the dying woman farewell to seek happiness in a life of poverty, helping the peasants. Like the pensioners they, too, must leave Ekeby (become a "home for happy labor") and in toil for others atone for the past.

# CHAPTER XII

## THE NINETEENTH AND TWENTIETH CENTURIES

### 1. *The Restoration*

In a hundred and one various ways nineteenth century subjects reflect the movements and trends of the changing years, the emotional, social, and political life of the century whose beginnings already are so far removed from intimate twentieth century consciousness that they have the strange and picturesque quality of older historic epochs. In Europe generally, despite Revolution and Empire, much of the eighteenth century in the way of thought, idea, and custom was carried over into the early nineteenth. The Restoration endured from 1816 to 1830 in France; and in literature Balzac's *Comédie humaine* presents French life during the Restoration (and under King Louis-Philippe) in an immense cycle of ninety-seven serious novels. In opera the Restoration setting has motived few scores. *Véronique* (*Brigitte,* Paris, 1898) by André Messager, a comic opera with delicate, attractive melodies, the tale of aristocratic Hélène de Solange who becomes Véronique, the shopgirl, in a florist's establishment, to win her lover's heart from the genuine shopgirl, Agathe Coquenard, is set in the Paris of King Louis XVIII. Auber's *La neige ou le nouvel Eginhardt* (*The Snow or the New Eginhardt,* Paris, 1823), an opera based on a secret sleigh ride of two lovers (Longfellow's poem "Charlemagne" will explain the "Eginhardt" to those whom it mystifies), and his *Léocadie* (Paris, 1824) with a tender romance, "Pour moi dans la nature," are characteristic of their time. Léocadie is a young Lisbon girl whose babe is a mystery, for she wots not who its father may be. She manages to keep secret the fact it is hers till the child falls into the Tagus; and betrayed by maternal anguish as she leaps to rescue it, Carlos, her betrothed, at once jilts her, believing her unworthy. Later, however, to his own surprise, he finds *he* is the child's father, forgives Léocadie and they are happily wedded.

Various operas reflect the period in Germany. *Regina* (*The Marauders,* Berlin, 1899) by Lortzing, posthumous, is considered his most dramatic work and was called "revolutionary" in its day because it contained several choruses praising liberty. Wolfram, an intriguing forester, leads a robber band to abduct a steward's daughter, only to be shot by the heroine. *Der Wildschütz* (*The Poacher*) by Lortzing, book after Kotzebue (Leipzig, 1842) is a comedy of the *Junker* Germany of 1803. Baroness Freimann, disguised as the village schoolmaster Baculus' sweetheart, pleads the pedagogue's cause with Baron Eberbach, about to dismiss him for poaching, and then, winning Baron Kronthal's heart in peasant dress, wedding bells chime in the feudal castle for her and for the schoolmaster's real love, Gretchen. The early nineteenth century spirit of servility toward royal and princely personages in Germany is satirized in Heuberger's *Das Abenteuer einer Neujahrsnacht* (*The Adventure of a New Year's Night*, Leipzig, 1886) whose Ballet (Act II) includes a "Dance of Halberdiers," *alla turca*, and a graceful waltz. The plot (after Zschokke's novel) is a comedy of errors resulting from an exchange of clothes between a prince and a night watchman. The latter, in the Prince's domino plays a noble part in the intrigues which mar a court ball; the former, the boisterous hooligan in the streets, to the annoyance of peaceful burghers.

*Lorle* (Dresden, 1891) by Alban Förster, a melodious score after an Auerbach novel of early nineteenth century life, makes Lorle's painter marry and neglect her for a countess. Heartbroken, the poor girl returns to die beneath a favorite village oak, to be sweetly surprised when her repentant husband folds her in his arms. *La Borghesina* (Lisbon, 1909) by Augusto Machado, Portugal's outstanding composer, who writes in Massenet's manner, is a tragedy of French society life in 1830, in Paris, based on Frederic Soulié's novel *Le lion amoureux* (*The Lion in Love*). *Versiegelt* (*Sealed*) by Leo Blech, book by Batka and Pordes-Milo (Hamburg, 1908) is a score rich in caressing melodies, with a happy climaxing waltz. "There is no false note, no transposition of emotions . . . the score is a series of musical dainties" (Bie). Braun, small-town German burgomaster (1830) loves Frau Schramm; his daughter Else loves Bertel, the town clerk, of whom her father disapproves. When Lampe the bailiff sees Frau Willmer's great wardrobe carried into Frau Schramm's to avoid seizure for taxes, Braun is kissing the pretty widow and as the official enters the burgomaster is hastily hidden in the wardrobe which Lampe innocently seals with the town seal. The lovers Else and Bertel take advantage of the chance and refuse to let Braun out till he consents to their marriage. When Lampe, who has heard stifled cries, returns, Bertel pretends it was he who was "sealed" by accident, and the comedy ends with a double wedding foreshadowed. *Adélaide ou le langage des fleurs* (*Adelaide or the Language of Flowers*, Paris, 1912) by Maurice Ravel is the ballet version of his symphonic Schubertian *Valses nobles et sentimentales,* set in the reign of Charles X, the last Restoration King of France, when flower symbolism had been revived as part of the Gothic romanticism of the 1830's. Penniless young Loredan and an old duke, rolling in gold, court lovely Adelaide, saying what they have to say with flowers till Loredan's red, red rose ("I love you!") triumphs.

## THE TIME OF THE "CITIZEN-KING"

Romanticism is the dominant note of French culture during the reign of Louis-Philippe, "the Citizen-King" (1830-1848), and is reflected in opera by settings of Scribe tales, and of subjects drawn from the works of Hugo, Lamartine, Chateaubriand, De Vigny, Soulié and others.

*La fête chez Thérèse* (*The Fête at Theresa's,* Paris, 1910), by Reynaldo Hahn, a ballet, shows a fashionable *modiste's* shop in Paris (1840) where the Duchess Theresa and her friends choose gowns for the fête the former means to give. Mimi Pinson—whom we meet later in Puccini's *Bohème*—a little shop slavey, hides with her lover Theodore behind a screen to watch the society folk, among whom is Carlotta Grisi, the famous *danseuse*. Theodore, stricken with the Duchess's beauty, upsets the screen, and Mimi, realizing with love's intuition what has happened, bursts into tears as he runs away.

A Watteau park is the scene of the Duchess' fête. When Theresa, after a minuet with Theodore, hears poor Mimi beg her amid tears to restore her lover, she pushes him into his little seamstress' arms (he really loves Mimi) and as though to cele-brate their reconciliation (night has stolen on) fireworks fill the skies with golden and jeweled radiance. The French folk song "Mimi Pinson est une blonde," a "Violent Dance" with *basso osti-nato* and a "Pompous Minuet" stand out. The Mimi Pinson of *La fête chez Thérèse* is the Mimi Pinson of Murger's *Vie de Bohème,* who is the Mimi Pinson of Puccini's opera. Murger's *Scènes de la vie de Bohème* (pub. 1848) relates the fortunes and misfortunes, amusements, loves, and sufferings of impecunious artists and men of letters of the Paris *Quartier Latin* and their feminine companions (Rodolphe being Murger himself). In Puc-cini's opera these types of Paris artistic Bohemian life have found their most popular musical expression.

## "LA BOHÈME"

GIACOMO PUCCINI. Book by Giacosa and Illica, after Murger's novel (Turin, 1896; New York, 1898). Mimi, "beautiful but frail," another

"Traviata" dies as tragically of love and consumption as the "Lady of the Camellias." The score is generally considered Puccini's masterwork. Mimi's tender, pathetic melodies run through it like a connecting thread and outstanding are, besides her "Mi chiamano Mimi" and the impassioned Love Duet (Act I), her "Addio, senza rancore" (Act III), and dying invocation of early days of love, "Te lo rammenti." Also should be mentioned Musetta's gay, joy-perfumed Waltz of the Paris pavements "Quando m'en vo" ("As through the streets I wander," Act II) ; Rudolfo's Air, "Che gelinda manina" (Act I) and his Duet with Mimi at the end of Act III, "Our time for parting"; Colline's "Song of the Coat" (Act IV) ; and the Quartet, "Addio, dolce svegliare" (Act III).

In his Latin Quarter studio Marcel paints at "The Passage of the Red Sea," while Rudolph kindles a fire with a rejected MS. Colline, who enters, could not pawn his books; but Schaunard has secured a three-day musical engagement from an eccentric Englishman. Two boys bring in food and fuel, purchased with his advance, and the landlord is fobbed off with a drink of wine. After the feast, Rudolph, staying to finish his writing before he meets them at the Café Momus, hears Mimi knock. She faints at the threshold. Rudolph, moved by her beauty, frailty, and little white hands, gropes for the key she has dropped, and finds and hides it in his pocket, to have an excuse to keep her. They tell each other of their life (the melting Love Duet) while moonlight silvers the garret floor and his impatient friends hail the poet from the street.

Christmas Eve in the Café Momus. Rudolph has bought Mimi a bonnet (gay scene with students, work girls, street vendors, a holiday crowd out for a good time) and together with Colline, Schaunard, and Marcel they sit at a table before the Café. Musetta, Rudolph's old flame, comes in with de Mittoneaux, old but rich. Rudolph when Musetta gets rid of Alcindoro becomes reconciled to her. In the artless Latin Quarter way the entire party then leaves both Café and bill—the latter settled by Alcindoro when he returns from the cobbler shop where Musetta had sent him.

Rudolph and Mimi, living together, know the happiness and the wretchedness of more regular unions. One February morning Mimi, her tubercular cough worse, calls Marcel from his tavern lodging, tells him of Rudolph's jealousy, and Rudolph, in turn, explains what torture their life in common is to them; that he loves Mimi, but thinks she is marked for the grave. They agree to part, without rancor. Marcel and Musetta, who have pooled their emotional resources, also quarrel and dissolve partnership.

Rudolph and Marcel are writing, painting and frolicking in their attic studio, when Musetta comes in to say that Mimi, weak and ill is outside, unable to walk further. She has asked to be allowed to die in the attic where she has been happy. A couch is prepared and Mimi embraces Rudolph tenderly and begs him not to leave her. While the others hurry out they recall their dream of love together; but Mimi soon falls back fainting. As Musetta and the other Bohemians return with medicine, she once more whispers her love for Rudolph and dies, while he flings himself sobbing on her lifeless form.

*La Bohème* (Milan, 1897) by Leoncavallo, book after Murger, varies the same tale in four acts. Outstanding in Act I (Café Momus) where the Bohemians, about to be thrown out, are saved by Barbemache, who pays their bill, is the canzonetta "Mimi è il nome di mia biondina." In Act II—bohemian celebration and fight in the court of Musetta's Latin Quarter tenement—is Marcello's air, "I have only a little room." In Act III, where Marcello and Rudolfo drive Mimi and Musetta out of their garret and lives, the melody "Adored One" deserves mention; while in Act IV, where Mimi dies in Rudolfo's arms to the chime of Christmas bells, the Death Scene stands out. *La petite Bohème* (Paris, 1877) by Henri Hirschmann, an operetta after Murger, substitutes a happy for a tragic ending; Mimi instead of coughing out her life falls happily on Rodolphe's neck, cured by his kisses. *Le Bonhomme-Jadis* (Paris, 1906; 1925) by M. E. Jacques-Dalcroze, book by Franc-Nohain after a Murger comedy, is an intimate little score in which "Goodman Once Upon A Time" a kindly old man in whose heart spring reigns eternal, finds happy pretexts to unite two lovers, timid Octave and candid, artless Jacqueline. The little opera is rich in charming airs, treated with great variety of rhythm. Gérard de Nerval, Murger's contemporary, wrote an autobiographical novel *Sylvie,* which has called forth a delicate modern score in the idiom of Debussy and Fauré, *Sylvie* (Paris, 1923) by Fred Barlow, book by Bertin. François, a young aristocrat, learns to love innocent Sylvie during vacations spent at the ancestral château. A gay Parisian life makes the country girl a memory; but Adrienne the actress so resembles Sylvie that François falls in love with her only to find her a mere reflection of his love's first dream. Hurrying to Sylvie he finds she— divining she could not hold him—has married a worthy farmer. François' despair is vain. With an evocation of "the saddest word of tongue or pen" Sylvie tenderly denies his suit and bids him farewell.

Paul de Kock, whose spicy novels once were popular, is represented by a score in which the novelist, borrowing La Fontaine's version of a Boccaccio tale, shocked the Parisian public of his day. The score is Hèrold's *Le Muletier* (Paris, 1823), full of movement and expressive melody, which Arthur Pougin, the distinguished French critic, does not hesitate, speaking musically, to call "an exquisite work." Similar in type is Adolphe Adam's *Le Toréador* (Paris, 1849), light and graceful, in which Caroline, the

Barcelona toreador Don Belflor's wife, deceives him with Trocolin, the flutist, and proving by the cards that her innocent husband deceives *her*, has her lover taken into the home as the ostensible guardian of her husband's morals. One of its clever musical effects is the use of broken horn-tones to imitate the beat of the human heart.

## "LA TRAVIATA"

### (*Violetta*)

GIUSEPPE VERDI. Text by Piave (Venice, 1853) after *La Dame aux Camélias* by Alexander Dumas *fils*. Dumas' novel (1848) reflects the world in which he lived (the notorious courtesan Marie Duplessis was the original of the author's heroine, Marguerite Gauthier). A forerunner of the veristic opera, realism had not yet stooped to the slums: it is a "drawing-room tragedy," a study in courtesan psychology, whose music still touches the heart in the portrayal of two fated human beings, for all they are oversentimentalized. The Prelude anticipates the sadness of the Death Scene; Violetta's great solo scene (Act I), the farewell Love Duet, and dramatic Finale (Act II) lead to the lyric pathos of Act III, in which "melodic blossoms" fall on the deathbed "and Violetta dies in ecstasy." *La Traviata* often is wrongly presented in Louis XIV costumes and setting.

The *demi-mondaine* Violetta Valery allows a new admirer, Alfred Germont, to stay when other guests leave (she is attacked by a coughing spell, a consequence of her life) and when he begs her to spare herself talks friendship to his love, and gives him a camellia she wears on her breast. On their meeting the following morning the courtesan for the first time realizes the miracle of true affection. Too late—she must let her life current carry her to the whirlpool of dissolution!

With Alfred as her lover she lives quietly on a farm near Paris till his father comes to beg her to release his son—otherwise his son-in-law will repudiate *his* wife. Violetta does not mention the interview; but shortly after a servant hands Alfred a letter—Violetta has left him. Deaf to his father's plea to return home, taking for granted Violetta is untrue (a letter asking her to a masquerade given by one of her companions suggests the thought), he hurries to Paris, intent on revenge. (change of scene.) At Flora Bervoix's ball (background of Spanish dance and waltz music) he casts his winnings at the card table at her feet when she falsely admits she loves Baron Dauphal, telling her it is to pay for her favors. The poor girl falls unconscious into Flora's arms while his father, eyewitness of the scene, reproaches him.

Violetta, on her sickbed, knows herself doomed and bids farewell to life while Paris resounds to Carnival merriment. Her one hope is to die in Alfred's arms. It is realized, for Alfred, repentant (he has learned of her sacrifice), hastens to her. Their love finds touching expression in painting the delights of an illusory future and Violetta (Alfred's father comes too late to accept and embrace her as a daughter) dies at the moment when life holds out to her all for which she had so vainly longed.

## ARTISTIC PORTRAITS

Often we find some celebrity of the "Age of Romanticism" himself appear as the hero of an operatic score. In *La bonne aventure* (*The Lucky Adventure,* Monte Carlo, 1925) by Camille Kufferath, a lyric score, the outstanding song "Chanson de Mimi," Alfred de Musset finds a princess instead of the *grisette* Mimi awaiting him at an amorous rendezvous, with complications which have a happy ending. *Die Bäder von Lucca* (*The Lucca Baths,* Berlin, 1904) by Bogumil Zepler, after Heine's *Reisebilder,* throws into sympathetic relief the figure of the great German poet during his stay in Lucca (1828); and Meyer-Helmund's *Traumbilder* (Berlin, 1912) may be mentioned in the same connection. The same composer's *Taglioni* (Berlin, 1912) glorifies the great dancer whom Théophile Gautier admired; while François Auber's *L'Ambassadrice* (Paris, 1836) book by Scribe, whose heroine, a singer married to a noble and who yearns to return to the stage, was regarded as a portrait of the composer's contemporary, the famous singer Henrietta Sontag, who sang the title rôle in Berlin, and at the same time was the wife of Count Rossi, the Sardinian ambassor to that Court. Chopin, friend of Heine and Balzac, and lover of George Sand (who painted an unfriendly picture of him in her novel *Lucrezia Floriani* under the name of "Prince Karol") also is the hero of an opera.

*Chopin* (Milan, 1901) by Giacomo Orefice, book by Orvieto, borrows themes from the composer's Nocturnes, Mazurkas, Berceuse, Barcarole, the Grand Fantaisie, Op. 13, etc., to tell the story of his love life. (1) It is winter in Poland. Peasants dance on the ice and Chopin and Stella, his first love, seated on a stone bench sing their fondness for each other. (2) In Paris Eli, Chopin's friend, tells the children of a private school tales of Poland's glory, so exciting Chopin's patriotism that he goes into the house and improvises a Nocturne on the piano. There he charms the teacher, Flora, and they sing *their* love in a duet. (3) This is the Majorcan idyl, full of mystic melancholy. Chopin and Stella (not George Sand) are on the island with their daughter Grazia. The child perishes in a thunderstorm and her parents and sorrowing Majorcans bewail her in an effective Finale. (4) In Paris, Chopin not wishing to die alone, Stella comes from distant Poland, bringing with her the breath of his native heath, to allow him to die in her arms. *Les Sylphides,* a Ballet Russe, with a poetic dance action, like a Lamartine poem visualized to Chopin melodies, might be mentioned; and also, as a poetic dance interpretation of a famous composition, the Ballet Russe *Spectre de la rose* (*Phantom of the Rose*). It gives the life of motion to Théophile Gautier's exquisite poem of the same name, in which the spirit of the rose she has worn on her breast appears to a young girl who has fallen asleep in the chair in her room after the ball, and in a dream dance relives with her the joy of the departed hour to the music of Weber's "Invitation to the Dance."

## 2. *Italian and Spanish Vistas*

### "FRA DIAVOLO"

#### (*The Inn at Terracina*)

FRANÇOIS AUBER. Book by Scribe (Paris, 1830). In this score, as in *Marco Spada* (Paris, 1852), the composer created the type of romantic Italian brigand in comic opera, in which realistic adventure is developed to piquant music. It has a brilliant military Overture and a bravura tenor rôle; Zerline's Romance (Act I), "Behold on mountain heights," is a favorite number. It was not without good reason that Auber made Terracina, in the old Papal States, the scene of a score which gave the Italian bandit operatic reality. For in 1830, the time of its action, the Papal States, worst governed in all Europe, were overrun with banditti, their highways and byways unsafe to travel.

Bandit-hunting Roman dragoons carouse in Matteo's inn at Terracina, while Lorenzo, their captain, makes love to Zerline, mine host's daughter, betrothed to a rich peasant. With loud outcries Lord Cockburn and Lady Pamela arrive. They have been robbed—of course by Fra Diavolo and his band—and the Englishman's reward of 10,000 lire for the recovery of his jewels sends Lorenzo and his dragoons off posthaste. Lord Cockburn is scolding his wife for coquetting with a traveling companion, the Marquis of San Marco (Fra Diavolo in disguise) who shared their coach for a time when—the latter descends at the inn! After listening to Zerline tell him his own legend, Fra Diavolo renews his flirtation and when Lorenzo, having slain most of the robbers, returns with the traveler's diamonds, the bandit has stolen a jewel-set medallion from the Englishwoman under cover of loving protestations. Lorenzo waives the reward in Zerline's favor.

Zerline goes to bed with her bank notes (Act II) while Fra Diavolo and his men, Giacomo and Beppo, wait to stab her as she sleeps. Fra Diavolo gains the girl's bedside but Cockburn and Lorenzo discover him hiding behind Zerline's bedroom curtain. The supposed Marquis explains he is keeping a rendezvous, and Lord Cockburn thinks it is with his wife, Lorenzo that it is with Zerline. The lie passed between Lorenzo and Fra Diavolo, a duel is arranged, to the brigand's satisfaction, since he plans to capture Lorenzo and his dragoons and avenge the slaughter of his band.

In picturesque robber costume Fra Diavolo pins his orders on a tree while peasants and dragoons celebrate the Easter festival. Beppo and Giacomo find their orders but, jokingly repeating some of Zerline's pleas of the preceding night, she denounces them. Fra Diavolo's letter is found in Beppo's pocket, and they are forced to lead their captain into a trap. Coming down the mountain, the bandit chief is slain by the bullets of the dragoons. While Lord Cockburn and his wife make up their difference, and Matteo joins Zerline's and Lorenzo's hands, the villagers rejoice because the terror of the countryside is dead.

*Le brigand de Terracine* (Paris, 1837), danced by Fanny Elssler, was the ballet version of *Fra Diavolo;* aside from many lesser operas of the type, Offenbach's burlesque *Tromb-Alcazar* (*The Robber Captain,* Paris, 1865), turns on the fact that an innkeeper on the Bohemian frontier mistakes a theatrical manager for a robber chieftain; while Franz von Suppé's *Banditenstreiche* (Vienna, 1867) idealizes the eighteenth century Neapolitan bandit Malandrino, a noble fellow who fits out a young girl with a thousand stolen ducats so she can marry her lover. Here, too, might be mentioned *Der Karneval in Rom* (Vienna, 1873) by Johann Strauss, a mid-Victorian romance in which a deserted village girl, a pretty Countess, her jealous husband, and three young painters figure in a humorous development of incident including an "American duel," ending with a universal reconciliation amid the merry masquerade of the Roman Carnival.

*Anima Allegra* (*The Joyous Soul,* Rome, 1921; New York, 1923) by Franco Vittadini, book by Adami, after the Fratelli Quintero comedy *El genio alegre.* A slight, colorful score, in which the Spanish gypsy dances, notably the Malaguena (Act II), stand out. In the ancestral country house at Alminar de Reina (Andalusia, 1830) Doña Sacramento lives gloomily with her morose major-domo Elijio, unable to understand why Don Pedro, her boy, spends his time in Granada where there are gay cafés and pretty girls. Suddenly Doña Sacramento is startled by a visit from her niece Consuelo, who arrives with frills and furbelows, canary and parrot and—to her aunt's horror—makes the gray walls of the house re-echo to laughter and song. When Don Pedro turns up on a brief visit home, he has no mind to leave the old mansion for the city again. In the camp *flamencas,* wandering gypsies, have set up near the village (Act II), Consuelo appears, followed by the younger household servants, enjoys the wild dances of the strollers, scatters money right and left and stands godmother to a gypsy babe. Pedro, sent by his horrified mother to rescue Consuelo from her low environment, instead of so doing finds himself scattering largesse to the gypsies who crowd around them. Doña Sacramento and Elijio deplore the atmosphere of gayety which pervades the house and lament the dear gloomy days of the past. Don Pedro's return from Granada, however, surprises his mother, but the cause of his swift homing is near at hand. Consuelo is the magnet which has drawn him. He declares his love to her, finds it is returned, and the curtain falls on the kiss which binds the betrothal of Don Pedro and "The Joyous Soul."

*Le domino noir* (*The Black Domino,* Paris, 1837) by François Auber, book by Scribe, is an *opéra comique* of Madrid at the period. A "Cachucha," the Aragonese song, "D'où venez-vous, ma chère," and the aria, "Ah, quelle nuit," stand out. At a *bal masqué* in the royal palace, Angela, a convent inmate, kept from returning to the cloister before closing time by Horatio di Massarena, rushes off in despair. Admitted to the home of gay Count Juliano after straying through the dark streets (Act II), the housekeeper lets her wait on the table and dance for the revelers as her country niece Inesille, shocking Massarena, who is upset to see his lovely Black Domino in such company when he arrives. But when she has at last entered the convent (Act III) by means of the steward Gil Perez' key, out of which she tricked him in Juliano's house, Massarena follows after to offer his hand and the Queen allows her to marry him instead of becoming the convent's abbess.

### 3. *The Second French Empire*

The Second French Empire, born of the "Napoleonic Legend" which the first great Bonaparte evolved in his years at St. Helena, already is a brilliant, picturesque "historical" epoch of that past into which the immediate present so swiftly and imperceptibly turns. Many of its operatic reactions are considered under other heads, but some which specifically reflect it are here gathered.

Émile Zola (1840-1902) in his tremendous novel sequence, the *Rougon-Macquart* undertook to do for the society of the Second Empire what Balzac had done for that of the First Empire and the Restoration—create a picture of French social life during that epoch in a succession of novels devoted to the fortunes of one family, the Rougon-Macquart, basing them on the supposed operation of the law of heredity. The operatic setting of *Le Rêve* has been considered as well as operas called forth by *La faute de l'Abbé Mouret*. The operas suggested by Zola's pictures of Second

Empire society are supplemented by lighter scores in which Jacques Offenbach parodied the social life and conditions of his day.

*La vie Parisienne* (Paris, 1866) introduces the millionaire Brazilian pleasure-seeker, aristocratic Paris loungers, male and female, and a typical *demi-mondaine* of a day when *filles de marbre,* "ladies of the Camellias," were idolized by painter, poet, and musician. *La Diva* (Paris 1869) is a musical biography of Hortense Schneider, the famous singer of Offenbach rôles. *Les deux aveugles* (*The Two Blind Men*) made all Paris laugh at two counterfeit street beggars, alternately blind and lame, who lie to each other about their imaginary ills and dice for "customers." *Monsieur et Madame Denis* (Paris, 1862), which contains one of Offenbach's choicest waltzes, tells the flight of a convent pupil with her young lover and how masquerading in the clothes of the lover's old aunt and uncle they escape the police. *No. 66* brings in a lottery prize winner, who wastes his wealth, but finds happiness in love in the end. *La princesse de Trapézunt* (Paris, 1869) introduces a traveling showman with mid-Victorian "waxwork figures," one of them, the "Princess," being impersonated by his daughter, whose beauty wins her a princely hand. *Princesse de Théâtre* (Paris, 1878) reflects the musical stage life of the time; and *Vert-Vert* (1869) reverts to the elopement of a convent girl with a lover. In *Toto* (1868) we have the impecunious old nobleman who must sell his ancestral castle to satisfy his creditors. In *L'île de Tulipatan* a piquant situation arises owing to an interchange of sex, a youth being brought up a girl by a mother who "did not raise her boy to be a soldier," while a girl is brought up as a boy. *Les dames de la Halle* (*The Ladies of the Market,* Paris, 1858) put the huckster women of Paris on the stage in a roaring farce. *La grande-duchesse de Gérolstein* (Paris, 1867) in which Private Fritz (who sings the famous air "Le sabre de mon père) reaches the highest military honor at the Court of a German grand duchess because she falls in love with him, delighted Parisians as a caricature of the Prussian soldiers who had just defeated Austria, France's friend, at Sadowa. Napoleon III, Thiers, the Princess of Wales, Bismarck, Czar Alexander III, and the Kings of Bavaria, Portugal, and Sweden were present at the first performance. The military pomp and circumstance of the Second Empire, the uniforms and prestige of the veteran regiments of Algerian, Crimean, Italian and Mexican campaigns are stressed in Offenbach scores like *La fille du tambour-major* (Paris, 1879) and *Le sorcier au régiment* (1864.)

Offenbach himself has been set to music and his scores utilized to reincarnate the spirit of the Second Empire for twentieth century music lovers in *The Love Song* (New York, 1925), a comic opera whose music, drawn from his own works, brings the composer of *Hoffman's Strange Tales* on the stage as the hero of an historically impossible affair of the heart with the Empress Eugénie together with Napoleon III, the dancer Taglioni, the *diva* Hortense Schneider and other artistic figures of the times. In *Capriccio Offenbachique* (Paris, 1924), a Russian ballet, however, the composer's music accompanies a pantomime picture of the elderly gourmand Rossini at Passy, at one of the famous luncheons when the works of unknown young composers and delicious food competed for consideration; while *La nuit ensorcelée* (*Enchanted Night*, Paris, 1923), a ballet, is Vuillermoz' adaptation of Chopin waltzes and mazurkas to a Bakst book which presents Chopin, Taglioni, Paganini and other celebrities in a Second Empire setting.

*Excelsior* (Milan, 1881) by Romualdo Marenco, book by Manzotti, a spectacular ballet with tuneful but negligible music, is an exposé of nineteenth century ideas in the dance. A later Vignano, Marenco secured his effects—the "story" the conflict of light and darkness, progress and superstition, invention and reaction—by massed dancers, combining and merging in a riot of color on an artfully lighted stage. "It filled a whole evening with spectacle, glitter and movement" (Brander Matthews). Among distinctively nineteenth century scenes were: the apotheosis of the original Italian *risorgimento* movement, the idea of a "place in the sun" of United Italy, with dances of Fame, Valor, Love, Union, etc.; and "the gigantic works of our century," the age of machinery idealized in the appearance of "The First Steamboat" (on the Weser river, Germany); the completion of the Suez Canal, an "Omaggio à de Lesseps," in which jugglers and dancers "from all parts of Egypt" assisted; the building of Mount Cenis tunnel; and a scene showing the "Piazza of the Electric Telegraph" in Washington, D. C., with the Genius of Electricity. About the only thing missing was "The Great Eastern."

Sentimental aspects of French Second Empire life are reflected in *La Rondine* (*The Swallow*, Monte Carlo, 1917) by Giacomo Puccini, a flowing lyric score along *opéra comique* lines. Magda, a Second Empire "Traviata," kept by the Parisian banker Rambaldo, gives up luxury for sentiment on meeting Ruggero, a poor young student at a *Bal Bullier,* and deserts her rent-free apartment for love in a cottage at Nice. Alas, his parents couple with permission to marry Magda the stipulation that she be virtuous! Unable to recall the past, the high-souled *demi-mondaine* resigns her lover rather than have him disobey his parents. *Lodoletta* (Rome, 1917) by Pietro Mascagni, after Ouida's *Two Little Wooden Shoes,* is *salon* verism in a Second Empire setting.

Flammen, a gay Parisian painter who comes to a Dutch hamlet, gives Antonio a gold piece to let his pretty Lodoletta pose for a Madonna. Antonio buys the girl a pair of little wooden shoes, then falls from a tree and dies. Soon painting is not Flammen's only passion but Lodoletta, after refusing village Gianetto, finds the love the painter offers is one virtue cannot accept and runs away. The scene shifts (Act II) to Flammen's Paris villa on New Year's night. Glasses clink to the laughter of evening-gowned women as poor Lodoletta, who has crept from Flanders through ice and snow in her little wooden shoes, crouches in the frozen garden and peers through the window to realize Flammen is not for her. But, happy in the illusion his lips are pressed to hers she freezes to death, and Flammen, entering the garden after his guests have gone, stumbles over the wooden shoes and discovering their wearer, flings himself on her body swearing that he will die for love of Lodoletta. Zola, apostle of realism, in the two opera books he wrote for Bruneau (though they appeared long after the Second Empire had passed) idealizes the working class and introduces socialistic and humanitarian ideas current in connection with the toilers of that time.

*Messidor* (Paris, 1897) by Alfred Bruneau, book by Zola, mingles allegory and socialism in a tale whose music has outstanding dramatic pages and a fine symphonic Ballet. Caspar, the capitalist, has installed hydraulic mining machinery in a village on the river Arriège, and made the miners destitute. Veronica tells her worthless nephew Mathias, a rolling stone returned, that she knows the secret spring which brings the golden grains into the river. But her son Guillaume loves Caspar's daughter, Hélène, so she waits to seek it till Hélène (Act II), thinking Guillaume cares only for her fortune, breaks with him as the starving miners gather to destroy Caspar's machines. "The Legend of the Gold" (Ballet). In a vast subterranean cathedral beneath the river the Christ Child sits in the Virgin's lap, laughing as the sand which streams through his baby fingers turns to grains of gold to fall into the fountain-head of the Arriège. Mathias is urging on the *saboteurs* when Veronica appears. She has found the spring, turned it aside, and Caspar is ruined. While Mathias, confessing he murdered Veronica's husband, flings himself over a cliff, Guillaume and Hélène fall into each other's arms. *L'enfant-roi* (*The Child King*, Paris, 1905) by Alfred Bruneau, book by Zola, using popular Parisian tunes, outstanding François' "Entrance Song" (Act II), is a working woman's tragedy treated as seriously as a society leader's might be, in a drama of Parisian life in the style of Charpentier. A baker's wife is confronted with a choice between her boy or the husband who is not its father.

When the husband finds she has been true to him since marriage, he pardons and accepts her earlier mistake.

## "LE ROI CAROTTE"

### (*King Carrot*)

JACQUES OFFENBACH. Book by Victorien Sardou (Paris, 1873). A political fairy opera announced for October 15, 1870, at the Paris *Gaîté* whose prophecy was realized before the event. *Le roi Carotte*, allegorically predicting the overthrow of the Second Empire by the "Reds" of the time, was not produced on October 15 because on July 15, 1870, France declared war on Prussia. The Franco-Prussian War over, *Le roi Carotte* was only a fantastic copy of what actually had happened. Sardou, a confirmed Bonapartist, was convinced that the Empire would be restored, and the opera was produced with moderate success. It contains delightful melodies and is musically a piquant and attractive score.

King Fridolin (Napoleon III) has married a foreign princess (Spanish Eugénie) who sets the fashion, is leader of the social world, and holds the reins of government. But though he invokes the memory of his great ancestor (Napoleon I) he does not imitate his virtues nor suspect the enemy, an evil fairy, his sworn foe (the "Red" or Communist Republicans) plans to overthrow him. One night the evil fay rouses the roots (radix—radicals) in the palace garden to life with magic wand. Among them is the Carrot, whom the others elect king. In Fridolin's palace all is festivity. Never was his glory greater, never did his power seem more firmly established (Paris Exposition, 1867) when suddenly King Carrot appears with his grotesque following. About to be ousted in disgrace a movement of the fairy's wand reveals to all that he possessed the virtues King Fridolin lacks. Then people, courtiers, and ministers of state bow low before the red apparition and Fridolin, thrust from his throne, wanders through the world while his rival is crowned. But soon all see that the new ruler possesses the old one's faults magnified a hundredfold. A horrid tyrant, he thinks only of stuffing himself, and when the people revolt King Carrot creeps underground and becomes a mere vegetable as before, while King Fridolin, who has turned over a new leaf, returns to rule his realm (Poor Napoleon III died in 1873).

*La Valse* (concert form, Paris, 1920), choregraphic poem by Maurice Ravel, using the Viennese waltz idiom of Strauss and Lanner in modernist transmutation, evokes with tragic underlying irony in a suite of waltzes, an imperial court (1855) revealing an immense ballroom filled with dancers under the blaze of great chandeliers, quite possibly the Court of St. Cloud, where the brilliant society of the Second Empire danced on a volcano.

The Franco-Prussian War has motived *Bei Sedan* (Leipzig,

1895) by Heinrich Zöllner, an episode from Zola's grandiose novel of the war, *Le Débâcle*. Honoré Fouchard, the French artillerist, meets his love Silvine in Father Fouchard's house near Sedan; and leaves her ("Und ich geh' freudig zum Kampfe," a good dramatic song) to fight for France. After a symphonic Intermezzo describing the Battle of Sedan and a German "Camp Scene," Honoré is brought in (Act II) mortally wounded, to die in Silvine's arms. *L'attaque du moulin* (*The Attack on the Mill*) by Alfred Bruneau, book by Émile Zola (Paris, 1893), an effective dramatic score, is an 1870 war episode. Miller Merlier's daughter, Franchette, is to marry young Dominic when the drums of war beat. A month passes and (Act II) defending the Merlier mill against Prussians, Dominic, caught with powder-blackened hands, is ordered shot as a *franc tireur*. He refuses to turn traitor to earn a pardon, but, after he had sung his swan song in prison, Franchette points out a means of escape. Dominic, climbing through the window (Act III), kills a sentry with Franchette's knife but Merlier, who will not tell where he is concealed, is ordered shot in his stead. When Dominic (Act IV) leads French soldiers to the rescue a volley rings and Merlier, riddled with bullets, falls dead.

*Der Überfall* (*The Surprise Attack*, Dresden, 1895) by Heinrich Zöllner is the tale of a French peasant girl (1870) who betrays her native village to the Prussians for love of a Uhlan and, unable to forgive herself, thrusts a knife into her heart before her lover's eyes. The year 1870 saw the fall of the Second French Empire, and the year 1871 in Austria a political ideal called forth the noblest score Smetana ever wrote. *Libussa* (Prague, 1881) by Bedřich Smetana, book by Wenzig, is the Bohemian national legend of the foundation of the old dynasty of Czech kings by the marriage of Queen Libussa to a heroic peasant. A vast musical fresco, the opera presents in succession Libussa's judgment; her marriage; and her invocation, the climax of the work. She presages the historic greatness of Bohemia, visions walls and towers of the golden Hradschin palace rising above the city of Prague, and calls forth the "Hussite Chorale" which voices the hymn of Czech independence. In 1871 the Czechs, aflame with enthusiasm, believed the Emperor Franz Josef would have himself solemnly crowned King of Bohemia in Prague as he had King of Hungary in Budapest. For this coronation which never took place Smetana wrote his score. However, the work was not given until ten years later, at the opening of the new National Opera House in the Czech capital. An operatic glimpse of Viennese social life in the third quarter of the nineteenth century is offered in a celebrated comic opera by Johann Strauss.

## "DIE FLEDERMAUS"

### (*The Bat*)

JOHANN STRAUSS. Book by Haffner (Vienna, 1874). This score is regarded, musically, as the best of all Viennese operettas, of which it is the classic model. Among the charming musical themes are: Rosalinda's "Farewell Air" (Act I), the Ballet, a brilliant chain of dances, and the Choral Waltz, "Ha, what a feast" (Act II); and the Entr'act (waltzes and banquet music) and Final Chorus (Act III).

Gabriel von Eisenstein has beaten up a police officer. Sentenced to jail, he is induced by his friend Falke ("Dr. Bat") to go to an "after the show" supper party at Prince Orloffsky's before surrendering. Eisenstein at Orloffsky's, Alfred, former lover of Rosalinda, Eisenstein's wife, installs himself at her home (Act II) and makes love to her, only to be taken to jail by the governor of the prison, who mistakes him for Eisenstein. When Rosalinda (lured there by "Dr. Bat") appears at Orloffsky's, she sees her husband flirt with pretty ballet girls and her own maid, Adele. The whole thing is Dr. Bat's revenge on Eisenstein who once made a mock of him by tricking him out with bat claws and wings when overcome with wine. But Rosalinda, masquerading as a Hungarian countess, so enchants her husband, who never suspects her identity, that he gives her his splendid gold repeater watch. Before the guests disperse the governor of the jail joins the gathering, courts Adele and becomes friendly with Eisenstein, who should be his prisoner. In the governor's private office in the prison, the tangled web of mistaken identities is finally unwound (Act III) and all ends happily.

*Die Kohlhaymerin* (*Kohlheimer's Widow* (Vienna, 1921) by Julius Bittner, is a fantastic musical apotheosis of the Vienna nineteenth century woman, outstanding the Prelude (Act I), Dionysiac Ballet, Intermezzo (Act III), the Final Duet between Franz and Hélène (Act II) and the "Widow's Theme," a waltz melody which serves as a widow's cruse to supply the whole opera with melodies. Kohlhaymer's widow longs for love (it is spring) and yielding to neighbor Von Pichler's plea, goes with him to a masquerade ball. There (Act II) she meets Karl Nowak, a Don Juan of the underworld who, as the Marchese di Salvatorre, dances with her and, taking her home, has well-nigh made her yield to his love-making when a glimpse of her dead husband's picture recalls her to virtuous resistance. The police arriving apropos, the chivalrous scoundrel admits a burglary he had no intention of committing and at the police station (Act III) after Franz Hofbauer, the Commissioner, has dismissed the case with a sympathy rare in police magistrates, Hélène and Hofbauer discover they love each other. As they leave, after singing their affection in moving folk-wise strains the Dionysiac Ballet (Act II), rushes on once more in a merry pandemonium of music and movement.

### 4. *Victorian England*

The reign of Queen Victoria began in 1837 and Dickens' *Sketches by Boz* appeared two years before her accession. Dickens' monumental novels reflect the age, the times, the people among whom he lived and had his being and have motived various scores. Best known are the operas on *The Cricket on the Hearth*.

### "DAS HEIMCHEN AM HERD"

#### (*The Cricket on the Hearth*)

KARL GOLDMARK. Text by Willner after Charles Dickens' tale (Berlin, 1896). The novelist's poetic idealization of simple village virtues: love of home, of parents, and of husband and wife, handled in "song-play" style, with German folk-tune material. Among many charming melodies, the song "Cricket, cricket, guess what this may be?" stands out.

The Cricket (after an off-stage elfin chorus) explains itself as the guardian spirit of John Tackleton's home. Then Dot, his wife, confides her sweet secret—a babe is expected. May (fated to marry old Tackleton, the rich toy maker, on the morrow) laments, thinking herself jilted by her sailor lover, Edward Plummer. Enter John (not as Dickens' carter, but in postilion's uniform) with a stranger (Edward in disguise, returned from South American ports), who distributes letters and parcels to flocking villagers. Edward first proceeds to rouse the old toy maker's jealousy at supper (Act II) by offering May a jewel—he has informed her elderly admirer he has returned from ocean wanderings to find his father dead and his sweetheart lost to him—then makes his friend John jealous. A tender garden tête-à-tête between Edward and Dot (to whom he reveals his identity) nearly drives John to suicide. But the voice of the Cricket, promising the joy of fatherhood, lulls him asleep, and in dreams he dandles his boy on his knee. May and Edward, reunited, drive off to be married in the infuriated toy maker's carriage as Dot's confession of her interesting situation to John motives their reconciliation, and the Cricket's song triumphantly celebrates the sacred joys of the hearth.

*Cricket on the Hearth* (London, 1914) Sir Alexander Mackensie, book by Sturgis after Dickens, is a sentimentally tuneful setting; and Zandonai's *Grillo del focolare* (*The Cricket on the Hearth*, Turin, 1908), is one of the composer's minor scores. Charles Kensington Salaman wrote a successful comic opera *Pickwick* (London, 1889) and the German, Grelinger, a *Nicholas Nickleby* (Berlin, 1900).

The "Trilby" operas and ballets which precede the publication of Du Maurier's famous Victorian novel, reproducing his own reminiscences of the Latin Quarter life of Paris in 1856 are settings of a tale by Charles Nodier. Nodier's "Trilby" is a will-o'-the wisp; Du Maurier's a dumb artist's model who becomes a prima donna. *Trilby* (Moscow, 1925) by Alexander Yourassovsky (d. 1922), book after Du Maurier's novel, is a lyric "twentieth century score, musical yet not ultramodern," without the conventional overture. The book departs from Du Maurier's original in the closing scene in Svengali's studio. Sitting at the piano playing Chopin's "Impromptu in A Flat," he falls dead with the last note struck by his fingers, instead of dying when brought face to face with his picture. Louis-Antoine Jullien (supposed to be the actual living musician who suggested the idea of his demoniac conductor to Du Maurier) a pupil of Halévy and one of the most popular dance orchestra conductors of his day, produced an opera, *Pietro il Grande* (Peter the Great) in Paris in 1852, at ruinous expense, and went insane when jailed for debt.

*Tess* (Naples, 1906) by Baron Frederic d'Erlanger, book by Illica after Thomas Hardy's novel, *Tess of the D'Urbervilles*. Modern lyric music, outstanding the Prelude to Act III. Hardy's tale is necessarily synoptic. The characters are "placed" (Act I); Tess Durbeyfield, locked out of the D'Urberville mansion, is led astray by Alec D'Urberville (Act II); she weds Angel Clare (Act III); and when her husband, after learning the story of her past and from her own lips that she is no innocent girl refuses to forgive her, the tale reaches its tragic climax (Act IV).

Oscar Wilde's "æsthetic movement" initiated during his undergraduate years at Oxford (1874-1878) with its pose of scorning athletic sports, wearing the hair long, filling rooms with peacock's feathers, lilies, sunflowers, blue china, and other "art objects" and proclaiming Whistler's gospel of "art for art's sake," was practically killed by the ridicule provoked by a comic opera, Gilbert and Sullivan's *Patience* (London, 1881) though, to use Streatfeild's words *"Patience* embalmed it in odors and spices of the most costly description, so that it has remained a thing of beauty to our own day."

Tennyson is remembered in an operatic setting of *Enoch Arden* (Leipzig, 1905) by Rudolf Raimann. Ouida, that characteristically Victorian novelist (aside from scores elsewhere mentioned) wrote a story which motived Frederic Cowen's opera *Signa* (London, Milan, 1893); while in more recent years Anthony Hope's *Prisoner of Zenda* (1894) started the vogue of the "Ruritanian romance" which has been variously reflected in opera. The most direct reaction is Herbert Bunning's opera *La Princesse Osra*

(London, 1902) after Hope's novel *The Heart of Princess Osra.*
Other "Ruritania" include an American score, *The Legend* (New
York, 1919) by Joseph Breil, book by J. Byrne. In Muscovadia,
a mythical Balkan land, dwells Count Stackareff, penniless noble by
day, Black Lorenzo the bandit by night. Stephen (ostensibly coming to see Carmelita his sweetheart, Stackareff's daughter, really
to capture Black Lorenzo) comes from Vienna, and Carmelita is
about to elope with her lover when her father enters. As Stephen
mentions his mission Stackareff leaps through the door, betraying
his less respectable identity. Stephen prepares to leap after and
Carmelita stabs him. A shot is heard without. Enter two soldiers
who carry in Black Lorenzo's body and seeing Stephen's corpse
on the floor shoot Carmelita. *La Reginetta delle rose* (Rome,
1912) by Leoncavallo tells how Max, Crown Prince of Portowa,
meets pretty Lilian the flower girl at a London charity bazaar
(Act I), imprisons her when she is brought to Portowa by a trick
(Act II), and marries her, making her his "Little Queen of Roses"
because (having broken his pen) the girl supplies the rose stem
with which he signs his act of accession.

Other nineteenth century subjects include *Fennimore und Gerda*
(Frankfurt, 1919) by Frederick Delius, based on the Danish novelist Jacobsen's *Niels Lyhnes,* a modern score in tableaux. Niels
and Erick love Fennimore. She marries Erick. Three years later,
her husband addicted to actresses and drink, Fennimore betrays
him in Niels' arms when he visits her; but when Erick is brought
home dead she realizes she loved him only, and turns with loathing from Niels who, after world wanderings, returns and finds
an ideal wife in Gerda. *Ingrid* (Dresden, 1894) by Gramman,
is an effective musical picture of Norwegian country life. Helga,
the rich Varö farmer Wandrup's daughter, betrothed to her cousin
Godila, meets and loves Erhard, a young German. Jealous Godila
tries to push Helga from a precipice where she and Erhard had
been pulling daisies but Ingrid, an orphan girl who also loves
Erhard brings him back in time to save Helga, while Godila falls
to his death. When Ingrid discovers Erhard is her brother, instead of committing suicide she devotes herself to living for her
newly found father Wandrup. *Kleider Machen Leute (Fine
Feathers Make Fine Birds)* by Alexander Zemlinsky, book after
Keller's studies of Swiss life, *Die Leute von Seldwyla* (Vienna,
1910) tells of the tailor's apprentice taken for a nobleman by the
villagers of Goldacher who, after manifold adventures, resumes
his true personality as a knight of the needle and gains the hand
of the girl who first had been captured by his title. Outstanding
is the Heine song, sung to spinet accompaniment. *Mam'zelle
Carabin* (Paris, 1893) by Émile Pessard, reflects in graceful music

the Paris Latin Quarter of its day and—a strange departure—ends with Olga (Mam'zelle Carabin), a "good girl," saving Ferdinand, her student lover, from a hussy and *marrying* him.

## 5. *The Twentieth Century*

Various phases of twentieth century life and thought as reflected in opera will be found under other heads (*The New World Opera Stories; The Verist's Rosary; Symbolic Operas*, etc.). Since the phrase "Time, the present" in connection with operas whose action takes place in the twentieth century, generally speaking means the year of its first performance, or a year or so before, the sequence of the years from 1900 on has been preferred for the arrangement of the operas included in this section. The year 1900, the first of the twentieth century, is marked by the appearance of a successor to those famous scores which like *La Bohème* and *Traviata* are intimate musical reflections of certain phases of Paris social life.

### "LOUISE"

GUSTAVE CHARPENTIER. The book by the composer (Paris, 1900), a "Musical Romance," is an autobiography illustrating the *vie de Bohème* at the beginning of the twentieth century. According as the auditor may react it is: (1) "The lyric impression of the sensations I reap in our beautiful, fairy-like modern life" (Charpentier); (2) "a mixture of 'humbug' and affected and silly sentimentalism giving infinite pleasure to the multitude, yet ringing false to more delicate ears" (Landormy); (3) "a realistic opera, too exact a copy of certain harrowing scenes from life" (Combarieu); or (4) a work whose music "lacks all mad, flaming, devouring passion . . . a *bourgeois,* not a Bohemian tale, with some literary points, no temperament and much that wearies" (Bie). Paris street cries (scavengers', ragpickers', street hawkers') are a feature of the score, and the lyric air, "Depuis le jour," in which Louise sings the happiness of her love, is one of the most popular of modern opera arias.

While Louise, the tenement seamstress, talks love with Julian, the shiftless painter whose room is in the garret across the alley, her mother scolds. When her father, a day laborer, comes in, shakes his head over Julian, his disorderly life, his unsettled habits, the poor girl promises to forget her lover.

Early morning in the Montmartre section. Night hawkers, street sweepers, ragpickers, peddlers, are vocal in the street. Intercepting Louise on her way to work, Julian begs her to elope with him, but she hurries to her sweatshop, where above the clatter of sewing machines and clack of gossip Julian is heard singing outside. The shop-girls throw him kisses, tease Louise, and at last she leaves her work to cast her lot with him.

In the garden of Julian's Montmartre cottage—Paris lights twinkling below—as gay bohemians, students, and grisettes crown Louise "Queen of Montmartre," Louise's mother appears. The mother has not come to reproach her child. Her father is dying, she says. Only Louise's return can save him. As a ragman's doleful song sounds in the street Louise leaves Julian, promising to return.

In the tenement, the broken old workman, somewhat recovered, while his wife tells Louise she shall not return to a "life of misery set to tunes," begs her to give up Julian. Louise refuses. He becomes brutal; she turns defiant, and makes for the door. When her father hinders her leaving, she grows hysterical, screaming for her Julian, and finally, he flings the door wide and cries "Get out!" As the mother tries to soothe his rage, Louise with a cry of terror runs down the stairs—and out of their lives. The poor old man calls after her in vain, then, shaking his fist at the lights of the vicious city beneath, he shouts "Oh, Paris!" in a tone which makes the words a curse.

*Julien* (Paris, 1913), a lyric drama, is the sequel to *Louise*. In it—Charpentier continued his "idealization" (?) of the freedom of artistic life. It is Julian's history after Louise's death, when he recognizes her in turn in five different women, going down the scale of decency and ending as a drab of the gutters. Julian finally dies in misery. The work is subtitled "Scenes from a Poet's Life." Musically the opera is chiefly noteworthy for its fivefold leading woman's part.

## "ZAZA"

RUGGIERO LEONCAVALLO. Book by Simon after P. Berton's play (Milan, 1900). A vulgar tale of Parisian concert-hall life set to a score of considerable passion which has been more popular in the United States than in Italy. The music is theatrically and sentimentally effective. The air "Buona Zaza, del mio buon tempo" has been praised.

Zaza, a *café chantant* singer, wagers with Bussy the playwright, she will overcome the coldness of Milio Dufresne, and wins her wager. In the process (Act II), she falls in love with Dufresne in earnest and abandons the stage for idyllic love-making in a cottage in Paris suburbs. When her distressed manager Cascart, who wants her to work, visits her, he tells Zaza that he has seen her lover in Paris with another woman, and the jealous *artiste* takes the next train into town. While Dufresne—it was his wife whom Cascart saw on his arm—takes the train back to his love nest (Act III), Zaza, admitted to his Paris home by the butler's mistake, discovers Dufresne is married and has a child. Listening to the artless prattle of Toto, her lover's little daughter, the lady of the half-world bravely controls herself and leaves without creating a scene. When in their cottage (Act IV) Zaza tells Dufresne she has seen little Toto and knows all, he flies into a rage. Zaza, angry in turn, declares she has betrayed their relations to his wife and finds—that Dufresne's love for his wife is real, and she is merely a toy of his idle moments. It is then that the frail fair rises to a lofty spiritual height of renunciation, and tearing all thought of Dufresne from her suffering heart sends him nobly back to his home.

*L'Aveugle* (*The Blind Woman*, Antwerp, 1901) by Valentine Neuville, is by a Belgian modernist. Marc, younger son of a blind mother, is called for military service. Yves, his crippled older brother, as well as his mother, is dependent on him. Knowing his own death will free Marc from military duty, Yves climbs to their tenement window ledge and flings himself into the black depths below. *La fille de Tabarin* (Paris, 1901) by Gabriel Pierné after Sardou's drama, touches the melodramatic in an ingeniously written score. About to marry his daughter to a gentleman who loves her, Tabarin is recognized, and, on the point of having his past on the boards disclosed by a theatrical troupe, rather than be an obstacle to his daughter's happiness, he kills himself. *Eva* (Vienna, 1911), by Lehar, whose music touches grand opera levels, uses operetta as a vehicle for presenting phases of proletarian life in a European metropolis.

## "LE CHEMINEAU"

### (*The Vagabond*)

Xavier Leroux. Book by Jean Richepin (Paris, 1907; New Orleans, 1911). A melodramatic excursion into French tramp life, by a pupil of Massenet, whose characters are not altogether convincing. The Preludes to Acts II and III have genuine symphonic worth.

It is harvest time in provincial France. Toinette confesses that she loves the Vagabond, a tramp who has been taken on as a hand. And she refuses staid and older François only to learn that the Vagabond, having had his will of her, is about to heed the call of the road. François has to prevent her from following her tramp into the "gay-cat" life by main force. Then he induces her to marry him. Twenty years have passed (Act II). Toinet, Toinette's son by the tramp, has been brought up by his mother's husband, François, as his own; but when he wins the love of the rich Pierre's daughter Aline, the girl's father comes to François' wretched home and reveals Toinet's parentage to the man who thinks himself his father. A paralytic stroke fells sick François as he staggers from his armchair to strike his tormentor. At a crossroads tavern the Vagabond learns Toinet is his own (Act III). Seeking out poor Toinette he promises in return for her forgiveness to force Pierre's consent to the match, and makes his son's acquaintance as his mother's friend in days before he was born. The Vagabond, successful in his mission (Act IV) returns to François' cottage as the young lovers hurry to Christmas midnight mass. All—Toinette, Pierre, dying François himself—want him to settle down and marry the widow presumptive. But he is homesick for the open road. While chime of Christmas bells, chant of choristers, and carols of waits ring out over the snow, the tramp, with a blessing for those he leaves, picks up his shapeless hat and strides off along the winter highway.

## "LE COQ D'OR"

### (*The Golden Cockerel*)

NICOLAS RIMSKY-KORSAKOFF. Book by Bielsky after Pushkin (Moscow, 1910). Completed in 1907, the Russian censorship forbade performance till three years later. A political meaning was read into the text, a "tragi-comedy of unhappy consequences following on mortal passions and weaknesses." The opening scenes of the council of war between King Dodon and his officers was thought to satirize well-known occurrences of the Russian-Japanese War (1904-05) and suspicion existed that King Dodon was a musical portrait of the late Czar Nicholas II. An "opera-ballet," with two distinct casts (singers, and mimes and dancers) the score is rich in glowing lyric pages.

King Dodon, a witless glutton, holds counsel with his boyars in his palace hall and conflicting opinions offered him by the young princes (in whom Russian censors recognized Romanoff grand dukes) lead to uproar and confusion. Suddenly an Astrologer enters with a Golden Cockerel, a magic bird that can foretell coming events and which, when King Dodon has placed it on the highest weather vane sends the citizens scurrying to arms when danger threatens. Relieved of responsibility King Dodon has his feather bed brought in and is put to sleep (the "Berceuse" is one of the loveliest numbers of the score) only to wake when the Golden Cockerel gives a frantic alarm. King Dodon's sons set out with the host for the enemy's country, followed later by Dodon himself. He reaches the spot where his sons and their army have been slain (Act II) and finds them lying cold and stark, but at dawn, from the tent he thought occupied by the enemy general issues the lovely Queen of Shemaka. She sings and dances (Ballet: the "Oriental Dance" is a glowing exotic page) her way into the doddering monarch's heart, and consents to be his bride after having forced him to dance till he drops to the ground exhausted.

The entry of the Queen of Shemaka and King Dodon into his royal city (Act III) is followed by the reappearance of the Astrologer. As his reward for the Golden Cockerel he asks—lovely Shemaka herself! In a rage Dodon kills the Astrologer with a blow of his scepter while the Golden Cockerel pierces Dodon's skull with its beak, instantly killing him. Sudden darkness falls and through the crash of thunder rings Shemaka's silvery mocking laughter. When light returns Queen and Bird are gone. The stupid people sing a chorus of regret for the King they have no reason to bewail: "Prudent, wise and peerless was our King! He treated us like dogs, yet where shall we find another like him!" Then (Epilogue) the Astrologer steps before the curtain and tells his audience to shed no tears since Dodon's kingdom held but two sentient human beings, the Queen of Shemaka and himself.

*Il segreto di Susanna* (*Susanne's Secret,* Munich, 1909) by Ermanno Wolf-Ferrari, book by Golisciani, a graceful one-act score, is the slight tale of Piedmontese Count Gil who smelling cigarette smoke in his newly wed wife Susanna's boudoir, suspects her of a lover and after a furious quarrel and quasi-reconciliation, coming in unexpectedly to seize Susanna's paramour, finds himself clutching her cigarette instead, and strikes a match for her to light a fresh one in token of reconciliation. *Liebelei* (*Love Affair,* Frankfort, 1910) by Franz Neumann, book after Schnitzler's play, a colorful score with emotional pages, shows Fritz Lobheimer, a Viennese, deeply in love with Christine, daughter of a theater violinist, challenged to a duel by the husband of a married woman with whom he has had a love affair. Christine, after an idyllic hour he has spent with her, alarmed when her lover does not return the next day (Act II) goes in search of him only to learn he lies six feet underground. *Rhena* (Brussels, 1912) by Van der Eeden, a semi-veristic, semi-psychologic score, is the tale of a murderer who, telling a priest his crime in the confessional, forces the latter to sacrifice himself to keep his vows. *Jeux* (Paris, 1913) by Claude Debussy, pantomime ballet by Nijinsky, "a plastic apologue of the man of 1913," showed a tennis player pursuing the ball in tremendous leaps to chromatic glissandi and after a dance flirtation with two girls, six lips meeting in a triple kiss. Debussy's programmatic music tried to express the "amatory play motive" in modern life. *Les Préludes* (New York, 1913), a ballet after Lamartine's *Méditations poétiques,* uses Franz Liszt's symphonic poem to comment a pantomime action showing Man struggling against the Phantoms of Darkness, Love his guiding star, succombing undefeated to Death in the consciousness of Immortality. *Parade* (Paris, 1917) by Erik Satie is a ballet whose music paints the empty melancholy of a crowded modern fair.

## "IL TABARRO"

### (*The Cloak*)

GIACOMO PUCCINI. Book by Adami after Didier Gold's *La Hauppelande* (New York, 1918). The "tragedy" score of the composer's tryptich is a realist's idyl of the Seine instead of the Bay of Naples, in which the composer "has indulged in the most reprehensible verist mannerisms" (Kapp).

At sunset the longshoremen Tinca and Luigi leave Michele's Seine barge, aboard which they have been working. Luigi, lover of Michele's wife Giorgetta, whispers to her to strike a match to let him know when he may safely return to her arms. Michele comes aboard but when he recalls to Giorgetta how she used to snuggle beneath his coat, his stirring of affection's dead ashes wakes no answering glow and Giorgetta, pleading weariness, goes down into the cabin. Michele strikes a match—to light his pipe—and Luigi climbs aboard. Michele, earlier suspicions verified, strangles Luigi, covers his body with his coat and—relights his pipe. Giorgetta, who has heard a thump, comes on deck her heart in her mouth, only to find Michele calmly smoking his briar. But when she reverts hypocritically to their love's young dream, Michele jerks away his coat and brutally flings her face down on the corpse.

## "DIE TOTE STADT"

### (*The Dead City*)

ERICK WOLFGANG KORNGOLD. Book by Paul Schott after Rodenbach's novel *Bruges la Morte* (Vienna, Hamburg, Cologne, 1920; New York, 1921). Georges Rodenbach, in *Bruges la Morte,* evoked the city as a living thing, associated with the moods of the spirit. The music of the score has that quality of fantastic romance which is opera's very own. Passionate, glowingly colorful, two symphonic Preludes (Act II, III) stand out, the favorite vocal number is Marietta's "Lute Song."

In Bruges, a "city of the past," the room in which Paul's wife, Marie, died is a shrine. There hangs her picture, there he keeps a lock of her golden hair. Frank, coming to visit his friend, finds he has seen the dead woman, reincarnated in a young girl who enters, Marietta, Marie's living image. Paul met her out walking, a dancer, sent for her, and she has come; but she leaves for a rehearsal when her visit promises no result. Paul sinks into a chair: Marie appears to him in a vision, stepping out of her picture frame, and the dream pictures born of Paul's love and longing take shape on the stage.

The moon shines in Bruges streets. Paul walks before Marietta's house. Suddenly a merry party comes along the canal in boats, dancers male and female, with Count Albert from Brussels, their Maecenas. They improvise a serenade and champagne party in the middle of the street, and Marietta gives a ghostly performance of the scene of the dead nuns in Meyerbeer's *Robert the Devil.* Paul rushes forward and tears the winding sheet from Marietta's body. The others intervene but Marietta sends them away, and she rouses Paul's baser instincts until he takes her home.

There Marietta triumphs over her dead rival before the latter's picture in Paul's shrine. When he pleads with her to leave the room,

Marietta's hatred for the dead woman breaks out in curses. Seeing the golden lock of hair she winds it around her neck, and dances shamelessly before Paul's horrified eyes till he flings her on the ground and strangles her with the shining strand she has desecrated. . . .

Waking from his horripilant dream Paul finds himself alone in the room. At that moment the flesh and blood Marietta returns. There is an inviting smile on her lips as she pretends to have forgotten some trifle, but Paul lets her go in silence. And Frank now finds it easy to persuade Paul to leave the "Dead City." His love Marie is dead for all time: he has no illusions left. It is his part to begin a new life elsewhere.

Raoul Pugno's *La Ville Morte* (*The Dead City*) completed by Nadia Boulanger, is based on a drama by D'Annunzio.

*Cocardes* (Paris, 1920) by Francis Poulenc, dance action by Jean Cocteau, calls up "the spirit of the Paris crowds at fairs and *bals publics* on July 14, "Bastille Day," with voice, horn, trumpet, and side-drum. *Le bœuf sur le toît* (*The Bull on the Roof*, Paris, 1920) by Darius Milhaud, action by Jean Cocteau, takes its name from a supposititious "American Bar" in Paris and is a pantomime satire on American Prohibition. The tunes used as a background for a farce action are rhythmic and contrapuntal developments of Brazilian folk tangos written on "simultaneous harmonic planes," that is, in several keys at the same time; and the action, without a plot, showed clowns in a "slowed-up" motion picture burlesque of what the atmosphere of an American bar in Paris might be, with trapeze and cocktail balancing. *Maison de fous* (*The Madhouse*, Paris, 1920) Swedish Ballet to veristic music by Viking Dahl, is a repulsive scene from a Paris insane asylum. A young girl, recently committed, is first swept away in a wild sarabande of hallucination by other inmates, then, left alone with a madman who thinks himself a prince, falls dead of shock when he tries to strangle her. As a charming climax a horrible hag, crouching in a corner, crawls gibbering to the corpse and expectorates in its face. *Les mariés de la Tour Eiffel* (*The Newly-Weds on the Eiffel Tower*), music by Taillefer, Auric, Honegger, Milhaud, and Poulenc, book by Jean Cocteau (Paris, 1921), is a burlesque of the Paris *bourgeoisie,* a musical farce—caricature of the type.

*Surprise* (Naples, 1921) by Marinetti is a futurist, "tactilate" opera. After a few measures of the "music"—Luigi Russolo's *bruiteur,* "noisemaker," a new futurist instrument producing sounds of ghastly power was a feature of the orchestra—such a shower of rotten tomatoes greeted the artists at the Roman performance that the police had to intervene.

*Das Wandbild* (*The Picture on the Wall,* Halle, 1921) pantomime scene by Othmar Schoek, a modern Swiss impressionist,
book by Ferrucio Busoni, offers exotic music to a symbolic stage
action.  In a Paris antiquarian shop a two-thousand-year-old
mummy from Thebes moves to the tick of a Dutch seventeenth
century clock and a young Oriental girl in a "picture on the wall"
steps from her frame to dance.  The confused action ends with
symbolic allusions to the interrelation of Life and Death in all
epochs. *L'homme et son désir* (*Man and His Desire,* Paris, 1921)
by Darius Milhaud, book by Claudel, is a symbolic pantomime to
French ultramodernist music of "strange and strident tonal combinations."  A nude male dancer dances "The Dance of the Soul,"
while temptations amatory and sadistic assail him.  Thus Man submits to the tortures of pleasure and the eternal rebirth of the soul
as true happiness evades him.  Above his head (decorative frieze)
the black hours refuse to yield to the white until Death, "the seductive deliverer" (?) wraps Man in the winding sheet she draws
from her own body.

*Isabelle* (Paris, 1922) by Manuel-Roland, uses the old Italian
*opera buffa* as vehicle for a modern musical setting, staging Dr.
Pantalon's hydropathic institute where he bleeds his patients literally and figuratively, and leaves Isabelle about to escape with
either Arlequin, her husband, or Pierrot, her lover. *Skating Rink*
(Paris, 1922) by Arthur Honegger, book by Canudo, Swedish
Ballet, expresses the mechanical dreariness of modern life in a
bored throng joylessly revolving around a skating rink.  Suddenly
a poet (or madman), personifying the natural instincts of mankind, bursts into the crowd and snatching up a woman for a partner, carries her off triumphantly while the human cogs resume
their monotonous glide.

## "LA CRÉATION DU MONDE"

### (*The Creation of the World*)

DARIUS MILHAUD. Swedish Ballet. Book by Cendrars (Paris, 1924).
An original and picturesque, if cacophonic ultramodern score. "Dis-
cordant jazz" (Lepommeraye) accompanies. a dance pantomime depicting the Creation *en noir,* in a Polynesian archipelago since covered by
the waters of the Indian Ocean, and with a Papuan Adam and Eve in
a cubist decorative scheme.

From the separation of earth and the heavens emerge three negroid
masters of creation: Nzame, Mebere, and N'kwa.  Their magic formulas
raise from inchoate matter fetishes, monkey-*djinns,* crocodiles, and reptile birds, *malakas,* which circle around the creative center.  Out of

the confusion of forms, when the gods have disappeared, emerges the first living man, Sekoumé, and the first living woman, Mbongwe. The original ancestors, black as the ace of spades, "isolate themselves in a kiss which bears them up like a wave" (we quote the book) and the moon rises and illumines "the springtime of life" which has begun.

*La brébis égarée* (*The Strayed Lamb,* Paris, 1923) by Darius Milhaud, an earlier Debussyan opera in twenty-four scenes, is the tale of an honest man's wife, the "Strayed Lamb," who runs away with his friend, but whom wretchedness drives back into her husband's forgiving arms.   Music singing flannel shirts, rubbers, and umbrellas, lends actuality to the romance.

*Within the Quota* (Paris, 1923) music by Cole Porter, orchestrated by Koechlin, ballet-sketch by Gerald Murphy, visions American Immigration Laws from a European angle and depicts the successive shocks produced on an immigrant who meets an American heiress, a modern girl, a gentleman of color, a cowboy—the encounters serving as a pretext for various blue developments in music and dance.   *Salade* (Paris, 1924) is a glorified Pulcinello choral pantomime, music by Darius Milhaud, book by Massine; and Erik Satie's *Relâche* (*Released,* Paris, 1924) book by Picabia, an "instantaneist ballet," with a motion picture interlude, expresses with figures from everyday life aimless movement and the thoughtless joy of the moment.   Nature's abhorrence of a vacuum is symbolized by a fireman who, decorated with the ribbon of the Legion of Honor, endlessly fills, then empties a bucket with water. The negligible music employs "popular tunes" to secure actuality of mood.   *Le tournoi singulier* (*The Strange Tourney,* Paris, 1924) a French ballet to an ultramodern score by Roland-Manuel, explains "why Love is blind" in a modernized La Fontaine fable. Cupid meets Folly.   Folly tries to teach him *golf,* but a poorly putted ball wrecks Cupid's optic nerve and Venus condemns Folly to serve as blind Cupid's guide forevermore.   *Die Nächtlichen* (*The Noctambules,* Berlin, 1924), dance fantasy, music by Egon Wellesz, book by Terpis, allegorically translates the "nocturnal" experiences of the soul, from delicate psychic dreams to wildest outbursts of passion, in a physical dance pantomime to ultramodern music.

*Intermezzo* (Dresden, 1924) by Richard Strauss, book by Bahr. A *bourgeoise* comedy of the day in which the composer exposes his private life in a two-act operatic pendant to his orchestral "Symphonia Domestica."   The score uses the vocal *parlando,* "song speech" and the expressive content rests mainly in the orchestral Intermezzos.   Court Conductor Storch (Strauss) and his wife have quarreled.   He goes to Vienna in a huff, to forget domestic troubles playing Skat with friends. Christine (Mrs. Strauss) goes to Rundelsee, where she flirts with a young baron who tries to borrow money. Returning home she finds a love letter to her husband signed "Your Mizzi Meier." It has been delivered by mistake to Storch instead of *Stroh!* Stroh is one of the Vienna skatplayers. Suddenly Storch learns Christine wants a divorce, but explanations result in a reconciliation.

*La chanson de Paris* (Paris, 1924) by Francis Casadesus is "a kind of rustic *Louise.*" Rosette, a Paris orphan girl, marries a Bressan farmer boy. Her aunt's hostility augments the homesickness she feels seeing an album of Parisian views; Jean, her husband, thinks she has tired of him, reproaches her, and she returns to Paris. On his sick bed he writes and she comes back on wings of love, though the peddler of the album views suggests the "Song of Paris" is one not easily forgotten. The musical score contains charming Bressan *noëls* and dances, and Puccinian as well as individual pages.

*Le train bleu* (Paris, 1925), music by Darius Milhaud, book by Jean Cocteau, is a ballet "take-off" on the fashionable French watering place, Deauville, in which the sports, fashions, and affectations of modern high society are cleverly satirized in dance and pantomime. To "film pictures" of life at a Continental seaside resort, the music travesties musical comedy songs, ragtime, and jazz and "plays up" human types such as the tennis champion, golfer, the "Bright Lad" who displays the power of his biceps to admiring flappers, beauties with chiming garters, and the "shore bathing" girl.

*135th Street* (New York, 1925) by George Gershwin, clever book by B. G. de Silva, a "jazz opera," locale, a Harlem cellar "colored" café, tells the tragedy of "a woman's intuition gone wrong" with realistic effect. Gambler Joe leaves town to see the Georgia mother for whom his "hard-boiled" heart guards a soft spot. Tom tells Vi, Joe's girl, he is faithless. When Joe will not show Vi his mother's letter, lest the "gang" laugh, she kills him.

*Gagliarda of a Merry Plague* (New York, 1925) by Lazare Saminsky. A "chamber opera" version of Edgar Allan Poe's tale of "The Red Death." The "Gagliarda" is the dance to which the Red Death enters the castle. High concentration compresses a complete opera in twenty minutes' time, and iron chains, strings of oyster shells, and a tom-tom filled with buckshot figure among the orchestral percussives. *Der rote Tod* (*The Red Death*) after Poe, by Franz Schreker, has not yet been set to music. Lora, a prostitute, symbolizing nature and undegenerate sexual impulses, survives the brilliant revelers in Prospero's castle, and calmly winds up the clock which stopped when the Red Death entered.

*Schlagobers* (Vienna, 1925) by Richard Strauss is a pantomime presentation of the nightmare of a first communicant whose parents, according to the Viennese custom, have "treated" him too freely in a pastry shop to the famous whipped cream puffs of his native town. The "hit" of the ballet is the appearance of all the dancers as successive snowy puffs of white cream, whipped up in an enormous "practicable" bowl by a gigantic cook.

## Opera and Ballet as a Means of Communistic Propaganda

A perversion is (1925) the prostitution of famous operas as the carrying medium for communistic doctrine in Soviet Russia, since the arbitrary separation of the music of an opera from its original story to make it a vehicle for the exploitation of political, economic, or any other form of propaganda is opposed to the fundamental ethics of musical art. The official decree of the Russian Commissar of Public Art (1924) declares "the *bourgeois* opera of the capitalistic epoch must be transformed into the proletarian opera of the present day." The government program involves "rewriting" of standard operas in the light of the communistic gospel. Those already presented include the following scores:

*Scythe and Hammer or a Life for the Country* (Moscow, 1925), formerly Glinka's *A Life for the Czar.* Ivan, instead of a moujik of 1663, is a moujik of the Red Revolution of 1917. Instead of saving his Czar he saves the Bolshevists by leading astray the foreign invaders: and the last act climaxes with the entrance of the Red regiments into the Kremlin, to the accompaniment of Russian revolutionary songs.

*Carmen* (Moscow, 1925). Carmen's cigarette factory stands in Polish Lodz where, while "rolling them"—she is a bright Jewish Communist girl instead of a gypsy—she uses her charms to win converts to Communism's cause. Her political instead of amatory activities get her in trouble with the authorities. Captain Joseph (once Don José), a police officer, is won over at the futuristic exhibition grounds where he is sent to arrest her, and lets her escape. He joins the smugglers (Act II) bringing contraband ammunition into Russia; but when the girl loses her heart to a Polish wrestler instead of Spanish bullfighter, Joseph stabs him— and her, after she has uttered a fiery eulogy of Communism.

*Faust* (Moscow, 1925) becomes "Harry," an American millionaire who, in his luxurious Berlin apartment, tells "Mr. Mephistopheles" life is vain unless he wins Margaret, a Hungarian moving picture actress, poor but pretty. Margaret, Siebel her lover, and Valentine, her brother, all communistically inclined, are tracked by the malefactor of great wealth to a Bavarian village (Act II) where the girl's noble ideals succumbing to the lure of an enormous package of thousand-dollar bills laid temptingly on her window sill, she breaks out into a "Money Waltz" ("Jewel Song") and allows Faust to lead her from the straight and narrow Marxian path while Mephistopheles, evil spirit of capitalism, laughs hideously. She is deserted by "Harry" (Act III) and condemned to death for the murder of her babe. When the millionaire, stung by remorse, comes to prison to rescue her, she kills him and is saved by the timely arrival of revolutionary troops. Gounod's music has been "pepped up" by the interpolation of jazz tunes (Acts II, III) to lend it "modern color."

*Lohengrin* (Moscow, 1925) is an American, John Reed (American socialist, d. Moscow, 1918), while Elsa, daughter of a nobleman of Pskoff, a revolutionist, is suspected of having made away with her brother, a loyal imperialist, who has mysteriously disappeared. Her accuser is Ortrud, wife of a German merchant of Pskoff, who says Elsa poisoned her brother, her husband, Telramund, confirming her tale. The Prince of Pskoff court-martials Elsa and when he allows her to appeal to the judgment of God, an American Red Cross officer drops down in an airplane to the music of "The Star Spangled Banner" (interpolated). He defeats Telramund and making Elsa promise never to ask his name or origin, informs the court-martial her brother is alive and happy in the United States. But Ortrud sows the seed of doubt in Elsa's mind (Act II) and she asks the ace the fatal question (Act III), after which, handing her a red flag, he mounts his airplane to the sound of the Russian "Marseillaise" and leaves her desolate, sadly shaking her bobbed head as his khaki-clad form disappears in the skies. *The Golden Calf* (Leningrad, 1925), music by Kordenko, a neo-Russian composer, book by Riabzov, is a symbolic pantomime representing the struggle between the proletariat and capitalism and ending in a proletarian triumph.

# INDEX

## A

# INDEX OF COMPOSERS